# LITTLE, BROWN AND COMPANY

## Law School Casebook Series

*The Employment Relation and the Law.* Edited by BENJAMIN AARON, Professor of Law and Director, Institute of Industrial Relations, University of California at Los Angeles

*Antitrust Analysis: Problems, Text, Cases.* PHILLIP AREEDA, Professor of Law, Harvard University

*Land Ownership and Use: Cases, Statutes, and Other Materials.* CURTIS J. BERGER, Professor of Law, Columbia University

*International Law: Cases and Materials.* Second Edition. WILLIAM W. BISHOP, JR., Professor of Law, University of Michigan

*Federal Income, Estate and Gift Taxation.* Third Edition. BORIS I. BITTKER, Southmayd Professor of Law, Yale University

*Materials on Reorganization, Recapitalization and Insolvency.* WALTER S. BLUM, Professor of Law, University of Chicago, and STANLEY A. KAPLAN, Professor of Law, University of Chicago

*Jurisdiction and Judgments: Cases and Statutes.* WILLIAM WIRT BLUME, Professor of Law, University of California, Hastings College of Law, and Dean CHARLES W. JOINER, Wayne State University, School of Law

*Pleading and Joinder: Cases and Statutes.* WILLIAM WIRT BLUME, Professor of Law, University of California, Hastings College of Law, and JOHN W. REED, Professor of Law, University of Michigan

*Civil Procedure: Cases and Comments on the Process of Adjudication.* PAUL D. CARRINGTON, Professor of Law, University of Michigan

*Estate Planning.* Third Edition. A. JAMES CASNER, Weld Professor of Law, Harvard University

*Cases and Text on Property.* Second Edition. A. JAMES CASNER, Weld Professor of Law, Harvard University, and W. BARTON LEACH, Story Professor of Law, Harvard University

*International Legal Process.* ABRAM CHAYES, Professor of Law, Harvard University, THOMAS EHRLICH, Professor of Law, Stanford University, and ANDREAS F. LOWENFELD, Professor of Law, New York University

*Cases and Materials on Debtor and Creditor.* VERN COUNTRYMAN, Professor of Law, Harvard University

*The Lawyer in Modern Society.* VERN COUNTRYMAN, Professor of Law, Harvard University, and TED FINMAN, Professor of Law, University of Wisconsin

*Law and Medicine: Text and Source Materials on Medico-Legal Problems.* WILLIAM J. CURRAN, Frances Glessner Lee Professor of Legal Medicine at Harvard Medical School, Harvard School of Public Health

*Trade Regulation: Cases and Materials.* FRANK ELKOURI, Professor of Law, University of Oklahoma

*Political and Civil Rights in the United States.* Third Edition. THOMAS I. EMERSON, Lines Professor of Law, Yale University, DAVID HABER, Professor of Law, Rutgers University, and NORMAN DORSEN, Professor of Law and Director of the Arthur Garfield Hays Civil Liberties Program, New York University

*Select Cases and Other Authorities on the Law of Trusts.* AUSTIN W. SCOTT, Dane Professor of Law, Emeritus, Harvard University, and AUSTIN W. SCOTT, JR., late Professor of Law, University of Colorado

*An Introduction to Criminal Justice: Text and Cases.* ORVILL C. SNYDER, Professor of Law, Emeritus, Brooklyn Law School

*The Civil Law System: Cases and Materials for the Comparative Study of Law.* ARTHUR TAYLOR VON MEHREN, Professor of Law, Harvard University

*The Law of Multistate Problems: Cases and Materials on Conflict of Laws.* ARTHUR TAYLOR VON MEHREN, Professor of Law, Harvard University, and DONALD THEODORE TRAUTMAN, Professor of Law, Harvard University

*Labor Relations and the Law.* Third Edition. Edited by JERRE WILLIAMS, Rex G. and Edna Heflin Baker Professor of Constitutional Law, University of Texas, and BENJAMIN AARON, Professor of Law and Director, Institute of Industrial Relations, University of California at Los Angeles

*Cases on Contracts.* SAMUEL WILLISTON, late Dane Professor of Law, Harvard University, Revised Sixth Edition by WILLIAM T. LAUBE, A. F. and May T. Morrison Professor of Law, University of California at Berkeley

## Law School Textbook Series

*American Civil Procedure.* WILLIAM WIRT BLUME, Professor of Law, University of California, Hastings College of Law

*Readings in Jurisprudence and Legal Philosophy.* MORRIS R. COHEN, late Professor of Law, City College of New York, and FELIX S. COHEN, late Visiting Professor of Law, City College of New York, and Visiting Lecturer, Yale University

*The Elements of Law.* THOMAS E. DAVITT, S.J., Professor of Jurisprudence, Marquette University

*Handbook of Modern Equity.* Second Edition. WILLIAM Q. DE FUNIAK, Professor of Law, McGeorge School of Law

*Judicial Control of Administrative Action.* Abridged Student Edition. LOUIS L. JAFFE, Byrne Professor of Administrative Law, Harvard University

*Civil Procedure.* FLEMING JAMES, JR., Lafayette S. Foster Professor of Law, Yale University

*Trial Tactics and Methods.* ROBERT E. KEETON, Professor of Law, Harvard University

*Securities Regulation.* Student Edition. LOUIS LOSS, William Nelson Cromwell Professor of Law, Harvard University

*Effective Legal Research.* Third Edition. MILES O. PRICE, late Professor of Law and Law Librarian, Columbia University, and HARRY BITNER, Professor of Law and Law Librarian, Cornell University

*Scott's Abridgment of the Law of Trusts.* AUSTIN W. SCOTT, Dane Professor of Law, Emeritus, Harvard University

*Handbook of Law Study.* FERDINAND FAIRFAX STONE, W. R. Irby Professor of Law and Director of Institute of Comparative Law, Tulane University

*Materials on the Lawyer's Professional Responsibility.* WILLIAM M. TRUMBULL, Professor of Law, Emeritus, Northwestern University

# Effective Legal Research

## THIRD EDITION

### MILES O. PRICE, B.S., B.L.S., LL.B., LL.D.
*Late Law Librarian Emeritus and Professor of Law Emeritus,*
*Columbia University*

### HARRY BITNER, A.B., B.L.S., J.D.
*Law Librarian and Professor of Law,*
*Cornell University Law Library*

LITTLE, BROWN AND COMPANY
*Boston*          1969          *Toronto*

*Published simultaneously in Canada*
*by Little, Brown & Company (Canada) Limited*
PRINTED IN THE UNITED STATES OF AMERICA

*To*
*F. J. P. and A. B.*

# Foreword to the Law Student

According to England's King George III, a lawyer is not a person who knows the law, but one who knows where to find it. This is not entirely so, but let us assume for the moment that it is. The lawyer finds the law principally in books housed in law libraries, so that a lawyer and a law library are inseparable.

Law books, as you may have already observed, are as multitudinous as they are voluminous. Their contents are revealed in still another voluminous host of specialized books of index, which the lawyer consults regularly in attempting to find the law. Once he has succeeded in his search, he is then able to perform another function of the lawyer; namely, evaluating the law and utilizing his conclusions in counseling clients and persuading courts. Hence, the well-equipped lawyer is one who, first of all, is thoroughly familiar with the tools of his profession. He has a priceless advantage over the one less so equipped.

What is true of the lawyer in this respect is even more so of the law student. He is in a strange world in his first year of law school. However much or little he may have read books in his undergraduate days, he has no choice in law school. He must live with a high, wide and sometimes frightening mountain of reading materials. At first they may seem to be put together in such an illogical manner as to defy successful attack. But the lawyer's very necessity of finding the law has brought order out of this seeming chaos by calling forth from the publishers the guides, indexes and other means of approach to the law not found so abundantly in any other literature.

It is the function of courses in the use of law books to acquaint law students, as embryonic lawyers, with the tools of their profession. As such, these courses truly epitomize the "bread and butter" approach in the law school curriculum.

# Preface to the Student Edition Revised (1962)

This Student Edition Revised, of Price and Bitner's Effective
Legal Research, has been written to meet the requests of those
teachers using Price and Bitner, who desire a book for instructional purposes which, while covering thoroughly the ground of
the parent book will do so in somewhat more simplified form.
Accordingly, certain text materials of a historical nature or more
intensive coverage than is perhaps needed for student instruction
have not been included within the scope of this edition. The
bibliographical appendices have also been omitted. The manual
of citation forms has been abridged and the list of abbreviations
used by lawyers and law students has been abridged; the student is
advised to consult for these materials the parent book, or, for citations, Miles O. Price's Practical Manual of Standard Legal Citations (2d ed. 1958).

The many changes in legal publications in the nine years since
the publication of Effective Legal Research are reflected in the
text of this revision. In both the original edition and revision,
the authors have received unstinted help from many colleagues.
These included, among others assisting in the composition of the
first edition, Fred B. Rothman, Meira Pimsleur, Charles J. Zinn,
Minnie Wiener, Jean Ashman, James B. Childs, Maurice Maxwell,
John Burke, Howard Drake, George A. Johnston, Leonard G.
Wrinch, William T. Hibbitt, Pauline E. Gee, and, especially,
many members of the Columbia Law Library staff. To these
should be added, as making valuable suggestions in the writing of
the Student Edition Revised, Professor Cyril McDermott, of St.
John's University Law School, and Anne Brown and Georgina
Broad, of Osgoode Hall, Toronto. Professors Albert Blaustein,
of the South Jersey branch of the Rutgers University Law School,
and J. Myron Jacobstein, of the University of Colorado Law
School, have made many valuable suggestions. Especial thanks go
to Professor Mortimer Schwartz, of the University of Oklahoma
Law School, who read and criticized the manuscript. Miss Edith
Hary and her staff at the Maine State Law Library were especially
helpful, as has been Pauline G. Wildman.

The following publishers have graciously permitted the reproduction in this book of material published by them, and have

been helpful in other ways: American Law Book Co.; Butterworth and Co.; Carswell Co., Ltd.; Commerce Clearing House, Inc.; Annotated Reports System; Little, Brown and Co.; Prentice-Hall, Inc.; Shepard's Citations, Inc.; Sweet & Maxwell Ltd.; the West Publishing Co.; and the Allen Smith Co. Extra special appreciation is due Miss Marjory P. Herrick, whose meticulous but kindly copy editing has contributed much.

To all others who have so generously helped the authors with both editions of Effective Legal Research, they say a blanket "Thank You!"

MILES O. PRICE
HARRY BITNER

*Columbia University*
*Yale University*

# Preface to the Third Edition

Miles O. Price passed away August 18, 1968. Prior to his death, he had completed his work of revision for the third edition. A few minor changes and the inclusion of some recent publications have been made by the co-author.

In addition to the acknowledgments for the previous editions, all of whom deserve continued recognition, others deserve special mention for this new edition: Professor Balfour Halevy, York University School of Law, Toronto, Canada, and Mr. D. C. Eberhart, Director, Office of the Federal Register. The members of the staff of the Cornell Law Library deserve mention for their help, particularly my secretary, Miss Crystal Bolton, for many hours of typing and general assistance.

HARRY BITNER

*Cornell University*
*April, 1969*

# Summary of Contents

## *Appendixes*

# Table of Contents

CHAPTER 5

LEGISLATIVE HISTORIES

CHAPTER 6

INDEXES AND TABLES FOR WORK WITH
FEDERAL STATUTES

CHAPTER 7

STATE LEGISLATION

CHAPTER 8

RULES OF COURT AND ADMINISTRATIVE
AGENCIES

CHAPTER 9

LAW REPORTS: RATIONALE, FORMAT
AND USE OF AS PRECEDENT

CHAPTER 10

## LAW REPORTS: DECISIONS OF FEDERAL AND STATE COURTS

CHAPTER 11

## LAW REPORTS: THE NATIONAL REPORTER SYSTEM

CHAPTER 12

## LAW REPORTS: SELECTIVE AND SPECIAL-SUBJECT SYSTEMS

CHAPTER 13

## LAW REPORTS: TABULAR MEANS FOR FINDING

CHAPTER 18

CITATORS

CHAPTER 19

TREATISES AND AMERICAN LAW INSTITUTE
RESTATEMENTS OF THE COMMON LAW

CHAPTER 20

# LEGAL PERIODICALS

CHAPTER 21

# DICTIONARIES; WORDS AND PHRASES; MAXIMS

CHAPTER 22

# FORM BOOKS; APPEAL PAPERS; DIRECTORIES

CHAPTER 23

# LOOSE-LEAF SERVICES OR TOPICAL REPORTS

CHAPTER 24

# ENGLISH AND CANADIAN MATERIALS

CHAPTER 25

COORDINATING THE RESEARCH TECHNIQUES

CHAPTER 26

STANDARD LEGAL CITATION FORMS

## Appendixes

# Effective Legal Research

# Introduction[1]

**§1.1.   Law books and their use as affected by the nature of law.**
Lawyers and law students cannot function away from a working
law library.   In law books are found the statutes and judicial
opinions which are the actual and indispensable source materials
of the law, as well as the various types of reference works and
indexes which aid in finding the law and in interpreting and
appraising its weight as authority when found.

Law books differ greatly in form and use from those in other
fields.   This difference is based upon the mutable nature of law
itself, which demands far greater promptness of publication and
supplementation of its repositories, and more precise indexing
than does the literature of other disciplines.   A practical definition
of the law is that it is the aggregate of rules recognized and acted
upon by courts of justice.   These rules, in the Anglo-American
system, are found both in the common law embodied in the decisions of courts, and in legislation.   Since there are few constants in
law, but continual change, these changes and the means for
keeping abreast of them vitally affect law books' composition,
publication and use.   Changes may be slow, as in a common-law
rule gradually modified by judicial decision; or sudden and drastic,
as in the overruling of a long-established judicial precedent, or the
enactment of a statute changing a common-law rule.

The rules of the common law are stated in decisions of courts of
competent jurisdiction, and grow by a process of synthesis from
these decisions.   As social conditions change, decisional law tends
to change with them, thus modifying and changing the common
law.   But it is a slow process.   Classic examples of this slow
process are the overruling of *Swift* v. *Tyson,* 16 Pet. 1, 10 L. Ed.
865 (1842), by the decision in *Erie Railroad* v. *Tompkins,* 304
U.S. 64, 58 Sup. Ct. 817, 82 L. Ed. 787, 114 A.L.R. 1487 (1938),

---

1 The authors acknowledge with thanks the counsel of Professor Cyril McDermott,
of St. John's University Law School, in preparing this introduction.   See also Note,
page 10.

upsetting a doctrine which throughout its nine and one-half decades of existence had been an established precedent; and of *Haddock* v. *Haddock,* 201 U.S. 562, 26 Sup. Ct. 525, 50 L. Ed. 867 (1906), by *Williams* v. *North Carolina,* 317 U.S. 287, 63 Sup. Ct. 207, 87 L. Ed. 279, 143 A.L.R. 1273 (1942). The *Haddock* case had been for nearly two generations undisputed authority for the proposition that the divorce decree of a state in which the plaintiff only is resident and in which the parties have never cohabited or had their matrimonial domicile is not entitled to recognition in the courts of other states under the requirements of the Full Faith and Credit Clause of the Constitution, where the defendant is served constructively.

Some landmark precedents of long standing, though they have been hacked at and eroded by subsequent decisions, law revision commission reports and highly critical law review articles, nevertheless remain at the core unchanged. Notable among this type of cases are those in the majority of states which deny liability for injuries or death brought on exclusively by fright to the injured or deceased person, without any impact. The classic illustration of this is *Mitchell* v. *Rochester Railway,* 151 N.Y. 107, 45 N.E. 354 (1896), which, though frequently excepted to, circumvented and criticized by the courts of New York, was never squarely overruled until the case of *Batella* v. *State,* 10 N.Y.2d 237, 176 N.E.2d 729, 219 N.Y.S. 2d 34 (1961).

Legislation is the product of legally constituted bodies authorized to make rules governing future conduct. These rules are binding within the competence and jurisdiction of the body creating them. For example, federal, state and municipal legislative bodies create statutes and rules of a substantive nature, while courts and administrative agencies make adjective rules which regulate procedure before them. None of these rules remain constant. They are subject to interpretation by courts to determine their meaning, and they may be further amended, repealed or extended by the particular body which promulgated them.

Thus there is an enormous and constantly changing mass of decisions and legislative enactments and rules from which the lawyer must speedily and accurately extract the law applicable to his specific problem, so as to be able to predict with some degree of certainty the action of a court to which the problem may be presented. His task is immeasurably increased because these decisions as made and these rules as enacted are not published in a subject or classified arrangement, but, instead, by jurisdiction and date of decision or enactment.

**§1.2. Aim of the search: Authority.** Always, the lawyer searches for authority; that is, something which he can use to convince a court and which the court is bound to respect. Accordingly, practically all law books are either repositories of authority, indexes to authority, or some means for appraising the present value and status of authority.

1. *What is authority?* Anything which a court says or cites in its opinion, as leading to its decision in a given case, is authority of a kind, but the weight to be given it varies. Some is only persuasive and may be disregarded; other authority is mandatory and heed must be paid to it. Legal writers frequently classify legal authority as primary or secondary, further subdividing primary authority into mandatory and persuasive categories with respect to legislation and judicial decisions; and persuasive with respect to other legal writings. It is simple and accurate to place all legal authority within the framework of the two categories, mandatory and persuasive. Law books not falling within either of these frames of reference are considered as no authority at all, but merely indexes and tables to aid in finding and appraising authority.

2. *Mandatory authority.* This is authority which the courts must heed, though they may under the circumstances shown below sometimes find reason for not following it. It is found in both statutes and in judicial decisions.

a. *Legislation as mandatory authority.* Legislation in effect in the jurisdiction where enacted by legislatures or promulgated legislatively by other competent bodies (as are the rules of courts or administrative bodies) is mandatory within the jurisdiction. Outside a jurisdiction which lacks any legislation on a given subject, other legislation from other jurisdictions covering the subject is not even persuasive authority. The decisions of the courts of other jurisdictions interpreting their own legislation are, however, persuasive authority. An example of the latter is when a statute which has been copied from a similar law in another jurisdiction comes before a court for the first time for interpretation. There are, of course, no precedents in the court of the forum. Then a well-considered decision on a like statute from a court of another jurisdiction, interpreting its similar statute, may be highly persuasive by force of its good reasoning, though it is in no way binding or imperative. If a court in one jurisdiction follows the reasoning of other state courts and reaches the same conclusion, such out-of-state decisions thus clearly constitute persuasive, though not binding, authority.

Furthermore, the legislation of other states may well be considered persuasive where the constitutionality of a new statute is challenged and is in issue, and the courts of other states have construed like legislation.    Thus the United States Supreme Court cited statutes limiting hours of labor for women, from nineteen states and seven foreign countries, in upholding the constitutionality of an Oregon statute limiting the hours of labor for women.    *Muller* v. *Oregon,* 208 U.S. 412, 419, 28 Sup. Ct. 324, 52 L. Ed. 551 (1908).

Other persuasive authorities in interpretation of statutes are documents bearing on the legislative history and background of a statute, as indicative of legislative intent.    Similarly persuasive may be the reports of law revision commissions, judicial councils and the opinions of attorneys general related to a statute in issue before the court.

Outstanding examples of legislation completely superseding and replacing the common law rule are the widespread enactment of workmen's compensation laws; terminating the common law liability of a husband for his wife's torts; and the abolition of the old "heart balm" suits for breach of promise of marriage.

b. *Judicial decisions as mandatory authority.*    These, when direct or "square" holdings, are mandatory authority when from a higher court in the same jurisdiction or from the same court itself.    This is because, when a court of competent jurisdiction hands down a decision, that decision establishes a precedent binding upon the court rendering it and upon courts subordinate to it, until and unless it is reversed on appeal to a higher court, or is overruled by the same court in another and later case (as the *Tyson* and *Haddock* cases in §1.1), or the subject matter is changed by statute.    The fact of subordination binds the lower court; the policy of uniformity binds the court making the decision.    In the latter situation, however, the court has both the right and the duty to overrule a former decision which it now deems, for any reason, to have been erroneous or not applicable to present conditions.    When the status of a decision as authority is affected by later decisions or legislation, the fact is noted in a citator, described in Chapter 18.

3. *Persuasive authority.*    Persuasive authority persuades, it does not command.    Because of the cogency of its reasoning, or the high standing of the court deciding a case, or of the author of a treatise or legal periodical article, it may tend to sway the court, even though it is in no way binding upon it.    Legislation from another jurisdiction is of itself, as noted above, of no authority, but a decision construing it may be.

Decisions may be persuasive authority when (1) they are from coordinate courts of the same jurisdiction (as from one or more of the Circuits of the United States Court of Appeals, or of the four Departments of the Appellate Division of the New York Supreme Court); (2) they involve dictum from any court in any jurisdiction; (3) they are from courts of another jurisdiction, both as to decisional law and the interpretation of statutes similar to those of the forum, as noted above. New York courts, for example, cite Texas decisions and American courts cite English decisions — but only as persuasive makeweights to support their own views. When a court in one jurisdiction necessarily construes the law of another, however, the decisions of that other jurisdiction as to its own law are controlling; but even here the court of the forum does not really hold that authority to be fully mandatory, but reserves an "escape hatch" (such as the existence of different conditions or policies) to enable it to get out from under if it so desires.

4. *Authority as between federal and state courts.* A decision of the United States Supreme Court interpreting federal legislation, including the Constitution, is mandatory on state and federal courts alike as to the principle stated. In matters of local state law, however, a Supreme Court decision is mandatory only on federal courts; it is only persuasive in the state courts. Conversely, the pronouncements of the highest state courts as to their own law are binding on federal courts unless a federal constitutional question is involved. In the absence of rulings by the highest state courts, those of the intermediate state courts are at least of persuasive authority, but those of a state trial court which does not publish or index its reports are not binding precedent upon federal courts. *King* v. *Order of United Commercial Travelers,* 333 U.S. 153, 68 Sup. Ct. 488, 92 L. Ed. 608 (1948). For a good discussion of the relation between federal and state courts as to this question, see 1 Moore, Federal Practice ¶0.402 (1959).

5. *Dictum as authority.* Dicta are remarks made by a court in an opinion, concerning a rule of law not necessarily involved in the case or essential to its determination. They are for background or illustration; they are not adjudications. (See §9.7 for a discussion of this point.) Strictly speaking, dictum has no authority at all, but this is too academic a view to take of it. In actual practice, well-considered dicta are often persuasive, some so much so that after many years their original status as dicta is often overlooked or forgotten, and they are cited as authority.

6. *Secondary authority: Treatises, encyclopedias, Restatements of the American Law Institute, law review articles.* Commentaries on the law by authors not acting at the time in a judicial capacity, sometimes called "secondary authority," may nevertheless be

highly persuasive. Although they are only statements of the opinion of their authors, based upon their analysis of legislation and judicial decisions and as such not binding in any way upon the courts, they are frequently cited by the courts in their opinions, and in other legal writing.

**§1.3. Role of stare decisis in law book making.** The significance of the various degrees and kinds of authority stems from the rule of stare decisis which under our common law system so largely controls judicial decisions. A brief statement about this rule — concerning which more is said in §9.7 — is that, under a precise set of facts, "a deliberate or solemn decision of a court or judge, made after full argument on a question of law fairly arising in a case and necessary to its determination, is an authority or binding precedent in the same court, or in other courts of . . . lower ranks within the same jurisdiction, in subsequent cases where the very same point is again presented. . . ." The aim of the doctrine is certainty.

The doctrine functions somewhat as a graph, upon which every decision in point is represented as a dot. When a figurative line is drawn through all of these dots, a curve or trend of decision is discernible, enabling the lawyer to predict with some degree of certainty judicial action upon a like set of facts in the future. The curve or trend is the statement of a legal principle, distilled from the decided cases and applicable in like future cases.

**§1.4. Law book characteristics.** Because mandatory authority is usually published in the law books in chronological order for each jurisdiction — that is, by the date of a statutory enactment or the handing down of a judicial decision — rather than in classified or subject order; and because the latest statute or decision may substantially affect a legal rule, law books have quite definite characteristics. A knowledge of these is essential to the searcher. Most law books strongly resemble one another. Thus the familiar National Reporter System "advance sheet" is to a considerable extent the epitome of law books. It has a *table of cases* — the most nearly universal of all law book features; a *table of statutes construed* — a form of citator found in many law books; a *list of words and phrases judicially defined;* and a *digest* in miniature of the cases reported in a particular issue of the advance sheet — which is an elaborate index forming the lawyer's most necessary tool for extracting the rules of case law. Another useful feature of some law books is the *transfer* or *parallel conversion table.* Almost always, where there is a change from one form of statute to another (as from session law to the compiled, subject matter arrangement), or where there is more than one series of law reports (as official, National Reporter System or American Law Reports Annotated), there is such a table, giving all forms of citations so that the lawyer who has access to only one form in his library can find it from the citation given from the other form.

1. *What to look for when consulting a law book.* First, ascertain what the book covers — both as to subject matter, legislative session, law report volume and page, and dates — and how it is put together. The *title page* tells who wrote or edited the book, what it is about, and the date of publication. Supplements to the main work note the dates of later statutes and volumes of law reports covered by them. *Tables of contents* furnish clues to the organization of the book. *Tables of abbreviations* sufficient for the purposes of the individual work covered are frequent and useful features.

2. *Publication dates and their importance.* The *date* of a statute, case, treatise or citator is one of its most vital elements in legal research. Superseded authority is not only not useful but dangerous when relied upon. A digest, practitioners' treatise, or a citator depends for much of its value upon how recent it is. The searcher should, therefore, acquire the invariable habit of looking at both the date of publication and the dates covered by the material in the book — both usually noted on the title page. Nearly all types of law books aim to keep up with the very latest developments of statute or case law. Therefore, law books are geared to speed of original publication and to frequency of supplementation.

Make it an invariable habit to see whether what is wanted by you is covered by the *main work* or by a *supplement*. The supplement is quite likely to be a "pocket part," inserted in the back of the main volume and keyed to that volume so as to bring its sections up to date and also to add new sections or other material as needed. Often the new material totally revises or repeals much that is in the main volume. It should become second nature to you to check both the main volumes and the supplements in your search, to make certain that you have covered the ground.

3. *Tools for using law books as a means for finding and appraising the law.* Statutes and reported cases are by far the best and most promptly indexed of all professional literature. Without books of index you would be helpless in your search for the law; with them it is possible to extract the legal principles set forth in every reported American case, down to within a few days; to find

such a case by its name, its subject matter and its place of publication; and to tell whether it is still good authority. This can also be done for statutes and for English and Canadian material. These tools are variously known as indexes, tables, digests, citators, form books, treatises, legal encyclopedias, periodicals and dictionaries. Their makeup and use are described in this book. They are the necessary tools of your trade.

4. *Note on Computerized Means of Search.* A revolutionary search technique has appeared: the use of the computer, as applied especially to statutes and law reports. Several such subscription services are available. So far, they supply statutory or case references through extremely detailed subject indexes but do not Shepardize the references cited. While these services are not yet widely used, there can be no doubt of their eventual importance. An example is the Automated Statutory Reporter, a publication of Aspen Systems Corporation, Pittsburgh, Pennsylvania. In this connection, the CCH Advance Session Laws Reporter (one for each state) offers speedy copies of the actual text of laws of business interest.

The Law Research Service, Inc.: Legal Service by Computer, covers 17 different main topics, such as domestic relations, patents, trade-marks, etc. Each "thesaurus" is a loose-leaf affair, arranged as a descriptive-word index, references being to a ten-digit number, which the searcher sends to the New York office, which then sends him his references by Telex, telephone, or mail.

# CHAPTER 2

# Types and Importance of Legislation

**§2.1. "Conventional" and "subordinate" legislation and their importance.** A major category of primary legal authority is legislation, and the search for the law usually begins with the effort to find applicable legislation; later the search turns to the cases. Nearly every case now reaching the Supreme Court of the United States is concerned with a statute. While legislation is usually thought of by the laymen as the enactments of the federal Congress and of the various state legislatures, it also includes "subordinate" legislation, much of which has a considerably more direct impact upon the average citizen than the product of the legislatures.

1. *Conventional legislation.* This is usually thought of as the output of the legislatures, but it comprises also constitutions, treaties and interstate compacts. Municipal ordinances are regarded in some states as conventional legislation (as "local" laws), and in others as subordinate, delegated legislation.

2. *Subordinate legislation.* Authorized by delegating conventional legislation, subordinate legislation comprises rules and regulations of administrative bodies, executive orders and proclamations of the President of the United States and of the governors of states, municipal ordinances (in some states), and the rules of courts. The most important subordinate legislation is put out under the authority of specific enabling legislation — that is, it is delegated legislation — but much of it is under the inherent authority of an administrative or judicial body to get its work done, such as to promulgate rules for the transaction of its business. In the aggregate, this subordinate legislation is vastly important and has given rise to law books (loose-leaf services, for example) unknown to earlier generations of lawyers.

**§2.2. Classes of conventional legislation and their authority.** Nearly all that is written here on federal legislation applies equally to state legislation, for which see Chapter 7.

1. *Constitutional provisions as to federal laws.* Provisions relating to federal legislation are Article I, §8, clause 18; Article I,

§7, clause 2; and Article VI, clause 2. Judicial interpretation of these three paragraphs restricts the designation "law" to three categories of legislation: the act, the joint resolution, and the treaty. The approval of an interstate compact is by joint resolution. There is some question as to whether or not the reorganization plan, a form discussed in Chapter 14, may be formally designated as law. However, there can be no doubt that when approved under the terms of a reorganization act such a plan has the force of law.

2. *Conventional federal legislation below the constitutional level.* Federal conventional legislation in this category comprises the following forms, most but not all of which are duplicated in state legislation:

Simple, concurrent and joint resolutions; acts, treaties and interstate compacts. The last two forms might be designated as hybrid legislation, since they require the action of an agency outside the Congress. Acts and joint resolutions, for convenience, are further subdivided into "public" and "private," but legally there is no distinction, as both have equally the force of law.

a. *Congressional legislation not having the force of law.* Three categories of Congressional legislation are called resolutions: the "resolution" (commonly called "simple resolution"), the "concurrent resolution" and the "joint resolution." The first two named do not have the force of law.

(1) *Resolutions or simple resolutions.* These have no legislative effect outside the house in which they originate. They concern only the business of the one house passing them. Creation and appointment of committees (other than joint, which are created by concurrent resolution), inquiries addressed to government departments, and directing an investigation by a committee (other than by a joint committee) are by simple resolution.

The text of many but not all simple resolutions, as passed, is found in the Congressional Record as of the day of passage, and they are also printed in the Journal of the house passing them. They are indexed in the Congressional Record index, and, by subject only, in the Congressional Record Daily Digest.

(2) *Concurrent resolutions.* The concurrent resolution is, in form, one passed by both houses of Congress. It is binding upon neither house until agreed to by both, and it is not signed by the President. Its purpose is to create and appoint joint committees and to arrange for joint sessions of the two houses. A modern use is to disapprove of reorganization plans submitted by the President. An important and frequently exercised function is to recall a bill from enrollment, subsequent to passage by both houses but

86TH CONGRESS
2D SESSION

# H. RES. 399

---

## IN THE HOUSE OF REPRESENTATIVES

JANUARY 6, 1960

Mr. CANNON submitted the following resolution; which was considered
and agreed to

---

# RESOLUTION

1    *Resolved,* That the Clerk of the House inform the Senate

2  that a quorum of the House is present and that the House is

3  ready to proceed with business.

V

---

86TH CONGRESS
2D SESSION

# S. RES. 205

---

## IN THE SENATE OF THE UNITED STATES

JANUARY 6, 1960

Mr. DIRKSEN submitted the following resolution; which was considered and
agreed to

---

# RESOLUTION

1    *Resolved,* That the Secretary inform the House of Rep-

2  resentatives that a quorum of the Senate is assembled and

3  that the Senate is ready to proceed to business.

V

Exhibit 1

86TH CONGRESS
2D SESSION

# H. CON. RES. 443

---

## IN THE HOUSE OF REPRESENTATIVES

JANUARY 6, 1960

Mr. McCORMACK submitted the following resolution; which was considered and agreed to

---

## CONCURRENT RESOLUTION

1     *Resolved by the House of Representatives (the Senate*

2     *concurring)*, That the two Houses of Congress assemble in

3     the Hall of the House of Representatives on Thursday, Jan-

4     uary 7, 1960, at 12:30 o'clock postmeridian, for the pur-

---

86TH CONGRESS
2D SESSION

# S. CON. RES. 80

---

## IN THE HOUSE OF REPRESENTATIVES

FEBRUARY 10, 1960

Referred to the Committee on House Administration

---

## CONCURRENT RESOLUTION

1     *Resolved by the Senate (the House of Representatives*

2     *concurring)*, That there be printed for the use of the Com-

3     mittee on Armed Services one thousand additional copies of

4     part 1 of the hearings held by that committee on an inquiry

Exhibit 2

prior to Presidential approval, for correction. Concurrent resolutions are printed in the United States Statutes at Large.

b. *Acts of Congress.* Acts are the most common form of Congressional legislation. They are referred to as bills in the house in which they originate, in contrast to the designations of the various forms of resolutions. Bills are designated simply as H.R. 8238 (for House of Representatives) or S. 19 (for Senate) of the respective Congresses. See Exhibit 3 below. After passage as bills by the originating house, they are called acts upon introduction or re-introduction in the other house. Bills become acts of Congress when they have passed both houses, have been prepared for the President's signature and then have been approved by him or passed over his veto by a two-thirds vote of quorums present in *both* houses.

c. *Joint resolutions.* In federal legislation the joint resolution is a law, just as is an act. Joint resolutions proposing constitutional amendments, having passed both houses, do not have to be submitted to the President for his signature like other joint resolutions. It is said that the joint resolution has a preamble more often than does an act, but both acts and joint resolutions have equally the force of law in federal legislation. In some states, however, the joint resolution has a lesser status than the act. See Exhibit 4 below.

d. *Interstate compacts.* These are sanctioned by Article I, section 10, clause 3 of the Constitution, to the effect that "No state shall, without the Consent of Congress, . . . enter into any agreement . . . with another state . . ." The compacts themselves are not enacted by Congress as a separate form of federal legislation, but are created by the states concerned. What Congress does is to give its consent by an act or joint resolution, or by its approval of a state constitution embodying the compact. Consent may also be inferred from Congressional acts recognizing the validity of the agreement. Approval may be given either before or after the states have entered into their compact. The compact is effected by parallel enactments by the several state legislatures involved. Such compacts are commonly used to settle boundary disputes and to provide for various kinds of cooperative state action, particularly in the development of natural resources and of interstate transportation facilities. As public laws, the texts of compacts are in the United States Statutes at Large and in the session laws of the states concerned; the consents of Congress are printed in the United States Code Congressional and Administrative News. Not being of general interest, compacts are not codified in the U.S. Code. A list of all interstate compacts entered into up to 1956 is contained in Interstate Compacts, 1783-1956, published by the Council of State Governments.

---

86TH CONGRESS
2D SESSION

# H. R. 12262

---

### IN THE HOUSE OF REPRESENTATIVES

MAY 17, 1960

Mr. SANTANGELO introduced the following bill; which was referred to the Committee on the Judiciary

---

# A BILL

To amend section 353 (3) of the Immigration and Nationality Act.

1      *Be it enacted by the Senate and House of Representa-*

2   *tives of the United States of America in Congress assembled,*

3    That section 353 (3) of the Immigration and Nationality

---

86TH CONGRESS
2D SESSION

# S. 3230

---

### IN THE SENATE OF THE UNITED STATES

MARCH 18, 1960

Mr. BUTLER introduced the following bill; which was read twice and referred to the Committee on the Judiciary

---

# A BILL

To amend section 35 of title 18 of the United States Code so as to increase the punishment for knowingly giving false information concerning destruction of aircraft and motor vehicles.

1      *Be it enacted by the Senate and House of Representa-*

2   *tives of the United States of America in Congress assembled,*

3    That section 35 of title 18 of the United States Code is

---

**Exhibit 3**

86TH CONGRESS
2D SESSION

# H. J. RES. 541

## IN THE HOUSE OF REPRESENTATIVES

JANUARY 6, 1960

Mr. LOSER introduced the following joint resolution; which was referred to the Committee on the Judiciary

# JOINT RESOLUTION

Authorizing and requesting the President to set aside and proclaim the Tuesday following the second Monday in June of each year as "National Fraternal Day".

1    *Resolved by the Senate and House of Representatives*

2    *of the United States of America in Congress assembled,*

3    That the President is authorized and requested to issue a

---

86TH CONGRESS
2D SESSION

# S. J. RES. 196

## IN THE SENATE OF THE UNITED STATES

MAY 23, 1960

Mr. MAGNUSON introduced the following joint resolution; which was read twice and referred to the Committee on the Judiciary

# JOINT RESOLUTION

To provide for the designation of June 20, 1960, as "National Academy of Television Arts and Sciences Day".

1    *Resolved by the Senate and House of Representatives*

2    *of the United States of America in Congress assembled,*

3    That the President is authorized and requested to issue a

Exhibit 4

e. *Reorganization plans.* Although reorganization plans are printed in the Statutes at Large and require action by the Congress, they are nearer to administrative law than to conventional legislation, and so are discussed in Chapter 14.

f. *Treaties.* Treaties are discussed in Chapter 4.

g. *Pre-Constitutional period federal legislation.* Federal legislation begins with the Constitutional period, 1789, but there was legislation under the Articles of Confederation from 1784 to 1788, preceding the adoption of the Constitution. The enactments were called Ordinances, and are to be found in the·Journals of the Continental Congress. The Ordinance of 1787 is significant today because it set up the governmental and legal system of the states north of the Ohio River and had a profound effect upon the laws of many of the states then called the Northwest Territory. It is printed in all editions of the United States Code and in the compiled statutes of some of the above states.

3. *Confederate States of America legislation, 1861-1865.* The Confederacy legislated throughout its existence. It is mentioned here because there has been litigation on some of it, as noted in the Table of Statutes Construed in the Digest of the United States Supreme Court Reports.

# CHAPTER 3

# Publication of Conventional
# Federal Legislation

**§3.1.   Federal Constitution.**   The Federal Constitution is readily available in many editions.   Although the unannotated text of the Constitution is found in many statute books, an annotated edition — digesting cases construing the Constitution — is essential for the lawyer who is seeking an interpretation of a particular section or clause.   There are three such editions in common use.

1. *Library of Congress edition.* The Constitution of the United States of America; Analysis and Interpretation.   Annotations of Cases Decided by the Supreme Court of the United States to June 22, 1964. . . . Washington, D.C., U.S. Government Printing Office, 1964.

This is a useful edition for those seeking a good basic knowledge of the Constitution rather than every case which has construed it. It is in effect an encyclopedic treatment of the Constitution.   It contains a "literal print" of the text and amendments, convenient for those who need only a speedy finding of the bare text.   A useful feature is a detailed account of the ratification of the several amendments by the various states.   The Constitution is then annotated, word for word.   This edition is virtually a Constitutional history, annotated to the leading cases.   Under each clause or section is set forth not only the current interpretation, but also a history of the legal route which the courts have traversed in arriving at their present interpretation.   The range of source materials in the annotations includes citations to and quotations from both federal and state court decisions, as well as from commentaries and treatises, arguments of counsel, and occasionally federal statutes.   A unique citator function, to the edition's publication date, is performed by three tables: (1) federal and (2) state acts held unconstitutional in whole or in part by the

Supreme Court, and (3) earlier Supreme Court decisions subsequently overruled. This edition is an updating and partial reorganization of the Corwin edition of 1952. It is not regularly supplemented.

2. *Federal Code Annotated edition.*

3. *United States Code Annotated edition.* When the practicing lawyer requires a complete picture of the law of the Constitution relating to his precise problem, he consults a fully annotated edition which cites not only *all* the United States Supreme Court cases reasonably in point, but also those of the state courts. He wants also references to all relevant material such as opinions of the Attorneys General of the United States, Presidential executive orders and proclamations, Board of Tax Appeals and Tax Court decisions, and even occasional law review articles. These he will find in the Federal Code Annotated and in the United States Code Annotated, which have the added virtue of annual pocket part supplementation and frequent interim service pamphlets referring to the latest cases.

4. *State annotations to the Federal Constitution.* Some state statutory compilations annotate not only their own constitutions but also the Federal Constitution, to the decisions of their own appellate courts.

§3.2.  **Slip laws.** The first officially published form of Congressional legislation is in a separate pamphlet for each law, termed a slip law. This is the same text form as is later bound and indexed for each year as the United States Statutes at Large. The purpose of slip law publication is speed. Slip laws are published in two series, as Public and Private laws, containing, together, both the acts and joint resolutions of the Congress. Through the Seventy-sixth Congress (1939-1942), the Public and Private Joint Resolutions were published as two series, separate from the acts, but since then they have been merged as above, as public and private laws.

Public and private laws have equal legal status as law. The student, however, is likely to be little concerned with private legislation, which includes for the most part that passed for the benefit of an individual or group, not of direct or immediate interest to the government or to the public. Assignment as "public" or "private" is a matter of editorial discretion on the part of the Editor of Laws of the Administrator of General Service. A slip law is shown below, with numbered arrows pointing to its various parts.

The information given above "An Act" is for index or identification purposes only and is not a part of the enactment. As such it is useful and is repeated when published in the Statutes at Large.

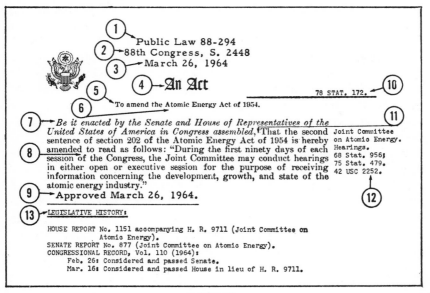

**Exhibit 5**

1. Law number.
2. Congress and bill number.
3. See 9.
4. Kind of legislation (here an Act).
5. Preamble.
6. Popular name or short title. See page 77.
7. Enacting clause; "Resolved" in a resolution.
8. Examples of two forms of statutory amendment: "perpetual revision" and that of inserting additional text. See page 103.

9. Approval date. If effective on a different date, that date is specified in the Act. When passed over the President's veto, that is indicated.
10. Statutes at Large citation for the Act as it will appear in bound form.
11. The first section of any act is unnumbered, but in legal writing it is cited, nevertheless, as "Section 1."
12. Editorial matter in the margin.
13. Legislative history. New, beginning with 88th Congress.

Until the issuance of the bound volume of the Statutes at Large — usually about fourteen months after the slip law publication — the law and bill numbers together are the law's identification tag.

In the example above, the matter in the margin has been inserted in slip laws only since mid-1951. It corresponds to similar rubrics in the Statutes at Large edition. The Statutes at Large citation given there for each act, while subject to correction in the published volume, is undoubtedly correct. When this citation on the slip law appears ahead of the preamble to the act, it means that the entire law is on the page given; thus all of Public Law 88-294 is printed on page 172 of volume 78 (the index material above the preamble being, in the Statutes at Large, printed in the margin at the same level as the preamble). When the text of an act begins elsewhere on the page, the exact place of beginning and the words at the tops of the second and succeeding pages of the law as in the Statutes at Large are indicated. Thus, in citing from a slip law, the Statutes at Large citation should be given. This is a matter of convenience to the reader of the citation, since so many will have the Statutes at Large on their shelves but not the slip law form. The full volume and page citation to the Statutes at Large is given also in the United States Code Congressional and Administrative News print of the slip laws.

Prior to the Eighty-fifth Congress, chapter numbers were used to indicate the order of approval of bills during a session of Congress. Chapter numbering was consecutive, with public and private laws in a single series. These chapter numbers will still be found in the Statutes at Large covering Congress preceding the Eighty-fifth. Now, all *public* laws are numbered consecutively in order of approval in *one* series, with *private* laws similarly numbered in *another* series.

It is still important to note that through the Seventy-fourth Congress all bills and their resulting enactments were renumbered at the beginning of each *session* of a two-year Congress, so that not only the number of the Congress but also the session were necessary parts of the citation. Beginning with the Seventy-fifth Congress in 1937, however, all bills and acts are numbered consecutively through an entire Congress.

The public laws are available by subscription from the United States Government Printing Office. They are published also in the unofficial United States Code Congressional and Administrative News, in semimonthly pamphlet issues which are much more convenient for the average user than are the official slip laws. These pamphlet issues are later cumulated into an annual volume. In both the official and unofficial publication forms above, the slip law is available about three weeks after date of approval. Some laws of great importance are also published in the unofficial United States Law Week within a week of approval.

Regarding the authority of official prints of slip laws, the courts take judicial notice of slip laws, without certification as positive law. 1 U.S.C. 113, as amended by 89-497, 80 Stat. 271 (1966).

**§3.3. United States Statutes at Large.** Slip laws representing the federal laws enacted during a session of Congress are cumulated into a permanent bound set known as the United States Statutes at Large. This is the first permanent version of federal legislation.

1. *Contents of the Statutes at Large.* Beginning with volume 65 in 1951, the Statutes at Large have contained only public and private laws, joint and concurrent resolutions, proclamations (but not executive orders) of the President, reorganization plans, and

Constitutional amendments.  The treaties and executive agreements of international import, formerly published in the Statutes at Large, are now printed in a new series called United States Treaties and Other International Agreements.

2. *Status of the Statutes at Large as legal authority: Four things to emphasize.*  The practicing lawyer is chiefly interested in public laws, and for him four things are emphasized:

a. *Best evidence.*  With the exception of sections of the United States Revised Statutes which are still in force, and those titles of the United States Code which have been reenacted into positive law (about one third of them), the Statutes at Large are still the "best evidence," to be cited in legal writing.  Those titles of the Code not so reenacted into positive law are only prima facie the law, which means that, in case of repugnance of text between the Code form and the original Statutes at Large, the Statutes at Large form governs.  This was pointed out by the court in *Royers, Inc.* v. *United States,* 265 F.2d 615, 618 (3d Cir. 1959), in reversing a judgment below based upon the Code text:

"We do not know what source of United States laws is used in the Commissioner's office but we would be surprised if they were not the same as that commonly used by a judge, namely, United States Code or United States Code Annotated.  The mistake, therefore, is perfectly natural.  But no one denies that the official source to find United States laws is the Statutes at Large and that the Code is only prima facie evidence for such laws."

In legal writing of all types, unless a statute has been reenacted as positive law in a code which thereby repeals it in its original form, it is as a Statute at Large that it is cited, together with its popular-name title, if any (as Immigration and Nationality Act of 1952).  The United States Code citation is usually added, merely for the convenience of those who have only the Code form at hand and not the Statutes at Large.  The section numbers cited in legal writing are those of the *original act, not of the Code,* unless the Code section has been reenacted as positive law, expressly repealing the original act from which derived.  The Code is so much more convenient to use that law students tend to forget that, with the exception of the titles which have been reenacted into positive law, the Code is only prima facie the law.

b. *Original form of the act.*  If the original form of an act — including the numbering of its sections — is desired, the Statutes at Large is the place to find it, not the Code.  Section numbering between the two forms is different and the order of the sections may be, also.  To be sure, there are conversion tables from the original act and its sections to the Code title and sections, but they often lead to error in the transfer.

c. *Uncodified acts in the Statutes at Large.* Many acts are not codified at all, not being of "public, general and permanent interest." Some which have been codified are only partly so, with other sections uncodified; that is, they have not been incorporated in the compilation of acts in subject arrangement which is entitled the United States Code. Revenue acts are examples of the latter.

d. *Tracing into the corresponding Code section.* Tracing a Statutes at Large section into its corresponding Code section is achieved through the use of Table III of the Code (for which see §6.6). Thus the Act of May 26, 1942, Chapter 319, §11, 56 Stat. 303 (1943), is in 12 U.S.C. §1743 (1964 ed.), as shown by that table.

Although for convenience the lawyer consults the Code for most purposes in his work with federal statutes, he may not ignore the legal evidence from which it was derived, the Statutes at Large.

3. *Form of the Statutes at Large.* The material in the Statutes at Large is copied verbatim from the original acts, reorganization plans, etc. The public and private laws are reprints of the slip laws, except that the identification material (bill number, etc.) is in the margin instead of at the top of each separate act. See Exhibit 6.

a. *Public law numbers.* The public law number indicates the chronological order of approval of the laws of each Congress by the President or passage over his veto. The first number stands for the Congress and should always be given when citing by public law number; thus, Public Law 86-366, not merely Public Law 366, as is often done. Every Congress has a Public Law 366. Private laws are also numbered consecutively in their own series.

b. *Index material in the margin.* This material is, as with the slip law form, intended for identification and index purposes. Therein are found the bill and public or private law numbers, and the date of approval. The approval date is the one used in citing federal acts. Also in the margin are rubrics comparable to the headnotes of a case, in that they index the matter in the paragraphs they adjoin. They may save much time when the searcher is interested in only one or a few sections of a long act and does not know the section number, since they lead swiftly to what he wants. They also identify by exact citation amended acts mentioned in the adjoining text only by name or date, and thus save the searcher from forced recourse to transfer tables.

c. *Tables and Index.* Preceding the Table of Contents of each volume is the authentication of legislation contained therein. This is a common feature of statute volumes, a statement indicating the authority of the publication of the laws printed therein. Then follow the List of Public Laws [or Private, in another table]

**156**                  **PUBLIC LAW 86-73—JUNE 30, 1959**          **[73 STAT.**

Public Law 86-73

June 30, 1959
[H. R. 2256]

AN ACT

To amend chapter 37 of title 38, United States Code, to provide additional funds for direct loans; to remove certain requirements with respect to the rate of interest on guaranteed loans; and for other purposes.

Veterans.
Home, farm and
business loans.
72 Stat. 1203.

*Be it enacted by the Senate and House of Representatives of the United States of America in Congress assembled,* That section 1802(d) of title 38, United States Code, is amended by (1) striking the word "or" before "(2)" in the first sentence thereof, and (2) inserting before the period at the end of such sentence a comma and the following: "or (3) by any Federal Housing Administration approved mortgagee designated by the Federal Housing Commissioner as a certified agent and which is acceptable to the Administrator".

72 Stat. 1205.
Guaranties.

68 Stat. 591.
12 USC 1709.

SEC. 2. Paragraph (1) of section 1803(c) of title 38, United States Code, is amended (1) by striking out ", but the rate of interest so prescribed by the Administrator shall not exceed at any time the rate of interest (exclusive of premium charges for insurance, and service charges if any), established by the Federal Housing Commissioner under section 203(b)(5) of the National Housing Act, less one-half of 1 per centum per annum"; and (2) by striking out "4¾ per centum per annum" and inserting in lieu thereof "5¼ per centum per annum".

72 Stat. 1206.
Restrictions.

68 Stat. 610.
12 USC 1731a.

SEC. 3. (a) Section 1804(b) of title 38, United States Code, is amended by adding at the end thereof a new sentence as follows: "The Administrator may also refuse to appraise any dwelling or housing project owned, sponsored, or to be constructed by any person refused the benefits of participation under the National Housing Act pursuant to a determination of the Federal Housing Commissioner under section 512 of that Act."

72 Stat. 1206.

68 Stat. 610.
12 USC 1731a.

(b) Section 1804(d) of title 38, United States Code, is amended by adding at the end thereof a new sentence as follows: "The Administrator may also refuse either temporarily or permanently to guarantee or insure any loans made by a lender or holder refused the benefits of participation under the National Housing Act pursuant to a determination of the Federal Housing Commissioner under section 512 of that Act."

72 Stat. 1214.
Direct loan re-
volving fund.

SEC. 4. Section 1823(a) of title 38, United States Code, is amended by inserting immediately after the second sentence the following new sentence: "In addition to the sums authorized in this subsection the Secretary of the Treasury shall also advance to the Administrator such additional sums, not in excess of $100,000,000, as the Administrator may request, and the sums so advanced shall be made available without regard to any limitation contained in this subsection with respect to the amount which may be advanced in any one quarter annual period."

Approved June 30, 1959.

Exhibit 6

Contained in This Volume, by number, title, approval date and page where printed; and a list of reorganization plans, if any, is included. *This is the place to search when the citation is to the law by law number* for the respective Congresses. Beginning with volume 77 there is a Guide to Legislative History of Bills Enacted Into Public Law, arranged by *public law number,* and thereunder giving for each law the approval date, bill number, committee report numbers, and dates of congressional consideration and passage. Each annual volume has its *own subject index*.

Beginning with volume 70, Eighty-fourth Congress, Second Session, the tables were greatly expanded in a separate Tables of Laws Affected by enactments in each volume. Herein are tables of Amendments and Repeals of Prior Laws and other instruments referred to in the text. This new table appeared as a separate pamphlet for volume 70; subsequently it has been published as part of each volume. The tables for volumes 70-74 of the Statutes at Large were cumulated into a single paper-back volume. In late 1967 a new edition appeared covering volumes 70-79. According to the General Services Administration, volumes 80-84 will be cumulated followed by a cumulation of volumes 80-89 as a supplement to the cumulation covering volumes 70-79.[1] The arrangement of the cumulations is as follows: General Legislation by date of approval, Revised Statutes, Internal Revenue Codes, U.S. Code Positive Law Titles (with parallel tables to their pre-codification sections), Reorganization Plans, Executive Orders and Proclamations, and Treaties and Other International Agreements. It will be seen that the above tables give what Shepard's Citations (see Chapter 18) calls the "subsequent legislative treatment" (amendments and repeals) of statutes listed; but though such *enactments* from 1789 are listed, enactments *affecting* are only for the period covered by the period of the list consulted.

Thus, in a particular Statutes at Large volume, it is easy to *trace a bill number to its law number,* and a *public law number to its bill number;* and for various periods, to trace enactments and repeals affecting legislation from 1789 to date, as included in the cumulated Tables of Laws Affected.

§3.4. **Statutory compilations.**

1. *Need for compilations.* The session law form of conventional legislation, as in the Statutes at Large, is the "best evidence" in published form of those federal and state enactments which have not been reenacted in code form, expressly repealing the session law form, as was done in the original Revised Statutes. For four good reasons, however, it is not the form most frequently consulted by the lawyer or student. *First,* the session laws, in all but two states are printed in volumes arranged chronologically by the approval dates of the various enactments, not by subject. *Second,* session laws commonly include private acts and those of only local interest. *Third,* and most important, a high percentage

---

[1] Letter to authors, dated February 23, 1968, by D. C. Eberhart, Director, Office of the Federal Register.

of enactments are soon repealed, amended, or expire by some date or event limitation within themselves — as the end of an appropriation period or of a war — or an act with such a limitation may be extended by later legislation. *Finally,* the session laws take up a vast amount of room.

The net result of this, after a very few sessions of a legislature, is a hopeless mass of legislation, the extent, meaning and operative force of which it is not possible to determine. A lawyer cannot operate under such conditions. For his benefit the laws of public, general interest, in force, must be republished in a usable arrangement which is constantly kept up to date by reference to later legislation. This is done in several ways, referred to generically as Revisions, Consolidations, Compilations, or Codes. These are not, however, legal words of art and have no definite meaning as applied to compilation form.

The common form in the United States, both for federal and state legislation, is to omit repealed and temporary acts, incorporate the changes made by amendments, and then to *combine and rewrite as necessary the remaining acts or parts of acts, arranged in a classified, subject order.* This is the form of the U.S. Revised Statutes, the United States Code and of most state compilations.

The resultant legal authority of these compilations varies from that of "positive law," repealing and superseding the original session laws from which derived, to the status of "certified as true copies" of the original by a commission or other state official, and to that of being a purely unofficial compilation having no authority at all except that conferred by a private publisher's job well done, as in Pennsylvania. If not reenacted as positive law by the legislature itself and merely compiled by a commission delegated to do the job, such compilations are only prima facie the law, rebuttable in case of textual variance by reference to the original session laws. This authority is usually shown in compilations by an enacting clause covering a reenactment or by a certificate of a legislatively employed commission that the text is a true copy which may be offered in evidence. The matter of statutory authority is so vital that the careful lawyer, unless there has been formal reenactment of the compilation, cites the original session law form, but with the compilation title and section numbers in parallel, for convenience of the user.

1a. *Revised, Compiled and Consolidated Laws and Codes Distinguished.* The multiplicity of designations of the collections of laws described above so confuses law students and others — the terms "Revised Laws," "Compiled Laws," "Consolidated Laws," and "Codes" have been used so interchangeably and indiscriminately to designate the same types of collection — that a brief paraphrase of the definitions of the noted English authority on legislation, Courtenay Ilbert, will be attempted here, taken from his *Mechanics of Lawmaking* (London, Froude, 1901). The definitions are presented here for what they are worth.

*Revised Laws* originally meant the elimination of superseded or dead statutes, and the reprinting, verbatim, of those remaining in force, in chronological order, without comment or annotation. This is the form of the English *Statutes Revised.*

*Compiled Laws* are also verbatim copies of the original text, but arranged by broad subject (as pamphlet editions of veterans' laws, patent laws and the like), published without annotation and usually not indexed.

*Consolidated Laws,* by the Ilbert definition, are by far the most common type of American statutory collections, under whatever name. In this form, a survey of existing and past statutory law is made by a legislatively-appointed commission; the provisions in force are preserved (and often rewritten to some extent); arranged according to an elaborate subject classification scheme, with detailed indexes, parallel reference tables and other aids to their use. The acid test of their status as authority is whether they are merely "authenticated" as true copies of the original laws, or whether they have been *reenacted* in their consolidated form, expressly repealing the original statutes from which derived. The fact that the publication is "official" is irrelevant; most statutory compilations of this kind are published under official auspices, whether by the legislatures concerned, or by arrangement with a commercial publisher.

*Codes,* as defined by Ilbert, are rare or nonexistent in the United States, though common in Civil law countries. Theoretically, for each code all existing statutory and case law is distilled into a statement which then comprises the entire law: if it is in the code, it is law; if not there, it is not law. In the United States, the nearest approaches to the true code are in areas where great precision of definition is required, as in procedure and in criminal or probate law. Such uniform state laws as the Uniform Commercial Code are "codes" only in so far as they attempt to restate the essence of statutory and case law.

2. *United States Revised Statutes.* This is the only compilation of the "public general laws of permanent interest" covering federal legislation which the Congress reenacted as positive law. Its title is Revised Statutes of the United States . . . in Force on the First Day of December, One Thousand Eight Hundred and

Seventy-Three (1875 edition). In it, the existing mass of legislation from 1789 on was carefully analyzed, laws of temporary, private or local interest — or those parts thereof which were of such limited interest — discarded; the remainder was arranged in classified order, rewritten as necessary, and reenacted as the law, repealing and superseding those Statutes at Large from which it was derived. This revision aroused so much dissatisfaction, however, because of errors in it and of the feeling that the revisers in many instances had exceeded their authority, that a second edition was published in 1878.

a. *Legal status of the first and second editions.* Although the Revised Statutes is very old, much of it is still the law of the land, either as enacted or, usually, as amended by later enactments. Therefore, though the lawyer or law student may first learn of the existence of the Revised Statutes upon which a United States Code section is based from the parallel citation to authority always given in that Code section, the unrepealed sections of the Revised Statutes, as amended, are the best authority, not the Code sections based upon them. Many sections of the Revised Statutes are still very much alive. The *first edition* was reenacted as the law, repealing and superseding the Statutes at Large or parts thereof from which derived. In citing it, therefore, it is neither necessary nor proper to cite the Statutes at Large sections, which are no longer in force. Later amending enactments should, of course, be cited.

The *second edition* of the Revised Statutes, in so far as it corrects the errors in the first, has a different status. The new sections or parts are, as published in the second edition, only prima facie the law, rebuttable by reference to the amending statute published in the Statutes at Large from which derived. Because of the way corrections and repeals are printed in the second edition, however, there is no difficulty in determining which is which. As shown in Exhibit 7, the distinction is made by the use of brackets [ ] and italics. Material contained in the first edition but later repealed is bracketed in italics, and the repealer cited in italics in the margin. New material is bracketed, however, in roman type. Therefore, in consulting the second edition, particular attention should be paid to the brackets and to italicized matter, whether in text or margin.

b. *Form and makeup of the Revised Statutes, 1875.* The arrangement is in 74 titles, and most titles are further subdivided into two or more chapters. The sections are numbered consecutively, from Section 1, Title 1, to Section 5601, Title 74. This useful feature simplifies citation, since only the section

**216**                          TITLE XIV.—THE ARMY.—CH. 1.

Civil employ-        SEC. 1224. [*Officers of the Army on the active list shall not be separated*
ment prohibited.    *from their regiments or corps for employment on civil works of internal im-*
 5 July, 1838, c.   *provement, nor be allowed to engage in the service of incorporated companies,*
162, s. 31, v. 5, p. *or be employed as acting paymaster, or disbursing agent of the Indian depart-*
260.                *ment, if such extra employment require that he be separated from his regiment*
 27 Feb., 1877, c.  *or company, or otherwise interfere with the performance of the military duties*
69, v. 19, p. 243.  *proper.*] [No officer of the Army shall be employed on civil works or
                    internal improvements, or be allowed to engage in the service of any
                    incorporated company, or be employed as acting paymaster or disburs-
                    ing-agent of the Indian Department, if such extra employment requires
                    that he shall be separated from his company, regiment, or corps, or if
                    it shall otherwise interfere with the performance of the military duties
                    proper.] [See § 2062.]

Exhibit 7

number is required. The margins contain identification and
index material: the subject matter of the section, the Statutes at
Large citation from which the section was derived (and, in the
second edition, later repealers or modifying statutes), and some
citations to cases interpreting either the original statute or the
Revised Statutes section. There is a *subject index*. There are
indispensable *parallel transfer tables* from the original statute
to its Revised Statutes number. These tables serve also as *tables
of repeals* of statutes reenacted in the Revised Statutes.

c. *Tracing a Revised Statutes section into the United States
Code.* Many Revised Statutes have been incorporated in the
Code. Table II of the Code — Revised Statutes 1878 — shows
which ones have been so incorporated, and where in the Code
they went. A "Status" column in this table indicates whether or
not the section concerned has been eliminated or repealed. Thus,
R.S. §2938 became 19 U.S.C. §378, but the "Status" column of
the table shows that it has been repealed.

d. *Repeals of Revised Statutes sections.* The "Status" column
in the above table, lists repealed R.S. sections, whether they were
ever in the Code or not. This table of the Code, and its counterparts in the Federal Code Annotated and the United States Code
Annotated, provide the only direct means (except, piecemeal, session by session, through the Table of Laws Affected in the Statutes
at Large from volume 70 on), of tracing a Revised Statutes section
into its corresponding Code section, or of determining — through
the Status column — whether a given section is still in force; but
when a Code section number is found through the above table,
it may then be Shepardized — as a Code section — in the usual
way.

3. *United States Code: Official edition.* The lawyer as a

practical matter consults the United States Code (cited as U.S.C.) more often than any other form of federal statute. If he merely wants to read the text, he will be content with the official, unannotated edition. If, on the other hand, he wants to consult decided cases in point which interpret the various Code sections, he will read the digest paragraphs extracting the legal rules from these cases in an annotated edition of the Code, to determine which cases to read in full.

a. *Authority of the Code.* The Code is the current official compilation by subject of the "public, general and permanent laws of the United States in force. . . . No new law is enacted and no law is repealed. It is prima facie the law. It is presumed to be the law. The presumption is rebuttable by production of prior unrepealed Acts of Congress at variance with the Code." (Preface to the United States Code.) In other words, the Code is an arrangement by subject of the federal legislation of a public and permanent nature, from 1789 to date in force today; it discards repealed and expired acts and those not of general interest, and all but a few private acts. Treaties are not included, except as editorial matter to explain a text section where needed.

b. *Editorial selection of statutes included.* Inclusion of legislation in the Code is purely an editorial matter, under the supervision of a committee of the House of Representatives. Other editorial features are compiled under contract by a commercial publishing firm employed by the committee for the purpose. Code sections included in one edition may be omitted from the next, or may be changed from one title of the Code to another by editorial fiat. That is one reason why the date or supplement number of the Code edition cited should be given, to avoid possible confusion as to text. Sometimes, as when an act included in the Code affects a plurality of government agencies, a section may be repeated in toto in several Code titles, except for the omission of the names of such agencies as are not pertinent to the title wherein printed.

c. *Editorial notes in the Code.* Printed with the Code but not technically a part of it, is various editorially added material, some of which is shown in Exhibit 8. This material, set out in fine print beneath the respective Code sections to which applicable, has the purpose of aiding in the understanding of those sections. Notes often refer to uncodified parts of a statute from which a Code section was derived. Others may explain the effect of the parenthetical citations to authority following each section or group of sections, or may cross-reference to related Code sections, or comment upon a transfer of agency functions under a reorganization plan — perhaps printing the reorganization plan in full.

d. *Tables of contents to Code titles.* Each of the fifty titles into which the Code is divided is preceded by a table of contents, consisting of a table of chapters in that title, by number and caption, and at the beginning of each chapter there is a similar expanded table for that chapter. (There is no Title 34, as of 1968.)

e. *Section numbering in the Code.* Sections are not numbered consecutively through the entire work in one numerical sequence, as in the Revised Statutes. Instead, the material is divided into fifty titles, such as Agriculture, Patents, Transportation, and the like, and for each title the section numbers begin anew with number 1. That is, there are 1 U.S.C. §1, 29 U.S.C. §1, and so on. Accordingly a citation to a section of the Code must include the title number. Depending upon the amount of material in a given title, it may be subdivided as follows: (1) Title, (2) Part, (3) Chapter and (4) Section. In citation only the title and section numbers, along with the edition date or supplement number, need be given, as 35 U.S.C. §187 (1964 ed.).

f. *Text of Code sections.* Sections are copied from the original enactment, but often with changes such as are shown in Exhibit 8 below. The changes, except as noted below, are of form, not of substance. Introductory words of the act, such as "Provided," or "That," at the beginning of the original statute section may be omitted; and the Code title and section numbers are substituted in the body of the text for the official title and sections of the act from which derived, when these are mentioned in the act. Substantive provisions, such as tariff rates, of some statute sections may be altered by a Presidential executive order under an enabling statute, with the changes incorporated in the Code sections. Again, only parts of a statute may be included, not the entire statute. Reorganization plans, as in the exhibit below, are frequent bases of agency title or function changes in the Code text. It is important to note that statutory authority is cited in parentheses at the end of each Code section or group of sections. Such authority may be Congressional acts or joint resolutions, Presidential executive orders, or reorganization plans.

g. *Index and tables for the Code.*

(1) *Subject index.* The subject index is voluminous, being quite full as to legal concept, governmental agency and fact situation or catchword involved in a statute. There is also a table of acts by popular name — as the National Labor Relations Act — whether or not they are or ever were in the Code. It is one of the best of such tables for federal legislation.

(2) *Tables of statutes included or repealed, and of Code Titles*

*revised in later editions of the Code.* The Tables volume of the Code contains six parallel reference tables which are invaluable in federal statutory research. These tables are included, in substantially identical form, in the Federal Code Annotated and in the United States Code Annotated. Table I is of Revised Titles — those Titles of the Code which have been revised since the original adoption of the Code, showing the former and the new section numbers, and indicating any omissions or repeals of the original sections. Table II is of Revised Statutes sections, whether or not they ever were in the Code; the Code Title and section of those in the Code; and their present status — whether in a revised Title, or eliminated or repealed. Table III is of Statutes at Large incorporated in whole or in part in the Code, with, in parallel, the Code Title and section and the present status of the enactment. Tables IV, V and VI cover, respectively, Executive Orders, Proclamations and Reorganization Plans.

The former tables of repeals of Revised Statutes sections and Statutes at Large have been dropped, as such, their repealer information now being incorporated in the Status columns. The tables are described more fully, with exhibits, in §6.6 of this manual.

h. *New editions and supplements to the Code.* The first edition of the Code appeared in 1926. New editions have been issued approximately every six years since, the 1964 one being in fourteen volumes. Cumulative supplements are issued annually.

i. *Authority of the Code.* See page 31, par. a; page 38, par. 4.

4. *Unofficial, annotated editions of the Code.* The lawyer using the Code will, as a practical matter, ordinarily consult an annotated edition, so that he can find out how its sections have been interpreted in court decisions. The text of the Code sections of the annotated editions is identical with that of the official, and the editorial matter is substantially so, but each section of the annotated Code is followed by digests of judicial opinions and of opinions of the Attorneys General interpreting it — these forming the annotations. The annotated edition thus combines the functions of a statutory digest with those of a citator, informing the lawyer of the statute's meaning and present value as authority.

a. *United States Code Annotated.* This publication, cited as U.S.C.A., was the first annotated edition of the Code.

(1) *Text of the U.S.C.A.* The text is identical throughout with that of the official edition, with the same section numbering and substantially the same notes and other editorial material. Speedier publication of the U.S.C.A. will sometimes result in a variance of the material in its pocket parts and other supplementation from

63 Stat. 864, to give effect to former provisions of section 778 of this title.

**1** → § 778. Administration by Secretary of Labor; delegation of powers.

**2** → Sections 751–756, 757–791 and 793 of this title shall be administered by the Secretary. The Secretary is authorized to delegate to any officer or employee of the Department of Labor any of the powers conferred upon him by said sections. (As amended

**3** → Oct. 14, 1949, ch. 691, title II, § 205 (a), 63 Stat. 864; 1950 Reorg. Plan No. 19, § 1, eff. May 24, 1950, 15 F. R. 3178, 64 Stat. 1271.)

AMENDMENTS

**4** → 1949—Act Oct. 14, 1949, cited to text, amended section generally to give effect to section 3 of 1946 Reorg. Plan No. 2, cited to text, which abolished the United States Employees' Compensation Commission and transferred its functions to the Federal Security Administrator.

TRANSFER OF BUREAU, APPEALS BOARD, AND FUNCTIONS

The Bureau of Employees' Compensation, established within the Federal Security Agency by Agency Order 58 of July 16, 1946, set out under this section, was, together with its functions, transferred to the Department of Labor to be administered under the direction and supervision of the Secretary of Labor, and the functions of the Federal Security Administrator, and of the Federal Security Agency, with respect to such Bureau and with respect to employees' compensation (including workmen's compensation), were transferred to the Secretary of Labor, all of such functions, except those not included in the transfer, to be performed by such Secretary or, subject to his direction and control, by such officers, agencies, and employees of the Department of Labor as he shall designate, by section 1 of 1950 Reorg. Plan No. 19, cited to text and set out below. Section 2 of such Plan transferred to the Department of Labor the Employees' Compensation Appeals Board which had also been established within the Federal Security Agency by said Agency Order 58, and transferred the functions of the Federal Security Administrator, with respect to such Board, to the Secretary of Labor. Such section 2 further provided that said Board shall continue to have authority to hear and, subject to applicable law and the rules and regulations of the Secretary of Labor, to make final decision on appeals taken from determinations and awards with respect to claims of employees of the Federal Government or of the District of Columbia.

REORGANIZATION PLAN NO. 19 OF 1950

15 F. R. 3178, 64 Stat. 1271

EMPLOYEES' COMPENSATION FUNCTIONS

§ 1. BUREAU OF EMPLOYEES' COMPENSATION

The Bureau of Employees' Compensation of the Federal Security Agency, together with its functions, is transferred to the Department of Labor and shall be administered under the direction and supervision of the Secretary of Labor. The functions of the Federal Security Administrator, and of the Federal Security Agency, with respect to the Bureau of Employees' Compensation and with respect to employees' compensation (including workmen's compensation) are transferred to the Secretary of Labor: Provided, That there are not transferred by the provisions of this reorganization plan (1) any function of the Public Health Service; (2) any function of the Federal Security Agency or the Federal Security Administrator under the Vocational Rehabilitation Act, as amended (including the function of assuring the development and accomplishment of State rehabilitation plans affecting beneficiaries under the Federal Employees' Compensation Act); nor (3) the function of developing or establishing rehabilitation services or facilities. The functions transferred by the provisions of this section shall be performed by the Secretary of Labor or, subject

1. Section number.
2. Text proper, showing an example of "rewriting" in the Code: the original act reads "This Act shall be administered by the Administrator."
3. Statutory authority for the Code section, including a reorganization plan. This section is an example of "perpetual revision," in which the latest amendment cited combines all the earlier forms in one current superseding enactment. The parenthetical citation affords an accurate means of determining the exact section of the original act (§205a here) from which the Code section was derived. This may also be done through Table I(b), "Statutes Included," of the Code.
4. Editorial matter, identified by its smaller type than the Code proper.

Exhibit 8

the official, because the earlier printed U.S.C.A. supplements, tables and indexes often contain material not yet printed in the official edition, but which will be incorporated therein later, when the annual cumulative supplement to the Code is published. For convenience in use and revision the U.S.C.A. is published in many small volumes, one or more to each of the fifty Code titles and four for the Constitution.

(2) *Material in the U.S.C.A. not found in the official editions of the Code.* The verbatim texts of pertinent statutes are printed for some Code titles. For example, the revenue acts, in their original session law form, from 1924 to date are printed as a supplement to Title 26, the Internal Revenue Title. For some titles, particularly those which have been revised as a result of substantial legislative changes, there is a historical or critical essay by a member of the Bar, explaining the probable impact of the new legislation, or congressional committee reports containing explanatory revisers' notes. Annotated court rules are in a separate volume. Indexes and tables are substantially identical with those of the official edition, but for some titles there are also separate indexes.

(3) *Annotations in the U.S.C.A.* The annotations are said to digest every opinion interpreting each Code section, from both official and unofficial federal and state law reports and the opinions of the Attorneys General of the United States. The digest paragraphs are arranged, following each Code section, according to a subject scheme which may be very elaborate when the section has been frequently interpreted by the courts. Where there have been many interpreting cases, an alphabetical subject and fact index is provided for each such section for greater convenience in locating decisions involving specific points of law or fact situations. Statutes constantly change, and when Code titles are revised and renumbered, often greatly expanded. An extreme example of this was in the Internal Revenue Code of 1939, in which the approximately 900 sections of the earlier statutes covered were expanded to 5011. When this occurs, annotations to the old, renumbered sections are transferred to the comparable revised section, if any, in the new edition. It sometimes happens that there is no comparable section in the revision, so that old editions of annotated statutes are often saved to preserve the source of decisions formerly in point.

(4) *Indexes and tables for the U.S.C.A.* These aids are prepared by the compilers of the indexes and tables for the official edition of the Code and are very similar to them. Not infrequently, however, there are added entries in the U.S.C.A. indexes and tables, not found in the official, so that if a search in the official edition is fruitless it may be worth while to consult the unofficial.

(5) *Supplementation and recompiled volumes.* One substantial advantage of the private, annotated editions of the Code over the official ones is the much greater frequency of supplementation.

The U.S.C.A. is supplemented four times a year — by a thrice-yearly pamphlet service, cumulating at the end of the year into the annual pocket parts. The supplements now contain new enactments, in Code form, and supplement the annotations, tables and indexes of the complete U.S.C.A. Except for the annotations, the U.S.C.A. may be said to be supplemented during sessions of Congress by the semimonthly issues of the United States Congressional and Administrative News. This promptly prints the public laws as approved, and also conversion tables from the session law form of enactment to the Code form. When new legislation of a particularly important character is enacted, a special pamphlet edition confined to that act, in Code form, may be issued by the U.S.C.A. within a few days of the enactment, containing also all revisers' notes and other editorial matter. This has been done for some entire titles when reenacted into positive law; e.g., Title 5.

Recompiled replacement volumes are printed as needed, as, for example, whenever the pocket parts become unwieldy in size or when a massive legislative revision of the subject matter of the title concerned has taken place. The recompilation combines all existing pocket supplement material for a given title or part thereof into one or more new volumes, to be supplemented in their turn by later pocket parts and the pamphlets issued three times a year. Whatever the form of supplementation, the matter supplemented is indicated on the title page, leaving no reason for the searcher to omit any of the units necessary for a complete search. This connecting up is a typical law book publishing technique. *Always look at the publishing date and indicated coverage of any unit or pocket part consulted in any law book.*

b. *Federal Code Annotated.* This edition of the Code differs from the official chiefly in that it is annotated by the cases and certain other opinions.

(1) *Text of the F.C.A.* The complete text of the organic documents and of the several titles and sections of the Code, as well as the various agency rules of practice as found in the official edition, are printed, but the editorial notes of the official edition are not. Where the compilers of the official edition have in their rewording of the statutes altered (in the opinion of the compilers of the F.C.A.) the true meaning of the original, the F.C.A. "is either made to conform literally to the authoritative enactments, or explanatory notes are placed under all objectionable sections calling attention to what is editorial language as distinguished from the true wording of the enactment." In practice, these notes are for the most part explanatory rather than critical or corrective.

(2) *Material in the F.C.A. not found in the official edition of the*

*Code.* Magna Carta is printed in the volumes of organic laws. Uncodified laws, treaties and proclamations (that is, legislation never placed in the Code) are annotated in a separate and unique volume. Citations include "superseded and repealed sections of the Revised Statutes, Public Acts and Resolutions of Congress which were not carried either in the United States Code or Federal Code Annotated, and Private Acts; treaties with Indians and foreign governments; Proclamations of the President." The arrangement of statutes and treaties is chronological, with separate tables for each category. United States court rules are in separate volumes.

(3) *Annotations in the F.C.A.* Annotations are to official and unofficial federal and state reports, Attorney Generals' and Judge Advocate Generals' opinions, Presidential executive orders and proclamations, and occasionally to law review articles.

(4) *Indexes and tables.* These are similar to those of the official edition of the Code, as above described.

(5) *Supplementation and recompiled volumes.* Current Public Laws and Administrative Material (monthly) reprints legislation (including some administrative orders and notices), cumulating into annual volumes of facsimilies of the official slip laws. For especially important new legislation, pamphlet editions are issued promptly. Recompiled volumes are issued as necessitated by the bulk of the annual pocket parts.

§3.5.  **Authority of statutes as publications.** The authority of the various forms of statutes has already been discussed in describing those publications. A summary at this point seems convenient, however.

1. *Slip laws.* Slip laws are properly citable authority only until the Statutes at Large or state session laws containing them are published. This matter is now largely academic, however, since the slip law form of federal enactments and that in the United States Code Congressional and Administrative News now contain the Statutes at Large citation in the margin, so that the permanent or Statutes at Large form of citation can be made from the slip law.

2. *Statutes at Large and state session laws.* These are cited as such until and unless they are expressly repealed by a later codifying statute reenacted into positive law. After that they are no longer in force and so should no longer be cited as present authority. On the other hand, when such a reenacted code section has later been amended or a new section added, cite both the code and the amending session law, with "as amended by" following the reenacted code citation. Where, as is the case with two thirds of the United States Code titles and most of the state statutory compila-

tions, the statute has been made part of a compilation which is only prima facie the law — that is, it is only certified as a true copy of the session law form — and not reenacted into positive law, cite the session law form, as found in parentheses at the end of the code section cited, followed by the compilation form, in that order. Thus Florida Laws 1941, c. 20954, §15, F.S.A. §694.08 (1944). You are then citing your "best evidence" first, followed by the convenient but not the best form.

3. *United States Revised Statutes.* Cite simply as Revised Statutes, without the statute from which derived, because that statute was repealed with the enactment of the compilation and so is no longer in force; if it has since been amended or added to, cite the R.S. section "as amended by" the amending statute. If the R.S. section has been included in a later codification of its material into positive law — i.e., in a reenacted Code title — it was repealed by that codification and should no longer be cited. Repeals of Revised Statutes sections are noted in tables in all editions of the United States Code.

4. *United States Code.* The official statement of the Congressional committee under whose auspices the Code is compiled is found in the Preface in each volume of each edition and cumulative supplement of the Code. It states that "no new law is enacted [by it] and no law is repealed. It is prima facie the law. It is presumed to be the law. The presumption is rebuttable by production of prior unrepealed Acts of Congress at variance with the Code." In other words this compilation, though official, has not been reenacted as a whole by Congress as was the Revised Statutes, thereby expressly repealing those acts or parts of acts from which the Code was derived. On the other hand, it was the original intention of Congress when authorizing the Code of 1926 to take up its fifty titles one by one and reenact them piecemeal as positive law, as had been done wholesale in the Revised Statutes. To date, about a third of the titles have been so treated, the number so reenacted being listed in the Preface to each Code volume or supplement and in the tables in the latest volume of the Statutes at Large.

Reenacting a Code title is done in each instance by an act of Congress. In order to avoid confusion between the section numbering of the act so reenacting the title and those of the Code so reenacted, the section numbers of the *codifying act* itself, as published in the Statutes at Large, are spelled out in abbreviated form (as Sec. 2, Sec. 3), while those of the reenacted *codified title* of the Code as printed in that act are designated by the symbols (as §1, §2, etc.). The entire codified and reenacted title is set out in the single, unnumbered Section 1 of the codifying act. It may be noted here that practically never is the first section of a federal act numbered; the visible numbering begins with Section 2, though in citing or Shepardizing the first section it is always recognized as Section 1. Section 2 and following of the codifying act itself, as distinct from the reenacted Code title, consist of saving clauses, the repealers of prior legislation, etc., but are not part of the Code title at all. In order to understand this legislative technique better, the student will do well to examine P.L. 86-682, 74 Stat. 578 (1961), reenacting Title 39, Postal Service, as positive law.

In citing the Code, cite first the Statutes at Large and section from which derived, followed by the Code citation, unless the Code title has been reenacted into positive law, expressly repealing the original enactment in the process. That is, Act of June 2, 1946, c. 373, §4, 62 Stat. 286, 15 U.S.C. §328 (1964 ed.). Where, however, the cited section has been so reenacted into positive law, the session law from which derived has thereby been repealed and should not be cited, but amendments should be cited as such. Thus, "39 U.S.C. §28, as amended by . . . ."

Citation of statutory material in legal writing is therefore to the original statutes with parallel references to the Code, unless the Code title has been reenacted into positive law. On the other hand, not to be academic about it, the work of the codifiers is so well done that the Code for most purposes of daily use has largely supplanted the statutes which are the real authority. Nevertheless the proper citation form is a mark of the careful lawyer.

*C H A P T E R   4*

# Treaties and Other International
# Acts of the United States[1]

§4.1.  **Importance of treaties and other international agreements in law practice.**  To many people the treaty is an esoteric
affair, reminiscent of high protocol and peace conferences.  It is,
however, also a matter of the disposition of the effects of a deceased
national of Greece, domiciled in Iowa; the extradition to Missouri
of a criminal from the Netherlands; the right of a Chilean to sue
in a New York court on a contract; or the validity of a California
statute prohibiting certain aliens from holding real property in
that state.  As long as the nationals of one country travel to, do
business in, or settle down in another country, the treaty defining
their rights will be of interest, not only to the diplomat but to the
common man.  Most of the cases interpreting treaties are from
state courts, not federal.  For example, the Treaty of March 2,
1899, with the United Kingdom, has been adjudicated twenty-one
times, sixteen of them by state courts.  At home, the relations of
the United States with most of the American Indians are still
governed by treaty.  Recent cases arising from the efforts of New
York and Pennsylvania to remove certain Indian tribes from their
reservations in order to make water power developments possible
are evidence of that.

§4.2.  **Place of treaties and other international agreements in
the legislative hierarchy.**  Whether or not both treaties and executive agreements are properly to be considered as conventional
legislation is academic.  As a practical matter, they are used interchangeably for many purposes and so are treated together here.

1 The authors acknowledge the valuable assistance of the late Mrs. Florence
Zagayko, international law librarian of the Columbia University Law Library, in
the preparation of this chapter.

While this manual of legal research is not a book on legal or political theory, enough background of international acts is given to serve as a basis for understanding the makeup and functions of this material.

1. *"Treaty"* and *"executive agreement"* defined. Article II, Section 2 of the Constitution provides that "The President . . . shall have the power, by and with the consent of the Senate, to make treaties, provided two-thirds of the Senators present concur. . . ." The term "treaty" denotes an international compact concluded by the President with a foreign power, with the approval of the Senate, but it may be designated as a treaty, convention, protocol, contract or by another term. "Executive agreements" are entered into by the President with a foreign state, in his capacity as United States representative with foreign nations, and require no action by the Senate. These agreements in turn may be under authority of specific acts of Congress, such as those which appoint the President as a fact finder with power to act; or they may be agreements entered into purely under those constitutional powers possessed by the President as the Chief Executive of the United States.

2. *As the law of the land: Under international law.* Both treaties and executive agreements are contracts between the United States and foreign nations having requisite power to carry out the terms thereof. At international law — the law of nations — they are equally binding. While such an international pact may be invalid as part of the municipal law of the United States, it may still be binding as a contract between the United States and the other signatory. This is true of both executory and self-executing treaties, and under the later decisions seems to be true of executive agreements as well. A self-executing pact is one which needs no Congressional legislation for its effectiveness; an executory one does require Congressional implementation.

3. *As the law of the land: At municipal law.* A formal treaty, negotiated and signed by the President and approved by the Senate, has the force of a federal statute, no more, no less. Article VI of the Constitution provides that ". . . all treaties made, or which shall be made, under the authority of the United States, shall be the supreme law of the land; and the judges of every state shall be bound thereby, any thing in the Constitution or laws of any state to the contrary notwithstanding." A court has said: ". . . there is no principle of law more firmly established by the highest court of the land than that, while a treaty will supersede a prior act of Congress, an act of Congress may supersede a prior treaty. The latest expression controls, whether it be a treaty or

an act of Congress." *United States* v. *Thompson,* 258 **Fed.** 268 (E.D. Ark. 1919). Like any other statute, a treaty is subject to constitutional limitations and to judicial review, but the courts strive to avoid finding repugnance. It has been said that no treaty has ever been held unconstitutional. Executive agreements may be upheld as the law of the land, even when opposed to the internal policy of a sovereign state. They are probably not, however, the "law of the land" to the extent that they can supersede an act of Congress, except when made under the authority of a later act. To this extent, at least, they are not interchangeable with treaties.

**§4.3. Publication of the international acts of the United States.**

1. *Press releases.* The first publication of a treaty or executive agreement may be in the form of a mimeographed press release of the Department of State, but not all agreements are so published. It is usually issued at the date of signing, which, in the case of a formal treaty, is thus in advance of its presentation to the Senate for approval and its later ratification by the President. (Note the nomenclature: The Senate "approves" or "recommends ratification" of treaties; the President then "ratifies.") The text may be preceded by a departmental statement tracing the history of the agreement.

2. *Department of State Bulletin.* Statements concerning the negotiation, signing, ratification, etc. of treaties are published in the Bulletin, and texts of exchanges of notes and of some treaties, if issued as press releases, are sometimes published therein. This information is made accessible through the tardily published annual indexes.

3. *"Slip law" form.* The next form of publication is comparable to the slip law. In this form treaties are listed in the official Monthly Catalog of Government Publications, and may be purchased separately from any series in which they may appear. There have been three numbered series of these slip agreements, all issued by the Department of State.

a. *Treaty Series.* The first series was the Treaty Series — cited as T.S. — and bibliographically it is a peculiar series. It began in January 1908, with number 489, and through number 814 published both formal treaties and executive agreements. Beginning with number 815 through number 994, which ended the series, only formal treaties were published. The numbers preceding 489 were unnumbered as published and there is no complete set; many were never printed at all.

b. *Executive Agreement Series.* Before 1929 some executive

agreements were included in the Treaty Series, as mentioned above, but others were to be found only in such sources as Foreign Relations of the United States, or the volumes of Malloy (page 43, par. 7), particularly in volumes 2 and 4, or in press releases. No collection includes them all, *nor is there any complete list of them.* From October 1, 1929, through March 16, 1945, executive agreements were published as the Executive Agreement Series — cited as E.A.S. — ending with number 506, when a combined series was resumed as described below.

c. *Treaties and Other International Acts Series.* This series — cited as T.I.A.S. — began with number 1501, as of December 1945. This number was arrived at by adding the 994 numbers of the Treaty Series to the 506 of the Executive Agreement Series. It was "inaugurated to make available in a single series the texts of treaties and other instruments (such as constitutions and charters of international organizations, declarations, agreements affected by exchanges of diplomatic notes, etc.) establishing or defining relations between the United States and other countries. Official prints are judicially noticed as positive law, without certification. 1 U.S.C. 113, as amended by 89-497, 80 Stat. 271 (1966).

These three series are indispensable for intensive work with United States treaties and executive agreements, especially currently. They present the full texts of the various acts, in English and any foreign language involved, and include the President's proclamations, if any, of these acts. The title page gives the title and critical dates.

d. *Unofficial treaty publication.* Both the United States Code Annotated and the United States Code Congressional and Administrative News publish a limited number of formal treaties and executive agreements which, in the words of the publisher of the latter, "affect U.S. Code provisions of a relatively permanent duration and general interest. . . . In 1956, an informal agreement was reached whereby the State Department representative would suggest treaties and agreements or references thereto for inclusion — final determination as to use and form would be made by the editorial department of the publishers. . . . For examples of full-text coverage . . . the following may be pointed out:

> "Title 17, §9 — Unesco Universal Copyright convention.
> "Title 22, §287, note — Agreement between United Nations and U.S. on U.N. Headquarters.
> "Title 22, §1372, note — Revised agreement between U.S. and Philippines." [2]

2 West Publishing Company letter to the authors, of October 17, 1960.

Tax Treaties is a Commerce Clearing House loose-leaf reporter, printing the full text of the United States treaties covering income and estate taxes.

4. *Statutes at Large publication.* Treaties were published in the Statutes at Large from volume 8 (which included the treaties from 1776 to 1845) through volume 64, covering 1949. From volume 47 (1931-1933) through volume 64, executive agreements of international import were also included.

5. *United States Treaties and Other International Agreements.* This series — cited as UST, by volume, page and year — takes the place of the former publication of treaties and agreements in the Statutes at Large, as noted above. It is, moreover, now the annual, bound form of publication of the Treaties and Other International Acts Series, beginning with T.I.A.S. number 2010, January 27, 1950. Each volume is indexed by both country and subject. There are usually several volumes a year.

6. *League of Nations and United Nations Treaty Series.* Although the United States never became a member of the League of Nations, most of the international acts of the United States from 1920 through 1945 were published in the League of Nations Treaty Series. They are now published in the successor United Nations Treaty Series. Both series are well indexed, though the indexes appear rather tardily.

7. *Other collections of United States treaties.* Several collected editions of United States treaties, other than those noted above, have been published, but for most practical purposes those described below are the ones currently consulted. William M. Malloy's Treaties, Conventions, International Acts, Protocols and Agreements Between the United States of America and Other Powers[3] is the most important compilation for the period covered. It prints the English text only of the acts, without background comment, though the first two volumes give some citations to cases interpreting them. Parallel citations to the various treaty series and to the Statutes at Large where these acts are published are given. Volume 3 of Malloy, covering the years 1910-1923, was compiled by C. F. Redmond, and is often cited as 3 Redmond; similarly, the fourth and final volume to date, covering 1923-1934, was compiled by Edward J. Trenwith, and is often cited as 4 Trenwith.

David Hunter Miller's compilation of Treaties and Other International Acts of the United States of America[4] started out as a most ambitious and useful project, but has been discontinued

3 Washington, D.C., U.S. Govt. Printing Office, 1910-1938, 4v.
4 Washington, D.C., U.S. Govt. Printing Office, 1931-1948, 9v.

after covering only the period through July 1, 1863. For this period it supersedes Malloy for scholarly purposes, though Malloy is still the most convenient for the English text. Miller annotates each act by extensive notes. Its volume 1 is introductory, outlining the plan of the series and giving tables of documents from 1778 to 1931, inclusive. There is no index.

8. *Indian treaties.* Indian treaties were originally collected and published in volumes 7 through 16 of the Statutes at Large. Together with laws relating to the American Indians, they were compiled by Charles J. Kappler in Indian Affairs, Laws and Treaties[5] and are well indexed. The work is best used in conjunction with Federal Indian Law, compiled by the Solicitor of the Department of the Interior,[6] the official commentary on Indian law. This brings up to date the earlier compilations by Felix S. Cohen, Handbook of Federal Indian Law (1945). Texts of treaties and relevant statutes are printed.

§4.4. **Lists and subject indexes of international acts.** There are no good general indexes covering all international acts, but the information can be pieced together with the aid of certain lists and indexes.

1. *Treaties in Force.* By far the most essential and useful for various purposes is the list Treaties in Force, published annually by the Department of State since 1950. As the title indicates, it includes only treaties currently in force. Part I of the list contains bilateral treaties, arranged by country, and under country by topic; Part II lists multilateral treaties by topic. Citations are given to texts as published in the various sources; i.e., Statutes at Large, UST, T.I.A.S., United Nations Treaty Series, Malloy, etc.

2. *Numerical lists.* A numerical list of the T.S., E.A.S. and the T.I.A.S. through December 1950 (T.I.A.S. number 222), is in United States Treaty Developments, Appendix II. The publication of this loose-leaf service was suspended as of that date. This is a good list and is still useful because it gives not only the titles of the treaties, but also cross references to other citations of the texts in the Statutes at Large, Miller, Malloy, etc. More recent numbers of the T.I.A.S. are listed numerically only in the cumulative catalogs of the Publications of the Department of State. While these Publications are primarily subject catalogs, they include indexes by series number.

3. *Alphabetical indexes by subject and country.* The only detailed analytical subject index to United States treaties was published in 1931, the Subject Index of the Treaty Series and the

---

5 Washington, D.C., U.S. Govt. Printing Office, 1904-1941, 5v.
6 Washington, D.C., U.S. Govt. Printing Office, 1958.

Executive Series, July 1, 1931. This covers only T.S. numbers 1-839, and E.A.S. numbers 1-18, of which there is also a numerical list with citations to the Statutes at Large. Subject indexes in the volumes of UST since 1950 are analytical.

An old list of Treaties in Force, 1941, is still occasionally useful because of its classified arrangement and its subject index. It was the last such list before the annual Treaties in Force commenced in 1950.

Volume 4 of Malloy has an alphabetical index by subjects and countries and is about the most convenient for this approach for the period covered. It is a cumulative index to the four volumes of Malloy, covering the years 1789-1937.

The List of Treaties and Other International Agreements Contained in the United States Statutes at Large is printed in 64 Statutes at Large, Part 3 (1953), which is the last volume of the Statutes at Large to contain international acts. It is a list by country, and under each country the acts are arranged alphabetically by topic. Citations are given to series number, if any, as well as to the Statutes at Large. Indian treaties, as found in volumes 7 to 18, inclusive, of the Statutes at Large, are not included.

The only up-to-date alphabetical lists are those in the latest Treaties in Force, and in each volume of UST. A special list on copyright relations is published as an appendix to Treaties in Force.

4. *Lists of treaties submitted to the Senate.* Information as to actions on treaties by the Senate is found in several publications, none complete and up to date. The two Lists of Treaties Submitted to the Senate, 1789-1944, are chronological lists of treaties which give the date of submission to the Senate, the Senate document number, and type of action taken by the Senate, whether acceptance, acceptance with reservation, rejection, withdrawal by the President, no action, or submission only for information. Footnotes give further details on some of the treaties. A useful list of dates of all sessions of Congress is appended. A similar treaty list without the notes is published in 4 Malloy, but covers only 1789 to 1937. Unfortunately, neither list has been brought up to date. It was intended that United States Treaty Developments, below, would continue giving the information on treaties pending before the Senate, but this publication has been suspended. The only convenient compilation now of such information is in the Commerce Clearing House Congressional Index, in its section on treaties pending in the Senate during the current session. This list gives the status of such treaties, whether in committee, reported out, ratified or rejected, and gives references

to published hearings and reports. The Calendar of the Senate Committee on Foreign Relations also has such a list, but it is less convenient to use and not generally available.

5. *Treaties by popular name.* Several lists translate the popular name of a treaty (as the Hay-Pauncefote or Ashburton-Webster, etc.) into its official Statutes at Large or other citation. Volume 4 of Malloy does this in its index, as do the table of Statutes by Popular Names in the Digest of the United States Supreme Court Reports, and the Shepard's Acts and Cases by Popular Names. Similar lists in the United States Code are not satisfactory for treaties.

6. *Citators for international acts.* Treaties and executive agreements of international import are federal statutes; as such they are subject to much the same process of amendment, repeal or extension as are other federal statutes; and they are interpreted by the federal and state courts in the same manner. Consequently, the lawyer will Shepardize them ordinarily through Shepard's Citations as noted below. There are, however, other means of Shepardizing to a limited extent when access to Shepard's itself is lacking. These citators are noted below.

a. *United States Treaty Developments.* The best citator for developments occurring during the period 1944-1950 was the Department of State loose-leaf service bearing this name. For each international act it gave, in one place, the following information: ". . . notes respecting the date and place of signature, effective date, duration, citations to text, signatories, ratifications, adherences, accessions, reservations, amendments, extensions, terminations, authorizing and implementing legislation, executive action, administrative interpretations, opinions of the Attorney General, court decisions, and other relevant action." It is most unfortunate that this admirable publication has been discontinued. It is still useful for the period covered.

b. *Subsequent legislative history of treaties.* The present status of treaties in force is indicated by three publications.

(1) *Treaties in Force.* This publication notes supersedings or terminations of articles or clauses of treaties still in force, and lists amending, extending or supplementing treaties. Treaties which have been terminated in full, whether by expiration, denunciation or replacement, are not included in the list. It is an annual.

(2) *Shepard's United States Citations.* These citators are described in detail in Chapter 18. Supersedings, amendments, supplementings, extensions, terminations and revisions of international agreements are noted in the United States unit, exactly as for any other uncodified United States statutes, if the treaty or

agreement was published in the Statutes at Large before 1950. Upon the inauguration of United States Treaties and Other International Agreements in 1950, Shepard's Citations added a special table for UST citations. These include citations in federal courts, in later Statutes at Large or UST volumes, and in the Journal of the American Bar Association, even if cited only by name of the treaty. State units of Shepard's Citations also cover the UST and state cases involving treaties before 1950.

It is important to note in Shepardizing treaties that their listing in Shepard's United States Citations and in the state Shepard's Citations as well, is, as with all uncodified federal acts, by date and not by volume and page of the Statutes at Large. That is, they are listed by the *date when signed*. For example, a treaty with France, on double taxation, was signed on October 18, 1946, ratified by the President on June 18, 1948, and proclaimed on October 27, 1949. This treaty was not noted in Shepard's United States Citations until in the 1956-1960 red-paper supplement, in which it was listed as an act of October 18, 1946, the signing date. Shepardizing treaties and agreements published in UST, beginning with 1950, however, is simple, since in Shepard's United States Citations and in the state Shepard's Citations they are listed by volume and page of UST, as 6 UST 4117.

(3) *Department of State Bulletin.* This weekly publication reports all current treaty action in its section on treaty information. From 1929 to 1939 such information was published separately in the Department's Treaty Information Bulletin and is covered by two cumulative indexes.

c. *Judicial history of treaties in federal courts.*

(1) *Treaty Developments.* During its short life, this publication was the simplest source of such information.

(2) *Shepard's United States Citations.* This is, for judicial as well as subsequent legislative history, the tool most lawyers would use, since all treaties to date are covered, if printed in the Statutes at Large or in United States Treaties and Other International Agreements. The citing cases from federal courts only are noted here, but *all* federal cases mentioning the treaty are listed, not just those directly construing it.

(3) *Federal Code Annotated.* This edition of the United States Code has a separate volume entitled Annotations to Uncodified Laws and Treaties, which, as its title indicates, includes treaties and other agreements of international import. The citing cases include both federal and state cases, but only those actually construing the treaty. Treaties are listed, however, whether cited by

cases or not.   The lists in F.C.A. are by country, then by date, and include treaties with the American Indians.

(4) *Digest of the United States Supreme Court Reports.*  The table of Laws Cited and Construed in this digest cites United States Supreme Court cases only.   The table includes foreign treaties to which the United States is not a party, if construed by the Court.   These and other treaties are listed alphabetically under the names of the foreign countries, and chronologically in a special treaty table (the latter table, however, not including treaties to which the United States is not a party).   There are also special lists of Indian treaties.

(5) *Supreme Court Reporter.*  Beginning with volume 37 (1916), this Reporter has a Table of Statutes Construed, which includes treaties.   State court cases construing treaties are listed as well as those of the Supreme Court.   It is not cumulative.

d. *Judicial history of treaties in the state courts.*  Each state Shepard's Citations has a section citing federal statutes construed by the courts of the state covered.   This section includes treaties and executive agreements, either as published in the Statutes at Large or in United States Treaties and Other International Agreements.   As noted above, the Federal Code Annotated cites state cases construing treaties, even when not appealed to the United States Supreme Court.   Another source of information about state courts construing treaties is in the table of Statutes Construed in the National Reporter System volumes.   In these tables, treaties interpreted are listed, following Statutes at Large citations, under Treaties, Conventions, and International Agreements.   Treaties are more often construed by state than by federal courts.

e. *Indian treaties.*  Federal and state relations with the American Indians are still largely regulated by treaty.   Particularly in the condemnation by states of Indian land for public purposes — such as power development — these treaties are often very important.   Indian treaties are annotated by United States and state cases in the Annotations to Uncodified Laws and Treaties volume of the Federal Code Annotated, wherein they are arranged first by date and under that alphabetically by tribe.   The Digest of the United States Supreme Court Reports lists, under Indian Tribes, the treaties between them and foreign nations by tribe (these antedating our nationhood), and, in another list, treaties and agreements of the United States with Indian tribes, arranged chronologically since 1778.   The most complete statutory citation of Indian treaties and statutes to 1958 is in Federal Indian Law, compiled by the Solicitor of the Department of the Interior.[7] The last Indian treaty was signed in 1904.

7. *Digests of international law.* There have been three United States digests of international law. These in essence are digests of treaties, court decisions interpreting them, and other official documents, together with a great deal of explanatory comment.

John Bassett Moore's A Digest of International Law . . .[8] is still an indispensable analysis of international law from the point of view of the United States, as embodied in official documents. Volume 8 comprises an index by subject, country and person; a list of cases cited; and a list of documents cited.

Francis Wharton's A Digest of the International Law of the United States[9] is the old standard digest, though now largely superseded. The supplement to the third volume consists of material omitted from the first edition, either inadvertently or because discovered after that edition went to press.

Greene H. Hackworth's Digest of International Law[10] is an analysis of international law as applied by the United States, based upon material made available since the publication of Moore. The material in Moore is not duplicated in this later work, but with a few exceptions the order and style of treatment are the same. Volume 8 is a general index and table of cases.

Marjorie M. Whiteman's Digest of International Law (Washington, D.C., U.S. Govt. Printing Office, 1963-, v.1-), in turn succeeds but does not duplicate Hackworth, to which, along with references to other predecessor digests, it makes cross-references in footnotes at the beginning of each chapter. Topics covered by Hackworth are, because of World War II and its aftermath, greatly expanded; for example, in one topic covered by Hackworth in 562 pages, Whiteman uses two large volumes. The increase is primarily due to World War II, reflecting the vast growth of international law, causing not only the expansion of Hackworth topics but the addition of new ones, such as air space and outer space — which are treated practically de novo in Whiteman. There are many new headings, such as "interdependent independent states." Emphasis is placed on the ever-changing nature of international law (including its definition). This is considerably more than a digest or paraphrase of rules; for example, there are copious digest quotations from Department of State publications, U.N. Security Council resolutions, conventions,

---

7 Washington, D.C., U.S. Govt. Printing Office, 1958.
8 Washington, D.C., U.S. Govt. Printing Office, 1906, 8v.
9 2d ed., Washington, D.C., U.S. Govt. Printing Office, 1887, 3v. and app.
10 Washington, D.C., U.S. Govt. Printing Office, 1940-1944, 8v.

etc., tied together by the compiler's editorial comment. This Digest will be completed during the next several years. The final volume will contain a comprehensive index, but in the meantime users of the volumes may find it helpful to consult the Table of Contents in each volume. The remaining volumes will appear as they are completed, not necessarily in numerical order.

8. *Dates of treaties and other international acts.*

a. *Date of treaty.* There are or may be five critical dates in the progress of a formal United States treaty to adoption: those of the *signature* by plenipotentiaries of the powers concerned, the *approval* by the Senate by a two-thirds vote of those present, the *ratification* by the President, the *exchange of ratifications,* and the President's *proclamation* of the treaty. The *date when signed* is that by which a formal treaty is cited by the Department of State and by international lawyers, and that by which it is listed in Shepard's Citations. The *effective date,* unless otherwise indicated in the treaty itself, is that of United States ratification by the President (or, if exchange of ratifications is called for, that date). The effective date can almost always be determined from the printed text. It may be and often is specified in the body of the treaty itself, though for domestic purposes that date is not binding upon the United States courts. In published treaties, the effective date is usually indicated at some point extraneous to the body of the treaty itself, as in a syllabus or on the title page.

b. *Date of executive agreement.* This is the *date of the signature.* The *effective date,* since such agreements do not require Congressional consent, is the one stated in the agreement itself. These dates are indicated on the face, title page, or in a syllabus to the printed publication, and in the official indexes.

§4.5. **Working with the international acts of the United States.** To the lawyer or law student, working with treaties and executive agreements is likely to be less satisfactory than with other forms of legislation. In the first place, there is no one single series which publishes them all. Similarly, tracing changes in form or status of these acts requires consulting more than one citator in some instances, as does also determining their judicial interpretation.

The procedure of the searcher's work depends quite largely upon whether he is a municipal lawyer, working in a conventional Anglo-American law library; or an international lawyer, with access to an international law collection which includes the various treaty series. As earlier noted, state courts more often construe treaties in connection with some local matter, than do the federal courts. Most Anglo-American law libraries have some volumes on international law, but the lawyer feels more at home with conventional law books. The municipal lawyer prefers to consult the Statutes at Large and its successor for the publication of international acts, United States Treaties and Other International Agreements. The international lawyer, on the other hand, tends first to turn to the various other treaty collections, like the Treaty Series, Executive Agreement Series, Treaties and Other International Acts Series, Malloy or Miller, or those of the League of Nations or United Nations. The municipal lawyer is familiar with Shepard's Citations, the international lawyer with the various official publications of the Department of State described in this chapter, as well.

A factor here is that the date by which the municipal lawyer may know a treaty is its effective date (see page 51, par. 8), which is not the date of signing; whereas the international lawyer as well as compilers of the various citation books discussed in this chapter think of it by the date of signature. In United States Treaties and Other International Agreements there is no such problem, since references in Shepard's Citations are by volume and page of that series.

  1. *Finding the text of an international act of the United States.*
    a. *For the municipal lawyer.*
      (1) Statutes at Large (through list in volume 64) or through F.C.A. volume for uncodified statutes.
      (2) Treaties in Force (latest annual list) gives citations to all treaty collections.
      (3) Separate volumes of UST (consulting index in each).
      (4) U.S. Code Congressional and Administrative News (for some treaties).
      (5) CCH Congressional Index (for Senate document numbers of treaties before the Senate and not elsewhere published).
    b. *For those with access to international law collections.*
      (1) Treaties in Force (latest annual, cumulative edition). If citation is not found there, use Malloy index in volume 4, or turn directly to country in volume covering period of treaty, for treaties to 1937.
      (2) Subject index to the Treaty Series and Executive Acts Series (for treaties, etc., to 1931).
      (3) List of Treaties in Force, 1941 (with subject index).
      (4) U.S. Treaty Developments (covering treaties on which action was taken during 1944-1948).
      (5) Indexes in UST volumes (for treaties since 1950). This is available in law libraries generally.

(6) Publications of the Department of State (through the semiannual indexes of this cumulative catalog, for treaties not found elsewhere, being not yet in force, etc.).

c. *Special aids for translating citations, when date, country or title of treaty is unknown.*

(1) If searcher has the citation to series number (T.S., E.A.S., T.I.A.S.) only, see page 45, par. 2, Numerical Lists.

(2) If citation is to popular name only, see page 47, par. 5, Treaties by Popular Name.

(3) If citation is to Statutes at Large only, it is possible to find other citations through:

(a) List in 64 Stat. B1104, where all international acts published in the Statutes at Large through 1949 are listed by country.

(b) Subject List of Treaties, 1931. (Statutes at Large citations are conspicuously placed in right-hand column of the numerical list, and generally they occur more or less in order, so that a reference to a T.S. number may be obtained. It is feasible in the Numerical List of Treaties in Treaty Developments to carry this through 64 Stat.

(4) If citation is to U.S.T. only, there is so far no direct tabular means to translate to other forms of citations; if a treaty has been cited in a case, it can be tracked down through Shepard's United States Citations, or, if construed by a state court, through the appropriate state Shepard's Citations.

2. *Shepardizing international acts.*

a. *Information on the status of a treaty.* See page 47, par. 6.

(1) Consulting the latest Treaties in Force, plus checking the Department of State Bulletins after that date, gives the best record of the status of treaties in force.

(2) Lawyers would prefer Shepard's Citations (the section of United States Statutes at Large Not in United States Code, or, for acts beginning with 1949, the following section of United States Treaties and Other International Agreements). The Treaties in Force method is quicker; the Shepard's Citations method brings the search down to a later date.

b. *Judicial citation or interpretation of an international agreement by United States or state courts.*

(1) Shepard's Citations: Shepard's United States Citations,

for federal court cases, and the various state units for state court cases, are the best places of search.

(2) Federal Code Annotated uncodified laws volume for both federal and state cases.

(3) Digest of United States Supreme Court Reports for Supreme Court cases only.

(4) Supreme Court Reporter, Statutes Construed tables, for both federal and state court cases.

(5) National Reporter System, Statutes Construed tables, for both federal and state cases.

(6) State Shepard's Citations for state cases, including those appealed to the federal courts.

(7) U.S. Treaty Developments, for action during 1944-1948, is probably the best source for the years covered.

3. *A simple treaty problem.* Decedent, a resident of Wisconsin, makes the President of the Federal Republic of Germany his residuary legatee, the funds to be used for charitable purposes in Germany. Wisconsin levies an inheritance tax, but the President of Germany resists, claiming exemption under a treaty of friendship and commerce with the United States. Wisconsin asserts that the treaty does not apply.

a. *Finding a treaty which might apply.* The latest edition of Treaties in Force lists under Germany a treaty of friendship and commerce, of December 8, 1923, modified on June 3, 1953, and in part replaced by a treaty of October 29, 1954, and cites four different series in which the treaty and its modifications were published. The 1923 treaty, being of an earlier date than 1950, will also be listed in the table in 64 Stat. B1107-1182. Reading the treaties, you discover that you are interested in Section 1 of the 1923 treaty and in Article 29, Section 2 of the 1954 treaty. Search of the Wisconsin Statutes Annotated reveals that the Wisconsin statute in point is W.S.A. 72.04(1), and that it digests a number of cases by Wisconsin courts interpreting that section — so many that it might take some time to determine the one in which you are interested in. To check further, you search Shepard's Wisconsin Citations, because its quarterly supplementation brings it closer to date than the annotated statute supplements. You know that the 1923 treaty was published in the Statutes at Large, so in the Wisconsin Shepard's Citations you search the section covering United States Statutes at Large Not in the United States Code, where you find that the treaty has been construed by the Wisconsin Supreme Court in 5 Wis. 2d 363, 92 N.W.2d 819 (1958).

The 1953 and 1954 modifications of the treaty, being of later date than 1949, are published in United States Treaties and Other

Agreements, and so you search that section of the Wisconsin citator covering UST, where you are cited to the same case. As a further check, you then search Shepard's United States Citations in the same manner for cases construing the treaty. There you are cited to the same Wisconsin case, though it has not been appealed to the United States Supreme Court as yet. You will note that the state court's interpretation of the treaty is covered in both the United States and Wisconsin Shepard's Citations units. You search all units of these two Shepard's Citations, including all bound and unbound supplements. Then you bring your search several weeks beyond the latest Shepard's Citations by consulting the Statutes Construed tables in the advance sheets of the Supreme Court Reporter and the North Western Reporter (which reports Wisconsin cases), covering later cases than those found in the latest Shepard's supplement. A long comment is in 1960 Wis. L.R. 74.

As you will discover in your study of cases and encyclopedias, the topic of conflicts between state statutes and federal treaties is covered at length, with citations to the decisions and comments thereon, in A.L.R. annotations, in American Jurisprudence and in Corpus Juris Secundum.

# CHAPTER 5

# Legislative Histories

**§5.1.   The need for legislative histories.**   "The custom of re-making statutes to fit their histories has gone so far that a formal Act, read three times and voted on by Congress and approved by the President, is no longer a safe basis on which a lawyer may advise his client or a lower court decide a case.   This has very practical consequences for the profession.   The lawyer must consult all the committee reports on the bill, and on all its antecedents, and all that its supporters and opponents said in debate, and then predict what part of the conflicting views will likely appeal to a majority of the Court. . . ." [1]   The implications are very clear in law school courses, which increasingly demand extensive and intensive work with statutes, both to learn their substantive content and to train the student in the techniques of statutory research and evaluation.

**§5.2.   The two aspects of legislative histories.**   Legislative histories have two aspects.   The first is to follow every step of a bill's progress in Congress, from its introduction to final passage, rejection or abandonment.   The aim here is to ascertain the status of a pending bill at any given time, which may be done with the aid of status tables.   The second aspect is the determination of what Congress meant in enacting a statute.   The lawyer here seeks to convince the court that Congress had a certain intent in enacting this legislation, and he does this by means of evidence from hearings held and reports made by committees in charge of the legislation concerned, and by debates on it as recorded in the daily Congressional Record.   A major activity in many law firms and governmental agencies today is the recording of every detail bearing on the legislative intent of laws in which their clients or their agencies may be concerned.

**§5.3.   Steps in the passage of a bill through Congress.**   How Our Laws Are Made, by Charles J. Zinn, Law Revision Counsel

---

[1] Mr. Justice Robert H. Jackson of the Supreme Court of the United States, 34 A.B.A.J. 535, 538 (1948).

of the House Committee on the Judiciary, is the best brief description of this process, and it may be secured free upon application to your Congressman. As outlined therein, a bill may take any of the following steps before becoming a federal law. The state legislative process is so similar as not to need further comment here.

1. *The bill is introduced.* The bill is drafted, usually by experts employed by the respective houses of the legislature for that purpose. Several private agencies specialize in bill drafting to order, and many states now have such bureaus, which members of their legislatures may consult for expert advice on the techniques and factual backgrounds involved. Revenue bills in the Congress must originate in the House of Representatives, though this restriction is often avoided by "riders" attached to Senate bills. When introduced the bill is first dropped into the "hopper," then read by title, given a serial or bill number, assigned to its proper legislative committee and ordered to be printed. In the House few bills are read even by title at this point.

2. *The bill is considered in committee.* Ninety percent of bills introduced are not considered in committee at all, but die there without further action. When the standing or special committee of the house in which the bill is introduced does decide to study and report the bill, it may hold public hearings on it, at which time those who are interested are heard to advocate or oppose it, in person or through briefs, or both. Thereafter the committee submits to the Congress a printed report, recommending passage or nonpassage of the bill. This committee report, stating the reasons for committee recommendations, is important in the lawyer's search for legislative intent.

3. *The bill is placed on the calendar.* The calendar — whether of House or Senate or of individual committees of either house — shows the order of business. When a bill is reported out of committee, it is placed on the calendar — corresponding somewhat to a court docket — of the house wherein it is introduced. In the House, "bills raising revenues, general appropriation bills, and bills of a public character directly or indirectly appropriating money or property" are placed on the *Union* calendar. Here are placed most public bills, but there is also a House calendar for public bills not raising revenue or appropriating money or property. Bills may be removed from the above calendars if there is no objection by a member, and placed on the *Consent* calendar. If there is still no objection when brought up for consideration, bills on the Consent calendar are passed without debate, by unanimous consent. In this manner about 90 percent of all enacted bills are passed. The *Private* calendar is for bills for claims

against the United States, and private immigration bills, the latter usually for the admission of non-quota immigrants.  When a bill's turn is reached on the calendar, it is read in full, section by section — unless, as is usually the case, by unanimous consent the reading is dispensed with and the entire bill printed in the Congressional Record — and is then debated.  This is the critical stage of a reported bill.

4. *Third reading of the bill, and vote.*  The bill is then read for a third time, by title, and voted upon.  Ninety percent of all enacted bills are voted by unanimous consent.  After passage in one house, the bill is sent to the other house for action.

5. *Procedure in the other house.*  After passage of the bill in one house, much the same procedure is followed in the other house, where, however, the erstwhile "bill" is designated as an "act."  If the bill is amended in the second house, it is returned to the first, after passage, for further consideration.

6. *Conference procedure.*  In case of disagreement between the two houses on any part of the bill, each house appoints a conference committee to determine its final form.  Conferees may compromise differences, but no new matter may be added by them, nor may matters already agreed upon by both houses be touched.  Conference reports are then submitted to each house, together with the printed conference bill, which retains its original number.  The conference report is printed in the house in which the bill originated, and occasionally in the other house also.  To the practicing lawyer it is useful to know that most conference reports on public bills are also printed in the unofficial United States Code Congressional and Administrative News, and so are readily accessible to him.  Conference reports may be debated but not amended.  Many are accepted and the bill is passed by unanimous consent.  Conference bills are usually printed in the Congressional Record at this point.

7. *The bill is signed by the Speaker and the Vice-President.*  After passage of a bill by both houses, it is signed — no matter in which house it originated — first by the Speaker of the House of Representatives, and then for the Senate by the Vice-President.  It is then "engrossed" or copied — in the process of which errors may creep in — and forwarded to the President for approval.

8. *The approval or veto of the bill by the President.*  A bill becomes law upon approval by the President, which may be by his signature or by his failing during ten days within a session to veto it.  A veto is affirmative, as when the President returns a bill to Congress with a message of disapproval; or it may be a "pocket veto," as when he fails to sign a bill which was received by him

less than ten days before adjournment of Congress. An affirmative veto can be overriden only by a two-thirds vote of a quorum voting in both houses, which seldom occurs. The President thus possesses a strong negative power over legislation.

9. *The fate of bills at the end of a Congress.* Bills which have not become law at the end of a Congress die and must be introduced anew in a subsequent Congress if further action is desired. They retain their status from session to session of the same Congress, however. Treaties pending in the Senate remain in the Foreign Relations Committee until disposed of, which may take many years. (See CCH Congressional Index Treaty Table.)

§5.4. **Materials for legislative histories.**

1. *Before the bill is introduced.* Legislation usually evolves from a demonstrated need for it. This need or desire may be shown by the pressure of interested groups, or, increasingly, develops as the result of legislative investigation into various areas of the law, to see if changes are advisable. The results of these preliminary investigations are usually published as Hearings.

2. *The bill in its various forms.* For the form of a typical bill see Chapter 2. All bills have serial or bill numbers, assigned at the time they are introduced. Bills are numbered consecutively through an entire Congress and not renumbered beginning with each session. The bill number, important in tracing legislative history and particularly status on the bill's way through Congress, uniquely identifies the bill and all hearings and reports on it. The number also appears, as has been seen, as an identification tag on the slip law and in the Statutes at Large.

Identical or "companion" bills may be introduced simultaneously in each house in order to speed passage through Congress. Amendments to bills are each separately printed in the Congressional Record. When such amendments are accepted by the committee in charge of a bill, the bill is then reprinted, matter to be omitted from the original bill having a horizontal line through it, new matter being printed in italics. When there have been so many amendments offered that the original content is lost, the bill may be scrapped in favor of an entirely new one, embodying all agreed upon changes, and then is called a "clean" bill.

a. *Publication and distribution of bills.* Bills are printed and distributed individually as *slip* bills, which may be subscribed to from the Government Printing Office or obtained individually from Congressional committees. *Committee prints:* These are especially prepared for the committees in charge of the respective bills and are obtainable only, if at all, from committee members.   They often show in parallel columns, section by section, the provisions of the bill as compared to existing statutes, together with notes giving the purpose of changes made by the new bill. They are thus excellent for showing legislative intent.   *Hearings print of a bill:* The bill is always printed as a part of the record of a hearing held on it.   *Congressional Record print of a bill:* The Congressional Record prints the text of some bills, in original or amended form, such printing being a matter of editorial discretion. *Resolutions in bill form:* These are printed and distributed in slip form as introduced.   Concurrent and simple resolutions are printed in the Congressional Record and, as passed, in the House and Senate Journals.   Concurrent resolutions are printed in the Statutes at Large.

b. *Synopses of bills.*   The Digest of Public General Bills and Resolutions has been prepared by the Library of Congress since the 74th Congress "to furnish in the form of a brief summary, the essential features of public bills and resolutions and changes made therein during the legislative process."   Each issue shows the status of all bills acted upon, and lists public laws and resolutions enacted, with corresponding bill numbers.   The digests are often quite full, and short of the full text of a bill, provide the best information as to its content.   It is available in most law libraries. Beginning with the 90th Congress (1967), the scope of the Digest has been considerably enlarged, especially as to the information in the subject-index.   There are five cumulative issues a year, with biweekly supplementation.   The cover page shows which bills are covered.   The digest is a status table for bills of the current session which have been acted upon, with date reported and report number and date of passage in each house.   Private bills are listed but not summarized.   Code sections affected are noted.   In the subject-index, measures acted upon are starred (*), and some popular-name acts are listed.   There is also an author (sponsor) index.

The Commerce Clearing House Congressional Index (described at page 68, par. b) lists and indexes public general bills, but at most gives a brief digest of the bill, usually only the title.

3. *Legislative calendars.*   Calendars are the Congressman's inventories of business on hand and its present status.   Each house, and almost every standing committee, has its own calendar.   They contain excellent status tables, both in the amount of information given and in their frequency and promptness of publication.

Calendars of the House of Representatives and History of Legislation is the title of perhaps the most useful single tool for the tracing of the legislative history of a bill, whether House or Senate.

It is cumulative and appears daily during term time, except on the day following a day when the House was not in session. It is free. It lists bills which have been reported or passed by either the House or Senate. The following are regular features.

*Bills in conference.* These are listed by *date*, not bill number. Information includes the title of the bill, conference report number, and action taken by each house; for bills through conference the above information is given, plus public or private law number and date of approval.

---

**55**

**NUMERICAL ORDER OF BILLS AND RESOLUTIONS WHICH HAVE PASSED EITHER OR BOTH HOUSES, AND BILLS NOW PENDING ON THE CALENDAR**

Complete history of all actions on each bill follows the number in chronological order. For subject of bill see index, using index key following bill number in this section

Note.—Similar or identical bills, and bills having reference to each other, are indicated by number in parentheses

| No. | Index Key and History of Bill | No. | Index Key and History of Bill |
|---|---|---|---|
| | **HOUSE BILLS** | | **HOUSE BILLS—Continued** |
| H.R. 10. | Self-Employed Individuals Tax Retirement Act of 1961. Reported from Ways and Means May 9, 1961; Rept. 378. Union Calendar. Rules suspended and passed House June 5, 1961. Reported in Senate Sept. 13, 1961; Finance; Rept. 992. | H.R. 132. | Education by television. Reported from Interstate and Foreign Commerce Aug. 21, 1961; Rept. 999. Union Calendar _____ Union 411 |
| H.R. 29. | Merchant Marine Academy, appointing of U.S. nationals. Reported from Merchant Marine and Fisheries Aug. 15, 1961; Rept. 918. Union Calendar. Passed House Aug. 21, 1961. Reported in Senate Aug. 24, 1961; Commerce; Rept. 785. Passed Senate Aug. 29, 1961. Approved Sept. 6, 1961. Public Law 87–199. | H.R. 157. | Playa del Rey Inlet and Harbor, change name. Reported from Public Works Aug. 28, 1961; Rept. 1052. House Calendar. Passed House Sept. 6, 1961. |
| | | H.R. 176. | Judicial Conference of the United States, representation. Reported from Judiciary July 10, 1961; Rept. 680. Union Calendar. Passed House July 17, 1961. Reported in Senate Sept. 7, 1961; Judiciary; Rept. 887. Passed Senate Sept. 11, 1961. |

**Exhibit 9**

---

*Numerical Order of Bills and Resolutions Which Have Passed Either or Both Houses, and Bills Now Pending on the Calendar.* This is a status table, as shown by Exhibit 9.

This is one of the best of the status tables, and the most frequently issued of the cumulative tables. There is also a separate status table of major bills, by number, title, and steps through Congress. Other features are the union, House, private and consent calendars; a list of public and private laws and resolutions enacted; and a subject index to the calendars.

*Final Edition for a Congress.* This issue is prepared after the final adjournment of a Congress, in readiness for the convening of the first session of the next Congress. It is perhaps the most useful repository of legislative history for a given Congress, especially since its complete résumé of actions on all House and Senate bills and resolutions during the entire Congress comes out in advance of the History of Bills and Resolutions, issued by the Congressional Record, which covers only a *session* of a Congress. It is less useful than the History of Bills and Resolutions, in that, unlike that status table, which lists all bills introduced, whether or not they were acted upon, this calendar lists only bills on which some committee or house action was taken. There is an index, and also a complete statistical résumé of the activities of the last five Congresses. There is also a Status of Major Bills table for each session of the Congress covered. Vetoes are noted.

4. *Committee hearings.* Hearings are held by legislative committees in order to acquire information about the need for new legislation or to permit proponents or opponents of pending bills to state their views. Thus hearings may relate to specific pending bills or they may be held pursuant to a House or Senate resolution calling for the investigation of some condition which may require corrective legislation. Advance notice of hearings is given in the Daily Digest of the Congressional Record. Not all reports of hearings are printed, by any means. The CCH Congressional Index and the Daily Digest History of Bills Enacted table (through v. 107 only) tell which hearings were printed, as does the Monthly Catalog of Government Publications. Although elaborate briefs and even entire books are reprinted in some of the hearings, a great deal of the text consists of impromptu and biased statements of opinion, and the whole must be read with this in mind. Nevertheless, they are important and much used factors in legislative histories. They are available in most law libraries.

5. *Committee reports and memoranda.* Like committee hearings, reports of legislative committees may relate to pending legislation or they may have to do with the possible need of corrective legislation for which no bills have as yet been introduced. Each report bears an identifying serial number, as H. Rept. No. 19, 81st Cong., 1st Sess., or S. Rept. No. 163, 72d Cong., 2d Sess.

a. *Reports on pending bills.* Each bill reported to the House or Senate by the committee in charge is accompanied by a report setting forth the recommendations of the committee that the bill should or should not pass, and giving reasons therefor. In some cases there may be a dissenting or a minority report. The Legislative Reorganization Act of 1946 gave each committee a professional staff and adequate clerical help. Since then committee reports have tended to be highly factual studies of the background of the bills and the reasons for new legislation. The official prints of committee reports are somewhat difficult to obtain, but the unofficial United States Code Congressional and Administrative News

prints the report of either the House or Senate Committee, which-
ever the editor deems the more useful report, on bills of general
interest enacted into public law.

b. *Reports of exploratory and investigating committees.*  Congressional committees are continually investigating such widely
divergent topics as small business, subversive activities, juvenile
delinquency, baseball as a monopoly, and the like, to discover
whether or not corrective legislation is needed.  The reports of
these investigations are often embodied in what in effect are extensive treatises on the subject matter involved, of considerable
intrinsic value outside their intended purpose of aiding Congress.
Examples of such reports are Congress and the Monopoly Problem: Fifty-six Years of Antitrust Development, 1900-1956, in 662
pages; and Documentation, Indexing, and Retrieval of Scientific
Information; a Study of Federal and Non-Federal Science Information Processing and Retrieval Programs, in 283 pages.

c. *House and Senate Documents.*  "Documents," so called,
contain reports of Congressional investigatory committees other
than those printed as committee "Reports," as described above,
and Presidential messages.  Communications which governmental
agencies frequently send to Congress relating to pending bills
affecting them are printed as documents, and usually in the Congressional Record as well.

6. *Legislative debates and proceedings.*  From 1774 on there has
been some sort of official or unofficial publication of the minutes
and debates of Congress.  Of current interest are the Congressional
Record and its Daily Digest, and the House and Senate Journals.

a. *Congressional Record.*  This newspaper is probably the most
useful single publication for the purpose of legislative history.
Published daily during sessions of Congress, Monday through
Friday except on days following a Congressional recess, it is popu-
larly supposed to be a full and faithful record of all that takes
place in Congress.  For various reasons it is rather far from being
that, because Congressmen may revise their remarks made on the
floor, before publication in the Record; but in general it is substantially accurate.  It covers the following:

    Introduction of all bills, resolutions and amendments
    Debates, supposedly verbatim, but subject to revision
    Text of many bills and joint resolutions; Simple and con-
       current resolutions are printed as passed
    Presidential messages
    Treaties, when debated

In addition, there is an appendix in which may be printed communications from government departments concerning pending

legislation in which they are interested; extensions of remarks supposed to have been made by Congress on the floor but in fact never made; and much miscellaneous material, such as a poem by the six-year-old son of a Congressman's constituent.

*Index to the Proceedings.* Issued every ten days and cumulated *annually,* it comprises a combined Index to the Proceedings, and a History of Bills and Resolutions for both House and Senate. Entries are by subject matter of pending legislation and by Congressman — the latter entries covering every bill and amendment offered and every motion or remark made on the floor. The History of Bills and Resolutions is probably the most widely available status table there is for legislation. It is also a finding guide to the text of simple and concurrent resolutions as passed. All bills and resolutions are listed by number, with title and every action taken on them noted, up to and including approval by the President or passage over his veto.

It is difficult, however, to follow debate on a bill through the "History," because it tends to list the first page where a bill was taken up on the floor but to ignore the skipping over of many pages because of intervening motions or "yielding" by a Congressman debating the bill. Checking debates fully is thus a laborious task.

A specimen entry is shown in Exhibit 10. The paging of the daily edition of the Congressional Record and of the Daily Digest differs from that of the bound volume. The text may differ also, since Congressmen are permitted to revise their remarks prior to final printing. *In legal writing, cite the bound volume if it is avail-*

H.R. 8601—To enforce constitutional rights, and for other purposes.
Made special order (H. Res. 359), 5192.—Debated, 5199, 5295, 5441, 5635, 5752, 5897, 6009, 6159, 6277, 6369.—Amended and passed House, 6509.—Referred to Senate Committee on the Judiciary with instructions, 6452.—Reported with amendments (S. Rept. 1205), (S. Rept 1205, pt. 2), 7187.—Debated (in lieu of H.R. 8315). 6931, 6945, 6954, 7023, 7049, 7051, 7053, 7129, 7137, 7208, 7213, 7219, 7244, 7312, 7343, 7344, 7354, 7401, 7408, 7409, 7417, 7448, 7497, 7536, 7558, 7563, 7578, 7728, 7746, 7763, 7803.—Amended and passed Senate, 7811.—Pursuant to H. Res. 503 House concurs in Senate amendments, 8491.—Examined and signed, 8574, 8581.—Presented to the President, 8677.—Approved [Public Law 449], 9796.

**Exhibit 10**

## HISTORY OF BILLS ENACTED INTO PUBLIC LAW (86TH CONG., 2D SESS.)—Continued

| Title | Bill No. | Date introduced | Committees—hearings House | Committees—hearings Senate | Date reported House | Date reported Senate | Report No. House | Report No. Senate | Page of Congressional Record of passage House | Page of Congressional Record of passage Senate | Date of passage House | Date of passage Senate | Public law Date approved | Public law No. |
|---|---|---|---|---|---|---|---|---|---|---|---|---|---|---|
| To set aside certain lands in Oklahoma for the Cheyenne and Arapaho Indians. | H.R. 816 | Jan. 7, 1959 | IIA | IIA | May 25, 1959 | June 20 | 378 | 1617 | 9461 | 14221 | June 1, 1959 | June 24 | Sept. 14 | 86-791 |
| Relating to the disposition of certain U.S. lands in Alaska. | S. 3267 | Mar. 23 | IIA | IIA | Aug. 29 | June 21 | 2196 | 1628 | 18762 | 14669 | Aug. 31 | June 28 | Sept. 14 | 86-792 |
| To protect farmers making certain land use changes under the Great Plains conservation program against loss of acreage allotments. | S. 3533 (H.R. 12849) | May 11 | Agr | Agr | Aug. 18 | June 29 | 2100 | 1773 | 18406 | 15619 | Aug. 30 | July 2 | Sept. 14 | 86-793 |
| Authorizing a compact between Maryland, Virginia, and the D.C. for the the regulation of mass transit in the metropolitan area. | H.J. Res. 402 | May 27, 1959 | Jud* | Jud* | May 18 | Aug. 23 | 1621 | 1906 | 11750 | 19000 | June 2 | Sept. 1 | Sept. 15 | 86-794 |
| To provide a temporary suspension of duty on heptanoic acid. | H.R. 12659 | June 15 | WM | Fin | June 29 | Aug. 25 | 2033 | 1913 | 15813 | 17857 | July 2 | Aug. 26 | Sept. 15 | 86-795 |
| Relating to holding world sport parachuting championships at Orange, Mass. | H.J. Res. 723 | June 1 | FA | | Aug. 26 | | 2169 | | 18387 | 18587 | Aug. 30 | Aug. 31 | Sept. 15 | 86-796 |
| To promote fish and game conservation and rehabilitation in military reservations. | H.R. 2565 | Jan. 15, 1959 | MMF* | IFC | Aug. 5, 1959 | May 27 | 767 | 1492 | 6132 | 13995 | Mar. 21 | June 23 | Sept. 15 | 86-797 |
| Authorizing grants-in-aid to nonprofit institutions to strengthen health research programs. | H.R. 10341 | Feb. 10 | IFC* | | Aug. 26 | | 2174 | | 18394 | 18593 | Aug. 30 | Aug. 31 | Sept. 15 | 86-798 |
| To establish a price support level for milk and butterfat. | S. 2917 | Jan. 27 | Agr* | Agr* | Aug. 29 | June 15 | 2182 | 1392 | 18748 | 16784 | Aug. 31 | Aug. 19 | Sept. 16 | 86-799 |
| To amend the Tariff Act of 1930 to place bamboo pipestems on the free list. | H.R. 10841 | Mar. 2 | WM | Fin | July 1 | Aug. 25 | 2079 | 1912 | 15814 | 18602 | July 2 | Aug. 31 | Sept. 16 | 86-800 |

* The starring of printed items is discontinued. See page 62.

NOTE.—The bill in parentheses is companion measure.

### TABLE OF COMMITTEE ABBREVIATIONS

| | | | | | |
|---|---|---|---|---|---|
| AE | Joint Committee on Atomic Energy | EdL | Education and Labor | IIA | Interior and Insular Affairs |
| Aer | Aeronautical and Space Sciences | FA | Foreign Affairs | IFC | Interstate and Foreign Commerce |
| Agr | Agriculture | FR | Foreign Relations | Jud | Judiciary |
| App | Appropriations | Fin | Finance | LPW | Labor and Public Welfare |
| AS | Armed Services | GO | Government Operations | MMF | Merchant Marine and Fisheries |
| BC | Banking and Currency | HA | House Administration | POCS | Post Office and Civil Service |
| DC | District of Columbia | | | | |

| | |
|---|---|
| PW | Public Works |
| R Adm | Rules and Administration |
| R | Rules |
| SA | Space and Astronautics |
| VA | Veterans' Affairs |
| WM | Ways and Means |

Exhibit 11

*able; otherwise give volume, page and exact date of the daily issue.*
Thus the same material from the daily edition is cited as 94 Cong.
Rec. 9917 (Aug. 4, 1948), and 94 Cong. Rec. 9761 (1948), when
cited from the bound volume.

b. *Daily Digest of the Congressional Record.* This is a supplement contained in each issue of the Congressional Record but
cumulated at the end of a session into a separate bound volume.
It is a sort of newspaper within a newspaper for Congressmen's use,
enabling them to brush up quickly on what went on the day before,
is scheduled for today and for tomorrow.   It notes bills introduced
the preceding day, bills and resolutions reported or passed, a
résumé of business transacted, of committee appointments, votes
and debates, and of committee hearings scheduled or held.   The
first issue of each month contains a cumulative statistical survey
of the business transacted by Congress to date and a table of appropriation bills passed.   The annual index, in addition to cumulating the daily indexes, has a useful table of bills enacted into public
law during the session, and a History of Bills Enacted Into Public
Law, in which, arranged by law number, are given the bill title
and number, date of introduction, hearings held, date reported,
committee report number, and Congressional Record page noting passage and approval.   See Exhibit 11 above.

There is also a subject index which serves as a status table for
each bill and resolution acted upon during the session.   A typical
index entry follows.   Page references are to the Daily Digest, which
in turn refers to the pertinent Congressional Record pages.

> LIBRARY SERVICES ACT (H.R. 9812, H.R.
>   12125, S. 2830)
>       Committee, Senate D263, 283
>       Senate D298
>       Committee, House D156, 176, 180,
>           255, 260, 274, 318
>       House D453
>       Public Law 86–679

Exhibit 12

c. *House and Senate Journals.* These record the proceedings
and votes of each house, with the debates omitted.

d. *Presidential messages.* Messages from the President are employed to suggest the need of new legislation or to veto bills passed
and submitted to him for approval by the Congress.   Since 1873
they have been printed in the Congressional Record, the House
and Senate Journals (veto messages only in the Journal of the house

in which the bill originated), as House or Senate Documents, and, since 1939, selected ones in the unofficial United States Code Congressional and Administrative News.

7. *Unofficial aids in compiling legislative histories.* Two of the most useful and frequently consulted aids are unofficial, though one of them publishes the official text of federal legislative documents of various kinds. As is typical of private law publications, greater promptness of issuance than of the official is an important feature.

a. *United States Code Congressional and Administrative News.* This periodical is accessible and indispensable in keeping the reader abreast of current federal fundamental legislative documents. It aims at supplying in one place verbatim copies of federal legislative materials less easily found in official form, or not so promptly. It is a very good tool not only for the collection and use of current federal conventional and subordinate legislation but for legislative history in the form of Congressional committee reports. It is issued semimonthly during sessions of Congress, cumulating into annual bound volumes covering a session, corresponding in coverage of public laws to the volumes of the Statutes at Large. Each issue contains some or all of the following departments.

(1) *Public laws of general interest in verbatim text.* This is one of the most convenient forms in which to collect such public laws. Statutes at Large citations are included.

(2) *Congressional committee reports.* For the public laws of general interest published in this periodical, one committee report is printed, it being that one, whether House or Senate, which the editor deems more useful. This is the "Legislative History" referred to in parentheses preceding the text of the corresponding public law printed in the same pamphlet issue.

(3) *Presidential messages, proclamations and executive orders, verbatim.*

(4) *Federal court rules as amended, verbatim.*

(5) *Administrative rules and regulations.* A selection of these rules and regulations and proposed regulations is printed. Of particular general interest are those of the Internal Revenue Service, and of the Immigration and Naturalization Service, and those relating to Social Security.

(6) *Tables.* These largely duplicate those in the United States Code Annotated, serving, since they are issued semimonthly during sessions of Congress instead of quarterly, as supplements to the U.S.C.A. tables. These tables cumulate for each issue so as to cover the entire session of Congress to date. They are of great

value in checking the present status of Congressional legislation of a given term. They cover: (a) public laws so far enacted during a session, with Statutes at Large citations; (b) United States Code classification assigned to public laws or parts of them incorporated in the Code, as printed in the current pamphlets; (c) United States Code sections affected — whether amended, repealed, etc. — by new legislation; (d) bills enacted into law, by bill number; (e) proclamations and executive orders, listed by number, date and title.

The above tables are of such utility that the student should examine them carefully so as to familiarize himself with them and their uses.

(7) *Index to all material printed during the session.* This is a cumulative index, covering the entire session to date, so that it is necessary to consult only the latest pamphlet issue of the periodical.

(8) *Index-Digest of Bills Introduced.* The yellow pages of each issue form a not very useful status table, which is omitted from the bound volumes. Its purpose is to point up legislative highlights of the preceding half month in Congress.

(9) *Annual cumulated volumes.* At the end of each session of Congress, the material in the pamphlet issues of the United States Code Congressional and Administrative News, is cumulated into bound volumes under the preceding categories. The bound volumes thus serve some of the purposes of the Statutes at Large, as supplements to Code tables, as convenient repositories of committee reports on newly enacted public laws, and as a collection of selected administrative rules and Presidential Documents.

b. *Commerce Clearing House Congressional Index.* This is perhaps the most frequently used index to the current legislative history material of a Congress. It is in loose-leaf form, taken from diverse official sources and so arranged and published as to be more usable than the official indexes. Purely an index, it contains no texts or abridgments of bills, committee reports or debates. As is typical of loose-leaf services and reporters, some of its separate indexes are chronologically in two parts; one for the material as a whole, the second supplementing the first by reference to the latest bills. *A complete coverage thus requires consultation of both indexes.* As is also true of all loose-leaf services, there is a sheet with a tab at the beginning of this service which tells in detail what is contained in it and how to use it. Following the instructions there given will save the user a good bit of time and insure better results than blind hunting. Following are features of the Congressional Index:

(1) *Pending public measures indexed.* These are covered under

such headings as Headline Legislation, Name Bills (as the Landrum-Griffin bill), Companion Bills, and by subject, with bills acted upon indicated by an asterisk. The introducer of the bill is also listed. Only public bills are indexed.

(2) *Bills and resolutions.* These are listed by number.

(3) *Bill status tables.* This is perhaps the most convenient of all federal legislative status tables, though the House Calendar (for which see §5.4(3)) is more complete and current in its coverage. Only *reported public bills* are covered, but for them every Congressional action is shown. Approved bills for the current session are indicated by a large star. Information is given about hearings on bills listed, and committee reports are noted, with serial number of the reports.

(4) *Special reports.* Those not relating to pending bills are listed.

(5) *Public laws enacted so far during the session.* These are listed by number and subject.

(6) *Treaties pending at the beginning of each session.* These are listed, with any action taken indicated.

(7) *Members of Congress listed.* Biographical information is given, including committee assignments. This is useful when writing to a Congressman for information or copies of publications. The same information is given in the Congressional Directory, an official publication issued for each session of Congress.

(8) *Voting records of each Congressman given.* This table covers a Congressman's action on any bill subject to a roll-call vote. Listing is (a) by bill number and (b) by Congressman, thus showing both who voted for and against a given bill, and how a given Congressman voted on all roll-call bills.

§5.5. **Compiling a legislative history.** In large law firms and in many government agencies the compiling of legislative histories relating to clients' or agencies' interests is a major activity, with the data collected going into extreme detail both as to content and indexing. The law student, while he ordinarily will have a more circumscribed interest directed probably to a specific bill involved in a problem he is studying in law school, must nevertheless understand much of the procedure and technique involved.

It is evident that the compiler of a federal legislative history has at his disposal a wide variety of materials. How he will proceed depends largely upon the precise objective of his search.

1. *Finding the specific bill.* Assuming that the law student is tracing the history of a pending bill, he will seek to collect the bills, House, Senate, and companion, in both original and amended form. He may find these bills, verbatim, filed by Congress and session, in his law school library; or, more likely, in the

form of good abstracts or abridgments in the Digest of Public General Bills.

2. *Status tables.* His next step is to consult a status table — under whatever title — to see what, if any, action has been taken on his bill since its introduction. There are numerous such tables, as outlined in §6.4. The most complete of these is the History of Bills and Resolutions, in the fortnightly issues of the Congressional Record and supplemented daily in part by the Daily Digest of the Congressional Record. This History cumulates in an annual index volume to the Congressional Record, covering each session of Congress. It is also the most complete federal status table there is, because it covers *all introduced bills and resolutions, both public and private, whether further acted upon or not.* Other status tables, on the contrary, cover only bills which have at least been reported out of committee, and this excludes 90 percent of all bills introduced. The Congressional Record History notes every action of any kind relating to all bills, from introduction to approval as laws or final rejection. Other status tables except the House Calendar do this only for public bills which have been acted upon.

An excellent status table, kept up to date by weekly loose-leaf supplements, is in the CCH Congressional Index, which also notes the votes of each Congressman on pending legislation. A too-little-known but most excellent status table is in the legislative Calendars of the House of Representatives, which covers Senate bills also. This is a daily, cumulative index, by bill number, setting forth every action to date on the bill. If your law school library does not have this index, it can probably have its name placed on a free mailing list.

3. *Legislative intent.* If the searcher is concerned also with legislative intent — what the Congress probably intended by legislation it has enacted — he has access to hearings of legislative committees, committee reports, and the debates on the bill on the floor of the House and Senate before enactment. Hearings may have been held before bills were introduced — to determine whether or not new legislation was called for — or after introduction, to permit interested parties — individuals, foundations or government agencies — to oppose or favor the bill by personal testimony or by briefs submitted to the committee handling the bill and incorporated in the hearing text. If the hearings are printed — and often they are not — as determined by reference to some status tables or in the annual table of public laws in the Daily Digest index volume, they can probably be found through the law school library. Reports of legislative commit-

tees are also available in most university libraries, but here the searcher probably has at hand the committee reports published in the United States Code Congressional and Administrative News.

Debates in Congress are a most fruitful source of legislative intent determination. They are reported at length in the Congressional Record, which in turn is indexed fortnightly, cumulating into an annual index. The index is by subject matter, introducer of the bill and by bill number, showing every action on the bill or resolution introduced.

4. *Finding the bill number of a law.* It often becomes necessary to trace the legislative history and intent of an existing law. To do this it is first necessary to learn its bill number, which may be done easily by two methods.

a. *Statutes at Large or slip laws.* Both the official, the unofficial United States Code and Administrative News, and the Federal Code Annotated compilations give the bill number preceding the text of the statute.

b. *From indexes.* When only the subject of a law is known, the above citations are obtainable through the statute subject index. A more laborious method is to trace the law through the table in the annual volume of the Congressional Record Daily Digest, which under the public law number gives the desired information. The CCH Congressional Index table of enacted laws may be similarly used, but neither of these methods would be employed if the slip law or Statutes at Large were available.

By the use of these same tables the searcher can find (1) committee reports on the subject matter of the legislation; (2) hearings; (3) debates on the floor of Congress; and (4) Presidential messages setting forth reasons for vetoing such a bill. If he is lucky, the searcher may find a committee print of his bill, in which, in parallel columns, are set forth the legislation existing when the bill was introduced, and corresponding provisions of the bill, the legislative history of which he is investigating. The committee print may also give the committee's rationale. When there has been extensive revision of existing legislation, as was the case when the patent laws were revised and reenacted into positive law as Title 35 of the United States Code, the revisers' notes may be published in full. This was done for some Code titles by the United States Code Annotated.

5. *Law office or governmental agency procedure.* Compiling histories here is a continuing chore, with much the following routine observed.

Digest the Congressional Record and Federal Register (the latter is described in Chapter 14) daily, reporting on all legislation of interest to the agency or firm, noting both new bills, the progress of previously noted bills and regulations, new or proposed, touching agency or clients' activities.

For each new bill of interest, start a file; until the bill becomes a law or dies, initial entries are made on a large index card calling for the following information: bill number, companion and related bill numbers, name of introducer, title and subject matter of bill, hearings, action in Congress (dates, pages in Congressional Record where noted committee reports, etc.), Presidential

## FIRST SUPPLEMENT SURPLUS APPROPRIATION
### RESCISSION ACT, 1946
Public Law 301 — 79th Congress
Ch. 30 — 2d Session
*(H.R. 5158)
Approved February 18, 1946.

An act reducing certain appropriations and authorizations ................1
Communication from the President transmitting . . . (H. Doc. 394) ......2
H.R. 5158 as introduced . . . and referred . . . January 17, 1946 ........3
H.R. 5158 as reported in House, January 29, 1946 .....................4
Report . . . to accompany H.R. 5158 . . . (H. Rept. 1500) ..............5
H.R. 5158 as passed House January 30, 1946, and referred ...............6
H.R. 5158 as reported in Senate with an amendment, Feb. 4, 1946 ........7
Report of Senate committee . . . (S. Rept. 919) .......................8
    *REFERENCES IN THE CONGRESSIONAL RECORD* ......9
1946
Jan. 17.    H.R. 5158 introduced . . . and referred ..................p.117
Jan. 29.    H.R. reported in House . . . (H. Rept. 1500) ............p.571
Jan. 30.    H.R. 5158 considered in House ................p.605, 606-7, 611
            Passed House .......................................p.619
            Proposed Reductions in Appropriations ..............p.616
            Proposed Reductions in Contract Authorizations ......p.617
Jan. 31.    H.R. 5158 referred to Senate Committee on Appropriations p.368
Feb. 8.    H.R. 5158 considered, amended, and passed by Senate ....p.1181
Feb. 13.    H.R. 5158 signed by the Speaker of the House ............p.1328
            Signed by the President pro tempore of Senate ........p.1281
            Signed by the President ..........................p.1328
            Approved by the President February 18, 1946; became Public
            Law 301

###### APPENDIX A.

H.R. 4103, a bill reducing certain appropriations. . . . [the history of this companion bill is given as above]

* This bill supersedes H.R. 4103 . . . and H.R. 4407 . . . H.R. 4407 . . . was vetoed . . . because it contained a rider to return . . . See appendixes for histories on H.R. 4103 and H.R. 4407.

H.R. 5604, a bill reducing or further reducing . . . was reported in the House on February 27, 1946.

**Exhibit 13**

action, public or private law number. All bills, hearings, reports, Congressional documents and Congressional Record clippings of debates are collected, with the act as finally approved.

From the index card you prepared, make a calendar or table of contents in final form, numbering each item in the margin. Collect, arrange by number all material listed, in order, and bind or file for permanent preservation.

Cross references should be made to all companion and related bills, and the same process followed with regard to them.

Above, in Exhibit 13, is part of a very simple legislative history, greatly abridged both as to number and fullness of entries, printed through the courtesy of its compiler, Miss Minnie Wiener, while Librarian of the General Services Administration.

§5.6. **State legislative histories.** One of the most frequent inquiries of the law librarian is for materials showing the legislative history of state legislation, paralleling those available in the federal field. The answer which must, unfortunately, be given nearly always is that it does not exist, though a good many state legislatures publish status tables during their sessions, in some form or other. Bills are not usually available, but in some states they are distributed, either generally or singly upon application to the legislature. Digests of pending legislation are more frequent and may be cumulated at session's end. Some unofficial legislative services for state annotated statutes series give information relating to pending legislation, including reports of commissions and administrative agencies proposing or opposing pending legislation. Legislative journals are usually published, but with the exception of those for California, Maine and Pennsylvania — which attempt some approximation of the Congressional Records content — they give only the minutes of the sessions, including votes on various measures, and little else.

Perhaps the most fruitful source of background information on state legislation is found in the reports and bulletins of the numerous state law revision commissions, legislative research bureaus, legislative councils, and state university bureaus of government and public administration. State law librarians are usually glad to be of service as far as their facilities permit.

# CHAPTER 6

# Indexes and Tables for Work with
# Federal Statutes

**§6.1. Subject indexes to statutes generally.** A major factor in successful work with statutes is facility with indexes and tables. Because of constant change in statute law, both in content (as traced through subject indexes) and in form (as followed by means of transfer tables from one form of legislation to another) by amendment, repeal and judicial interpretation (as shown in annotations and citators), tabular means of keeping abreast of legislation are a necessity.

Statutory indexes tend to be less complete and satisfactory than those for cases. The reason is this: The word indexes to decided cases cover not only every legal principle but every fact situation in every reported case. Their entries concern actual situations which have been brought into court for decision. The statute subject indexes, on the other hand, are to hypothetical situations as envisioned by the lawmakers when enacting the law and specifically referred to in the text of their enactments. They are not to facts involved in cases actually interpreting the statutes. Their coverage, therefore, is vastly less detailed than would be the coverage of cases interpreting the statutes, as they are in case digest word indexes.

Each session law volume indexes the laws contained in it, through which those statutes may be located in the volume. Because of subsequent amendment, repeal and death of statutes (as appropriation bills expiring at the end of the appropriation period), these indexes are of little value in ascertaining the present state of statute law.   For that, one must consult the indexes supplied with compilations of statutes, federal or state.

**§6.2.  Subject indexes to federal statutes.**  Statutes at Large individual volumes index by subject all enactments published in each volume, but their value is limited to what is so contained at the time of enactment, and they do not present a true picture of the entire federal legislative content.   The index to the United States Code covers public general laws of permanent interest in force at the time of publication and is the index commonly used by lawyers.   Two indexes, one by Beaman and McNamara, and the other by McClenon and Gilbert, described below, cover up to 1931 all federal laws of public general interest which have *ever* been in force, and these indexes still have some value for historical purposes.   See also *Note,* page 10.

1. *Constitution.*  The Constitution is indexed separately in all editions of the United States Code and in separate annotated editions of the Constitution.   It is also separately indexed in some state statutory compilations.

2. *All federal statutes ever enacted.*  There is no general index with this wide coverage.

3. *All private federal laws ever enacted.*  No cumulative index of present value exists, but these laws are indexed in the individual volumes of the Statutes at Large.

4. *All public federal laws ever enacted.*  There is no cumulative index of this kind, covering all public laws.   Such laws are indexed in the individual volumes of the Statutes at Large.

5. *All public general laws of a permanent nature ever enacted.* There have been only two indexes of this kind, each now of only historical value.   They are, respectively, the Index Analysis of the Federal Statutes . . . 1789-1873, compiled by Middleton G. Beaman and A. K. McNamara; and the Index to the Federal Statutes, 1874-1931, compiled by Walter H. McClenon and Wilfred C. Gilbert.   Together, they cover all federal legisation of a public, general and permanent nature through 1931, whether in force or not at the time the indexes were compiled.   Although both these indexes have lost much of their value through not being kept up to date after 1931, they are invaluable in tracing the history of

earlier legislation. For example, the history of federal legislation concerning banks, courts, railroads, etc. through 1931, is readily followed.

6. *Public general laws of a permanent nature in force.* This is the common type of statutory subject index for both federal and state compilations of public laws, and every general statutory compilation has such an index. Although many sections of the United States Revised Statutes are still in force, its index is now of limited interest because those sections which are in force are practically all incorporated in the United States Code, and indexed therein, together with any later amendatory legislation. Lawyers ordinarily will consult the subject index to the United States Code, in either an annotated or unannotated edition. This type of index must be used with an awareness that *only acts actually in force as incorporated in the compilation indexed* are covered. For earlier codified material, since repealed, superseded or expired, the index to the latest edition of the compilation still containing such enactments must be consulted. Also, some statutes indexed may since have been amended, repealed or superseded, requiring recourse by the searcher to the latest pamphlet supplements of the compilations or to Shepard's United States Citations, to make certain that the present picture is complete and accurate.

7. *United States Code.* The indexes to the Code, either in the official, unannotated edition or in the privately published, annotated editions, are the currently useful indexes of the type which index permanent federal laws of a public general nature. It is important to note that *all material printed in the Code volumes is indexed, editorial matters as well as Code sections.* Entries are both by large topic (as Agriculture, Patents), by governmental agency (as Department of Agriculture, Court of Claims), and by fact or catchword (as High Schools, Jurisdictional Amount), all integrated in a single alphabetical order as in a dictionary. Acts by popular name are occasionally indexed, but there is a separate and more complete table of such acts in all Code editions. The Federal Rules of Civil and of Criminal Procedure are indexed, as are those of some courts. Agency rules of practice which prescribe the conduct of business before these agencies, are often printed in the Code as appendices, and when this is done they are indexed.

The United States Code Annotated indexes are prepared by the compilers of the United States Code indexes and the indexes are substantially identical; occasionally, however, the former indexes are somewhat fuller in content, and it may therefore be wise to search them when the official edition indexes fail. Recompiled volumes of the U.S.C.A. now have their own separate indexes, but the general index, since it covers overlapping subject matter from all titles of the Code, is often more satisfactory to use. The Federal Code Annotated has both a general index and one for each separate volume. It is important to bear in mind that citations in the Code indexes are to Code titles and sections and not to the original or Statutes at Large form of enactment.

8. *Administrative rules and regulations.* The indexes to the Federal Register and the Code of Federal Regulations are described in Chapter 14. Some of these rules are indexed also in loose-leaf services described in Chapter 23.

9. *Court rules.* These rules are indexed in any volume printing them, whether in the Code, digests, the Federal Rules Service or in separate treatises or manuals on federal procedure. They are described in Chapter 8.

**§6.3. Popular-name tables for federal acts.** Many acts are known by a popular name — as the G.I. Bill of Rights — and almost every edition of federal statutes lists enactments by such titles. This may be done by a separate table by popular name, or, less frequently, the popular name may be an entry in the general subject index, with no separate table. Following are listed some of the most frequently used tables.

1. *Shepard's Acts and Cases by Popular Names, Federal and State . . . to January 1, 1968.* This is the title of a new publication combining, in one hard cover volume, two previous paperback pamphlets, *Federal Acts by Popular Names or Short Titles* and *Federal and State Cases by Popular Names.* The new volume will also include popular names of state acts which were found previously only in the state editions of Shepard's Citators. Shepard's will continue to publish this information in the state editions as well. A paper-covered cumulative supplement will be issued to keep *Shepard's Acts and Cases by Popular Names* up-to-date. In the case of federal acts, citations are given to the Statutes

| Hou | FEDERAL AND STATE ACTS CITED BY POPULAR NAMES | |
|---|---|---|
| **Housing Act (Shipping Board)**<br>U. S., Mar. 1, 1918, c. 19, 40 Stat. 438 | | **Housing Act of 1961**<br>U. S. Code 1964 Title 12, §§371, 1701 et seq.<br>U. S. Code 1964 Title 15, §§631, 633, 636<br>U. S. Code 1964 Title 40, §§461, 462<br>U. S. Code 1964 Title 42, §1401 et seq.<br>June 30, 1961, P. L. 87-70, 75 Stat. 149 |
| **Housing Act (State)**<br>Del. Code of 1953, Title 31, §4101 et seq.<br>Kan. Laws 1933, Ch. 225 | | |
| **Housing Law (State Board)**<br>Pa. 1937 Pamph. Laws 1705, No. 359 | | **Housing Act of 1964**<br>U. S. Code 1964 Title 12, §1703 et seq. |

**Exhibit 14**

at Large and to the United States Code; while in the case of state acts, citation is usually to the state compilation if there is one, if not then to the session law citation.  See Exhibit 14.

2. *Digest of the United States Supreme Court Reports: Table of Statutes by Popular Name.*  This is probably the most complete list of its kind, and is contained in volume 14 of the digest.  It is useful also as a subject index, since all federal legislation in many categories can be easily traced in it.  For example, listed is all federal legislation concerning national forests, monuments and parks; all naturalization, pension, Indian, tariff and merchant marine acts; as well as general peace treaties.  Legislation relating to government departments and other agencies is listed, as are neutrality proclamations.  The supplementation of this table is by annual pocket parts.

3. *United States Code popular-name tables.*  Both official and annotated editions of the Code contain such lists, including statutes which *at any time* have been part of the Code.  The two tables described above cover statutes not in the Code, giving them a broader coverage than the Code table.

4. *Current-year tables by popular name.*  Shepard's United States Citations, as noted, supplements its list during the year.  The pamphlet supplements of the U.S.C.A. and F.C.A. do the same.  The United States Code Congressional and Administrative News has a popular-name table, supplemented twice a month; the CCH Congressional Index lists Name Bills, Headline Legislation, and acts by official short title as given in the preamble.  The general index of United States Law Week and the American Digest System Descriptive-Word Index frequently list litigated statutes by popular name.

5. *United States Statutes at Large Tables of Laws Affected.*  Each cumulation of this title publishes a "List of Popular Name Acts Affected" by the enactments of the Statutes at Large in the period covered.

§6.4.  **Bill status tables.**  These tables and their indispensable function in tracing the current status in Congress of individual bills and resolutions have been described in Chapter 5.  The following, accordingly, is intended only to correlate that information.

1. *Coverage of bill status tables: All bills introduced.*  Status tables generally ignore unreported bills, estimated at 90 percent of the total introduced.  Omission of a bill from a cumulative status table indicates that it was never reported out of committee.

a. *Congressional Record History of Bills and Resolutions.*  This is the one status table which lists *all* bills and resolutions.  As introduced, they are indexed in the fortnightly noncumulative indexes to the Congressional Record. Thereafter they are listed only as action is taken on them during the period covered by the index. At the end of each session, all this information is cumulated in a History of Bills and Resolutions for each the House and the Senate, in which *every bill and resolution introduced*, whether acted upon or not, is listed, and its legislative history given. This is the only complete status table for Congressional legislation, and it is a good one, widely available. (But see §5.4(3).)

2. *Coverage of bill status tables: Bills acted upon.*

a. *Congressional Record Daily Digest.* The subject index of bills acted upon serves as a status table. See page 66, par. b.

b. *CCH Congressional Index.* This table lists reported public bills only; for them, every action taken is reported. See page 68, par. b.

c. *Digest of Public General Bills.* This publication (see page 60) digests bills which have been acted upon and serves as a status table for them. The final issue for each *session* of a Congress is a very useful tool, giving at once rather good abridgments of bills acted upon and noting any action taken in Congress on them.

d. *House of Representatives Calendars.* The daily Numerical Order of Bills and Resolutions Which Have Passed Either House, and Bills Now Pending on the Calendar, as noted at page 61, par. 3, is a very good status table of reported bills, private as well as public, for both House and Senate. The Final Edition for a Congress, since it covers an entire Congress instead of only a session (as does the Congressional Record History of Bills), is one of the most useful single status tables.

e. *Treaty status tables.* See Chapter 4.

3. *Procedure in using bill status tables.*

a. *Bill number and Congress known.* When the searcher has the bill number and the Congress, he need only check that number in a current status table in order to determine what, if any, actions have been taken on it, and the dates and nature of such actions. Some tables note the publication of hearings and reports (with the report number). Which table to use depends upon its availability, latest date of coverage, and whether the searcher is interested only in the bill's status in Congress, or wishes also to check debates and amendments offered on the floor of Congress. If texts of debates are required, he can find citations to them directly from the Congressional Record History of Bills and Resolutions indexes (remembering that the fortnightly indexes cite to the unbound paging of the daily issues, which differs from that of the bound volumes to which the annual index cites). For the period between fortnightly Congressional Record indexes, the searcher can check the Daily Digest caption noting Chamber Action, House and Senate.

b. *Bill number and Congress not known.* If the bill is pending and the subject matter is known, any of the status tables above listed should turn up its number. If the bill is known to have been enacted into law and its subject matter or the Public Law number is known, the law can be found through means described in Chapters 3 and 5, such as the subject indexes of the United States Code Congressional and Administrative News, the Statutes at Large, and the CCH Congressional Index. In the margin of each of these, the bill number is shown.

c. *Introducer's name is known.* If the introducer's name is known, the bill number can best be found through the subject index of the Congressional Record and in the CCH Congressional Index.

d. *Searching all required units of tables.* As a matter of routine, the searcher makes certain that he has examined *all* pertinent units of indexes consulted. Thus the fortnightly indexes of the Congressional Record's History of Bills and Resolutions list only bills *as introduced* and, thereafter, any *subsequent* action during a *session* of Congress. In this and other status tables, absence of a bill number in the table means no action has been taken on it. Since the History of Bills and Resolutions fortnightly index is not cumulative, a complete search during a session requires examination of each such fortnightly unit. Because the History of Bills and Resolutions annual cumulation covers only a session of a Congress, a complete search of a bill acted upon but not enacted into law during the first session requires also a search of that bill in the second or later session indexes.

The same procedure as to the latest index is routine for the other status tables listed above, except that the House of Representatives Calendars covers an entire Congress, not just one session.

**§6.5. Parallel conversion tables: Bill or chapter number to law number, or reverse.** If the bill or the law text is at hand, conversion is easy, as all this information appears on its face. When, however, the slip law is not available, it becomes necessary by other means to translate a bill to a law number, or the reverse; a law number to a Statutes at Large citation; or a law number to a United States Code title and section. There are tables to perform most of these tasks for public laws.

1. *Bill number to public law number.* That is, as *from* H.R. 6538, 81st Congress, *to* Public Law Number 495 of the same Congress. This information is found as follows:

a. *Face of the slip law or Statutes at Large.*

b. *Status tables.* These tables give this information for enacted public laws.

c. *United States Code Congressional and Administrative News.* The table of Senate and House Bill Enacted gives this information.

2. *Public law number to bill number.* That is, as *from* Public Law Number 496, 81st Congress, *to* H.R. 6538 of the same Congress. The information is found as follows:

a. *On the face of the slip law.*

b. *On the face of the Statutes at Large.* In the Statutes at Large volumes public law numbers are indexed from the List of Public Laws, arranged by law number.

c. *Digest of Public General Bills: Public Laws table.*

d. *Daily Digest of Congressional Record:* annual History of Bills Enacted into Public Law, arranged by law number.

e. *United States Code Congressional and Administrative News:* Table of Public Laws.

f. *CCH Congressional Index:* Table of Enactments — Public Laws.

g. *House Calendar.* Tables of Laws.

3. *Bill or law number to chapter number.* That is, as *from* H.R. 6539, 81st Congress, Public Law Number 495, *to* Chapter 139, 81st Congress, 2d Session. Beginning with the 85th Congress, chapter numbers have been abandoned. Formerly they appeared on the face of the slip law or Statutes at Large.

4. *Bill or law number to Statutes at Large.* That is, as *from* the above bill and law number *to* 64 Stat. 96 (1952). The information is found as follows:

a. *On the face of the slip law.* The Statutes at Large citation has appeared here since mid-1951.

b. *Statutes at Large: List of Public Laws.*

c. *United States Code Congressional and Administrative News and Federal Code Annotated.* In the slip law reprint and in the Table of Public Laws.

5. *Bill or public law number to Revised Statutes or Code.* That is, as *from* H.R. 451, Public Law 86-171, 86th Congress, *to* 33 U.S.C. §933 (Supp. I, 1959). The information is found as follows:

a. *United States Code Congressional and Administrative News tables.* In the Table of Classifications, which is arranged by public law number.

b. *All editions of Revised Statutes or U.S. Code.* This requires the additional step of translating the bill or law number into the Statutes at Large citation, as in par. 4, *supra.* Then the equivalent

Revised Statutes or U.S. Code citation is found through the tables of Statutes Included in the compilations.

**§6.6. Parallel transfer tables from one form of statute to another: Where these tables are published and how they are used.** In many statutory research operations it is necessary to translate a citation from one form of enactment to another, as from session law to code, or the reverse. Almost always in legal publishing a parallel transfer table is provided where needed, and this is particularly true for statutes. Such tables for the United States Code, in both the official and private annotated editions, are very complete and simple to use, as shown in Exhibits 15a, 15b and 15c, which follow. The law student will save himself endless trouble if he learns the simple techniques of their use. With the exceptions noted below, Code tables in all editions are substantially identical, including those for popular names.

1. *United States Code Tables.*

a. *Table I. Revised Titles.* This is a parallel reference table of those Code titles which have been reenacted into positive law, giving first the former section, and then the new section number or numbers. See Exhibit 15a below.

*Table II. Revised Statutes 1878.* This table lists all R.S. sections, whether or not they were ever in the U.S. Code, and gives their present status — whether now in force, and their use as authority for U.S. Code sections. Thus, R.S. 18 is shown to be 2 U.S.C. §1a (1964 ed.); while §74 was repealed without having achieved Code status. This table and similar ones in the privately printed Federal Code Annotated and U.S. Code Annotated provide the only tabular means of "Shepardizing" Revised Statutes sections as such; this is, they show whether a section never in the Code is still in force, and, for those in the Code, translate the R.S. section into its corresponding Code section, under which it may be Shepardized in the usual manner through Shepard's United States Citations. See Exhibit 15b below.

*Table III; Statutes at Large included in the Code.* This table now includes under "Status" the old Tables of Statutes Repealed, and Statutes Eliminated. See Exhibit 15c below.

b. *Tables IV to VI. Executive Orders, Proclamations and Reorganization Plans Included in the Code.* Here are listed Presidential documents, such as executive orders, proclamations or reorganization plans which in any way *affect* or *implement* Code sections, together with citations to sections so affected or implemented. Where the executive act causes a change in the text of the Code section (as Proclamation, 15 U.S.C. §637-(d) specifying the effective date of an act), it is cited without the "note," as one

## TABLE I—REVISED TITLES

The following tables represent those titles of the United States Code that have been revised and renumbered since adoption of the Code in 1926. These tables show where former sections of the revised titles have been incorporated in this edition of the Code.

| Title | Page | | Title | Page |
|---|---|---|---|---|
| 1. General Provisions | 9799 | | 17. Copyrights | 9811 |
| 3. The President | 9799 | | 18. Crimes and Criminal Procedure | 9812 |
| 4. Flag and Seal, Seat of Government, and | | | 23. Highways | 9815 |
| the States | 9800 | | 26. Internal Revenue Code of 1954 | 9816 |
| 6. Official and Penal Bonds | 9800 | | 28. Judiciary and Judicial Procedure | 9827 |

• • •

## TITLE 1—GENERAL PROVISIONS

[*This title was enacted into law by Act July 30, 1947, ch. 388, § 1, 61 Stat. 633. This table shows where sections of former Title 1 have been incorporated in revised Title 1*]

| Title 1 Former Sections | Title 1 New Sections | | Title 1 New Sections | Title 1 Former Sections | | Title 1 New Sections |
|---|---|---|---|---|---|---|
| 1 | 27 | | 107 | 54 | | 204 |
| 2 | 28 | | 108 | 54a | | 205 |
| 3 | 29 | | 109 | 54b | | 206 |
| 4 | 29a | | 110 | 54c | | 207 |
| 5 | 29b | | 111 | 54d | | 208 |
| 6 | 30 | | 112 | 55 | | 209 |

Exhibit 15a

## TABLE II—REVISED STATUTES 1878

Showing where sections of the Revised Statutes of the United States of 1878 will be found in this edition of the United States Code.

### Abbreviations

Rep.—Repealed. Where "Rep." appears in the status column following a U.S.C. reference an explanation of the repeal can be found under such U.S.C. title and section. Where no U.S.C. reference appears the Rev. St. section was repealed prior to the adoption of the United States Code (1926) or for other reasons was not included in the Code but was subsequently repealed.

Rev. T.—Revised Title. Where "Rev. T." appears in the status column the U.S.C. reference is to title and section where the Rev. St. section was originally allocated in the U.S.C. To locate the Rev. St. section in the U.S.C. new title, see the Table (Pages 9799 to 9841, this volume).

Elim.—Eliminated. Where "Elim." appears in the status column following a U.S.C. reference the reason for the elimination of the text can be fo md under such U.S.C. title and section.

I.R.C. '39—Internal Revenue Code of 1939. Where I.R.C. '39 appears in the status column, it is an indication that the provision was repealed or otherwise superseded by the Internal Revenue Code of 1939.

| R.S. Sec. | U.S.C. Tit. | U.S.C. Sec. | Status |
|---|---|---|---|
| 1 | 1 | 1 | Rev. T. 1 |
|  | -- | -- | I.R.C. '39 |
| 2—5 | 1 | 2—5 | Rev. T. 1 |
| 6 | 1 | 31 | Rev. T. 1 |
| 7—11 | 1 | 21—25 | Rev. T. 1 |
| 12,13 | 1 | 28,29 | Rev. T. 1 |
| 14—17 | -- | -- | Rep. |
| 18 | 2 | 1a |  |

| R.S. Sec. | U.S.C. Tit. | U.S.C. Sec. | Status |
|---|---|---|---|
| 74 | -- | -- | Rep. |
| 75—78 | -- | -- | Rep. |
| 79 | 44 | 321 |  |
| 80 | 2 | 131 |  |
| 81 | 2 | 132 |  |
| 82 | 2 | 132a |  |
| 83 | 2 | 134 |  |
| 84 | 2 | 135 |  |

| R.S. Sec. | U.S.C. Tit. | U.S.C. Sec. | Status |
|---|---|---|---|
| 152, 153 | 3 | 41, 42 | Rev. T. 3 |
| 154 | 3 | 44 | Rev. T. 3 |
| 155 | 3 | 45 | Elim. |
| 156, 157 | -- | -- | Rep. |
| 158 | 5 | 1 |  |
| 159 | 5 | 2 |  |
| 160 | 5 | 3 | Elim. |
| 161 | 5 | 22 |  |

Exhibit 15b

# TABLE III—STATUTES AT LARGE

Showing where the Acts of Congress will be found in the United States Code

## Abbreviations

**Rep.—Repealed.** Where "Rep." appears in the status column following a U.S.C. reference, an explanation of the repeal can be found under such U.S.C. title and section.

**Rev. T.—Revised Title.** Where "Rev. T." appears in the status column, the U.S.C. reference is to title and section where the section of the Act of Congress was originally allocated in the U.S.C. To locate the section of the Act in the U.S.C. revised title, see the Tables (Pages 9799 to 9841, this volume).

**Elim.—Eliminated.** Where "Elim." appears in the status column following a U.S.C. reference, the reason for the elimination of the text can be found under such U.S.C. title and section.

**Exec.—Executed.** Where "Exec." appears in the status column, it is an indication that the provisions are directory and that Codification changes in the text of various sections have been made in the Code as a result of such directions.

**I.R.C. '39.—Internal Revenue Code of 1939.** Where I.R.C. '39 appears in the status column, it is an indication that the provision was repealed or otherwise superseded by the Internal Revenue Code of 1939.

| | | | | U.S.C. | | |
| Stat. | Chapter | Section | Page | Title | Section | Status |
|---|---|---|---|---|---|---|
| **2 Stat.** | | | | | | |
| 1802—May 3......... | 51............. | 5......... | 193 | 24 | 11a......... | Rep. |
| 1814—Dec. 1......... | 7............. | ......... | 248 | 44 | 88......... | |
| 1820—Feb. 10......... | 11............. | 14,15......... | 543 | -- | 307......... | I.R.C. '39 |
| 1822—May 7......... | 96............. | 3......... | 692 | 40 | 307......... | Elim. |
| 1836—July 4......... | 352............. | 4......... | 111 | 43 | 5......... | Elim. |
| 1837—Mar. 3......... | 33............. | 1......... | 163,164 | 43 | 5......... | Elim. |
| **9 Stat.** | | | | | | |
| 1846—Aug. 6......... | 84............. | 5......... | 55 | -- | ......... | I.R.C. '39 |
| 1850—Sept. 28......... | 80............. | ......... | 515 | 34 | 868......... | Rev. T. 10 |

Exhibit 15c

of the statutory sections listed in parentheses following the text section in the Code. See Exhibit 15d below.

c. *Repeal tables.* The Repeal Tables found in official editions of the Code through 1958, have now been incorporated in the "Status" columns of Table II or Table III, and so are not in later official editions. Similar or identical tables to the official are printed in the Federal Code Annotated and the U.S. Code Annotated.

2. *United States Code Annotated tables.* These tables are com-

---

### TABLE IV.—EXECUTIVE ORDERS

This Table lists the Executive Orders that implement general and permanent law as contained in U.S.C.

| Exec. Ord. | | U.S.C. | | Exec. Ord. | | U.S.C. | |
|---|---|---|---|---|---|---|---|
| Date | No. | Title | Sec. | Date | No. | Title | Sec. |
| 1918 | | | | 1941 | | | |
| May 11 .......... | 2859 | 36 | 253 nt | June 14 ............ | 8785 | 12 | 95a nt |
| 1929 | | | | July 26 ............ | 8832 | 12 | 95a nt |
| | | | | Dec. 9............. | 8963 | 12 | 95a nt |
| Oct. 1 ........... | 5200 | 7 | 452 nt | 26............. | 8998 | 12 | 95a nt |

---

### TABLE V.—PROCLAMATIONS

This Table lists the Proclamations that are referred to in U.S.C.

| Proc. | | U.S.C. | | Proc. | | U.S.C. | |
|---|---|---|---|---|---|---|---|
| Date | No. | Title | Sec. | Date | No. | Title | Sec. |
| 1938 | | | | 1950 | | | |
| Oct. 25........... | 2307 | 16 | 450r nt | Mar. 24............ | 2879 | 26 | 4731 nt |
| 1939 | | | | Oct. 6............. | 2906 | 50 App. | 454 nt |
| Jan. 25 .......... | 2320 | 16 | 441e nt | Dec. 16............ | 2914 | 50 App. | Prec. 1 nt |
| Sept. 5........... | 2348 | 50 App. | Prec. 1 nt | 28............. | 2915 | 50 App. | 454 nt |
| | 2350 | 50 App. | Prec. 1 nt | 1951 | | | |
| 8........... | 2352 | 50 App. | Prec. 1 nt | June 22............ | 2931 | 50 App. | 2314 nt |
| | 2353 | 50 App. | Prec. 1 nt | Aur. 1 ............ | 2935 | 19 | 1362 nt |
| 10........... | 2359 | 50 App. | Prec. 1 nt | 31............. | 2942 | 50 App. | 453 nt |
| Nov. 4............ | 2374 | 50 App. | Prec. 1 nt | Oct. 12............ | 2948 | 19 | 1318 nt |
| | | | | 25............. | 2950 | 50 App. | Prec. 1 nt |

---

### TABLE VI.—REORGANIZATION PLANS

This Table lists the Reorganization Plans that are set out in U.S.C.

| Statutes at Large | | | U.S.C. | | Statutes at Large | | | U.S.C. | |
|---|---|---|---|---|---|---|---|---|---|
| Section | Vol. | Page | Title | Section | Section | Vol. | Page | Title | Section |
| | | 1939 Plan No. 1 | | | | | 1950 Plan No. 5 | | |
| All.............. | 53 | 1423 | 5 | 133t nt | All.............. | 64 | 1263 | 5 | 133z—15, 591 nts |
| | | 1939 Plan No. 2 | | | All.............. | 64 | 1265 | 16 | 792 nt |
| All............. | 53 | 1431 | 5 | 133 nt | | | 1950 Plan No. 6 | | |
| | | 1940 Plan No. 3 | | | All.............. | 64 | 1263 | 5 | 133z—15, 611 nts |
| All.............. | 54 | 1231 | 5 | 133t nt | | | 1950 Plan No. 8 | | |
| | | | | | All.............. | 64 | 1264 | 5 | 133z—15 nt |

**Exhibit 15d**

piled by the same staff which compiles the official edition tables, and are substantially identical in all respects. They appear in a single volume, with annual, cumulative pocket supplements, and to a considerable extent are continued by the Cumulative Tables in the United States Code Congressional and Administrative News.

a. *Index to legislative history.* The Legislative History table of the U.S.C.A. Index, covering the Seventy-seventh through the Eightieth Congresses, is continued by the cumulative tables of the United States Code Congressional and Administrative News during each year. These tables translate the Public Law number to approval date, Statutes at Large citation, bill and report numbers, and date passed in Senate and House.

3. *Federal Code Annotated tables.* These tables are substantially like those of the official edition in content and arrangement. Positive law titles are listed in parallel with the original Code form. There is a table of acts by popular names. Supplementation is by annual pocket parts. The monthly (cumulated annually) Current Public Laws and Administrative Material lists Code Sections Amended or Repealed.

4. *Slip law or Statutes at Large to Code of Federal Regulations.* See §14.6, Tables for the Federal Register System.

5. *Use of parallel transfer tables from one form of statute to another.*

a. *Slip laws to Statutes at Large.* The Statutes at Large citation is given on the face of the slip law in all editions.

b. *Slip laws to United States Code; Statutes at Large to United States Code.* That is, as *from* Act of July 15, 1965, §9(b), Public Law 89-74, 79 Stat. 234, *to* 21 U.S.C. 321 (Supp. I, 1965).

This transfer is made in two ways. The first, during the year in which the legislation was enacted and thus before the publication of the United States Code annual tables, is made through the Table of Classifications in the United States Code Congressional and Administrative News, in which the appropriate Code classification is assigned in the above table at the back of each pamphlet. The second method employs United States Code Table III, the U.S.C.A. Chronological Tables, or the F.C.A. Key to United States Statutes at Large.

c. *Statutes at Large to Revised Statutes.* That is, as *from* the Act of September 2, 1789, c. 1, 1 Stat. 65, *to* R.S. §161. This transfer is made by the Reference Index to the Revised Statutes . . . from Statutes to Sections in the Revised Statutes.

d. *Revised Statutes to United States Code.* That is, as *from* R.S. §4178 *to* 46 U.S.C. §46 (1964 ed.). Table II of the Code lists all sections of the Revised Statutes which have been incorporated in the Code.

e. *Revised Statutes to Statutes at Large: United States Code to Statutes at Large.* This information is given with the text of the compilation section itself, and so no table is necessary. Thus, in the Revised Statutes, the original Statutes at Large citation is shown in roman type in the margin of the page. In the Code, the citations to statutory authority are in parentheses at the end of the Code section or group of sections. See Exhibit 8, page 34.

f. *Executive acts affecting Code sections.* Presidential executive orders and proclamations and reorganization plans frequently affect legislation incorporated in the Code sections or cited in notes relating to these sections. Tables IV-VI of the Code, Executive Acts Included, lists those instruments, together with the section affected or implemented, as shown in Exhibit 15d.

g. *Executive acts: Finding statutory authority for.* Many Executive orders and proclamations are issued under authority of specific enabling acts. Table V in Title 3 of the Code of Federal Regulations, Statutes Cited as Authority for Presidential Documents pairs the executive act with its statutory authority.

h. *Executive acts: As authority for Code of Federal Regulations sections.* That is, as *from* Executive Order No. 5644 *to* 5 C.F.R. §301.61 (1961). See Exhibit 33, page 176.

**§6.7. Original and compiled forms of statutes distinguished.** This matter has been discussed at length in §3.5 and so will only be summarized here.

Compilations of public general interest, arranged by subject, are so much more convenient to use than the slip or session law form that lawyers and students prefer to work with the compilations. In doing so, they are prone to forget that the compilation is usually only prima facie the law, and that the original form is still the real, the "best" authority. Therefore, in legal writing of all kinds, the session law form of a statute is best cited, not the compilation, *unless the latter has been reenacted as the positive law,* expressly repealing the original session law. Thus the statutory provision that human labor is not a commodity is cited as Section 6 of the Clayton Act, Act of October 15, 1914, c. 323, §6, 38 Stat. 731, 15 U.S.C. §17 (1964 ed.), and not merely as 15 U.S.C. §17 (1964 ed.). If the original act has not been amended, the Code text of an individual section (but not the arangement of sections within the Code) is probably identical with that of the original, but safe procedure is to check with the original to make certain.

**§6.8. Finding the earliest printing of new enactments.** Slip laws in their various forms as described in §3.2 are commonly the promptest form of publication, except that loose-leaf services, described in Chapter 23, may reach their subscribers still earlier.

**§6.9. Finding a particular federal statute.** This may be done in a variety of ways depending upon the information available.

1. *By subject.* Subject indexes are available, both for bills pending in Congress and for enacted legislation. Indexes to the status tables described in §6.4 enable the searcher to find bills when their subject matter is known. In searching for a specific statute when only the subject matter is known, it must be borne in mind that for private laws there is no cumulative index of present value. On the other hand, these laws are indexed by subject in each of the volumes of the Statutes at Large in which they are printed.

Public laws are normally approached through a subject index of public general laws in force, such as are found in all statutory compilations, federal and state. If the law, though a public law, was not of sufficient general interest or permanency to be incorporated in a compilation such as the United States Code, there are only two categories of subject indexes available, neither very satisfactory currently.

The first is in the individual volumes of the Statutes at Large, indexing material found only in those volumes and not cumulative. If the date of the enactment or the approximate date is known, the search is narrowed to the volumes of such date. The other index is of public general laws, even though uncodified, which had at any time been in force through 1931. This is the McClenon and Gilbert index, described at page 75, par. 5. As the coverage of this index extends only through 1931, it must be supplemented for later years by searching the volumes of the Statutes at Large covering 1932 to date. Certain broad subjects by category, such as appropriation acts for the various government agencies, railroad legislation, and so forth, are listed under those headings in the Shepard's Citations and Digest of the United States Supreme Court Reports popular-name tables. In any search, care must be taken that all applicable statutes are consulted, as more than one may be pertinent to a given set of facts.

In searching multi-volume unofficial editions of the United States Code, the indexes to individual titles are more convenient to use than the much larger general index to the entire Code, but search should not be restricted to them. The reason is that legislation very often overlaps in its coverage, so that a given topic may be covered by more than one title of the Code. This is particularly true where adjective and substantive law impinge upon each other; often what seems logically to be substantive law is covered wholly or in part by a procedural provision in a different Code title. The general index to the whole body of the law covered by the Code should be consulted, because it coordinates these various overlapping entries.

2. *By title.* Many acts are known and cited by a popular name, as the Taft-Hartley Act, the G.I. Bill of Rights, etc. The popular-name indexes described in §6.3 give the various forms of citations under the name.

3. *By bill, law or chapter number.* Tracing an act when this information is known is described in §§6.5 and 6.6. The number of the Congress or the approximate date of the act are necessary parts of the data, because bills and law numbers are renumbered at the beginning of each Congress. Chapter numbers, not assigned since the close of the Eighty-fourth Congress, are renumbered with each session. These necessary data are printed on each slip law and in the margin of the Statutes at Large.

4. *Transfer tables from one form of statute to another.* See §6.6.

5. *Treaties.* As described in Chapter 4, these are indexed both by number and by subject.

6. *Statutes no longer in force.* The only complete coverage is through search of the indexes of all volumes of the Statutes at Large. Indexes to compilations all omit something — private laws, uncodified laws, temporary, repealed and superseded laws; they index only public general laws in force, excluding appropriation acts. A law indexed in one compilation of the sort may be omitted from a later one because it is no longer in force.

Search normally would begin with the index of a compilation of laws in force. If the desired law is not found there, a game of legal ticktacktoe ensues, in which the searcher works back through various editions until he finds his statute covered. If his law is found in the 1952 Code but not in the 1956 edition, a table of repeals in the 1958 edition probably will show when and by what act the desired law was repealed. Whenever a law is found in a compilation, each section will contain a reference to the original session law from which copied. For indexes to all public general acts from 1789 to 1931, see the McClenon and Gilbert index described at page 75, par. 5.

**§6.10. Finding federal administrative rules and regulations.** This material is described in Chapter 14, together with all tables and indexes.

**§6.11. Finding federal court rules.** This material is described in Chapter 8.

**§6.12. Work with the United States Revised Statutes.** This compilation must not be overlooked, as much of it is still the law of the land; and this though it covers only codified laws through December 1, 1873. Although the lawyer seldom sees the volume containing this compilation, he should still check the text of its sections cited as authority for such sections of the United States Code as have not been reenacted into positive law and which base their text upon the Revised Statutes sections. Its makeup and use are described at page 28, par. 2. Revised Statutes sections which have been incorporated in the United States Code are listed in Table II of the Code. Those which have been repealed, whether or not they were ever in the Code, are listed in Table II of the Code.

**§6.13.   Work with the United States Code.**  The makeup of the Code and its indexes have been described in Chapter 3, with a discussion of its legal status. It is the form of federal statute most used by the lawyer, though he will cite the original Statutes at Large in legal writing as his authority, unless the particular title cited has been reenacted as positive law, expressly repealing the original statute from which derived. Which edition of the Code — official unannotated or unofficial annotated — to consult depends largely upon whether only the text of a section is wanted, or whether case annotations also are required.

1. *Official editions of the Code.*  If only the text of a Code section is wanted, the official edition is more convenient than the unofficial annotated editions, since it is not buried in page after page of digest paragraphs of cases interpreting it. Notes, tables and indexes are largely the same in all editions. Except for the smaller initial cost of the official edition, however, the advantage is all with the unofficial editions, which are the ones the lawyer customarily uses.

2. *Unofficial annotated editions of the Code.*  The added value of the unofficial editions, as described in Chapter 3, lies in the case digests interpreting each section of the Constitution and Code, and also in their more frequent supplementation.

3. *Finding the required Code sections.*  When a specific Code section is desired but the citation is to a slip law or to the Statutes at Large, recourse must be had to the indexes and tables noted in the description of the Code at page 30, par. 3 of this book, and in the Chapter and Law Number Tables (§6.5) and Parallel Tables for Statutes From one Form to Another (§6.6). Care should always be taken to ascertain by scanning the publication date of the volume or supplement used, that it covers the desired dates and that the sequence of parts is complete.

**§6.14.   Citators for federal statutes.**  Having found a statute section in point, the lawyer must yet determine two things: (1) whether the section is still in force and in the form found, not having been amended, repealed or superseded by later legislative action; and (2) whether it has been construed by a court of competent jurisdiction. Elaborate devices called citators or citation books aid the lawyer here. They are described in Chapter 18.

§6.15. **Elementary considerations in work with statutes.** The following is an informal check list of things the searcher should ask himself when embarking upon the solution of a statutory problem.

Most important is to determine what is wanted. Is it the text of a bill or its present status in Congress? Is it desired to find the intent of Congress in enacting a given piece of legislation, and if so, what are the available means? Is a particular statute or section sought? In its original or in codified form? What is the authority as legislation of a given form of statute? What is known about the statute — its date, subject matter, bill or law number? Are case or other annotations wanted, or just the text? Has a certain governmental agency regulation been amended since promulgation? Once the desired goal is determined, the rest is largely a matter of knowing the resources of statutory publication.

The next most important factor in an efficient search is to ascertain that the right materials are being used. Does the publication date of the volume being consulted exclude the particular statute, regulation or annotation sought? Are all the required units and supplements at hand? Is it certain that the statute is still in force, or should an earlier compilation be consulted?

Finally, has the statute been fully Shepardized, using materials and techniques described in Chapter 18?

§6.16. **Code of Federal Regulations outlines.** The reader is urged to consult the Code of Federal Regulations Title 1, Appendix C — Guide to Federal Register Finding Aids — and its four tables: Researching: (1) Agency Materials; (2) Presidential Materials; (3) Statutory Materials; and (4) Special Information Lists. These are printed in the annual revision of Titles 1, 2, 3. Pertinent publications of the Office of the Federal Register are listed, including statutes, indexes, etc., together with where they may be found. The information provided forms an excellent checklist of the official resources relating both to conventional federal statutes and to administrative materials — Agency and Presidential. The tables will solve many research problems.

§6.17. **Computerized searches in statutes and law reports.** See note on page 10.

# CHAPTER 7

# State Legislation

§7.1.  **Similarity to federal legislative forms.**  What has been written in this book about federal legislation and its publication is essentially true also of state legislation.  Such differences as there are relate chiefly to the chronological period covered, frequency of statutory compilations, and availability of legislative history sources.  Long before the establishment of the Union in 1776, the Colonies had published their legislation regularly, but the lawyer and law student are little concerned with Colonial legislation.  That for the statehood period from 1776 on is readily available, both in session law and compiled forms.  The states have been less conservative than the United States in compiling their statutes in subject arrangement, and in most states there have been many editions.  Legislative history sources are chiefly notable by their absence, though in most states some sort of status table is published during legislative sessions.  See §5.6.

§7.2.  **Constitutions.**  Each state publishes its constitution as part of the various editions of its statutory compilations.  Where, as is usual with the states, there have been several different constitutions, all are published.

Research with constitutions is facilitated by (1) Constitutions of the United States, National and State (Dobbs Ferry, N.Y., Oceana Publications, Inc., 1962, 2v., loose-leaf), which publishes the full text of the *latest* constitutions and amendments, with brief notes on the history and sources of each constitution; (2) Index Digest of State Constitutions (2d ed., Edwards, New York, 1959), which is very detailed; (3) A Selective Bibliography on State Constitutional Revision; Compiled by Balfour Halévy (New York, c.1963); and (4) A Selective Bibliography on State Constitutional Revision; Compiled by Myron Fink for the New Mexico Constitutional Revision Commission (September, 1966) (which is, in effect, an updating of Halévy for 1963-1966).

1. *Amendments to state constitutions.* Amendments are frequent. Their text is printed in all state statutory compilations. As submitted to the voters in most states the text of proposed amendments is printed in the session laws, reference being made in Shepard's Citations for the respective states. As most amendments so submitted are not ratified, a careful check must be made of the status of proposed amendments. Shepard's Citations state units cover constitutions just as they do other legislation, including both amendments and proposed amendments and their adoption. Citations to later revisions and amendments of state constitutions are given in the biennial Book of the States, published by the Council of State Governments, with a list of late treatises and documents.

2. *Judicial history of state constitutions.* Constitutions are covered by the various kinds of citators described in Chapter 18, including Shepard's Citations, certain Supreme Court digests, and the Table of Statutes Construed in all units of the National Reporter System.

§7.3.   **State session laws.**   Every state publishes its session laws under such titles as Acts and Resolves, Laws, Public Laws, or Acts and Joint Resolutions, etc.   These are not legal words of art, but all designate the enactments of the state legislature concerned at a regular or special session.   Regular session periods vary from annual to biennial, with special sessions as necessitated by emergency conditions in war, times of financial stress, etc.   Customarily, the laws of a special session are combined with those of a regular session, in a single volume.

1. *Slip laws.*   Very few states officially publish their slip laws. In an increasing number of states, however, the publisher of the annotated edition of the state statutes publishes an advance sheet "session law service," in which are printed, in session law form, the latest enactments.   This is in addition to the pamphlet supplements to the compiled statutes, containing the latest annotations to cases interpreting statutes existing in code form.

2. *Session laws proper.*   Enactments — public, private and local laws and resolutions — are usually published in a single volume, but some states publish local, public and private laws in separate volumes.   Usually the resolutions — which in some states lack the force of law — follow the acts and are separately numbered. In some states the current enactments are published in classified order (as in Kansas), following as far as feasible the classification

of the statutory compilation. By far the greater number, however, arrange the session laws in the bound volumes in chronological order, by date of approval, as in the United States Statutes
at Large.

a. *Content of session law volumes.* All have subject indexes;
tables of chapters or acts in numerical order are included; many
have tables of statutory revisions or code titles and sections
amended and repealed; other tables may include amendments
and repeals of uncodified laws, allocation of session laws into the
state code, bills maturing into laws during the session, and data
concerning the legislature and legislators.

b. *Unofficial editions of session laws.* In some states, in connection with the publication of their annotated laws and current
pamphlet law service, commercial publishers compile volumes of
the laws enacted during a session, including allocation tables
to the compilation, texts of communications by state officials or
private institutions or individuals favoring or opposing legislation
enacted during the sessions. Since these volumes usually precede
the publication date of the official session laws by several months,
and since the communications are at least some aid in legislative
history research, they serve a useful purpose.

c. *Authority of session laws.* See §7.9.

**§7.4. State statutory compilations.** State compilations follow
in form and content the United States Code pattern of "public
general and permanent" laws, arranged by subject. Their status
as legal authority varies from state to state, according to whether
they have been reenacted as positive law or are only certified copies
of the original session laws. They may variously be called Codes,
Revisions, Compilations, Consolidations, General Statutes, or
Statutes, according to the preference of the legislatures, but these
are not legal words of art and their status depends upon the
authority conferred upon them by the legislature in each case.

1. *Status of the compilations as law.* See §7.9.

2. *Content of state compilations: Statutes and court rules.* All
the state statutes needed by the lawyer in his practice are included.
These comprise statutes of public general and permanent interest,
omitting obsolete material, appropriation acts and statutes of no
general interest. Court rules are commonly included. Constitutions, federal and state, together with pre-statehood organic charters, are usually found at the beginning of the compilation.
Magna Carta is fairly common here. Uncodified laws, mostly
relating to the business of government, may be published in a
separate volume, as are McKinney's New York Unconsolidated
Laws.

3. *Content of state compilations: Editorial matter and case*

*annotations.* Editorial matter in *official compilations* is likely to be brief, a notation of the origins of the various statute sections, with an occasional cross reference or note of amendment or repeal. These notes are apt to be of limited value and for most purposes must be supplemented by an unofficial annotated edition. This is particularly true when the searcher is tracing the history of a statute section, its evolution from the original session law and its subsequent amendment.

a. *Editorial matter.* This usually includes the derivation of each statute section from its earlier forms, and perhaps excerpts from revisers' notes, explaining why changes were made. Pertinent law review articles may be cited, as well as legal encyclopedia and American Law Reports comment. Essays on the law of the state by members of the local Bar are found in some annotated editions. Some compilations print a compilation of rules of practice of official and unofficial boards, and statutory forms.

b. *Case annotations.* These vary from none at all to full-dress case digests, which may cover both federal and state courts and the opinions of the state attorney general. West Publishing Company and affiliated company editions copy or paraphrase National Reporter System case headnotes, but without the Key-Number. The classification schemes for state statutory compilations frequently change, sometimes radically, between editions. In such instances, case digests under the old classification system are taken over into the new, if there is a place there for them. It sometimes happens, however, that a presumably obsolete old section is omitted altogether in the new, in which case the old annotations are dropped entirely. This occurs when a provision has been entirely repealed and not merely shifted to another part of the statute classification.

4. *Indexes to state compilations.* See §7.6.

5. *Parallel conversion tables from one form of statute to another.* Conversion tables for federal legislation have been discussed in §§6.5 and 6.6. The functions of state statutory conversion tables are identical, but the problems are complicated by the much more frequent changes in statutory form of state legislation, particularly as brought about by the changes in or complete revamping of classification schemes. The parallel conversion table is thus even more important for state than for federal legislation.

The table's purpose is to enable the searcher to trace an earlier form of legislation — as a session law section into a compilation section, or a compilation section of an earlier compilation into its corresponding section of later compilations — into its place in the current compilation, and to determine if it is still law. Tracing backward to the legislative antecedents of a current code section is, as in the United States Code, done through the citations to authority following each compilation section. Shepard's Citations cover the latest form of compilation, as amended by later enactments.

The lawyer or student, however, often is cited to an earlier form, and in order to Shepardize that section he has to translate it into the current form as covered by the current Shepard's Citations. This is often a difficult process, since the pertinent section may have been repealed, with no provision for its subject matter to be found in the new classification scheme. Thus, while the conversion tables are indispensable, they do not always cover all enactments cited in earlier cases. If the earlier Shepard's Citations are available, the earlier cases may then be found; if not, the searcher must go through obsolete editions of state compilations for such case annotations as may be available there.

a. *Types of state statutory conversion tables.* One type, the most useful but seldom found, traces the original session law through all earlier compilations to the current one. Arranged under the session law citation, this type of table notes, in addition to the latest classification designation, sections no longer in the compilation because repealed or obsolete. A more common type lists only those session laws which have at any time been codified. An example of the first type is shown in Exhibit 16, from the New Mexico Statutes Annotated (1953).

TABLE OF CORRESPONDING SECTIONS

| Ch. | Section | Herein | Ch. | Section | Herein | Ch. | Section | Herein |
|---|---|---|---|---|---|---|---|---|
| 45 | 1 | 73-15-8 | 76 | 5 | 67-11-5 | 97 | 15 | 75-13-15 |
| | 2 | Sep. Cl. | | 6 | 67-11-6 | | 16 | 75-13-16 |
| | 3 | Rplg. Cl. | | 7 | 67-11-7 | | 17 | 75-13-17 |
| | 4 | Emer. Cl. | | 8 | 67-11-8 | | 18 | 75-13-18 |
| 46 | 1 | 14-5-1, n. | | 9 | 67-11-9 | | 19 | 75-13-19 |
| | 2 | Sep. Cl. | | 10 | 67-11-10 | | 20 | 75-13-20 |
| | 3 | Rplg. Cl. | | 11 | 67-11-11 | | 21 | 75-13-21 |
| | 4 | Emer. Cl. | 77 | 1 | R. 1953, | | 22 | Sep. Cl. |
| 47 | 1–5 | Appn. | | | ch. 138, § 123 | | 23 | Emer. Cl. |
| 48 | 1 | Temp. | | 2–6 | R. 1953, | 98 | 1 | Spec. |

Exhibit 16

The more common conversion table goes back from the current compilation to one or more earlier revisions. The most elaborate one of this type is for the Iowa Code Annotated (1951), as shown by Exhibit 17.

Tracing the original session law into the revision carries the

## TABLE 2

## CORRESPONDING SECTIONS

**Abbreviations**

| | |
|---|---|
| Om. _ _ _ _ | Omitted |
| R. _ _ _ _ _ | Repealed |
| R.C.P. _ _ _ | Rules of Civil Procedure |
| Rep.Cl. _ _ _ | Repealing Clause |
| Sav.Cl. _ _ _ | Saving Clause |
| Sep.Cl. _ _ _ | Separability Clause |
| U. _ _ _ _ _ | Unconstitutional |

| Code 1924 Sec. | Code 1927 Sec. | Code 1931 Sec. | Code 1935 Sec. | Code 1939 Sec. | I.C.A. and Iowa Code Sec. |
|---|---|---|---|---|---|
| 1 | 1 | 1 | 1 | 1 | 1.1 |
| 2 | 2 | 2 | 2 | 2 | 1.2 |
| 3 | 3 | 3 | 3 | 3 | 1.3 |
| 4 | 4 | 4 | 4 | 4 | 1.4 |
| | 4–a1 | 4–a1 | 4–a1 | 4.1 | 1.5 |
| | 4–a2 | 4–a2 | 4–a2 | 4.2 | 1.6 |
| | 4–a3 | 4–a3 | 4–a3 | 4.3 | 1.7 |
| | 4–a4 | 4–a4 | 4–a4 | 4.4 | 1.8 |
| | | | 4–f1 | 4.5 | 1.9 |
| | | | 4–f2 | 4.6 | 1.10 |

Exhibit 17

searcher back to the table of statutes included in the *earliest revision following the session law's enactment.* If such revision is not available, recourse must be had to the subject index of the current edition, but this is an inexact process.

In New York there is at present no tabular means by which the searcher may trace a session law into the Consolidated Laws, not knowing the subject matter of the law. This is a tabular blind spot.

Some states, after reenacting a compilation as positive law, do not follow it up by later compilations of the same authority, but instead adopt compilations which are only prima facie the law. This is the process exemplified by the United States Revised Statutes (enacted into positive law), and the United States Code (prima facie the law except as to individual titles later reenacted). Some state codes, as in Exhibit 18 below, carry the latest positive law compilation into the current prima facie revision, showing the disposition in the revision of session laws enacted since the latest positive law compilations in the later prima facie compilation.

| Code 1930 §§ | Code 1942 §§ | Code 1930 §§ | Code 1942 §§ | Code 1930 §§ | Code 1942 §§ |
|---|---|---|---|---|---|
| **Table A** | | 1930 CODE TO 1942 CODE | | | |
| 5231 | 5745 | 5298 | 5812 | 5365 | 3363 |
| 5232 | 5746 | 5299 | 5813 | 5366 | 3364 |
| 5233 | 5747 | 5300 | 5814 | 5367 | 3365 |
| 5234 | 5748 | 5301 | 5815 | 5368–5387 | R 1940 ch. 135 |
| 5235 | 5749 | 5302 | 5816 | 5388 | 6210 |
| 5236 | 5750 | 5303 | 5817 | 5389 | 6211 |

Exhibit 18

b. *Subsequent amendments, repeals, etc.* With a few exceptions, conversion tables enable the searcher to trace the provisions of a session law or earlier compilation into the latest compilation, including information as to subsequent legislative action.

6. *Supplementation of state statutory compilations.* Few state official compilations are supplemented at all, thus relegating the searcher to the unofficial editions for later information. Supplementation otherwise is typical of law books generally, being by annual pocket parts, cumulative bound supplements, recompiled individual volumes, etc. The most satisfactory type, because of its frequency, is by advance sheet service supplying the text of new session laws, together with tabular material giving their statute classification, citations to repeals, amendments, and so forth, supplementing like tables in the bound set. The student should acquaint himself with the characteristics of the supplementation for his own state compilation, which may print legislative history material otherwise not readily available. This may include governors' messages and recommendations concerning pending legislation, and like documents from other official and unofficial bodies.

*Noting the date of publication.* This is routine with regard to any statutory material to assure that the full sequence or original parts and all later supplementation are covered.

§7.5. **Municipal charters, ordinances and codes.** The creation of municipal corporations is a function of the state legislature. The modern practice is to enact a general law setting up standards and conditions for the creation of such corporations, and then to assign the duty to some officer or official body to determine whether these have been met in specific instances. Incorporation may be by special act, however, if not forbidden by the state constitution, or by the adoption of a home rule charter in states permitting such charters.

1. *Charters.* The charter granted by the legislature constitutes

a limited delegation of its power over the government of the area covered.   In form, it may follow a special or general statute; or may be one selected from among a number of legislatively authorized forms (optional charters); or the commission or city manager form may be adopted.   The charter is the city's fundamental document, judicially noticed by the courts.   Unless contrary to the state constitution, the legislature may amend or repeal a municipal charter.   Constitutional or home rule charters may, in some states, be amended by a vote of the electors.

2. *Ordinances.*   These are the local laws of the municipalities, enacted by the duly constituted board of aldermen, council or commission, under authority delegated by the state legislature, for application within the narrow limits of its jurisdiction.   An ordinance must be in writing and enacted according to all the prescribed formalities.   It may be in furtherance of the police power of the municipality and prescribe penalties for its violation; or it may grant franchises and special privileges; or be for the improvement of the physical facilities of the corporation, for the doing of public works or abatement of nuisances; or may correspond to a code of laws laying down rules for the conduct of public business.   If duly voted an ordinance is as binding upon those concerned as the general laws of the state are upon its citizens.

In some states, a general statute provides for the enactment by the cities, counties and villages of the state of local laws which are in effect ordinances but are published with the session laws of the state, often in separate volumes.   In many localities ordinances are referred to as resolutions.

In states where there is an "upstate" community overshadowed by a "downstate" overwhelmingly large city, the legislature is apt to keep more than usually close control over the ordinances of the metropolis.   An example is New York City, operating under a home rule charter but governed through a huge administrative code enacted by the state legislature, and amended by subsequent acts of the legislature.

3. *Citators for charters and ordinances.*   Charters and ordinances are amended, repealed and adjudicated just as is conventional legislation, and are covered by the usual statutory citation books.   The coverage is incomplete, however, because of the failure of the municipalities to provide the necessary information as to amendments and repeals.

a. *Shepard's Citations.*   In all state Shepard's Citations, charters and ordinances are covered, both as to amendments and repeals (with the above limitation) and as to adjudication.   For some state citators there is a separate subject index of ordinances cited, because most ordinances are not numbered and must therefore be cited by subject and date. Otherwise the tabular treatment in Shepard's Citations is exactly as for other statutes.

b. *National Reporter System.* The Table of Statutes Construed in the regional units cites charters, but apparently not ordinances, construed by cases in the various jurisdictions.

c. *Digest of the United States Supreme Court Reports.* City ordinances and codes construed by the Supreme Court of the United States are covered in the tables of this digest and of the Lawyers' Edition of the United States Reports.

§7.6. **State statutory indexes.**

1. *Subject indexes to state statutes.*

a. *All laws ever enacted in a state.* As with federal statutes, no state has an index covering all of its statutory enactments, though New York has one covering the period 1777-1901, with a supplement through 1907 which goes quite far in this respect. This is the General Index to the Laws of the State of New York, 1777-1901. Each session law volume of a state has its own subject index, but these are not cumulative.

b. *All public laws presently in force.* Such an index would, in a single alphabet, index both codified, uncodified and procedural laws. The nearest present approximation of such an index is the Larmac Consolidated Index to the Constitution and Laws of California, but this does not index private laws or appropriation acts.

c. *All public general laws presently in force.* Every general state statutory compilation has such an index, on the plan of that for the United States Code. In some states the constitution and the procedural laws are separately indexed from the substantive laws, which is confusing.

In using an index of laws in force to trace a particular enactment when the date is unknown, one starts in with the current index and works back and forth through indexes to earlier editions, until an entry covering the desired law is found. The section of the statute, when found, will tell from what session law it was derived, so that the original text may be found there. When the citation to source is only to another, earlier edition, that compilation must be searched for the desired session law citation.

d. *Indexes to laws of more than one state.* There is no such index covering public general laws. From 1925 to 1948 the Library of Congress published a State Law Index. Partial coverage is often found in indexes to limited compilations, usually made by government agencies or in treatises. These are noted in §7.10.

2. *Popular-name indexes to state statutes.* As separate tables state popular-name statutory indexes are uncommon, though some of the general indexes to state compilations note statutes by popular name occasionally, as entries in their normal place in the combined alphabet. The Iowa Code Annotated has a separate table. Shepard's Citations for all the states have popular-name tables for statutes.

3. *Parallel conversion tables from one form of state statute to another.* See §7.4. The problem is more difficult in work with state statutes than with federal, because in most states there have been so many different editions of statutory compilations, often changing the numbering systems of the sections radically or discarding entirely the old system. This makes it difficult or impossible in many cases to match up the old statute section with its current form.

a. *Session law to code.* Transfer tables of this kind are uncommon, either in session laws or in official editions of the codes, but are fairly common in the private annotated editions.

b. *Code to session law.* Code sections cite the original session law from which derived, so that if the code section is found, the rest is simple. The citation is commonly in parentheses at the end of the text of the section, but may be in small print below it. If, as often occurs, the citation to authority is merely to an earlier compilation, then that compilation must be searched for citation to the session law source.

c. *Code tables translating from one edition to another.* Most state statutory conversion tables make it possible to trace an older section number into the current form, or the reverse, as described at page 96, par. 5.

4. *Bill status tables.* The chapter and law numbers of an act are noted on the face of the session law as published, and in tables in each session law volume. Many state legislatures or other state agencies publish status tables during a session, which are often cumulated and printed also at the close of a session. For some states there are private services during the sessions of the state legislature which indicate the progress of a bill through the legislature.

§7.7. **Citation books for state statutes.** The conventional forms are Shepard's Citations and, for judicial interpretations, also the Tables of Statues Construed in the various units of the National Reporter System, as described in Chapter 11. The tables of amendments and repeals of existing legislation by new laws, found in each volume of most state session laws, are of limited utility because noncumulative. Annotated statutes give the judicial history — what the courts have done in construing legislation printed therein.

**§7.8. Legislative intent.** The means for determining this for state legislation are disappointing. Such as they are, they are noted in §5.6. Communication with the state law librarian or legislative reference librarian may elicit governors' messages, legislative committee reports and other legislative history material, much of it in manuscript and otherwise unavailable. It is generally an unsatisfactory process, however.

**§7.9. Authority of state statutes.**

1. *Session laws.* State session laws are the "best evidence" of the laws in printed form, unless and until superseded by a codification which has been reenacted into positive law, expressly repealing the session laws from which derived. Compilations not so reenacted are merely prima facie the law, certified as true copies and receivable in evidence, but rebuttable in case of repugnance of texts by reference to the original session law from which derived. Some states, as New York, have "perpetual revision" of code sections, in which each enactment amending or adding to a section is enacted as positive law by the session law itself. Thus, "Section 211 of the General Corporation Law is amended to read as follows: . . . ." In that form of enactment, the latest amendment supersedes all that has gone before, and is the definitive form of the statute. In such cases, the session form of citation is seldom used, but only that of the consolidation. For example, the above, in New York, would not ordinarily be cited as New York Laws 1956, Chapter 381, but as New York General Corporation Law §211.

As a practical matter, even in states which have a compilation enacted as positive law, it is usually unannotated or only sparsely annotated in the official edition, and not frequently supplemented, so that it is not of as much use to the lawyer as is the unofficially published, annotated edition. In practice, therefore, the lawyer consults the unofficial edition; in case of amendment of a reenacted compilation he cites the compilation section "as amended by" the amending act. Where the compilation has not been reenacted and the session law is still the "best evidence," the session law is cited, with the compilation title and section following in parallel for convenience.

2. *Statutory compilations.* The status of state compilations of the laws as legal authority varies from state to state, according to whether they have been reenacted as positive law, or are only certified as true copies of the original session laws, entitled to be received in evidence, but rebuttable by the original session law in case of repugnance of texts.

a. *Enactment of the compilation into positive law.* This reenactment of the compilation makes it the highest form of authority, superseding the original session law from which derived and expressly repealing that law. It is something *the legislature has done directly*, not acting through a commission or the Secretary of State. *The test is the presence or absence of an enacting clause.* If it has such a clause, as "It is enacted by the General Assembly as follows," or "Be it enacted," it is of the highest authority. Later amendments to its sections are cited as such; that is, the compilation is cited by title and section, "as amended by" the amending session law. An exception is the "perpetual revision" type of amendment noted under Session Laws, *supra,* in which the amending session law either entirely supersedes the section amended, or adds a new section. In such cases, the amendment may be said to be cumulative in effect, the latest form superseding all earlier ones.

b. *Official compilation of laws in force, in classified order, but without reenactment as positive law.* This is the United States Code form and the one commonly adopted by the state compilations. The resulting text is prima facie the law, rebuttable by reference to the original form from which derived, no new law being enacted by the compilation or old one repealed by it. Usually the legislature delegates the work of compilation to a state reviser, by a "revision statute."

Students often confuse positive law and prima facie the law compilations with official and unofficial compilations. An official compilation is merely one put out under governmental auspices of some kind — either directly published by the government or sponsored by it. It may or may not be positive law or only prima facie the law. The United States Code, for example, is certainly fully official, since it is published under the auspices of the Congress and printed by the Government Printing Office. Almost two thirds of it, however, is only prima facie the law. The Wisconsin legislature authorizes a "reviser" to compile a subject arrangement of the laws, which is published by the state. This is certainly official, but, since it is merely an editorial job by an appointed agent of the legislature and not reenacted as such by the legislature, it is only prima facie the law. See par. 1a, page 27.

c. *Unofficial and annotated edition of an official compilation.* Official publications tend to be one-shot jobs, not kept up to date regularly and not annotated, or not fully so. After publication, therefore, they become out of date and of diminishing value to the lawyer. The private publisher steps in here with an annotated edition, frequently supplemented, which the lawyer uses to the exclusion of the official edition, except to cite the latter as his authority, "as amended" by later enactments. This is the type of McKinney's New York Consolidated Laws.

d. *Entirely unofficial compilations.* Purdon's Pennsylvania Statutes is, from beginning to end, an unofficially published, classified arrangement of the laws of Pennsylvania. It has no official status of any kind, but is so well done as to be cited by and to all courts. It is a typical annotated edition of the statutes. The student should bear in mind that in citing Purdon's, P.L. does not mean Purdon's but Public Law of Pennsylvania.

3. *Municipal ordinances.* These are delegated legislation, in that the state legislature has empowered the municipal authorities to enact certain measures for the governance of their corporate areas. To the extent that they do not exceed this authority, municipal ordinances are binding upon those subject to them. The same is true of local laws.

**§7.10. Subject collections of statutes covering more than one jurisdiction.** One of the most frequent calls from law students is for collections of the laws of all states on various subjects. Although there have been some attempts at supplying this need, it is simply too great a task and there is no general collection of present value. When such compilations are made for a specific subject, they are likely to suffer from two weaknesses: (1) the compilers here have included the obvious laws but failed to include many which have an important peripheral effect; (2) the collections are not kept up to date. There is no royal road for the researcher in working with such statutes and the safest procedure is to make a careful and laborious search of the statutory compilations of all states in the legislation of which he is interested. Such collections as have been made vary greatly in treatment. Some print the entire text of legislation. Others provide merely digests or paraphrases of legislation, with citations to the full text.

1. *Directories paraphrasing laws.* The Lawyers' Directory[1] and the Martindale-Hubbell Law Directory[2] paraphrase at considerable length business and family laws of all states and most foreign countries, and are kept up by annual new editions. They are described in Chapter 22.

2. *Compilations on one subject only.* Such collections are occasionally made by official agencies, or may be included as an important part of treatises, or may be published by foundations.

3. *Trade or professional organization compilations.* Some organizations sometimes provide compilations of statutes or of abridgments of them for their members.

---

1 Philadelphia, Pa., Sharp & Alleman.
2 New York, N.Y., Martindale-Hubbell Law Directory, Inc.

4. *Uniform Laws Annotated.* The Uniform Laws are promulgated by the National Conference of Commissioners of Uniform State Laws to meet the need of uniformity as between states, of their laws in business, domestic relations and criminal laws. One such law, the Negotiable Instruments Law, has been adopted by all states, with or without modifications. Some have been adopted by none as yet. The annual Handbook of the Conference lists adopting states by name. Furthermore, because adopting states have to fit the law into their own classification schemes and so cannot ordinarily enact the Uniform Laws in either the same exact sequence or the same section numbers, there is a parallel conversion table from the Uniform Act sections to those of each state adopting it. Enacting statutes of the various states are cited with dates of adoption. Tentative drafts of laws not yet promulgated by the Conference are printed in the Handbook, as are the texts of certain obsolete uniform Laws. The Uniform Laws can be Shepardized as such through the National Reporter System tables of Statutes Construed, and in Shepard's Citations by means of the state statute adopting them.

The Uniform Laws Annotated is a typical annotated statute, one or more laws to the volume, kept up to date by annual pocket supplements.

*Uniform Commercial Code.* This Code, dating from 1952, in effect supersedes most prior Uniform Laws on business, as the Negotiable Instruments and Sales Laws. As of 1967, it had been adopted by 49 states, with modifications to suit local practice. States so adopting it have provided parallel references from Code sections to their own corresponding state sections. There are available from several sources reprints of the "official" edition, with parallel reference tables from superseded Uniform Laws, and with invaluable compilers' explanatory "Comments." Many state annotated statutes have issued special U.C.C. pamphlets, with explanatory notes and, in some, annotations to the decided cases. A voluminous literature on the Code has sprung up, much of it rendering obsolete predecessor publications, including some treatises. There are several loose-leaf services covering the Code.

5. *Current state session laws pertaining to business.* The CCH Advance Session Laws Reporter is a loose-leaf reporter offering speedy publication of verbatim texts of current session laws "of general business interest," one binder for each state. Laws are listed by bill number and are subject-indexed.

# Rules of Court and Administrative Agencies

**§8.1. Function, authority and nomenclature of rules of court and administrative agencies.** Rules of practice govern the procedure of getting into court or before administrative agencies, and the conduct of business when there. They assist in the proper and expeditious transaction of business before these busy entities; so much so that failure to proceed in accordance with them may defeat the nonobserver of them. Successful practice before government agencies like the Patent Office or the Interstate Commerce Commission often depends more upon a thorough knowledge of their rules of practice than of the substantive law involved.

1. *Rule-making power generally.* There has been much question as to the power to make court rules — whether and to what extent it resides in the legislatures or in the courts themselves. The courts stress their inherent powers and assert that the doctrine of separation of powers in this country limits the legislatures' control. The weight of judicial authority is that the courts do have inherent power to make reasonable rules. On the other hand the rules must conform to and be subordinate to legislation which is constitutional in the jurisdiction where enacted. It is notable that the federal rules of civil procedure (effective September 16, 1938) and of criminal procedure (effective February 1, 1941), for the guidance of the district courts, were promulgated under an enabling act of Congress.

2. *Authority of rules of court.* Rules of court, not inconsistent with enactments of the legislature, have the force and effect of stat-

utes, but any rule inconsistent with a statute is inoperative. Rules prescribed for district courts by the United States Supreme Court by virtue of 18 U.S.C. §§3771 and 3773 and 28 U.S.C. §§2072 and 2073 (1958 ed.) supersede existing statutes repugnant to them. Rules of court made and published are said to have the force of law and are binding on the court and the parties to the action. *District of Columbia* v. *Roth,* 18 U.S. App. D.C. 547, 553 (1901).

3. *Nomenclature of rules of court.* Rules of court may be called rules of practice or rules of procedure. The term is often used interchangeably with federal or state codes of procedure which are direct enactments of the legislature, not promulgated by the courts. In some jurisdictions the court rules are incorporated in the procedural codes, though adopted by the courts pursuant to a legislative directive providing for subsequent legislative approval before becoming effective. The distinction should be maintained, however, between a code of procedure enacted by law, and the rules of courts operating under that code and implementing it.

§8.2. **Federal court rules.** The statutory authority for federal court rules has been noted above. The Supreme Court of the United States has promulgated rules for its own court and the separate lower federal courts; civil procedure and criminal procedure rules for use in federal district courts; and admiralty rules. The former equity rules have been merged with those for civil procedure.

1. *District court rules and Courts of Appeals rules for individual courts.* The federal court rules promulgated by the Supreme Court are for the general guidance of the courts. Since the individual Courts of Appeals in their circuits and the federal district courts throughout the country encounter special local conditions and circumstances, these courts are empowered by 28 U.S.C. §2071 (1964 ed.) to make their own special rules, not inconsistent with the rules of general application laid down for them by the Supreme Court. Such rules as are promulgated by the several circuits are easily found, but those of the district courts are not. See §8.5.

§8.3. **State court rules.** State courts follow much the same procedure as the federal in promulgating rules not inconsistent with the constitutions and enactments of the state legislatures. As authorized by the United States Code provisions mentioned above, many states have, since 1939, adopted rules of procedure modeled after the federal rules.

§8.4. **Rules of practice of quasi-judicial agencies and their tribunals.** Agency rules prescribe procedure before examiners or other agency officials in the transaction of business before their agencies and for appealing from adverse office decisions to one or more quasi-judicial tribunals within the office.  Knowledge of the rules and compliance with them are presumed as to suitors before the agencies, and many agencies have their own administrative bars, regulating the admission and conduct of agents or attorneys representing clients before them.  While qualifications for admission to some of these administrative bars are usually only good character, they are very strict for others, such as that of the United States Patent Office.  The impact of the rules of practice has two aspects, illustrated by the Patent Office practice.

The first regulates the routine operation of getting the applicant's business done in the Office: the form of application for a patent, the oath and fees, correspondence with the Office concerning the application, and the like.  The second provides for appeal from adverse decision of patent examiners to the quasi-judicial tribunals of the Office, from which tribunals appeals lie to the Court of Customs and Patent Appeals, which ranks as a United States Court of Appeals.

Administrative agencies promulgating rules of practice include such agencies as the Interstate Commerce Commission, the Tax Court (an administrative agency, not a true court), the Federal Trade Commission and most state public utility and tax commissions and labor relations boards.  While procedure before these quasi-judicial tribunals is apt to be somewhat less formal than in the courts, it is parallel in nearly all respects.  The rules are often detailed and voluminous, occupying as many as 150 pages of text for some agencies.  The power to promulgate rules of practice is granted federal agencies by Section 3a of the Administrative Procedure Act.  They are published in the Federal Register.  State statutes setting up administrative agencies confer similar power.

### §8.5.  Availability of published court and agency rules.

1. *Federal Register.*  Federal agency rules are not binding upon persons affected unless they have actual notice or unless the rules have been published in the Federal Register.  This official newspaper, described in Chapter 14, was established for the publication of administrative rules and orders of general effect.  Court rules are not published in the Register, because courts are not administrative agencies.  At the end of each year rules originally published in the Federal Register are cumulated in the Code of Federal Regulations, described in §14.3, but they are not court rules.

2. *Court or agency distribution.*  Many courts and quasi-judicial administrative agency tribunals distribute their rules in pamphlet form, free on application.  For local federal district court rules this is often the only source, aside from the Federal Rules Service, an unofficial publication described in §8.6.

3. *In statute compilations.*  Federal court rules are printed in

the United States Code, where they may be found through the general index. The U.S.C.A. and F.C.A. both publish court rules. Rules for specific courts as well as the general rules are included, excepting local court rules as above noted. Rules of practice of some quasi-judicial administrative tribunals are printed and indexed. Much historical and other editorial matter is supplied, and the U.S.C.A. and F.C.A. annotate the rules to the cases and Attorney Generals' opinions. Some state statutory compilations print the rules of the circuit of the United States Court of Appeals and of the district court or courts covering the state. State court rules are found in more than half the state statutory compilations, usually annotated.

4. *In law reports.* Federal court rules, except those for the Courts of Appeals and for individual district courts, are printed in the United States Reports, the Supreme Court Reporter and the Supreme Court Reports, Lawyers' Edition, including amendments as adopted. The Federal Rules Decisions, a unit of the National Reporter System, prints federal court rules and amendments of general application, but not those of individual courts other than the Supreme Court.

State court rules are printed in the official editions of the law reports of about two thirds of the states, though in a few states only amendments are printed. Rules are printed in the advance sheets, but not in the bound volumes of the National Reporter System units, and furnish in most cases the promptest available printing of these rules. ("Statutes Construed" Tables cite them.)

Shepard's United States, Federal, and state Citations cover court rules and indicate where in the law reports they are printed.

5. *In loose-leaf services.* The Federal Rules Service, described in §8.6, collects the texts of local federal district court rules, this being the most convenient repository of such rules as a whole. Agency rules are published in Pike and Fischer's Administrative Law Service, described in §14.9.

6. *In commentaries on the rules.* Separate treatises on the rules, and encyclopedias of procedure which comment on the rules, include the texts. Local practice rules commonly print them for their jurisdictions.

7. *In volumes collecting the rules.* Federal court rules, including those of the circuits of the Courts of Appeals but not for the individual district courts, are published as separate volumes of the Digest of the United States Supreme Court Reports[1] and the United States Supreme Court Digest.[2] An annotated manual, in-

[1] Rochester, N.Y., Lawyers Co-operative Publishing Co.
[2] St. Paul, Minn., West Publishing Co.

cluding state court decisions on federal court rules, is the Federal Court Rules Annotated.[3]

8. *Finding lists of court and agency rules.* The index below refers to the paragraphs in §8.5 in which the places of publication of the mentioned rules are noted directly or by implication. The relative values of these sources are largely a matter of the frequency and fullness of supplementation.

Administrative Agencies, 1, 2, 3, 5  
Admiralty, 2, 3, 5, 7  
Civil procedure, federal, 3, 4, 5, 6, 7  
Copyright, 2, 3  
Court of Claims, 2, 3, 7  
Courts of Appeals, local rules, 2, 3, 5  
Criminal procedure, federal, 3, 4, 5, 6, 7  
Customs Court, 2, 3, 7  

District Courts, local rules, 2, 3, 5  
District of Columbia Court of Appeals, 2, 3, 7  
Emergency Court of Appeals, 2, 3, 7  
Equity (merged with Civil Procedure rules)  
General Orders in Bankruptcy, 3, 4, 7  
Military Appeals Court, 2, 3, 7  
Tax Court of the United States, 2, 3, 7  

**§8.6. Decisions construing court rules.** Commonly decisions of federal, state and quasi-judicial tribunals construing their rules of procedure are printed in the same law reporters that cover the decisions of such tribunals generally. There are two special reporters which print decisions on federal court rules.

1. *Federal Rules Decisions.* The decisions of federal courts construing rules of civil and criminal procedure are printed in this unit of the National Reporter System. Decisions printed are only those not printed in the Federal Reporter or the Federal Supplement. Each advance sheet and bound volume of this reporter, however, cites the cases in all federal courts construing each rule. Articles on the federal rules are printed or reprinted from other sources in this reporter.

2. *Federal Rules Service.* This is a loose-leaf service, published by Pike & Fisher, devoted entirely to decisions construing the federal rules of civil procedure and combining in one unit the functions of a law reporter, a digest and a citator. Approximately annually the material for that period is cumulated into a bound volume of decisions, but indexing is from the beginning of the service in 1939. A second series began in 1958.

The service is organized around a copyrighted device called the Federal FindeX, serving somewhat the same functions for this service as does the copyrighted Key Number of the West Publishing Company for case digests generally. The service organized around the FindeX comprises a weekly news release, a cumulative table of cases, the text of federal decisions construing the rules, the

---

[3] Indianapolis, Ind., Bobbs-Merrill Co., Inc., 2d ed., 1963, 2v.

Local Court Rules in Force, a word index giving a fact approach, and a Federal Rules Service Digest covering all federal court cases decided since the adoption of the Federal Rules of Civil Procedure in 1938. As already noted, the Local Court Rules collection is the most convenient repository of the local rules of the various federal district courts. The Digest is arranged by Rule number.

**§8.7. State court rules modeled after federal rules.** Since 1938 many states have adopted rules of civil procedure modeled after the federal rules promulgated in that year. The Federal Rules Service Digest contains comparative tables of such state rules and the corresponding federal rules upon which they are based, and points out the differences existing between them.

**§8.8. Citation books for court rules.** Court rules are treated as statutes in citators. That is, two aspects are or may be covered: (1) amendments to and repeals of existing rules are noted, and added new rules as well; and (2) cases construing the rules are cited and, in some citators, digested.

1. *Shepard's United States, Federal and state Citations.* Shepard's United States, Federal and all state units of the Citations treat court rules as they do statutes, noting changes in text and citing to cases construing the rules. Comments on the rules by law journals within the jurisdiction and some fifteen representative ones chosen at large from other jurisdictions are also noted. As with other forms of statutes, cases annotating earlier forms of rules are, as far as possible, brought over to annotate the corresponding current form. The place of publication in the official reports of the jurisdiction in which the latest revision of the rules is published is noted.

2. *Statutory compilations printing rules of court.* Amendments, repeals and new rules are customarily noted. Annotated editions of statutes digest decisions construing each rule.

3. *Commentaries on the rules.* These serve some of the purposes of the citator, though usually not in tabular form, as in Shepard's Citations.

4. *Loose-leaf services.* The Federal Rules Service FindeX is a citator.

5. *Tables of statutes construed.* These tables, in all units of National Reporter System advance sheets and bound volumes, cover the interpretation of court rules. They are not cumulative, covering only each particular volume.

6. *United States Supreme Court Bulletin.* This is a Commerce Clearing House loose-leaf publication which, among its other functions, annotates Supreme Court rules.

### §8.9.    Suggested routine for search of court rules.

1. *Finding the rules of a given court or agency.* The rules will be found either as a part of a statutory compilation covering the appropriate jurisdiction, or in a separate manual of court rules. Where there is doubt consult the list at page 111, par. 8. Rules of quasi-judicial tribunals are often part of the rules of practice of the agency served. Those for federal agencies are published, if of general application, both in the United States Code, in the Federal Register and in the Code of Federal Regulations. The latter two publications are described in Chapter 14.

2. *Ascertaining the latest form of a rule.* The current form of a court rule will ordinarily be found through the supplementary service to annotated editions of the statutes, or in editorial notes in unannotated editions. Shepard's Citations note amendments, repeals and additions to the rules, citing the official law report in which court rules are published. National Reporter System advance sheets print federal court rules and amendments of general application, as does the Federal Rules Service in its current supplementary sheets.

Finding the latest form of a federal administrative rule is somewhat more complicated. It is done through the Code of Federal Cumulative List of Parts Affected (Codification Guide) in each issue of the Federal Register. (See page 178, par. 7.)

3. *Finding citations to decisions construing a rule.* This may be done through Shepard's Citations, the Table of Statutes Construed in the National Reporter System, annotated rules which are usually found in annotated statute compilations, the Federal Rules Service, and, as commentaries, in treatises covering the rules.

4. *Finding a textual discussion of a rule.* There are numerous means of doing this. Probably practice books are the best. For example, Moore's Federal Practice[4] and Barron and Holtzoff's Federal Practice and Procedure, with Forms[5] discuss at length all the federal rules of civil procedure (and criminal rules in Barron and Holtzoff's, as well), with exhaustive comment based upon the cases. Shorter treatments do the same thing in smaller compass. Local practice books are written to cover the law of many states or regions, and these include the court rules. Law reviews are a source of learned discussion of court rules. The Federal Rules Decisions prints or reprints articles on various aspects of the Federal Rules of Civil Procedure.

4 Albany, N.Y., Matthew Bender & Company, Inc., 7v.
5 St. Paul, Minn., West Publishing Co., 7v.

# CHAPTER 9

# Law Reports: Rationale, Format and Use of as Precedent

**§9.1.  Importance of law reports.**  What a lawyer wants most is a case squarely in point with his legal problem, decided by a court of competent jurisdiction, which has not been reversed on appeal, but is still in good standing as a legal precedent.  The most important material in a reasonably complete American working law library, accordingly, is its collection of published reports of judicial decisions, English and American.  Except for statutes and the tools for their use, practically all other books in a law library are means for unlocking the store of rules found in these reports, or for ascertaining whether the rule of law of a given case is still good law.  The elaborate machinery for making accessible these printed reports is necessary because the reports are bound up in the books according to decisions dates, not subject matter.  The legal purist goes so far as to maintain that case law is the only real authority, in that a statute's meaning is fixed and determined only by a judicial decision construing it.

**§9.2.  Definition and purpose of a law report.**  A printed law report is not the minutes of a trial, recording the evidence, examination and cross-examination and other proceedings before the court.  It is, instead ". . . the production of an adequate record of a judicial decision on a point of law, in a case heard in open court, for the subsequent citation as a precedent.  A law report is a report of law, and not of fact.  Only the issues and the facts relevant to the point of law should be recorded, since every judgment is founded on a decision of fact." [1]

"The purpose of a law report is the exposition of the law.  It

[1] Moran, The Heralds of the Law, London, Stevens, 1948, pp. 13, 14.

should show the parties, the nature of the pleadings, the essential facts, the arguments of Counsel, the decision, and the grounds for the judgment." [2]

§9.3.   **What judicial decisions are reported.**   With some exceptions, the printed law reports found in law libraries are of appellate cases, those appealed from a trial court or from an intermediate appellate court on a point of law, to correct an error which the appellant believes was committed to his hurt in the court below. The exceptions are the printing of selected cases from the federal district courts, the United States Customs Court — all trial courts — and of those of some of the lower courts in a few states such as California, New York and Pennsylvania.   Even in the courts of first instance mentioned, the cases reported have to do with the weight or admission of evidence, pleadings, or other matters of law rather than of fact.   Not even all appellate cases are reported. Reported cases are confined to those which make new law or are of general interest to the public, excluding those which are merely routine.   The selection of cases to be reported and printed is usually a matter of editorial discretion on the part of the reporter.

The value of decisions of state trial courts as precedents is dubious; it is practically nonexistent if the reports are not printed but are of record only in the clerk's office of the court where decided.   See South Carolina Court of Common Pleas for Spartansburg County, Judgment Roll No. 33,454, July 19, 1946; *King* v. *Order of United Commercial Travelers*, 333 U.S. 153, 68 Sup. Ct. 488, 92 L. Ed. 608 (1948).   The reason is chiefly that such unprinted reports are in effect secret, not being available to the profession generally but only in the clerk's office, with likelihood of their being upset on appeal.

Selective printing of reports has perhaps excluded too many cases which should have been reported and is one of the reasons leading to the establishment of the National Reporter System, which publishes many thousands of otherwise unreported appellate decisions.

§9.4.   **Reporting judicial decisions.**   In the United States, contrary to English practice, opinions of courts are read from the bench instead of being delivered orally, and there are official reporters who are responsible for making a record of all proceedings, including the opinion and judgment of each case.   Some reports are designated as official and others unofficial, the difference being that the official are published under statutory direction and the unofficial usually are not.   Both use identical texts of opinions and

---

[2] Great Britain, Lord Chancellor's Department, Report of the Law Reporting Committee, London, H.M.S.O., 1940, p. 3.

judgments, as supplied by the courts, but the editorial matter, such as tables, indexes and, usually, headnotes, is different as between official and unofficial. Both official and unofficial reports are citable in court, but the courts prefer the citation of their own official reports, with the permissible additional citation in parallel of the unofficial reports. The official is to be cited first, followed by the unofficial. Thus, *Wynn* v. *Sullivan*, 294 Mass. 562, 3 N.E.2d 235 (1936).

1. *Why there are unofficial law reports.* The principal reasons for unofficial law reporting are the greater speed of publication and the inclusion of reports which the editors deemed worthy of publication, but which the official reporter did not.

Before the National Reporter System was instituted, the publication of the official reports might lag anywhere from one to three or four years after the decision was handed down. This played hob with the rule of stare decisis, because the latest cases were unavailable. The National Reporter System published its state reports weekly, in its "advance sheets," and federal court reports semimonthly.

Other reasons for unofficial reporting are the selection of cases across jurisdictional lines which the editors deem of general interest to the profession, and their extensive annotation to cases in all jurisdictions. Special-subject series, like public utilities, labor, taxation, etc., are published for lawyers' interest in those fields.

2. *"Star paging" of unofficial editions.* Paging in unofficial editions, often is not identical with that of the official. This is because, while the opinion text is identical, editorial features are different and usually the type style and size of page are not the same. The lawyer, however, may find it necessary to cite the exact page of the official, though he has at hand only the unofficial. The device of "star paging" is employed to make this possible, as follows, to indicate the precise word or letter on one page of the official with which that page ends, and the one with which the next page begins. Thus:

> . . . of competition. From
> **\*464**
> its findings, the Com- . . .

Here, the last word on page 463 was "from" and the first on 464 was "its."

Some of the older reports have been reproduced in facsimile, making unnecessary the star paging device. Because the National Reporter System reports — excepting its Supreme Court

Reporter — are printed before the official reports, they are not star paged, with the above exception.

**§9.5.   Law reports cited by the name of the reporter.**   Up to about the middle of the nineteenth century, the law reporter commonly gave his name to his series of reports, such as Hun, Pickering or Brevard, regardless of the name of the jurisdiction reported.   This caused so much confusion with its multiplicity of meaningless personal names, that the practice was abandoned, with the name of the jurisdiction thereafter forming an integral part of the series title, as United States, South Carolina, etc.   In those official series still current at the time this change in nomenclature took place, the existing volumes were renumbered consecutively from the earliest ones on.

At that time the ninety volumes of the United States Reports, reporting the Supreme Court cases from Dallas through Wallace, and the ninety-six Massachusetts Reports, which reported Williams through Allen, were so renumbered.   Further confusion has resulted in citing these early "nominatives," however.   One reason is that the cases in the reports antedating the renumbering cited these renumbered cases by their old form, as nominatives. Another reason, and a correlative one, lies in the conservatism of lawyers: They just prefer the original form.   Thus, 90 U.S. is still cited as 23 Wallace, but 91 U.S. is not 1 Otto (its reporter), but 91 U.S., because that is where the break came, and Otto and his successors never were cited by their names.   A similar procedure was followed for state nominative reports.

In bibliographic manuals on law books, such as Price and Bitner's Effective Legal Research (1953), and in Shepard's Citations red-paper pamphlet issues for the United States Reports and for some of the early state nominatives, parallel tables from the nominative citation to the renumbered volumes are provided.

Those early series which were not current when renumbering became the rule were not renumbered at all and are still cited by the name of the reporter.   Since their titles are always abbreviated in citations, tables of abbreviations are necessary in order to identify the reports.   Digests and encyclopedias of law frequently contain tables of abbreviations; the most complete such table is probably that in Price and Bitner's Effective Legal Research (1953), available in most law libraries, and somewhat shortened in this edition.   See Appendix III.

**§9.6.   Parts of a reported case.**   A reported case may consist of the following parts:

1. *Title.*   The title or case name designates the parties, such as *Smith* v. *Jones,* In re *Pimsleur, Matter of Cohen, People* v. *Clar-*

*ence* (a criminal case), *The Elizabeth* (an admiralty case, giving the name of the vessel involved), or *United States* v. *34 Cases of Square-face Gin.*

The plaintiff-defendant order as above is usually kept throughout, but in some courts the order is reversed on appeal when the defendant in the court below has lost and thus becomes the "Plaintiff in Error" in the court above. Tables of cases customarily follow the official case designation in listing cases, but a growing number of case tables are also by "Defendant-Plaintiff," enabling the cases to be found when only the defendant's name is known.

2. *Docket number.* When a case is filed in the court clerk's office, it is assigned a serial number, called a docket number, which serves as an identification tag in its progress through the court. This number is usually printed in a law report, following the title of the case; the term of court and the dates of argument and decision are noted here.

3. *Headnote or syllabus.* This index to the law in the reported opinion is extremely important as the foundation of the case digests which enable the lawyer to find cases in point in the United States — if they exist — from 1754 to date. The headnote is made up of brief statements of the law involved in the reported case, usually each paragraph comprising a single sentence. The headnote may be propositional in that it is purely a statement of legal principle, or factual, containing sufficient facts to tie it to the case reported. In some states it is written by the judge or court, when it will usually bear the notation "syllabus by the court," but it is usually written by the reporter. The official headnote by the reporter thus differs in text from that of the unofficial, and the latter is apt to be more detailed. Where, as in Georgia, Ohio and Oklahoma, the court is required by law to write a syllabus, it is the personal statement of the law by the judge. The National Reporter System reports customarily carry both the syllabus of the court, if any, and their own; their syllabus also numbers the individual paragraphs of the headnotes in boldface type, with corresponding numbers in the text of the opinion. This is to make it easier and quicker to find the text statements upon which the headnote paragraphs are based. These boldface type numbers should not be confused with the Reporter Key Number which is also attached to each headnote paragraph and which is a classification number employed in compiling case digests.

With the possible exception of the syllabi by the courts, headnote paragraphs are not authority but only indexes to it. They contain both the reasoning leading inevitably to the holding —

the ratio decidendi — and dictum, which is useful background material in the opinion but not necessary to the decision. The case itself must be read if the headnote points to it as possible precedent to be relied upon.

4. *Statement of facts of the reported case.* Formerly a statement of facts preceded the opinion of the courts, but it is now seldom found except briefly at the beginning of the opinion itself. New York official reports still have it, however, and also the American Law Reports Annotated, an unofficial, selective case series.

5. *Statement of how the case arose.* A brief statement of how the case came to the court which is deciding it is found in practically all published case reports. It may precede the opinion or, more often, be in the opinion itself, a statement by the court preliminary to its discussion of the issues. It is important, because how a case arose is often decisive of its value as precedent to the searcher. For example, a case coming up on a prayer for a preliminary injunction is unlikely to be authority on the merits of a point of substantive law, though such a point may be discussed as background for the decision. In the latter instance it will be dictum, perhaps persuasive but not mandatory.

6. *Names of counsel.* Counsel are often willing to supply inquiring lawyers or law students with briefs. Also they may be willing to detail the arguments, the questions asked by the courts and other possible factors influencing the decision and affecting its value as precedent, where the case report has not been published. Law students sometimes take advantage of this in preparing moot court briefs.

7. *Synopses of briefs of counsel.* Formerly these commonly preceded the opinion, but are seldom found any more.

8. *Opinion of the court.* This is the real meat of the law report to which all else except the actual decision with which the report closes is incidental and subsidiary. In it the court explains why it decided as it did. The opinion begins with a statement of the facts involved, sufficient to set the issues, the parties concerned and the relief sought. Errors charged to the court below are detailed. Judicial technique then usually applies the method of the syllogism, as classically expressed by Professor Eugene Wambaugh:

"(1) When the circumstances surrounding the parties are thus and thus, the rights of the parties are thus and thus; (2) in this particular case such circumstances do surround the parties; (3) in this particular case the other circumstances are not material; and (4) in this particular case the rights of the parties are as indicated in the first proposition. (In the phraseology of logicians, the first of these propositions is the major premise, the second and third taken together are the minor premise, and the fourth is the conclusion.") [3]

Following this technique, the opinion commonly consists of a general statement of the points of law involved, and this is likely to be pure dictum. Then the law is applied to the specific circumstances of the case being decided, the statement of which involves the reasoning or ratio decidendi which is the statement of an underlying principle leading inevitably to the decision. It is this last which is most prized by the lawyer seeking judicial precedents.

Opinions of the court may be unanimous. Or there may be concurring opinions, when the concurrer agrees with the result but not altogether with the reasoning leading to it. Dissenting opinions are the minority's statement of its reasons for disagreeing. Per curiam or memorandum decisions report routine decisions and commonly lack any statement of the reasoning behind them, thus somewhat diminishing their value as precedent. Frequently, when a written opinion has been read but the court orders only the decision to be printed, the National Reporter System report of the case supplies the headnotes to the opinion as actually delivered, and the case is thus digested.

9. *Decision of the court.* This is the court's statement that the decision below is "Affirmed," "Reversed," that "There is no error," etc. This is what the court *does,* as distinguished from what it *says* in its opinion. The decision is final, but the opinion as delivered by the court may be revised and, occasionally, even withdrawn before publication.

### §9.7. Stare decisis in case law.

1. *The doctrine defined.* The theory of Anglo-American law is *stare decisis et non quieta movere,* "to adhere to precedent and not to unsettle things which are settled"; that the principle underlying the decision in one case will be deemed of imperative authority, controlling the decisions of like cases in the same court and in lower courts within the same jurisdiction, unless and until the decision in question is reversed or overruled by a court of competent authority. A single decision does not necessarily create a precedent to be followed.

Decisions relied upon as precedent are commonly those of appellate courts, since the decisions of trial courts may be appealed to higher courts and are probably not the best evidence of the rule of law laid down. A detailed discussion of the rule of stare decisis on the weight of decisions of the various hierarchies of courts is found in 1 Moore, Federal Practice ¶¶4017, 4051-95 (1959).

[3] The Study of Cases, Boston, Little, Brown and Co., 1892, p. 16.

2. *Res judicata distinguished.*   Res judicata has nothing to do with precedent.   It merely operates as an estoppel between the parties to a specific case, so that ". . . a right, question of fact distinctly put in issue and directly determined by a court of competent jurisdiction, as a ground of recovery cannot be disputed in a subsequent suit between the same parties or their privies." *Southern Pacific Ry.* v. *United States,* 168 U.S. 1, 48, 18 Sup. Ct. 18, 27, 42 L. Ed. 355, 377 (1897).

3. *Reasons for the doctrine.*   Following is Chancellor James Kent's statement:

"A solemn decision upon a point of law arising in any given case, becomes an authority in a like case, because it is the highest evidence which we can have of the law applicable to the subject, and the judges are bound to follow that decision so long as it stands unreversed, unless it can be shown that the law was misunderstood or misapplied in that particular case.   If a decision has been made upon solemn argument and mature deliberation, the presumption is in favor of its correctness, and the community have a right to regard it as a just declaration or exposition of the law, and to regu-late their actions and contracts by it.   It would, therefore, be extremely inconvenient to the public, if precedents were not duly regarded and implicitly followed.   It is on the notoriety and stability of such rules that professional men can give safe advice to those who consult them; and people in general can venture with confidence to buy and trust, and to deal with each other.   If judicial decisions were to be lightly disregarded, we should disturb and unsettle the great landmarks of property.   When a rule has been once deliberately adopted and declared, it ought not to be disturbed unless by a court of appeal or review, and never by the same court, except for very cogent reasons, and upon a clear manifestation of error; and if the practice were otherwise, it would be leaving us in a state of perpetual uncertainty as to the law." [4]

4. *Analysis of the doctrine of stare decisis.*

a. *The point must have been raised and considered.*   This must have been done both by counsel and court.   If raised by counsel but not treated by the court, it is not a precedent.

b. *Identity of essential circumstances.*   No two cases are identi-cal, and nonessential circumstances such as parties, time and place, may be stripped from a fact situation and still permit the case to be used as precedent.   But at the point where elimination of an element changes the legal principles involved the cases are no longer "like."

[4] 1 Commentaries on American Law, 14th ed., Boston, Little, Brown and Co., 1896, p. 476.

c. *Doctrine of the case.*   There must be a rule in the case without which that case could not have been decided as it was; and this rule must be of general application to the class of cases under consideration.

d. *Ratio decidendi or reasoning.*   This is the legal reasoning of the court which leads inevitably and necessarily to the decision; it is a statement of a doctrine precisely applicable to the case being decided and necessarily involved in the decision.   As reasoning from a rule to its specific application it is broader than the decision.

e. *Dictum.*   Dictum is an expression of opinion as to the state of the law, not necessarily raised by the case or necessary to its decision; dicta are not regarded as precedents within the rule of stare decisis, because, not having been at issue before the court, they have not been argued by counsel or investigated fully.   Only the specific case before the court is the basis of a precedent.   Well-considered dicta, nevertheless, are often highly persuasive and are frequently cited.   When this is done, however, it should be with full awareness.[5]

5. *Illustrative case.*   The opinion in *Hoffman* v. *Le Traunik,* 209 Fed. 375 (N.D.N.Y. 1913), illustrates the distinction between dictum, *ratio decidendi* and decisions.   It is also a good example of the decisive effect on precedent of the manner in which a case reaches the appellate court.   This particular opinion is also proof that an opinion need not be dull.

In Equity.   Suit by Aaron Hoffman against Sam Le Traunik, for alleged infringement of copyright in the use of monologues.   On motion for preliminary injunction pendente lite.   Denied.

*P* charged *D,* a burlesque comedian, with using his copyrighted monologues.   The opinion reproduced one monologue and discussed certain similarities of *D's* material; it then proceeded as follows: (see Exhibit 19 below).

Casting the proposition extracted from the excerpt in Exhibit 19, in the form of a syllogism, we have:

(1) Preliminary injunctions will not issue except in the clearest cases.   [A general rule.]

(2) Where, on a motion for a preliminary injunction, complainant makes affidavit one way, defendant the other; and the substantive issue will be tried on its merits within two months; no public interest being involved; and the damage to the complainant will not be very serious, no clear and satisfactory case is made.   [Illustrating the rule.]

---

[5] Paraphrased from Wambaugh, The Study of Cases, Boston, Little, Brown and Co., 1892, pp. 16 et seq. passim.

378                    209 FEDERAL REPORTER

378                    HOFFMAN V. LE TRAUNIK

It may be proved on the trial that the complainant originated all these expressions, and the court may be of the mind that no one but the author and his licensees should be permitted to use them; but, so long as the defendants aver under oath that they were not new with complainant but common-property and used on the stage prior to the writing of complainant's monologues, it seems to me that a preliminary injunction should not issue. No public interest is involved, and the damage to the complainant will not be very serious. The answers are served, and a term of court will be held at Albany February 10th, when the suit can be tried if the parties desire.

[2] To be entitled to be copyrighted, the composition must be "original, meritorious, and free from illegality or immorality." And "a work, in order to be copyrighted, must be original in the sense that the author has created it by his own skill, labor, and judgment, without directly copying or evasively imitating the work of another." However, "a new and original plan, arrangement, or combination of materials will entitle the author to a copyright therein, whether the materials themselves be new or old."

[3] But here the defendants have not copied substantially the plan, arrangement, or combination of materials found in complainant's monologues or in any one of them. Conceding literary or artistic merit in the complainant's monologues growing out of some original matter combined with old matter in a new and an original plan, arrangement, or combination, the defendants do not infringe, not having used that plan, arrangement, or combination, unless they have abstracted and used some of the complainant's new matter and so much of it as to authorize the finding that there has been a copying or a taking.

"Copying the whole or a substantial part of a copyrighted work constitutes and is an essential element of infringement. It is not confined to literal repetition or reproduction but includes also the various modes in which the matter of any work may be adopted, imitated, transferred. or reproduced with more or less colorable alteration to disguise the piracy. But, on the principle of de minimis non curat lex, it is necessary that a substantial part of the copyrighted work. be taken." 9 Cyc. 939, 940.

If there is any piracy in this case, it consists in the taking and use of these isolated expressions or "gags," as they are called, and to constitute infringement it must be established by the complainant that they were original with him. The burden is on him to show this, and with complainant making affidavit one way and the defendants the other, and a sworn answer also interposed, a clear and satisfactory case on such a subject is not made for the drastic use of a preliminary injunction.

The motion is denied, but the defendants must be ready for trial at the Albany term of this court or the motion may be renewed on the same and additional papers.

Exhibit 19

(3) Therefore, these conditions existing here, the motion for a preliminary injunction to restrain D from using his monologues is denied.

All that is said above by the court about copyright and infringement is dictum, not required for the decision. The case decides nothing on the merits of any copyright infringement issue, but for reasons given refuses a preliminary injunction.

### §9.8. Publication of law reports: Promptness and format.

1. *Promptness of publication and the rule of stare decisis.* Application of the rule of stare decisis demands access to the latest cases if the lawyer is to advise his clients properly. This is because any late case may affirm, modify or overturn an existing rule of law. Accordingly case law publishing is geared to speed, speed of publishing the case report itself and of all indexes and other tools necessary to their effective use.

2. *Chronological arrangement of published law reports.* Law reports are published in the order of the decision date, and so arranged in the publications making them available to lawyers. Exceptions to this rule are cases published in a few special-subject periodicals and special-subject law reports series, such as those for labor, public utilities, taxation, etc. Because of this chronological arrangement, elaborate indexes, such as case digests, legal encyclopedias and treatises are necessary to enable the lawyer to find the law in the approximately 3,500,000 American cases reported to date, and in the English cases.

3. *Slip decisions.* Some courts, both federal and state, issue slip decisions on their decision days or close to them. Each such decision is in the form of a separate pamphlet, with complete text but no syllabus or headnote. Unofficial slip decisions for the Supreme Court of the United States are published in the CCH United States Supreme Court Bulletin, a weekly loose-leaf service, and in the United States Law Week. In each case the reports are facsimile reprints of the official decision. Ordinarily they reach their subscribers in from one to five days after decision date, depending upon the distance from Washington.

4. *Advance sheets.* Oustanding examples of speed in law publishing are the advance sheets. Each is a pamphlet collecting all reports decided within the jurisdiction or jurisdictions covered by the individual advance sheet, as reported since its preceding issue. All units of the National Reporter System are covered by advance sheets and there are official editions for the Supreme Court of the United States and for several state courts.

Advance sheets appear weekly for the National Reporter System units (semimonthly for the Supreme Court Reporter), as against an average of once a year for the official bound reports. Since the pagination and volume numbers of all National Reporter System advance sheets are identical with their form when cumulated into bound volumes, citation to them is as to the bound volumes — the same volume and page.

The National Reporter System advance sheets are the epitome of law book format, containing as they do almost every typical feature. They have tables of cases, tables of statutes construed, words and phrases of legal meaning as defined by the courts in reports printed in the respective sheets, law reports, and a digest which cumulates progressively into the digest in the bound volume of the Reporter, into the General Digest covering all Reporter units, and eventually into the Decennial Digests.

a. *Corrections in advance sheets.* Advance sheets, because of their speed of publication, are subject to error. The judge writing the opinion can at any time prior to final publication in bound form withdraw an opinion for revision, or even from publication entirely.

5. *Legal newspapers and periodicals publishing law reports.* Daily newspapers for practitioners, such as the New York Law Journal and its prototypes in other large cities, usually publish highly selected reports of cases decided within the jurisdiction served by them. The publication may be a full report, or, usually, one minus the headnote, or an abridged report. Practitioners' periodicals of less frequency of publication also publish law reports. Although the chief value of such reports is their promptness of publication, they also frequently publish reports not printed elsewhere. Thus the New York Law Journal publishes some reports not published in the New York Miscellaneous Reports or in the New York Supplement.

6. *Loose-leaf services publishing law reports.* Special-subject series of reports in labor, tax, public utilities and other regulatory fields are found in loose-leaf services. The reports, which appear first in loose-leaf form, to be inserted in the service's binders, are, for some series, collected later and published in bound volumes.

7. *Bound volumes of law reports.* All the forms of law reports described above have as their principal asset speed of publication. For convenience of finding and use, however, the bound volume, which is the final form of publication of law reports, is superior and is the form commonly found and consulted on library shelves. It contains, for the material published in each individual volume, the tables, digests and other features mentioned above for advance sheets. Often, as noted in Chapter 8, it prints court rules and amendments.

8. *Governmental agency publication of law reports.*  Governmental agencies, including especially those having quasi-judicial functions, collect and bind for various purposes both judicial and quasi-judicial decisions affecting them and the laws they administer.  An example is the Federal Communications Commission Reports.  While these agency decisions vary in format and authority, they tend to resemble in most respects those of formal courts.

# CHAPTER 10

# Law Reports: Decisions of Federal
# and State Courts

§10.1.   **The federal court system as it affects law report publication.**[1] That the federal court system is complicated is reflected in the multiplicity of series reporting the decisions of the courts comprising it.   At the present time there is a hierarchy of three steps of federal Constitutional courts, plus several specialized statutory or legislative courts.   In addition there have been courts for the insular possessions of the United States, now reduced in number and jurisdiction with the admission of Alaska and Hawaii to statehood and Puerto Rico to commonwealth status.

The lowest courts in this federal hierarchy are the district courts, which are general trial courts of original jurisdiction. There is at least one federal district court in each state, and in many states there are two or more.   The district courts for the Canal Zone and the Virgin Islands have also local jurisdiction approximating that of state courts, which was true of the district courts of Alaska prior to statehood.   Appeal from the district courts ordinarily lies to the Courts of Appeals, but in some instances is directly to the Supreme Court.

The second rung of federal courts comprises the Courts of Appeals, formerly the Circuit Courts of Appeals.   These courts hear appeals from the district courts mentioned above.   There are ten numbered circuits, covering geographically the United States

[1] The United States Court (H. Doc. No. 233, 86th Cong., 1st Sess., 1959) in twelve pages describes the United States court system.   Fannie J. Klein, A Guide to Court Systems (New York, N.Y., Institute of Judicial Administration, 1957) in fifty pages outlines the federal and state court systems and their relation to each other, with special reference to the courts of New York State.   Both pamphlets contain schematic diagrams of court systems.

and its insular possessions. The respective territorial jurisdictions of these numbered circuits are shown on a map printed in each Federal Reporter advance sheet and bound volume. In addition there are several other courts ranking for certain purposes as courts of appeals, in that appeals from them lie to the Supreme Court. The Court of Appeals for the District of Columbia ranks as a court of appeals, and there are three statutory courts from which appeals lie directly to the Supreme Court. These are the Court of Customs and Patent Appeals, the Emergency Court of Appeals and the Court of Claims. The latter achieved this status only in 1960.

There were various other categories of federal trial and intermediate appellate courts before 1880, reported in so very many different series that it would be impossible for the lawyer to have all of them in his library. For practical purposes the cases so reported have been combined in a series entitled Federal Cases, described in §10.3.

At the top of the ladder is the Supreme Court of the United States — its official title, commonly shortened to United States Supreme Court, or simply Supreme Court. In addition to a limited original jurisdiction, as over suits between the states, it hears appeals from the Courts of Appeals and from some classes of decisions of the district courts.

The statutory or legislative courts mentioned in §10.5 occupy a somewhat different status, which need not concern us here. This difference in status between Constitutional and legislative courts is discussed at length in 1 Moore, Federal Practice 53-60 [2] and in other works on federal practice.

1. *Inclusiveness of publication of federal court decisions.* Not all decisions of any federal court, even of the Supreme Court, are reported. On the other hand all written and nearly all per curiam decisions of the Supreme Court are reported either officially or unofficially. This is true also of the reports of the intermediate appellate courts and those of the special courts. Only selected decisions of the district courts are published.

**§10.2. United States Supreme Court reports.** All decisions for which written opinions were rendered are published both in the official United States Reports and in the unofficial Lawyers' Edition and Supreme Court Reporter. Most but not all per curiam reports of decisions are printed also; a good many are reported in the two unofficial series which are not in the official. These latter are of a routine nature, for the most part simply noting the probable jurisdiction of the Court, extending time for filing

[2] Albany, N.Y., Matthew Bender & Co., Inc., 1959.

various petitions, fixing the compensation of special masters, permitting the filing of briefs as amici curiae and similar matters not affecting the merits.

1. *Opinions of Supreme Court Justices in chambers.* Each Supreme Court Justice is assigned to a circuit of the Courts of Appeals, and as such sits in chambers to hear petitions and motions of various kinds, such as for stay of execution, continuance of bail pending appeal from conviction, etc. While the opinions rendered are usually brief, some are not. A notable example of the latter is the opinion of Mr. Justice William O. Douglas in granting a stay of execution to Julius and Ethel Rosenberg, from their conviction of espionage. 73 Sup. Ct. 1152, 1173; 97 L. Ed. 1607, 1629 (1953). These opinions are printed in the privately published Supreme Court Reporter and the Lawyers' Edition, but usually not in the official United States Reports. The Douglas opinion in chambers in the *Rosenberg* case was printed as an appendix to his dissent in the order vacating the stay of execution. 346 U.S. 273, 313 (1953). The practice of printing these opinions has grown up up only since about 1950. They are discussed by Frederick Bernays Wiender in 49 Law Library Journal 2 (1956).

2. *Slip decisions.* A slip decision is one in which each separate report is a separate pamphlet which is usually, but not always, handed down on Mondays during term time. It has as its only virtue speed of publication, because it lacks headnotes and may be corrected in text later. It does contain the docket number, the title (as *Chamberlain* v. *Pierce*), how it came to the Court (as by writ of certiorari, etc.) and the date of the decision, together with the text of the opinion and of the decision. The official edition, which includes both written and per curiam decisions, is mailed from the Government Printing Office in Washington to subscribers, whom it reaches anywhere from two days to two weeks after decision date. Facsimile editions are published unofficially in the CCH United States Supreme Court Bulletin and in the United States Law Week, both described later in this section. These unofficial editions reach their subscribers somewhat earlier than the official edition. Loose-leaf services frequently mail decisions of outstanding interest to their subscribers on decision day.

3. *Advance sheets.* Advance sheets are published during term time for the official United States Reports, the Lawyers' Edition and the Supreme Court Reporter. Since the volume numbering and pagination are identical with those of the bound volumes into which the respective series cumulate, the advance sheets are cited as bound volumes, not as advance sheets.

4. *United States Reports.*  This is the title of the official edition of the reports of the Supreme Court of the United States, a series dating nominally from 1774 but reporting Supreme Court cases only from the August term of 1791.  It is a typical law report series, with advance sheets, called Preliminary Prints, which appear at irregular intervals of from a month to six weeks during term time.  Thus the lag from decision to receipt date may be up to two months, so that if time is of the essence the searcher should seek a slip decision.

As earlier noted, the first ninety volumes of the reports, entitled Reports of Cases Argued and Adjudged in the Supreme Court of the United States, are still cited by the names of their official reporters, in spite of the fact that in 1875 they were renumbered serially from volume 1 to 90.  In 1876, beginning with volume 91, the series title was changed to United States Reports, its present title.  Citation to the first ninety volumes is by the name of the reporter, not by the renumbered designation.  Below is a transfer table from the reporter citation to the renumbered consecutive volume citation:

| Reporter | Nominative Citation | United States Reports | Dates Covered |
|---|---|---|---|
| Dallas | 1-4 Dall. | 1-4 U.S. | 1790-1800 |
| Cranch | 1-9 Cr. | 5-13 U.S. | 1801-1815 |
| Wheaton | 1-12 Wheat. | 14-25 U.S. | 1816-1827 |
| Peters | 1-16 Pet. | 26-41 U.S. | 1828-1842 |
| Howard | 1-24 How. | 42-65 U.S. | 1843-1860 |
| Black | 1-2 Black | 66-67 U.S. | 1861-1862 |
| Wallace | 1-23 Wall. | 68-90 U.S. | 1863-1874 |
| United States Reports | | 91-date | 1875-date |

5. *Lawyers' Edition of the Supreme Court Reports.*  This unofficial edition covers the entire series of reports of the Supreme Court, from its volume 1 to date.  It contains many decisions not reported originally in the early official volumes.  The report text is that of the official volumes, except that errors in the official are pointed out and parallel statutory and case citations are supplied when lacking in the official.

The editorial matter, however, is quite different.  In the Lawyers' Edition, Second Series, a rather full summary of each case precedes the report of the case itself.  The headnotes, by the publisher's staff, are keyed to the Digest of the United States Supreme Court Reports, described on page 211.  Through them, annotations of cases involving similar legal principles are found.  The principal difference between this series of United States reports and others is that most of the cases are carefully and often elaborately annotated in the manner of the American Law Reports Annotated (A.L.R.), published by the same firm.

An annotation like those in the Lawyers' Edition takes up the points of law involved in a decided case, notes or discusses all cases in point, indicating the general rules applicable, majority and minority rules, jurisdictional factors and the impact of the present case upon the existing law. Extensive tables of foreign, federal and state statutes construed by the Supreme Court are included in each volume, for that volume, thus performing some of the functions of a conventional citator. The coverage of foreign statutes construed by the Supreme Court in these tables is unique. They are cumulated in volume 14 of the Digest of the United States Supreme Court Reports.

Since volume numbers and pagination of the Lawyers' Edition are different from those of the official United States Reports, a parallel cross-reference table in each volume refers from the official citation to the Lawyers' Edition. The Lawyers' Edition publishes some reports not officially reported, though none with written opinions. Per curiam orders comprise most of these, along with the occasional reports of Justices in chambers, sitting as Circuit Judges.

The first series of the Lawyers' Edition ended with 351 U.S. Reports. Beginning with the first volume of the Second Series, briefs of counsel and annotations are printed in a separate section at the end of each bound volume (covering, usually, three volumes of official U.S. Reports). Briefs of counsel and annotations are printed in a separate section thus permitting identical pagination and citation of advance sheet and bound volume. The annotations correspond to the A.L.R. annotations discussed in Chapter 12, and are often elaborate. The annotation of the *in rem* case entitled *A Book Named "John Cleland's Memoirs of a Woman of Pleasure"* v. *Attorney General of Massachusetts* (383 U.S. 413, 16 L. Ed. 2d 1, 86 Sup. Ct. 975(1966)), the Fanny Hill case, occupies twenty-six pages of discussion of the right of free speech and the press, indexed in detail, and cross-referenced to A.L.R. annotations and American Jurisprudence sections in point.

6. *Supreme Court Reporter.* The coverage of this unit of the National Reporter System is only from 106 U.S. (October Term, 1882) to date. It is a typical Reporter, with the usual features, including the Key-Numbering of headnote paragraphs. The advance sheets appear semimonthly, with a time lag of receipt by the subscriber of from ten days to three weeks after decision date. The bound volumes into which the advance sheets cumulate are

"star paged" to the official. While the text of the opinions is identical with that of the official edition, corrections in the official may be pointed out and additional per curiam opinions printed. The headnotes and other editorial matter are different, however, being written by the publisher's own editorial staff.

In addition to features common to all Reporters, federal court rules and amendments are printed as adopted — not including local rules of federal district courts — and there are tables of rules construed by cases reported. A transfer table from official to Reporter citation is supplied, and there is in each advance sheet and bound volume a digest, identical in classification with that of the American Digest System (§16.5), covering the reports published in the advance sheet or bound volume. A Statutes Construed table, described in §11.3, is significant for its citation of state court decisions interpreting federal statutes.

7. *Services covering the United States Supreme Court.* Three services cover the work of the Supreme Court, two of them printing the slip decisions unofficially.

a. *Journal of the Supreme Court.* This is a daily, official publication issued during term time, noting the business transacted by the Court, such as the admission of attorneys to practice, decisions and orders handed down, etc. It lacks an index, making search in it difficult. It is reprinted in the United States Law Week, described *infra.*

b. *CCH United States Supreme Court Bulletin.* This loose-leaf reporter, mailed to subscribers on decision day, provides a very elaborate coverage of the business of the Supreme Court. It contains: (1) a statement of all official actions taken by the Court for the preceding week; (2) facsimile reprints of decisions and orders, which usually reach subscribers before the official prints; (3) a subject index to cases on the docket or decided during the term; (4) a table of cases on the docket; (5) rules of the Supreme Court; (6) the docket, with a summary of docketed cases; (7) a weekly United States Supreme Court Docket, with highlights of recently docketed cases and cases awaiting decisions; and (8) a tentative calendar for arguments before the Court. It will be seen that this is a very detailed status table for the Supreme Court, plus a repository of slip decisions for the current term.

c. *United States Law Week.* This is a service in periodical form, of which two important sections are devoted to the work of the Supreme Court and the printing of facsimile copies of its latest decisions. Mailed on decision day, it usually reaches the New York area, for example, the next day, with its Supreme Court news and case reports. It contains the complete docket, with summaries by topic of cases on it, and a Review of Supreme Court's Work. The Review is a unique treatment of various aspects of the Court's work. Exhaustive arguments of the more important cases recently heard by the Court and awaiting decision, and questions by the Court are presented for various categories of cases. Frequently the term's cases awaiting decision are reviewed.

The indexes to the Supreme Court sections of the United States Law Week are elaborate, by subject, case and docket number, and are cumulated at irregular intervals of from four to six weeks during the term, with a final cumulated issue at the end of the term.

The services mentioned above give a detailed picture of the pending work of the Supreme Court, the docket, the cases argued and awaiting decision, and the text of the term's decisions to date.

§10.3.   **Lower federal court reports.**   It is commonly said that the decisions of the federal courts below the Supreme Court have not been officially reported, but only in a multitude of unofficial series before 1880 and in units of the unofficial National Reporter System since then. This is only partly true, however. Each of the ten circuits of the Courts of Appeals, the Court of Appeals for the District of Columbia and the special courts of appeal noted in §10.5 prints and distributes its slip decisions. Unfortunately, these decisions for the numbered circuits of the Courts of Appeals are not bound for distribution and few libraries have them. Reversing the usual practice — that the unofficial reports print decisions not officially reported — the above slip decisions *may print per curiam decisions not printed in the unofficial Federal Reporter.* The special courts of appeal are said to prefer to be cited to their own official reports rather than the unofficial. All courts, however, accept citations to the unofficial only, and this is law review practice generally, as well. One reason is the very practical one that the unofficial reports are much more generally available in law libraries than the official.

1. *1789-1880: Federal Cases.*   In the period preceding the establishment of the Federal Reporter in 1880, some 233 different reporters at various times printed lower federal court decisions. This was an impossible situation for the practicing lawyer. Between the years 1894 and 1897 a unique series, Federal Cases,[3] appeared, combining and reprinting the cases so diversely published originally. This set is now used to the exclusion of the original reports it reprints.

a. *Arrangement of Federal Cases.*   The arrangement of cases is not chronological, as in other reports, but by title and arbitrary

[3] St. Paul, Minn., West Publishing Co., 1894-1897, 30v.

case number. That is, Case No. 1 is *The Aalesund;* Case No. 26 is *Acker* v. *The Rainbow;* Case No. 18,222 is *In re Zug,* etc. By the time the last volume was ready for printing, ninety-one additional cases were found, which were put in an alphabetically arranged supplement in the last volume, and, continuing the consecutive numbering, were given numbers 18,223 to 18,313. This rendered a table of cases necessary to take care of the two alphabets. As nearly as possible the cases included were copied verbatim from the originals, together with the original citations, the court deciding the case, the decision date and a headnote. Unreported cases cited to certain points in other decisions are noted by title, e.g., 30 Fed. Cas. No. 17,856. This case is not reported textually in Federal Cases, but because it is cited for certain points of law in 2 Wharton's Digest 408-410, Federal Cases reprints the Wharton Digest statements of these points.

b. *Citation of cases printed in Federal Cases.* As in all series in which there has been a change in numbering or other designation, cases citing the reprinted cases before the change in numbering was made, perforce cite the original form, and it is necessary to translate these citations into the Federal Cases citation. If the citation contains the case name, it is only necessary to go to Federal Cases, to the 18,222 cases arranged in the main alphabet by case number; or, if not found there, to the 91 cases arranged by case name under Additional Cases in the appendix. If, however, the citation is only by the original series volume and page, then a blue-paper parallel transfer Table of Citations, as shown in Exhibit 26 at page 161, refers to the Federal Case location. Thus, 2 Benedict's U.S. District Court Reports (2 Ben.) 76 is 26 Fed. Cas. No. 15,626.

2. *1880 to date: National Reporter System reports.* For practical purposes the reports of lower federal courts consulted today for the years 1880 to date are units of the National Reporter System entitled the Federal Reporter, Federal Supplement, and Federal Rules Decisions; that is, with the exception of the reports of the special courts described in §10.5. With the exception of the reports designated as official by those courts, there are no technically official reports for the lower federal courts today. The distinction is only technical, however, and perhaps not even that, since the Judicial Conference of the United States, which regulates administrative matters concerning the federal courts, by its requests to the West Publishing Company concerning the content of its Reporters of federal courts, may be said to have conferred at least semi-official status. For example, on March 11, 1960, the Conference approved the following resolution: "Resolved, that

the Judicial Conference of the United States approve a request by the United States Court of Claims that its opinions be published hereafter in the Federal Reporter, 2d Series."

These Reporters are typical units, containing all the features common to the National Reporter System.

a. *Federal Reporter.* From its beginning in 1880 through volume 60, Second Series (October Term, 1931), the Federal Reporter reported cases from the federal district courts and the then Circuit Courts of Appeals, and selected cases, principally tax cases, of the United States Court of Claims. With the beginning of the Federal Supplement, the Federal Reporter reported only cases decided by the intermediate courts of appeals; that is, the Courts of Appeals, the Court of Appeals for the District of Columbia, patent, trade-mark and customs cases from the United States Court of Customs and Patent Appeals, and the United States Emergency Court of Appeals. All written opinions of the federal courts below the Supreme Court, with the above exceptions, are said to be reported. Since the status of the Court of Claims has been changed, with appeal lying directly to the Supreme Court, its decisions are again reported in the Federal Reporter, beginning with volume 276, second series. Cases reported for this court are principally tax cases. There are weekly advance sheets for this Reporter.

b. *Federal Supplement.* This Reporter covers the federal district courts. From volume 60, second series (October Term, 1931) until volume 275, second series (October Term, 1959), it reported also the decisions of the Court of Claims, but as noted above, that court is once again reported in the Federal Reporter.

c. *Federal Rules Decisions.* This Reporter reports decisions construing the federal rules of civil and criminal procedure, for the most part from the federal district courts, not elsewhere reported. It began publication in 1940, following the adoption of the Federal Rules, and is a typical National Reporter System unit, except that it prints also speeches and articles on federal practice. These latter are indexed in each volume of the set (for that volume), with occasional cumulative indexes in addition; for example, those covering volumes 1-12 (in volume 12) and 13-20 (in volume 20). Federal rules are annotated to the cases published in all standard report series. New revisions and amendments of court rules are printed as adopted. There are monthly advance sheets.

§10.4. **"Consent" decisions in antitrust cases.**[4] The Department of Justice Antitrust Division in its prosecution of antitrust

---

[4] The authors acknowledge with thanks the assistance of Miss Marie L. Resweber, of the Department of Justice Library; now retired.

cases frequently negotiates what are called "consent decrees," under which the party proceeded against agrees to take or to desist from certain action. These decrees currently are published in the CCH Trade Regulation Reports, first in loose-leaf form and later cumulated in bound form. The Department included them in a compilation of Decrees and Judgments in Federal Anti-trust Cases, July 2, 1890-January 1, 1918. This compilation has been brought up through 1949 in a compilation of four additional volumes, but these are not available to the public.

**§10.5.  Lower federal courts for which there are official reports.** There are official reports, printed by the government, for all the special federal courts or quasi-judicial tribunals listed below. In form these reports are typical law reports. Although the courts concerned prefer to be cited to their own official reports, it is proper and indeed customary to cite instead the Reporter series in which they are reported.

1. *Court of Claims.* Now a Constitutional court by Act of September 3, 1954, c. 1263, §39(a), 68 Stat. 1240, 28 U.S.C. §171 (1964 ed.), it has jurisdiction to hear statutorily defined claims against the United States, and its decisions have been reported in the Federal Reporter and Federal Supplement as noted above. There are official slip decisions and there have been two consecutive series of official reports, covering from 1855 to date.

2. *Court of Customs and Patent Appeals.* This is a legislative court, hearing appeals from the Customs Court and Patent Office tribunals, and on questions of law from certain findings of the United States Tariff Commission. It is officially reported in two separate, parallel series, the Court of Customs and Patent Appeals Reports (Patent Cases) and the Court of Customs and Patent Appeals (Custom Cases). Its patent and customs cases are also reported in the Federal Reporter. The patent decisions up to 1967 were reported in the official Commissioner's Decisions, but are now reported only in the unofficial United States Patents Quarterly.

3. *Customs Court.* There has been some confusion as to the status of this court, although it was called a true court of the United States in *Brooks* v. *Mandel-Witte, Inc.,* 84 F.2d 922 (2d Cir. 1932), *cert. denied,* 286 U.S. 559, 52 Sup. Ct. 641, 76 L. Ed. 1292 (1932). It was formerly the Board of General Appraisers of the Treasury Department, but was transformed into a legislative court by the Act of May 28, 1926, c. 411, §1, 44 Stat. 669, 19 U.S.C. §1518 (1964 ed.).

4. *Emergency Court of Appeals.* This is a legislative court having limited jurisdiction to hear cases reviewing orders of the

Emergency Price Control Administration and successor agencies. Its decisions were reported in the Federal Reporter.   For a history of its 19 years, see 299 F.2d 1 (1962).

5. *Court of Military Appeals.*   In spite of its name, this is not a court but a quasi-judicial tribunal, located for administrative purposes in the Department of Defense.   Official slip decisions are printed, but are not reported in the Federal Reporter, which reports only true courts.   Together with the holdings and decisions of the Judge Advocates' General Boards of Review, these are cumulated into an unofficial reporter, Courts-Martial Reports.[5]

6. *Tax Court of the United States.*   This also is an independent executive agency, not a true court.   Its decisions are officially reported in advance sheets and cumulated in bound volumes. Loose-leaf tax services print and annotate the reports.

§10.6.   **Digests of cases decided in federal courts.**   The reported cases of all federal cases are digested in conventional case digests of varying scope.   They are described in Chapter 16.

§10.7.   **Citators for federal court reports.**   These are described in Chapter 18.

§10.8.   **State court reports.**   Every state has its system of courts, with a supreme court — by whatever title — at the top.   Some, like California, Illinois, Indiana, Missouri, Ohio, and New York, have intermediate appellate courts as well.   For some states, like New York, Ohio and Pennsylvania, selected reports of certain courts of first instance are printed.

1. *Official state reports.*   Formerly every state had its official court reports, to which its courts preferred to be cited rather than to the unofficial.   Now their number is diminishing, with a trend toward discontinuing the official reports and relying, instead, upon reports published by private publishers.   The following states have discontinued the publication of official reports: Alaska, Florida, Kentucky, Maine, Mississippi, Missouri, North Dakota, Oklahoma, Texas, and Wyoming.   Louisiana discontinued the Louisiana Appeals Reports, but continues to publish the Louisiana Reports through the West Publishing Company.   A count at the end of 1967 showed that the law reports of sixteen states are prepared for publication, wholly or in part, by the West Publishing Company, Callaghan, or the Lawyers Co-operative Publishing Company.   In some instances, one or more editorial features of, for example, the National Reporter System, are incorporated; in others, the official form is discarded entirely, in favor of National Reporter System volume numbering and format, but with the state's name on the spine, as Wyoming Reporter.

---

[5] Rochester, N.Y., Lawyers Co-operative Publishing Co., 1951-1952 to date.

Few states publish slip decisions, but there are many advance sheets. The citation form for state law reports is discussed in Chapter 26.

2. *Unofficial editions of state reports.* The distinction between official and unofficial state reports is significant only in that state courts prefer, sometimes as specifically indicated by their rules, to be cited to the official reports rather than to the unofficial. In legal writing the official should be cited first, if published, with the unofficial citation in parallel following. The unofficial reporters print many reports of decisions not printed in the official. This often bothers the first year law student, who has been quite properly instructed to cite always the official and in some instances can find no official, though he has before him an unofficial report.

There are several means of determining whether there ever was an official report for a given case. The table of cases in a digest covering the appropriate jurisdiction will give citations to all forms of standard reports — official, National Reporter System and A.L.R. If the table of cases was printed before the official volume was published, however, this test fails. A further check, and usually the most accurate, is through the regional Shepard's Citations — Atlantic, Southwestern, etc. If it fails to cite the official report in addition to the unofficial, then, subject to the above reservation, which applies only to fairly recent cases, there is no official report.

3. *Digests of state and territorial cases.* In one form or another the reported decisions of all federal and state appellate courts and of some courts of first instance from 1658 to date are said to be covered by conventional digests. These are described in Chapter 16.

4. *Legal encyclopedias covering individual states.* Legal encyclopedias generally are described in Chapter 17. Both the Lawyers Co-operative Publishing Company and the West Publishing Company issue encyclopedias covering the law of some of the individual states.

# CHAPTER 11

# Law Reports: The National Reporter System

**§11.1. Scope.** The National Reporter System is a privately published edition of law reports, covering all true federal courts but the Customs Court; the appellate courts of all states and of some state courts of first instance; and two special series, the New York Supplement for the courts of record of New York, and the California Reporter, covering the lower courts of California. It is by far the most comprehensive of all unofficial report series, and as noted in §10.8 a growing number of states have abandoned their own official reports, relying instead on the Reporters. The National Reporter System was begun in 1879 with the North Western Reporter, and within a decade had spread to all the courts indicated above. Two later series have been the Federal Rules Decisions, added in 1940, and the California Reporter, begun January 4, 1960. The Federal Rules Decisions reports federal court decisions construing the federal rules of civil and criminal procedure for the district courts, which are not printed in either the Federal Reporter or the Federal Supplement.

Intermediate state appellate courts have not always been reported. The Illinois Appellate Court reports appeared for the first time in the North Eastern Reporter in 1936, beginning with cases reported in volume 284 of the official reports.

1. *State editions of the Reporters.* A rather recent innovation has been that of state editions of the regional reporters. The Atlantic, California, New York Supplement, North Eastern, North Western, Pacific, South Eastern, South Western and Southern units of the System are called regional reports, as distinguished from the United States, Federal, Federal Supplement and Federal Rules Decisions, covering federal courts. In the text of the state

Reporters, the text of the regional Reporter is unchanged, including all tables and other subsidiary features, but there are additional tables, on colored paper, for an individual state reported in that particular Reporter. Thus the Massachusetts edition of the North Eastern Reporter has a table showing the sections of the Massachusetts General Laws of 1932 (the latest edition reenacted as positive law) amended or repealed by the Massachusetts legislature during the session of the current year. There are also parallel conversion tables, from the official Massachusetts Reports to the corresponding North Eastern Reporter citation; from the Massachusetts Advance Sheets of the current year to the North Eastern Reporter; and from the North Eastern Reporter citation to the official Massachusetts Reports citation.

2. *Court reports and years covered by Reporters and Reporter digests.*[1]

*Atlantic Reporter* (1885 to date): *52 Connecticut; 12 Delaware (7 Houston); 6 Delaware Chancery; *77 Maine; *63 Maryland; *63 New Hampshire; *47 New Jersey Law; *40 New Jersey Equity; *108 Pennsylvania State; *102 Pennsylvania Superior; 15 Rhode Island; 58 Vermont; District of Columbia, 31 Atl. 2d (1942).

*Atlantic Reporter Digest* (cases 1764 to date): All Connecticut, Delaware, Maine, New Jersey and Rhode Island cases from the earliest time as reported in standard reports; Maryland, New Hampshire, Pennsylvania and Vermont cases only from 1 Atlantic Reporter to date.

*California Reporter* (1960 to date): Supreme Court, District Courts of Appeal, Appellate Department Superior Court. Begins with 53 Cal. 2d 187; 176 Cal. App. 2d 1, but includes some cases in 175 Cal. App. 2d.

*New York Supplement:* 1 New York (Court of Appeals), 1847 to date; lower courts of record (including the Appellate Divisions), 1888 to date.

*North Eastern Reporter* (1885 to date): *112 Illinois; 284 Illinois Appellate; 102 Indiana; 1 Indiana Appellate; 139 Massachusetts; 99 New York; 43 Ohio State; 20 Ohio Appellate.

*North Eastern Digest* (cases 1817 to date): All Indiana cases from the earliest time as reported in standard reporters. Illinois, Massachusetts, New York and Ohio cases only from 1 North Eastern Reporter to date.

*North Western Reporter* (1883 to date): 1 Dakota; 51 Iowa; 41 Michigan; 26 Minnesota; 9 Nebraska; 1 Nebraska Unofficial; 1 North Dakota; 1 South Dakota; 46 Wisconsin.

---

[1] The asterisk indicates that only part of the volume is covered.

*North Western Digest* (cases 1836 to date): All North Western Reporter cases from the earliest time as reported in standard reporters.

*Pacific Reporter* (1883 to date): 1 Alaska, 348 P.2d; 1 Arizona; 64 California; 1 California 2d; 1 California Appellate; 1 California Appellate 2d; 2 California Unreported; 7 Colorado; 1 Colorado Appellate; 44 Hawaii in 351 P.2d; 2 Idaho; 30 Kansas; 1 Kansas Appellate; 4 Montana; 17 Nevada; 3 New Mexico; 1 Oklahoma; 1 Oklahoma Criminal Appeals; 11 Oregon; 3 Utah; 1 Washington; 2 Washington Territory; 3 Wyoming.

*Pacific Digest* (cases 1850 to date): All Pacific Reporter cases; see also California Reporter, *supra*.

*South Eastern Reporter* (1887 to date): *77 Georgia; 1 Georgia Appellate; *96 North Carolina; *25 South Carolina; *82 Virginia; 29 West Virginia.

*South Eastern Digest* (cases 1729 to date): All South Eastern Reporter Cases.

*Southern Reporter* (1887 to date): *80 Alabama; 1 Alabama Appellate; *22 Florida; 104 Louisiana; 39 Louisiana Annotated; 9 Louisiana Appellate; 64 Mississippi.

*Southern Digest* (cases 1809 to date): All Southern Reporter cases and also early decisions of Florida prior to Southern Reporter.

*South Western Reporter* (1887 to date): 47 Arkansas; *84 Kentucky; *8 Kentucky Law Reporter; 1 Kentucky Decisions; 89 Missouri; *93 Missouri Appellate; *84 Tennessee; 16 Tennessee Appellate; 66 Texas; 21 Texas Appellate; 1 Texas Civil Appeals; 31 Texas Criminal Reports; 4 Willson Civ. Cas. Ct. App. (Texas).

*South Western Digest* (cases 1887-1958): only from volume 1 of the South Western Reporter to volume 309 of the South Western Reporter, Second Series, inclusive, except all Texas prior to South Western Reporter.  Suspended with 309 South Western Reporter.

*Supreme Court Reporter* (1882 to date): 106 United States Reports to date.

*United States Supreme Court Digest* (1954 to date): All cases from 2 Dallas (2 U.S.) to date.

*Federal Reporter* (cases 1880 to date): U.S. Circuit Court to 1912 (when abolished); U.S. Circuit Courts of Appeal (1891-1948), continued by Courts of Appeals (Sept. 1, 1948 to date); U.S. District courts to 1932; U.S. Commerce Court, 1910-1913 (entire life); U.S. Court of Customs and Patent Appeals (Patent Cases), 1929 to date; U.S. Court of Claims 1930-1932, 1960 to date; U.S. Court of Appeals for the District of Columbia Circuit, 1919 to date.

*Federal Digest* (1754 through 1938 term): Federal courts, except

Customs Court cases, including cases from all federal courts for Alaska and Hawaii and U.S. Court of Appeals for the District of Columbia.

*Modern Federal Practice Digest* (1939 term to date): Continuing Federal Digest.

*Federal Supplement* (1932 to date): U.S. District Courts; U.S. Court of Claims, 1932-1960.

*Federal Rules Decisions* (1940 to date): Federal court decisions, not elsewhere reported, interpreting the federal Rules of Civil and Criminal Procedure.

§11.2. **Rationale of the National Reporter System.** The National Reporter System is described in considerable detail in a free pamphlet distributed by the publishers, the West Publishing Company. What follows here is intended only to point up several important features of these Reporters.

1. *Speed of publication as exemplified by advance sheets.* Proper application of the rule of stare decisis or precedent requires the speedy availability of the latest reports of decided cases in point. At the time the National Reporter System was inaugurated in 1879, however, the official state reports made a farce of this rule, because they were published from one to several years later than the decision date. In most states today the situation is little improved. The reason is plain enough: Law report publication must pay its way through sales, and in few states are sufficient cases decided during a year to justify the publication of more than a single volume. The contribution of the National Reporter System here was the lumping together of the reports of several contiguous states, providing thereby sufficient text to justify the expense of publishing them weekly. The result was the "advance sheet," published weekly for all Reporter units except the semimonthly Supreme Court Reporter and monthly Federal Rules Decisions. Each advance sheet issue is a reporting and digesting system in miniature, covering the cases reported in it, with nearly all the features which later cumulate into the bound volumes of the Reporter.

2. *Combining the reports of contiguous states.* A part of the Reporter publishing philosophy is that the law in certain fairly large groups of contiguous states has common elements of interest to all in each such group. That is, the states in the North Eastern or Atlantic Reporter areas may operate under quite different rules of water law, for example, than do those in the Pacific Reporter area.

3. *Reporting more cases than reported in the official reports.* Not all the reports of cases decided in any court are published.

Whether or not they are is for most courts a matter of editorial discretion on the part of the official reporter; if the latter decides that a given case is merely routine and adds nothing to the state of the law, in most jurisdictions such a case is not reported.  The National Reporter System editors, while realizing that comparatively few important cases were deprived of the light of day in this way, did believe that too many were.  The Reporters, accordingly, have printed thousands of cases not officially reported.  Since the Supreme Court has questioned the value as precedent of unreported cases — because of their unavailability to the public and likelihood of appeal — it will be seen that the Reporters have added a good bit of otherwise neglected authority to the literature by their policy.

It must be emphasized that the fact that certain Reporter cases have not been officially published in no way lessens their authority as precedents.

4. *Key Number system.*  While the copyrighted Key Number logotype (  ) is not of itself a classification device, any more than would be a section symbol, it serves to identify the very elaborate classification system of points of law in the decided cases which is the basis of the West Publishing Company system of digests.  By this system, the individual headnote paragraphs of the cases reported in federal and state appellate courts from 1897 to date are readily found; and by means of conversion tables to the earlier Century Digest, cases back to 1658.  The philosophy and application of the Key Number system and its application to digests are described in Chapter 16.

### §11.3.   Content of material in the Reporters.

1. *Opinions and headnotes.*  Since courts as a matter of public record provide the written texts of the opinions they read in open court, these are identical with those of the official reports, with two occasional exceptions: (a) The court may, at any time up to the printing of its opinions in the official reports, revise them; sometimes they have even been withdrawn and others substituted. In the Reporters this is always caught before the bound volume is printed, and the revised text then printed.  Such revision happens very seldom, but it has happened.  (b) The Reporter editors may discover errors in the text of the opinion supplied.  They then point out, but do not correct, the errors, in their reports.  The headnotes of the Reporter and the official reports, while covering the same material, do not exactly coincide either in number of paragraphs or in text.  There are apt to be more paragraphs in the Reporter than in the official, to serve as the basis of the infinitely detailed American Digest System classification.  Where, as is

CITY OF TOLEDO v. JOHNSON     Ohio    675
50 N.E.2d 675

72 Ohio App. 46
**CITY OF TOLEDO v. JOHNSON, Appellant.**

Court of Appeals of Ohio, Lucas County
June 1, 1938.

**1. Criminal law ☞304(21)**

Court of Appeals cannot take judicial notice that the "number game" is a "game or scheme of chance" or gambling.

See Words and Phrases, Permanent Edition, for all other definitions of "Game of Chance" and "Number Game"

**2. Gaming ☞94(1)**

In a prosecution for operating a "number game" as a game of chance for money in violation of ordinance, there must be proof that a number game is such a game or scheme of chance or gambling in absence of statute or ordinance recognizing the number game as being in such classification.

**3. Gaming ☞98(1)**

Where there was neither statute nor ordinance defining the number game as a game of chance for money, and court was unauthorized to take judicial notice that the number game is a game of chance, evidence that defendant was maintaining the number game was insufficient to sustain a conviction under ordinance of maintaining a game of chance for money.

At the left of this page is a typical application of the Key-Number to a National Reporter System case report, taken from 50 N. E. 2d 675 (1938). (Where it is available at press time, the official citation is supplied, as here, rendering the use of conversion tables to find such citation unnecessary. Such is the time lag of official reporting, however, that this official citation is usually undetermined when the bound *Reporter* volume is made up.) The example is from a state requiring the court to prepare a syllabus, and so the two sets of headnotes, official and *Reporter*, afford an opportunity to compare headnote writing techniques. Usually there are more *Reporter* paragraphs than official, and the *Reporters* try to connect each note as directly as possible to the case reported, by including facts. Each note is a single sentence. In some cases a *Reporter* headnote is given, even though the opinion is not printed as part of the report, as in *Schmidt v. Langer*, 336 Ill. App. 158, 83 N. E. 2d 35 (1948).

In the example, the bold-face numerals (1, 2, 3) are not part of the headnote or Key-Number classification, but refer to like numerals, in brackets [1], in the text of the opinion, where the headnoted rule is stated. Criminal Law ☞ 304(21) is the Key-Number, each such number always being composed of *both a word or words (the main topic heading), and a number (indicating the sub-topic).* In the digest at the back of the *Reporter* in which our case is

---

676    Ohio     50 NORTH EASTERN REPORTER, 2d SERIES

*Syllabus by the Court.*

1. A court may not take judicial notice that a "number game" is a game or scheme of chance or gambling.

2. In order to sustain a conviction on a charge of unlawfully engaging "in a game of chance for money, to wit, number game," in violation of an ordinance making it unlawful to engage in a game of chance, there must be proof that a "number game" is a game or scheme of chance or gambling, there being no such "game of chance" recognized by statute or ordinance as a "number game."

George Johnson was convicted of engaging in a game of chance for money, and he appeals.—[Editorial Statement]

printed, this subhead is defined as *Evidence: Judicial Notice, Presumptions, and Burden of Proof: Nature of certain games and terminology thereof.* This particular paragraph, verbatim, is printed in 13 *Fifth Decennial Digest* 668, along with six other paragraphs on the same topic, from six states. It is also printed in the *North Eastern Reporter Digest* under the same classification. By means explained in Chapter 19 like cases in point, if any, from 1658 to date may be found through this same Key-Number.

Exhibit 20

directed by law in some states, the court writes its own headnotes, which state the law of the case, the National Reporter System regards them as part of the official text of the decision, and incorporates them verbatim in addition to its own headnotes.

2. *Words and phrases.* The courts' definitions of either words of common use or of legal terms of art, as stated in their opinions, are collected in each advance sheet and bound volume of the Reporters, and then taken from them to form a very large dictionary of such definitions. This is described in Chapter 21.

3. *Court rules.* New rules, both revisions and amendments, are printed in the appropriate Reporter units at the time of adoption.

4. *Tables of cases.* There are two case tables in the bound volumes of all units except the Supreme Court Reporter, which reports only one jurisdiction. The first table lists in a single alphabet all cases in all states or federal court circuits covered by the Reporter. Then, as a further convenience, when the individual state or federal circuit is known, there is a second index by state or circuit. The advance sheet tables of cases, however, are all in a single alphabet.

5. *Tables of statutes construed.* These tables, found in each advance sheet and bound volume, serve an interim citator function, in that they list conventional and administrative legislation which has been construed by the courts in the cases reported. As citators they are described in Chapter 18.

6. *Digests.* Each advance sheet and bound volume contains a digest in miniature, formed from the Key-Numbered digest paragraphs of cases reported therein.

7. *Miscellaneous features.* Judges in the courts reported are listed in each bound volume by jurisdiction. Judicial Highlights are occasionally found in advance sheets, containing a "synopsis of state and federal cases of current interest and importance."

**§11.4. Citation books for Reporters.** Shepard's Citations covers all Reporter units, as described in Chapter 18.

**§11.5. Parallel transfer tables from official to Reporter citations or the reverse.** These tables are described in §13.5.

# CHAPTER 12

# Law Reports: Selective and Special-Subject Systems

### §12.1.   Annotated reports systems.

1. *Rationale.* The selective, annotated case system is a device whereby the legal researcher, be he practicing lawyer or student, is enabled to pick the brains of an expert editorial staff as an aid to solving his problems.  It is based upon two propositions: first, that out of the thousands of new cases reported each year there are some which are of interest to lawyers of all jurisdictions, not just the one in which the cases were decided; second, that these same lawyers will find useful a careful and precise lining up of all American cases in point, with a discussion based upon them of a point of law involved, stating the majority and minority rules and the impact of the annotated case upon the law.  It is a recognition of the fact, also, that a case in point in another jurisdiction may be highly persuasive when cited to your own courts, even if not of mandatory authority.  These cases, comprising but a small fraction of the total decided cases in all jurisdictions, merit expert selection and annotation for the use of lawyers everywhere.

2. *Selective case series, past and present.* There have at various times been some seven principal selective reports series in the United States, of which only the American Law Reports Annotated (cited as A.L.R.) is still current.  The earlier series were not annotated to any important degree and had as their purpose making available to lawyers generally and cheaply a limited selection of cases of interest in all jurisdictions.  In the days before law libraries were as complete and generally accessible as they now are, this served an important function.

Three early series, known collectively as the "Trinity Series," were the American Reports, American Decisions and American State Reports, printing a selection of American cases from the earliest times through 1911.  They were not truly annotated cases in the full sense, but did contain some notes helpful to the lawyer at the time. American and English Annotated Cases (1906-1911), merging into American Annotated Cases (1912-1918), and Lawyers Reports Annotated, in two series from 1888 to 1918, were, as their titles indicate, annotated, but in varying degrees of completeness, all short of the fullness of the present A.L.R. All of these competing series were merged in 1918 into the current American Law Reports Annotated. Of these early law reports series, only the Lawyers Reports Annotated (L.R.A.) may be said to serve a presently useful purpose, and the others are now seldom found on law library reading room shelves. The only present value of these series is that they print the text of the decision, but it would be better for the searcher to go to the American Digest System table of cases and find the official citation and read his report from it, as that is the series he will have to cite in legal writing anyway. Lawyers Reports Annotated, though of diminishing value, is on the reading room shelves of most law school libraries.

The Lawyers' Edition of the United States Reports is selective only in that it prints only Supreme Court reports. It is described in §10.2.

3. *American Law Reports Annotated* (cited as A.L.R.). This reporter prints and annotates cases from 1918 to date, in three units: A.L.R., First Series, in 175 volumes covers from 1918 to 1947; the Second Series, from 1947 to the early 1960's; and A.L.R., Third, thence to date. There is some overlapping of dates covered.

a. *Selection of cases for A.L.R. reports.* Cases from all American jurisdictions are selected. While Supreme Court cases are not excluded, very few are included, because all such cases are printed in the annotated Lawyers' Edition of the Supreme Court reports, issued by the same publishers. Such Supreme Court cases as are reported in A.L.R. are apt to be those of interest to lawyers whose principal practice is in the state courts. On the other hand a good number of United States Courts of Appeals reports are printed in A.L.R.

Cases for inclusion and annotation are selected on the basis of utility to the profession, rather than as leading cases. They may perhaps be broken down into two broad categories of subject matter:

(1) *Cases lending themselves to an exhaustive treatment of an important subdivision of the law of a major topic.* Such subject matter might include contracts, torts or evidence, which, the editors feel, needs to be brought more up to date than has been done in legal encyclopedias or treatises. An example is the case upon which the 113-page annotation in 55 A.L.R.2d 6 was written,

on the "implied or apparent authority of an agent to purchase or order goods or merchandise."

(2) *Cases treating limited areas of the law, not covered at all, or insufficiently, in other law books.* Examples of this type are cases on which are written annotations such as the 305-page annotation in 164 A.L.R. 8, on "liability for accidents at street or highway intersection as affected by reliance upon or disregard of traffic sign, signal or marker"; the 63-page annotation in 55 A.L.R.2d 129, on "liability for injury or death by electrification by guy wire"; the 28-page annotation in 57 A.L.R.2d 569, on "rights of fishing, boating or bathing or the like in inland lakes"; the 58-page annotation in 65 A.L.R.2d 342, on "carbon copies or other written instruments as evidence"; or the 155-page annotation in 100 A.L.R.2d 16, on apportionment of damages caused by successive impacts of motor vehicles.

Sometimes a group of cases illustrating different aspects of a single topic will be annotated in a single A.L.R. volume. Examples are four annotations in 68 A.L.R.2d, on group insurance termination (totaling 257 pages); and three in 13 A.L.R.3d, on a union's rights as to members' dues and fines (totaling 53 pages).

b. *Content of A.L.R. reports.* Every opinion is printed in full from the official text. Parallel official, Reporter and A.L.R. citations are supplied. The decision is summarized at some length in the Second and Third Series, as illustrated by Exhibit 21 below. The subject of the annotation is noted. Headnotes are written by the editors, but any "syllabus by the court," being regarded as a part of the official record of the case, is printed verbatim also. The headnotes are classified according to the Permanent A.L.R. Digest classification. A.L.R. is tied in with the text of American Jurisprudence, a legal encyclopedia, issued by the same publishers, based largely upon A.L.R. cases. Accordingly, Am. Jur. topic titles and section numbers are included in the A.L.R. headnotes, to make finding similar cases in point in the encyclopedia a simple matter. Conversely, there are Am. Jur. cross references to A.L.R. annotations. Headnotes are numbered and keyed to corresponding numerals in the text of the opinion, as is done in the National Reporter System digests from the Key Numbers of the syllabi. A.L.R. is one of the very few remaining report series in which the statement of facts and summaries of arguments of counsel are supplied.

c. *The A.L.R. annotation.* The varied subject matter of A.L.R. annotations has been indicated above. All A.L.R. cases are now

1355

## EDYTHE B. BURNS, Appt.,
v
## ROBERT H. BURNS, Respt.

Montana Supreme Court — February 2, 1965
145 Mont 1, 400 P2d 642, 13 ALR3d 1355

---

### SUMMARY OF DECISION

In divorce proceedings in the Sixth District Court, Sweet Grass County, Montana, George J. Allen, J., both parties sought a divorce. The trial court's judgment consisted of a decree of divorce granted to each party, and an award of child custody and alimony to the wife.

On appeal by the wife, the trial court's judgment was affirmed by the Supreme Court of Montana, which, in an opinion by Doyle, J., held, inter alia, that when the trial court in a divorce action wherein both parties sought a divorce found that both parties established grounds for divorce, and further found that the legitimate objects of marriage were destroyed, it could, in its discretion, award a divorce to both parties, notwithstanding statutory provisions for the denial of a divorce upon showing recrimination.

John C. Harrison, J., and Adair, J., dissented.

---

### HEADNOTES

#### Classified to ALR Digests

**Divorce and Separation § 62 — divorce to both parties — recrimination statutes**

1. When the trial court in a divorce action wherein both parties seek a divorce finds that both parties have established grounds for divorce, and it further finds that the legitimate objects of marriage have been destroyed, it may, in its discretion, award a divorce to both parties, notwithstanding statutory provisions that divorces must be denied upon showing recrimination, and that recrimination was a showing by the defendant of any cause of divorce against the plaintiff, in a bar of the plaintiff's cause of divorce.

[Annotated]

**Divorce and Separation § 87 — propriety of alimony award — divorce awarded to both parties**

2. An award of alimony to a wife in her divorce action wherein the husband also

---

### SUBJECT OF ANNOTATION

Beginning on page 1364

Power of court to grant absolute divorce to both spouses upon showing of mutual fault

---

**Exhibit 21**

annotated, unlike some of the earlier ones. Annotations vary in length from a half-page note to an encyclopedic treatment of 300 pages or more.

An annotation is organized in much the same manner as a case digest or legal encyclopedia topic, as described in Chapters 16 and 17. It tends to proceed from the general to the specific, and often ends with procedure and remedies. The Introduction defines the limits of the annotation, states broadly the existing law and points out the main and subsidiary topics to be considered. Often earlier annotations or other materials are referred to. Then, as in a digest or encyclopedia, the main topic is broken down into increasingly narrow subtopics. Each of these is considered, in turn, with majority and jurisdictional rules stated and analyzed, with discussion of supporting cases. Variations and departures from the various rules and the reasons therefor are pointed out. Where the result depended upon a statute, that fact is noted. The final structural breakdown of an A.L.R. annotation is into numbered sections. These have an important subsidiary function with respect to keeping the annotation up to date by references to later cases in point. Later cases supplementing annotations are noted differently as between A.L.R. First, and Second and Third Series. The various aids for updating are described below in §12.1(f) and Exhibits 23 and 24.

Preceding each annotation of substantial length is an alphabetical index, which may consist of several pages of catchwords relating to both legal principles and fact situations (Discretion of the court, Store account book, Boating accident) noted in the text. The Word Index, described below, offers one of the most fruitful approaches to the law. A Table of Jurisdictions Represented in the annotation is also provided for Second and Third Series annotations.

These features of an A.L.R. annotation are illustrated by Exhibit 22, below.

d. *Authority citation in A.L.R. annotations.* All American cases in point are said to be considered in the annotation, and also occasional British cases. Following the statements of the general rules, all cases in point are cited by jurisdiction; then for the textual analyses following the general statements individual supporting cases, including the case being annotated, are analyzed and majority and minority rules and variations are stated and discussed. Although there are no formal case digests, as in headnotes, the cases cited as authority are discussed at some length in many instances, which in effect does digest them. Citation is by jurisdiction, in a typography which renders it simple to pick out the juris-

ANNO.—INTEREST RECEIVED BY OFFICER     257

## ANNOTATION

**Liability of public officer for interest or other earnings received on public money in his possession**

[See ALR Digests, Officers, § 131.3.]

---

### INDEX

---

### I. Introduction

**§ 1. In general.**

This annotation deals with the question whether a public officer who, having custody of public funds, receives interest from the use of such funds, may retain the interest as his own or has to account for it in the same manner as for the principal.

In order that the question as to the accountability of a public officer for interest received on public funds in his possession can arise, it must be assumed that the money in his possession is public money[1] and that the officer

[1] The general rule stated above has no application where the fund in the hands of the public officer is not a public fund. This limitation of the general rule was well brought out in United States v. MacMillan (1913; DC) 209 F 266 (affd (1917; CCA 7th) 251 F 55, which is affd (1920) 253 US 195, 64 L ed 857, 40 S Ct 540). It was held in this case that the Federal government had no claim to interest which had accrued on a fund

✦ Consult ALR2d BLUE BOOK SERVICE for cases subsequent to publication date ✦
    [5 ALR2d]—17

Exhibit 22

dictions desired. Thus the series name part of a report citation is printed in boldface type, as 43 **Del.** 494. As a further aid, a table of jurisdictions cited in each annotation precedes the annotation — this feature having begun with 57 A.L.R.2d.

There are no advance sheets. Cases printed in A.L.R. are usually over a year old at publication, because it takes considerable time to prepare the annotation. For this reason, parallel A.L.R. citation is often omitted from digest tables of cases, which are frequently made up before the selection of a case for annotation is made. The digest table of cases, accordingly, is not always a reliable test of whether or not a case has been published in A.L.R. A more certain method is to check the appropriate unit of Shepard's Citations in the cumulative red-paper supplement or later bound volume. See page 243, par. a.

e. *Utility and citation of A.L.R. annotations.* The annotated cases do not cover legal or fact situations as all-inclusively as does a digest; too few cases are annotated for that. On the other hand, since all cases in point are said to be considered in the annotations themselves, the subject matter covered is much wider than the limited number of annotations might indicate. The annotations are so carefully done that they are widely used by both practicing lawyers and law students. If these searchers can find annotations in point and update them by supplements or other means, they have had preliminary, arduous tasks of case finding and analysis done for them. Annotations are particularly effective in analyses of narrow subjects not yet adequately treated in textbooks or encyclopedias. They are also effective where a new decision has upset an old rule, and treatises and encyclopedias have not yet adequately discussed its probable effect. The annotation may treat at considerable length a facet of a subject only touched on in passing in textbooks. An example is the two successive annotations by W. E. Shipley in 16 A.L.R.2d 3 and 393 (1951) on the topics of (1) excessive and (2) adequate damages for personal injuries not resulting in death. Together these two annotations occupy 453 pages and consider 162 types of injury. They are subject-indexed to the extent of fifteen pages.

Annotations are not authority of themselves, but only indexes to authority. In citing the annotation, the *page upon which the annotation begins, not that of the reported case* is the one to give. Supplementary references in the A.L.R. Blue Book of Supplemental Decision and the A.L.R.2d and 3d Later Case Service are to the annotation, not to the reported and annotated case.

Annotated cases are cited in federal court briefs or in law reviews only as cases, not as annotations, but are frequently cited for their

annotations in state courts.   The proper form of citation is as
follows:

> *Lively* v. *Munday,* 201 Ga. 409, 40 S.E.2d 62, 173 A.L.R. 1295 (1946)
> [when cited as a case]
> *Lively* v. *Munday,* 201 Ga. 409, 40 S.E.2d 62, 173 A.L.R.1295 (1946).
> See Annotation, 173 A.L.R. 1309, 1318 (1948) [meaning that part
> of an annotation beginning on page 1309 which is at page 1318,
> and which was written in 1948]

f. *Supplementing A.L.R. annotations by later cases in point.*
Cases cited as authority for A.L.R. annotation sections are the
latest available at press time, but later ones in point keep appearing, of which the searcher must be made aware if his search for
authority is to be complete and up to date.

A.L.R., First Series takes care of this with its Blue Book of Supplemental Decisions for Annotations in American Law Reports.
To the extent of noting these later cases in point, it is a citator.
All annotations are listed in the Blue Book by A.L.R. volume and
the page upon which the annotation begins, not that of the annotated case.   Thereunder are cited all later cases in point with the
annotation, by jurisdiction, as noted in Exhibit 23.

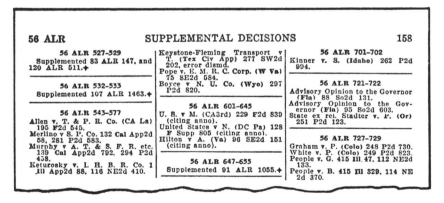

Exhibit 23

If the number of supplemental cases in point becomes unwieldy,
a supplemental of superseding annotation is often compiled, incorporating all these cases and commenting on them as in the original annotation.   As noted in Exhibit 23, such supplemental annotations are indicated by a star under the citation to the original
annotation, and searches for future cases are made under the
starred citation, not under the original annotation.   Since the Blue
Book list of additional citations is by case only, with no indication

of which section of the annotation it applies to, determining whether a given additional case cited in it is pertinent involves a slow and laborious matching up if there are very many cases cited. The Blue Book has appeared in four "permanent" volumes covering later supplementing cases through 1967, kept up to date by a pamphlet Blue Book Service, issued semiannually. This service is confined entirely to supplementing cases annotated in A.L.R., First Series.

Second and Third Series Annotations are updated by a Later Case Service. In the Second Series, a separate set of volumes has been published to cover the supplementation of the annotations in A.L.R.2d. Each of these volumes is arranged by volume and page of the annotation affected and is further updated by annual pocket parts.

The annotations in the Third Series will be kept up to date with annual pocket parts in each volume of A.L.R.3d; again the arrangement will be by the volume and page of the annotation affected.

---

# AMERICAN
# LAW REPORTS

### THIRD SERIES

Later Case Service

## VOLUME 13 ALR3d

### 13 ALR3d 140–223

**§ 6**   [13 ALR3d 165]

[c]  **View that insured must sue in own name**
When insurer pays only part of loss, insured must bring suit for entire loss in his own name. Hardware Dealers Mut. Fire Ins. Co. v Sheek, 272 NC 484, 158 SE2d 635.

**§ 8**   [13 ALR3d 183]

[a]  **Where insured sues for whole loss**
Insurance companies were proper, although not necessary, parties where insured sued for whole loss, although division of any recovery was neither any concern of defendant nor proper question for submission to jury, purpose of joinder of insurance companies being

paid entire loss.  Hardware Dealers Mut. Fire Ins. Co. v Sheek, 272 NC 484, 158 SE2d 635.

### 13 ALR3d 284–302

**§ 3**   [13 ALR3d 288]

[a]  **Generally; discretion of trial court, probative value**
Records of creditor were admissible in discretion under Uniform Business Records as Evidence Act, to show amount owing by debtor, even though action was against guarantor of debt, rather than debtor itself.  D. N. & E. Walter & Co. v Van Domelen (Or) 425 P2d 166.

---

Exhibit 24

This latter service is a great improvement over the Blue Book in two respects. As in the Blue Book all annotations for which later cases in point are cited are listed by volume and page of annotation, but there the resemblance ceases. The cases are not merely listed by jurisdiction. Instead, they are listed, where pertinent, also under the *precise section number* of the annotation which they supplement; the citation being, then, by A.L.R.2d or 3d volume, page and *section number,* together with the title heading of that section. Not only that, but each listed supplemental case is digested and commented upon, sometimes at considerable length. Where later cases present distinct new subject matter, new sections and headings are added. Where an A.L.R.2d annotation has been supplemented or superseded by a later one, that fact is noted by a statement. Thus, 13 A.L.R.2d 191-252, supplemented in 58 A.L.R.2d 865. An Annotation History Table in the A.L.R. Quick Index lists annotations in A.L.R., First and Second Series annotations. Thus, 160 A.L.R. 1406-1416, superseded by 43 A.L.R.2d 632. First Series case annotations are still traced only through the Blue Book. See Exhibit 23.

There may be closer supplementation through the Key Number System advance sheets and General Digest reporting or digesting cases later than those cited in the Annual Later Case Service. Thus, if the searcher knows either the name of a supplemental case or its subject matter and finds the report in the National Reporter System, he will there locate the pertinent Key Number classification for his point of law; then he can look in the National Reporter System advance sheets and the General Digest reporting or digesting later cases, bringing his search down past the Later Case Service to within a very few weeks of the latest decision.

g. *Citators for selective cases system cases.* Neither L.R.A. nor A.L.R. cases are covered in Shepard's Citations as such, but are Shepardized under their official and National Reporter System citations. If the name of the case is known, its citation forms may be found in the usual way through the American Digest System table of cases, or the tables of cases for L.R.A. or A.L.R. in their respective digests. To the extent of noting later cases in point with an annotation, the Blue Book and the Later Case Service serve as citators.

4. *Approaches to the law through L.R.A. and A.L.R.* There are three approaches, standard for all digests and the tools for their use: the table of cases, the fact approach through the descriptive-word index, and the analytical, through topic analyses in the digests; or, for A.L.R.2d and A.L.R.3d, the Quick Index. These approaches generally are described in §26.1. Specific A.L.R. aids are described below.

a. *The Complete Digest of Lawyers Reports Annotated 1888-1918.* This conventional digest is now little used.

b. *Permanent Digest of American Law Reports Annotated.*

This otherwise conventional digest, covering volumes 1-175 of A.L.R, First Series, stresses A.L.R. annotations, but the points of law digested are wider in scope and there are more of them than in the annotations. This is because, while all points in an A.L.R. case are fully *digested*, only a few closely connected ones are *annotated*. Thus, *Egner* v. *States Realty Co.*, 170 A.L.R. 500, has twenty-nine headnotes (all reflected in the Digest). But only the first six, relating to the termination of partners' agency by partnership dissolution, are the subject of the annotation and are so indexed in the Word Index. The function of the usual descriptive-word index is performed by the Word Index to Annotations and the Quick Index, below.

c. *The A.L.R.2d 1-100 Digest, Cases and Annotations,* covering the 100 volumes of the Second Series, is a typical case digest as described in Chapter 16. Access to the law is through the table of cases (by both Plaintiff and Defendant), the scope note and cross-references to and from pertinent topics, and the Word Index and the Quick Index described below.

d. *The A.L.R. Word Indexes to Annotations,* covering, together, the first two series of A.L.R. are the usual point of departure in an A.L.R. search. They are the descriptive-word indexes to the annotations, with references to the annotations, not to the digests. They are easily distinguishable on the shelves by their bright red binding.

e. *A.L.R. Quick Index to Annotations.* Both A.L.R. First and Second Series are now covered by a new A.L.R. Quick Index; A.L.R.3d is covered by pocket supplements to the A.L.R.2d bound volume. This index is designed to combine most of the functions of the digest and of the descriptive-word index. References are to the more accurate *exact titles* of the annotations, rather than the former cryptic subject condensation type of entry. The pocket supplement has a table of cases (by plaintiff only) of A.L.R.3d cases to date. A new feature is the Annotation History Table, referred to above at page 155. The publishers indicate that the Quick Index may supplant both the former A.L.R. Digest and the Word Index to Annotations format.

§12.2. **Special-subject reporters.** Several series of law reports select decisions relating to special and limited subjects in which their subscribers are interested. They may collect labor, tax, public utilities, trade regulation or bankruptcy cases, and usually the cases contained in them are also published in the regular official and unofficial reports series. Occasionally, however, as in the antitrust consent decisions in the CCH Trade Regulation Reports, they make available material not otherwise printed for general distribution.   Most such current series are issued as loose-leaf services, collecting and binding in permanent form the reports first printed in the services in loose-leaf form.

§12.3.   **Loose-leaf reporting services.**   These are described in Chapter 23.

# Law Reports: Tabular Means
# for Finding

**§13.1.   Need for tables.**   If all case reports from all jurisdictions were published in a single, all-inclusive series arranged in alphabetical order by case name, there would perhaps be little need of tables as aids to finding individual case reports.   In fact, however, there have been many hundreds of different, parallel series in which, except in Federal Cases, the reports are printed in chronological, not alphabetical, order, by jurisdiction.   Therefore tables to aid in locating cases are indispensable.

**§13.2.   Copying case citations fully and accurately.**   Always copy down the very fullest information about each case you read and select for reference.   When you have a law report in front of you giving the name of a case and the citation in at least one form, or when you have in front of you some other kind of law book giving a citation to a case in which you are interested, do not skimp in setting down the information identifying it.   The five seconds you save in writing down an abridged and hasty citation may cost you many minutes of detective work before the correct citation is found.

For example, if the case is *Bordy* v. *Smith,* 150 Neb. 272, 34 N.W.2d 331, 5 A.L.R.2d 250 (1948), write all that down while you have the actual report or other law book citing it open in front of you.   There are at least two sound reasons for this.   First, each element of that complete citation is an important clue if you or the person whose citation you are copying has made an error in it somewhere, so that you have an incorrect citation to begin with. If, however, all elements — title, official and unofficial reporter volume and page, and date of decision — were written down, some are bound to be correct and will lead speedily to the correct full citation.  Second, if the official report containing your case is off the shelf at the time, you have the citation to the unofficial or vice versa, and you have given yourself two chances to find your case. Or if you are citing the case to somebody else and you do not know which reporter — official or unofficial — he has in his library, you have given him two chances without forcing him to use a parallel conversion table.  That is a matter of courtesy.

§13.3.   **Tables of abbreviations.**  In order to save time and space, legal writers employ many hundreds of abbreviations in their citations of case series, statutes, encyclopedias, etc.  Some of these are obvious, like U.S., N.Y., Harv. L. Rev., but many are not and would be incomprehensible without tables of abbreviations to identify them.  Many such tables are available in digests, loose-leaf services, citators, dictionaries, encyclopedias, etc.  Probably the most nearly complete is in Price and Bitner, Effective Legal Research (1953), at the loan desk in your law school library.  An abridgment of that list, sufficient for most purposes, is printed as Appendix III of this book.

§13.4.   **Tables of cases.**  Almost every law book which prints or cites cases has a table of such cases.  The table of cases approach is one of the most fruitful of all, but because its full utilization involves case tables or some materials not yet studied in this book, its detailed discussion is postponed to Chapter 25.

§13.5.   **Parallel citation tables from official to unofficial reports and reverse.**  As already noted, law reports may be published officially or unofficially in various and usually duplicating forms, such as the National Reporter System, selective annotated case series, special-subject series, or loose-leaf services.  Reports from more than two hundred different series were combined in the single Federal Cases, for example.  Because few libraries have all forms of every report, and because, even if the official is at hand, the searcher may desire to utilize the Key Number approach to a digest through a National Reporter System headnote, or to see if a case has been annotated in A.L.R., parallel citation tables from one form to the other are supplied by law publishers.  These permit the translation from the official to the unofficial or the reverse. Thus, *from* 41 Ohio App. 169 *to* 180 N.E. 659; or *from* 139 So. 509 *to* 19 La. App. 19, or *from* 150 Neb. 272, 34 N.W.2d 331, *to* 5 A.L.R.2d 250.  There are several means for doing this, the best one to employ at the moment depending upon the circumstances.

The parallel listing of cases in case tables is in this form, official citation first, Reporter next, followed by selective case series, if any: *Kritzer* v. *Moffat,* 136 Wash. 410, 240 Pac. 355, 44 A.L.R. 681 (1925).  Some tables include the date of decision, some do not.

In legal writing it should be included, because it usually is an important element of the value of the case cited.

1. *Tables of cases.* The name of the case is a prerequisite to the use of these tables, which are alphabetically arranged lists of cases by name or title. All such tables have a Plaintiff-Defendant alphabet; increasingly, there is also a listing by Defendant-Plaintiff, either in a separate table or in the same alphabet with the Plaintiff-Defendant listing. The American Digest System Decennial Digests have only the Plaintiff-Defendant listing, but other National Reporter System digests increasingly incorporate also the Defendant-Plaintiff tables, as do the digests of other publishers.

All plaintiff-defendant tables give the complete parallel citations *as known at the date the tables were compiled.* This reservation is necessary because sometimes the table may have been compiled before a case listed was selected for annotation by A.L.R. The A.L.R. citation would then be omitted, though, in fact, the case is annotated in that series. Similarly the official may not have been published at the time the table was compiled, though it is rare that by the time a digest case table is printed the official has not also been published. A further advisable check on this is through Shepard's Citations.

2. *Official citation to Reporter citation.* As *from* 142 Tex. 589 *to* 180 S.W.2d 135.

a. *National Reporter Blue Book.* This transfer table is "A complete table showing volume and page of the Reporter for every case found in the corresponding state [and United States Supreme Court] reports." As seen by Exhibit 25, it is a very simple table, listing the official report by volume (above the line) and page (below the line), with the unofficial Reporter citation in parallel. The Blue Book is in units covering, respectively, years to 1928, 1929 to 1936, 1937 to 1948, and 1949 to 1960, with cumulative pamphlet supplements.

b. *State Blue and White Books.* These are no longer published,

### 156 TEXAS REPORTS

| Tex. Pg. | S.W.2d Vol. | S.W.2d Pg. | Tex. Pg. | S.W.2d Vol. | S.W.2d Pg. | Tex. Pg. | S.W.2d Vol. | S.W.2d Pg. | Tex. Pg. | S.W.2d Vol. | S.W.2d Pg. | Tex. Pg. | S.W.2d Vol. | S.W.2d Pg. | Tex. Pg. | S.W.2d Vol. | S.W.2d Pg. |
|---|---|---|---|---|---|---|---|---|---|---|---|---|---|---|---|---|---|
| 1 | 291 | 673 | 139 | 293 | 488 | 238 | 294 | 385 | 329 | 294 | 795 | 455 | 295 | 901 | 561 | 297 | 817 |
| 7 | 291 | 697 | 148 | 293 | 484 | 252 | 294 | 377 | 334 | 295 | 890 | 456 | 295 | 894 | 570 | 297 | 811 |
| 18 | 291 | 721 | 154 | 293 | 493 | 262 | 293 | 841 | 340 | 295 | 412 | 467 | 296 | 233 | 574 | 297 | 813 |
| 28 | 291 | 926 | 158 | 293 | 758 | 267 | 295 | 654 | 365 | 295 | 408 | 474 | 296 | 517 | 580 | 298 | 108 |
| 36 | 291 | 693 | 168 | 293 | 753 | 269 | 294 | 712 | 371 | 295 | 405 | 484 | 297 | 112 | 584 | 298 | 119 |
| 44 | 291 | 677 | 176 | 293 | 639 | 277 | 294 | 706 | 376 | 295 | 902 | 488 | 296 | 757 | 587 | 298 | 93 |
| 61 | 291 | 689 | 185 | 293 | 736 | 282 | 294 | 705 | 382 | 295 | 642 | 492 | 296 | 750 | 593 | 298 | 97 |

Exhibit 25

the need for them having largely ceased.[1]   There was a separate one for each state, sold for use only in the state covered.   A Blue Section was, for the one state only, a counterpart of the National Reporter Blue Book, translating the official state report citation to the Reporter.   The White Section reversed this process, translating the Reporter citation to the official, for the one state only.

c. *State editions of Reporter advance sheets.*   For those states, as Massachusetts, for which there are special editions of the Reporter advance sheets, a colored-sheet table is provided in each advance sheet which translates from the official to the Reporter. Conversely there are tables translating from the Reporter to the official.

d. *Original report series to Federal Cases citation.*   A blue-page table in the digest volume of the series makes this translation, as *from* 1 Ben. 15 *to* 27 Fed. Cas. No. 16,510.   This table is shown in Exhibit 26, below.

Vols. 1–30.]                    TABLE OF CITATIONS.

**BANNING & ARDEN'S PATENT CASES—Cont'd.**

**Vol. 5, Ban. & A.—Cont'd.**

| Page. | F. C. No. | Page. | F. C. No. |
|---|---|---|---|
| 484 (2 F. 899) | — | 572 (3 F. 222) | — |
| 486 (3 F. 338) | — | 575 | 17,579a |
| 488 (3 F. 335) | — | 577 (3 F. 143) | — |
| 491 (2 F. 855) | — | 584 (3 F. 151) | — |
| 509 (3 F. 95) | — | 586 (3 F. 298) | — |
| 511 (3 F. 636) | — | 590 (3 F. 509) | — |

**BENEDICT'S UNITED STATES DISTRICT COURT REPORTS.**

**Vol. 1, Ben.**

| Page. | F. C. No. | Page. | F. C. No. | Page. | F. C. No. |
|---|---|---|---|---|---|
| 1 | 5,339 | 225 | 13,202 | 397 | 17,474 |
| 8 | 2,617 | 226 | 6,416 | 398 | 7,892 |
| 15 | 16,510 | 228 | 1,556 | 402 | 6,189 |
| 19 | 4,472 | 234 | 12,218 | 406 | 8,577 |
| 19 (note) | 8,412 | 241 | 14,012 | 407 | 1,543 |
| 23 | 2,642 | 264 | 9,796 | 408 | 11,834 |

Exhibit 26

e. *Shepard's United States and state citations.*   If either the official or the Reporter citation is known, it is very simple to translate from one to the other by means of the appropriate Shepard's Citations unit.   This is now done in two ways, depending upon which unit must be consulted.   In the older Shepard's units, which do not stand as tall on the shelves as the later ones, this translation was made by an "s" immediately following the page citation, meaning "same case in the other series."   Thus, in the Massachusetts case in Exhibit 27, 174 Mass. 212, the "s" refers to this same case as printed in 54 N.E. 539 and 75 American State Reports 300.

In the parallel citation in Exhibit 27, the "s 161 Mas. 558" refers to the same case at its first hearing before the Supreme Judicial Court, while the "174 Mas. 212" is the rehearing of that case, as here listed.   Thus 161 Mas. 558 is not a parallel citation to 174 Mas. 212, as are 54 N.E. 539 and 75 American State Reports 300.

[1] Letter dated April 8, 1959, from West Publishing Company to one of the authors.

**MASSACHUSETTS REPORTS**                                        **Vol. 174**

| | | | | | | |
|---|---|---|---|---|---|---|
| **—570—** | **Vol. 174** | 6MQ(2) 20 | **—129—** | 195Mas$^2$115 | **—212—** | 259Mas 2462 |
| s 54NE 257 | | 16MQ(5)224 | s 54NE 338 | 196Mas 220 | s 54NE 539 | 265Mas $^8$386 |
| 177Mas$^1$193 | | **—68—** | 33AIR 1748n | 197Mas$^2$483 | s 75AS 300 | 267Mas 2522 |
| 180Mas 119 | **—1—** | s 54NE 358 | | 199Mas$^1$572 | s161Mas 558 | 269Mas 393 |
| 180Mas$^1$147 | s 54NE 339 | s176Mas 433 | **—132—** | 201Mas$^1$300 | j184Mas$^1$155 | 275Mas $^5$335 |
| 184Mas$^1$129 | 178Mas 463 | 183Mas$^1$556 | s 54NE 502 | d204Mas 227 | d226Mas$^1$491 | 228US $^8$274 |
| 190Mas 183 | 194Mas$^4$180 | 186Mas 42 | 206Mas 568 | 215Mas 135 | 100AS 520n | 57LE $^8$833 |
| 192Mas 144 | 210Mas$^7$156 | 195Mas 54 | 231Mas$^5$581 | f219Mas 190 | 45Lns $^1$305n | 33SC $^8$460 |
| 193Mas 166 | 211Mas$^4$133 | 210Mas$^1$298 | 14Lns 102n | 219Mas 291 | AC'18D 5n | 229US$^{12}$377 |
| 206Mas 179 | 226Mas$^8$453 | **—74—** | **—144—** | 250Mas$^1$371 | **—216—** | 57LE$^{121}$235 |
| | | | s 54NE 490 | | | |

Exhibit 27

In the more recent compilations of Shepard's Citations, the taller volumes, the parallel translation is done in another manner and the "s" has a different meaning. This is illustrated in Exhibit 28.

**UNITED STATES SUPREME COURT REPORTS**                        **Vol. 362**

| | | | | | | | |
|---|---|---|---|---|---|---|---|
| — Or — | Formula- | s363 US 858 | f190 FS 681 | f283 F2d 485 | **—574—** | s 3 LE 76 | 195 FS 751 |
| 364 P2d1011 | tion–Trial | s 4 LE1739 | | f286 F2d 922 | (4 LE963) | s 79 SC 66 | 4 Æ 667s |
| **—456—** | Court Dis- | s 80 SC1605 | — CA2d — | ('61 MC | (80 SC909) | s 4 LE 53 | 23 Æ21419s |
| (4 LE874) | cretion | ('61 MC | 12 CaR334 | 1135) | s350 US 971 | s 80 SC 50 | **—901—** |
| (80 SC874) | 366 US 322 | 1923) | 67 NM 246 | 288 F2d 806 | s100LE 843 | s362 US 99 | (80 SC608) |
| s361 US 874 | 6 LE 322 | s264 F2d 289 | 354 P2d 537 | ('61 MC | s 76 SC 444 | s 4 LE 584 | No. 130 |
| s 4 LE 113 | 81 SC1248 | s286 F2d 875 | 11 Æ 646s | 1172) | s359 US 924 | s 80 SC 543 | s361 US 808 |
| s 80 SC 137 | j366 US 372 | s155 FS 442 | **—539—** | 290 F2d 398 | s 3 LE 627 | s257 F2d 885 | s 4 LE 57 |
| s 6 NY 788 | j 6 LE 351 | ('58 MC978) | (4 LE941) | ('61 MC | s 79 SC 610 | s161 FS 702 | s 80 SC 62 |
| s188 S2d 184 | j 81 SC1274 | 192 FS 450 | (80 SC926) | 1087) | s359 US 951 | s164 FS 107 | s361 US 947 |
| s159 NE 677 | Sherman | ('61 MC712) | s361 US 808 | 290 F2d 430 | s 3 LE 759 | **—609—** | s 80 SC 400 |
| s 6 NY 881 | Act–Vio- | Nav. Wat. | s 4 LE 57 | ('61 MC | s 79 SC 741 | (4 LE1009) | s363 US 817 |
| s188 S2d | lation–De- | Obstruc- | s 80 SC 70 | 1177) | s258 F2d 937 | (80 SC960) | s 4 LE1157 |
| [100] | cree–Ade- | tions–In- | ('59 MC | d291 F2d 97 | cc276SW533 | s 86 Az 275 | s 80 SC1245 |
| s160 NE 128 | quacy of | dustrial | 2665) | j291 F2d 98 | Hab. Corp. | s345 P2d 202 | s265 F2d 825 |
| | Relief | Solids–In- | s265 F2d 426 | 291 F2d 419 | Sentence | | s148 FS 106 |

Exhibit 28

In the listing of 362 U.S. 456, the parallel citations to the Lawyers' Edition and the Supreme Court Reporter, respectively, are in parentheses. The "s's" here, referring to 361 U.S. 874 (and, in parallel, 4 L. Ed. 2d 113 and 80 Sup. Ct. 137), and to various New York reports, are to the same case at other stages in the Supreme Court, or in the New York courts from which appealed to the Supreme Court. They do not refer to the identical report in 362 U.S. 456.

The parallel citation in Shepard's Citations is given only in the paper-bound supplements which lead up to the first bound volumes following the listing of the case, and in that first bound volume following the publication of the report cited. It is not repeated in later supplements or bound volumes. If one form of citation is known, Shepard's Citations is perhaps the most satisfactory parallel translation table from official to Reporter or reverse.

f. *Official to A.L.R. citation.*   This translation may not be made by any A.L.R. Table.   The official Shepard's unit, however, makes the translation by means of the "s" or parenthetical citations to the "same case in another series" citations noted above.

3. *Unofficial citation to official citation.*   As *from* 281 P. 728 *to* 75 Utah 6.

a. *Shepard's Reporter Citations.*   This procedure is precisely the reverse of that described above for translating from official to unofficial citation and is carried out through the Reporter Citations.   The Reporter Citations will reveal that there are many citations to cases in the Reporters for which there are no official reports.   This is probably the most nearly infallible test for such non-publication of official reports of a given decision.

b. *State editions of Reporter advance sheets.*   Those states, as Massachusetts, for which there are special state editions of the Reporter advance sheets covering them, provide in each advance sheet a colored-sheet table which translates from the Reporter to the official.

Whenever the official form of citation has been determined by the time the bound volume of the Reporter is published, it is included, preceding the case name in the Reporter, but usually the Reporter is printed before the official citation is known.

## CHAPTER 14

# Administrative Law

### §14.1. Administrative rules and regulations.[1]

1. *Impact and functions of administrative law.* Administrative agencies were called by Mr. Justice Robert H. Jackson a "veritable fourth branch of the government," in his dissent in *FTC* v. *Ruberoid Co.*, 343 U.S. 470, 477; 72 Sup. Ct. 800, 805; 96 L. Ed. 1081, 1089 (1952). Certainly, administrative law has a more direct impact upon the lives of most of us than conventional statute law. It tells us how to make out our income tax returns, what hours our post offices will be open, sets the rates we pay for telephone and electric light service, licenses our teachers and barbers and prescribes the kind of paper and ink to be used when applying for a patent. By a somewhat less direct contact, it licenses our radio and television stations, promulgates operating regulations for airlines and umpires labor relations.

Administrative law is based upon the common-sense recognition that business has to be transacted with reasonable expedition; that Congress must delegate some of its authority to the agencies and people who actually transact business; and that state legislatures must do the same. An important part of that delegation is for rule making and the power to make preliminary decisions and orders in carrying out the purposes of the legislation under which the rules are made. Both rule-making powers and the preliminary power to enforce decisions under the rules are, within wide limits, given to the various agencies of the executive branch of the federal and state governments, to counties and municipalities, and to courts.

[1] See § 6.16, page 92.

2. *Scope and basis of administrative regulation.* Administrative law or sublegislation includes rules and regulations made by the President and state governors, heads of lesser government agencies and by courts. Some of the rules thus promulgated are by virtue of the inherent power of such agencies to take the necessary measures to get work done, matters with which the legislatures do not wish to be bothered or with which they do not have the necessary expertise to deal. These concern matters of orderly procedure within the agency in the transaction of its business. Most sublegislation, however, is by authorization and direction of specific legislation which delegates the power to the officers and bodies designated to put it into effect and administer it.

§14.2. **The President as lawmaker.** Both directly and indirectly the President is an important lawmaker. On the negative side the President's veto is rarely overridden, and fear of it prevents the passage of many bills likely to be vetoed. On the positive side Congress, within the very wide Constitutional limitations of the doctrine of separation of powers, may authorize the President to conclude reciprocal trade treaties with other nations, raise or lower tariff rates, withdraw public lands from private entry, fix certain prices and realign or create new federal agencies below the rank of department, etc. Much of his rule-making power is delegated to various executive agencies under his jurisdiction, this being done by authority of the Act of August 8, 1950, c. 646, 64 Stat. 419, 3 U.S.C. §§301-303 (1964 ed.). Under the Constitution the President has wide power over foreign relations, and he is Commander in Chief of the Armed Forces.

1. *Forms of Presidential legislation.* These are treated in considerable detail in Price and Bitner, Effective Legal Research (1953), available at the loan desk of your law school library, and will be mentioned only briefly here. They include:

a. *Treaties and executive agreements.* These are discussed in Chapter 4, and at greater length in the corresponding chapter of Price and Bitner, Effective Legal Research (1953).

b. *Reorganization plans.* These are, in effect, Presidential executive orders which go into effect as law unless disapproved by either house of Congress within a stated time, which is sixty days under present law. Under these plans the President may combine, shift and even abolish designated agencies of the executive branch of the government, below the rank of department. The reorganization plan is an old device, but its free use is modern. The plans, from the earliest time, are collected in Title 5 of the United States Code. They are published as approved in the Statutes at Large and in the United States Code Congressional and Administrative

News.   As offered by the President, they are printed as House and
Senate documents, in the Weekly Compilation of Presidential
Documents, and in the unofficial United States Code Congressional and Administrative News.   These are the only places of
publication of *plans proposed but not approved,* as well as those
which are later approved (by Congress' failure to disapprove).
After approval, they are printed in the Federal Register on the
day after their effective date.   The Code of Federal Regulations
prints them as Presidential documents in Title 3.   They appear
as annotations to the codified sections of the enabling act under
which they were issued, in Title 5 of the United States Code.
This latter is the place where the search will normally begin, since
it is the only place where *all adopted reorganization plans, of whatever date, are collected in one spot.*   And only here are all pertinent documents, such as the enabling act, text of the plan, Presidential messages pertaining to the plans, any necessary executive
orders implementing them, and editorial notes and cross references, for all plans in force.   Where a function of a governmental
agency has been transferred from an agency by a plan, that fact is
noted, together with all necessary editorial matter, in a Transfer of
Functions note relating to the agency from which the functions
were transferred, in its appropriate Code title or section.

   c. *Proclamations and executive orders.*   The President exercises
a great deal of authority, especially that delegated to him by Congress by specific legislation, through proclamations and executive
orders.   In importance they vary from an order authorizing the
appointment of a minor government employee without regard to
Civil Service rules, to those establishing war emergency agencies,
such as the Office of Price Administration during World War II,
and fixing their functions.   Proclamation No. 3355, of July 6, 1960,
"Determining the Cuban Sugar Quota," has great effect on our
foreign relations.   Revocation, superseding or amendment of an
order is by another such order.   There is no difference in legal
effect between the proclamation and the executive order.

   (1) *Indexes to executive orders.*   The orders are indexed in the
Federal Register, the Weekly Compilation of Presidential Documents, Title 3 of the Code of Federal Regulations (beginning with
Executive Order No. 7906), and in the U.S. Code Congressional
and Administrative News.   When an executive order has directly
affected a United States Code section, it is indexed also in the
general index of the Code, as a statute, but this seldom occurs.

   (2) *Determining the present form and effect of an order.*
Amendment, revocation, termination, superseding, etc., of executive orders is noted in tables described in §14.5.

(3) *Judicial history of executive orders.* See §14.5.

(4) *Publication of Presidential documents.* These are published in the Federal Register and in the Weekly Compilation of Presidential Documents (which has a weekly cumulative index). Proclamations are published in the Statutes at Large; all are published in the unofficial United States Code Congressional and Administrative News.

2. *Shepardizing Presidential legislation.* See §14.5.

**§14.3. Publication of administrative rules:**[2] **The Federal Register System.** Under the Federal Register Act of 1935, as amended by the Administrative Procedure Act of 1946, no person is bound by the terms of an administrative federal rule of general application unless he has actual notice or unless the rule has been published in the Federal Register. The Federal Register System, established pursuant to the act, is the most inclusive repository of federal administrative legislation. The publications comprising this system are the Federal Register, the Code of Federal Regulations, the Weekly Compilation of Presidential Documents, the Government Organization Manual, and the Public Papers of the President of the United States.

1. *Federal Register.* The function of the Federal Register is to publish the literal text of official documents officially promulgated under the law, documents whose validity depends upon such publication. It is published daily, Tuesday through Saturday except on the day following a legal holiday; in other words, it is published on each day following a government working day. It is in effect the daily supplement to the Code of Federal Regulations. It began publication on March 14, 1936.

a. *Content of the Federal Register.* The following kinds of documents are required or authorized to be filed and published: (1) Presidential proclamations and executive orders of general interest in the numbered series, and any other documents which the President submits or orders to be published. (2) Every document issued under proper authority, prescribing a penalty or a course of conduct, conferring a right, privilege, authority or immunity, or imposing an obligation, and relevant or applicable to the general public, the members of a class or the persons of a locality. (3) Documents or classes of documents required by Act of Congress to be filed and published. (4) Other documents deemed by the Director of the Federal Register to be of sufficient interest. The text as published in the Federal Register is prima

---

[2] The authors acknowledge with thanks the valuable suggestions made on the Federal Register System by Mr. D. C. Eberhart, Director, Office of the Federal Register.

facie evidence of the filing and text of the original document, and courts are required to take judicial notice of it. The Federal Register covers only Presidential orders and administrative regulations. It does not include the rules of Congress or of courts.

b. *Arrangement of material in the Federal Register.* The first two pages of the Federal Register are devoted to (1) a subject index of material in that particular issue, and (2) the Codification Guide covering that issue. The function of the Codification Guide is to note changes in the form or status of published rules. See §14.6.

Beginning on the third page of each daily issue, the documents published are arranged under four principal headings, and each of the headings is begun on a new page. They are, in order:

> The President (Presidential documents have a page or pages to themselves, no other documents being printed on the same page)
> Rules and Regulations
> Proposed Rule Making
> Notices

Following the documents is the Cumulated Codification Guide (List of Sections Affected) for the current month.

(1) *Presidential documents.* The text of proclamations, executive orders and reorganization plans is printed. Beginning August 2, 1965, these and a wider variety of other Presidential documents — lists of Acts approved, appointments, communications to Congress, letters, etc. — are also printed in the Weekly Compilation of Presidential Documents, to which there is a weekly cumulative index.

(2) *Rules and regulations.* The aim is to arrange these in the Federal Register according to the numbered Titles of the C.F.R., but this is not always possible. (Letter of Director of Federal Register to authors, July 6, 1967.)

(3) *Proposed rule making.* See par. c(2) below.

(4) *Notices.* See par. d below.

c. *Compilations of rules in the Federal Register.* Rule revision and change are constant. A rule is made, amended and expanded. Then the chapter or title of which it is a part becomes so cumbersome that the chapter is completely revised; whereupon the process begins anew. There is now a policy of publication of revised titles annually. There has been constant improvement of publication, as exemplified in the C.F.R. (for which see 2 below). Rule changes are one of the *raisons d'être* of the loose-leaf service, which keeps track of them for its subscribers.

(1) *Rules of practice.* These prescribe the procedure which must be followed in transacting business before administrative

agencies. Failure by the practitioner or petitioner to observe them may prejudice or defeat the cause. The rules printed in the Federal Register are, if in force at the end of the calendar year, reprinted in the Code of Federal Regulations. Some are also printed in the United States Code, and most agencies concerned print them separately and send them free on request, though these pamphlets are not kept up to date very well. Perhaps the most complete and current collection is that published in Pike and Fischer's Administrative Law, Second Series. Some of the loose-leaf services described in Chapter 23 also print agency rules of practice pertinent to their subscribers. Treatises on such subjects as taxation or patents frequently print the rules of practice as appendices.

There is no general heading for Rules of Practice in the index to the Federal Register; even under the agency concerned the rules are not always so listed. They have been indexed under such odd heads as Organization and Procedure, or Records and Procedure.

(2) *Proposed rule making.* Proposed changes in rules of general application, including rate changes, are published in the Federal Register in a separate section following the publication of new rules. These are published in advance of adoption so as to permit those affected to register protests or suggest changes. Such proposed changes are listed in the Codification Guide (List of Sections Affected).

d. *Notices.* Changes in statements of agency organization and functions are printed in this section, as are notices of agreements filed for approval, notices of opinions and orders.

e. *Cumulated Codification Guide for the current month.* A change inaugurated in 1960 greatly shortens the search during the current month for the status and form of a rule, by printing a daily *cumulative* codification guide for the entire month to date, so that it is now necessary to search only the latest daily issue following the index for the preceding month.

f. *Indexes and tables for the Federal Register.* These are described in §§14.4 and 14.5 in the discussion of indexes and tables for the Federal Register System as a whole.

2. *Code of Federal Regulations.* This code bears somewhat the same relation to the Federal Register as the United States Code does to the Statutes at Large, in that the rules *actually in force* at the end of a calendar year are incorporated in the code (cited as C.F.R.). That is, if there has been more than one change in a rule during the year, as is frequently the case, only the form in force at the end of the year is printed in the C.F.R. If, as sometimes happens, it is necessary to consult the intermediate form or forms the

rule has had during the year, that must be done through the Federal Register itself, by means of the Codification Guide (List of Sections Affected) in it showing such changes, and by the annual List of Sections Affected in the pocket supplements to the respective titles of the C.F.R., described in §14.5.

The C.F.R. is not as inclusive as the Federal Register in some other respects: (a) Most descriptions of agency organization are omitted in favor of digests only of such statements in the United States Government Manual, which gives citations to the full statement in the Federal Register. (b) Many miscellaneous rules are omitted or cited in the C.F.R. only by reference. (c) Preliminary statements of policy reasons for the adoption of certain rules are omitted, though these often contain statements useful to the public concerned. (d) Proposed rules are omitted.

a. *Format of the Code.* Like the United States Code, the C.F.R. is divided into fifty titles, the first five of which concern the organization of the government. The remaining titles are arranged alphabetically, many of them corresponding in number to those of the United States Code, though the internal organization is quite different and the section numbers do not in any way coincide.

The basic subdivision is into chapters, parts and sections. The chapters usually bear the names of the agencies administering the rules included therein, such as the Civil Aeronautics Board. The section numbers are formed from the part numbers, plus a decimal point and a subsection number. Thus §202.13 is subsection number 13 of Part 202. A full citation would include the title and the section number.

As a part of its constant efforts to improve the format, the C.F.R. now has annual revision and publication of the various titles; and the pamphlets published as inserts are reduced in number of pages to form "use-units" which more nearly fit the needs of users. Individual pamphlets, covering only a small part of a complete title, can now be purchased separately. An American Bar Association committee recommended against publication in loose-leaf form, and such format is not contemplated. (Letter of Director to authors, July 6, 1967.)

b. *Current status and statutory basis of Code sections.* It should be emphasized that the C.F.R. is a compilation of *rules actually in force at the date of publication* of the annual compilations. Any sections which have been amended, superseded, terminated or repealed during the calendar year covered by the annual pamphlet are cited therein in a brief note, together with the page in the Federal Register printing the original. See Exhibit 29 below.

A List of Sections Affected (described in §14.5) at the end of

§ 1483.250      **Title 7—Chapter XIV**

as specified in the above provisions of this section, CCC may accept such other evidence of export as will establish to the satisfaction of the Vice President that the exporter has fully complied with his obligation to export.

(e) The exporter shall furnish such additional evidence of export as the Director may require in order to determine that there has been compliance with the export requirements hereof.

[Rev. I, 25 F.R. 5820, June 24, 1960, as amended by Amdt. 2, 25 F.R. 10758, Nov. 11, 1960; Amdt. 4, 27 F.R. 4863, May 24, 1962; Amdt. 5, 27 F.R. 10351, Oct. 24, 1962; Amdt. 7, 29 F.R. 12012, Aug. 22, 1964; Amdt. 8, 30 F.R. 6772, May 19, 1965; Amdt. 10, 31 F.R. 7818, June 2, 1966; Amdt. 11, 31 F.R. 14505, Nov. 11, 1966]

(e) Refunds shall not be required on exportations of flour by or to a United States Government agency as defined in § 1483.295.

(f) **The terms "domestic prices"** as used in the refund provisions of the regulations means domestic prices as determined by CCC including the cost to the exporter of any marketing certificates required under applicable legislation.

[Amdt. 6, 29 F.R. 4668, Apr. 1, 1964]

§ 1483.251    **Refunds on flour.**

(a) Except as otherwise provided in these regulations, the exporter shall refund to CCC a portion of the conditional payments previously received by him if

**Exhibit 29**

each annual edition cites all sections of regulations which were affected either directly or indirectly during any preceding calendar year. Since January 1, 1964, a separate C.F.R. volume covers the period 1949-1963. Statutes which are the authority for the rules are cited with the rules in the C.F.R. The rules' first place

# CHAPTER XII—STATISTICAL REPORTING SERVICE
# (AGRICULTURAL STATISTICS)
# DEPARTMENT OF AGRICULTURE

**PART 1300—PEANUT STATISTICS**

Sec.
1300.1   Scope of regulations.
1300.2   Definitions.
1300.3   Persons required to submit reports; forms to be used; where available.
1300.4   Time when reports are due.

AUTHORITY: The provisions of this Part 1300 issued under sec. 6, 49 Stat. 1899; 7 U.S.C. 956.

SOURCE: The provisions of this Part 1300 appear at 23 F.R. 2375, Apr. 11, 1958. Redesignated at 28 F.R. 4788, May 14, 1963.

§ 1300.1   **Scope of regulations.**

Under the act of June 24, 1936, as

of the United States who is authorized to exercise the powers and to perform the duties of the Secretary of Agriculture under the act.

§ 1300.3   **Persons required to submit reports; forms to be used; where available.**

(a) The following persons are required to submit monthly reports, as follows:

(1) Peanut cleaners, shellers, crushers and manufacturers of crude peanut oil, peanut cake and meal are required to report on Form C. E. 6-18 "A", Peanut Stocks and Processing Report, inventories, receipts and disposition of

**Exhibit 30**

of publication — which is usually in the Federal Register — is also cited, as in Exhibit 30, under Source.

3. *Weekly Compilation of Presidential Documents.* The third member of the Federal Register System, the Weekly Compilation of Presidential Documents, has been published each Monday since August 2, 1965. The issues contain Presidential items released up to 5 p.m. of the preceding Friday.

All items to be published in the Public Papers series (see §14.5) are first published in the Weekly Compilation. However, many items are published only in the Weekly Compilation. Such items include announcements of appointments, letters and reports *to* the President, and news conferences and remarks by administration officials other than the President.

Appended materials include (1) a digest of other White House announcements, (2) a list of nominations submitted to the Senate, (3) a checklist of White House releases, and (4) a list of acts approved by the President. For indexes see §14.4.

4. *United States Government Organization Manual.* This Manual is the fourth member of the Federal Register System. Its purpose is to keep its users abreast of the current organization, functions and major personnel of government agencies and of selected quasi-official agencies and international organizations. It is the place to which you go to find out how government agencies are set up and operated — how the federal government keeps house. An understanding of the mechanics of the government, a knowledge of the names of officials, and the statutory authority and limitations of a government agency are often of great assistance in starting a search. The Manual prints digests of more complete statements already printed in the Federal Register. It sets forth for each agency its mode of creation and its authority — whether under statute, executive order or reorganization plan — and its organization, including major personnel, organization charts and functions. It is an annual publication.

5. *Public Papers of the Presidents of the United States.* The last unit of the Federal Register System is the Public Papers series. This is a series of bound volumes, issued annually beginning with the Truman administration in 1945 and continuing through the terms of subsequent Presidents. Their function is to provide a uniform and systematic publication of the Presidential messages and papers essential to an understanding of the laws and the administrative rules of the year covered.

Included in each volume are the State of the Union address, the budget and the economic messages, and other formal communications to the Congress. Also included are the President's news conferences, his addresses and informal remarks, letters to Congressional leaders and to have the heads of Federal agencies, all "statements by the President," and the public record of his meetings with foreign leaders.

The text is based on original sources, where available. All items are in the public domain, usually by virtue of release by the White House Press Office. Appended tables list (1) White House press releases, (2) Presidential proclamations and Executive orders, and (3) Presidential reports to the Congress. Each annual volume is separately indexed (see §14.4).

§14.4. **Indexes to the Federal Register System.** The indexes include the following:

1. *Federal Register indexes.* The indexes are daily, cumulated monthly, quarterly and annually. The daily index is printed on the first and second pages of the daily issue. These indexes have not been satisfactory to use, because they have required too detailed a preliminary knowledge of government organization by the searcher. Up to 1959 the entries were listed alphabetically by agency, thereunder by subagency and function, rather than by subject. There were, to be sure, catchwords indexing fact situations, like "Bond," "Installment Credit," and "Subversive Organizations," but too often, instead of leading directly to the appropriate title and section number, they led to the organizational index, wherein the same process must be carried out again. There were no catchwords in the daily issue index, which was really a table of contents.

Beginning with 1959 the philosophy of the index was changed somewhat, with more emphasis on catchwords. The new index is more inclusive in documents covered than is the C.F.R. index, because it covers all material published in the Federal Register, while the C.F.R. indexes only regulations adopted and presently in force. The Codification Guide (List of Sections Affected) described in §14.5, is a vital part of the Federal Register index. The annual index contains a Parallel Table of Statutory Authorities and Rules, supplementing the table in 2 C.F.R. (see §14.5).

2. *Code of Federal Regulation Indexes.* There has been great change and improvement in C.F.R. indexing, with present stress upon catchwords rather than agency, though agency entries are not neglected. The index now approaches the digest descriptive-word index in style. It is much smaller than the old General Index and is issued annually in pamphlet form.

3. *Weekly Compilation of Presidential Documents.* An Index of Contents appears at the beginning of each issue. At the end, a Cumulative Index to Prior Issues covers all items since the begin-

ning of the calendar quarter. Cumulation begins anew with each quarter. Thus Quarterly Indexes are published in issues numbers 1, 14, 27, and 40 of each year. There are also separate Semi-Annual and Annual Indexes.

The method of indexing is similar to that of the Public Papers of the Presidents.

4. *United States Government Organization Manual Index.* There are really several indexes to the Manual. The Index proper, which is the subject index to government organizations and applicable statutes, is an index not only to active organizations, but also to Appendix A, Executive Agencies and Functions . . . Abolished, Transferred, or Terminated Subsequent to March 4, 1933. This index is the best starting place in the search for the statutory origin, organization, functions and principal personnel of government agencies. Personnel are indexed in a separate List of Names of all persons mentioned by name in the Manual.

5. *Public Papers of the Presidents of the United States.* Each volume contains a complete subject index. Names of persons and places are listed alphabetically together with analytical entries covering the text of all items. Special categories group classes of items, such as "Veto Messages" or "Statements by the President."

**§14.5. Tables for the Federal Register System.** Conversion tables make it possible (1) to determine what rules have been promulgated under the authority of a given statute, proclamation or executive order; (2) to determine what the statutory basis is for any rule; (3) to determine what changes have been made in the form of any established rule; and (4) to some extent to Shepardize (using the word as generic for citators) Presidential proclamations and executive orders, and some administrative regulations. The reader is urged to examine the detailed checklists of Title 1, Appendix C, the Guide to Federal Register Finding Aids.

---

**8 U. S. C. 1227**        **Title 2—Chapter I**

| United States Code | Code of Federal Regulations |
|---|---|
| 8 U. S. C. 1227_____ | 8 CFR Part 235<br>Part 237<br>Part 280 |
| 1228_____ | 8 CFR Part 212<br>Part 231<br>Part 235 |
| 1229_____ | 8 CFR Part 231<br>Part 239<br>Part 280 |

Exhibit 31

1. *Statute to rule.* As *from* 49 U.S.C. §921 *to* 19 C.F.R. §333. This conversion is made by a table in Title 2 of the C.F.R. and in the monthly and quarterly indexes to the Federal Register. It is arranged by United States Code citation, with parallel citation to the C.F.R. rule for which the U.S. Code is cited as authority. Exhibit 31 gives examples.

2. *Statute to executive order or proclamation.* In Table 5 of 3 C.F.R. is a table entitled Statutes Cited as Authority for Presidential Documents. See Exhibit 32.

3. *Presidential proclamations, orders or reorganization plans to*

### Title 3—The President

#### Statutes at Large—Continued

| Date | Citation | Title of Act | Document |
|------|----------|--------------|----------|
| **1932** | | | |
| June 30 | Sec. 204, 47 Stat. 404____ | _____ | EO 10512, 10569. |
| **1933** | | | |
| _____ | Sec. 22_____ | Agricultural Adjustment Act. | Proc. 3048, 3070, 3073, 3075. |
| Mar. 3 | 47 Stat. 1520_____ | Buy-American Act_____ | EO 10582. |
| May 20 | 48 Stat. 73_____ | _____ | Proc. 3055. |
| **1934** | | | |
| Apr. 30 | 48 Stat. 657_____ | _____ | Proc. 3068. |
| June 12 | 48 Stat. 943_____ | An Act to amend the Tariff Act of 1930. | Proc. 3053. |

Exhibit 32

*C.F.R.* As *from* Executive order No. 11,038 *to* 15 C.F.R. Parts 368–399. In three separate tables in Title 3 of the C.F.R., these Presidential documents are listed by number, with their subject matter, C.F.R. title and section number, and comment as to the nature of the reference. See Exhibit 33.

4. *Presidential proclamations, orders or reorganization plans to U.S. Code.* As *from* Executive order No. 6084 *to* 12 U.S.C. §1026. This is done, not through a Federal Register System table, but through Tables IV-VI of the United States Code, and similar tables in the United States Code Annotated and Federal Code Annotated.

5. *Code of Federal Regulations to statutory or Presidential authority.* As *from* 16 C.F.R. §226.0 *to* 38 Stat. 721, 719; 15 U.S.C. §46, 45; 20 Fed. Reg. 613.

a. *Footnote citation to authority.* Authority is cited for C.F.R.

| | | | Title 3—The President | Chapter II—Executive Orders | |
|---|---|---|---|---|---|
| E. O. No. | Date | F. R. Citation | Subject | Reference | Comment |
| | 1952 | 17 F. R. | | | |
| 10326 | Feb. 11 | 1381 | Authorizing inspection of income, excess-profits, declared value excess-profits, capital stock, estate, and gift tax returns by the Senate Committee on Expenditures in the Executive Departments. | 26 CFR (1939) 458.307a | Cited in text and in footnote. |
| 10328 | Feb. 20 | 1645 | Prescribing a portion of the Selective Service Regulations | 32 CFR Part 1660 | Codified. |
| 10331 | Mar. 4 | 1963 | Authorizing inspection of income tax returns by the Senate Committee on Interior and Insular Affairs. | 26 CFR (1939) 358.311 | Cited in text and in footnote. |
| 10335 | Mar. 28 | 2741 | Provisional Intergovernmental Committee for the Movement of Migrants from Europe; designation as a public international organization entitled to enjoy certain privileges, exemptions, and immunities | 19 CFR 10.30a | Cited in table. |
| 10336 | Apr. 3 | 2957 | Amendment of Executive Order 9586 of July 6, 1945, establishment of the Medal of Freedom. | 32 CFR 578.17 / 878.16 | Interpreted or applied and cited in text. Cited in text. |
| 10341 | Apr. 8 | 3143 | Discontinuing the Rose Island and the Tutuila Island Naval Defense Sea Areas and Naval Airspace reservations. | 32 CFR 761.3, 761.21–761.24 | Do. |
| 10343 | Apr. 12 | 3259 | Authorizing inspection of tax returns by Committee on the Judiciary, House of Representatives. | 26 CFR (1939) 458.312 | Cited in text and in footnote. |

Exhibit 33

sections, either as a footnote for a single section, or as a note preceding a group of sections. See Exhibit 30, page 171.

b. *Title 3 table of first edition of C.F.R.* A table in Title 3 of the first edition of the C.F.R., arranged by the C.F.R. title and section number, gives in parallel columns the proclamation or executive order included or cited in the regulation. No statutory authority is cited, and this table was omitted from all supplements and from the second edition, since the same information now accompanies the text of each regulation. Thus Title 3 of the first edition should be retained for reference purposes.

6. *Changes in form or status of published rules: Revisions, revocations.* Tables performing somewhat the role of the Shepard's Citations legislative history notations are necessary and have been provided.

a. *List of Sections Affected.* Although the C.F.R. itself prints only those regulations presently in force as of the publication date of the respective bound volumes and cumulative annual pocket supplements, cognizance is taken of the numerous changes in regulations which may have taken place during a calendar year. This is done through the List of Sections Affected, in which references are made to those pages in the Federal Register in which all actions during a calendar year affecting a given section are recorded. These include any revisions or revocations, and also references to proposed rules.

As shown in Exhibit 34, the List of Sections Affected includes all documents which were effected from 1964 to the date of revision. It should be noted that with the exception of some seven titles, revisions of titles are now on an annual basis. Annual pocket-part supplements following the revision date of these seven titles list further actions affecting title sections, arranged by calen-

### List of Sections Affected

All sections in this volume of the Code of Federal Regulations which were affected by documents published in the Federal Register since January 1, 1964, are enumerated in the following list. Entries indicate the nature of the changes effected. Page numbers refer to Federal Register pages.

For the period before January 1, 1964, see the "List of Sections Affected, 1949–1963," which is published in a separate volume.

| 1964 17 CFR | 29 F.R. Page | 17 CFR—Continued | 29 F.R. Page |
|---|---|---|---|
| Chapter I: | | Chapter II—Continued | |
| 150.10 | | 201.7 | |
|   Added | 15571 |   (e) revised | 9487 |
| Chapter II: | | 201.8 | |
| 200.11 | |   (b) and (c) revised | 9487 |
|   (b) amended | 11579 | 201.9 | |
| 200.15 | |   (d) revised | 9487 |
|   Revised | 5276 |   (b) redesignation as (b)(1); | |
| 200.18 | |   (b)(2) added | 13422 |
|   Revised | 15282 | 201.11 | |
| 200.20 | |   Heading and (d) and (e) revised | 3567 |
|   Revised | 15282 |   (d) and (e) revised | 9488 |
| 200.21 | | 201.12 | |
|   Amended | 5276 |   Heading and (a) revised | 3567 |
| | |   (d) added | 9488 |

Exhibit 34

dar year. A single volume contains a compilation of the List of Sections Affected for all titles of the Code of Federal Regulations for the years 1949 through 1963; 1949 being the date of the second edition of the Code.

During the year following the latest one covered by the List of Sections Affected, the search for the most recent form of a rule, or of proposed rules, will be made directly in the Federal Register by means of the Codification Guide (List of Sections Affected) described below.

b. *Codification Guide (List of Sections Affected).* This is the most important tool for tracing the present text of a given C.F.R. title and section and for finding changes made since the publication of the text in the volume covering the title. It is a checklist, by title and section number, of all C.F.R. sections which have in any way been affected by later action. It lists not only regulations in force which have been published or modified, but also those revoked, terminated or superseded, as well as proposed rules. All forms of a regulation in effect at any time during the period covered are listed, showing their disposition and where they are published in the Federal Register. It is thus more inclusive than the current form of the C.F.R. section as published at the end of a year in the C.F.R.

There has been a distinct improvement in the publication of this index, in that the daily indexes (published on the first and second pages of each issue of the Federal Register) have, beginning in 1960, been cumulated at the end of each issue so as to cover *all changes made during the current month*. It is not, therefore, necessary to check each of the daily issues for changes made during the current month, as it formerly was.

The Codification Guide (List of Sections Affected) appears in the following forms: daily, on the second page of each issue; cumulative for the current month, showing changes since the preceding month, printed at the back of each daily issue; monthly, quarterly and annual cumulations. Usually the annual table appears well in advance of the pocket supplement tables in the C.F.R., but there are occasional errors in it. Exhibit 35 shows a specimen entry.

---

10       LIST OF CFR SECTIONS AFFECTED

| 7 CFR—Continued | Page | 7 CFR—Continued | Page | 7 CFR—Continued | Page |
|---|---|---|---|---|---|
| Chapter III—Continued | | Chapter IV—Continued | | Chapter VII—Continued | |
| 331 | | 408.1 | | 709.12 | |
| Added | 9544 | Appendix amended | 13589 | Revised | 15791 |
| 331.1 | | 408.6 | | 709.16 | |
| Revoked | 14925 | Amended | 9711 | (b) amended | 15791 |
| 354.1 | | 409.1 | | 709.20 | |
| Revised | 10311 | Appendix amended | 7554 | Amended | 15791 |

ANNUAL 1966       11

| 7 CFR—Continued | Page | 7 CFR—Continued | Page | 7 CFR—Continued | Page |
|---|---|---|---|---|---|
| Chapter VII—Continued | | Chapter VII—Continued | | Chapter VII—Continued | |
| ˜18.16—Continued | | 722.417 | | 724.35m—724.35o | |
| Amended | 7393 | Revised | 13529 | Subpart added | 703 |
| Amended | 9677 | 722.429 | | 724.35p, 724.35q | |
| (b) amended | 10881 | (b) added | 13205 | Subpart added | 2414 |

Exhibit 35

---

c. *U.S. Code tables of Presidential documents repealed or eliminated.* Table 4 in the annual supplement to Title 3 supplies this information, which the U.S. Code tables did formerly but do no longer.

7. *Determination of the present form of a federal rule or regulation.* This is one of the most important and frequent tasks the worker with federal administrative rules and regulations has to perform. It is now less laborious than formerly, because of the cumulation from day to day during a month of the Codification Guide (List of Parts Affected) in the back of each Federal Register issue.

The search would normally begin with the volume of the appropriate title of the C.F.R. containing the desired rule or regulation; proceeding then to the List of Sections Affected in this volume; thence forward to the quarterly, monthly, current month and current day's Codification Guide (List of Parts Affected) in the latest issue of the Federal Register.  This will give the searcher not only the latest text of the rule, but references to volumes and pages of the Federal Register on which any intervening form of text was printed.

Loose-leaf services, particularly tax services, note these changes for their subscribers.

8. *Citators for rules: Subsequent judicial history.*  Changes in form of rules, corresponding to the conventional citators' "legislative history" notations, were discussed in the preceding section. To find the "judicial history," that is the interpretation or construction of such a rule by a court, is impossible or at least impracticable by tabular means, with a very few exceptions.

a. *Shepard's Citations.*  If a rule is cited in connection with a Statutes at Large or Code section in a judicial decision, it is covered — but as a Statute at Large or Code section — in Shepard's United States Citations, but that rarely occurs.  Presidential proclamations and reorganization plans and executive agreements may be identified through Tables IV-VI of the United States Code and in like tables in unofficial editions of the Code.  The procedure here is to consult the table listing Presidential documents which are included in the Code, and then to Shepardize the Code section with which the document is identified.

b. *National Reporter System Tables of Statutes Construed.* Presidential executive orders and proclamations and such administrative regulations as are the subject of litigation are covered by these tables as found in the advance sheets and bound volumes of the National Reporter System.

c. *Digest of the United States Supreme Court Reports.*  Supreme Court decisions construing the orders and rules noted above are covered in the table of statutes construed in this digest. See §16.9.

d. *Loose-leaf services.*  Loose-leaf services not only note changes in form, such as amendments and revocations of rules, but cite and discuss decisions concerning them.  See Chapter 23.

§14.6.  **Dissatisfaction with the Federal Register System.**  The system has an impossible task, because of the enormous volume of materials to be taken care of daily, the changes of form, and the speed with which the printed results must be made available. Since the late 1950's the persistent efforts of the Director have born fruit in many changes, some of which have been noted in the preceding sections.  Indexing has improved; the Codification Guide simplifies finding the present format of a regulation; titles are now published annually in small "use-units" to fit the needs of users, and are sold separately through the Superintendent of Documents. A frequently proposed loose-leaf format was contrarecommended by a committee of the American Bar Association and is not in contemplation.

§14.7. **Other sources of federal rules publication.** Printed copies of regulations and rules of practice are distributed by some federal agencies, covering their own activities. Loose-leaf services do the same for the subject matter covered by them. The most complete current unofficial publication of Presidential proclamations and executive orders is in the United States Code Congressional and Administrative News, which also publishes some administrative regulations of general interest.

§14.8. **Administrative agency rulings and opinions.** Written opinions and orders through which administrative agencies construe and apply the laws and regulations they administer parallel in form those of conventional courts. The procedure of the agencies and their quasi-judicial tribunals, though less formal than that of the courts, closely resembles it.

1. *Scope of administrative rulings.* In any given agency its rulings may relate only to the internal affairs of the agency itself in the transaction of its business, or may regulate the relations of the government with private citizens, or of citizens with each other. A ruling may be an office opinion or memorandum, effective only as to matters of internal agency procedure. Or the chief law officer of the federal or state government may lay down advisory interpretations for outside application, such as the opinions of the federal or a state attorney general. Decisions and orders effective outside the government proper range from patent grants, on through public utility rate making, to regulatory decisions under specific statutes.

2. *Publication of administrative agency rulings.* By no means all agencies, particularly state, publish their rulings. When printed in full, they so closely resemble reported court decisions in form as to require little additional comment here. They may appear in any or all of the following forms.

a. *Press releases.* These are mimeographed, ordinarily, and circulated to newspapers and others interested, within a day or two of the decision. They commonly contain a brief statement of facts, followed by a paraphrase of the arguments of counsel, an abridgment of the opinion, and the decision.

b. *Mimeographed reports of decisions.* These reports, usually issued within a day or two of the decision date, give either long abridgments of the full opinion, or more commonly the complete decision and order, minus syllabus but with all footnotes. There is some serial designation by which they may be cited, which usually includes the volume number of the report series in which the reports will eventually appear and a case number, since the page number of the printed report is as yet undetermined. Thus 97 N.L.R.B. No. 72.

c. *Printed slip decisions.* These are usually in final complete form as found in the later-published bound cumulations. They are not common.

d. *Advance sheet pamphlets and bulletins.* The content and frequency of rulings in this form vary from agency to agency. Some contain both agency and court decisions; others, agency decisions and rules of practice, dockets of impending hearings, etc.

e. *Bound volumes of agency rulings.* The preliminary, unbound form of agency ruling is almost always superseded by a bound volume, duplicating in all essential features the bound volumes of court reports.

f. *Unofficial publication of agency rulings.* The impact of administrative law is such that those affected, or their attorneys, must have speedy access to all aspects of it — the law, the rules and regulations, and the decisions. Loose-leaf services, as described in Chapter 23, are the best answer to this need, as in labor law, taxation, public utilities law, etc. At the end of a year the decisions reported in these services may be cumulated and bound, as in labor and tax cases.

Legal periodicals frequently publish federal or state (or both) court and agency adjudications. For state regulatory agencies these may be the best or even the only printed reports available. Examples are the Public Utilities Fortnightly, the Journal of the Federal Communications Bar Association, and Taxes.

g. *Administrative law digests.* Court decisions involving administrative law are digested under appropriate subject headings in conventional case digests covering these courts.

(1) *American Digest System.* (See §16.5.) Cases involving administrative law are collected, beginning with the Fifth Decennial, in the Administrative Law and Procedure title, but these are only court decisions, not agency rulings. Since not all material deemed by the searcher as classifiable under this title may in fact be digested here, the searcher should still consult the Descriptive Word Index.

(2) *Agency special-subject digests.* Most official and unofficial publication series of agency rulings have digests of some kind. Often it is only the index digest found in each bound volume, so that a complete coverage requires the examination of numerous

single volumes. Some federal agencies cumulate this digest material at irregular intervals, and for the periods covered such digests are extremely useful. The most useful digests of official agency decisions are apt to be commercial ventures. Such are the Consolidated Digest of Decisions Under the Interstate Commerce Act,[2] and supplements, covering decisions from 1887 to date, and the Lois G. Moore, Tax Court Digest and annual pocket supplements.[3]

More common are the digests which are part of unofficial editions of agency rulings. Examples are the cumulative digests of the United States Patents Quarterly and the Labor Relations Cumulative Digest and Index of the unofficial Bureau of National Affairs.

(3) *Pike & Fischer Administrative Law Service.*[4] This is a service for the procedural, not the substantive, aspects of administrative law. While it covers the decisions of six federal courts and twenty-four administrative agencies (beginning with 1948), the approach is to procedure generally, rather than to that of specific agencies. The four-volume Consolidated Digest covers both series, and has annual pocket supplements. Beginning with the Second Series of the Service in 1951 there are annual bound volumes of new cases, collecting reports of both courts and agency decisions on administrative procedure. All material is keyed to the Administrative Procedure Act, but its scope is somewhat wider. Current Material (loose-leaf) contains the text and headnotes of current opinions and decisions of courts and agencies. A loose-leaf Desk Book contains the digests of current cases not yet incorporated in the Consolidated Digest supplements; the text and legislative history of the Administrative Procedure Act; the text of other relevant acts; and rules of practice of some twenty-four agencies. There is also a newsletter.

§14.9. **State aspects of administrative law.**

1. *Importance.* The impact of administrative law upon the average citizen is perhaps greater in state than in federal relations. The barber, the plumber, the teacher — all practitioners of the many trades or professions subject to licensing — the housewife who uses electricity and telephone, the man who drives an automobile, the farmer selling milk, the laborer injured on a job or out of work — all these and many more are affected in one way or another by rules, regulations, rate schedules and decisions of state administrative agencies and commissions.

---

2 Fowler, Ind., H. C. Lust Co.

3 Indianapolis, Ind., Bobbs-Merrill, 1951 to date.

4 Albany, N.Y., Matthew Bender & Co., 1941-1948, 5v.; New York, Pike & Fischer, Second Series, 1952 to date. Decisions, Digest, Current Material, Desk Book.

2. *State administrative rules and regulations.* The publication and promulgation of state rules has been much less satisfactorily handled than in the federal field. Most state licensing or regulatory agencies and commissions publish the regulations governing licenses and distribute them free. Similarly tax and equalization boards, workmen's compensation hearing officers, etc., are apt to print their regulations. There have been and continue to be efforts to put the compilation, editing and publication of these rules on a systematic basis, similar to that exemplified by the Federal Register System. Some fourteen states now publish compiled regulations.[5]

3. *State administrative agency opinions and decisions.* State agency decisions follow the pattern of the federal, but official publication of them is somewhat rare, except in the two categories below.

a. *Attorney General's opinions.* The advisory opinions of the chief law officer of the state usually follow closely the form and technique of the judicial opinion; when they comment on cases or statutes they are noted in some of the state Shepard's Citations units as "citing cases." They are similarly noted in the annotated statutes in some states. Every state publishes its attorney general's decisions. The Council of State Governments has published since March 1937, a Digest of Opinions of Attorneys General, formerly weekly, now monthly, to which there is an annual index.

b. *Public utilities commission decisions.* State public utilities commissions approve or initiate rate schedules, grant certificates of convenience and necessity, and issue orders to effectuate their decisions. The opinions and orders closely follow the form of judicial opinions and are published, usually in conjunction with the routine periodical reports of the respective commissions. Public Utilities Reports, First and Second Series,[6] have published both court and agency decisions. There is an annual digest.

c. *Loose-leaf services.* The most convenient, expeditious and complete collection of state administrative rules and decisions on any given subject is usually in loose-leaf services. As described in Chapter 23, they cover such varied topics as labor, insurance, taxation and public utilities.

**§14.10. Citation books.** See Chapter 18.

[5] Cohen, Publication of State Administrative Regulations — Reform in slow motion. 14 Buffalo L. Rev. 410, 421 (1965). This is an excellent survey and contains a table of publications by state.

[6] Washington, D.C., Public Utilities Reports, Inc.

*CHAPTER 15*

# Law Reports: Index and Search Books

**§15.1.   Need and kinds of indexes and search books in case law.**
Although, as far as is known, nobody has ever made a complete and accurate count of published reports of American judicial decisions, there are said to be in existence between three and three and one-half million of them, with over 30,000 being added each year. Assuming, conservatively, that for each of these cases there are six headnote paragraphs, these statements of principles of law involved in the decided cases would mount up to over 18,000,000, with annual additions of over 180,000. The law reports to which these headnote paragraphs apply are published in chronological, not subject, order.

The need of some workable device or devices to enable the lawyer to locate among this enormous, growing and unclassified mass of statements those which are in point with his own problem, and to appraise the value as precedent of the cases in which they were made or decided, is obvious. To meet this need several different kinds of law books have been developed. Generically they are called books of index and search books. They include case digests, treatises, cyclopedias, annotations, restatements of the law, legal periodicals, dictionaries, form books, loose-leaf services and citation books. They are the necessary means which the lawyer must employ to find, appraise and apply legal authority.

**§15.2.   Authority of index and search books.** Under the definition of authority in Chapter 1, treatises, encyclopedias, annotations, restatements of the law, and legal periodicals may be designated as persuasive authority, to the extent that they are cited by courts. Judges frequently cite them because of the excellence and completeness of their analyses of the statutes and cases which *are* mandatory authority. Such persuasive authorities themselves are, however, in no sense mandatory, in that a court would be bound by any statement of the law in them. No matter how excellent the reasoning and cogent the conclusions, they are nevertheless only unofficial statements unless delivered from the bench as part of an opinion. While undoubtedly persuasive in many cases, they are cited because the citer approves and adopts them as a convenient analysis and statement of that which is authority.

Accordingly when a judge in his opinion says that a certain rule of law is as stated in American Jurisprudence, Corpus Juris Secundum, Wigmore, or a Columbia Law Review article by Chafee, he is merely saying that the authors or editors of the works cited above have read and analyzed the cases and statutes carefully and have written down a statement of the law extracted from them which he, the judge, believes to be a proper interpretation of this authority. In view of the frequency with which these secondary materials are cited by courts, the distinction is perhaps academic, but it does exist and should always be kept in mind. Their primary function is to direct the searcher to the sources relied upon.

Search books and books of index such as digests and the various tables and other tools aiding in their use, and citation books, have no authority of any kind under any definition. The statement of a rule of law in a digest is not to be accepted as applicable to any given situation, without careful study of the case digested. Index books are not an end in themselves, but only means to an end. As such they are indispensable.

A detailed and, at times, highly critical analysis of such secondary materials as annotations, encyclopedias and treatises is by Professor John Henry Merryman. Authority of Authority, 6 Stanford L. Rev. 613-673. While directed specifically at authority cited by the California Supreme Court, it has general applicability.

See also Note in Computerized Means of Research, page 10.

Most publishers of law search books and indexes, as West, Lawyers Co-operative Publishing Company and Shepard's Citations, publish and distribute free, elaborate and graphically illustrated descriptions of their publications and how to use them. They are very useful.

§16.1.   **Function of digests.**   The case digest is the lawyer's indispensable tool.   It is a vastly detailed subject index to the law as set forth in the reported cases.   Its text is composed of the headnote paragraphs — verbatim or paraphrased — which form the syllabi or headnotes of the published law reports, without connecting comment.   In the American Digest System, described in §§16.5 and 16.6, these paragraphs are, for cases reported in the National Reporter System, the actual Key-Numbered headnote paragraphs as taken from the various Reporters, with added citator material showing the subsequent judicial treatment of the cases digested. Exhibit 36, below, shows a digest paragraph from the Fifth Decennial Digest.

The reports of the cases from which these headnotes are taken are arranged in their respective bound volumes in chronological order by date of decision, not in subject order.   To form the digest it is necessary to arrange these millions of headnote paragraphs by subject, under an elaborate classification which brings digests of like cases together.   Although the subject classification schemes employed by the various publishers of digests differ from each other somewhat in detail, they are so similar to each other in organization and effect that only the American Digest System need be described here, as representative of them all.

§16.2.   **Distinguishing features of digests.**   The digest is a collection of separate paragraphs, each of which is related to its fellows only because they belong in the same subject class, as stating like principles of law as extracted from the reported cases.   They are

**Wis. 1938.** The state court had jurisdiction to proceed to confirm foreclosure sale
and execute judgment of foreclosure even
though farm debtor's petition under Frasier-
Lemke Act was pending, where there was no
stay of proceedings granted, since the stay
of proceedings provided by the Frasier-Lemke
Act is a "judicial stay" not a "statutory stay"
and requires application to state or federal
court in which foreclosure proceedings are
pending for a stay. Bankr.Act § 75(n), as
amended, 11 U.S.C.A. § 208(n).—Kalb v. Luce,
279 N.W. 685, 228 Wis. 519, rehearing denied
280 N.W. 725, 228 Wis. 519, appeal dismissed
59 S.Ct. 107, 305 U.S. 566, 83 L.Ed. 356, followed in 285 N.W. 431, 231 Wis. 186, reversed
60 S.Ct. 343, 30 U.S. 433, 84 L.Ed. 370, man-
date conformed to 291 N.W. 841, 234 Wis. 509.

Exhibit 36

linked together by no editorial comment on the case or cases involved; there is no synthesis of rules from a group of cases, no
statements as to jurisdictional rules, historical developments, majority and minority views, etc., as in a treatise, encyclopedia or law
review article. Each stated rule is there on its own. The digest
thus leaves to the reader the task of determining for himself for
each statement its present place within the hierarchy of decisions
on the point, and its applicability to his own specific problem.
This presupposes possession by him of all the skills and techniques
necessary for the digest's proper use; that is why the digest is
peculiarly the lawyer's tool.

In using this tool, however, even the lawyer must be constantly
on the alert to note the law's changes, both by decision and by
statute. When a decision or line of decisions seriously modifying
or overturning the existing rule is digested and the digest paragraph takes its place under the proper digest classification, no
statement is made in the digest itself of the probable effect of this
new decision or decisions on existing law, and the older, perhaps
overruled or modified decisions must be relegated to their proper
place only by the alertness of the searcher; the digest will not
apprise him of the changes in so many words.

An example is the 1942 case of *Williams* v. *North Carolina*, 317
U.S. 187, 63 Sup. Ct. 207, 143 A.L.R. 143. When this case expressly overruled the 1906 case of *Haddock* v. *Haddock,* 201 U.S.
562, 26 Sup. Ct. 525, 50 L. Ed. 867, which had for a generation
been settled law on the question of full faith and credit as related

to decisions involving matrimonial domicile, there was no editorial comment in the digest to this effect. Indeed, the old *Haddock* case digest paragraphs, and the digests of the many cases following the doctrine of that decision, are still in the digest. This illustrates the necessity of reading and relying upon the authority of a decided *case,* not merely the *digest* of the case.

§16.3. **Authority of digests.** It follows that a digest is not authority of any kind, even persuasive, but only a guide or index to finding such authority. There is no presumption that the rule of law as stated in a digest paragraph is the rule of the case digested; this is particularly true because not only reasoning and square holding are digested, but pure dictum as well. An editor can only rarely compress in the single sentence of the conventional digest paragraph the entire rule of the case, including the fact situation, how the case arose, relevant statutes and the other factors which go to determine the value of a given case as authority. There is no indication in the digest as to whether the rule of law stated in a given paragraph is square holding, reasoning or dictum, and in practice the majority of cases taken from the digest by the searcher will have to be discarded as unsuitable after careful examination. Human errors are another factor affecting the use made of digests. While errors occur only infrequently, they do occur. The inadvertent omission of a "not" may cause the digest to state exactly the reverse of the rule of the case. The digester may have misunderstood the case, particularly if a technical or scientific rule was involved.

§16.4. **Scope of digests.** Digests vary greatly in scope. The American Digest System is the most comprehensive of all in its coverage. Since the National Reporter System reports many cases not elsewhere covered, the American Digest System also digests cases not elsewhere digested. Other digests cover the various units of the National Reporter System — such as the Atlantic, Pacific, or Federal — separate states, or individual courts, such as the Supreme Court of the United States or the United States Court of Claims; or single topics, such as patents, labor relations or taxation.

§16.5. **American Digest System.**[1] The American Digest System is the most comprehensive of all American case digests, and its various units are said by its publisher to cover all standard law reports from appellate courts rendering written decisions from 1658 to date. It also digests selective opinions from certain courts of first instance, such as the federal district courts and some lower state courts.

[1] St. Paul, Minn., West Publishing Co.

1. *Units of the American Digest System.* The System is composed of the Century Edition and the various Decennial Digests, as supplemented by the bound volumes and monthly pamphlet issues of the General Digest. These units are shown in the table in Exhibit 37.

TABLE
SHOWING PERIOD OF TIME

COVERED BY EACH UNIT OF THE

# AMERICAN DIGEST SYSTEM

TOGETHER WITH

## VOLUMES OF DIGEST WHERE TABLES OF CASES WILL BE FOUND

| YEARS | DIGEST UNIT | TABLE OF CASES WHERE FOUND |
|---|---|---|
| 1658–1896 | Century | First Decennial, vols. 21–25 |
| 1897–1906 | First Decennial | First Decennial, vols. 21–25 |
| 1907–1916 | Second Decennial | Second Decennial, vol. 24 |
| 1916–1926 | Third Decennial | Third Decennial, vol. 29 |
| 1926–1936 | Fourth Decennial | Fourth Decennial, vol. 31 |
| 1936–1946 | Fifth Decennial | Fifth Decennial, vols. 48–49 |
| 1946–1956 | Sixth Decennial | Sixth Decennial, vols. 35–36 |
| 1956–1966 | Seventh Decennial | Seventh Decennial, vols. 37–38 |
| 1966–to date | General Digest, Fourth Series | General Digest, vol. 1–to date |

Exhibit 37

Note that each Decennial begins and ends in midyear, in a year whose final digit is a six, covering the terms of court and not the calendar year. The table shown is to be found immediately following the title page of each bound volume of the General Digest into which the Reporter advance sheets cumulate and which, in term, cumulates into the Decennials.

The Century Edition, the predecessor of the Decennials, covers the years 1658-1896. Its class subdivisions are called sections as in other digests, and do not correspond precisely in coverage to the Key Numbers adopted in the First Decennial and continued to date. As is shown in Exhibit 43, page 197, a parallel conversion table in volume 21 of the First Decennial translates from the Century section numbers to the Decennial Key Numbers.

The Decennials, as their name indicates, cumulate every ten

years from the General Digest.  The General Digest is, first, a monthly pamphlet supplement to the Decennial, and itself cumulates approximately every four months into a bound volume which in turn is superseded every ten years by the Decennial compiled from it.  Each National Reporter System advance sheet has its own Key Number digest in miniature for cases printed in it, cumulating each month in the pamphlet General Digest, as noted above. The routine of a complete American Digest System search, therefore, may carry through the Century, the Decennials, the bound and unbound General, and the various advance sheets later than the latest General pamphlet.

a. *Table showing reports digested in each unit.*  In order to pinpoint a search chronologically it is necessary to determine that all pertinent report volumes have been covered in the digest consulted.  This is easily done for the General Digest and the Decennials, beginning with the Third Decennial, by a table on the page following the table of contents in each volume.  As will be noted in Exhibit 38 below, not only are all the Reporter System units digested in the present Decennials, but also official reports.

2. *Classification scheme of the American Digest System.*  The seven great subdivisions of the rules of law announced in the cases — that is, the law of persons, property, contracts, torts, crimes, remedies and government — are expanded into chapters or main topic headings.  These, e.g., "Abandonment," "Aviation," "Chattel Mortgages," may be said to correspond somewhat to the division of a treatise into chapters, except that the order of placement in the digest is alphabetical by chapter heading instead of by logical progression of subjects.  These headings correspond to the lawyer's conventional conception of the divisions of the law as taught in law school.  A list of these main topics is found in the front of every volume of the digests, beginning with the Fourth Decennial, and the breakdown affords a useful elimination process for topics to be or not to be searched.  There are some blind spots. For example, there is no topic or subtopic for conflict of laws, and the cases involving conflicts, as scattered through the various main topics, are best found through "Conflict of Laws" in the Descriptive-Word Indexes of the digest.

3. *Scope-Note and Analysis.*  Each of the main topics of the digest has a "Scope-Note" and an "Analysis," as shown in Exhibit 39 below.

a. *Scope-Note.*  This has the obvious function of listing the principal subject matter included in a given main topic, and, by implication, of excluding subject matter not treated.  The use of this device avoids waste of time in searching in appropriate topics.

# REPORTERS AND REPORTS

### COVERED BY

## SIXTH DECENNIAL DIGEST

| REPORTER OR REPORT | From | To |
|---|---|---|
| Atlantic | 46 A.2d 1 | 121 A.2d 728 |
| Federal | 153 F.2d 305 | 230 F.2d 792 |
| Federal Rules Decisions | 5 F.R.D. 108 | 18 F.R.D. 517 |
| Federal Supplement | 64 F.Supp. 233 | 138 F.Supp. 959 |
| New York Supplement | 60 N.Y.S.2d 185 | 149 N.Y.S.2d 896 |
| North Eastern | 65 N.E.2d 417 | 133 N.E.2d 256 |
| North Western | 21 N.W.2d 881 | 75 N.W.2d 840 |
| Pacific | 166 P.2d 593 | 295 P.2d 400 |
| South Eastern | 37 S.E.2d 1 | 92 S.E.2d 88 |
| Southern | 25 So.2d 57 | 86 So.2d 368 |
| South Western | 192 S.W.2d 577 | 288 S.W.2d 320 |
| Supreme Court | 66 S.Ct. 686 | 76 S.Ct. 558 |
| Alaska | 10 Alaska 1 | 15 Alaska 688 |
| U. S. Court of Customs and Patent Appeals | 33 C.C.P.A. Customs 1 | 41 C.C.P.A. Customs 246 |
| U. S. Court of Claims | 103 Ct.Cl. 1 | 131 Ct.Cl. 800 |
| Hawaii | 37 Hawaii 1 | 40 Hawaii 738 |

**Exhibit 38**

For example, if a guardian and ward problem related to the marriage or divorce of the ward, a trust for him, or workmen's compensation awards, you would look in vain under "Guardian and Ward" for precedents. The procedure would be either to look under the main topics of "Marriage," "Divorce," "Trusts," or "Workmen's Compensation," or to look in the Descriptive-Word Index (described at page 200, par. e) under "Guardian and Ward," with subentries under the above subjects. The relationship of a ship's captain to his crew would also be found under either "Guardian and Ward" in this index or as a spot reference in it under "Ship's Captain."

16-6th D—959

# GUARDIAN AND WARD

*Scope-Note.*

INCLUDES general guardianship, particularly of the persons and estates of infants, by nature or under parental or judicial appointment; rights, powers, duties, and liabilities of guardians in respect of the persons and property of their wards; and legal proceedings relating thereto.

**Matters not in this topic, treated elsewhere, see Descriptive-Word Index.**

*Analysis.*

I. GUARDIANSHIP IN GENERAL, ☜1–7.

II. APPOINTMENT, QUALIFICATION, AND TENURE OF GUARDIAN, ☜8–27.

III. CUSTODY AND CARE OF WARD'S PERSON AND ESTATE, ☜28–74.

IV. SALES AND CONVEYANCES UNDER ORDER OF COURT, ☜75–115.

V. ACTIONS, ☜116–136,

VI. ACCOUNTING AND SETTLEMENT, ☜137–165.

VII. FOREIGN AND ANCILLARY GUARDIANSHIP, ☜166–172.

VIII. LIABILITIES ON GUARDIANSHIP BONDS, ☜173–182.

---

I. GUARDIANSHIP IN GENERAL.
    ☜1. The relation in general.
    2. Power to control guardianship.
    3. What law governs.
    4. Guardians by nature.
    5. Guardians in socage.
    6. Volunteer and de facto guardians.
    7. Estoppel to deny guardianship.

II. APPOINTMENT, QUALIFICATION, AND TENURE OF GUARDIAN.
    ☜8. Jurisdiction of courts.
    9. Family meetings.
    9½. Persons for whom guardians may be appointed.
    10. Persons who may be appointed.
    11. Appointment by deed or will.
    12. Appointment of undertutor.
    13. Proceedings for judicial appointment.
        (1). In general.
        (2). Inventory.
        (3). Application, parties, and notice.
        (4). Evidence.
        (5). Discontinuance.
        (6). Temporary guardian.
        (7). Findings and order.
        (8). Review.

Exhibit 39

b. *Analysis.* This device splits the main topic into workable smaller concepts by which the searcher skilled in the law is enabled to arrive speedily at the proper Key Number. In any fairly large topic the main analysis is subject to a further breakdown into sub-analyses and, as in "Guardian and Ward ☜ 13(1)" in Exhibit 39, even into sub-subanalyses. In such large topics as "Evidence," "Internal Revenue," or "Patents," there may be as many as 2500 subdivisions or Key Numbers. It is this detailed analysis, leading to the appropriate Key Number, that forms the basis of the so-called "analytical approach" to the case law, as described in §16.6.

c. *Application of the Analysis to other Key Number digests.* All National Reporter System case reports syllabi or headnote paragraphs are Key Numbered. The Key Number thus assigned is uniform throughout the West Publishing Company digests, so that when a pertinent Key Number is found in any Reporter case, like subject matter will be found under it in any West digest. Thus, in the "Guardian and Ward" example, the case in 80 N.E.2d, as shown in Exhibit 39, is digested under the Key Number "Guardian and Ward 126, Parties" in the North Eastern Reporter. Under that identical Key Number, cases involving like subject matter from all jurisdictions are digested in all Decennial Digest units, in the monthly General Digest units supplementing the latest Decennial, in the North Eastern Reporter Digest, and in all West state digests for cases decided as far back as 1896.

Cases decided before mid-1896 are digested in the Century Digest, covering from 1658 to 1896. Since the *section* numbers of the Century Digest do not agree precisely with the Decennial Digest *Key Numbers,* a simple additional step is necessary to find the earlier cases corresponding to those digested under "Guardian and Ward 126." A boldface cross reference immediately under the Key Number heading in both the First and Second Decennials cites the appropriate Century Digest section number or numbers. Thus the Key Number above is covered in the Century Digest by §§430-432 and 434-437. An example of this cross reference is shown in Exhibit 44, page 198.

Although the digests mentioned as part of the West system are substantially uniform in makeup, a given West state digest may contain additional features of local interest; the same is true, of course, of digests by other publishers. There are individual state digests for nearly every state.

4. *Digest paragraphs.* The digest paragraphs themselves are the meat of the digests, containing as they do the statements of rules of law taken from the decided cases. They are arranged by subject under the Key Number classification. Under each Key Number the paragraphs are arranged by jurisdiction, and under jurisdiction by date of decision. Through the Fifth Decennial this date in boldface type was given with the digest paragraph, but in later issues it is rarely seen in the Decennial or General Digests, though

it is retained in the Modern Federal Practice Digest.   This seems an unfortunate omission.

United States Supreme Court cases come first; then come Courts of Appeals cases, followed by those of the federal district courts, alphabetically by state district; then the state court cases, alphabetically by state, with the digest paragraphs in each state arranged in the descending order of court rank.   These digest paragraphs differ from the original syllabi or headnotes of the Reporter cases from which they are taken, only in that they often contain additional citator information (affirmances, reversals, etc., on appeal) not available when the case was first printed and digested.   That is, if the case digested has been the subject of later court treatment on rehearing or appeal before the publication of the digest in which it is digested, that fact is noted with citation to the rehearing or appeal cases.   Exhibit 40 illustrates this.

5. *Auxiliary tables and indexes.*   The digests are so voluminous and complex as to require a variety of tables and indexes to render them workable.   American Digest System tables and indexes, typical of them all, are described below.

a. *Tables of cases.*   The table of cases provides one of the most effective of all approaches to the law because, as shown in Exhibit 40 below, it lists for each case all Key Numbers under which that case has been digested.   Thus, when in some manner — as in a footnote citation in a treatise, encyclopedia, law review article or in another case — a case in point has been cited, recourse to the table of cases will lead through the Key Number listings to all other cases in point.

Each digest unit has its own table of cases, giving the information shown in the exhibit below.

**Lane v. Endicott Johnson Corp,** Sup,
75 NYS2d 171, aff 274 AppDiv 833,
80 NYS2d 639, app den 274 App
Div 855, 82 NYS2d 387, aff 299 NY
725, 87 NE2d 450, cert den 70 SCt
243, 338 US 892, 94 LEd 548—Arb
& Aw 36; Labor 263, 433, 436, 453;
Mast & S 3(2).

**Exhibit 40**

It will be noted that, in addition to listing the pertinent Key Numbers under which the digest paragraphs are classified, later court action, if any, on this *identical* case is noted.   To this limited extent the Decennial tables serve as case citators.   See also Exhibit 41 below.

# TABLE OF CASES

### ABBREVIATIONS

| | | | |
|---|---|---|---|
| aff | ..................... affirmed | mod | ................. modified |
| am | ..................... amended | rearg | ................. reargument |
| cert | ................. certiorari | reh | ................. rehearing |
| den | ..................... denied | rev | ................. reversed |
| dism | ................. dismissed | transf | ................. transferred |
| foll | ................. followed | vac | ..................... vacated |
| gr | ..................... granted | | |

---

### References are to Digest Topics and Key Numbers

---

## A

A v. B, Ark, 233 SW2d 629—Adop 7, 14.

A A Bennett, Inc v. Minneapolis Gas Co, CAMinn, 227 F2d 665. See Arena Co v. Minneapolis Gas Co.

Aaberg v. People, Colo, 183 P2d 260 —Larc 40(2), 68(1); Sales 11, 208.

A A Bush, Contractor v. Watkins, Miss, 80 So2d 19. See Bush v. Watkins.

Aaby v. Better Builders, Minn, 37 NW 2d 234—Mech Liens 5, 157(4, 5), 290(4); Trial 401.

Aaby v. States Marine Corp, CANY, 181 F2d 383, cert den 71 SCt 66— Ship 38, 42(1, 7), 58(2¾).

Aaby v. States Marine Corp, DCNY, 80 FSupp 328, aff 181 F2d 383, cert den 71 SCt 66—Ship 38, 42(1), 51 (7), 58(1, 2¾).

A Arena & Co v. U S, DCCal, 103 F Supp 505—Evid 574; Int Rev 951.

Aarnes v. Aarnes 172 La 648, 135 So 13—Divorce 411, 416(2).

Aaron v. Agwilines, Inc, DCNY, 75 F Supp 604—Courts 274(13), 276; FedCivProc 492, 500.

Aaron v. Bay Ridge Operating Co C CANY, 162 F2d 665, mod 68 SCt 1186, reh den 69 SCt 19 and Huron Stevedoring Corp v. Blue 69 SCt 11—FedCivProc 2281, 2744; Labor 1278.

Aaron v. Bay Ridge Operating Co, CANY, 204 F2d 88. See Addison v. Huron Stevedoring Corp.

Aaron v. Bay Ridge Operating Co, D CNY, 69 FSupp 956. See Addison v. Huron Stevedoring Corp.

Aaron v. Bay Bridge Operating Co, DCNY, 96 FSupp 142. See Addison v. Huron Stevedoring Corp.

See Com ex rel Aaron v. Court of Quarter Sessions of Westmoreland County.

Aaron's Estate v. C I R, CA3, 224 F 2d 314—Int Rev 1000.

Aarons v. Board of Medical Examiners, CalApp, 176 P2d 706, subsequent opinion 187 P2d 8—Phys 4.

Aarons v. Local 32-E, Bldg Service Emp Intern Union, Sup, 52 NYS2d 262—Labor 455, 456, 482; Mast & 8 7.

Aarons v. U S, CAMo, 200 F2d 828 —Courts 361; Land & Ten 200.74, 200.76; War 219, 220.

Aaronson v. U S, CAMd, 175 F2d 41— Crim Law 29, 59(5), 200(3); Larc 27; Rec 8 Goods 6.

Aaronson Bros Paper Corp v. Fishko, Sup, 144 NYS2d 543, aff 148 NYS2d

Exhibit 41

This table's citator function is supplemented by a monthly table in the General Digest, as shown in Exhibit 42.

The case tables always give the Reporter citation when there is one. If, at the time the Decennial table is prepared for the press, the official report and the A.L.R. reports have been published, their citations also are included. Unfortunately these reports, with their volume and page numbers, are frequently not then available, so that the alternative citations may be lacking. The Decennial case tables, therefore, are not always the best means by which to determine the parallel citations — official, Reporter and A.L.R. — for a given case. If only the Reporter citation is given, take it for checking to the appropriate Shepard's Reporter Citations (Atlantic, Pacific, etc.) which will give the official and A.L.R. citations, if available.

The Decennial case table is supplemented by the monthly General Digest pamphlets, which cumulate approximately every four months into a bound volume with its own cumulative case table

# TABLE OF CASES

**References are to Digest Topics and Key Numbers**

## A

**Abel v. Board of Works of City of Elizabeth,** NJSuperAD, 164 A2d 764—App & E 169, 170(1), 181, 756, 757(1), 773(2); Courts 82, 85(1); Judgm 665, 715(1, 3); Zoning 29, 153, 193, 484, 653, 654, 743.

**A B Lewis Co v. Robinson,** TexCivApp, 339 SW2d 731—Corp 498; Evid 543(4), 553(1); Plead 139; Princ & A 169(3); Sales 477(5), 481; Tresp 45(5), 67; Trial 395(7).

**Absher v. Illinois Cent R Co,** Ky, 339 SW2d 874—Judgm 185.3(17); Mast & S 78.4(1); Trusts 105.

**Acker v. Karosen,** Sup, 207 NYS2d 16. See Leventhal v. Acker.

**Alford v. Emory University,** Ga, 116 SE2d 596—Plead 214(1); Tax 242 (2), 498.

**Allen v. Coal Operators Cas Co,** LaApp, 124 So2d 344—Evid 574; Work Comp 1420, 1652.

**Allen v. Travelers Ins Co,** LaApp, 124 So2d 367—Work Comp 64, 105, 110, 111, 134, 155, 159, 1319.

**Allison v. Ely,** Ind, 170 NE2d 371—App & E 882(11); Autos 181(2), 244(20), 245(24); Trial 176.

**Allison v. Unemployment Compensation Bd of Review,** PaSuper, 165 A2d 125—Social S 388, 584, 655, 662, 665.

**Amato v. R R Heywood Co,** AD3d, 206 NYS2d 626—Work Comp 1509.

**Ambrose v. Singleton,** Colo, 356 P2d 253—Wills 840.

**Archer-Daniels-Midland Co v. Paull,** DCArk, 188 FSupp 277—Bankr 145 (1), 146, 150, 152; Contracts 28(3), 322(3), 350(1); Damag 40(2), 125; Joint Adv 8.

**Archuleta v. Landers,** NM, 356 P2d 443—App & E 919; Judgm 460(4); Jury 25(2), 28(3, 9); Proc 96(4); Quiet T 35(3), 36, 37(1); Ven & Pur 242.

**Argroe v. Marinaccio,** NJSuperAD, 164 A2d 809—Work Comp 662, 766.

**Argroe v. Morris Plains Amoco Service Station,** NJSuperAD, 164 A2d 809. See Argroe v. Marinaccio.

**Aris Gloves, Inc v. U S,** CustCt, 188 FSupp 50—Cust Dut 10; Notice 9.

**Arkansas Real Estate Co v. Fullerton,** Ark, 339 SW2d 947—App & E 262

Exhibit 42

for the period covered, which in turn cumulates at the end of ten years into a new Decennial case table.

Reporter advance sheets list the cases reported in each issue. A complete table of cases search, then, depending upon the period to be covered, may include the Decennials, the bound volumes of the General Digest since the latest Decennial, the monthly pamphlet issues since the latest bound volumes of the General Digest, and the advance sheets of the appropriate Reporter units for the month subsequent to the latest pamphlet issues of the General Digest.

The same case may be listed several times in a table, each appearance representing a different stage of the case's progress through the courts. In such a listing the case on appeal to the Supreme Court of the United States is listed first, even though decided later than some of the state actions. Thus *Kalb* v. *Luce,* a Wisconsin case, is listed six times in the Fifth Decennial table of cases because of a variety of appeals and rehearings, culminating in an appeal to the United States Supreme Court. Care must be taken, therefore, in searching the table, to ascertain the final disposition of the case being searched. This is particularly true of a case decided in a year ending with the digit 6, because the Decennial coverage follows the court term period of that year; a case decided in April 1946 might be listed in the Fifth Decennial, while one decided in October would be in the Sixth Decennial.

The name of a case may be changed on appeal if the defendant in the case below lost and appeals to a higher court. Thus *Colver*

v. *Skeffington* in the federal district court may be listed as *Skeffington* v. *Colver* in the table of cases covering the U.S. Court of Appeals report of that case on appeal.

(1) *Defendant-Plaintiff case tables.* Decennial Digest case tables are Plaintiff-Defendant tables only. Most digest tables now, however, including many by West, have Defendant-Plaintiff tables also; that is, the cases are listed alphabetically by defendant's last name. Usually these tables refer back to the Plaintiff-Defendant table, where full information is given.

(2) *Popular-name case tables.* Beginning with the table of cases volume of the Second Decennial Digest, each table of cases volume has a table of cases which are known or cited by popular name, such as the *Apex* case, *Danbury Hatters'* case, and *Hot Oil* case. Customarily these tables give the same information as do the other case tables described above. For other popular-name tables, see page 353, par. e.

b. *Parallel transfer tables from Century to Decennial Digest or reverse.* The Century Digest, covering 1658 to mid-1896, is classified by *section numbers,* the Decennials by *Key Numbers.* To facilitate search, however, there are parallel conversion tables from the Centennial to the Decennials, so that, having found a Centennial section number, the searcher can easily find the equivalent Key Number in the Decennial. Pink-paper Tables of Key Number Sections for Century Digest are found in volume 21 of the First Decennial, which cite in parallel from the Century topic and section number to the corresponding Decennial Key Number. Thus "Contribution 20" of the Century is here seen to be equivalent to "Contribution 9(5)" of the Decennial.

CENTURY DIGEST SECTIONS WITH CORRESPONDING KEY–NUMBERS A 51

CONTRIBUTION

| Dec. & Cent. Key No. | | Dec. & Cent. Key No. | | Dec. & Cent. Key No. | | Dec. & Cent. Key No. | | Dec. & Cent. Key No. | | Dec. & Cent. Key No. | | Dec. & Cent. Key No. | |
|---|---|---|---|---|---|---|---|---|---|---|---|---|---|
| Sec. | Sec. | Sec. | Sec. | Sec. | Sec. | Sec. | Sec. | Sec. | Sec. | Sec. | Sec. | Sec. | Sec. |
| 1 | 1 | 5 | 3 | 9 | 5 | 13 | 7 | 17 | 9(3) | 18 | 9(2) | 21 | 9(6) |
| 2 | 3 | 6 | 5 | 10 | 6 | 14 | 9(1) | | Lim. of | 19 | 9(4) | 23 | 9(8) |
| 3 | 4 | 7 | 5 | 11 | 6 | 15 | 8 | | Act. | 20 | 9(5) | | |
| 4 | 4 | 8 | 5 | 12 | 6 | 16 | Eq. 44 | | 49(1-8) | | | | |

Exhibit 43

Going from Key Number in the Decennial to section number in the Century is even simpler. In both the First and Second Decennials there is a "See" reference beneath each boldface Key Number, referring to the corresponding Centennial section number.

21. Operation and effect.
See 11 Cent. Dig. Conversion, §§ 56-65.
Effect on right to maintain partition, see Partition, 21.

Exhibit 44

If the case to be pursued into the Century Digest is found in the Third or later Decennials, there is simply the added step of taking the Key Number reference into the Second Decennial, where the "See" reference to the Centennial will be found. With the exceptions noted below for certain new or expanded Decennial main topics, it is thus a simple mechanical matter, once a case in point is found and its Key Number or section numbers in point ascertained from the headnote paragraphs, to work back and forth through both the Centennial and the Decennials, finding all cases in point from 1658 to date.

c. *Key number change: Tables of new or expanded classification of topics.* Law changes, and digest classifications must change with it. In the Sixth Decennial, there were eight new or expanded topics; in the forthcoming Seventh there will be four. These new topics constitute, to the extent of requiring one additional step, an exception to the rule that, once having found a Key Number in point, the searcher merely needs to check all units of the American Digest System under that Key Number to find all other cases in point. When such changes are made in the Key Number classification for a topic, the editors reexamine all the reported cases from earliest time to date, regardless of the Key Numbers or sections under which they were originally reported. The classification scheme of the new topic is then developed and all pertinent cases are reclassified under the new topic. The digest paragraphs are then republished in the next pocket parts of the various state, regional and federal digests. In the American Digest System proper they are published in the next General Digest volume and are eventually merged into the next Decennial Digest. It is not possible, for example, having found the aviation case of *Montijo* v. *Samuel Goldwyn, Inc.,* 13 Cal. App. 57, 297 Pac. 949 (1931), and the Key Number of "Negligence 105" in the headnote of the Pacific Reporter report of that case, to go directly to the digest of the case and of like cases under the same Key Number in the Sixth and later Decennials. This is because digests of all aviation cases of whatever date have been reclassified in the Sixth Decennial, in a single volume, in a new topic, "Aviation." To find the new Key Number of the *Montijo* and like cases, the searcher merely consults the Sixth Decennial Table of Cases for the *Montijo* case, which tells him that the new Key Number covering the assumption of risk or contributory negligence of a stunt aviator is "Aviation ☞ 152."

In "Workmen's Compensation," in the Fourth Decennial, and in "Administrative Law and Procedure," in the Fifth Decennial, a special table of cases for each of the respective new volumes was supplied, listing all cases collected under the new topic, no matter what their publication dates, together with their newly assigned Key Numbers. Once having the name of the earlier case, therefore, the only step was to consult this supplementary table of cases, which would supply the new Key Number. Many lawyers, however, overlooked the existence of these special tables of cases and they failed of their purpose.

The Decennial Digest practice now is to *list all cases, old and new, of whatever date,* which are collected in the new or expanded digest topic, *in the general table of cases for the Decennial unit in which the new topic first appears.* For example, the names of all aviation cases of whatever date, reported through mid-1956, are listed in the Sixth Decennial table.

In either situation — whether a special table of cases is provided or all cases of whatever date up to the inclusion of their digests in the new Decennial Digest topic are listed in the general table of cases for that decennium — there is just the one additional step, that of going forward from the old to the new Key Number through the table of cases in the Decennial for the decennium in which the new or expanded topic first appeared.

As a rule *there is no cross-reference table from the former Key Number to the new one.* This leaves it to the alertness of the searcher to discover that the old Key Number is no longer appropriate and to search in the case tables of later Decennials under the old case name for the current Key Number.

*Parallel transfer tables between the old and new Key Numbers have been provided,* however, in the Seventh Decennial for the revised Insurance topic and the new Secured Transactions topic. The latter topic stems from the adoption of the Uniform Commercial Code. In both instances, tables from the new to the old and from the old to the new Key Numbers are provided.

d. *Key Number tables in the General Digest.* These are tables cumulated in the bound volumes of the General Digest Descriptive-Word Index and supplemented at irregular intervals by a pamphlet, Cumulative Table of Key Numbers. The tables are designed to avoid the necessity of searching through as many as thirty interim volumes of the General Digest for which there are no digests under a given Key Number therein. In Exhibit 45, for example, the Key Number "Abatement and Revival ☜ 63" appears only once, in volume 7, in the first ten volumes of the General Digest; hence it would be fruitless to search the other volumes.

# TABLE OF KEY NUMBERS
## GENERAL DIGEST, VOLUMES 1–10 3d

---

**A Time Saver for Locating The Latest Cases**

---

**Example:** Having found a proposition of law under the topic Abandonment ☜6, refer to the same topic and Key in this table which will show that other cases appear in the General Digest, Third Series, Volumes 1, 3, 5, 6, 9, 10. Search is therefore unnecessary in Volumes 2, 4, 7 and 8 of the General Digest, Third Series.

---

| ABANDONMENT | ABATEMENT AND RE-VIVAL—Cont'd | ABSTRACTS OF TITLE | ACCOUNT—Cont'd |
|---|---|---|---|
| ☜ | ☜ | ☜ | ☜ |
| 2—1, 2, 3, 4, 5, 7, 9, 10 | 57—2, 4, 8, 10 | 1—7 | 7—7, 10 |
| 3—3, 7, 9 | 58—1, 3, 5, 6, 9 | 3—3, 7, 8, 10 | 9—7 |
| 4—3, 9, 10 | 58(1)—1, 2, 6, 7, 10 | | 11—2 |
| 5—2, 3, 5, 6, 7, 8, 9, 10 | 58(2)—1, 2, 7, 9 | ACCESSION | 12—3, 4, 6, 7 |
| 6—1, 3, 5, 6, 9, 10 | 61—7, 9 | 1—3, 4 | 14—1, 2, 3, 4, 5, 6, 9 |
| 7—1, 9 | 63—7 | 2—5, 6 | 15—4, 8 |
| | | | 16—8 |

Exhibit 45

e. *Descriptive-Word Index.* This is an enormous dictionary-like table, listing in alphabetical order words and phrases describing just about every fact situation arising in every case reported during the respective periods covered by each unit of the American Digest System.

Thus, if your case involves tomato paste adulteration, for example, you can find the principle involved through this table under "Tomato Paste." Or you may be interested in such terms as "war surplus," "sudden stopping," a tractor clutch gone wrong, etc. Worms-in-jam cases may be found under both "Worms" and "Jam."

In addition to the above catchwords, this table breaks up each of the 426 main topics of the Digest into workable, alphabetically arranged fact situations.

To provide for flexibility and ease in finding pertinent Key Numbers through the various units of this table, there is a great deal of duplication and overlapping of entries. Thus a situation involving an airplane passenger injured in a jumpy plane during rough weather is covered in the main topical headings of "Aviation" and "Carriers," and also through such fact situation entries as "Airlines," "Airplanes," "Passengers," etc.

The tables for the First and Second Decennials were combined, as were those for the Third and Fourth, but each of the subsequent ones has its own table. Each bound volume of the General Digest supplementing the latest Decennial has its own blue-paper Descriptive-Word Index, and for every ten volumes of the General Digest during a decennium there is a blue-cloth-bound supplement.

Every case digest, by whatever publisher, has such an index, under whatever name the publisher chooses to give it. It is the means employed in the fact approach to the law described at page 286, par. 4, and page 356, par. 4.

§16.6. **Techniques of use of the American Digest System.**

1. *Preliminary problem analysis.* First, analyze the facts of your situation so as to clear away deadwood and restrict consideration to those elements necessary to the solution of your problem:

What parties are involved?

How did the case arise, how did it find its way to this court?

What is the subject matter — tort, contract, crime?

Is a statute involved?

What is the cause of action?

What remedy is sought?

Not all these elements are likely to be vital in any single problem. In a contract case the fact that the plaintiff is an infant may be controlling, whereas it might be of no importance in a tort. Whether a case involves the admissibility of evidence, want of jurisdiction, or an improper charge to a jury may determine the applicability of digested cases to the problem at hand. A case decided on a statute is unlikely to be useful precedent if no such statute is involved. Nor is a prayer for a preliminary injunction apt to lead to a decision on the merits of a substantive fact situation.

2. *Approaches to the law through the digest.* There are four standard modes of procedure for finding cases in point through the American Digest System or any other standard digest. The specific illustrations given in the discussion below, while simple, are typical of the reasoning and routines to be followed in pursuing the respective techniques. On the other hand, the student should remember that in actual practice a case exactly on all fours

as to the facts and law of his own problem is uncommon and that he must usually be content with a reasonable approximation of the fact situation as applicable to the rule of law involved. Very often the cases in several different Key Number classifications must be fully searched before the right one is found.

a. *Table of cases approach.* This is one of the most effective and the simplest of the approaches to the law. When by some means or other — a footnote citation in a treatise, encyclopedia or casebook, or in a law report — you have found a case in point, you are well on your way. Tracing the case by name in the table to cases leads you immediately to the Key Numbers under which your case has been digested, and through them to all other cases in point. If you have the Reporter containing the case, you can get from the headnote paragraphs the exact Key Numbers you want, and will not need to consult the case table. If not, and you do not know the date of the case, it may be necessary to search through several of the Decennial Digests units. But see §16.5c

Since the table of cases technique is common to nearly all books which print or discuss law reports, and since there are a number of problems common to all, it is described in greater detail in Chapter 25, Coordinating the Research Techniques.

b. *Fact or Descriptive-Word Index approach.* Legal questions arise out of fact situations. Accordingly all digests provide exhaustive indexes to fact situations as found in the reported cases. The one in the American Digest System, the largest in size and scope, is called the Descriptive-Word Index. By means of this index the searcher for Key Numbers in point can usually so analyze the pertinent facts of his case as to be able to seize upon one or more words which tie in so significantly with the legal consequences involved as to lead him to the desired Key Numbers.

Thus a dining-car waiter whose duties require him to polish the silver sues his railroad under a workmen's compensation statute because of resulting dermatitis. Various pertinent facts call for attention here: dining car, waiter, silver polish, railroad, workmen's compensation, and dermatitis, among others. Of these, "Railroads" and "Workmen's Compensation" are main topics in the Digest, legal words of art or legal concepts. The others are strictly fact words, or catchwords. The least common denominator of these various words is "dermatitis," and under it in the Descriptive-Word Index Key Numbers in point will be found. The same Key Numbers in point will also be found under some of the other words above, but perhaps requiring one or more additional steps. Thus:

WORKMEN'S COMPENSATION
DERMATITIS, SEE DERMATITIS

The Descriptive-Word Index is an enormous dictionary-type affair; that is, with all words and terms arranged in a single, great alphabet, and not systematically by legal concept. In this single alphabet are found both catchwords and main topic heads. The arrangement under the main topic heads — which are almost always legal words of art — is very largely by catchwords, as in the "Workmen's Compensation" example above, rather than by legal concepts. Thus the catchwords — like "Dermatitis," "Quonset Huts," "One-legged Race" — are found under the main legal topic involved and as separate entries. The problem below, illustrated by Exhibit 46, taken from the Fifth Decennial Digest, shows how the fact-index approach works.

(1) *Problem illustrating the fact approach.* A woman brings an action to recover for injuries received when she jumped from a stalled automobile at a railroad crossing and was struck by one of a line of boxcars which was suddenly discovered to be backing toward the automobile. Several main topics are involved here — railroads, torts, negligence, automobiles, and damages — but they are all very large and the analysis to the desired point is not very obvious, though it can be made. However, two special facts are present — that the accident occurred at a *railroad crossing* and that a train *backed* into the plaintiff at that crossing. Further thought reveals that the totality of crossing accidents is greater than those caused at such crossings by backing trains. Therefore, by a process taking much less time to carry out than to describe, "backing" is determined to be the smallest significant fact, the least common denominator. Examination of "backing" in the Fifth Decennial Digest Descriptive-Word Index leads to the subentry "Trains," with a further subdivision under "Crossing accidents," where fact situations are noted, with pertinent Key Numbers. See Exhibit 46.

The Descriptive-Word Index so meticulously picks out all pertinent fact situations, however, that the probable Key Numbers could have been found in the example above through several different entries under "Automobiles," "Crossings," "Railroads," etc., but not quite so quickly as under "Backing."

The above is purely a catchword problem, depending upon the unusual situation of "backing" for its easy solution. In numerous instances, however, no such decisive catchword is available and a closer scrutiny of the facts must be made, requiring the examina-

**BACKING** (Cont'd)

TRAILER into highway, contributory negligence of motorist. **Autos 245(67)**

TRAINS—
  Contributory negligence of motorist crossing. **R R 327(1), 333(1)**
  Crossing accidents, **R R 310**
    Absence of license signals as negligence as jury question. **R R 350(8)**
    Amendment of pleading affecting limitations. **Lim of Act 127(14)**
    Contributory negligence of—
      Automobile guest. **R R 350(21)**
      Motorist, reliance on precautions on part of railroad. **R R 330(1–3)**
    Gross negligence. **R R 310**
    Instruction, conformity to pleadings and issues. **R R 351(2)**
    Last clear chance. **R R 338**
    Question for jury. **R R 350(8)**
      Darkness. **R R 350(26)**
      Proximate cause. **R R 350(32)**
    Pleading cause of action under last clear chance doctrine. **R R 344(10)**
  Duty as to lookout for employees in yard. **R R 369(3)**

Exhibit 46

tion of the detailed alphabetical analyses under the main topics in the Descriptive-Word Index. For example, the guest knowingly riding in an automobile driven by an intoxicated driver, to his consequent injury in an accident, seeks recovery. The significant words here are "passenger," "guest," "intoxicated driver," and "automobile," and under these words, directly or indirectly, the proper Key Numbers can be found. Proper legal analysis, however, shows that the real point at issue is the passenger's contributory negligence in knowingly riding with an intoxicated driver. Under the main topic of "Contributory Negligence," the pertinent Key Numbers are given under half a dozen subheads — "Automobiles"; "Intoxicated Driver, driving with"; "Guest, driving with intoxicated host"; "Intoxicated Persons, riding with" — with cross references to other pertinent topics. The proper Key Number is thus speedily found.

Since there are several different units of the Descriptive-Word Index, covering as many different periods of time, common sense must be employed in using them. For example, as few people were purchasing radios and automobile tires on the installment plan between 1896 and 1916, the period covered by the Descriptive-Word Index for the first two Decennials, a search in this unit for a case involving such transactions would probably be useless.

However, in the next unit, covering the Third and Fourth Decennial during the next twenty years, such a search would be fruitful. Similarly, atomic energy was not involved in any cases digested in the Fifth Decennial, but the Descriptive-Word Index covering a later period does include such entries.

In searching the Descriptive-Word Index, remember that the Index for the latest Decennial is supplemented by a blue-paper supplement for each volume of the General Digest, and that for every ten volumes of the General Digest these paper supplements are cumulated into a bound volume.

c. *Analytical or topical approach.* It is often quicker to find the Key Numbers in point through legal analysis than by the fact approach.

Having a set of facts but no case in point and with no salient catchword pointing to the Descriptive-Word Index, how is the pertinent Key Number to be found analytically?

First, a preliminary analysis should be made to determine whether the problem is one of persons, property, contracts, torts, crimes, remedies, or government. The next step will further break your problem down into a much smaller subdivision of the law, as admiralty, damages, husband and wife, or tenancy. These are recognizable as logically belonging to one of the 426 subjects in the List of Digest Topics found in the front of each volume of the Decennials, beginning with the Fourth. Most such topics are fairly obvious. For example, a contract of insurance leads to "Insurance" rather than to "Contracts," because insurance is a smaller and more workable subdivision of the law of contracts. Similarly, a problem on the admissibility of evidence falls within the topic "Evidence." Others may not be so obvious and require more careful analysis. The proper recipient of the proceeds of a deceased's life insurance might be a problem in insurance, equity, or marshaling of assets. Perhaps your pertinent Key Numbers can be found under all. In this the Scope-Note and the Analysis at the head of each main topic help. The following is a simple, but typical, example of how the analytical approach works.

(1) *Problem illustrating the analytical approach.* Your client, who occupies a loft building for manufacturing purposes, has had some of his goods damaged by the overflow of water from that part of the premises in the same building occupied by the defendant and under his control. The defendant admits the overflow. Damages are involved, but liability must first be established. Since the parties are both tenants of a building, the Digest topic "Landlord and Tenant" seems obvious. Checking the main analysis of that topic enables the searcher to discard all subtopics but

"VII. Premises, and Enjoyment and Use Thereof," as shown in Exhibit 47, page 207.

Most large topics, such as Landlord and Tenant, have also a subanalysis to afford a further breakdown of the main topics. A check of subtopic VII in the subanalysis speedily suggests that "E. Injuries from Dangerous or Defective Conditions" be examined, for which see Exhibit 48, page 208.

It will be noted that this subanalysis leads to the ultimate analysis, which is the actual Key Number itself. Thus this subanalysis under E suggests Key Numbers ☞ 163 and ☞ 166, especially ☞ 166(9). Searching under this latter Key Number, all the way backward through the First Decennial and forward through the General Digest bound volumes and blue monthly pamphlets, locates all cases in point from 1896 to date. Examining "Landlord and Tenant ☞ 166(9)" in the Second Decennial reveals a notation in boldface type that this subject matter is collected in the Century Digest, covering cases back to 1658, in "Landlord and Tenant, §§657 and 658." The Table of Key Numbers shown in Exhibit 45, covering the bound volumes of the General Digest, discloses the only volumes of that digest which include any cases under either number shown. This makes it unnecessary to search any others of these interim volumes for cases in point. A complete search would include also the advance sheets of Reporters not yet covered by the monthly pamphlets of the General Digest.

d. *Words and phrases approach to the law.* Courts are often called upon to define words or terms, the meanings of which are in dispute. These judicial definitions are printed as headnote paragraphs in the Reporter and then collected in alphabetical order in a dictionary of many volumes, called Words and Phrases. The words so defined may be legal words of art, like "fine," "forced heir," or "forgery," but frequently consist of words in common use, like "flat stones," "flax," "flight crew," or "food." Such dictionaries and the approach to the law through them are discussed in Chapter 21.

3. *Progress from unit to unit of the Digest, for full coverage.* In practice, since most lawyers are more interested in the latest cases in point than in a historical survey, they are likely to begin their search with the General Digest and work backward to the First Decennial and thence to the Century. It should be remembered that a full search may include: (1) the Century Digest; (2) all Decennial Digests; (3) all bound volumes and monthly pamphlets of the General Digest; and (4) National Reporter System advance sheets to date.

29–5th D—197

# LANDLORD AND TENANT

*Scope-Note.*

INCLUDES nature and incidents of estates for years and tenancies from year to year, at will, or at sufferance; leases and agreements for the occupation of real property in general, the relation between the parties thereto, and their rights and liabilities as between themselves and as to others incident to such relation; and remedies relating thereto.

**Matters not in this topic, treated elsewhere, see Descriptive-Word Index.**

*Analysis.*

I. CREATION AND EXISTENCE OF THE RELATION, ☞1–19.

II. LEASES AND AGREEMENTS IN GENERAL, ☞20–49.
    A. REQUISITES AND VALIDITY, ☞20–36.
    B. CONSTRUCTION AND OPERATION, ☞37–49.

III. LANDLORD'S TITLE AND REVERSION, ☞50–69.
    A. RIGHTS AND POWERS OF LANDLORD, ☞50–60.
    B. ESTOPPEL OF TENANT, ☞61–69.

IV. TERMS FOR YEARS, ☞70–112½.
    A. NATURE AND EXTENT, ☞70–73.
    B. ASSIGNMENT, SUBLETTING, AND MORTGAGE, ☞74–81.
    C. EXTENSIONS, RENEWALS, AND OPTIONS TO PURCHASE OR SELL, ☞81½–92.
    D. TERMINATION, ☞93–112½.

V. TENANCIES FROM YEAR TO YEAR AND MONTH TO MONTH, ☞113–116.

VI. TENANCIES AT WILL AND AT SUFFERANCE, ☞117–120.

VII. PREMISES, AND ENJOYMENT AND USE THEREOF, ☞121–180.
    A. DESCRIPTION, EXTENT, AND CONDITION, ☞121–125.
    B. POSSESSION, ENJOYMENT, AND USE, ☞126–144.
    C. INCUMBRANCES, TAXES, AND ASSESSMENTS, ☞145–149.
    D. REPAIRS, INSURANCE, AND IMPROVEMENTS, ☞150–161.
    E. INJURIES FROM DANGEROUS OR DEFECTIVE CONDITION, ☞162–170.
    F. EVICTION, ☞171–180.

VIII. RENT AND ADVANCES, ☞181–274.
    A. RIGHTS AND LIABILITIES, ☞181–216.
    B. ACTIONS, ☞217–238.
    C. LIEN, ☞239–262½.
    D. DISTRESS, ☞263–274.

IX. RE-ENTRY AND RECOVERY OF POSSESSION BY LANDLORD, ☞275–318.

X. RENTING ON SHARES, ☞319–333.

Exhibit 47

17—3d Dec.Dig.,Page 1139     LANDLORD AND TENANT

**VII. Premises and Enjoyment and Use Thereof—Continued.**

   (E) INJURIES FROM DANGEROUS OR DEFECTIVE CONDITION.

        ⟜162. Nature and extent of landlord's duty to tenant.

        163. Mutual duties of tenants of different portions of same premises.

        164. Injuries to tenants or occupants.

            164 (1). Injuries due to defective or dangerous condition of premises in general.

            164 (2). Injuries due to failure to repair.

            164 (3). Injuries due to negligence in making repairs.

            164 (4). Injuries due to unlighted passageways.

            164 (5). Liability for injuries to subtenant.

            164 (6). Liability of landlord as dependent on knowledge of defects.

            164 (7). Notice to or knowledge of tenant as to defects.

        165. Injuries to employé of tenant.

            165 (1). Injuries due to defective or dangerous condition of premises in general.

            165 (2). Injuries due to failure to repair.

            165 (3). Injuries due to unlighted passageway.

            165 (4). Liability of landlord as dependent on knowledge of defects.

            165 (5). Failure to guard dangerous places.

            165 (6). Operation or condition of elevators.

            165 (7). Notice to or knowledge of tenant as to defects.

        166. Injuries to property of tenant on premises.

            166 (1). Nature and extent of the duties of landlord and tenant respectively.

            166 (2). Injuries due to defective condition of premises in general.

            166 (3). Injuries due to failure to repair.

            166 (4). Injuries due to negligence in making repairs.

            166 (5). Injuries due to defective water pipes or drains.

            166 (6). Injuries due to negligent acts of landlord.

            166 (7, 8). Injuries due to negligence of third persons in general.

            166 (9). Injuries due to negligence of cotenant.

            166 (10). Liability of landlord as dependent on knowledge or notice of defects.

        167. Injuries to third persons and their property.

            167 (1). Duties of landlord and tenant to third persons.

            167 (2). Injuries due to defective or dangerous condition of premises in general.

Exhibit 48

**§16.7. Digests of lesser scope than the American Digest System.** Nearly all the reported cases digested in the American Digest System are, in the aggregate, included in other digests of lesser scope. A few digests, like Clark's Digest Annotator[2] for certain New York lower court cases, cover cases not included in the American Digest System. Since in construction and use these smaller digests closely resemble the American Digest System in organization and tables, no detailed description of them individually is needed. Some of their specialized features, however, are pointed out below. If you know how to use one digest, you know how to use them all.

**§16.8. Digests of cases decided in the federal courts.** As stated earlier, all reported cases with few exceptions are covered by

2 Boonton, N.J., Kimball-Clark Pub. Co., 1938 to date.

the American Digest System. However, if only a federal court decision in point is being sought, considerable time is saved by searching a digest whose coverage is wholly confined to federal cases.

**§16.9. Digests covering federal courts.** Two digests, together, cover all the federal courts. Several other digests, by covering individual courts, combine to effect complete coverage.

1. *Federal Digest and Modern Federal Practice Digest.*

a. *Scope of coverage.* All federal constitutional and legislative courts of record are covered. The Federal Digest, 1940 edition, is the repository of the federal case law through the year 1938. This set includes the permanent bound volumes only, excluding any supplements. Because of the federal rules governing district courts in civil and criminal matters promulgated in 1938 (the Criminal Rules became effective in 1941), federal practice was changed so radically that the publishers of the Federal Digest felt that there should be a clean break between the older digested cases and the newer ones, and consequently inaugurated the publication of the Modern Federal Practice Digest. All case law in the supplements to the Federal Digest is included in the Modern Federal Practice Digest, and those supplements and parts were dead upon the completion of the new digest. All federal case law subsequent to the publication date of each main volume of the Modern Federal Practice Digest, even if originally included in the pocket parts of the Federal Digest, is in the 1961 pocket parts of the new digest, and the Federal Digest is no longer supplemented. All future pamphlets and pocket parts will supplement only the new digest.

The Descriptive-Word Index for the Modern Federal Practice Digest covers all federal case law from the earliest times to date, superseding the index for the Federal Digest.

Thus all federal case law, with the completion of the Modern Federal Practice Digest, is covered in the following:

(1) Federal Digest bound volumes, not including the bound cumulative supplements and Descriptive-Word Indexes, but including the tables of cases. All cases through 1938 are here.

(2) Modern Federal Practice Digest, supplemented by quarterly pamphlet supplements and annual pocket parts, for cases beginning with 1939.

Certain administrative tribunals which bear the title of "court," but are not true courts, are not covered in these digests. An example is the Tax Court of the United States. The reports of the federal courts of Alaska and Hawaii, which, during the territorial period, served also some of the functions of state courts, and the United States Court of Appeals for the District of Columbia (which has the status of a circuit of the United States Court of Appeals), are covered. Cases originating in Puerto Rico, now a commonwealth, are reported in the Federal Supplement and Federal Reporter, respectively.

The Federal Digest and Modern Federal Practice Digest are typical Key Number digests, as described earlier in this chapter. They have the usual features, such as the descriptive-word index, case tables and lists of adjudicated patents and trade-marks. They also have some features not found in the Decennials. There is a Defendant-Plaintiff case table, also an index to words and phrases judicially defined in the digested cases. Court rules construed are listed in a separate table.

New or expanded digest topics usually appear in these digests before they do in the Decennials. For example, in the Sixth Decennial there is no main topic of "Zoning," but this new topic is included in the Modern Federal Practice Digest and will be incorporated in the Seventh and succeeding Decennials.

b. *Steps in a complete search of reported federal cases.*

(1) *Cases decided through 1938.* The search here is in the Federal Digest except in so far as the pertinent topic has been expanded or superseded by a new topic in the Modern Federal Practice Digest. In that case the procedure described at page 198, par. c is in order.

(2) *Cases decided since 1938 to date.* These are digested in the Modern Federal Practice Digest, and for them the Federal Digest is not consulted at all. This set is supplemented by three quarterly cumulated pamphlets, each covering the entire digest. These in turn cumulate at the end of the year into annual pocket supplements for each individual volume.

(3) *New topics in Modern Federal Practice Digest.* Many main digest topics either have been started as new topics (e.g., Administrative Law and Procedure and Labor Relations) or have been greatly expanded since the beginning of the Federal Digest. These new or expanded topics constitute exceptions to the rule that Key Numbers cover identical material in all Key Number digests. The modified search procedure for them has been described at page 198, par. c.

(4) *Search for latest cases in the General Digest and Reporter advance sheets.* Since supplementation of the Modern Federal Practice Digest is only quarterly, a digest search may include two additional steps to produce the latest cases: examination of the monthly General Digest pamphlets later than the latest quarterly digest supplement, and of the advance sheets of the various Reporter units covering still later cases. An accurate check of the

reports covered in these respective units is supplied by the tables at the beginning of each quarterly and annual digest supplement, and of each monthly General Digest issue. These tables give the precise volume and page coverage of the reports digested in each supplement.

2. *State digests digesting federal court reports.* State digests commonly digest all federal court decisions involving their state or cases up on appeal to the Supreme Court of the United States from state courts.

3. *Supreme Court of the United States cases.* Supreme Court cases are digested both in the American Digest System and in the Federal Digest and Modern Federal Practice Digest, but there are two special digests for the Supreme Court alone.

a. *Digest of the United States Supreme Court Reports.* This is an excellent digest, in eighteen volumes, published by the Lawyers Co-operative Publishing Company and cross-referenced to that company's American Law Reports Annotated, American Jurisprudence and Lawyers' Edition of Supreme Court Reports. Although it is a typical case digest, with the usual tables and indexes, it has some special features of its own.

(1) *Table of cases.* This table is in a single alphabet for both plaintiff-defendant and defendant-plaintiff and popular name (e.g., *Hot Oil* case). References to additional cases and discussions in point are made in it through citations to American Jurisprudence and American Law Reports annotations and digest. Annotations in the Lawyers' Edition are indexed in a separate volume. Dissenting and separate concurring opinions are separately listed in the tables. The Table of Federal Statutes by Popular Name (e.g., Morrill Act, Taft-Hartley Act) is perhaps the most complete of all such tables. Words and phrases judicially defined are not listed in the Tables volume, but under "Words and Phrases" in the digest proper as a main topic of the digest.

(2) *Court rules.* Rules covering all federal courts (but not those covering specific district courts) are printed in two separate volumes.

(3) *Citator information.* Such information includes some not readily available elsewhere. As part of the digest paragraphs, whenever a point of law noted has been modified or commented upon by a later Supreme Court decision, that fact is noted together with the holding of the later case. This is kept up to date by annual pocket parts. The extensive Table of Cases Affirmed, Reversed, Reheard, Etc. in volume 14 covers rehearings in the Supreme Court of lower court cases, both federal and state, considered by the Court. The arrangement is by volume and page of

the report reconsidered, not by case name, with the precise action by the Supreme Court stated. *This table supplies perhaps the speediest means of determining whether a specific federal or state case or group of cases has been appealed to the Supreme Court, and the disposition there.* A complete search here would cover the table in volume 14 and its annual pocket supplement, and in the later bound volumes (but not the advance sheets) of the Lawyers' Edition.

(4) *Table of Laws Cited and Construed.* This table of laws cited and construed by the cases digested is unique in some of its coverage. It includes constitutions, statutes, treaties, proclamations and regulations construed by the Supreme Court, not only of the federal and state governments, of the Confederate States of America, but also those of foreign countries. Treaties of the United States with the American Indians and interstate compacts are also listed when construed by the Court. A useful feature of the citation of both state and federal statutes is that the form of the statute is listed as of the date of the original action, so that the title and section of an earlier code do not have to be translated into an uneasy equivalent to the current code, as must be done in working with other citators.

b. *United States Supreme Court Digest.* A typical West Publishing Company Key Number digest, this has the various features of such digests, such as tables of cases, of words and phrases judicially defined, cases listed by popular name, and a descriptive-word index. Court rules are printed (not including those for the individual district courts). Both the digest paragraphs and the table of cases give such citator information as to actions on appeal of the precise cases digested as is available at publication time of the digest.

4. *Digests covering lower federal courts.*

a. *Federal Cases.* The digest to Federal Cases is of no current interest as a digest, but it is useful for the conversion table bound with it, which translates the original citations of the lower federal court cases up to 1880 to the Federal Cases citation, as, for example, from 7 Blatchf. 555 to Fed. Cas. No. 602.

b. *Federal Digest and Modern Federal Practice Digest.* These two digests cover all federal courts of record, past and present. They are described at page 209, par. 1.

c. *Court of Claims Digest.* This digest, covering cases from 1855 to date, is a typical Key Number digest and can be used as are other Key Number digests.

d. *Customs Court Digest.* This digest covers all Customs Court decisions and those of the Court of Customs and Patent Appeals from 1910 to date. For customs reports there are also small, officially published digests covering volumes 1 to 45. Since so much of the Customs Court's function relates to the interpretation of the law relating to specific types of imports, the Words and Phrases section of this digest is useful. Such terms as shrines, bricks, regulus of copper are defined.

e. *Digests for "courts" which are not true courts.* There is a Tax Court Digest[3] in 16 volumes. The Tax Court is not a true court but an administrative tribunal. Similarly the United States Military Court of Appeals, though nominally a court under Article 67 of the Code of Military Justice, is an agency of the Department of Defense. Its decisions are published and there is a Citator and Index covering the first twenty-five volumes. It is not a true digest, but an "index-digest," in that, under rather broad subject headings, there is further descriptive-word analysis.

**§16.10. State and territorial court digests.** In one form or another the reported decisions of all federal and state appellate courts and of some courts of first instance, from 1658 to date, are covered by conventional case digests. The American Digest System, already described, covers state courts. State and territorial courts are also covered by Reporter regional digests (e.g., Atlantic, Pacific) and, for most states and the territories before statehood, by separate digests for each such political division.

1. *Reporter digests.* These are typical Key Number digests. The South Western Reporter Digest has been discontinued. The coverage of the other regional units varies from the Reporter period only (about 1880) to date for some, to complete statehood period coverage for others. See §11.1.

2. *Individual state digests.* The West Publishing Company publishes separate digests for nearly all of the fifty states, and others are in preparation. Other publishers cover a good many states. For your own purposes, check with your law librarian to see which states are covered by individual digests in your library.

The West state digests are typical Key Number digests, with the digest paragraphs taken from the American Digest System (which means, in effect, from the Reporter advance sheets with added citator information available when the state digest went to press). For most states there are local materials also, not found in the American Digest System. Examples are the enumeration and description of all New York state courts from the beginning, and the description of their reports, in 2 Abbott's New York Digest; and the Table of Statutes Construed in the Massachusetts Digest Annotated.

3 Indianapolis, Ind., Bobbs-Merrill Co., 1952 to date.

There are many state digests other than those which are published by West and some of them by permission copy the Key Number classification without the key symbol. Their composition, tables and methods of use so nearly coincide in all significant respects with other digests that the lawyer or student who can work with one digest is soon at home with them all. All of course seek to emphasize their local character. The Indiana Decennial Digest is keyed to Burns's Indiana Statutes, which in turn is keyed to the Digest. Page's Ohio Digest, in addition to some other citator data, has a separate alphabetical table of Cases Judicially Noticed. Callaghan's Wisconsin Digest cites A.L.R. annotations, local practice treatises and all law review comments on Wisconsin cases.

Abbott's New York Digest, jointly published by the West Publishing Company and the Lawyers' Co-operative Publishing Company, employs the Key Number classification of the former company and refers to pertinent A.L.R. annotations of the latter. Volume 2 of the Consolidated Edition lists and describes all New York courts and their reports. Two other New York digests cover selected lower court opinions of the First and Second Judicial Departments of New York (the Greater New York metropolitan area), as published in the New York Law Journal, a legal newspaper. While most of these opinions are published also in the standard New York official and Reporter system reports and so are digested in the American Digest System and in Abbott's, the New York Law Journal publishes some opinions not found in other report series. Therefore a New York case search covering cases decided in the lower courts of the First and Second Departments may require a search of New York Law Journal cases. Clark's Digest Annotator (1937 to date) appears monthly, cumulating into an annual bound volume. It has its own classification scheme, table of cases and subject-matter index. The New York Law Journal coverage is now more selective than formerly, and there is selective inclusion of digests of the New York Court of Appeals and Appellate Division cases, and also of the United States Supreme Court and Courts of Appeals decisions.

§16.11. **Coordinating the digest with other case finders.** Digests, while the most comprehensive and generally useful of all case finders, are by no means the only ones. Treatises, legal encyclopedias, legal periodicals, annotations and citators are also fruitful sources of cases in point and provide starting points for searchers.

The simplest technique of coordinating the various indexes to cases in point is to find a single case and then go on from there.

This starter case may be found in a treatise, law review article footnote, legal encyclopedia, or as a citation by the court in another case. Then, either by checking a Key Number digest table of cases or by going directly to the Reporter containing the case, Key Numbers in point are found, thus opening up the entire resources of American case law. With the name of the case you may find, through the Index to Legal Periodicals tables beginning with 1917, that the case has been discussed in a law review article or case comment. Through the parallel citations of your case in case table or footnote citations or a search in the A.L.R. case table, you will discover whether your case has been the subject of an A.L.R. annotation. These annotations are cited also in American Jurisprudence, a legal encyclopedia discussed in the next chapter. Further checking with Shepard's Citations, described in Chapter 18, will reveal citations to all cases which have acted in an appellate capacity upon your case or have cited it in some way as precedent. It is a snowballing process, starting from one or more cases in point and building up.

It is also a process which turns up more chaff than wheat, requiring the examination and discarding of many cases of no use to you, before you find those which are helpful. It is a process bringing into play all your skills and discriminatory ability to appraise and to cull the cases found, but that is the way legal research is done.

# CHAPTER 17

# Legal Encyclopedias

**§17.1.  Function, scope and content of legal encyclopedias.**
Ideally the legal encyclopedia provides within its announced scope
the following material: (1) a complete and integrated statement of
all the applicable law; (2) citation to the authority relied upon,
which may include not only references to cases in point but also
digests of cases and excerpts from standard treatises and American
Law Institute Restatements; (3) exhaustive analytical and subject
indexes; and (4) frequent supplements, in which the main text
may be rewritten in view of later cases than those forming the basis
of the original discussion.

The encyclopedia is best used as a starting point in a search for
the law, to provide a frame of reference.  The cases cited act as
conduits between the encyclopedia and the brief paragraphs in
the digests which tell the searcher whether or not he should read
the entire case.  By giving the reader an elementary statement
of the law applicable to his problem, as extracted from the cases
cited as supporting the text, the encyclopedia places those cases
selected for reading in their proper perspective.

The text in the encyclopedia begins with a general and elementary statement of the law, proceeding thence to more detailed
consideration of all aspects of the substantive law concerned, and
ending with a discussion of the available remedies.  Special-subject
encyclopedias commonly contain annotated substantive and procedural forms.  The encyclopedia provides a useful starting point
in a search.  It serves the double purpose of giving the searcher
a good treatment of a topic of which he is relatively ignorant and

of brushing him up on a subject in which he may have become somewhat rusty. By citing its authority the encyclopedia serves as a casefinder. Once the searcher has cases in point the whole field of search through the digests, treatises, legal periodicals, annotated cases and citation books is opened up to him.

Since the primary purpose of the encyclopedia is to help judges decide and lawyers to win cases, it is, like the practitioners' textbook, the exponent of the law as it is. The men for whom it is designed are little concerned for the moment with the history of the past or speculation as to the future of the law; these they can glean, if desired, from scholarly treatises or law review articles on history or jurisprudence. The encyclopedia resembles student books, however, in that it is careful to state and explain majority, minority and jurisdictional rules, and in that its statements of the law begin with an elementary exposition of each point covered.

§17.2. **Authority of legal encyclopedias.** By a strict definition of "authority," the encyclopedia has none, for no court is bound in any way to regard its statements of the law as precedent. It is, rather, an index to the law, in textbook form, as set forth in the decided cases upon which its statements are based. On the other hand, not to be too academic about it, legal encyclopedias are frequently cited with approval in judicial opinions — not as authority in themselves, but as containing well-reasoned statements of the rules of law as extracted from the cited cases relied upon.

§17.3. **Form of legal encyclopedias.** Like the conventional treatise, the encyclopedia states the law in literary form as extracted from the authorities cited. Like the digest, the encyclopedia is alphabetically arranged by topics under a classification system almost exactly like that of the digest, even to the scope note, analysis, and subanalyses. The scope note is an eliminator. By stating briefly what is covered by a topic it also tells by implication what is not, and thus prevents the searcher from wasting time. The analysis may be compared to an unusually detailed table of contents. For the most part, the encyclopedia consists of about 400 alphabetically arranged treatises, which vary in length from a few lines to hundreds of pages. It resembles the digest in having a descriptive-word index, but no general encyclopedia has a table of cases, though some of the special-subject ones do. The digest page is typical of those of law books generally — the text discussion above the line, supported by citations below the line to authority relied upon.

§17.4. **Advantages and disadvantages of the encyclopedia form.** The encyclopedia aims to be a one-set law library, at a

considerable saving of both cost and space over a collection of individual treatises covering the same aggregate of topics of law.
It probably covers the totality of the law more precisely than such
a collection of treatises would and leaves fewer gaps.  Continuity
of editorial policy assures that changes in the law will be reflected
and that there will be regular and complete supplementation, so
that theoretically the encyclopedia is never out of date by more
than the time between annual supplements.  The comprehensive
indexes are said to offer a better guide to the body of the law than
the sum total of the indexes of individual treatises.

On the other hand, the compilation of an encyclopedia is such
an enormous task that it extends over many years, during which
time individual volumes are issued for sale, covering material
available up to the publication date.  It took sixteen years to
complete American Jurisprudence and twenty-four (including the
general index) for Corpus Juris Secundum.  During these years
a great deal of new law was made, and though the supplements
note these changes, complete rewriting of affected topics to reflect
them lags.  Indexing as between editions is difficult.

§17.5.  **The two current general legal encyclopedias.**  There
are two current general legal encyclopedias, that is, encyclopedias
aiming to cover all topics, both substantive and adjective, of our
American law.  While their scope of coverage is thus identical,
their approaches differ somewhat.  Their similarities and differences are outlined briefly here, as a preliminary to more detailed
descriptions of each encyclopedia separately.

These two encyclopedias are, respectively, American Jurisprudence[1] (cited as Am. Jur.) and Corpus Juris Secundum[2] (cited as
C.J.S.).

1. *Basic differences between the two encyclopedias.*[3]  The differences in policy in compiling the two encyclopedias are stated as
follows by the publishers themselves:

> *American Jurisprudence:* ". . . comprehensive text statement
> of American case law as developed in the cases and annota-
> tions in the annotated reports."

> *Corpus Juris Secundum:* ". . . a complete restatement of the
> entire American law, as developed by all reported cases."

---

1 San Francisco, Cal., Bancroft-Whitney Co., Rochester, N.Y., Lawyers Co-operative
Publishing Co., 1936-1952, 58v. and 4 General Index volumes, with annual cumulative pocket supplements and recompiled volumes as required.

2 Brooklyn, N.Y., American Law Book Co., 1936-1958, 101v. and 5 General Index
volumes, with annual cumulative pocket supplements and recompiled volumes as required.

8 This outline was suggested by Professor Albert J. Blaustein, of the Rutgers University School of Law, South Jersey Branch, whose students have found it useful.

## 2. *Mutual characteristics outlined.*

| Characteristics | American Jurisprudence | Corpus Juris Secundum |
| --- | --- | --- |
| Multi-volume | 58 text volumes | 101 text volumes |
| Arranged alphabetically by topic | 443 topics | 433 topics |
| Descriptive-word indexes | 4-volume General Index, plus index in each volume for topics covered in that volume | 5-volume General Index, plus index in each volume for topics covered in that volume |
| Table of cases | None | None |
| Scope note, analysis | Yes, as in a digest | Yes, as in a digest |
| Dictionary functions | Definitions under Maxims and Words and Phrases in General Index | Definitions through special index following main text in each volume, and in alphabetical order in main text volumes |
| Supplementation | Annual pocket parts; replacement volumes | Annual pocket parts; replacement volumes |

**§17.6. American Jurisprudence (Am. Jur.) and American Jurisprudence Second (Am. Jur. 2d).**[4] Am. Jur. will have been entirely superseded by Am. Jur. 2d by about 1972, but the two encyclopedias are so alike that they will be discussed here together, while pointing out such differences as should be noted. The Am. Jur. 2d text is largely rewritten, using such of the old text as requires no change, but expanding it as needed and incorporating all cases and other references later than Am. Jur. New Topics are introduced as necessary. A cross reference table in each Am. Jur. 2d volume leads from section in Am. Jur. to the corresponding but usually differently numbered sections in Am. Jur. 2d.

This encyclopedia aims at complete coverage of both adjective and substantive law of general application, as modified by statute. It also serves a dictionary function in defining legal maxims and words and phrases.

1. *Scope of citation to authority.* Am. Jur. relies heavily upon cases printed in the annotated, selective cases series, though other cases are cited, including all United States Supreme Court and some English and Canadian cases. While Am. Jur. 2d does not attempt to cite all cases in point and still cites A.L.R. annotations,

4 See the publisher's The Living Law, for a detailed account of Am. Jur. 2d and its use.

it cites many more non-A.L.R. cases than does Am. Jur., including foreign ones.    Pertinent American Law Institute Restatements are quoted or cited.    Am. Jur. 2d increasingly stresses federal statutes, rules and practice, the Uniform Laws (including the Uniform Commercial Code), and articles in legal periodicals and treatises.

2. *Arrangement of material; supplementation as affecting indexes and tables.*   The arrangement resembles that of the digests we have already studied, but the text pages, instead of being merely a collection of self-contained paragraphs independently stating principles of law without any connecting comment, discuss these principles for the topics covered, in literary form, with citations to the cases and other materials relied upon as authority. There are about 440 main topics or separate treatises, alphabetically arranged by broad topic.   Just as in the digest, analyses and subanalyses precede the text, forming the basis of the analytical approach to the law through the encyclopedia.

New cases causing changes in the law are reflected in the encyclopedias by annual cumulative pocket supplements to each text volume. In time, these pocket supplements become unwieldy, and a "recompiled" volume is issued, incorporating the supplementary material, rewriting the original text as required.   Until Am. Jur. 2d is completed, cross references to volumes of Am. Jur. not superseded are employed in the completed volumes of Am. Jur. 2d.    Thus, Abandoned, Lost and Unclaimed Property §28, note 11 (1 Am. Jur. 2d 24), relating to the tortious appropriation by a finder of lost property, is cross referenced to Larceny §28, note 11 (1 Am. Jur. 971), for a discussion of the criminal aspects. As Am. Jur. 2d supersedes Am. Jur., volume by volume, the pocket supplements to the superseded volumes are themselves superseded by the supplements in the superseding volumes, and are dropped.

The supplementary procedures are described in an Explanatory Note at the beginning of each pocket supplement, which should be read.

3. *Subject indexes to Am. Jur. and Am. Jur. 2d: the fact approach to the law.*   These indexes correspond to the descriptive-word indexes to A.L.R. digests and in the digests, as described in Chapters 15 and 16.   They illustrate the complication in simultaneously using a volume of an older encyclopedia while superseding volumes of the new edition replace the old, volume by volume.

For Am. Jur. — Am. Jur. 2d there are four different index units grown-up son not in the custody of the wife against the opposition or without the acquiescence of the husband.[16]

## § 843. — College education.

The view has been taken that the father may be required to provide his minor child with a college education in a proper case.[17] In a few of the college education cases the courts have had occasion to consider the effect of particular statutory provisions.[18] However, it should be shown that the child has sufficient intelligence or aptitude to justify enrollment in a college,[19] and that the child desires a college education.[20] And a father will not be burdened with expenses attributable to a college education if his financial condition is such that such expenditures would be unreasonable.[1]

---

**16.** Streitwolf v Streitwolf, 58 NJ Eq 570, 43 A 904.

**17.** Ogle v Ogle, 275 Ala 483, 156 So 2d 345; Allison v Allison, 188 Kan 593, 363 P2d 795; Johnson v Johnson, 346 Mich 418, 78 NW2d 216; Jackman v Short, 165 Or 626, 109 P2d 860, 133 ALR 887; Esteb v Esteb, 138 Wash 174, 244 P 264, 246 P 27, 47 ALR 110.

*Annotation:* 133 ALR 911, s. 56 ALR2d 1220, § 5[a].

The child need not be required to attend a college within the state where a college education in the college chosen by the mother and child, located in a neighboring state, will not cost more than an education within the state. Titus v Titus, 311 Mich 434, 18 NW 2d 883.

Under the rule that where there is an agreement to support and it is within the contemplation of the parties, a father may be liable to support and furnish his child with a college education, the fact that an educational insurance policy had been taken out 10 years previously, and that the defendant admitted that the policy was designed to send the child to college, established that a college education was within the contemplation of the parties and warranted an order requiring the payment of college tuition for an 18-year-old daughter from the proceeds of the policy. Commonwealth ex rel. Howell v Howell, 198 Pa Super 396, 181 A2d 903.

**18.** *Annotation:* 56 ALR2d 1231, § 6[a].

Where a statute gives the divorce court the power to make any reasonable order for the education of children "as may seem necessary and proper," it is evident that the court has a discretionary power to take the expense of a college education into account when awarding child support where the child desires to attend college and the father can reasonably be required to pay the sums awarded. Howton v Howton, 51 Cal App 2d 323, 124 P2d 837. Annotation: 56 ALR2d 1231, § 6[b].

Where a statute provides that the court may enter an order for the "nurture and education" of a child, it may be assumed that the legislature intended to make a change in the common-law scope of the father's liability for mere necessaries, with the result that he may be required to pay the expenses of a college education of a child. In the absence of evidence specifically showing the aptitude of a daughter, the court may award the expenses of a college education, where it appears that the daughter has completed her high school education, that she is willing to earn a part of her college expenses, and that her mother believes that she is entitled to a college education. Jackman v Short, 165 Or 626, 109 P2d 860, 133 ALR 887. Annotation: 133 ALR 911, s. 56 ALR2d 1220, § 5 [a].

**19.** Mapes v Mapes, 336 Mich 137, 57 NW 2d 471 (wherein it appeared that the son was an honor student in the eleventh grade in high school).

*Annotation:* 56 ALR2d 1225, § 5[c].

It is error to order a father to support two sons through college where they are only 8 and 14 years of age and no showing can be made as to their aptitude and desire for a college education. Johnson v Johnson, 346 Mich 418, 78 NW2d 216.

**20.** Rufner v Rufner, 131 NJ Eq 193, 24 A2d 180; Commonwealth ex rel. Ulmer v Sommerville, 200 Pa Super 640, 190 A2d 182.

**1.** Rufner v Rufner, 131 NJ Eq 193, 24 A 2d 180; Bernstein v Bernstein, 282 App Div 30, 121 NYS2d 818; Golay v Golay, 35 Wash 2d 122, 210 P2d 1022; Peck v Peck, 272 Wis 466, 76 NW2d 316, 56 ALR2d 1202.

*Annotation:* 56 ALR2d 1223, § 5[b].

Where a child is able and willing to successfully pursue a course of studies and the father has a sufficient estate, earning capacity, or income to enable him to do so, he may be ordered to support the child while attending college, but the father was not ordered to do so where an order for payment of $20 per week would have resulted in a total income to his 18-year-old daughter of approximately $70 and the father would have less than $60 per week. Commonwealth ex rel. Ulmer v Sommerville, 200 Pa Super 640, 190 A2d 182.

Exhibit 49

until the General Index for Am. Jur. 2d is printed, and it is important to keep them straight. They are:

a. *General Index.* This covers Am. Jur., except for the few recompiled volumes, each of which has its own separate index. Until the Am. Jur. 2d index is completed, this index will still be essential to complete research, even in the subject matter of Am. Jur 2d volumes. It is a vast, alphabetically arranged index to the material in the Am. Jur. text proper. Like the descriptive word index of a digest, it includes in a single alphabetical arrangement of entries three different categories: (1) main topics, a list of which is at the front of every text volume; (2) large subjects, such as "Unemployment Insurance," which are not main topics in the encyclopedia, with alphabetically arranged catchword subentries thereunder; (3) catchword entries, such as "Conductors," "Reserved seats" and "Vermin." Maxims are usually, but not always, listed both under the maxim itself (e.g., *De minimus non curat lex*), and under a general heading of "Maxims."

As in a digest descriptive-word index, there is extensive duplication of subject entries in the indexes, to lead the searcher more speedily to the object of his search — which is a main topic head and specific section number under it, corresponding in function to the Key Number — without too much analytical effort on his part.

For example, if the searcher seeks a discussion of the status of a greenhouse employee as a claimant for unemployment insurance, he can find the same reference in the index under the main topic of "Social Security," subhead "Greenhouse employee"; under the large subject of "Unemployment Insurance," subhead "Greenhouse employee"; and under the catchwords of "Greenhouse employee." There are many cross references from topics not used to topics used. The typography of these cross references tells its own story, as explained in a page immediately following the title page of each index volume. This page, Explanation of References, should be read.

*Dictionary function of General Index.* The General Index does not itself define maxims and words and terms. Instead, it refers to the text where they are defined. The use of the index is necessary because neither maxims nor words defined are to be found in alphabetical order in the main text. For example, "work horse" is defined in "Exemption §57"; "gorge" in "Waters §76" of Am. Jur.

b. *Recompiled volumes' separate indexes.* When a volume is recompiled and republished, the old section numbers of the original volumes are superseded, so that the General Index no longer applies for their subject matter. The indexes in the re-compiled volumes wholly supersede, for their precise subject matter, the bound volume of the General Index covering a specific title, except as noted below. For the period covered by the re-compiled volume, the bound volumes of the General Index are not consulted at all, except for coordinating references to material in other titles. A main function of the General Index is to co-ordinate citations to discussion of a given topic in all titles. For all material later than the date of the recompiled volume, the pocket supplements of the General Index must be consulted for peripheral material in unsuperseded volumes of Am. Jur.

For example, while the material on divorce and separation is covered generally in a volume devoted to that subject, many pe-ripheral aspects of this subject matter are commented upon in other titles, as "Adoption," "Adultery," "Appeal and Error," and "Income Taxes."

c. *Am. Jur. 2d indexes to each volume.* Each new volume is separately indexed. There are cross references from matter treated in other topics. There is also a Table of Parallel References in the front of each volume, from Am. Jur. sections to those of Am. Jur. 2d, from which, also, the reverse Am. Jur. 2d to Am. Jur. transition is easily made.

d. *Cumulative pocket supplements.* These are annual and cumulative. The reader is advised to read the detailed Explana-tory Note in the front of each supplement, which cite later cases, calling attention to new principles of law, noting the addition of new sections and of new text material. As noted above, the pocket supplements in superseded Am. Jur. volumes are dropped, the material formerly in them having been added to the recompiled volumes, for each of which supplements keep the text current.

e. *Problem in the use of Am. Jur. — Am. Jur. 2d.* How the new edition and the supplementation of both editions work to-gether is shown in the following illustrative problem. W obtains a divorce from H. The decree grants W custody of the children and directs H to supply funds for their education. When the first child reaches college age, W applies for an increase in ali-mony contributions to cover the added expense of sending the child to college, and H resists. If the increase for college educa-tion is granted at all, must the child attend a college in his home state?

(1) *Fact approach.* A search in the General Index under "Edu-cation" of a child results in a cross reference to "Parent and Child." Here, the subhead "Education" leads to situations per-taining to the education of a child residing with its married

parents living together.   So a reexamination of the problem is necessary.   You soon learn that few searches lead inevitably and speedily to the precise treatment of the problem which you desire; that it is necessary to use a great deal of imagination to put yourself *en rapport* with the indexer, whose concept of legal fact situations may differ from your own.

Starting over again, you find that "Alimony" in the General Index leads to a cross reference to the main topic of "Divorce and Separation."   Since this has now been rewritten in Am. Jur. 2d, in volume 24, you search in the index to that volume.   Here, under the subheads "Alimony or support," "Education," "Children," "College," and "Support of Children," among others, you are referred to Divorce and Separation §§842 and 843, with citations and digests of authority, including matter formerly included in the pocket supplements of Am. Jur. volume 17A.

---

DIVORCE AND SEPARATION                                    § 855

p 929, n 13—
Swindle v Swindle, 242 Ark 790, 415 SW2d 564.

§ 820. Factors or circumstances justifying or affecting modification

p 931, n 5
Wells v Wells (Ky) 412 SW2d 568.

§ 821. — Remarriage of parent

p 933, n 5—
Although the remarriage of the mother is not of itself a sufficient reason for changing an order of custody, it may have a bearing on change of custody.  Stingley v Wesch, 77 Ill App 2d 472, 222 NE2d 505.

p 933, n 6—
Guldeman v Heller (ND) 151 NW2d 436 (modification justified where, among other things, father was remarried, mother and stepfather were unstable).

p 933, n 11—
Wells v Wells (Ky) 412 SW2d 568.

§ 825. — Effect of agreement of parties

p 937, n 10—
Wells v Wells (Ky) 412 SW2d 568.

B. Support of Children

1. Support Orders in Divorce and Separation Cases

a. In General; Jurisdiction

§ 827. Generally

p 939, n 5—
Alimony cannot be awarded to the wife in the guise of child support.  Farwell v Farwell, 33 Wis 2d 324, 147 NW2d 289.

p 949, n 1—
But see Franklin Life Ins. Co. v Kitchens, 249 Cal App 2d 623, 57 Cal Rptr 652, holding that the court may order compulsory designation of minor children as beneficiaries of insurance, under a statute imposing a liability on both parents to furnish support, maintenance, and education of the children.

§ 839. Amount of allowance

p 952, n 9—
Woodward v Woodward (Wyo) 428 P2d 389.

§ 840. — Mother's or child's means or earning capacity

p 954, n 20—
There was no abuse of discretion in ordering the mother of an incompetent child to contribute to its support where she had joint custody and possessed a substantial estate.  Levy v Levy, 245 Cal App 2d 341, 53 Cal Rptr 790.

p 954—*Add after note* 3.5:  However, where the child has a separate estate, support money should not be paid from that estate unless and until it is established that the parents are unable to adequately support the child.[3.5]

n 3.5—Huff v Huff, 68 Wash 2d 501, 413 P2d 818 (trust fund established by grandfather for children's future education could not be invaded for their support).

c. Modification or Cancellation as to Future Payments

§ 847. Grounds for modification; what constitutes, and sufficiency of, change in circumstances

---

Exhibit 50

In this problem, you see the utility of the Am. Jur. General Index as a coordinator of like topics, even for coverage of a superseded volume: The topic under which the problem is treated is made clear only by considerable analysis. Note that the General Index reference is to "Divorce and Separation §855," in the old edition. The parallel reference table under the same volume of Am. Jur. 2d tells you that the new reference is to §§842 and 843. To bring your search down to date, you now consult the Am. Jur. 2d pocket supplements under these sections. See Exhibit 50 below. Note there are no additional citations for §§842 and 843 as of 1968.

(2) *Analytical approach.* This approach to Am. Jur. — Am. Jur. 2d is precisely the same as in a digest. The outline or table of contents of "Divorce and Separation" is in nineteen subtopics, each subtopic being further subdivided into the ultimate sections under which the subject matter is discussed. Scanning this outline speedily turns up the information shown in Exhibit 51.

(3) *Table of cases approach not available.* Since the Am. Jur.

---

24 Am Jur 2d    DIVORCE AND SEPARATION

XIII.—Continued
  D. TEMPORARY ALIMONY (§§ 548–570)
  E. SUIT MONEY, COUNSEL FEES, AND COSTS (§§ 571–599)
  F. PERMANENT ALIMONY (§§ 600–707)
  G. ENFORCEMENT OF JUDGMENT, DECREE, OR ORDER (§§ 708–771)
XIV. CUSTODY, SUPPORT, AND PATERNITY OR LEGITIMACY OF CHILDREN
  A. CUSTODY OF CHILDREN (§§ 772–826)
→ B. SUPPORT OF CHILDREN (§§ 827–875)
  C. DETERMINATION OF PATERNITY, LEGITIMACY, OR LEGITIMATION OF CHILD (§§ 876–878)
XV. OPERATION AND EFFECT (§§ 879–882)

---

      b. MODE AND AMOUNT OF ALLOWANCE; ALLOWANCES FOR SPECIFIC PURPOSES
  § 837. Mode of allowance; award of property
  § 838. — Trust to secure child support
  § 839. Amount of allowance
  § 840. — Mother's or child's means or earning capacity
  § 841. — Effect of agreement or stipulation of parties
  § 842. Awards for education and other specific purposes
→ § 843. — College education

**Exhibit 51**

system has no table of cases, this valuable approach to the law is not available.

*The Desk Book.* Another new feature of Am. Jur. 2d is the Desk Book: Historical and Legal Documents, Facts, Tables, Charts, and Statistics of Special Interest to Attorneys.[5]

This is a data book for lawyers. In addition to a complete listing of titles in Am. Jur. 2d, it is divided into seven parts, as follows: Part I prints the texts of sixteen classic documents — the Constitution, Magna Carta, United Nations Charter, etc. — organization charts of federal government agencies; officers and addresses of the principal federal administrative agencies; and a great deal of similar data for the states, territories and possessions. Part II concerns the courts and their organization. Part III relates to the legal profession: ethics, bar admission procedure, accredited law schools, American Bar Association organization, and the number of lawyers in the United States (by states and sex). Part IV prints the text of ancient English statutes and tabulates a wide variety of statutory materials across state lines — voting qualifications, limitation periods for common actions, marriage and divorce laws, Uniform Laws, etc. Part V is devoted to statistical matters, such as financial and mathematical tables, tax and annuity computation tables, mortality tables, price index charts, foreign exchange and foreign money, weights and measures, weather, population, and skid-speed charts for motor cars. Part VI is a table of American and major British law reports and of common abbreviations of legal materials, as law reports, statutes and periodicals. Part VII, Miscellaneous Records, gives such information as where to write for vital statistical records of the various states, tables of descent and distribution, mail time between cities, number of days from any date in one month to the same date in any other month, etc.

There is a subject index.

**§17.7.   Corpus Juris.**   This legal encyclopedia, the predecessor of Corpus Juris Secundum (cited as C.J.S.), has been entirely superseded by C.J.S. as a legal text and should no longer be read as a statement of existing law. Therefore it will not be described here. The cases and other authorities cited in the original C.J. volumes are, however, still cited by reference in the text and footnotes of C.J.S., so that the encyclopedia retains its place on law library shelves entirely for the sake of these citations.

**§17.8.   Corpus Juris Secundum.**   This general legal encyclopedia aims to be at once "a complete restatement of the entire

---

[5] Rochester, New York, Lawyers Co-operative Publishing Co., 1962. 659p.

American law, as developed by all reported cases," an annotated legal dictionary, and an annotated dictionary of legal maxims.

1. *Scope of citation to authority in C.J.S.* Citation is said to be to all cases in point. In addition C.J.S. cites and often quotes pertinent American Law Institute Restatements provisions, treatises and law review articles. The theory of legislation and of statutory construction generally is treated. Where a statute is involved in a decision cited as authority, that fact is brought out in the footnote citation of the case, but there is no attempt to treat local statutes generally; that is left to local practice books. Where statutes significantly affect the body of an area of law, their effect is analyzed in the main text. While there is no intention to serve as local practice books, the fundamentals of procedure are covered in detail.

The totality of citations to authority in C.J.S. includes also the cases cited in its predecessor, C.J., but the text of C.J. is entirely superseded by the C.J.S. text and should not be read. All citations in the C.J.S. Annotations volumes, issued annually until the completion of C.J.S., have been incorporated in C.J.S. and are not to be consulted. How the citation of C.J. cases by C.J.S. is handled is shown by Exhibit 52.

2. *Arrangement of material in C.J.S.* Since the internal arrangement of C.J.S. is like that of the Decennial Digests, as described in Chapter 16 — except that C.J.S. has no table of cases — little needs to be added here.

The significant difference is that C.J.S. carefully extracts the rules of law from the decided cases and other authorities cited below the line in a typical C.J.S. page and states the law in literary form instead of copying digest paragraphs without connecting comment, as does the digest. There are 480 different treatises of varying length in C.J.S., alphabetically arranged from "Abandonment" to "Zoning." There is also a dictionary function — defining words and phrases, and maxims — not found in the Decennials.

The Scope Note, Analysis and subanalyses perform the same function in both digest and C.J.S., and in the same way. In fact, except that the titles for the same subject matter in the Decennials and C.J.S. occasionally are different — e.g., "Agency" in C.J.S. and "Principal and Agent" in the Decennials — the titles in the two words are identical, but with the further exception that C.J.S. has many additional titles not found in the Decennials, such as "Architects," "Barratry," "Business Trusts," "Conflict of Laws." In a topic in which a statute is influential, as in "Forgery" or the "Statute of Frauds," the parallel in analysis is striking. Where the encyclopedia and the digest differ chiefly in analysis is that the encyclopedia always starts out with an elementary introduction, for which there is no digest parallel.

As in a conventional textbook the subject is developed in C.J.S.

---

**15 C.J.S.**      *CONFLICT OF LAWS*      **§ 14**

found in the cases where the positive law of the domicile makes void certain kinds of marriages by its citizens although celebrated elsewhere, and although they would otherwise be valid where celebrated,[29] in which case such a marriage is held to be void not only in the domiciliary state,[29] but in every other state.[30]

For an extended discussion of the foregoing and an exhaustive collection of the authorities, the C.J.S. title Marriage § 4, also 38 C.J. p 1276 note 24–p 1279 note 45, should be consulted.

A distinction should be made at this point between the creation and existence of the marriage status and the incidents attached thereto. Hence while a foreign contracted marriage will be recognized everywhere, the rights and duties flowing therefrom will be governed by the law of the place where the parties are[31] or by some law other than that of the state creating the status, depending upon the nature of the problem involved.[32] Appropriate sections of the title Husband and Wife should be consulted for the treatment of the law governing the particular rights growing out of the marriage relation.

See § 16 c infra for a discussion of the foregoing rules in so far as they involve the capacity of the parties to enter into the marriage status. See § 20 e

infra for a discussion of the law governing the formal requisites of a marriage.

#### d. Parent and Child

While ordinarily the relation of parent and child is governed by the law of the domicile of the parent having custody, any state in which a minor child is found has jurisdiction to determine questions of custody and control in the interest of the child.

As stated in the C.J.S. title Parent and Child § 1, also 46 C.J. p·1220 note 3, the term parent and child indicates the relation existing between husband and wife or either of them and their legitimate offspring. It is a status, not a property right.[33]

A Conflict of Laws problem involving this relationship may arise when the right to, and jurisdiction to determine, the custody and control of a minor child is involved. While basically the domicile of the parent having custody of the child is the place which has control of the status of parent and child, because the domicile of the parent is that of the child, see the C.J.S. title Domicile § 12, also 19 C.J. p 411 note 29, only such state having the right to adjudicate any change in the relationship,[34] because every state has an interest in the welfare of children within its confines, the law of the domicile of the parents is not necessarily a factor in determining questions of the custody and control of a child,[35] the state within which the child is found

---

Mass.—Atwood v. Atwood, 8 N.E.2d 916.

N.Y.—In re Seymour, 185 N.Y.S. 373, 113 Misc. 421.

Okl.—Eggers v. Olson, 231 P. 483, 104 Okl. 297.

**29.** Mass.—Atwood v. Atwood, 8 N. E.2d·916—Hanson v. Hanson, 191 N.E. 673, 287 Mass. 154,·.93 A.L.R. 701.

N.Y.—Bell v. Little, 197 N.Y.S. 674, 204 App.Div. 235, modifying 189 N. Y.S. 935, and affirmed 143 N.E. 726, ·237 N.Y. 519—Bays v. Bays, 174 N. Y.S. 212, 105 Misc. 492.

Okl.—Eggers v. Olson, 231 P. 483, 104 Okl. 297—Ross v. Bryant, 217 P. 364, 90 Okl. 300.

Wis.—Lyannes v. Lyannes, 177 N.W. 683, 171 Wis. 381.

**Prohibiting evasion of local law**
The legislature can declare out-of-state marriage of Massachusetts residents void in Massachusetts, if marriage was consummated in another state to avoid provisions of Massachusetts laws forbidding marriage in Massachusetts.—Atwood v. Atwood, Mass., 8 N.E.2d 916.

**Law of domicile governs**
Where citizens of one state go to another state, and there contract a marriage prohibited by the statutes

of the former state governing public policy as to persons competent to enter into such status, and return forthwith to the place of domicile, the validity of their marital status, be determined by the law of domicile under the rule that the law, n t of the place of contract, but of the domicile of the parties, governs.— Ross v. Bryant, 217 P. 364, 90 Okl. 300.

**"A marriage which is against the law of the state** of domicil of either party, though the requirements have been complied with, will be invalid everywhere in the following cases: (a) polygamous marriage, (b) incestuous marriage between persons so closely related that their marriage is contrary to a strong public policy of the domicil, (c) marriage between persons of different races where such marriages are at the domicil regarded as odious, (d) marriage of a domiciliary which a statute at the domicil makes void even though celebrated in another state."—Restatement, Conflict of Laws § 132.

**30.** Mich.—People v. Steere, 151 N. W. 617, 184 Mich. 556.

Wis.—Hall v. Industrial Commission,

162 N.W. 312, 165 Wis. 364, L.R.A. 1917D 829.

**31.** Wis.—Forbes v. Forbes, 277 N. W. 112, 226 Wis. 477.

12 C.J. p 459 note 25.

**32.** S.D.—Calhoun v. Bryant, 133 N. W. 266, 271, 28 S.D. 266.

"We believe a substantially correct statement of the proposition is that the law of the state where the marriage is consummated establishes the 'relationship' of one to the other as husband and wife or parent and child which is universally recognized, but that the mere incidents flowing from that 'status' or relationship are controlled by the law of the domicile of the parties or the situs of the property."—Calhoun v. Bryant, supra.

**33.** Pa.—In re Rosenthal, 157 A. 342, 103 Pa.Super. 27.

**34.** Iowa.—Kline v. Kline, 10 N.W. 825, 57 Iowa 386, 42 Am.R. 47.

Minn.—State v. Larson, 252 N.W. 329, 190 Minn. 496.

N.Y.—Finlay v. Finlay, 148 N.E. 624, 240 N.Y. 429.

Tex.—Lanning v. Gregory, 99 S.W. 542, 100 Tex. 310, 10 L.R.A.,N.S., 690.

**35.** N.Y.—Finlay v. Finlay, 148 N.E. 624, 240 N.Y. 429, 40 A.L.R. 792.

911

---

Exhibit 52

in logical fashion, from the general to the specific and to the remedial or procedural. Each section, the ultimate subdivision of subject matter in C.J.S., corresponding in that respect to the Decennial Key Number, begins with a paragraph in boldface type. This briefly distills and summarizes the applicable law, which the encyclopedia then expands into a full treatment in the following text, with citations to authority. This is a helpful device, somewhat analogous to the headnote paragraphs in a case report or to the boldface type statements in the Hornbook series of student texts, as Prosser on Torts.

The analytical solution of the overflowing water problem in the loft, on page 205, is precisely the same in C.J.S. as in the Decennials, as examination of 51 C.J.S. 488, 489 and 500 will demonstrate.

3. *Page format of C.J.S.* A typical C.J.S. page is shown in Exhibit 52. In the specimen page the boldface paragraph "d. Parent and Child" summarizes the conflicts rule, which is then expanded in the rest of this subsection. Points to be emphasized in the notes are also in boldface. The topic ("Conflict of Laws") and the section (§14), page (911), and note numbers (33 to 35) are keyed to like notations in the cumulative annual supplements, where later citations to authority on the precise points of law referred to are found under the same numbers. The supplementary citations may so modify the law as to require the rewriting of the original text in the pocket supplements.

Authority is customarily cited below the line — though sometimes also in the main text — and is often a direct quotation from an opinion, an A.L.I. Restatement, a treatise or a Reporter headnote. This authority may include citations — both in the main text and in footnotes — of earlier cases and comments cited below the line in C.J. Cross references to other pertinent titles in C.J.S. are also given.

4. *Dictionary and words and phrases function of C.J.S.* Maxims and legal words and terms are defined. However, it is much more convenient to consult a one- or two-volume conventional legal dictionary for these definitions than the 101 volumes of C.J.S. or the 58 volumes of Am. Jur. On the other hand, the encyclopedia definitions are more completely annotated and kept more up to date than are those in the dictionaries.

Maxims — as *Discretio est scire per legum quid sit justum* — are listed and defined in their regular alphabetical order in the respective volumes of C.J.S. In addition each volume has at the back a section of Words and Phrases and Maxims in This Volume, directing the searcher to the exact page where a definition is found in that volume. Maxims are not always listed in the General Index to C.J.S.

Legal words and terms as defined are found in two ways: first, through the General Index in regular alphabetical order as in any dictionary; second, through the list in the back of each volume covering definitions in that volume. These two sources complement each other. For example, under "Discretion" in the General Index we learn that the word is defined in titles "Appeal and Error," "Federal Courts," "Internal Revenue," and in volume 27 at page 289, under "Discretion." In the latter volume, under the subhead "In Phrases," many other phrases employing the word "discretion" are defined, such as "legal discretion" and "political discretion." Unfortunately this Words and Phrases list is not kept up in the pocket supplements.

Some definitions, with their citations to authority, are exhaustive. "At" and "Public," for example, occupy seventeen and sixteen pages respectively.

5. *Indexes for C.J.S.* At first glance the indexing of C.J.S. and its supplementation may seem complicated, but actually it is not. Here is how it works.

There are two indexes, the General Index with its annual cumulative pocket supplements, and the title indexes, one for each of the 480 C.J.S. titles as listed at the beginning of every volume of the set. Of these two indexes, the really *basic coverage is through the title indexes,* which the General Index coordinates and supplements. An index search, then, includes consultation of all the indexes mentioned above.

a. *Title indexes.* Each of the 480 main C.J.S. topics or titles is separately indexed in the volume in which it is printed, except that when a title begins in one volume and is completed in another, it is indexed only in the final volume containing that title. These indexes are referred to in the General Indexes as "title indexes."

The title indexes form the main subject indexing of C.J.S., and any index search should start with them for matter up to the date of their publication. For example, if the searcher is interested in notice as an element of fraudulent conveyances of corporate property, he should first consult the index to "Corporations" in volume 20 of C.J.S., subtitle "fraudulent conveyances," for any material up to 1940, the publication date of the C.J.S. volume covering that subtopic. For material from 1940 to date in this subtopic, the index search would be in the General Index and its annual pocket supplements under the same title and subtitle. There will be no additional index entry if the materials later than 1940 are only cumulative in effect and make no new law; if there are additional cases in point, they will be noted in the pocket supplement (not an index but a systematic noting of new material) in volume 20, containing the main text treatment of the topic. No additional index entry is made, because the new cases are precisely covered by the same title, subtitle and section designations as in the original text volume. Later citations will be noted in the index, however, whenever they constitute new law or for some other reason require additional comment or rewriting.

The title index coverage is limited to material in the actual title indexed, with no cross references to material in other titles. If, as frequently happens, *another title* does contain material pertinent in any way to the subject matter of this title, it is to be found through the General Index. For example, the index to "Wills" in 97 C.J.S. covers only material contained in volumes 94 to 97 of C.J.S. on the topic of wills, and there are in it no cross references to materials involving wills in other titles. This is where the General Index complements the title index: While specific legacies, devises and gifts, for example, are covered generally in "Wills" and indexed in volume 97 of C.J.S., an executor's or administrator's powers and duties under the will are discussed in the title "Executors and Administrators." The General Index, under "Wills — specific legacy, devise or gift," refers the searcher *generally* to the "title index to Wills," which is in volume 96, but for the powers and duties of executors and administrators, the reference is to the specific sections in "Executors and Administrators" covering the desired subtopic.

b. *Recompiled volumes indexes.* When the bulk of the pocket part supplementary material or substantial changes in the law of a given C.J.S. title require it, the entire title is rewritten to incorporate new material and to note the changes. The recompiled title or titles found in the expanded, recompiled volume are then reindexed and the original volume with its index discarded.

c. *General Index and its functions.* The five-volume General Index covers all of the C.J.S. titles. Large topics, which are not, however, "titles," are also covered in detail as in other descriptive-word indexes — e.g., Rivers and Streams, Social Rights and Standing. Separate words, e.g., "soapstone," "sweat," "uncut diamonds," and "vending machines," are listed in their regular word order as in a dictionary, but there is an additional table of Words and Phrases and Maxims in This Volume, at the back of each text volume just preceding the title indexes. In total, these separate indexes include more words and terms than are found in the General Index in the alphabetical listing of separate words.

> **SECURITY**
> Generally, see **Title Index to**
> **Chattel Mortgages**
> **Costs**
> **Mortgages**
> **Principal and Surety**
> Abandonment, discharge of indemnitor by, **Indem § 40,
> p. 635**
> Accord and satisfaction, new or additional security,
> **Accord § 25**
> Account stated,
> Given to settle, **Acct St § 44**
> Taking security on settlement affecting right **to**
> impeach, **Acct St § 51**

Exhibit 53

Maxims may be both in the General Index and in their proper alphabetical order in the text volumes.

The General Index, in so far as it indexes the titles or large subjects, has two principal functions: First, it is a title finder; second, it is a coordinator of subject entries which are found in two or more different titles. This is illustrated by Exhibit 53.

"Security," which is not a C.J.S. title, is covered generally in its various aspects by the indexes to the four titles mentioned in the index in the respective text volumes discussing "Chattel Mortgages," "Costs," "Mortgages," and "Principal and Surety." Items relating to security which are covered to some extent in other titles than these are made specific entries under "Security" in the index — e.g., "Indemnity §340," "Accord and Satisfaction §25."

Thus, while the student interested in a wife's power to acquire a separate domicile for divorce purposes would normally start his index search in the detailed index to "Divorce" in volume 27B of C.J.S., he would also, as part of his search, consult the General Index to C.J.S., and for two reasons: first, for references to new materials since 1959, the publication date of volume 27B; second, for references to other pertinent titles and sections, as, for example, "Domicile §12," page 26.

6. *Tables in C.J.S.*

a. *Tables of cases not supplied.* There are no tables of cases in C.J.S.

b. *Tables of abbreviations.* At the front of each volume of C.J.S. there is a table of abbreviations of reports, treatises and legal periodicals cited as authority. Though by no means a complete table of abbreviations, it is useful as such beyond the immediate confines of C.J.S. itself.

c. *Volumes and pages of reports covered by the annual cumulative pocket supplements.* These tables are found in each pocket supplement. Thus, if the student's problem is one of enforcing the payment of arrears in alimony and he wants to supplement his encyclopedia search by going to the digest or Reporter advance sheets for later cases, the pocket supplement tables will tell him exactly what volumes and pages of each standard report are covered in the C.J.S. supplement he has just consulted. He then needs to begin his search of recent materials only with specific later volumes and pages, thus avoiding much duplication of effort.

---

**§ 142  COMMERCE**
Page 512

15 CJS 104

In this example, the added text material shows that the cases relied upon in the original note have been reversed, states the new rule, and cites the reversing case, together (in note 99.1) with later cases in point. C.J.S. is thus to a limited extent a citator. Although C.J.S. makes such comments as this, often at considerable length, its policy is not to speculate (in the manner of law reviews) on the *probable* effects of new rulings or statutes.

**Grandfather proceedings**
U.S.—Sims Motor Transport Lines, Inc. v. U. S., D.C.Ill., 183 F.Supp. 113, affd. 80 S.Ct. 1076, 362 U.S. 637, 4 L.Ed.2d 1019.

99. U.S.—Schenley Distillers Corporation v. U. S., supra, n. 97—I. C. C. v. Isner, D.C.Mich., 92 F.Supp. 582.

Since the publication of Corpus Juris Secundum the case cited therein has been reversed and the court has been held not required to determine whether applicant is entitled to a certificate under other provisions of the Motor Carrier Act of 1935.99.1

99.1 U.S.—U. S. v. Maher, Or., 59 S.Ct. 768, 307 U.S. 148, 83 L.Ed. 1162, reh. den. 59 S.Ct. 831, 307 U.S. 649, 83 L.Ed. 1528—A. E. McDonald Motor Freight Lines v. U. S., supra, n. 97—A. B. & C. Motor Transp. Co. v. U. S., D.C.Mass., 69 F.Supp. 166.

**Exhibit 54**

7. *Supplementation of C.J.S.* Supplementation is of three kinds.

a. *Annual cumulative pocket parts.* The text material in the respective volumes is kept up to date by annual cumulative pocket parts. These supplementary entries are keyed to the original text of the bound volume by having exactly the same volume, title, section, page and footnote numbers. Matching up the original text and the supplement is done very simply. For example, to bring up to date the text and corresponding citations to authority for the topic "Commerce §142," note 99, which is on page 512 of volume 15 of C.J.S., it is necessary only to go to the pocket supplement of volume 15, under "Commerce §142," page 512, note 99, where later citations in point are collected, as seen in Exhibit 54.

When later decisions in point are merely cumulative in effect and do not change the law, no added comment is made in the supplements, even though hundreds of new cases have been cited for a single footnote, as in "Conspiracy §193," footnote 44. Every later case in point is said to be cited and, if necessary, commented upon in the supplements. Where, however, the later cases have modified the law as stated in the original C.J.S. text, comments are made in the pocket supplements, even to the extent of complete revision. An example of extensive rewriting in the supplements is in the "Bankruptcy" title, in which statutory amendments since publication of the original volume have substantially changed the law.

A table at the front of each pocket supplement lists the volumes and pages of reports covered in the supplementary materials.

b. *Recompiled volumes.* Where the mass of supplementary decisions makes the pocket parts noting them unwieldy, or where extensive changes have been made in the law covered by one or more titles included in a C.J.S. volume, the text of that volume is rewritten as necessary, incorporating the added materials. The original volume is then discarded, the expanded volumes inheriting that volume's number, plus additional "A" or "B" numbered volumes as required. Thus original volume 27 comprised "Discovery" through "Domesticated," including the large title of "Divorce." The law relating to divorce was so greatly changed by later decisions that a revision of the whole title was necessary, the expanded material in old volume 27 now being contained in new volumes 27, 27A and 27B. The respective titles in the recompiled volumes are completely indexed anew, and these indexes, not the General Index, should be a starting point for a descriptive-word search in these titles.

c. *General Index pocket parts.* The General Index is supplemented by annual cumulative pocket parts, as noted under Indexes for C.J.S., page 230, par. 5.

§17.9. **State legal encyclopedias.** The publishers of Am. Jur. have brought out several state "Jurisprudence" legal encyclopedias, which parallel Am. Jur. in purpose but emphasize the law of a single state (as influenced by federal law, of course). Other publishers have similar state legal encyclopedias.

§17.10. **Special-subject legal encyclopedias.** These are really very large textbooks, some of twenty or more volumes, which cover their subject matter — insurance, automobiles, corporations, oil and gas, federal and state procedure, etc., in great detail. Most of them differ from the general legal encyclopedia in having tables of cases; annotated legal forms are also a common feature. They are essentially casefinders with a running commentary on the law covered. While there are descriptive-word indexes, the analysis of topics at the beginning of each title is ordinarily not so detailed as in the general encyclopedias or digests.

§17.11. **Techniques of using legal encyclopedias.** As noted earlier in this chapter, the general legal encyclopedia serves both as a text commentary on the law and as a casefinder. The searcher who knows little or nothing about a topic of law can find in the encyclopedia an elementary statement of the law. The lawyer needing a brushup in a field in which he has become rusty can renew his acquaintance with it, or he can find the applicable rules covering any topic, substantive or procedural, set out in the most detailed manner.

A workman seldom can complete a job with the use of only a single tool; neither can a lawyer. We have, so far in this book, studied tools of various kinds, including annotations, and digests and encyclopedias. A lawyer would probably use all these in a search and also some legal tools we have not yet dealt with. The following illustrative problem employs some of the necessary techniques of integrating the materials studied so far.

1. *Problem.* At the time of their marriage, H took out a $15,000 life insurance policy in favor of W as named beneficiary. There was a double indemnity provision in case of accidental death. The policy also provided that "In the event of death of any beneficiary before insured, the interest of such beneficiary shall vest in the insured"; and "Double indemnity death benefits shall not be payable if death resulted . . . from having been engaged in aviation or aeronautics." H and W were killed in the crash of a regularly licensed carrier airplane in which they were passengers. What are the rights of the administrators and of the estates of H and W? The insurer denies liability for double indemnity, on the ground that as an airplane passenger H was "engaged in aviation or aeronautics." H's administrator claims that the "death of beneficiary before insured" provision entitles him to the proceeds, because of a presumption of H's longer survival in case of death by common disaster. Since both problems are solved by like processes in the encyclopedias, digests and A.L.R., only the first one will be solved here as an example. In order to save duplication, the solution will be first by the fact method through C.J.S. and then through the analytical approach in Am. Jur., with mention of two special-subject encyclopedias and of the digests. Each approach is, of course, equally available to users of any of these encyclopedias.

*The insurer denies liability for double indemnity, on the ground that H was "engaged in aviation or aeronautics."*

2. *Index approach.* On its face, this might be either an aviation or an insurance problem. A search under Aerial Navigation, however, in the General Index to C.J.S. and in volume 2 of C.J.S. under the same title, reveals that the subject matter here has to do with the licensing and operation of airplanes and the liability as between passenger and carrier; insurance as between

passenger and insurance company is not covered at all. Therefore, you think of "Insurance" as an index heading. Under this title in the index you are referred to the index to the title "Insurance" in volume 46 of C.J.S. This index yields the following applicable entries, all leading to "Insurance, §938," pages 1085-1086 of volume 45. See Exhibit 55.

**INDEXING**

Airplanes and aeronautics
  Life Insurance, death from engaging in aviation, § 938
Double Indemnity
  Death resulting from particular risks, § 938
  Passenger
    Double Indemnity for death, § 938
    Participating in aviation within exception, § 938
    Public conveyance, death of passenger riding in, § 938
Life Insurance
  Accidental death benefits, § 938
  Aviation, liability for death while engaging in, § 938
Passengers
  Airplane
    Double indemnity clause exception applicable to passenger of, § 938
    Double indemnity for death, § 938

Exhibit 55

Closer analysis of the specific pages cited leads to page 1086, where the precise question involved in the problem is discussed, with the citation in footnotes 91 and 92 to authority from all jurisdictions which have considered it. Normally at this point, the C.J.S. text would refer to earlier cases in point in C.J., but there is no such citation in this example. This is because, when the "Insurance" title of C.J. was compiled in 1924, people were not yet riding as passengers in commercial airplanes, and so there were no cases to refer to. Turning to the annual cumulative pocket supplement in the back of volume 45, a search under 45 C.J.S. 1086, §938, notes 91 and 92 will reveal any later authorities in point.

3. *Analytical approach.* In solving the same problem through the analytical approach, in Am. Jur. this time, the same preliminary analysis leads to the topic "Insurance." As in digests, there is first a main analysis with only the principal chapter headings, but with references to pages where each main head is expanded into a detailed subanalysis. "Insurance" is divided into twenty-four main heads. The searcher in scanning these main

heads discards as inapplicable such heads as "Insurance Companies," "Insurance Agents and Brokers," "Insurable Interest," etc. "XVI: Risks and Coverage," however, is encouraging, particularly subdivision "D-1: Aviation or Aeronautics," covering sections 1260 to 1271. Although perusal of the text under these section numbers gives a good general discussion of the matter of "engaging in" aeronautics, section 1270 seems to be the closest in point. Notes 16 to 19 cite authority and refer to two A.L.R. annotations in point, in 155 A.L.R. 1036 and 17 A.L.R.2d 1041, 1052. The latter annotation lists thirty-eight different exclusionary clauses in insurance policies, where death results from riding in an airplane. Of these Clause 10 is directly in point and lists and discusses several cases in which the clause was construed.

Later cases are found through the A.L.R.2d Supplement Service, and in the pocket supplement to volume 29A of Am. Jur. by the process of matching title, section, page and note numbers with those of the main text. New material may call for a new note to a given section or a revision of it.

Exhibit 56, showing a subanalysis under "Insurance," illustrates the use of the analytical method.

4. *Special legal encyclopedias.* The insurance problem above, and problems in other subject matter for which there are special-subject encyclopedias, are solved in exactly the same two ways as by a general legal encyclopedia, with the addition for some such

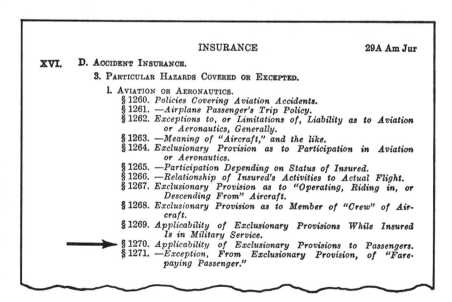

Exhibit 56

encyclopedias of the table of cases approach. The space devoted to a given topic in a special-subject encyclopedia is often considerably more than that in a general legal one. For example, each of two insurance encyclopedias devotes about four times as much space to our airplane passenger situation as do the general legal encyclopedias. The indexing is also apt to be much more detailed in the special-subject encyclopedia.

5. *Words and phrases approach.* This approach, described at page 286, par. 4, is frequently useful when the legal interpretation of a word or term is involved. In our insurance problem the chief point at issue is whether, within the terms of the insurance policy, H was "engaged in aviation or aeronautics." Notes 90 to 92 to "Insurance §938," on page 1086 of volume 45 of C.J.S. concern the construction of that term. The dictionary function of C.J.S. is demonstrated in 30 C.J.S. 246-248, where "engage" is defined as to its various uses. Footnote 80(5) on page 248 defines "engaged in aeronautics," with citations to cases. In Am. Jur. the Words and Phrases section of the General Index does not define the word in our connection, but in the index to "Insurance" in volume 29A the word is defined under "Insurance: Aviation: participation or engagement in."

6. *Integration of annotations and digests with encyclopedias.* Work with A.L.R. annotations has been described in detail at pages 148-155. They often complement the discussion of many points of law in the encyclopedias by considering at length minute aspects touched upon only broadly in the relatively limited space available in encyclopedias and treatises. Annotations are cited directly in Am. Jur. The parallel citations to cases in C.J.S. serve the same purpose by citing A.L.R. cases, all of which are now annotated.

The digest, in supplementing the encyclopedia, serves two useful functions: It digests cases in point, giving the searcher much more information than mere citations, and its supplementation is monthly instead of annually. Carrying the search into the Reporter advance sheets provides weekly supplementation as well.

Employing methods learned in the preceding chapter on digests, the searcher is speedily led to the Key Number "Insurance ☞ 515.8 — Aviation or aeronautics," where he will find all cases in point in the Decennials, the General Digest, and in the Reporter advance sheet digest sections.

## CHAPTER 18

# Citators

§18.1. **Functions of citators.** In his The Jerry Giesler Story,[1] the noted Los Angeles trial lawyer relates how in his early days he lost a case when he cited as authority in a trial a case which, unknown to him, had been reversed on appeal. The presiding judge then took him into his chambers and said, "I suggest you regard this as a useful lesson rather than a humiliating experience. Your lesson is: Always Shepardize your case."[2] The judge should have added "and your statute."

The citator or citation book tells the lawyer whether the statutes and cases to be cited by him as authority are in fact valid for that purpose. Through subsequent legislative or judicial action the status of this material as authority constantly changes, and there is no assurance on its face that the long-sought-for statute or case exactly in point is of any value whatsoever when found. The careful lawyer and student alike, therefore, check the present value of each authority they consider using.

1. *Evaluating a case as authority.* There are several facets in the examination of the availability of a case to be cited as authority, as pointed out below.

[1] New York, Simon and Schuster, 1960.
[2] The Jerry Giesler Story 282 (1960).

2. *Evaluating a case as authority: Same case on appeal.* A case on appeal may be affirmed, reversed, or modified, or the appeal may be dismissed. There may be rehearings by the same court. All these actions are noted in citators. In Shepard's Citations, the outstanding example of the citation book, this aspect of the citator is called the "history" of the case.

3. *Evaluating a case as authority: Citation of case in an action on an entirely different and later case.* Such a citation or action may affect the value of an earlier case as precedent. A court may *overrule* the earlier case, as stating a doctrine no longer valid as applicable to later cases. This in no way affects the *holding* of the overruled case as between the original parties to it, as an appellate decision does. Its action is purely prospective, not retroactive. More frequently, the court in the case it now has before it, may diminish or enhance the value of the earlier case cited to it as precedent or which it cites in connection with the present action. It may do this by *criticizing, distinguishing, explaining, following* or *questioning* the holding in the earlier case cited to it. This is what Shepard's Citations calls the "treatment" of the cited case.

4. *"Cited" and "citing" statutes or cases explained.* These terms are frequently employed in legal writing and in this book and need some explanation. A *cited* case or statute in a citator is simply the one which is being Shepardized (see §18.3); in Shepard's Citation this means the volume number of a case above the line on a Shepard's page and the page number in boldface type below the line. In a statute it is the enactment, the status of which as precedent you are testing. A *citing* case, on the other hand, is a different case which the court or a brief mentions as in some way constituting precedent in the case before the court. For example, the case of *Williams* v. *North Carolina,* 317 U.S. 287, 63 Sup. Ct. 207, 87 L. Ed. 279 (1942), considered the earlier case of *Haddock* v. *Haddock,* 201 U.S. 562, 26 Sup. Ct. 525, 50 L. Ed. 867 (1906), as precedent in the matter of one spouse establishing a separate matrimonial domicile for divorce purposes. *Haddock* had been cited to the Supreme Court as an established precedent, but the Court expressly overruled it. Here the Court in *Williams* cited the *Haddock* case; *Haddock* is, accordingly, the *cited* case by the Court, and *Williams* the case which cited it — the *citing* case. In a later case where *Williams* is offered as precedent in another case before the Court, it will be the *cited* case.

In the Massachusetts case shown in Exhibit 57 below, 296 Mass. 275, with its Reporter counterpart, 5 N.E.2d 720, is the *cited* case. Everything else, beginning, respectively, with 298 Mass. 500 and 11 N.E.2d 590, is *citing* material.

Citing material has a wide range, comprising for our Massachusetts example all Massachusetts and federal court reported decisions construing Massachusetts cases; opinions of the Attorney General of Massachusetts affecting existing cases; law review comments on the cited cases; and annotated reports system comments on Massachusetts cases.

5. *Collecting other cases in point.* Some citators, like Shepard's citations, by listing all cases commenting upon a case known by the searcher to be in point (the *citing* cases commenting upon the *cited* case), collect additional references of value. Since the courts have regarded a case as worthy of comment by them as to the point of law involved, such cases may assay high as precedent. By the same token, the cases commenting upon a case in point may themselves have value as precedent. Cases commenting upon a statute, even though not directly construing it, may aid the lawyer in ascertaining the statute's meaning.

6. *Providing parallel citations to other standard reports or editions of statutes.* Shepard's case citations are perhaps the most accurate and complete means of translating from one form of case citation to another. In the Massachusetts example in Exhibit 57, page 244, the citator translates from Massachusetts to Northeastern and from Northeastern to Massachusetts.

7. *Court rule publication indicated.* Citators may tell in which volumes of reports court rules and amendments to them are published.

8. *Tables of statutes and cases by popular name.* Statutes and cases are often cited by a popular name — as the Taft-Hartley Act or the *Hot Oil* case — which must be translated to the official citation before they can be Shepardized. Tables are provided for this purpose. See §25.1.

**§18.2. Scope of citators.** In one form or another, citators cover all federal and state statutes, adjudicated patents and trademarks, municipal ordinances, standard editions of reported court and administrative agency decisions, Uniform Laws, American Law Institute Restatements (for a third of the states), and 117 law reviews and legal periodicals.

**§18.3. Shepard's Citations.** By far the most complete American citator system, in both geographical scope and fullness of treatment, is Shepard's Citations.[3] It is so well known that it has given rise to the legal words of art, "Shepardize" and "Shepardizing," to describe certain essential operations in assessing the current value of statutes and cases as authority. These terms are used in this book by the express permission of Shepard's Citations, Inc.

[3] Colorado Springs, Colo., Shepard's Citations, Inc.

1. *Federal coverage.*

a. *Federal statutes and cases.*   United States statutes and Supreme Court cases are covered by Shepard's United States Citations.   Prior to 1967, this citator, in its Statutes division, also covered certain federal agency decisions now included in Shepard's United States Administrative Decisions.

b. *Federal lower court cases.*   Shepard's Federal Reporter Citations covers the federal courts (and their rules, except local rules for federal district courts) below the Supreme Court, including special bankruptcy, maritime, patent and trademark reports, both official and unofficial.   Its coverage was radically altered in 1967 by the new Shepard's United States Administrative Citations, which took over some of the Federal Reporter Citations' former field.

c. *Shepard's Federal Labor Law Citations,* which began in 1959, is described at page 263.

d. *Shepard's United States Administrative Decisions.*   This series, inaugurated in 1967, is described at page 264.

In all, the above federal citations units include fifty-four different statutory or case series, the precise coverage of which is not always obvious.   In order to lead the searcher quickly to the proper Shepard's unit, a *Table of Reports in Shepard's United States, United States Administrative, and Federal Reporter Citations* is printed near the front of each *red-paper* supplement to the above-named citators.   See Exhibit 60, page 249.

2. *State coverage.*   Each state has its own Shepard's unit for official statute and case coverage.   In addition, each unit of the regional Shepard's — as Atlantic or North Eastern — gives *case* coverage of the states included in that region.

3. *District of Columbia coverage.*   In October, 1968, Shepard Citation's published a separate volume for the District of Columbia covering all the reports and all the statutes relating to the District.

§18.4.   **Shepardizing a case: State Shepard's Citations.**   Ascertaining a case's present status as authority through Shepard's Citations is intrinsically simple.   It is made virtually error-proof for anybody who will read the explanatory material at the front of each cloth bound and red-paper bound Shepard's Citations volume.   This material explains the Shepardizing process itself.   A page of Abbreviations — Analysis: Cases explains the meanings of the abbreviations to the left of the various case citations in the tabular citators — "a" for affirmed, "r" for reversed, "o" for overruled.

Abbreviations used but not explained in this Analysis are

"App'l Pen'g" in Shepard's Federal Reporter Citations and "US Sup. Ct. App'l Pen'g," in the state and other Shepard's Reporter units. These abbreviations are used only in the red-paper pamphlet supplements, and as soon as the pending appeal has been disposed of the notation is removed.

1. *Example.* You have found a case in point, 296 Mass. 275, which you wish to cite as authority. First, however, you Shepardize it to ascertain whether it is still good law.

You consult the various cloth bound volumes and the paper bound supplements of Shepard's Massachusetts Citations. To do this you simply find your citation: Volume 296 (in large type above the line on a page in the Shepard's volume), and page 275 (in large, boldface type below the line, this being the page reference). On the other hand, if your citation is to the unofficial 5 N.E.2d 720, you consult Shepard's Northeastern Reporter Citations, where volume 5, Second Series, is found above the line, and page 720, in boldface type, below the line. The rest of the simple process is described in the instruction page, Exhibit 57 below.

2. *Information gleaned from Shepardizing.* In this Shepardizing process the searcher will glean any or all of the following information:

a. *Parallel citation from one report series to another.* (As from official to unofficial, or reverse.) Shepard's Citations provide one of the best means of translating an official citation to a Reporter citation, or the reverse. The parallel citation is supplied, whether or not other cases have later cited the main case.

"Same case in another report series" is denoted in the older Shepard's Citations by the "s" preceding the case citation. In most of the newer ones it is done by enclosing the case citation in parentheses; the "s" is then reserved for the main case in another stage of its progress through the courts. Note also that *once the parallel citation has been printed in a bound volume of Shepard's, it is no longer given in succeeding supplements.*

b. *Appellate disposition of main case.* This is what Shepard's calls the "history" of the case, that is, affirmance, reversal or dismissal on appeal.

c. *Courts' citation of the main case as authority in another and later case.* Under the main or *cited* case are listed citations to any cases which have subsequently commented on the main case and so affected its status as authority. This is the "treatment" of the case by the *citing* cases listed, whether they criticize, distinguish, explain, overrule, etc.

d. *Courts of other states citing the main case.* This information is available through the regional Reporter Shepard's units, the

# ILLUSTRATIVE CASE

**Massachu-
setts
Reports**

**Vol. 296**

Citations to the case of Howes Brothers Company v. Unemployment Compensation Commission reported in Volume 296 Massachusetts Reports at page 275 are shown in the left margin as they appear in this volume.

An examination of the history of this case shows that the same case "s" (see tables of abbreviations, *infra*) is reported in 5 Northeastern Reporter, Second Series "NE" page 720. Upon appeal to the United States Supreme Court, a petition for writ of certiorari was denied in 300 United States Reports "US" 657, 81 Lawyers Edition of United States "LE" 867, 57 Supreme Court Reporter "SC" 434. The arrangement of these citations is an example of the grouping that is used wherever there are parallel sets of reports covering the same citing case.

An examination of the treatment of this case indicates that it has been distinguished "d" and explained "e" in subsequent cases in the Massachusetts Reports and Federal Reporter, Second Series.

The first citation is found in 298 Massachusetts Reports "Mas" 500. The superior figure "2" appearing in advance of the citing page number 500 indicates that the principle of law brought out in paragraph two of the syllabus of 296 Mas 275 is also dealt with in 298 Mas 500. If you are especially interested in this paragraph of the syllabus, the citing authorities indicate that this point of law has been cited to in a case reported in 31 Federal Supplement "FS" 604.

There are references analyzed to other paragraphs of the syllabus of the cited case in cases reported in the Massachusetts Reports, United States Supreme Court Reports (three editions), Federal Reporter, Second Series "F2d", Federal Supplement and in the notes of the American Law Reports "AlR". Thus, the citations dealing with a point of law in any particular paragraph of the syllabus may be referred to instantly without examining every citation to the case.

This case has also been cited in the Opinions of the Attorney General of Massachusetts "AG", Boston University Law Review "BUR" and Massachusetts Law Quarterly "MQ".

By reference to the citations to the corresponding decision in the Northeastern Reporter division of this volume, which are reproduced in the right margin it is possible to trace the history and citations to this decision in the parallel Massachusetts decisions in the Northeastern Reporter and in cases in the United States Supreme and lower Federal Courts.

Thus, in the most compact and convenient form, the complete judicial history of every Massachusetts case is shown; where else reported; whether affirmed, reversed, dismissed or modified; and the mode of its citation, whether followed, explained, distinguished, overruled, etc., and the extent to which each of the points decided in the case has been regarded as an authority.

**North-
eastern
Reporter,
Second
Series**

**Vol. 5**

Exhibit 57

citations being, of course, to the Reporters and not to the official citing reports.

e. *Attorney Generals' comment on main case in their opinions.* When an attorney general has commented on the main case, his opinion is noted in Shepard's Citations.

f. *Law review comments on main case.* If law reviews of the state of the forum have commented on the case, that is noted. Since 1958, comments by fifteen "national" law reviews have also been noted.

g. *A.L.R. annotations mentioning main case.* When an A.L.R. annotation mentions the main case, that fact is indicated.

3. *Selecting the proper state Shepard's unit and volume.* There is possible difficulty here in only two instances: selection of the proper unit of the New York official case citators, and of the report volume number for those states which have renumbered their old "nominative" reports, i.e., reports cited by name of reporter instead of by jurisdiction.

a. *New York official reports citators.* Since New York has had eighty-eight different official series of reports from its numerous courts, there are three Shepard's units for this state (in addition to Shepard's New York Supplement Citations, which covers the unofficial series): (1) Shepard's Court of Appeals Citations; (2) Shepard's Miscellaneous Citations; and (3) Shepard's Supreme Court Citations.

A table of New York Reports in Shepard's New York editions, near the front of each red-paper supplement to each edition, lists alphabetically all eighty-eight reports series, with the Shepards' unit covering each. Parallel reference tables in Shepard's New York Court of Appeals Citations tell where each Court of Appeals case is printed in the New York Supplement, and all "nominative" series (as Abbott, Sanford) publishing Court of Appeals reports.

b. *State reports by name of reporter which have been renumbered consecutively.* Most official reports series in the older states, up to the mid-nineteenth century, were known and cited by the name of the official reporter, as Pickering, Randolph or Chipman. This proved so cumbersome that most such series then still current were renumbered consecutively and chronologically in a single numerical series for each jurisdiction, bearing the name of the state only. Shepard's Citations follows the renumbered order. In spite of such renumbering, however, these early nominatives are commonly cited by their original Pickering, Randolph, etc., volume numbers. Wherever this renumbering has occurred, Shepard's Citations provides a cross reference table, like the one shown in Exhibit 58, in the front of each appropriate unit. Where these

## MASSACHUSETTS REPORTS, Vols. 18–96

### CROSS REFERENCE TABLE

| | | | | |
|---|---|---|---|---|
| 1 Allen | ..............83 Massachusetts | | 15 Gray | ..............81 Massachusetts |
| 2 Allen | ..............84 Massachusetts | | 16 Gray | ..............82 Massachusetts |
| 3 Allen | ..............85 Massachusetts | | 1 Metcalf | ............42 Massachusetts |
| 4 Allen | ..............86 Massachusetts | | 2 Metcalf | ............43 Massachusetts |
| 5 Allen | ..............87 Massachusetts | | 3 Metcalf | ............44 Massachusetts |
| 6 Allen | ..............88 Massachusetts | | 4 Metcalf | ............45 Massachusetts |
| 7 Allen | ..............89 Massachusetts | | 5 Metcalf | ............46 Massachusetts |
| 8 Allen | ..............90 Massachusetts | | 6 Metcalf | ............47 Massachusetts |
| 9 Allen | ..............91 Massachusetts | | 7 Metcalf | ............48 Massachusetts |
| 10 Allen | ..............92 Massachusetts | | 8 Metcalf | ............49 Massachusetts |
| 11 Allen | ..............93 Massachusetts | | 9 Metcalf | ............50 Massachusetts |
| 12 Allen | ..............94 Massachusetts | | 10 Metcalf | ............51 Massachusetts |
| 13 Allen | ..............95 Massachusetts | | 11 Metcalf | ............52 Massachusetts |
| 14 Allen | ..............96 Massachusetts | | 12 Metcalf | ............53 Massachusetts |
| 1 Cushing | ............55 Massachusetts | | 13 Metcalf | ............54 Massachusetts |
| 2 Cushing | ............56 Massachusetts | | 1 Pickering | .........18 Massachusetts |
| 3 Cushing | ............57 Massachusetts | | 2 Pickering | .........19 Massachusetts |
| 4 Cushing | ............58 Massachusetts | | 3 Pickering | .........20 Massachusetts |
| 5 Cushing | ............59 Massachusetts | | 4 Pickering | .........21 Massachusetts |
| 6 Cushing | ............60 Massachusetts | | 5 Pickering | .........22 Massachusetts |
| 7 Cushing | ............61 Massachusetts | | 6 Pickering | .........23 Massachusetts |

Exhibit 58

old nominatives have been discontinued and have not been renumbered, they are listed in the tables of contents of the appropriate Shepard's units under their names. This is true of many New York early case series, as Barbour or Lansing.

4. *Comments on a state case by courts of another jurisdiction.* Although a decision in Illinois is not mandatory in Iowa or Oklahoma, it may be highly persuasive there. Therefore, well-reasoned and significant opinions by the courts of one state are often cited as persuasive authority by the courts of other states. For example, *Mitchell* v. *Rochester Ry. Co.,* 151 N.Y. 107, 45 N.E. 354 (1896), has been cited by the courts of thirty-five other states. As a practical matter such out-of-state citing cases are traceable only through their National Reporter System citations.

a. *Citation of cases decided before the National Reporter System.* Comments by out-of-state courts on cases of the forum are available only through their Reporter citations. Since the earliest Reporter dates from 1879, *citing* cases previous to that date cannot be found. However, *cited* cases from the very beginning, if cited by a Reporter at any subsequent date, can be found for more than half the states.

(1) *Citing cases listed by Reporter citation.* Some state Shepard's units like those for California, Delaware, Georgia and Illinois, list the citing cases by their Reporter citation immediately following the citation of the cited case by cases of the forum. How this is done is shown by Exhibit 59. Thus, 102 Ill. 359 has been cited by 362 Ill. 60 and by certain other cases, such as 198 N.E. 704 and 106 P.2d 175, the citing cases other than Illinois being listed by their Reporter citations.

ILLINOIS SUPREME COURT REPORTS     Vol. 102

—359—
362 Ill   160
198 N E¹704
106 P2d 175

Exhibit 59

(2) *Listing citing cases in the same Reporter area.* A few state Shepard's units like Shepard's Colorado Citations, list all the cases of the forum citing local state cases, followed by Reporter citations for states in the same Reporter area (Pacific as applied to Colorado cited cases).

(3) *Separate Reporter citation section in state Shepard's units.* For several states — Connecticut, Kansas, Massachusetts, Nebraska, Ohio and Wyoming — the state Shepard's Citations has a separate section covering all Reporter citations of cases of the forum decided up to the beginning of the Reporter for each state. An example is the separate section in Shepard's Massachusetts Citations, entitled Massachusetts Reports — Vols. 1-38 — Cited in the National Reporter System. This section notes every comment on these earlier, pre-Reporter, cases by National Reporter System cases in any jurisdiction.

b. *Citation of cases reported in the National Reporter System.* Every state Shepard's Citations except for New York (which state has its New York Supplement Citations) contains a section listing cases for that state under their Reporter volume and page numbers.

Again taking as an example 296 Mass. 275, Shepard's Massachusetts Citations contains a section called Northeastern Reporter (Massachusetts Cases), which lists this case under its Reporter citation of 5 N.E.2d 720 as a *cited* case. *Citing* cases, that is, those cases which have mentioned 296 Mass. 275 in their opinions, listed thereunder are Massachusetts cases (by their Reporter citations) and federal court cases (also by Reporter citations). Normally, because the official reports section of a state Shepard's unit lists citing cases by official citation, you would, if you had only the 5 N.E.2d 720 citation, translate it to 296 Mass. 275 by means of the Reporter citation's parallel official citation.   When a case is reported only in the Reporter and not in the official report — as many are — you will of course find it listed only in the separate Reporter section, in the state Shepard's unit having such a section.

c. *Citation of a state court case by courts of all jurisdictions.* Since the state Shepard's Citations lists only federal court and local court (Massachusetts here) citing cases, the approach to the courts of all jurisdictions must be through the appropriate Shepard's regional Reporter Citations.   In our Massachusetts example, taking the citation 5 N.E.2d 720 into Shepard's Northeastern Citations, you will find there every Reporter citation of cases mentioning this case, together with the state of the court making the decision.   The order of listing of these citing cases under the above citation is: United States Supreme Court cases affirming or reversing, Massachusetts commenting or citing cases, cases from other states in that Reporter unit (Northeastern here), and last, alphabetically by state, cases from other regional Reporters.

§18.5.   **Shepardizing a case: National Reporter System Shepard's Citations, covering United States, Federal and regional Reporter cases.**   Shepard's Reporter units include Shepard's United States Citations, Federal Reporter Citations, Federal Labor Law Citations, United States Administrative Citations, and those for the various regional Reporters, as, for example, Atlantic, Northeastern, New York Supplement, Pacific, etc.   Together, these cover all standard report series, but the regional Reporter Shepard's Citations coverage is for the Reporter period only, or from about 1880 to date.   There are special Shepard's Citations for the New York Supplement and the California Reporter.

1. *Process employed in Shepardizing.*   Shepardizing cases through the Reporter Shepard's Citations is exactly the same as when the state units are used, but the results are broader, in that the unit, in addition to citing the cases of the forum commenting on the case you are Shepardizing, also includes all commenting cases in all Reporters, thus giving nationwide citing case coverage. Our main case, 296 Mass. 275, is shown, through the 5 N.E.2d 720 citation in Shepard's Northeastern Reporter Citations, to have been cited by the courts of twenty other states.

No statutes are covered by Shepard's Reporter Citations, except by Shepard's United States Citations, which covers the Statutes at Large and United States Code.   No law review comments are noted, except in the four federal units, since they are in the state

Shepard's units, though mention of the main case in A.L.R. annotations is noted.

2. *Shepardizing state cases not officially reported.* Regional Reporters (like Atlantic or North Eastern) print many cases which are not officially reported, and so cannot be Shepardized in the state Shepard's Citations except in the section covering local state cases reported in the Reporter (e.g., the section of Northeastern Reporter — Massachusetts Cases). The absence of a parallel official citation in its proper place in a Reporter Shepard's Citations is almost infallible proof of the lack of an official report. For cases beginning with the National Reporter System, the Reporter Shepard's Citations is more complete in its listings than the state Shepard's official section, to the extent of the inclusion of cases unreported officially. Cases antedating the National Reporter System, if commented upon by Reporters at a later date, are listed in the Reports Cited in the National Reporter System section found in some state Shepard's units.

3. *Shepardizing federal court decisions.* Federal court decisions are covered by three different Shepard's units: Shepard's United States Citations, Shepard's Federal Reporter Citations, and Shepard's Federal Labor Law Citations (which covers, also, N.L.R.B. decisions). Since the series covered by these three units comprise some fifty-four different ones — not always easily distinguishable from their titles — Shepard's has provided in each red-paper supplement to the above units a Table of Reports covered in all federal units (see Exhibit 60). Federal administrative agency decisions are described at page 263.

---

# Table of Reports in Shepard's United States, United States Administrative and Federal Reporter Editions

Abstracted Protest Decisions ............................Administrative
Abstracted Reappraisement Decisions ....................Administrative
Abstracts ..............................................Administrative
Abstracts, New Series ..................................Administrative
American Bankruptcy Reports ............................Federal
American Bankruptcy Reports, New Series ................Federal
American Maritime Cases ................................Federal
Appeal Cases, District of Columbia Reports .............Federal
Application for Review Decisions .......................Administrative
Black's Reports (66–67 U. S.) ..........................United States

---

**Exhibit 60**

a. *Supreme Court cases.* These are covered by Shepard's United States Citations.

The procedure in Shepardizing Supreme Court cases is as described for state cases. Citing cases, those mentioning the case you are Shepardizing, include not only all state reports and units of the National Reporter System, but a wide variety of administrative reports series and A.L.R. annotations.

Citations to reports in Shepard's United States Citations are in three parallel series: (1) by United States Reports official citation, (2) by Supreme Court Reporter citation, and (3) by Lawyers' Edition citation. Since the first ninety volumes of the Supreme Court Reports are commonly cited by the reporter's name instead of by series volume number, a Parallel Reference Table in the front of the unit translates from the nominative — Dallas, Peters, etc. — to the United States Reports citation. To save space, *all actual Shepardizing information is given only under the official* — with the following exceptions: the unofficial listing of Supreme Court cases shows some cases not officially reported. If such cases have been the subject of action which is covered by Shepard's units, that action is indicated under the unofficial citation only, since there is no place for it under the official.

b. *Lower federal court cases.* Shepard's Federal Reporter Citations now cover those federal courts below the Supreme Court (including federal courts in the District of Columbia) as distinct from administrative agencies having the title but not the full status of "court" and federal court rules above the local federal district court level. It also covers certain maritime, bankruptcy, patent and trade-mark series, some of them unofficial. Since the coverage of this Reporter citator unit was radically changed in 1967, the comparative table shown in Exhibit 60 should be consulted when in doubt.

c. *Patents and trade-marks.* These are covered by Shepard's United States Citations, Patents and Trademarks. What might be called the history of a patent or trade-mark — whether declared valid, infringed, etc. — is also covered by the Federal Digest, the Modern Legal Practice Digest and the Decennial Digests, under "Patents" and "Trade-Marks" respectively. (See page 210.)

d. *Shepard's Federal Labor Law Citations.* This series, covering both statutes and court and agency decisions, is described at page 263.

e. *Shepard's United States Administrative Decisions.* This series is described at page 264.

**§18.6.  Case citators other than Shepard's Citations.**

1. *Digest tables of cases generally.*  Most case digests, through their tables of cases or in their digest paragraphs or both, state whether the cases digested therein have been affirmed, reversed or modified on appeal — corresponding to the Shepard's "history" of the case.

2. *Digest tables of cases affirmed, reversed or modified.*  Tables in the General Digest list cases which have been affected by later decisions, the history of the cases.  The Digest of the United States Supreme Court Reports has a similar table.  (See page 211, par. (3).)  This latter table affords the quickest means of checking on all cases in any jurisdiction, or over any given time span, which have been directly affected by subsequent decisions of the Supreme Court.

3. *Tables of cases judicially noticed.*  Several state digests have such tables, arranged as plaintiff-defendant case tables.

4. *Loose-leaf services and reporters as case citators.*  Especially in the tax and labor fields, loose-leaf services perform a citator function.  This is described in Chapter 23.

**§18.7.  Sheparding legislation: Generally.**  Legislation is somewhat more complicated to Shepardize than cases.  Once a case is decided and the opinion published, its form is fixed.  Subsequent judicial action may affect its value as precedent, but not its form.  Statutes, however, change in form: Constitutions are amended or new ones adopted; session laws are later codified into sections of codes or other compilations, and they are amended and repealed; codes themselves are revised at intervals.

The function of Shepardizing legislation, therefore, is a dual one: (1) To trace subsequent legislative action on a given law.  This may include amendments, repeals, additions, extensions of the term where an act is to end on a given date or event, revisions, etc.  (2) To trace subsequent judicial action construing the legislation.  This may include decisions as to constitutionality and validity.

**§18.8.  Sheparding legislation: Shepard's Citations coverage.**  The Shepard's system covers federal and state constitutions, session laws, compiled statutes, city charters and ordinances, and court rules.  For twenty-one states the American Law Institute Restatements as cited by the courts and commented upon by law reviews are covered.  Subordinate legislation has a limited Shepardizing coverage, for which see §18.15.

**§18.9.  Sheparding legislation: Arrangement of legislation in Shepard's Citations.**  Facility in finding the legislation to be Shepardized in the appropriate unit is increased by knowledge of the physical order in which the various types are arranged in these citators.

The arrangement depends upon the form of the legislation. This form may be changed by legislative action subsequent to the original enactment or promulgation. This is significant principally when a session law — for example, the Statutes at Large in federal legislation — is incorporated in a subject arrangement in a federal or state compilation of public, general and permanent interest, such as the United States Code and similar state compilations. Arrangement of legislation in Shepard's Citations is as follows:

1. *Constitutions.* The arrangement is by article and section and by amendment and section for the federal Constitution; state constitutions are listed by date of adoption, then by article and section.

2. *Session laws.* The federal form is the Statutes at Large. These are listed by date, chapter (or, beginning with the eighty-fifth Congress in 1957, by law number for the Statutes at Large) and section.

3. *Compilations of statutes.* These are listed by edition or date, then by title and section.

4. *Treaties.* Up to 1945, as Statutes at Large, by date of treaty; thereafter by volume and page in a special section in both Shepard's United States Citations and in the state Shepard's Citations, under United States Treaties and Other International Agreements.

5. *Municipal charters and ordinances.* These are arranged alphabetically by municipality, thereunder by date and section. There is a subject index of adjudications.

6. *Court rules.* The arrangement is by court, date, section.

7. *Presidential executive acts.* Executive orders, proclamations and reorganization plans can be Shepardized when they form integral parts of Code sections. To find out whether they are so included, check the tables of Executive Acts Included in the tables and volumes of the Code. See also §18.15.

§18.10. **Shepardizing legislation: Information supplied by Shepard's Citations.** The information includes notations as to subsequent amendments, repeals, etc., by the legislature, and judicial action construing the legislation as to constitutionality and validity. This is shown by the illustrative statute in Exhibit 61, below. The abbreviations employed for statutes in this example are explained in the Abbreviation — Analysis: Statutes at the front of every Shepard's unit covering statutes.

**§18.11. Sheparding legislation: The federal Constitution and conventional legislation in Shepard's Citations.** Shepard's United States Citations covers the Constitution and all conventional federal legislation. In addition, nearly all state Shepard's Citations list decisions of their own courts in construing the federal Constitution and statutes. The Table of Contents at the front of each state Shepard's tells whether or not it does this.

Arranging legislation by date in Shepard's Citations sometimes causes confusion in the United States Citations when — as in treaties, for example — a group of earlier but hitherto unpublished acts are collected in a later volume of the Statutes at Large. Since the date controls the order of listing, the Act of January 23, 1792, c. 5, which is 1 Stat. 229, follows in Shepard's Citations a treaty of July 2, 1791, published in a treaty compilation in 7 Stat. 39.

1. *Constitution.* This is covered by article and section, and by amendment and section. Citing cases are from the federal courts, but comments from the Journal of the American Bar Association and annotations from the Lawyers' Edition and A.L.R. are also noted. State court treatment of the Constitution is covered by the respective state Shepard's Citations.

2. *Statutes at Large.* Sheparding any session law is quite simple if the law has never been codified in a subject matter compilation of laws of public, permanent and general interest. The law is to be found in Shepard's Citations by exact date of enactment, chapter or law number, section and Statutes at Large volume and page, but the important factor is the date. Under this date all subsequent legislative and judicial action is noted.

Where the difficulty arises is with a session law which, being of public, general and permanent interest, has been incorporated into a subject matter compilation of such enactments, such as the United States Code or its state counterparts. Shepard's United States Citations covers as Statutes at Large only those enactments of Congress which have never been so incorporated. For those that have been, the Statutes at Large citation must be translated to the Code form and there Sheparded. This, for federal laws, is done through Table III, Statutes at Large, in the Tables volume of the U.S. Code. All state statutory compilations have similar transfer tables from the session law to the compilation form.

Accordingly the Act of February 21, 1871, c. 62, 16 Stat. 419, can be Sheparded as a Statute at Large because it was never codified. This is done in that part of Shepard's United States Citations entitled United States Statutes at Large (Not in United States

## ILLUSTRATIVE STATUTES

**Mississippi
Code,
1942
and
Supple-
ment, 1956**

**TITLE 40**

**Ch. 3**

**Div. 1
§ 10109**

A1955Ex
   [p 228 ⎤ 1
A1956 p 676 ⎦

C203Mis 716
C 35So2d 73
  36So2d 142
218Mis 303 ⎤ 2
  63So2d 80
  61So2d 276

C337US 664
C 93LE1618 ⎤ 3
C 69SC 1264

1955Ex p254 ⎤ 5

**Div. 3
§ 10146-
04**
See §10149

Rs1955Ex ⎤ 1
  [p 251§4 ⎦

**§ 10149**
S §10146-04

A1946 p 527
A1948 p 773 ⎤ 1
Rp1952 p667

203Mis 715
  35So2d 73
  36So2d 142 ⎤ 2
219Mis 390
  68So2d 473
Up43So2d185

Subd. d
203Mis 724 ⎤ 6
  35So2d 75
  36So2d 142

Citations to section "§" 10109 of Division "Div." 1 and to § 10146-04 and § 10149 of Div. 3 of Chapter "Ch." 3 of Title 40 of the Mississippi Code of 1942 and Supplement, 1956 are shown in the left margin in the same form in which they appear in this volume.

Where a cited section of the Mississippi Code of 1942 has been superseded by a section in a recompiled volume of that same code, Shepard's Mississippi Citations includes under the superseded section an "S" reference to the superseding section and under the superseding section a "See" reference to the superseded section. Thus the references "S § 10146-04" under § 10149 and "See § 10149" under § 10146-04 indicate that § 10146-04 has superseded § 10149.

Citations to each cited statutory provision are grouped as follows:

1. amendments, repeals, etc. by the Mississippi Legislature;

2. citations by the Mississippi Supreme Court analyzed as to constitutionality or validity;

3. citations by federal courts analyzed as to constitutionality or validity;

4. citations in legal periodicals;

5. citations in Acts of the Mississippi Legislature; and

6. citations to specific subdivisions.

For the purpose of illustration only, this grouping has been indicated by bracketing the citations accordingly. It will be noted that as yet there are no citations in group four.

In indicating the legislative and judicial operation of a cited statute, the letter-form abbreviations shown on page 15 are used.

The first illustrative statute, § 10109 of Div. 1, was amended "A" by acts appearing on page "p" 228 of the General Laws of Mississippi, Extraordinary Session "Ex" of 1955 and page 676 of the Laws of 1956. The section was held constitutional "C" by the Mississipi Supreme Court in a case reported in 203 Mississippi Reports "Mis" 716 and 35 Southern Reporter, Second Series "So2d" 73. Each reference to a citing case as reported in the Mississippi Reports is followed by any cross reference to the same case as reported in the Southern Reporter. The section was also cited by the Mississippi Supreme Court in a case reported only in 61 So2d 276. The United States Supreme Court held the section constitutional in a case reported in 337 United States Supreme Court Reports "US" 664, 93 Lawyers' Edition, United States Supreme Court Reports "LE" 1618 and 69 Supreme Court Reporter "SC" 1264. The section was also cited by the Mississippi Legislature in an act appearing on page 254 of the General Laws of Mississippi, Extraordinary Session of 1955.

The second illustrative statute, § 10146-04 of Div. 3, was repealed and superseded "Rs" by a subsequent act of the Mississippi Legislature.

The third illustrative statute, § 10149 of Div. 3, was amended twice and repealed in part "Rp" by subsequent acts of the Mississippi Legislature. The section was cited in two Mississippi cases and was held unconstitutional in part "Up" by the Mississippi Supreme Court in a case reported only in 43 So2d 185. Subdivision "Subd." d of § 10149 was specifically cited by the Mississippi Supreme Court in a case reported in 203 Mis 724, 35 So2d 75 and 36 So2d 142.

10

Exhibit 61

Code).  The Act of February 1, 1876, c. 6, 19 Stat. 2, however, can
not be Shepardized as a Statute at Large because, as an act of public, permanent and general interest it was codified as 22 U.S.C.
§178, a form of citation found through the above parallel transfer table.  It can be Shepardized through that part of Shepard's
United States Citations entitled United States Code (1964 Edition or later editions as they appear).

a. *Federal and state cases construing the Statutes at Large.*
Shepard's United States Citations and nearly all state Shepard's
Citations cover both federal and state cases construing the Statutes
at Large.  The state units, of course, note only their own state decisions construing the Statutes at Large.

3. *Revised Statutes.*  The United States Revised Statutes are
not covered as such by any Shepard's Citations, though many sections are still in force.  If, as is the case with most of these sections
still in force, they have been integrated with the United States
Code, they can be Shepardized under the Code sections for which
they are statutory authority.  The parallel transfer Table II, Revised Statutes, in the tables volume of the Code gives the Code
citation, which can then be Shepardized.

For example, R.S. §1827 is statutory authority for 40 U.S.C.
§216 and can be Shepardized as that Code section.  If the section
to be Shepardized never was in the Code, its session law citation
will be found at the end of the section of the Revised Statutes itself and can be Shepardized as a Statute at Large.  If the section is
no longer in force, that fact can be ascertained from Table II,
above in the tables volume of the Code.

The Statutes Construed tables in the National Reporter System
cover the Revised Statutes, but these tables are not cumulative, so
that a complete search would take in every bound volume and succeeding advance sheet of the Reporters.  All Supreme Court cases
interpreting the Revised Statutes are covered in volume 14 of the
Digest of the United States Supreme Court Reports, in a table of
Laws Cited and Construed, by Supreme Court decisions.

4. *United States Code.*  If an enactment has been incorporated
in the Code, it can be directly Shepardized only through the *latest
form* of its Code citation.  Indirectly, however, an earlier Code
form can be translated into its present form.  The Statutes at
Large citation, which is authority for any form of the section, is
given in Table III of the U.S. Code, as noted above, together with
the present Code section.  Furthermore, if the former Code section was in a Code title reenacted into positive law, and that title
has been revised since, so that the old section number is obsolete,
Title I in the Code Tables volume gives the present section num-

ber, by which it is now Shepardizable. In all state Shepard's units, Code titles and sections are covered, the citing cases being those interpreting the law of the forum.

Labor provisions of the Code can be Shepardized through Shepard's Federal Labor Law Citations, which has collected all provisions concerning labor regulation in this unit. As Code sections, these provisions are also covered by Shepard's United States Citations.

*No amendments or other statutory changes back of the latest Code edition and supplement are shown.* Changes subsequent to the latest Code supplement appear in the current paperbound Shepard's Citations supplement.

Thus, the Shepard's bound supplement covering 1943-1964, noted only changes since the 1958 edition of the Code and its Supplement IV (1962). The April 1967 red-paper Supplement to 1943-1964 covered later statutory changes through the 1964 Code, Supplement I (1965). As far as possible, all cases construing the present statute in any of its earlier forms are transferred to the current section, but there is not always an exact counterpart of the older form. A repealed statute is not so represented.

In practice this does not cause much difficulty, because the searcher is ordinarily interested only in the latest form of enactment. If, on the other hand, he does want to trace the earlier forms and the cases construing them, he can usually do so through the "history" comments in his annotated edition of the United States Code or of the corresponding state compilations.

5. *Treaties.* Through 1949 (64 Statutes at Large), treaties were published as Statutes at Large and can be Shepardized as such in both Shepard's United States Citations and, as construed by state courts, in state Shepard's Citations. They are listed by treaty date, which by no means always coincides with the Statutes at Large publication date, and this sometimes causes confusion. Beginning with 1950, treaties can be Shepardized through the same federal and state Shepard's Citations units in a special section entitled United States Treaties and Other International Agreements, by volume and page of this new treaty series publication. The Statutes Construed tables in the National Reporter System cover treaties. Supreme Court interpretations of treaties are covered in the Table of Laws Cited and Construed in volume 14 of the Digest of the United States Supreme Court Reports. This latter table is unique as a citator in that it construes foreign treaties to which the United States is not a party, if such treaties are involved in a Supreme Court case.

Other publications serving a citator function for treaties are discussed at pages 47 and 48.

6. *State court construction of federal legislation.* State courts construe the federal Constitution and statutes when these affect their own states. Nearly every state Shepard's Citations has a section listing federal legislation construed. Whether a particular state has such a section is always indicated by the Table of Contents of the unit covering that state.

§18.12. **Shepardizing legislation: State conventional legislation in Shepard's Citations.** The same difficulties arise in Shepardizing state legislation as in federal, and the attack is the same.

1. *Session laws.* The current Shepard's Citations practice is to cover as session laws only those laws not incorporated into the state subject matter compilation, thus following the policy described for the federal Statutes at Large and the United States Code. Tables of statutes construed in Reporter advance sheets cover session laws as such. Some state statutory compilations have tables showing all amendments, repeals, etc., for session laws for varying periods.

2. *Compilations of statutes.* The Shepard's Citations practice is to cover subject matter compilations of statutes only in their latest form, as of the date of publication of the particular Shepard's unit or supplement. However, all citations to cases construing the predecessor form of the statutes are transferred to the new form as far as possible. Here again it may be stated that in practice this causes the lawyer little difficulty, since for the most part he is interested only in the statute in its present form. For most states, tables are provided in the statutory compilations, which enable the searcher interested in an earlier form of statute to translate the present form into the earlier one, though it is not always possible to find an equivalent.

3. *Municipal charters and ordinances.* Municipal legislation is covered by the state Shepard's Citations in a special section which includes a subject index of the legislation construed. The Reporter Statutes Construed tables cover charters and ordinances, as does, for Supreme Court decisions, the Laws Cited and Construed table of the Digest of the United States Supreme Court Reports.

4. *Uniform state laws.* There is no Shepard's Citations unit covering the Uniform Laws as such. On the other hand, parallel transfer tables in the Uniform Laws Annotated volumes enable the searcher to find the corresponding official state law citation for any section. That law, being found, can be Shepardized in the usual manner. The recently published Shepard's Acts and Cases

by Popular Names, Federal and State permit a like translation to the official statutory citation which can be Shepardized. The Reporter Statutes Construed tables cover the Uniform Laws as such, but are not cumulated from volume to volume.

5. *Interstate compacts.* These can be Shepardized in the Shepard's Citations of the states concerned, as session laws. Each state enacts separately, as a conventional session law, the compact agreed upon. The Reporter Statutes Construed tables and the Laws Cited and Construed table of the Digest of the United States Supreme Court Reports list the compacts as interstate compacts.

6. *Federal court construction of state legislation.* Citing cases in nearly all state Shepard's Citations list federal court decisions construing the state's legislation.

§18.13. **Shepardizing legislation: Statutory citators other than Shepard's Citations.** Several publications which serve a citator function have been mentioned. They are best used to supplement a Shepard's Citations unit temporarily, until the latest supplement of that unit appears. Some of these publications are described below.

1. *Statutes Construed tables of the National Reporter System.* Each advance sheet and bound volume of each Reporter unit contains a table of federal and state statutes construed by decisions printed in that unit. Citation is not confined to decisions printed in the Reporter unit containing the table, but covers interpretations by decisions reported in other units for the same period. For example, the table in the Atlantic Reporter notes the interpretations of Maryland statutes by all federal courts covered by the Supreme Court Reporter, Federal Reporter and Federal Supplement, and by Maryland courts reported in the Atlantic Reporter.

The Statutes Construed table in the Reporters include not only federal and state constitutions, session laws and treaties, but municipal charters, court rules, Presidential proclamations and executive orders. Uniform laws are covered as well.

The principal value of this table is that it may temporarily bring your search closer to date for the statutes covered than does Shepard's Citations. This is because the advance sheets bearing the table appear weekly, whereas the most frequent publication of the Shepard's Citations is the six-week period between the issuance of the red-paper supplement and the white-paper supplement. (An exception is the monthly supplementation of Shepard's Federal Labor Law Citations.) The Reporter table notes only that a statute has been construed by a given case, not the nature of the action taken; for that, the cited case must be consulted. It. is a stopgap help, pending the publication of the Shepard's Citations unit which will cover the same statutory interpretation.

These tables are not cumulated.

2. *Table of Laws Cited and Construed of the Digest of the United States Supreme Court Reports.* This table is an adjunct of the Lawyers' Edition of the United States Supreme Court Reports. Through it cases can be found construing statutes covered by no other citator. Coverage includes foreign law (including Roman), Indian laws and treaties with foreign nations as well as with the United States, the Articles of Confederation, Acts of the Continental Congress and of the Confederate States of America. Treaties and executive agreements with foreign nations, interstate compacts, proclamations and executive orders of the President are covered, in addition to conventional federal and state legislation construed by the Supreme Court. It covers state and territorial statutes in their original forms, which Shepard's Citations no longer does. This table is supplemented by annual pocket parts.

3. *Compiled statutes as citators.* Some official unannotated editions and most annotated editions of statutes serve a citator function in connection with Shepard's Citations. This is in the coverage of forms of statutes which are earlier than the current one treated in Shepard's Citations. A certain amount of the history of each section or group of sections of a statute is given, and annotations cite or digest cases construing the statutes. Examples are the United States Code Annotated, the Federal Code Annotated, and Florida Statutes Annotated.

**§18.14. A complete citator search.**

1. *Shepard's Citations.* A complete Shepard's Citations unit consists of the following parts: (a) one or more bound volumes; (b) a quarterly red-paper cumulative supplement, which eventually matures into a bound supplement; and (c) for the United States, Federal Reporter and Labor Law Citations, and about one fourth of the state Shepard's Citations, a quarterly white-paper Advance

---

**WHAT YOUR LIBRARY SHOULD CONTAIN**

| CASES | STATUTES |
|---|---|
| 1963 Bound Volume | 1963 Bound Volume |

Supplemented with
September, 1968 Cumulative Supplement Vol. LVIII No. 3
October, 1968 Advance Sheet Vol. III No. 2

**DESTROY ALL OTHER ISSUES**

---

Exhibit 62

Sheet Edition. The Advance Sheet Edition appears six weeks after the red-paper cumulative supplement, so that for units containing this edition, supplementation is about every six weeks, except for the Labor Law Citations, for which there is a month's interval.

The exact coverage of a complete unit is indicated on the cover of the latest paper supplement, as in Exhibit 62.

2. *Statutes Construed tables.* These tables may supplement temporarily the various units of Shepard's Citations and cite later cases construing a given statute than are recorded in the latest Shepard's supplement.

a. *National Reporter System units.*

b. *Digest of the United States Supreme Court Reports Laws Cited and Construed tables.* These tables are described in §18.13.

3. *Cited cases or statutes of any date are included in all Shepard's units.* The oldest case may be cited or the oldest statute, if still in force, may be construed by the very latest case. Thus, to Shepardize 1 Mo. 1 completely, each unit of Shepard's Missouri Citations must be searched — the 1963 case edition, the latest red-paper supplement, and the white-paper Advance Sheet Edition to date. Each unit contains a tabulation of citing cases covered by it: "This Issue Includes Citations in . . . ." It tells you the precise volumes and pages of each citing series included. The latest white-paper supplement will cite the earliest statute or the earliest case, if it has been affected by a current decision.

**§18.15. Administrative law citators: Subordinate legislation and decisions.** The coverage is incomplete, though, for federal administrative decisions, Shepard's United States Administrative Citations has widened it. Some of the available material is noted below.

1. *Administrative rules and regulations changes.*

a. *Federal Register Codification Guide.* This table, described in §14.6, is the most complete index to changes in the form of federal rules of general application. It notes all changes in form in regulations printed in the Federal Register.

b. *C.F.R. List of Sections Affected.* Changes made between the form of regulation as in the bound C.F.R. volumes and in the Codification Guide are noted in this annual table found as a pocket part in each volume of C.F.R.

c. *Loose-leaf services.* Some regulatory and tax services note changes in and revocation of rules and regulations. See Chapter 23.

2. *Presidential legislation.* See §14.6.

a. *Proclamations.* In some degree these are covered by: (1)

Shepard's United States Citations, as Statutes at Large when a proclamation is listed as a statutory source affecting or authorized by a Statute at Large; (2) National Reporter System Statutes Construed tables, which cover the case law on proclamations; (3) Laws Cited and Construed tables in the Digest of the United States Supreme Court Reports, which notes Supreme Court decisions construing proclamations; and (4) Shepard's United States Citations when the proclamation is integrated with U. S. Code sections (to be found through Table V of the Code in its Tables volume).

b. *Executive orders.* Since these are not published in the Statutes at Large, they are not directly covered by Shepard's Citations. Many, however, are made integral parts of Code sections by enabling legislation and so are discussed or printed in the notes to the Code sections. Since all such sections are covered by Shepard's United States Citations, the executive order can be Shepardized to the extent that it becomes a Code section, but only if it can be directly related to the Code. Relating an executive order, proclamation or reorganization plan to a Code section is accomplished through Table III of the Code, or through similar U.S.C.A. and F.C.A. tables.

Thus, in Exhibit 63, below, if it is desired to Shepardize executive order number 6084, the various Code sections of which it is a part in any way are found through the table, and the sections are Shepardized. It is indirect and not altogether satisfactory, but it can be done. This is true whether the order becomes an integral part of the Code section or is only mentioned in an editorial note to the section.

See §14.5 for a discussion of the changes in executive orders.

Statutes Construed tables in the National Reporter System note whenever an executive order has been construed by the courts, and the similar tables of the Digest of the United States Supreme Court Reports do it for Supreme Court cases. "Finding lists" of some loose-leaf services act as citators for pertinent executive orders. See §23.4.

c. *Reorganization plans.* The same procedure is followed as for proclamations and executive orders. See U.S.C. (1964 ed.), Table VI.

3. *Statutes and regulations as construed by federal agencies.* There is little agency coverage of this kind.

a. *Shepard's Federal Labor Law Citations.* As described later in this section, these cover National Labor Relations Board interpretations of federal labor acts.

b. *Index Digest of the Comptroller-General's Decisions . . . With Statutes, Decisions and Opinions Cited Therein.* This lists

# TABLE IV.—EXECUTIVE ORDERS

This Table lists the Executive Orders that implement general and permanent law as contained in U.S.C.

| Exec. Ord. | | U.S.C. | |
| --- | --- | --- | --- |
| Date | No. | Title | Sec. |
| **1918** | | | |
| May 11 | 2859 | 36 | 253 nt |
| **1929** | | | |
| Oct. 1 | 5200 | 7 | 452 nt |
| **1933** | | | |
| Mar. 27 | 6084 | 12 | Prec. 636 nt |
| June 8 | 6161 | 16 | 831u nt |
| 10 | 6166 | 5 | 124-132 nt |
| July 30 | 6237-A | 50 App. | 12 nt |
| Aug. 28 | 6260 | 12 | 95a nt |
| Oct. 25 | 6359 | 12 | 248 nt |

| Exec. Ord. | | U.S.C. | |
| --- | --- | --- | --- |
| Date | No. | Title | Sec. |
| **1941** | | | |
| June 14 | 8785 | 12 | 95a nt |
| July 26 | 8832 | 12 | 95a nt |
| Dec. 9 | 8963 | 12 | 95a nt |
| 26 | 8998 | 12 | 95a nt |
| **1942** | | | |
| Mar. 11 | 9005 | 50 App. | 6 nt |
| Apr. 4 | 9126 | 50 App. | 601 nt |
| May 29 | 9176 | 22 | Prec. 611 nt |
| 30 | 9177 | 50 App. | 601 nt |
| July 6 | 9193 | 50 App. | 6 nt |
| Aug. 20 | 9230 | 5 | 63la nt |
| | 9232 | 50 App. | 601 nt |
| Nov. 5 | 9262 | 50 App. | 601 nt |

Page 2195     TITLE 12.—BANKS AND BANKING     § 636

## INTRODUCTORY

Ex. Ord. No. 6084. Reorganizing Agricultural Credit Agencies of the United States

Ex. Ord. No. 6084, Mar. 27, 1933, provided in part: . . . It is hereby ordered that:

(1) The functions of the Secretary of Agriculture as a member of the Federal Farm Board, and the offices of the appointed members of the Federal Farm Board, except the office of the member designated as chairman thereof, are abolished.

(2) The name of the Federal Farm Board is changed to the Farm Credit Administration.

(3) The name of the office of Chairman of the Federal Farm Board is changed to Governor of the Farm Credit Administration, and he is vested with all the powers and duties of the Federal Farm Board.

(9) The unexpended balances of appropriations to the Secretary of Agriculture, the Federal Farm Loan Bureau, and the Federal Farm Board for salaries, expenses, and all other administrative expenditures in the execution of the functions herein vested in the Farm Credit Administration shall be transferred to and vested in the Farm Credit Administration as a single fund for its use for salaries, expenses, and all other administrative expenditures for the execution of any or all of such functions without restriction as to the particular functions for the execution of which the same were originally appropriated. All other appropriations, allotments, and other funds available for use in connection with the functions and executive agencies hereby transferred and consolidated are hereby transferred to and vested in the Farm Credit Administration, and shall be available for use by it, for the same purposes as if the Farm Credit Administration

Exhibit 63

all statutes cited in the Comptroller General's decisions, as well as his own decisions cited in his later decisions. Opinions of the Attorney General and of courts, arranged by case name, are cited.

c. *Agriculture Decisions.* Each bound volume has a citator for statutes, regulations, orders and court decisions relating to matter printed in the Decisions.

d. *Cumulative Bulletin of the Internal Revenue Service.* This is an example of the publication of agency interpretations of an internal or intra-agency nature.

e. *Loose-leaf services.* In tax and regulatory fields these services, through formal citators or through "finding lists" arranged by statute or regulation perform a citator function.

4. *Administrative agency decisions.* A good many of these can be Shepardized.

a. *Shepard's Citations.* Three Shepard's units cover 48 different series of administrative agency decisions: Shepard's Federal Reporter Citations, Shepard's United States Administrative Citations, and Shepard's Federal Labor Law Citations. Until 1967, eighteen of these were in Shepard's United States Citations, but these are now in either the Federal or the Administrative editions. To tell which edition covers a specific series, see the Tables in the red-paper supplements, referred to above, except the Labor Law unit, which is not listed therein.

(1) *Shepard's Federal Labor Law Citations.* This 1959 publication, with monthly supplements, is an innovation by Shepard's Citations, a citator devoted entirely to a specific area of administrative law. It is in three sections, as follows:

(a) *Cases.* Decisions and orders of the National Labor Relations Board since its inception receive the usual Shepard's Citations treatment. Federal court decisions are listed in the following subsections: United States Supreme Court Cases (Labor Cases), Federal Reporter, 2d Series (Labor Cases), Federal Supplement (Labor Cases), and Federal Rules Decisions (Labor Cases). Citing or commenting cases include those from all federal and state courts, N.L.R.B. decisions and several unofficial reports series; and law reviews citing the main case are listed.

(b) *Statutes.* The labor provisions of the various titles of the United States Code can be Shepardized. A Table of Federal Labor Acts and Corresponding Sections of the United States Code provides both a table of such acts by popular name and a parallel transfer table from the original form of act to its Code title and section.

(c) *Cross references.* A unique feature of the new citator is a cross reference table from the Decisions and Orders of the N.L.R.B.

to the places in the loose-leaf services or reports of the Bureau of National Affairs, Commerce Clearing House, and Prentice-Hall where these are discussed.

(2) *Shepard's United States Administrative Citations.* Begun in 1967, this edition now serves several series formerly covered by Shepard's United States and Federal Reporter units, as well as several agency decision series never before Shepardizable. Although Shepard's keeps quite precisely in the new series to the demarcation line separating true court and administrative agency, the reader should consult the table in the red-paper supplements, for precise coverage. A preface in the citator describes in detail what is and what is not included in the coverage, and there are specimen pages doing the job graphically. All reports of agency decisions, whether or not formerly included in other Shepard units, and all series now included for the first time in any Shepard's unit, were collected in the first bound volume of the Administrative unit, so that it is unnecessary to search elsewhere. There are fourteen parallel reference tables between citations of official agency reports and the unofficial — as between the Federal Securities Law Reporter and the official S.E.C. Decisions and Reports. Supplementation is quarterly, with no white-covered Advance Citations.

(3) *Loose-leaf services or reporters.* Especially in the tax field, the services cover agency decisions, either through citators arranged by case name or through their tables of cases.

(4) *Patents and trade-marks.* These are covered by Shepard's United States Citations, Patents and Trademarks, and by tables in the Decennial, Federal and Modern Federal Practice Digests, as well as by the unofficial United States Patents Quarterly.

§18.16.  **Miscellaneous legislation which can be Shepardized.**

1. *A.L.I. Restatements.* About one third of the state Shepard's Citations include state court construction of the Restatements. The authors of this book are informed by Shepard's Citations, Inc., that this coverage is not likely to be extended to other states. The Statutes Construed tables of the National Reporter System cover them.

The American Law Institute Restatement in the Courts is a citator. It was first published in 1945 covering the years 1932-1944; supplements were issued in 1948, 1954, 1965, 1967, and 1968.

2. *Interstate compacts.* These are covered in Shepard's Citations as enactments of the states concerned — as session laws but not as a separate type of legislation. The Statutes Construed tables in the National Reporter System and the Digest of the United

States Supreme Court Reports cover them as interstate compacts.

3. *Court rules.* See §8.8.

4. *Uniform State Laws.* See §18.12.

5. *Foreign country laws.* As construed by Supreme Court cases these are noted in the statutory tables of the Digest of the United States Supreme Court Reports.

**§18.17. Legal periodicals which can be Shepardized.** In order to show where articles in legal periodicals have been cited in other law review articles or court decisions, Shepard's Citations published in 1968, its Shepard's Law Review Citations. This publication will cover 117 law reviews and legal periodicals. The coverage will be of articles written since 1947 and cited in later articles from 1957 to date, or in state or federal decisions. The volume will be kept up to date by cumulative supplements.

*C H A P T E R  1 9*

# Treatises and American Law Institute
# Restatements of the Common Law

### §19.1.  Treatises.

1. *Functions.*  The reader of a treatise usually has one or more of the following purposes: To brush up or refresh his memory on the present state of the law covered by the book, to study minutely an aspect of the law less thoroughly treated in any other medium, or to take from it citations to leading cases in point which will guide him to other cases in point.

The treatise, as an index to the law, applies the expert knowledge and research facilities of the author to an exhaustive consideration of the decided cases and statutes of competent jurisdiction in point, and then sets down in connected literary form an exposition of the law as found therein.  It thus goes a step beyond the digest, which supplies no comment.  The encyclopedia is said to be an alphabetically arranged collection of treatises, but, according to its scope and purpose, the treatise may be expected to do things that the encyclopedia does not usually attempt.  It traces the history of the law covered and its development along varying lines.  In its best form it is apt to be more assiduous than the encyclopedia in pointing out the effect of statutes or of cases overruling a line of earlier cases and in calling attention to majority, minority and jurisdictional rules, and trends or needed changes.  It is less a frame of reference from an elementary exposition to cited cases to be read, and more an exhaustive treatment of the law with a detailed study of the cases.  Whereas the encyclopedia is rarely critical, the treatise is quite apt to be so, and it thus exerts a definite formative influence upon the law.  In a student book the emphasis is likely to be heavily upon the elementary exposition of the law, with no attempt to cite all cases in point, or at supplementation.  Practitioners' books frequently provide for at least annual supplementation.

2. *Authority.*  Under a strict definition of authority, treatises are at most persuasive, never mandatory.  As a practical matter,

however, under a concept of authority as anything which a judge cites for any purpose in an opinion, the treatise may be said to have authority to the extent that its well-reasoned statements of the law as distilled from the cases and statutes are persuasive. Certainly, however, no treatise has any mandatory authority, that is, something which a court is bound to obey. When — and this frequently occurs — treatises are cited in opinions and briefs, it is because the judge or attorney citing them adopts their reasoning or statements as his own. But it is the cases and statutes cited in support of these statements which are the authority, not the author's analysis. Mandatory authority is the product of legislatures and of opinions officially delivered from the bench, not treatises.

Within these limitations treatises may be extremely useful. The law student will find them of real value in providing background in the law and clarification of knotty points. Treatises are often cited by both courts and attorneys. While no court is bound by a statement in Wigmore or Williston or any other treatise, it is just as true that it will often be influenced by a carefully reasoned analysis of a line of cases by such authors, especially if that analysis has stood up for a number of years.

3. *Varieties.* This topic is treated at considerable length in Price and Bitner, Effective Legal Research 192-198 (1953), and what is said there need only be summarized briefly here.

Treatises are written on every conceivable subject having any relation to the law, but they may be classified roughly according to their purpose as histories of the law, theoretical works on jurisprudence, commentaries and monographs covering a large or small topic in great detail, and textbooks proper. There is considerable overlapping of these categories, because authors do not write primarily according to technical classifications of subject matter.

a. *Student books.* The treatise written primarily for law school use offers an elementary exposition of the principles of the topic covered — such as contracts, torts or insurance — for the purpose of instructing its readers or refreshing their memory. It usually traces the historical development of the topic to some extent, discusses the divergent rules, criticizes cases and tries to provide an over-all picture of the law involved. Often it is a scholarly work, providing the best available book of any kind on the topic treated. Not being intended as an exhaustive casefinder, it makes no attempt to list all cases in point, but confines itself to a relatively few leading ones. Theory and trends are emphasized, elements which are commonly omitted from encyclopedias and practitioners' books. It is an excellent starting point, both for a brush-up and for citations of good cases in point. Furthermore, it often supplies the most convenient survey of the more scholarly aspects of the subject treated, since it tends to follow the techniques of modern law school instruction. A substantial part of some student books first appeared as leading articles in law reviews.

The student book's value for the student lies, not in substituting it for a careful reading of his casebook, but in putting him straight as to the meaning of a case in the over-all picture of the law when that case has not been clear to him when he read it. The table of cases in such a book serves as a casefinder, a starter on the road to a search of the sources of the law; more particularly in connection with any given course, the student may find that many of the cases in his casebook are cited or discussed in the student book, traceable through the table of cases. Other citations to authority may lead him to A.L.R. annotations, periodical articles, etc.

b. *Cram and bar review books.* The cram book is one which the student, upon graduation from law school, uses as an adjunct to taking his local bar examination. It is an outline of a restricted topic such as criminal law, family law or practice, for a single jurisdiction, and is intended only for review purposes, not as an exhaustive treatment. It mentions local peculiarities of the law, collects a minimum number of outstanding cases and statutes for its jurisdiction, is frequently revised to keep up with the latest local developments, but is worthless for general instructional purposes.

c. *Practitioners' books.* Most law books are written neither for students nor for scholars, but to help practicing lawyers win cases. Accordingly, they emphasize the casefinding function of the treatise and the practical aspects of the existing law, rather than historical development, theories or critical comment on the law. They assume more of a background in the law on the part of the reader than does the elementary student book. Some practitioners' books are little more than digests, worthless if not frequently supplemented. They are apt to disappoint the seeker after an adequate picture of the meanderings of the law or the reasons behind them, but if they cite all cases in point and extract from them a valid statement of the law as it now stands as a basis for prediction by judge or advocate, they serve their purpose if they are supplemented frequently enough to keep up with current developments and cases. On the other hand there is no hard and fast dividing line between the scholarly books and the practitioners' books; some of the better books are both.

d. *Student editions of practitioners' books.* It is not uncommon, to extract suitable material from the more scholarly of the comprehensive treatises, and to publish it separately for student use. In such a book most of the citations to cases in the larger work are omitted, and only leading historical cases are cited. An example is Austin W. Scott's Abridgment of the Law of Trusts,[1] in which much of the text but few of the case citations of his scholarly five-volume The Law of Trusts[2] are put into a single volume. George G. Bogert accomplishes the same result by writing a Hornbook Series Handbook of the Law of Trusts,[3] in which much of the material of instructional value from his The Law of Trusts and Trustees[4] is compressed into a single volume.

e. *"Local" books.* Many practitioners' books are designed for the lawyers of a specific jurisdiction or area. The most common of these are treatises on the procedure of such a state or area, and of necessity they are usually supplemented at least annually. They tend to become commentaries on the practice acts and court rules. Another type of local book covers substantive law, such as the New York law of real property or the oil and gas law in the states of the Southwest.

f. *Mechanics of the practice of the law.* The law student, in preparing his paper work in practice and moot court courses in law school, must know something of the practical side of a lawyer's office activities: How documents are drafted and typed in proper form; how to write fee contracts, etc. Listed below are a few of the many books published for the lawyer, but useful as well for the student:

Cantor, Daniel J., Managing the Law Office; Organizations, Systems, Records and Fees. Mundelein, Ill., Callaghan, 1964.

Horowitz, Jacob L., Lawyers' Manual, Explaining the Procedure and Routine Work Involved in the Practice of Law. 3d ed., New York, N.Y., Central Book Co., 1953. Supplemented.

McCarty, Dwight G., Law Office Manual. 3d ed., Englewood Cliffs, N.J., Prentice-Hall, 1955.

Shannon, William H., Accounting and the Law. St. Paul, Minn., West Publishing Co., 1957.

State Bar of California. Committee on Continuing Education of the Bar, California Law Office Handbook. Berke-

---

[1] Boston, Mass., Little, Brown and Company, 1960.
[2] 2d ed., Boston, Mass., Little, Brown and Company, 1956, 5v.
[3] 3d ed., St. Paul, Minn., West Publishing Co., 1963.
[4] St. Paul, Minn., West Publishing Co., 1935- , 12v.

ley, 1962. (While denominated a "California" book, it is widely applicable.)

g. *Law books for non-lawyers.* Works on law for the engineer, the farmer, the undertaker, the physician or the nurse are popular nontechnical discussions of elementary contract and tort law as applied to these callings. They are usually not intended to be used by lawyers, but are written to call attention of the people concerned to some of the problems which may confront them and some of the traps to be avoided by them. The principal value of these books to the lawyer is as casefinders. That is, by citing a few cases in point concerning their specialized problems, they afford a starting point in the search through the digests for all cases in point.

h. *Foreign law books for the law student.* More and more, the American lawyer's practice brings him into contact with foreign law. Because law courses reflect this trend, the student's research calls for works on foreign law, especially those in the English language. As for translations of the laws themselves, the law digests in the Martindale-Hubbell Law Directory cover, in digest form, the business and domestic relations laws of practically all foreign countries. A similar service is afforded by the Lawyers Directory, as described in §22.3. For Latin America, the Pan American Union synthesizes the laws in matters affecting business in a series entitled "A Statement of the Laws of . . . ," in which each number covers a specific country and each is written by a lawyer native to the country covered. The Bureau of Foreign Commerce, of the United States Department of Commerce, publishes a series of reports on "Investments in" various foreign countries. While these latter publications are primarily economic studies, each has sections on the commercial laws of the country involved.

By far the most complete source of information as to publications in English relating to foreign laws are the following by Dr. Charles Szladits, of the Parker School of Foreign and Comparative Law, of Columbia University (frequently supplemented):

Bibliography on Foreign and Comparative Law: Books and Articles in English. New York, N.Y., Oceana Publications, 1955.

International and Foreign Law Sources for the Business Lawyer, Business Lawyer, April 1960, p. 575.

i. *A.L.R. annotations as treatises.* Of late years many A.L.R. annotations have tended to assume the functions of treatises, particularly in their detailed treatment of relatively small areas of broad topics. For example, the annotation in 72 A.L.R.2d 6-183 is a discussion of the "Negligence of Driver of Motor Vehicle as Respects Manner of Timely Application of Proper Brakes."

Like a conventional treatise it has an author. It has a very detailed and analytical table of contents, a similarly detailed subject index and a table of jurisdictions represented by the cases cited. There is also a tendency to publish in a single A.L.R. volume several annotations relating to minute aspects of the same broad topic, such as compromise and settlement, evidence, wills, etc.

4. *Supplementation of treatises.* Bound or pamphlet supplements, usually annual, are customary, the most common type being the cumulative pocket supplement or "part." A recent development which overcomes some of the disadvantages of other kinds of supplementation is the loose-leaf binder, permitting the preparation and insertion of new pages or pamphlets in their proper places without reissuing the entire work.

5. *Techniques in the use of treatises.* Perhaps the most important factor in legal research through treatises is finding a text which covers the specific problem. The law school librarian will help in this: first, by placing the most-used books on reserve at the loan desk; and second, by maintaining the card catalog which lists all books in the library, both by author and by subject matter.

Acquaintance with the functions and use of the various tables and indexes of the conventional treatise is necessary.

a. *Tables in treatises.* The table of contents fulfills an obvious function and should be examined for the author's analysis. The subject index provides a much more detailed analysis by broad subject and catchword, but the reader must realize that indexers may not think the way he does and that considerable ingenuity is often required to find a topic's listing. The table of cases, found in nearly all law books, emphasizes the secondary nature of a treatise, and is a factor in the makeup of the text pages. In varying degree these pages are composed of text commentary, supported by citations to authority in the footnotes. In a book on legal history or the philosophy of the law, these footnote references are usually comparatively few; in a student text most of the leading cases in point are cited; while in a practitioners' work substantially all cases in point are cited, often taking up more space on a page than the main text.

The table of cases has two principal functions: It leads to the page, pages or sections in the treatise where the significant points of law in a case are discussed; and the case citations in the footnotes on the designated pages give parallel references to standard reports printing the case, thus leading the searcher to annotations or digests of other cases in point.

§19.2. **American Law Institute Restatements of the common law.**

1. *Function.* Although the Restatements are not treatises,

they aim "to present an orderly restatement of the general common law of the United States, including in that term not only the law developed solely by judicial decision, but also the law that has grown from the application by the courts of statutes that were generally enacted and were in force for many years."[5]

They are not codes: they are statements of the law, not as the Institute would like to make it, but as it believes the law is. The Restatements state "best rules" as agreed upon by the Institute, these being those applied in the United States generally. They attempt to achieve some degree of unity of the rules of the common law among the states. They try to give the judges — especially the rapidly changing trial judges — a statement of the common-law rules which has more scholarship and study behind it than is found in the conventional treatise or legal encyclopedia. To the lawyer they give a rule of decision backed by the prestige of the Institute and a high degree of acceptance by the courts. To the student they give a statement of principles, backed by commentaries and numerous illustrative examples to set him straight in his study.

Most of the work of compiling the Restatements was done by "Reporters" for each topic, men eminent in their respective fields, assisted by staffs of "advisers." After each group of specialists determined for itself the proper statement of the "best rule" of law in each instance, the tentative draft or parts of it were submitted to the Council of the American Law Institute for debate and final approval. The Reporters have been teachers of the law of the caliber of Williston, Powell, Hanna and Beale. The advisers were eminent teachers, practitioners and judges. No other study of comparable thoroughness and scholarship has ever been made of American law.

2. *Form and scope.* To date, Restatements have been adopted by the Institute for agency, conflict of laws, contracts, judgments, property, restitution, security, torts and trusts. In addition a code of criminal procedure and a model code of evidence have been promulgated, and (in conjunction with the National Conference of Commissioners of Uniform State Laws) a Uniform Commercial Code. The latter, as a uniform law, has been adopted, usually as amended, by a number of state legislatures.

Each Restatement begins with an introduction, describing the organization and purpose of the Institute, and an elaborate schematic table of contents showing the organization of the material. The treatment of this material closely resembles that of the Hornbook Series of treatises, in that it is in three distinct parts, as follows:

[5] Wolkin, Restatements of the Law: Origin, Preparation, Availability, 21 Ohio B.A. Rept. 663 (1940).

First, there is a boldface statement of principle (which may be more or less elaborately subdivided). This is the Restatement proper. Second, there is a comment for most sections. This is designed to explain the meaning of the boldface section and to limit its application. Third, there are illustrations of the various sections and subsections. These correspond to the footnote digests of cases supporting text statements in treatises, but are not citations to cases, though any law student will recognize many familiar cases described, though not cited, in the illustrations.

The Restatements state only the "best rule" and cite no authority. The rule stated, however, has been found to be applicable in nearly 98 percent of the decided cases mentioning the Restatements since their adoption.

3. *Indexes.* Each Restatement has its own detailed index, and there is also a General Index covering all Restatements. This combines the individual indexes in a single alphabetical arrangement, but contains many additional catchwords and cross references. If the searcher lacks a citation to a specific Restatement topic and section, the combined Index should first be consulted. Although each Restatement has its own index, there is overlapping of subject matter between Restatements, all of which is caught in the combined Index.

4. *Keeping the Restatements up to date.* Although there is no regular supplementation, effort is made to keep abreast of significant changes in the law. This is done in three ways. First, tentative drafts of proposed changes are circulated to the advisers, setting forth the changes and the reasons for and against making them. Second, the Restatement of the Law supplements published the text of changes adopted up to 1954. Third, some Restatements have been so thoroughly revised as to call for new editions called Restatement Second. These stress more the background, reasons, criticism and to some extent, statutory materials. Most changes have been made only to clarify language.

5. *Authority.* The authority of the Restatements is only persuasive, but they have been highly persuasive. As of December 1962 a total of 29,000 published appellate decisions had cited them. They had been cited by federal courts, including the Supreme Court of the United States, 3253 times during that period. Disagreement with the Restatements has been only about two percent. The practical effect has been that the Restatements are presumed to state the common-law rule, and that the party opposing them has the burden of proof to the contrary. It would seem that they are becoming accepted as the authoritative statement of the common law of the United States. On the other hand, many aspects of the law covered by the Restatements have not been

covered in state decisions citing them, so that categorical statements should be made with great caution. Courts often fail to mention the Restatements in their decisions.

6. *Shepardizing.* Although the Restatements are not statutes but only private statements of the rules of common law, they have achieved sufficient prestige to be covered, in the same manner as statutes, in more than a third of the state Shepard's Citations (but not Reporter, United States or Federal Reporter). For the states covered, this is the best means of completely tracing citations of cases commenting on the Restatements, though considerably more information is given in the Restatement in the Courts. The state Shepard's which do cover the Restatements also cite articles in law reviews published in the states covered, as well as by a selection of fifteen reviews published in other states.

The Restatement in the Courts (1945, 1948, 1954, 1965, 1967, 1968) is arranged by Restatement — e.g., Agency, Trusts — and section. Citations are in the form of digests of decisions, as in a digest. The first volume in 1945 cited thousands of law review comments also, but these are omitted from the supplements. Thus far Restatements Second have been published for Foreign Relations, Agency, Torts and Trusts. The latter three Restatements each have Appendix volumes containing digests of cases and citations to law review articles relevant to each section. In addition, the publisher gives cross references to West and A.L.R. digests. This last feature is not found in the Restatement in the Courts.

State annotations were undertaken by cooperative efforts of the various state bar associations and law reviews, in a very ambitious program in conjunction with the Institute. Although annotations for one or more Restatements have been published for nearly all states, and the project is still alive, it has not been kept up very well.

English courts, both trial and appellate, have cited the Restatements, but not very often.

7. *Glossary of terms defined in the Restatements.* A 68-page glossary of definitions included from all Restatements is printed in the Restatement in the Courts, Permanent Edition (1945), beginning at page 43.

# Legal Periodicals

**§20.1.   Function and authority.**   "Today, periodical writing plays a leading part in the shaping of our law.   While law reviews exert some influence over legislation and administration, their greatest impact in the formation of law is through the courts. Although objections to judicial reliance on legal periodicals and related sources have erupted in Congress and the press . . . such writing has generally been accepted now for several years as a central part of the judicial process.   In 1941 Mr. Chief Justice Charles Evans Hughes characterized legal periodicals as the 'fourth estate' of the law. . . .   The growth of legal writing has enlarged the knowledge available to the Court.   When they are aware of it, the Justices are compelled to take notice of such writing if they are to base their opinions on the best available knowledge.   This is true whether or not counsel in a case takes notice of such sources."[1]

Legal periodicals, especially the law school reviews, can be of the greatest assistance to the law student, particularly in his preparation of moot court briefs and seminar papers.   They often discuss in meticulous and scholarly detail aspects of the law nowhere else covered in print.   More often still, they write of these matters in advance of their publication in treatises.

The legal periodical is at once a student's book, a practitioner's book and the foremost outlet of the research scholar in the law. It is the most versatile of all the publications in a law library.   It is flexible, represents many points of view and discusses legal topics ranging from the elementary, through the eminently practical, to the most learned and abstruse.   New developments in the law are usually first discussed in legal periodicals and often only there.   As a forum for the critical analysis of legal topics it

[1] Newland, The Supreme Court and Legal Writings: Learned Journals as Vehicles of an Anti-Trust Lobby, 48 Geo. L.J., 105, 126, 142 (1959).

is preeminent. It discusses the law as it was, as it is, as it is tending and as it ought to be — with a thoroughness rarely found elsewhere.

The authority of legal periodicals is only persuasive. Although they are cited increasingly in courts from the Supreme Court of the United States on down, they are in no way mandatory. On the other hand, they certainly are persuasive as the "fourth estate of the law."

§20.2. **Varieties.** Legal periodicals are of many kinds, published under many auspices and for many purposes. The principal varieties are mentioned below.

1. *Scholarly periodicals, including law school reviews.* Although periodicals of a thoroughly scholarly character, such as the Law Quarterly Review and the Modern Law Review, are independently published, the typical scholarly legal periodical in the United States is the law school review, sponsored by a law school and edited by a student board.

The law student is more likely to be interested in the law school review than in any other type of legal periodical. Such reviews serve as outlets for the scholarly and technically expert writings of teachers, practitioners and judges. The student work in them is closely supervised for quality by the faculty of the sponsoring school. The typical law school review is divided into four parts.

a. *Leading articles.* About half the total space of any given law review issue is occupied by articles by law school teachers, practitioners and judges. These articles are likely to be exhaustive analyses of narrow topics, with full citations to authority. Often such a topic has been treated nowhere else, or at least not so fully.

b. *Notes or Comments section.* Student editors contribute the notes and comments, which are often of the utmost value. Although usually limited to eight or ten pages in length, some are much longer. Typical of their divergent subject matter are notes on such topics as entrapment, consequences of abstention by a federal court, expropriation of alien property, extraterritorial application of antitrust laws, and government officials' absolute privilege in libel and slander suits.

c. *Recent cases commented upon.* Five or six cases are usually selected from a reading of all advance sheets, for comment by a student editor in each issue of a review. The comments are valuable to the law student, as being a fairly exhaustive treatment of a minute point of law and explaining the meaning of particular cases. The cases so treated have been indexed since 1917 in the Index to Legal Periodicals.

d. *Book reviews.* While the reviews are useful, the time lag between publication of the book and of the review is so long as to impair their value to the law student.

e. *Special features of law school reviews.* Some law reviews in special annual issues review the work of the federal or state supreme court for the preceding term. A new type of law review, of which Duke University's Law and Contemporary Problems was the first, devotes all of its issues or all of an occasional issue to articles or symposia on a single topic. All but a few "national" law school reviews emphasize to some extent the law of their own state or region. Some of these, like the Oregon Law Review and the Indiana Law Journal, also serve as an organ of the state bar association. Other law school reviews specialize in a particular aspect of the law. The Louisiana Law Review, the Tulane Law Review and, to some extent, the Georgetown Law Journal emphasize civil law in America. The George Washington Law Review is now devoted entirely to administrative law. Other reviews, like those of Notre Dame, St. John's University and the Catholic University of America give more or less emphasis to canon law. Air law, tax law, criminal law and public law are the specialties of other law school reviews.

A variant where the law school review carries nothing but student work is the intramural law school review. This is composed entirely of student notes and case comments and is designed primarily as an outlet for the best work of students in legal bibliography and legal writing courses.

2. *Professional law reviews.* Some of the best legal periodicals are published by associations of scholarly specialists. For law teachers there are the Journal of Legal Education and the Journal of the Society of Public Teachers of Law. Bar association journals, though usually not of a particularly scholarly character, are important, and several are indexed in the Index to Legal Periodicals. Important to practitioners of administrative law are journals like the Journal of the Patent Office Society and the I.C.C. Practitioners' Journal.

3. *Practice periodicals and legal newspapers.* For the most part these have as their chief function keeping practitioners abreast of the legal business transacted in their areas. Commonly these print court dockets and some law reports of special local interest. Some legal newspapers are designated as the official organs for courts in their areas. Examples of local legal newspapers are the New York Law Journal, Washington (D.C.) Law Reporter and the Chicago Law Bulletin. Your law school librarian will tell you whether such a legal newspaper is published for your area.

4. *United States Law Week.*[2]　The law student should, by all means, be familiar with this publication, which has already been mentioned in connection with statutes and Supreme Court slip decisions.

a. *Sections of the United States Law Week.*　The U.S. Law Week is a loose-leaf (or, rather, a loose-pamphlet) periodical, consisting of an unnumbered federal statutes section and four numbered sections.　As stated by the publisher, "The *statute section* is issued only as laws of general interest or importance are passed by Congress."　Numbered Section 1, entitled Summary and Analysis, is a four-page news comment on recent statutes, federal and state court decisions and federal agency rulings.　Section 2 publishes digests and abridgments, of varying length, of selected new federal and state court decisions and of federal agency rulings.　Section 3 contains the "Journal of proceedings of the Supreme Court, summary orders of the Court, cases docketed and summary of cases recently filed, calendar of hearings scheduled, and special articles on Supreme Court work; including summaries of arguments in important cases, periodical reports on cases argued and awaiting decision, etc."　Section 4 contains "opinions . . . in full text, supplemented by Digest-headnotes, and with cumulative table of opinions for current term of the Court."

b. *Indexes.*　The U.S. Law Week has two indexes.　A green-paper one covers the statutes and section 2.　It is issued monthly and cumulates for six months, when the process starts over again; in other words, for the year there will be two six-month indexes, covering July-December and January-June.　A red-paper index covers sections 3 and 4 — the United States Supreme Court.　It is issued and cumulated in the same manner as the green index, except that a final single index covers the entire court term.　The index is by subject, docket number, case name, legislative acts and court rules, patents and trade-marks.　It is not limited to opinions of the Court, but contains also references to all cases filed.

§20.3.　**Abridgments of periodical articles.**　*The Law Review Digest*[3] is a bi-monthly periodical presenting quite long abstracts of articles from a wide variety of legal periodicals, with emphasis on the practical aspects of the practice of law.　In addition, there is a subject-matter index covering a great many articles not digested.　An annual index cumulates the bi-monthly subject indexes.

There are a number of periodicals abridging articles on special

[2] Washington, D.C., Sept. 5, 1933 to date.
[3] Boonton, N.J., v.1-, 1950-.

subjects. Commerce Clearing House publishes *Business Law Articles* and *Tax Articles,* each being arranged by arbitrary topics consisting of brief paragraphs. Both periodicals are indexed. The *Monthly Digest of Tax Articles*[4] prints fairly long abstracts of articles from various periodicals, and in addition indexes case comments from law reviews. There is an annual cumulative index.

**§20.4. Indexes to legal periodicals.** Nearly all legal periodicals publish indexes for each of their volumes. Usually, in addition, cumulative indexes for various periods are published. Another type of index covers a great many periodicals in a single subject, author and title alphabet. The latter index, because of the great expense involved in compiling and printing, is commonly less full than the individual indexes mentioned above or the descriptive-word indexes to the case digests and encyclopedias.

1. *Jones-Chipman Index to Periodical Literature.*[5] The first three volumes of this index, covering the period preceding the start of the Index to Legal Periodicals in 1908, are indispensable for their period, but the last three are little used in libraries possessing the latter work, which is considerably more inclusive in its periodical coverage and is better kept up to date. The Jones-Chipman Index is a subject and author index to the principal English language legal periodicals from 1803 to 1937. The arrangement of subject entries is alphabetical by rather large topics. Few notes or case comments and no book reviews are indexed.

2. *Index to Legal Periodicals.*[6] For the period covered, this is the most inclusive index to English language legal periodicals. Some 160 of the principal American, British and British Commonwealth periodicals, many bar association publications and some judicial council reports are indexed. Entries are alphabetical by subject, under a scheme based by permission of the West Publishing Company upon the copyrighted American Digest System scheme, though much less elaborate.

The indexing policy has varied somewhat over the years, the following statement setting forth the present policy: "Articles of less than five ordinary pages or less than two folio pages, and book reviews of less than two ordinary pages or less than one folio page are not indexed; case notes are indexed regardless of length and commencing with the October 1963 issue are indexed at the end of each subject under the sub-heading 'Cases.' . . . Insubstantial articles . . . annual surveys of the law of a jurisdiction . . . are

4 Albany, N.Y., Bender-Newkirk, v.1-, Oct. 1950-.

5 Various imprints, 1888-1939, 6v.

6 New York, N.Y., H. W. Wilson, 1908 to date.

not indexed. Articles on foreign, comparative and international law are indexed. . . ." Before this change, nearly all articles and book reviews were indexed, and cases were indexed in the same alphabet as leading articles.

Before September 1961, there were separate author and subject indexes, but as of that date they were combined in a single alphabet. The names of student authors are omitted (i.e., signed case comments).

Searching through the numerous units of the Index to Legal Periodicals may be laborious and often requires considerable ingenuity. Since not more than two or three subject entries are made for an article (because of the printing expense involved), indexing is not as close as it should be, and if it is known by the searcher that a certain article or type of article is published in a given law review, the separate indexes for that law review will provide considerably closer indexing than the Index to Legal Periodicals.

The Index to Legal Periodicals is divided into author, book review and (beginning with 1917) case indexes. In the case table, cases commented upon in both leading articles, notes and case comments are listed. Through 1925 the Index to Legal Periodicals cumulated annually, but beginning with 1926 it has cumulated both annually and triennially. From year to year the frequency of publication has varied, at present being monthly except September.

3. *Index to Periodical Articles Related to Law.*[7] This index, published quarterly, January to October, covers selected material from journals not included in the Index to Legal Periodicals or the Index to Foreign Periodicals and Collections of Essays. Number 4 of each volume is cumulative for the year. Some periodicals indexed are legal newspapers, others are bar association publications. Most, however, are periodicals in the fields of economics, sociology and political science, which publish occasional articles relating to law. The need of such an index for lawyers has long been felt but this is the first systematic attempt to supply it.

4. *Index to Foreign Legal Periodicals and Collections of Essays.*[8] This quarterly index is an activity of the Institute of Advanced Legal Studies of the University of London and of the American Association of Law Libraries. The fourth quarterly issue of each year cumulates the other three into an annual volume. Articles of at least three pages in length are indexed, and book reviews if

[7] Law Library, Stanford University, Stanford, California. Oct. 1958 to date.

[8] London, Institute for Advanced Legal Studies, University of London, Feb. 1960 to date.

they are two or more pages in length. Cases are not indexed. Indexes include an author index, a geographical index and a book reviewers' index. About 260 different periodicals are indexed. The entries are in the language of the periodical indexed, but languages not using the Roman alphabet are transliterated into that alphabet.

§20.5. **Approach to the law through legal periodicals.** Finding an article squarely in point with your needs is usually more difficult than finding cases or statutes, because there are relatively so few of the former compared to the number of the latter. The article's coverage is apt to be considerably broader in scope than the student's specific problem, requiring him in practice to locate one which looks promising and then to read it thoroughly for statements and authorities helpful to him. Fortunately, his sifting process is simplified somewhat, once he has found an article he wishes to examine, by authors' self-indexing techniques.

Most leading articles are divided and subdivided into small units, each with its own subject caption. Commonly the first division of an article is the introduction, which states the problem and gives an historical and perhaps a bibliographical summary of the topic. Legal writers are meticulous in giving credit to other writers for material used or suggested. This means that the finding of one article reasonably in point frequently leads to the best of the earlier literature, as cited in footnotes. This is particularly true at the beginning of an article, where citation to this earlier literature is likely to be collected, but it usually continues throughout the whole article. When the topic discussed is one upon which comparatively little has been written, especially where a new legal-technological development is involved, this can be a very useful technique. See, for example, Estep, Radiation Injuries and Statistics: The Need for a New Approach to Injury Litigation, 59 Mich. L. Rev. 259 (1960), which cites books, articles, hearings and other documents from a wide variety of legal and nonlegal sources.

There is now such a wide variety of specialized periodicals, in addition to those of pretty general subject matter coverage, that the student would do well before undertaking a periodical literature search to consult his law librarian, who can familiarize him with the periodical resources available and the techniques for utilizing them.

1. *Subject indexes.* Unless the student already has a direct citation to an article, the search normally begins with a periodical index, as described above. It is likely to be more difficult than the descriptive-word index search in the digest or encyclopedia be-

cause few articles are given more than two subject entries.  Also, within the subject headings, the articles are for the most part listed alphabetically by title, rather than being broken down systematically, so that several pages of listings may have to be scanned in an effort to locate titles of interest to the searcher.

In the Index to Legal Periodicals, some large topics like Constitutional Law have been broken down geographically, but for the most part you must follow the cross references from the large topic to smaller subdivisions.  For example, "Evidence: See also Admissibility of Evidence, Admissions, Burden of proof, Parol evidence, Witnesses, etc."  But it is still a laborious task to sift, all the titles for one which might be in point.  For example, in the 1961-1964 triennial cumulation, there are five pages of citations to articles on a wide variety of subtopics relating to patents.  An effort has been made to invert titles to the first significant word, so as to shorten the search, but this cannot be relied upon to pinpoint the subject matter, and a thorough search requires going down the entire list.  Although the rewards of periodical research are often most valuable, they are usually to be earned only through diligence and patience.

2. *Author indexes.*  Prior to the 1961-1964 triennial cumulation, there were separate subject-matter and author indexes; now these two types of index entries are combined in a single index.  In both the pre- and post-1962-1964 author indexes, the citation is to the main topic under which the authors' articles are indexed.  Thus:

Schwartz, Mortimer D.
Attorneys (H)

Professor Schwartz wrote an article entitled "How to Utilize the Talents of Retired Lawyers," which is indexed under "Attorneys."  There are four long pages of entries under "Attorneys," in the 1961-1964 cumulation, but only seven of them begin with "H."

3. *Shepard's Citations.*  Most state Shepard's Citations cite periodical articles or case comments on particular cases, that is, articles in legal periodicals published in the state in which the case was decided.  A later expansion of this purely local legal periodical coverage has resulted in listing case citations also in the American Bar Association Journal and in fifteen outstanding law reviews from various parts of the country.  No similar coverage is found in Shepard's Reporter Citations.  But now, for example, Shepard's Pennsylvania Citations show that 387 Pa. 548 was commented upon not only in the University of Pittsburgh Law Review in its

own state, but also in the Harvard and Virginia Law Reviews as well.

4. *Shepard's Law Review Citations.* In order to show where articles in legal periodicals have been cited in other law review articles or court decisions, Shepard's Citations published in 1968, its Shepard's Law Review Citations. This publication will cover 117 law reviews and legal periodicals. The coverage will be of articles written since 1947 and cited in later articles from 1957 to date, or in state or federal decisions. The volume will be kept up to date by cumulative supplements.

5. *Table of cases.* The useful table of cases approach is available through the Jones-Chipman Index, volume 3, page 536, covering 1898 through 1907. It is also available through case tables in the Index to Legal Periodicals from 1917 to date, and through the Legal Periodical Digest from 1928 to date. The individual law reviews index cases commented upon from their first volumes to date. The cases listed are for the most part only those discussed in individual Case Comments. But if a case is commented upon at any length at a later date in a leading article or note, that case is also listed, no matter what the date of the decision.

The law student also often finds these case comments useful in aiding his understanding of a case in his casebook or one cited by his instructor for outside reading. An important case may be commented upon by as many as thirty-five different law reviews.

6. *References from treatises, encyclopedias, and annotations.* Although there is no means, through tables, of checking citations to legal periodicals by the above materials, they are frequently so cited in footnotes, and when found, help show the process of thought of the citer, and thus help in understanding the subject matter discussed.

# CHAPTER 21

# Dictionaries; Words and Phrases; Maxims

**§21.1.  Function and value of law dictionaries.**  Law is, among other things, the science of the precise use of words. The law dictionary is, therefore, indispensable.  This is particularly so for the beginning law student, who is confronted not only by a vocabulary relatively new to him, but by requirements of semantic precision hitherto unsuspected by him.  He cannot afford to be mistaken or hazy as to the exact meaning of legal terminology.  Roscoe Pound has written: "My first advice to the beginner in the study of law has always been to buy a good law dictionary and turn to it constantly. . . .  The sure way of acquiring an enduring grasp upon legal terminology is to look up every word as it is encountered in the student's reading, get its meaning concretely in view of the context, and keep up this process until there is an assured conviction that it is no longer necessary." [1]

While unabridged general English language dictionaries define legal words of art, they do not do so with the detail and precision of a good law dictionary, nor do they cite authority for their definitions to anything like the extent customary in law dictionaries. The law dictionary defines and illustrates the meaning of words, terms and phrases which are legal words of art or have a legal slant. Most of these are English, but because the early language of the law was Latin and Law French, many words from these languages also are defined.  Many modern French and Spanish terms are plentiful in the law, too, as well as canon law terms.  All dictionaries, except some pocket ones, cite or quote authority for their definitions, law dictionaries probably more than any others.

**§21.2.  Authority.**  The law dictionary is not authority, though the cases or other sources that it cites may be.  On the other hand,

---

[1] Foreword to Ballentine, Law Dictionary with Pronunciations. 2d ed. Rochester, N.Y., Lawyers Co-operative Publishing Co., 1948.

to some extent it may serve as a casefinder through its citation of authority, leading to that snowballing process in legal research by which a single case in point so often leads to all like cases. The "words and phrases" type of dictionary quotes or paraphrases the actual language of the courts in defining words or terms, the meaning of which is significant in a decision.

**§21.3. Scope.** Law dictionaries vary in size and scope from the small pocket glossary or synonym dictionary to those which are almost encyclopedic in their discussion of the law and citation to authority. These latter define more words, more completely, and cite more authority than any other type of law dictionary and are the kind commonly consulted by student and lawyer alike.

Maxims, beloved of the old-time lawyer and still encountered, are defined by most law dictionaries and legal encyclopedias, either in special tables or in regular alphabetical order throughout the respective works. Legal encyclopedias serve a dictionary function, as noted in Chapter 17. Tables in most law dictionaries list common abbreviations, English regnal years, mortality and interest tables etc.

**§21.4. Some United States law dictionaries described.**

1. *Bouvier's Law Dictionary and Concise Encyclopedia.*[2] At one time this was the best known of all American law dictionaries, but it is now outdated and little used. It was first published in 1839. It grew from a dictionary into a small encyclopedia, so large that it was somewhat inconvenient to use as a dictionary and too small to serve as a current encyclopedia.

2. *Ballentine,*[3] *Black,*[4] *Shumaker.*[5] These are probably the most used American law dictionaries. Their makeup and functions are those described above and require no description here. All are of the semiencyclopedic type, defining words, phrases and maxims, with citations to authority and variorum definitions. Undoubtedly your law school library has one or all of them freely available for consultation.

3. *American Law Institute Restatement Glossary.* This is not a general legal dictionary, but glossary of terms defined in the Restatements and is printed in the Restatement in the Courts, Permanent Edition (1945), beginning on page 43. It is described in §19.2.

---

[2] 3d Revision (8th ed.), Kansas City, Mo., Vernon Law Book Co., 1914, 3v.

[3] Law Dictionary with Prononciations. 2d ed. Rochester, N.Y., Lawyers Cooperative Publishing Co., 1948; supplement 1954.

[4] Black's Law Dictionary . . . with Guide to Pronunciation. 4th ed. St. Paul, Minn., West Publishing Co., 1957.

[5] Cyclopedic Law Dictionary. . . . 3d ed. by Frank D. Moore. Chicago, Ill., Callaghan & Co., 1940.

4. *Words and phrases dictionaries.* Definitions in this type of dictionary are taken from judicial opinions wherein the word or phrase is defined by the courts. Sometimes the language is quoted verbatim, but usually it is paraphrased by the compiler. It can be a very useful approach to the law when the meaning of a word or phrase, whether of special legal import or in common use, is important. The words and phrases approach is frequently an effective starting point in the search for cases. In effect the dictionary of this type is a digest of words instead of points of law.

An example is Words and Phrases.[6] This work is kept up to date both by annual cumulative pocket supplements and by the various Reporter advance sheets from which the supplements are compiled. Each advance sheet has its own table of words and phrases, as do the Reporter bound volumes and Reporter digests (but not the American Digest System). The Reporter and digest tables, however, only list, but do not define, the words. These are defined in the headnotes and in the opinions on the pages referred to in the tables in the advance sheets and bound volumes of the Reporters.

5. *Dictionary function of legal encyclopedias.* This function is described in §§17.6 and 17.8.

### §21.5. British law dictionaries.

1. *Value.* Although our common law and many of our statutes stem from the English, the terminology often varies as between the countries. For that reason an English law dictionary is a useful adjunct to law study. Jowitt's Dictionary of English Law[7] has displaced Wharton's Law Lexicon[8] as the most useful for current purposes. It is of the semiencyclopedic type and is especially helpful in America for its definitions of medieval legal terms, those from several foreign languages which found their way into English legal usage, descriptions of old courts and of the functions of various officials, and of statutes.

2. *English words and phrases dictionaries.* Stroud's Judicial Dictionary[9] differs from its American counterparts in having tables of cases and of statutes which are involved in the judicial definitions. Cases on the construction of repealed statutes are listed, as well as some from Scottish, Irish and Dominion sources.

3. *Maxims.* As already noted, most law dictionaries and encyclopedias define maxims. Broom, A Selection of Legal Maxims,

---

[6] Permanent Edition. St. Paul, Minn., West Publishing Co., 1940-1952. 45 volumes and recompiled volumes. See Exhibit 64 below.

[7] London, Sweet & Maxwell, 1959, 2v.

[8] 14th ed., London, Stephens, 1938.

[9] 3d ed., London, Sweet & Maxwell, 1952, 5v.

## PARALLEL

**Parallel or nearly so—Cont'd**

theory that the quoted word required that transmission line be equidistant from gas pipe line in its entire course. Valente v. Atlantic City Elec. Co., 101 A.2d 106, 108, 109, 28 N.J.Super. 476.

**Railroads**

The term "parallel and competing roads," within the meaning of Const.Ky.1891, § 201, prohibiting the consolidation of a railroad with a parallel or competing road, applies to two roads which connect two important cities, and are natural competitors for the traffic between such cities. Louisville & N. R. Co. v. Commonwealth of Kentucky, 16 S.Ct. 714, 719, 161 U.S. 677, 40 L.Ed. 849.

The term "parallel line," in the clause of the Constitution forbidding any railroad corporation to in any way control any other corporation having in its control a parallel or competing line, is not limited in its operation to a railroad completely constructed, but includes a projected road surveyed, laid out, and in the process of construction. Pennsylvania R. Co. v. Commonwealth, Pa., 7 A. 368, 373.

"Parallel railroads," as used in Const. art. 15, § 6, providing that no railroad corporation shall consolidate with any other railroad corporation owning or having under its control a parallel or competing line, etc., means railroads running in one general direction, traversing the same section of country, and running within a few miles of one another throughout their respective routes, and does not include exact parallelism. State v. Montana R. Co., 53 P. 623, 627, 21 Mont. 221, 45 L.R.A. 271.

**Exhibit 64**

Classified and Illustrated [10] is a treatise or commentary based upon maxims.

*4. Development and history of British law dictionaries.*  The student interested in this subject is referred to Price and Bitner, Effective Legal Research 221-224 (1953).

[10] 10th ed., London, Sweet & Maxwell, 1939.

CHAPTER 22

# Form Books; Appeal Papers;
# Directories

§22.1.  **Form books.**  Drafting legal documents is a test of exact and formal knowledge.  The student, when he sits down to write out a document for moot court or other problem work in his law courses, is beset by doubts.  Is this clause too broad; does that proviso properly protect; does this declaration state a cause of action; and is the manuscript properly typed?

It is here that the form book is indispensable.  Your law school library has a collection of books containing printed forms.  Great care is essential in copying or adapting forms, however, to make certain that they fit exactly the precise situation for which they are being used.  A carelessly adapted form is potentially very dangerous.

1. *Annotated forms.*  A form which has not been adjudicated has somewhat the same weak status as an unadjudicated statute.  Therefore, it is customary to include in form books those forms which have withstood attack in court.  The fact that a form is not annotated does not necessarily condemn it, however.  It may be one of such age and universal acceptance that it is protected by a sort of judicial notice.  Statutory forms are almost always annotated.

American Jurisprudence Legal Forms Annotated[1] and American Jurisprudence Pleading and Practice Forms[2] are the most elaborate and most closely indexed collections of forms.  They are both keyed to the encyclopedia American Jurisprudence as well as to the cases construing individual forms.  A checklist of items to look out for in drafting a form is printed as an endpaper of the

---

[1] Rochester, N.Y., Lawyers Co-operative Publishing Co., 1935-1955, 14v.  Annual cumulative pocket part supplements.

[2] Rochester, N.Y., Lawyers Co-operative Publishing Co., 1936-1956, 21v.  Annual cumulative pocket part supplements.

binding of the American Jurisprudence Legal Forms Annotated. Other collections of somewhat lesser scope are described below under Encyclopedic Collections.

2. *Varieties.* Forms are broadly classified as either business or procedural and form books are usually one or the other, though some have both types of forms in them. An example of the latter is Medina's Bostwick,[3] in which three quarters of the forms pertain to procedure and the remainder to Common Forms of Instruments, which are business forms.

One reason for the separation of form books into distinct volumes is that practice forms change so rapidly, with changes in practice acts and rules, as to need more frequent supplementation or new editions than do the business forms. Most business forms other than statutory are of pretty general application; that is, many business forms may be used across jurisdictional lines. For example, many form books, though devoted predominantly to New York forms and case annotations, are published as of general applicability. Others are designed for specific geographical areas where special problems of law concerning, for example, irrigation or oil and gas, may be encountered. Such a form book is Stanley's Western Forms.[4]

3. *Sources.*

a. *Statutory forms.* These, both substantive and procedural, are commonly printed in state statutory compilations, where they can be found through the general index. Many statutory forms, including some from foreign countries, are printed in both the Martindale-Hubbell Law Directory and the Lawyers Directory, mentioned in §22.3. Procedural forms are usually applicable only in one jurisdiction. They are commonly adapted for frequent supplementation or new editions, to keep abreast of statutory changes. Business forms are much more standard over the years and normally do not call for such frequent revision.

b. *Encyclopedic collections.* The American Jurisprudence forms have been mentioned above. Modern Legal Forms,[5] and Nichols, Cyclopedia of Legal Forms, Annotated[6] print both standard and statutory forms, annotated to the decisions. They are well indexed and supplemented by new forms and new annotations. The arrangement is alphabetical by broad subject as far as prac-

---

[3] Medina's Bostwick's Lawyers Manual. 6th ed., New York, N.Y., Mathew Bender & Co., 1954.

[4] Albany, N.Y., Mathew Bender & Co., 1955, 2v. Annual cumulative supplements.

[5] Kansas City, Mo., Vernon Law Book Co., 1937-1957 11v. Annual pocket supplements.

[6] Chicago, Ill., Callaghan & Co., 1936-1964, 12v. Periodic supplements and recompiled volumes.

ticable. Within a subject topic, the first forms are usually of broad coverage (long form) followed by shorter forms. Then particular clauses are set forth. For example, you can find forms relating to such minute topics as attacks by a cat, injuries to a toe or heel, or injuries causing embarrassment. Raskin and Johnson, tax experts, have compiled Current Legal Forms with Tax Analysis,[7] which contains, as its title indicates, comments upon the tax aspects of the different forms in it.

c. *Single- and double-volume collections.* These print a good collection of standard forms, with less attention to special contracts and particular clauses than is paid in the larger collections.

d. *Special-subject forms.* Forms relating to a single topic may be published as separate works or as an integral part of a treatise on the subject covered. Examples of the first type are Warren and Markuson's Forms of Agreement: Business Forms,[8] a loose-leaf form book on contracts; Klipstein's Drafting New York Wills: Law and Clauses,[9] which is especially useful for its checklist of items to be included in drafting a will; and Menin and Herzog's Bankruptcy Forms and Practice.[10]

More commonly, however, special-subject forms are adjuncts of treatises on the special subject covered. It is so common for practitioners' treatises to print appropriate forms that these should be looked for as a matter of course. Often their presence is noted by the word Forms on the spine of the volume or volumes containing them.

e. *Practice or procedural forms.* Such forms are almost always statutory and thus restricted in scope to a particular jurisdiction, action or tribunal. They may appear as compilations of forms only. About one third of the states are specifically covered by their own procedural form books. Most frequently, however, these forms are published as integral parts of local practice treatises. Many treatises on practice include printed forms, usually annotated to the decisions. Treatises on substantive law which are peculiarly the creatures of statutes, such as bankruptcy or patents, usually print procedural forms.

f. *Foreign law forms.* Forms, principally business forms, in use in foreign countries, are printed in the Martindale-Hubbell Law Directory and in the Lawyers Directory.

g. *Form book for student use.* Professor Kenneth R. Redden,

7 Albany, N.Y., Mathew Bender & Co., 1960, 6v. Annual pocket supplements.
8 Albany, N.Y., Mathew Bender & Co., 1959.
9 New York, N.Y., Baker, Voorhis & Co., 1948. Pocket parts to date.
10 3d ed., New York, N.Y., Clark Boardman, 1954.

of the University of Virginia Law School, has compiled a Law Student's Form Manual,[11] which, though slanted to Virginia law, is useful as an example of how to handle forms.

4. *Typing legal forms.* A lawyer has a secretary trained to type legal papers in correct form, but the law student ordinarily is not so well favored. A neat and technically correct paper is important, and several books are available to help achieve this result. Horowitz, Lawyers' Manual[12] and McCarty, Law Office Management[13] are both good for the purpose.

5. *How to use form books.*

a. *Selecting the proper form.* The index to the collection of forms should first be consulted. The analytical tables of contents, often elaborate and systematic, also aid in this search. Supplements, as in all law books, should be searched, especially for procedural forms, where statutory changes are frequent. If a procedural form is copied from a general book of forms, care should be taken that it is applicable to the searcher's jurisdiction. Statutes and appeal papers are good sources to search for procedural forms.

b. *Selecting the applicable clauses.* Most form books, particularly the multi-volume type, help the searcher by presenting an introductory or preparatory explanation of the applicability and technique of finding for each topic the form desired. In fitting in particular clauses, care should be taken to avoid inconsistent or contradictory ones. If forms could safely be taken verbatim from a book or a stationery store's stock, the lawyer's function would be greatly reduced, but that is not the case. Few forms can be so taken and used, and common sense, caution and professional skill must be employed at all times in adapting forms for a specific set of facts. A form book is never a substitute for sound legal training.

c. *Checklists in the use of forms.* Nobody has an infallible memory, which is one reason why there are checklists. The careful will draftsman, for example, always has a detailed checklist of items to be included or discussed, and this technique is applicable to the use of forms generally. The most complete such list is probably that at the beginning of each volume of American Jurisprudence Legal Forms Annotated.[14]

Your law librarian can tell you what form books there are in your library and where to find them.

---

11 Charlottesville, Va., Michie Co., 1951.
12 3d ed., New York, N.Y. Central Book Co., 1953.
13 3d ed., Englewood Cliffs, N.J., Prentice-Hall, 1955.
14 See note 1 *supra.*

d. *Manuals for the use of forms.* Several books intended for the legal secretary are also useful for the law student and lawyer. Evangeline Sletwold's Manual of Documents and Form for the Legal Secretary [15] gives general and specific instructions for typing legal documents, with many actual forms. In addition, it has a good bibliography of form books and their use.[16] Mary Ann Altman's Self-Administering Course for Legal Secretaries ran through ten issues of *Law Office Economics and Management.* Wider in scope than *Sletwold,* it is intended for courses in law offices for instruction of the secretarial staff.

**§22.2. Briefs and records on appeal.** In most jurisdictions appellants and appellees must submit to the appellate court printed briefs and transcripts of the record from the court below. These printed papers represent the results of the best legal knowledge and research in the authorities on the part of counsel.

1. *Principal functions in a law library.* After they have served their original purpose, appeal papers have two principal functions: (1) Legal researchers with similar problems study them for their analyses, arguments and supporting authorities. (2) When a pleading used in an appeal paper has withstood attack on appeal, it is frequently studied for form and content by other lawyers in their own practice and by students in preparing moot court briefs.

**§22.3. Directories.** Legal directories list lawyers in active practice and give certain information about them. Some are general, for all lawyers; others are jurisdictional or list lawyers in a specified branch of practice, or members of a particular bar association.

1. *Martindale-Hubbell Law Directory.*[17] This directory performs several functions.

a. *Lawyers listed.* Practically all lawyers in active practice are listed. The directory is subdivided by states, with lawyers and firms listed alphabetically by city and town. It is thus necessary, in consulting the directory, to know the state and city of residence of a listed lawyer in order to find his name, since there is no alphabetical list of lawyers. The dates of birth, college and law school graduation, and of admission to the bar are given, together with any practice specialty, membership in the American Bar Association, and a "confidential" rating. Professional cards are printed both in the directory proper for individual lawyers and in a Biographical Section at the end of the main directory for law firms. In the latter the partners' names and some additional data are

15 Englewood Cliffs, N.J., Prentice-Hall, 1965.
16 Mundelein, Ill., Callaghan, 1962.
17 Summit, N.J., Martindale-Hubbell, Inc., 1931 to date. Annually.

given, with bank references, the nature of the practice and usually a list of clients. A selection of foreign lawyers is also listed.

A special listing is made of lawyers admitted to practice before the United States Patent Office.

b. *Law digests.* Laws of all states and territories and of foreign countries are digested, with citations to the statutes, with particular emphasis upon business and family laws. The digests are prepared by lawyers in each state or foreign country and are fairly detailed. Special forms of statutory instruments favored in the various jurisdictions are often included. Statutory forms are frequently a part of the text. The federal section is confined to digests of United States copyright, patent, tax and trade-mark laws. In many law libraries the Martindale-Hubbell Law Directory or the Lawyers Directory, below, are the only readily available sources of foreign law.

Uniform and model acts and codes are printed in full in an appendix.

c. *Court information.* The jurisdiction, important personnel, terms and calendars of federal, state, District of Columbia and Canal Zone courts are given.

2. *Lawyers Directory.*[18] This directory gives the same information as the one described above. More emphasis is placed upon the listing of foreign lawyers, and the foreign embassies and legations in Washington, and United States embassies, legations and consular offices throughout the world are listed. Forms are in a separate section, by jurisdiction.

3. *Miscellaneous legal directories.* Most bar associations, law school alumni associations and legal fraternities issue directories of their members. These are of interest principally to lawyers rather than law students.

[18] Cincinnati, Ohio, Lawyers Directory, Inc., 1883 to date. Annually.

# CHAPTER 23

# Loose-leaf Services or Topical

# Reports

**§23.1. Genesis and function.**[1] The loose-leaf service or topical report collects and explains all the law on a single topic in one place, supplementing it as often as once a week. It is the law publishers' answer to the lawyers' cry for help in their efforts to keep abreast of the vast amount of rapidly changing material — statutes, court decisions, administrative regulations and rulings, and government documents of many kinds — which today determines the course of the law, especially in tax and regulatory fields, both federal and state. An income tax amendment to the Constitution, world wars, a great depression and the increasing complexity of life in almost all areas have brought extraordinary changes in the laws governing our business and personal activities. In rapid succession a series of control and regulatory measures have created new problems and greatly increased government participation at all levels.

It is impossible for any lawyer to collect, organize and digest much of this material promptly and accurately. The loose-leaf service attempts to do so for him. It is the embodiment of that colloquial term, the "package deal," as applied to law book publication. It collects and reports all the pertinent material in a specialized field of law in which the continuous reporting of new developments is necessary, no matter how and where the material originates. It then coordinates — its special contribution — and presents all the essential data promptly, in a highly usable form. Editorial comment — so labeled — is added, backed by the latest pertinent authority in all fields.

**§23.2. Advantages claimed.**

1. *Speed of availability.* The loose-leaf form permits supplementation at will. The text of important statutes may be mailed

[1] Publishers distribute free elaborate instruction books describing the function, format and use of their products.

to subscribers on the day of enactment. When a new statute or regulation makes existing material obsolete, the editors analyze anew the topic or subtopic affected and immediately incorporate the result into the body of the reporter as new pages to replace the outdated ones. New statutes, amendments, regulations and proposed regulations are mailed out shortly after approval or promulgation.

2. *All the law in one place.* Each reporter attempts to be an exhaustive source of information in just one field, but to treat each separate topic thus covered in complete detail — statutes, court decisions, administrative regulations and rulings, editorial explanation — all together in one spot. The aim here is to reduce to a minimum the number of sources necessary to be consulted. Every type of law about any given topic is brought together in one unit, often on the same page, presented with editorial explanations and a common index for the whole.

3. *Cutting across jurisdictional lines.* Often, as in labor law, for example, there is interplay between federal and state statutes and decisions. The service aims to present the composite picture in one place.

4. *Editorial explanations.* The editors endeavor to illustrate, analyze and show the law in action. They explain apparent inconsistencies and tie the whole together.

5. *Expert and speedy indexing.* All this composite of materials is indexed and the indexes are frequently supplemented. Indexes are described in §23.3, par. 6 below.

**§23.3. Basic organization.** Although the organization varies considerably from publisher to publisher and from service to service of the same publisher, certain fundamentals are common to most of them, which are as follows:

1. *Binders.* Each service is delivered to the subscriber in one or more binders which permits removal of superseded pages and insertion of new ones.

2. *Instructions for use.* Because of the necessity of speedy supplementation and revision, as well as of the diversity of materials covered, loose-leaf services are arranged and constructed in a different manner from most other law publications. The publisher supplies with each service clear and detailed instructions on how to use it. These are carefully worked out, with specimen pages and problems, and a few minutes' perusal of them will save a great deal of time over aimless searching. A conspicuous tab at the front of each volume points out these instructions.

3. *Basic text or compilation.* The basic information on the topic covered by a service is usually, but not always, set forth in a

basic text, which is revised at intervals varying with the subject matter. Where, as in income taxation, the changes in statute and decision are frequent and drastic, the basic compilation may be revised annually. If, on the other hand, the topic is relatively stable, as in labor, wills or trusts, there is a continual partial revision, with complete revision only after several years' accumulation of changes.

4. *Arrangement within the basic compilation.* Services are usually based upon regulatory statutes and the rules and regulations promulgated by authority of the statutes. For purposes of quick reference, the basic statute and the regulations thereunder are generally printed in their entirety in one place in the service. Then, following the organic statutes and the regulations comes the basic compilation proper, as noted above, in which the entire text of the statute is broken down into small, workable subdivisions, following a logical scheme of subject arrangement. Each of these subdivisions is accompanied by the pertinent administrative regulations. Based upon and explaining this statutory material there are editorial commentaries. Accompanying all this are decisions, or digests thereof, and orders interpreting the statutes and regulations. Finally, there are various indexes, tables, and so forth. With each mailing of new material, a sort of newsletter is enclosed, pointing out new developments in the field covered by the service.

Two general plans of arranging the basic contents are encountered. The first of these is the statutory plan, so called because it follows the section sequence of the statute under analysis. This plan is used where the statute in question develops the field logically, as, for example, the Internal Revenue Code.

Where, however, as in labor law or trade regulation, there are numerous statutes of coordinate importance, often overlapping in coverage, the arrangement is usually by topic, with ample cross references to related topics. Similarly, where the subject matter of the service follows common law rules closely (as in trusts and estates), the material is developed by subject or topic.

5. *Paragraph number arrangement.* All material is identified and indexed by paragraph number, not page. These numbers are not fixed classification notations as in a digest, but merely serial numbers which are usually changed with each new edition of the service. In most cases paragraph numbers are enclosed in brackets to avoid confusion with official numbers assigned to laws and regulations. Each page of the service is also numbered for ease and accuracy in filing.

6. *Indexes.* Subject indexes serve the usual purpose and provide a major approach. They vary greatly from service to service,

but their format and use are described in detail in each service by How to Use tabs preceding each of them.

a. *Subject matter coverage.* There are — or may be, depending upon the number of volumes and complexity of the service or reporter — four or more types of subject indexes: (1) The co-ordinator of fairly broad topics, called variously the Answer Finder, Problem Solver, or Rapid Finder Index; (2) the basic index to the complete text of the service as compiled at the time the basic text was published; (3) the index to new matter — the supplementary, current index; and (4) special-subject indexes sometimes found, as the index to substances (heparin sodium, rice bran, fatty acid, etc.) in the CCH Food, Drug and Cosmetics Reporter. The Rapid Finder type of index is usually found only in multi-volume services. It has for its purpose the coordination of references to the complete service, and it is especially useful when the subject matter you are interested in may be organized logically under more than one main topic. For example, in the CCH Trade Regulation Reporter, under "Bad debts," are col-lected a dozen sub-topics, enabling the searcher to locate his prob-able interest in short order. The basic topical index may cover the entire service and be the only index to the basic compilation; or it may refer to topics in a more detailed topical index provided for each major subdivision of the service. The index to new mat-ters or the current index, is for matters covered by insertion pages in the main text, issued since the basic text was published and the basic index compiled. The special-subject index noted above is not common, but can be a great time saver when called for.

In practice, each index is likely to be used, beginning with the Rapid Finder, thence to the basic index under the indicated catch-word, thence to the current matter index. The use of the special-subject matter index will usually be obvious when the need arises. References in all indexes are to the serial numbers of paragraphs, not pages. The page references are almost always for the use of the person filing insertion pages.

b. *Date covered and supplementation.* It is not practicable to do over the basic index every time new material is added, but still the new material has to be indexed. The solution is to have two, or sometimes even three, indexes: the index to the compilation as a whole, indexing everything up to the time of publication of the service; a supplemental index to later published material; and, in some services, still a third index, to the very latest material. A complete index search would cover all of these. Auxiliary to these supplementary indexes are Cross-Reference Tables, or Supple-mentary Cross Reference Tables, referring from a paragraph

number in the basic compilation to later supplementary material
in point, collected in the current material file under a later paragraph number.  Thus, if the main compilation of material covers
your subject matter under ¶52.101, you can find later material in
point, if any, by going to the parallel reference tables under
¶52.101, which will tell you under what paragraph numbers the
later material is organized.

c. *Finding lists.*  Official material contained in services is usually listed under so-called finding lists.  Thus, in a federal tax
service these lists give paragraphs covering the respective Internal
Revenue Code sections, the Regulations, court and Internal Revenue Service rulings, etc., as well as Presidential Executive Orders
which have affected tax matters.  Thus Executive Order No. 10,
916 is noted in ¶5209.11 of the CCH Standard Federal Tax Reporter.  Revenue Ruling 60-321 is noted in ¶2944.115; Treasury
Decision 6506 in ¶5069B.001 etc.  The finding lists also usually
contain the tables of cases.

d. *Tables of cases.*  The case tables in services list all orders of
any kind affecting a party, not just court decisions.  They also
serve a citator function, as noted below.

§23.4.  **Citator function.**  Tax and regulatory services note
amendments, repeals and other legislative and judicial changes
affecting statutes and regulations covered by them and are annotated with judicial decisions and agency rulings.  With respect
to administrative regulations and rulings, this information is often
unavailable elsewhere.  The rulings themselves are listed in case
tables which also give the subsequent judicial history of each
ruling.  Finding lists lead to notations of amendments or repeals
of statutes and regulations.

Tax citators in loose-leaf services render a complete citator
service for court and Tax Court cases, Treasury decisions and
rulings, and executive orders commented upon.  Commonly, tax
citator case tables are divided into two sections: (1) court and Tax
Court decisions by case name; and (2) Treasury decisions and
rulings, and executive orders, by serial number.  While the Internal Revenue Code and Treasury Regulations have no loose-leaf
citator as such, changes in form are indicated, and case and other
comments upon them are made in the annotations to the Code
sections by which the services are arranged.

§23.5.  **How to use.**  While the approaches to the loose-leaf
services resemble closely those to digests, annotated statutes and
legal encyclopedias, each service has its own special features.  The
best advice, therefore, is to study carefully the "How to Use This
Service [or Reporter]" instruction sheets and tabs in the front of

each volume or subdivision of the service. This results in a real saving of time and in better understanding over the hit or miss approach. A much more complete demonstration of what is involved in the solution of a problem such as the following is found in these instructions.

*Problem.* The following simple problem is designed to demonstrate the variety of index tools provided by a typical loose-leaf service (or reporter, as Commerce Clearing House designates its products). For convenience, a number of illustrative exhibits taken from a "Reporter" are shown, keyed to the text. In this particular problem, to save space, the CCH Standard Federal Tax Reporter is used, but very similar tools and procedures are available through the Prentice-Hall Federal Taxes and the Research Institute of America Tax Coordinator.

*Statement of facts.* A captain of the Marines was assigned to a Far East post for eighteen months. His family was not permitted to accompany him. His quarters were provided, but not the cost of his meals. May he deduct the cost of the meals as traveling expenses away from home?

1. *Index or fact approach.*

a. *First step: the basic indexes.* This approach is just like the descriptive-word index approach to the digest or encyclopedia and requires the same preliminary problem analysis. Here the question is as to the situs of the taxpayer's "tax home," which governs his tax liability; and whether the same "temporary-permanent" job exception for deductions applies to a serviceman in the field as applies to a civilian in the United States.

First, consult the green-paper Rapid Finder Index (see Exhibit 65), just preceding the main Topical (or subject) Index of the reporter. This index is a coordinator leading to all subtopics treating a given fact key word, and gives a general coverage of various types of traveling expense deductions.

Since the reference from the Rapid Finder Index is not as detailed as you may need, you now examine the main Topical Index (see Exhibit 66), under Traveling Expenses. There you find many specific expenses noted, with a cross-reference to Meals and lodging, deductibility. The one you are most interested in seems to be §1350 generally.

b. *Second step: the basic text.* The index has referred you to ¶1350 of the basic text of the reporter, with further reference to Meals and lodging, expense of, deductibility. That subheading refers you to two paragraphs, 1350 and 1352.145. Going now from the index to the main text, you try ¶1350 first. See Exhibit 67. Here you find a "CCH Explanation," with a sub-

**10,101**

# Rapid  Finder  Index

| | Paragraph | | Paragraph |
|---|---|---|---|
| **A** | | Adjustments | |
| Abandonment losses ...............1535 | | amount and method of adjustment .....................4809-4814 | |

---

• CCH •                    **10,223**                    **YEA**

| Paragraph | Paragraph |
|---|---|
| Transferees ...................5649-5660 | "Unrelated trade or business" |
| . fiduciary's personal liability.......5662 | defined ....................3251-3257 |
| . liability for tax.............5649-5662 | |
| . notice of fiduciary relationship..5667-5670 | **V** |
| . suits to restrain assessment or | Valuation of inventories.............2938 |
| collection ...............5778-5779 | Virgin Islands, tax rebates......4370-4372 |
| Transfers to avoid tax, application | Voluntary demolition or removal |
| of excise tax.....................4896 | of buildings or equipment, losses..1546.012 |
| Transportation costs, employees'....717.03 | |
| Traveling expenses, deductibility..1350-1354 | **W** |
| Treasury bond exemption, trusts | Wagering losses ..............1580, 1581 |
| or partnerships ...................972 | |

**Exhibit 65**

section ¶1350.022, relating to meals away from home.  This Explanation is a careful editorial disquisition on the problems involved.  There may also be the full text or digest of pertinent I.R.S. Regulations.  See Exhibit 67.  Following the Explanation, you find digests of cases of all kinds (memoranda, Tax Court and court decisions, etc.).  Preceding these digests for many topics (as ours) is an alphabetical table of comments leading directly to cases which may be in point.  See Exhibit 68.

¶1350.1981 relates to meals and lodgings of servicemen away from home.  Going to this sub-paragraph, we find two cases digested, *Bercaw* and *Stidger,* which are apparently inconsistent with each other.  *Stidger,* exactly in point (which rarely happens in practice), cites agency and court decisions and tells where *Stidger* is printed in the CCH U.S. Tax Cases (USTC).

c. *Third step: Current Matter indexes.*  So far so good, but has *Stidger* been appealed, and is there any new material in point?

At this point, the first thing to do is to consult the Cumulative

**10,826** **Topical Index**

**MARKET QUOTATIONS**
. book values v., stock valuation . . 4430.259
. stock valuation . . . . . . . . . . . . . . . . 4430.257

**MARKET VALUE**
. absence of bids or buyers, worthless stock . . . . . . . . . . . . . . . . . . . . . . . . 1555.49
. defined . . . . . . . . . . . . . . . . . . . . . . . 2942.01
. inventories, method of . . . . . . . . . . . 2938.01
. inventory value, cotton and grain . . . . . . . . . . . . . . . . . . . . . . . . . . . . . . 2936.20

**Marks, German**—see Foreign currency and foreign exchange: German marks

**MARRIAGE**—see also Husband and wife
. payments in contemplation of . . . . 644.296
. proof of . . . . . . . . . . . . . . . . . . . . . . . 1266.07

**Marsh Foundation, exemption** . . . . . . 3033.26; 3035.05

**MARYLAND**
. accrual dates of taxes . . . . . . . . . 1449.0661
. estate's income
. . real estate . . . . . . . . . . . . . . . . . . 3605.5209
. ground rents—see also Ground rents . . . . . . . . . . . . 2830.402; 2831.8848; 2871.725
. . deductibility as interest . . . . . . . 1382.413; 1415; 1416.015; 1416.187; 4470.0103
. . income from . . . . . . . . . . . . . . . . . . 947.05
. . leases as real estate sales . . . . . 668.538
. income tax, year deductible . . . . 2907.1085
. reservation of ground rent . . . . . . . 2871.725
. state tax liens, priority . . . . . . . . . 5362.804
. taxes imposed by, deductibility . . . . . . . . . . . . . . . 1449.476; 1449.815; 2907.1085
. tenants by the entirety . . . . 303.14; 303.165
. waiver executed after dissolution of corporation . . . . . . . . . . . . . . . . . . 5447.905

**MASSACHUSETTS**
. accrual dates of taxes . . . . . . . . . 1449.0661

**MAUSOLEUM**—continued
. sale of space—continued
. . application of installment sale provision . . . . . . . . . . . . . . . . . . . . 2871.60

**Mausoleum space, depreciation** . . . . . 1715.30

**MEALS AND LODGING**
. compensation received
. . airline employee in Alaska . . . . . . 1191.04
. . cash in lieu of meals . . . . . . . . . . . 1191.01
. . cattle partnership . . . . . . . . . . . . . 1191.055
. . employer's convenience . . . . . . . 1191.01; 1191.059
. . entertainer . . . . . . . . . . . . . . . . . 1191.0597
. . fishermen and canners . . . . . . . . . 1191.06
. . government employees . . . . . . . . 1191.061
. . hospital employees . . . . . . . . . . . 1191.062
. . hotel employees . . . . . . 1191.01; 1191.063
. . Indian Bureau employees . . . . . . 1191.079
. . living expenses . . . . . . 1370.158; 1370.18; 1370.313
. . luncheon excepted . . . . . . . . . . . 1191.0652
. . plantation manager . . . . . . . . . . 1191.0655
. . Red Cross employee . . . . . . . . . 1191.0657
. . rehabilitation patient . . . . . . . . . 1191.0658
. . remote area . . . . . . . 1191.0585; 1191.0653
. . restaurant employees' meals . . . 1191.085
. . servants . . . . . . . . . . . . . . . . . . . . 1191.0673
. . state trooper, allowances of . . 1191.0682
. . state weight inspectors . . . . . . . 1191.0683
. convenience of employer . . . . . . . . 1191.01; 1191.059; 1191.063
. . boarding school faculty . . . . . . . . . 1191.05
. . Chamber of Commerce president . . . . . . . . . . . . . . . . . . . . . . . . . . . . . . 1191.056
. . funeral home . . . . . . . . . . . . . . . . 1191.0605
. . mining employees . . . . . . . . . . . 1191.0653
. expense of, deductibility . . . 1350; 1352.145; 1386.023; 2206.233
. . airline pilot . . . . . . . . . . . . . . . . . . 1352.146
. . bakery route salesman . . . . . . . 1352.1471

**Exhibit 66**

Index which coordinates new matters with the basic contents. To do this you use the paragraph numbers of the basic contents which are arranged in order in the Cumulative Index and in its Supplements. References were to the CCH Explanation at ¶1350.022 and to the decisions involving servicemen at ¶1350.198 and 1350.1981.

Reference to these paragraph numbers in the "Latest Additions" for the Cumulative Index shows no entries for ¶1350. See Exhibit 69. In the main part of the Cumulative Index reference to ¶1350 indicates a substantial number of new items including reversal of the *Stidger* case by the Supreme Court at ¶9309 and a comment on *Stidger* at ¶8551.

The Supreme Court's decision in the Stidger Case indicates that the Court of Appeals has been reversed and the serviceman cannot deduct expenses of meals and lodging. The current comment on this Supreme Court decision appears at ¶8551 and describes the effect of the reversal. See Exhibit 70.

*Research by Citator.* When you have the name of a case in point, you can also use the citator. See Exhibit 70a. The yellow

**21,008**   TRADE OR BUSINESS EXPENSES—Sec. 162 [page 21,007]

✔ • *Regulations*

[¶ 1350]  § 1.162-2.  **Traveling expenses.**—(a) Traveling expenses include travel fares, meals and lodging, and expenses incident to travel such as expenses for sample rooms, telephone and telegraph, public stenographers, etc.  Only such traveling expenses as are reasonable and necessary in the conduct of the taxpayer's business and directly attributable to it may be deducted.  If the trip is undertaken for other than business purposes, the travel fares and expenses incident to travel are personal expenses and the meals and lodging are living expenses.  If the trip is solely on business, the reasonable and necessary traveling expenses, including travel fares, meals and lodging, and expenses incident to travel, are business expenses.  For the allowance of traveling expenses as deductions in determining adjusted gross income, see section 62(2)(B) and the regulations thereunder.

(b)(1)  If a taxpayer travels to a destination and while at such destination engages in both business and personal activities, traveling expenses to and from such destination are deductible only if the trip is related primarily to the taxpayer's trade or business.  If the trip is primarily personal in nature, the traveling expenses to and from the destination are not deductible even though the taxpayer engages in business activities while at such destination.  However, expenses while at the destination which are properly allocable to the taxpayer's trade or business are deductible even though the traveling expenses to and from the destination are not deductible.

(2)  Whether a trip is related primarily to the taxpayer's trade or business or is primarily personal in nature depends on the facts and circumstances in each case.  The amount of time during the period of the trip which is spent on personal activity compared to the amount of time spent on activities directly relating to the taxpayer's trade or business is an important factor in determining whether the trip is primarily personal.  If, for example, a taxpayer spends one week while at a destination on activities which are directly related to his trade or business and subsequently spends an additional five weeks for vacation or other personal activities, the trip will be considered primarily personal in nature in the absence of a clear showing to the contrary.

¶ 1350   **Reg. § 1.162-2(a)**          © 1966, Commerce Clearing House, Inc.

---

Number 12—11     Sec. 162 [page 21,007]—TRAVELING EXPENSES     **21,009**
1-25-67

## Traveling Expenses

• • *CCH Explanation*_____

✔   .022  **"Away from home".**—Sec. 162 (¶ 1320) allows a deduction for traveling expenses while away from home in the pursuit of a trade or business.  This includes amounts expended for meals and lodging.  Traveling expenses incurred in earning income or in managing or conserving income-producing property also are deductible.  See ¶ 2006.475.  Travel expenses incurred in connection with income-producing property are allowable only if deductions are itemized on page 2 of Form 1040, that is, in lieu of the standard deduction, unless they are attributable to the production of rents and royalties.  Travel expenses attributable to a trade or business are deductible from gross income.  See ¶ 1350.054.

The Revenue Act of 1962 added Code Sec. 274(c).  This section authorized the Commissioner to allocate traveling expenses (including meals and lodging) between those which are for business and those which are for personal reasons.  Expenses for all travel after 1962 incurred in taxable years ending after 1962 were affected.  The Revenue Act of 1964 retroactively amended Sec. 274(c) so as to eliminate application of the allocation rules to domestic travel costs.  But the allocation rules still apply in the case of foreign travel.  See ¶ 2296.11-.13.

---

Exhibit 67

Sec. 162 [page 21,007]—TRAVELING EXPENSES    **2 1 , 0 1 1**

## Traveling Expenses

• • *CCH Explanation*

ample).  If the so-called traveling expenses paid on behalf of the
employee or officer constitute compensation, they are subject to the
requirement that they be reasonable in order that the employer be
allowed a deduction.  See ¶ 1320.—CCH.

• • • *Annotations by Topic*

| | | | |
|---|---|---|---|
| Actor's traveling expenses | .03 | Government officials and employees—continued | |
| Airline employees | .0348 | State legislator | .1293 |
| Airplane expenses | .035 | Prior law | .1231 |
| Apartment for business use | .0353 | Laundry expenses | .144 |
| Employee | .0803 | Lawyers | .145 |
| Insurance men | .0807 | Lawyer's traveling expenses | .081 |
| Legal secretary | .0815 | Lobbying distinguished | .147 |
| Merchant's expenses | .082 | Local transportation costs | .149 |
| Physician's expenses | .083 | Nonresident alien | .165 |
| Resort areas | .0835 | Officers and employees | .1657 |
| Secretaries | .0815 | Overnight trips | .166 |
| Teachers | .084 | Pari-mutuels | .167 |
| Corporation reimbursing officers | .09 | Partnership members | .17 |
| Disbarment proceedings | .094 | Railroad men | .175 |
| Executive | .098 | Reimbursement | .18 |
| | | Safeguarding investments | .195 |
| Fact finding (deductible expenses) | .10 | School transportation expenses | .197 |
| Fact finding (nondeductible expenses) | .1005 | Serviceman's expenses | .198 |
| Farmer | .105 | Ship company's grant of free trips | .1987 |

**2 1 , 0 3 4**    TRADE OR BUSINESS EXPENSES—§ 162 [p. 21,007]    Number 12—18
1-25-67

[¶ 1350.19]—Continued
that $12,000 was for traveling expenses
and that $10,636.96 of the amount so paid
him was income to him.
*Wind,* 3 TCM 376, Dec. 13,879(M).

.192  A taxpayer derived no income from
the repayment by his employer of
his traveling expenses.
*Cullinan,* 5 BTA 996, Dec. 2041 (Acq.).

.1921  An airline mechanic's $8-per-day
allowance for foreign travel did
not exceed the amount expended and, therefore, did not result in taxable income.
*Chianese,* 9 TCM 627, Dec. 17,784(M).

.1922  Where the expected reimburse-
ment was not made because of the
corporation's financial condition, the expenses did not become those of the corporate officer who incurred and paid them.
*H. A. Worth,* 20 TCM 218, Dec. 24,668(M),
TC Memo. 1961-39.
*W. Ockrant,* 25 TCM 333, Dec. 27,885(M), TC
Memo. 1966-60.

.1981  An Army captain could not deduct
the cost of his meals in an officers'
mess, a voluntary organization to which he
belonged, or the expense of a "striker fee"
(janitor service for his living quarters),
since he was not "away from home," his
place of business being his Army post.
*Bercaw v. Com.,* (CA-4) 48-1 USTC ¶ 9153, 165
F. 2d 521.

A Marine captain, assigned to a post in
the Far East to which his family could not
accompany him, was entitled to deduct the
cost of his meals as traveling expenses away
from home. He had no choice but to maintain a separate residence.
*H. A. Stidger,* (CA-9) 66-1 USTC ¶ 9161, 355 F.
2d 294, rev'g 40 TC 896, Dec. 26,286.

.1982  An Air Force officer who on two
occasions was assigned to temporary duty away from his home base for an
aggregate period of 154 days was allowed
to deduct $646 as living expenses for which
he had not been reimbursed by the Government.

Exhibit 68

Number 47—71
9-20-67

**70,351**

# Latest Additions for Cumulative Index to 1967 Developments (for Reports 44-47)

> See also Cumulative Index at page 70,401.

| From Compilation Paragraph (¶) No. | | | To New Matter Paragraph (¶) No. |
|---|---|---|---|
| 228 | .01 | *Kintner* Regulations are held invalid.—*Rewrite* | 8468 |
| 234 | .020 | IRS position on year-of-sale depreciation modified.—Rev. Rul. | 6776 |
| 301 | .01 | Corporation rather than stockholder was taxpayer.—*Ward*, TC | 7496 |
| | .40 | Corporation rather than stockholder was taxpayer.—*Ward*, TC | 7496 |
| | .40 | *Kittle* (¶ 9241).—Gov't will not appeal. | |
| | .76 | *First National* (¶ 7415(M)).—Taxpayer on appeal to CA-6. | |
| 1348 | .409 | Legal expenses for suits under Clayton Act are deductible.—TIR | 6732 |
| | .4156 | *Glimco* (¶ 7383(M)).—Taxpayer on appeal to CA-7. | |
| 1358 | .071 | *Wehrli* (¶ 9512).—Gov't on appeal to CA-10. | |
| | .105 | *Wehrli* (¶ 9512).—Gov't on appeal to CA-10 | |

677 CCH—Standard Federal Tax Reports     **¶ 1416**

---

**70,416**     Cumulative Index to 1967 Developments (For Reports 1-43)     Number 44—26
8-30-67

➡ *See also Cumulative Index at page 70,351.*

| From Compilation Paragraph (¶) No. | | | To New Matter Paragraph (¶) No. |
|---|---|---|---|
| 1350 | .146 | Fine and court costs in baseless litigation disallowed.—*Meredith*, TC | 7225 |
| | .166 | *Bagley* vacated and rem'd, CA-1.—Meal costs not deductible since taxpayer not away from home over night | 9300 |
| | .166 | *Bagley* (¶ 9300).—Cert. applied for by taxpayer 5/12/67. | |
| | .19 | Excess of reimbursed auto expense over cost is income.—*Hayes*, TCM | 7323 |
| | .1981 | *Stidger* rev'd, Sup. Ct.—"Tax home" of military personnel | 9309 |
| | .1981 | "Tax home" of military personnel for purposes of deducting traveling expenses.—*Rewrite* | 8551 |
| | .214 | *Gotcher*.—Gov't on appeal to CA-5. | |
| 1352 | .01 | Racetrack employee's tax-home was at permanent residence.—*Pierce*, DC | 9566 |
| | .01 | Tax home of professional baseball player is city where team he plays for is located.—*Wills*, TC | 7398 |

**Exhibit 69**

pages in the Citator volume lists by name all cases decided since 1913 to the current year, with agency or court action, and other cases citing them; also where in U.S. Tax Cases they are printed. Searching for still later cases, you consult the white-paged "Current Citator Table" in the Citator volume, preceding the yellow pages, where you find a Supreme Court reversal of *Stidger* with citations. You can also check the case table for the current year where you note the Supreme Court reversal and reference to the CCH comments or the reversal.

2. *Analytical approach.* This is somewhat more complicated than with digests, because the services vary in content and organization of material. As with the digests, however, the problem is analyzed through its legal implications rather than by fact or catchword situations.

a. *Tables of contents following permanent tabs.* The function and use of the tables of contents may be compared to the "Analysis" of the case digest. Taken as an example, a problem of the deductibility from income, of advertising as a business expense, specifically for promotion or advertising of good will, the CCH Standard Federal Tax Reporter has ten tables dealing with deduction, of which two deal with business deductions. The table

---

<table>
<tr><td>Number 20—165<br>3-22-67</td><td align="center">Court Decisions—Cited 67-1 USTC<br>Com. v. Stidger et ux.</td><td align="right">83,767</td></tr>
</table>

[¶ 9309]   **Commissioner of Internal Revenue, Petitioner v. Howe A. Stidger et ux.**

Supreme Court of the United States, No. 173, 3/20/67. Reversing CA-9, 66-1 USTC ¶ 9161, 355 F. 2d 294.

On Writ of Certiorari to the United States Court of Appeals for the Ninth Circuit.

### [*1954 Code Sec. 162(a)(2)*]

**Employee traveling expenses: "Away from home": Military personnel: Tax home.** —For income tax purposes, a member of the military services is not "away from home" when he is at his permanent duty station and, therefore, is not entitled to a deduction for travel expenses, including meals and lodging, incurred while at his permanent duty station, whether or not it is feasible or even permissible for his family to reside with him there. The court based its holding on the Commissioner's long-standing and judicially approved interpretation given to the permanent duty station as the "tax home" of military personnel, the knowledge of that interpretation by Congress, and the fact that Congress grants tax-free allowances as recognition of the financial problems peculiar to military life. Three justices dissented. Back reference: ¶ 1350.1981.

Mitchell Rogovin, Department of Justice, Washington, D. C. 20530, for petitioner. John A. Reed, amicus curiae.

[*Issue of Traveling Expenses for Military Personnel*]

Mr. CHIEF JUSTICE WARREN delivered the opinion of the Court: In this case we are required to determine whether, under the 1954 Internal Revenue Code, expenditures for meals by a military officer stationed at a post to which his dependents were prohibited from accompanying him were deductible "traveling expenses . . . (incurred) while away from home" within the meaning of § 162(a)(2)[1] or whether instead they were nondeductible "personal, living, or family expenses" within the meaning of § 262.[2] At

---

[1] "There shall be allowed as a deduction all the ordinary and necessary expenses paid or incurred during the taxable year in carrying on any trade or business, including—

"(2) traveling expenses (including the entire amount expended for meals and lodging) while away from home in the pursuit of a trade or business; . . ." § 162(a)(2) of the Internal Revenue Code of 1954, 26 U. S. C. § 162(a)(2).

[2] "Except as otherwise expressly provided in this chapter, no deduction shall be allowed for personal, living, or family expenses." § 262 of the Internal Revenue Code of 1954, 26 U. S. C. § 262.

1967 Standard Federal Tax Reports           **¶ 9309**

---

**Exhibit 70**

Number 21—121
3-29-67

**7 3, 9 3 5**

# REWRITE BULLETINS

MARCH 29, 1967

---

☛    [¶ 8551]    SUPREME COURT—PERMANENT DUTY STATION IS "TAX HOME" OF MILITARY PERSONNEL

A member of the Armed Forces, the Supreme Court says, is not "away from home" while at his permanent duty station and may not deduct traveling expenses, including meals and lodging, incurred at such location. This is so even though it is not feasible or even permissible for his family to join him.[1] In this six-to-three decision, the Court reversed the Court of Appeals for the Ninth Circuit which had maintained that a taxpayer's "home" is his residence and that traveling expenses are deductible unless it is reasonable to expect the taxpayer to move his residence to his place of employment.[2] The majority of the Supreme Court, however, sidestepped blanket approval of the Commissioner's interpretation of "tax home" as a taxpayer's place of employment and restricted its ruling solely to the "tax home" of military personnel. The dissenters, on the other hand, clearly accepted a taxpayer's residence as his "tax home," with the qualification that the taxpayer should establish his residence as near to his place of employment as is reasonable.

### Facts in Case

In the *Stidger* case, a Marine Corps cap-

payer's permanent duty station is his "home" for purposes of determining the deductibility of traveling expenses and that until the Ninth Circuit decision, neither the courts nor Congress had disturbed this interpretation. The High Court saw additional support for the Commissioner's view in the congressionally approved system of tax-free allowances for military personnel.

### Limited Application

The Supreme Court's decision quiets the disagreement among the lower courts in the limited area of the "tax home" of military personnel, but it leaves untouched the larger and more important disagreement as to the "tax home" of civilian taxpayers. The Fifth, Sixth and Ninth Circuits hold that a civilian taxpayer's "home" is his residence and that traveling expenses are deductible unless they stem from his unreasonable refusal to bring his home close to his work.[3] The Tax Court and the other Circuit Courts of Appeals sustain the Commissioner's interpretation.[4]

### Previous Actions of High Court

---

Exhibit 70 continued

of contents lists (under I.R.S. Regulation §1.162-14) the desired subject matter as being treated under ¶1392 of the Reporter. Finding this is made easier by the presence of a "Correlator," which is "a preliminary discussion introducing the subjects covered in this division. Use it for a quick review of the high points. . . ." The text of ¶1392 devotes six and one-half pages to a discussion of the problem, including an "explanation" of what is involved, the Commissioner's policy, pertinent regulations and court and agency decisions. By a like process, the same matter is found in the Prentice-Hall Federal Taxes Service, under ¶11,090.

3. *Table of cases approach.* Tables of cases fulfill the same function in loose-leaf services and reporters as in other law books. The following information may be given, though it varies somewhat from service to service:

    1. Full citation to the case, including parallel citations, if any, to standard reports series

———— CCH ————     **8 2, 6 4 1**     **STI**

STEWART, MYLES, TRUSTEE (PEABODY EST., ARTHUR): PHOENIX TITLE AND TRUST CO. v. (See Phoenix Title and Trust Co. v. Stewart, Myles, Trustee (Peabody Est., Arthur))

STEWART, NIELS ESPERSON....(Estate Tax)
    Sup. Ct., Cert. denied, 284 U. S. 658; 52 S. Ct.

STICKNEY, CHARLES L. v. SQUIRE............¶ 3920.302
    DC, Wash., 51-2 USTC ¶ 9443

✔ STIDGER, HOWE A..............¶ 1350.1981
    ● CA-9—(rev'g TC), 66-1 USTC ¶ 9161; 355 Fed. (2d) 294
    Cowger, Dec. 27,940(M), 25 TCM 513, T. C. Memo. 1966-95
    ● TC—40 TC 896; Dec. 26,286

STIEFEL, REUBEN ................¶ 3922.39
    ● TC—9 TC 576; Dec. 16,039; A. 1948-1 CB 3
    Offord, Dec. 24,874(M), 20 TCM 797, T. C. Memo. 1961-159
    Spada, Dec. 17,747(M), 9 TCM 941
    Carolin, Dec. 17,023(M), 8 TCM 548
    Rood, Dec. 17,013(M), 8 TCM 531

STILES, J. VERNON (See Taylor Oil & Gas Co.)

STILES, LESLIE E. (See Wells-Lee, William)

STILES, W. G. ......................¶ 5924.093
    DC, Ark., 44-2 USTC ¶ 9485; 56 Fed. Supp. 881

STILGENBAUR, ROY R. .............¶ 3973.04
    ● CA-9—(reversing and remanding DC), 40-2 USTC ¶ 9771; 115 Fed. (2d) 283

---

Number 40—171 ✔ Current Citator Table—Court, Tax Court and BTA Cases    **8 1, 0 8 7**
8-2-67

STEUART BROS., INC. .............¶ 4625.176
    *Cited in:*

    Seaboard Finance Co., 66-2 USTC ¶ 9707, 367 Fed. (2d) 646

✔ STIDGER, HOWE A................¶ 1350.1981
    Sup. Ct., (rev'g CA-9), 67-1 USTC ¶ 9309; Ct. D. 1914, 1967-23, 9; 386 U. S. 287; 87 S. Ct. 1065
    *Cited in:*
    McLendon, Dec. 28,481(M), 26 TCM 544, T. C. Memo. 1967-118
    Drinko, Dec. 28,475(M), 26 TCM 532, T. C. Memo. 1967-115

STIERWALT, L. H. .............¶ 5943.0985

STOEPLER, A. M.: RICE, BERNARD M. v. (See Rice, Bernard M. v. Stoepler, A. M.)

    USTC ¶ 9405

STREBLER, JOSEPH X..............¶ 5569.013
    *Cited in:*
    White, 67-1 USTC ¶ 9250, 372 Fed. (2d) 513
    Hill, 66-2 USTC ¶ 9736, 368 Fed. (2d) 617
    White, 667 CCH ¶ 8163, Ct. Cls. Commissioner's Report

STRINGHAM, L. KEEVER..........¶ 2019.801
    *Cited in:*
    Lucas, Dec. 28,184(M), 25 TCM 1312, T. C. Memo. 1966-253

---

**7 0, 8 2 2**     1967 Case Table     Number 27—74
       (Through Report 26)        5-10-67

| Tax Court (TC) District Court (DC) Court of Claims (Ct. Cls.) Court of Claims Commissioner's Report (Ct. Cls. Com. Rpt.) | Acquiescence (A.) Nonacquiescence (NA.) Appeal Action—Rewrites | Court of Appeals (CA) Court of Claims (Ct. Cls.) Supreme Court (Sup. Ct.) |
|---|---|---|
| Stern & Field (See Edling Electric, Inc. v. Peterson) | | |
| Stevens, H. K. (TC) Dec. 28,016........... | CA-6 (T) | |
| Stewart Est., J. D. (See Liberty Nat'l Bank & Trust Co.) | | |
| Stewart, P. M. (DC) ¶ 9174............... | Rewrite, ¶ 8581 | |
| ✔ Stidger, H. A. (TC) Dec. 26,286........... | Rewrite, ¶ 8551 | Rev'd, CA-9, 66-1 USTC ¶ 9161; Rev'd, Sup. Ct., ¶ 9309; |
| Stoepler, A. M. (Listed under taxpayer's | | |

Exhibit 70a

2. Number of paragraph where found in the service
3. Citator information
4. In some services (where the basic compilation is frequently revised because of statutory changes) citations to prior-year paragraph numbers in earlier editions of the service at which the case is printed in full text

4. *Finding list approach.* The finding list is just that, a means by which official material is found in the text of the service. It is a parallel conversion table from an official citation, to the paragraph number in the service where the item is printed or discussed. Case tables are usually designated in the services as finding lists.

Statutes, regulations, Presidential Executive Orders or proclamations, attorney generals' opinions, if treated in the service, are listed numerically by category, with citation to the paragraph numbers of the service at which they are discussed.

In other words, finding lists of official materials serve to co-ordinate information, no matter where in the service the materials are discussed. Since the statutes are by no means always printed in a service in the order of their original section numbering, and since regulations are commonly printed in connection with pertinent statutes rather than in the order of their original numbering, the value of finding lists is obvious.

Usually, finding lists are in tabular form, following the official statute or regulation as cited, but they are alphabetical when the material so indexed is not numbered.

Shepard's Federal Labor Law Citations serves as a finding list. The Cross References section in this citator shows where, in the Bureau of National Affairs labor services and in the CCH and Prentice-Hall labor law services and reporters, the decisions and orders of the National Labor Relations Board are reported or digested. The citation is by volume, decision or order number and page of the NLRB Decisions and Orders.

Working with finding lists is simple. If the searcher knows the section number of a part of a law, an article number of a regulation, the series and serial number of a Presidential Executive Order or of an administrative agency order or memorandum, or a similar citation, he matches that up with the number in the finding lists. This directs him to the appropriate paragraph number in the service. Alphabetical finding lists are arranged, of course, as in your dictionary or telephone directory. Not all services have finding lists; where present they are plainly labeled as such.

5. *Special-subject services by state.* Some topics, like taxation, corporations and labor, have separate state services or editions.

Here the services aim to index and annotate every state statute relating in any way to the main topic. Furthermore, a uniform arrangement within each of the states renders it simple to locate like material in any other state, once the pertinent section number for one state is found.

# CHAPTER 24

# English and Canadian Materials[1]

§24.1.  **Authority of English statutes and decisions in America.**
Every law student is constantly made aware in his courses, especially in first-year torts, real property, contracts and criminal law, of the contribution of English statutes and case law to the development of the basic concepts of the common law as applied in the United States.  This is no mere matter of history, either, since courts today are constantly being asked to decide questions of American law upon the basis of the English law from which it was so largely derived.

1. *English decisions interpreting the common law.*  The English common law, as modified by English statutes up to the time of the American Colonial settlement and as interpreted by English decisions up to the separation of the Colonies from England, is regarded as the basis of American jurisprudence.  These decisions, though still highly persuasive in the federal and state courts in the United States, are not binding as mandatory authority, but are frequently cited by and to the courts.  Since there is no national American common law, each state decides for itself the degree of adoption of the English common law within its borders, and with the exception of civil law Louisiana every continental state has a "reception statute," relating to the legal effect of English decisions or statutes, or both.

As to English decisions as evidence of the common law, most

1 The authors gratefully acknowledge the advice of Messrs. Maurice Maxwell and John Burke, of Sweet & Maxwell, Ltd.; and of Howard Drake, Secretary and Librarian of the University of London Institute of Advanced Legal Studies, who read and criticized this chapter in manuscript in the original edition of Price and Bitner, Effective Legal Research (1953); and of Balfour Halevy, Barrister of the Middle Temple, who did the same for the Student Edition Revised and for the present edition.  None of these gentlemen is, however, in any way responsible for the appraisals and other statements made herein.

reception statutes place July 4, 1776, as the limit up to which such decisions are authority here.   Others specify the date of the state's admission into the Union.   English statutes enacted after the settlement of the colony out of which a state was formed are generally stated in the reception statutes to be of no effect.

American courts, while holding English precedents to be binding, do so only to the extent that they are "suitable to American conditions" or are "not in conflict with American indigenous law," or where later changes in conditions here have not made them inapplicable.

2. *English decisions construing English statutes.*   These decisions are persuasive when the statutes they construe have formed the basis of specific American statutes, and a case of first impression involving them confronts an American court.   The court will then pay close attention to well-considered English decisions interpreting their own statute and will frequently adopt their reasoning. In conflict of laws situations, where the American court is asked to adopt an English court's construction of an English statute, the presumption is in favor of that construction.   It will not, however, be permitted to prevail against a plain and obvious American policy to the contrary.

§24.2.   **English statutes.**   Since American statute forms are largely copied from the English, the American searcher will have little trouble with English statutes.

1. *Slip laws.*   These have been available in one form or another since 1484.   They are issued by Her Majesty's Stationery Office as approved — each act a separate pamphlet, as in the United States. By the Acts of Parliament Numbering & Citation Act, 1962, all acts passed in 1963 and after are given chapter numbers within a calendar year and not by session; i.e., 1st piece of legislation passed in 1963 is 1963, c. 1, etc.

2. *Session laws: Public General Acts and Measures and predecessors.*   Corresponding to the United States Statutes at Large, the English slip laws are cumulated and bound annually in what is now the Public General Acts and Measures (the title having varied over the years).   Indexes are provided in each volume, including an alphabetical list of public general acts, a chronological list, and a citator table, the Effects of Legislation of the current year upon existing legislation: repeals, amendments, etc.

The public printer makes the laws available to other publishers, who commonly distribute them as part of a law report or other subscription service.

a. *Current Law Statutes Annotated*[2] binds the session laws into

2 London, Sweet & Maxwell, Ltd., 1947 to date.

an annual volume which contains a Statute Citator listing all statutes passed during the year; statutory instruments issued under rule-making powers; cases on the construction of statutes; and statutes amended, applied, repealed or otherwise affected by legislation.

b. *Halsbury's Statutes of England: Interim Service.*  This is a loose-leaf slip law service, issued about five times a year.

3. *Compilations of English statutes.*  There is no official English compilation by subject matter, corresponding to the United States Revised Statutes or the United States Code.  There have been numerous chronological collections of statutes in force, however, which are described in Price and Bitner, Effective Legal Research (1953), at pages 277 and 278.  Three of them are covered below.

4. *Statutes Revised,*[3] *1235 to date.*  This is an official publication, covering statutes from 1235 through 1948.  It prints all acts in force, exclusive of those of a local, personal or private nature.  They are arranged in chronological, not classified, order.  Acts relating exclusively to Northern Ireland are omitted.  There are extensive notes.  Although each volume has its own subject and chronological index, the set has no cumulative index of its own, relying for this upon the annual Index to the Statutes in Force and the Chronological Table of the Statutes, described in §24.3.  The set was out of date before it was printed, because England is in process of consolidating many of its acts (analogous to our codification process).  The set, therefore, must be carefully used in connection with the above indexes and the annual Public General Acts and Measures containing the consolidation acts.  In addition the annual noncumulative Annotations to Acts: Directions for Noting the Amendments Made by the Acts, Statutory Instruments, and Church Assembly Measures note for the year covered the exact changes in wording made by later enactments.  Gummed labels containing the text of longer passages of amending acts are supplied, to be pasted in the respective volumes of the Statutes Revised.

The utility of this set consists chiefly in providing in convenient form the text of all public, general acts in force (subject to the above amending process), together with some notes about them.

5. *Statutes of the Realm,*[4] *1225-1713.*  This is the fullest and most accurate edition of the statutes for the period covered.  There are an alphabetical subject index and a chronological index, though each volume has its own index.  Editorial notes

---

3 3d ed. rev., London, Her Majesty's Stationery Office, 1950, 32v. and 1 volume of Church Assembly Measures.

4 London, G. Eyre and A. Strahan, 1824-1828.  Reprinted edition by Dawson, London, 1963; Oceana, Dobbs Ferry, N.Y., 1963.

accompany many of the statutes.  The text of the statutes is in both the contemporary language (if different from modern English) and in modern English.  There are many statutes, long since repealed but of historical importance, which are not in the Statutes Revised or indexed in the Index to Statutes in Force.

6. *Acts and Ordinances of the Interregnum,*[5] *1642-1660.*  This collection covers the period of Cromwell's Commonwealth.  Volume 3 contains a chronological list of acts and ordinances printed in the set, a subject index, and an index of names, places and things legislated about, together with an essay on the content and validity of legislation of the Interregnum period.

7. *Halsbury's Statutes of England.*[6]  This is an encyclopedic treatment of the statutes of England and Northern Ireland.  In it statutes of public general interest in force are classified under 174 alphabetically arranged titles, as "Actions," "Husband and Wife," and "War Damage."  Each of these main titles begins with a table of contents, corresponding to the Analysis in a conventional American case digest or encyclopedia.  Then there is a Preliminary Note (an essay on the subject matter of the title), after which the texts of the various acts are printed verbatim.  Following the text of each section of an act are Notes, in small type, which Shepardize the act, both by subsequent legislative and by judicial action.  For an example of this, see the specimen page in Exhibit 71.

a. *Paragraph numbering.*  At the end of each statute paragraph there is a number in boldface brackets, e.g., [1037] in Exhibit 71. This is not a classification number, as in the United States Code, but merely a serial number.  The volume and bracketed number (3-1037 here) identify that statute paragraph in the main text and in all future cumulative supplements.  It is a very neat device for Shepardizing a statute, keying thus the main text to the supplements by a simple matching of volume and serial numbers.

b. *Tables.*  Each volume and supplement has a table of the statutes which are printed in part or in full therein, a table of cases interpreting such statutes, and a table of abbreviations employed in the volume.  Each volume has its own subject index also. The final tables volume of the set cumulates the chronological tables of statutes and adds an alphabetical list of statutes; it also cumulates and expands the subject index, but omits the table of cases.  That is, there is no consolidated table of cases for the entire set.

---

[5] Collected by C. H. Firth and R. S. Rait.  London, H. M. Stationery Office, 1911, 3v.

[6] 2d ed., London, Butterworth & Co., Ltd., 1948-1952, 27v. and annual "continuation" volumes, 28 to date, and annual cumulative supplements.

c. *Supplementation.*   There are three supplements, which serve different purposes and should not be confused with each other:

---

**518**                    VOL. 3—COMPANIES

(3) Where a company is ordered to add to its name the words " and reduced ", those words shall, until the expiration of the period specified in the order, be deemed to be part of the name of the company.   **[1037]**

**NOTES**

This section corresponds to s. 57 of the 1929 Act, which corresponded to s. 50 of the 1908 Act.

**May make an order confirming reduction.**   The court has a wide discretion to sanction a reduction (*Re Credit Assurance and Guarantee Corporation, Ltd.*, [1902] 2 Ch. 601), but will not sanction a reduction which would work unfairly as against any shareholders who do not consent to it (*Bannatyne* v. *Direct Spanish Telegraph Co.* (1886), 34 Ch.D. 287 ; 9 Digest 149, *843*).   The court will consider whether the sanction to the proposed reduction ought to be refused out of regard to the interest of members of the public induced to take shares in the company and whether the reduction is fair between classes of shareholders ; see *Poole* v. *National Bank of China, Ltd.*, [1907] A.C. 229, H.L.; 9 Digest 149, *842* ; and see also *Carruth* v. *Imperial Chemical Industries, Ltd.*, [1937] A.C. 707 ; [1937] 2 All E.R. 422 ; Digest Supp.   Where there are several classes of shareholders and there has been a loss of capital, the loss should be made to fall upon that class of shares which according to the constitution of the company ought to bear it (*Re Floating Dock Co. of St. Thomas, Ltd.*, [1895] 1 Ch. 691 ; and cf. *Re Direct Spanish Telegraph Co.* (1886), 34 Ch.D. 307; 9 Digest 148, *836*).   The court has refused to confirm a reduction by the surrender of paid up deferred shares, the holders of which were to receive a larger amount in paid up ordinary shares, by which amount the capital was to be increased (*Re Development Co. of Central and West Africa*, [1902] 1 Ch. 547 ; 9 Digest 153, *868*).   For further cases on this topic, see 9 Digest 148 *et seq.*

See also *Re Chatterley-Whitfield Collieries, Ltd.*, [1948] 1 All E.R. 911, C.A., where the court, having regard to the rights of the preference shareholders under the Coal Industry Nationalisation Act, 1946 (c. 59), s. 25, title Mines, Minerals and Quarries, Vol. 16, refused to sanction a petition by a company to reduce its share capital by returning to preference shareholders all capital paid up on their shares.

**Creditor entitled to object.**   See s. 67, p. 516, *ante.*   Generally with regard to proof of consent, see 9 Digest 165, 166.

**And reduced.**   Before the 1929 Act the addition of these words was obligatory, unless dispensed with by the court.   They need not now be added unless the court so directs.

**Company to publish reasons for reduction.**   For a case where the company was not required to publish the reasons for the reduction, see *Re Llynvi, Tondu and Ogmore Coal and Iron Co.* (1877), 37 L.T. 373 ; 9 Digest 155, *883*; for a case where it was required to do so, see *Re Truman, Hanbury, Buxton & Co., Ltd.*, [1910] 2 Ch. 498 ; 9 Digest 168, *1038.*

**Definitions.**   For " company " and " the court ", see s. 455 (1), p. 788, *post.*

**Northern Ireland.**   Cf. the Companies Act (Northern Ireland), 1932 (c. 7) (N.I.), s. 57.

---

                    COMPANIES               **Vol. 3—1037–1063**

**KEY NOS.**

**The Companies Act, 1948 (c. 38)**—*continued*

**1037     Section 68.**—*continued*

affirmed (*sub nom. Prudential Assurance Co., Ltd.* v. *Chatterley-Whitfield Collieries Co., Ltd.*) by the House of Lords, [1949] A. C. 512 ; [1949] 1 All E. R. 1094; 2nd Digest Supp.   See also *Scottish Insurance Corporation, Ltd.* v. *Wilsons and Clyde Coal Co., Ltd.*, [1949] A. C. 462, H. L.; [1949] 1 All E. R. 1068 ; 2nd Digest Supp., distinguished in *Re Old Silkstone Collieries, Ltd.*, [1954] 1 All E. R. 68.

Exhibit 71

The Cumulative Supplement (Exhibit 71) serves as a statutory citator, and in a yellow-paper section prints texts of amendments.

(1) Annotated Current Statutes. This is a loose-leaf annotated slip law service issued five times a year.

(2) Continuation Volume. This is the annual statutes volume for the preceding year, cumulating the year's slip laws and classifying and indexing them by subject as in the main set.

(3) Cumulative Supplement. This is an annual citator volume to the main set, to which it is keyed by volume and paragraph number, as shown in Exhibit 71. It brings the Notes of the main volumes down to date for each statute section number.

8. *Scottish statutes.* These consist of the following: Scots Statutes Revised, the Acts of the Parliaments,[7] 1424-1707; Public General Statutes Affecting Scotland,[8] 1707-1900; Scots Statutes,[9] 1901-1948, continued by Scottish Current Law Statutes,[10] 1949 to date; and, since the Act of Union in 1707, Scots Acts will be found also in the Public General Acts and Measure of Great Britain.

9. *Statutory Instruments.*[11] This is the counterpart of our Code of Federal Regulations. Through 1947 the regulations were known as Statutory Rules and Orders, but with 1948 they took their present title. They also include, Orders in Council made under "Prerogative powers of the Crown" and therefore not needing any legislative sanction. Generally these cover colonial matters.

The Statutory Instruments consist of rules, regulations and orders implementing formal legislation, including treaties. (Usually, unless the treaty covers a Prerogative matter, the statutory instrument will implement not the treaty as such, which has no legal effect within the United Kingdom, but will be made under the statute implementing the treaty. Treaties as such are not the law of the land in the United Kingdom.)

The statutory authorization and effective date of each instrument are stated. There are the usual tables and indexes in each annual volume, as well as additional tables showing, respectively, the effect of the new instruments adopted during the year on acts of Parliament, and of the year's legislation on previous instruments. Instruments are numbered serially by year. Thus, 1937 (No. 252); 1938 (No. 18). The headings of law correspond to those in the Index to the Statutes in Force. Under each subject entry — for example, "War Charities" — are listed, first the

---

7 Edinburgh, W. Green, 1908.
8 Edinburgh, W. Green, 1899-1902, 10v. (volume 10 is an index).
9 Edinburgh, W. Green 1901-1948, 12v.
10 Edinburgh, W. Green, 1949 to date.
11 London, H. M. Stationery Office, 1904 to date.

"Power" (that is, the act of Parliament under which the order is issued), then the "Exercise" (that is, the regulation or order issued under the power).

a. *Statutory Rules and Orders and Statutory Instruments Revised, to December 31, 1948.*[12] This official edition reprints all statutory instruments (with minor exceptions) of a "general and permanent character," and certain Orders in Council and Letters Patent. The first three volumes print both the original form of the instrument and any amendments, but in the remaining volumes only the current form, as amended, is given, with footnote citations to the amendments. It is kept up to date by the annual volumes of Statutory Instruments. The last volume of the set contains extensive tables, which include chiefly: a numerical table of instruments for finding a given instrument by year and number; and a Table of Government Orders, 1671 to date, which Shepardizes the instruments by noting all amendments, revocations and the like of earlier instruments by later ones.

10. *Treaties.* British treaties and agreements of international effect (including unratified treaties) are published as Command Papers, all of which appear in the bound volume of the Parliamentary Papers for each session, entitled State Papers. Treaties are indexed in the monthly and annual lists of government publications of Her Majesty's Stationery Office.

Those treaties which are ratified, and most of the agreements and exchanges of notes, are also numbered as a Treaty Series,[13] in which a new numbering commences every year. The last Treaty Series number of each year is an index, and the one preceding it is a List of Ratifications, Accessions, Withdrawals, Etc., for the current year. Biennial or triennial indexes are also issued within the series itself. The numbered series began in 1892.

British treaties are also included in the collection of British and Foreign State Papers,[14] covering the period from 1812; and in Hertslet's Commercial Treaties.[15] The first volume of each of these series included pertinent treaties in force at the time the set was begun. Hertslet was incorporated with British and Foreign State Papers, beginning with volume 116 (1922) of the latter.

**§24.3.  Indexes to English statutes.** These are superior to their American counterparts. Each annual volume of session laws has its own index; those noted below are to collections of statutes.

12 London, H. M. Stationery Office, 1948-1952, 25v.

13 London, H. M. Stationery Office, 1892 to date.

14 London, H. M. Stationery Office, 1812 to date.

15 London. Volumes 1-19 published by Butterworth & Co., Ltd., 1827-1895; Volumes 20-31 published by H. M. Stationery Office, 1898-1925.

1. *Chronological Table of the Statutes*,[16] *1235 to date*.  In this annual cumulative table all statutes are listed in chronological order — regnal year, chapter and section — together with short title, if any.  Repeals and modifications are noted in italics, with citations to the repealing or modifying act.  References to Irish acts since 1923 are italicized.

2. *Index to the Statutes in Force*.[17]  This annual (since 1870) cumulative subject index to public acts is a companion volume to the Chronological Table, above, and the two together form the indexes to the third edition of the Statutes Revised as well as to all annual statutes.

3. *Halsbury's Statutes of England*.  Each volume of this encyclopedia of English statutes has its own index, and there is a consolidated index to all volumes.

4. *Halsbury's Laws of England*.[18]  Each volume contains a table of the statutes cited, cumulated in a single one for the entire set.

5. *Statutes of the Realm*,[19] *1225-1713*.  There are two elaborate index volumes to these early statutes, the alphabetical and the chronological.  The value of these indexes today is that they include many statutes, long since repealed, which are not covered in the Index to the Statutes in Force, though they are noted in the Chronological Table.

6. *Statutory Instruments*.  The Index to Government Orders [Indexing S. R. & O.'s and S.I.'s in Force],[20] a biennial cumulative index, lists all statutes under which orders have been issued, with the subject heading under which the order is found in the index. It serves as the index to the Revised edition.

§24.4.  **Dates of English statutes.**  Although English statutes are conventionally cited by regnal year, that is, by the year of the sovereign's reign during which they were enacted (as 1 Geo. V, 15 Vict., etc.), by Section 35(1) of the Interpretation Act of 1889, an act may be cited by reference to the short title; and by the Law Revision Act, 1948, 11 & 12 Geo. VI, c. 62, s. 5, it is legal to cite an act by short title only.  British practice is increasingly to cite by short title and year only.  The volumes of statutes being annual, this is the most convenient form of citation.

[16] London, H. M. Stationery Office.  To 1949 issued as Chronological Table and Index of the Statutes; beginning in 1949 issued as Chronological Table of the Statutes.

[17] London, H. M. Stationery Office.  To 1949 issued as Chronological Table and Index of the Statutes; beginning in 1949 issued as Index to the Statutes in Force, to date.

[18] London, Butterworth & Co., Ltd. 3d ed., 1952 to 1962, 42v.; 2d ed., 1931-1939, 37v.  Annual cumulative supplements.

[19] London, G. Eyre & A. Strahan, 1824-1828.

[20] London, H. M. Stationery Office.  Annual, 1891 to date; title changes.

Nearly all significant statutes since 1875 bear a short title, part of which is the year of passage. Thus Housing Act, 1949, Medical Act, 1950. To be on the safe side, however, the regnal year and chapter are added in most legal writing. A list of regnal years is given below.

## TABLE OF REGNAL YEARS OF ENGLISH SOVEREIGNS

| King | Inclusive Dates |
|---|---|
| William I | 14 Oct. 1066 - 9 Sept. 1087 |
| William II | 26 Sept. 1087 - 2 Aug. 1100 |
| Henry I | 5 Aug. 1100 - 1 Dec. 1135 |
| Stephen | 26 Dec. 1135 - 25 Oct. 1154 |
| Henry II | 19 Dec. 1154 - 6 July 1189 |
| Richard I | 3 Sept. 1189 - 6 April 1199 |
| John | 27 May 1199 - 19 Oct. 1216 |
| Henry III | 28 Oct. 1216 - 16 Nov. 1272 |
| Edward I | 20 Nov. 1272 - 7 July 1307 |
| Edward II | 8 July 1307 - 20 Jan. 1327 |
| Edward III | 25 Jan. 1327 - 21 June 1377 |
| Richard II | 22 June 1377 - 29 Sept. 1399 |
| Henry IV | 30 Sept. 1399 - 20 March 1413 |
| Henry V | 21 March 1413 - 31 Aug. 1422 |
| Henry VI | 1 Sept. 1422 - 4 March 1461 (deposed by Edward V) |
| Henry VI | 9 Oct. 1470 - about April 1471 (regained Throne) |
| Edward IV | 4 March 1461 - 9 April 1483 |
| Edward V | 9 Apr. 1483 - 25 June 1483 |
| Richard III | 26 June 1483 - 22 Aug. 1485 |
| Henry VII | 22 Aug. 1485 - 21 April 1509 |
| Henry VIII | 22 April 1509 - 28 Jan. 1547 |
| Edward VI | 28 Jan. 1547 - 6 July 1553 |
| Mary | 6 July 1553 - 24 July 1554 |
| Jane | 6 July 1553 - 17 July 1553 |
| Philip and Mary | 25 July 1554 - 17 Nov. 1558 |
| Elizabeth I | 17 Nov. 1558 - 24 Mar. 1603 |
| James I | 24 March 1603 - 27 March 1625 |
| Charles I | 27 March 1625 - 30 Jan. 1649 |
| Charles II | 30 Jan. 1649 - 6 Feb. 1685 |
| Interregnum | 30 Jan. 1649 - 29 Jan. 1661 |
| James II | 6 Feb. 1685 - 11 Dec. 1688 |
| William and Mary | 13 Feb. 1689 - 8 Mar. 1702 |
| Anne | 8 March 1702 - 1 Aug. 1714 |
| George I | 1 Aug. 1714 - 11 June 1727 |
| George II | 11 June 1727 - 25 Oct. 1760 |
| George III | 25 Oct. 1760 - 29 Jan. 1820 (Regency 25 Oct. 1810 - 29 Jan. 1820) |
| George IV | 29 Jan. 1820 - 26 June 1830 |

| William IV  | 26 June 1830 - 20 June 1837 |
| Victoria    | 20 June 1837 - 22 Jan. 1901 |
| Edward VII  | 22 Jan. 1901 - 6 May 1910   |
| George V    | 6 May 1910 - 20 Jan. 1936   |
| Edward VIII | 20 Jan. 1936 - 11 Dec. 1936 |
| George VI   | 11 Dec. 1936 - 6 Feb. 1952  |
| Elizabeth II| 6 Feb. 1952 -               |

### §24.5.  English law reports.

1. *English court system as it affects law reporting.*  English law reporting reflects the court system under which it operates and can best be understood against the background of that system. English courts in effect combine in one hierarchy those courts which in the United States are federal and state tribunals.  The court system was greatly simplified by the Judicature Acts of 1873 and 1875, and further clarified by the Acts of 1881, 1885 and others.  The court system is briefly described at pages 281-283 of Price and Bitner, Effective Legal Research (1953).

2. *English law reports and their development.*  English law reports are of considerable importance to the American law student, even today; as you have already discovered in your first-year courses, much of torts, real property, contracts and criminal law derives from the English case law.  The English law reports are so similar in construction and purpose to the American that the American user is at once at home with them.

The law report as we now know it was substantially fixed in form by 1765.  There probably never has been official reporting of decisions in England, except for a few special courts, like patents and taxation, because English opinions are almost always delivered orally and not read from manuscript.  This has led to a multiplicity of duplicating and often inaccurate reports.  Reporting is selective, and though there have been some three hundred different series of reports, not only does no one of them report all decided appellate cases, but not all of them combined do so. The confusion, duplication and variance of law reports are furthered by the fact that any written report signed or initialed by a barrister present when the opinion was delivered, or any oral report vouched for by a barrister, is citable in court.

### §24.6.  English law reports: Through 1865.

1. *Year Books, 1282-1537.*  It is generally believed that these reports, such as they are, were originally written down by students or practitioners in open court, for educational purposes.  Most of the Year Books have now been printed, with extensive notes. Although the first-year law student may have little occasion to read them, they profoundly influenced the progress of the law for

over three hundred years through their use in treatises and digests.

2. *Named reporters, 1537-1865.* From the Year Books up to 1865 — the date of the English Reports, Full Reprint — there were more than three hundred different, duplicating reports series. Your law school library may have the originals of these, but you are more likely to read them in the much more convenient Full Reprint. Whenever you have a citation to a case by a named English reporter, try the Full Reprint first.

3. *English Reports, Full Reprint.*[21] For reports during the period 1378 to 1865, this reprint series is the one which you will almost always use. As noted above, the great majority of citations to named English reporters will be to cases reprinted in this set. Practically all reports of value for the years covered are said to be found here, as contained in some 274 different report series. About 100,000 cases are so reprinted verbatim (hence the title Full Reprint, which means that every case in the set is reprinted in full), with parallel citations to reports of the case in other series of reports. Some editorial notes are provided. The parallel citations to other reports not printed are in the following form (the "S.C." meaning "Same Case in Another Report"):

> *Mayor of Ludlow* v. *Charlton,* 6 M. & W. 815 (1840). [S.C. 10 L.J. Ex. 75; 3 Jur. 657; 8 Car. & P. 242. Followed, *Arnold* v. *Poole Corp.,* 4 Man. & G. 860; Referred to, *Wells* v. *Kingston-Upon-Hull,* 1875, L.R.C.P. 409]

The reprint volumes are arranged by courts — House of Lords, Chancery, Nisi Prius, etc. — and are star-paged to the original so that the exact paging of the original may be cited from the reprint. Many "unauthorized" series of reports were not reprinted at all, but most cases reported in the unauthorized reports were reprinted in the Full Reprint from authorized reports. A wall chart listing alphabetically all report series reprinted, with parallel references to the corresponding volumes of the Reprint, is provided, which in your law school library will be found adjacent to the shelves holding the Reprint. There is a two-volume table of cases, in addition to the 174 volumes of reports.

4. *Revised Reports.*[22] This set, covering 1785-1865, reprints most of the cases for the period covered. In general its coverage for these years duplicates that of the English Reports, Full Reprint, but in addition it reprints many collateral (unauthorized)

---

21 Edinburgh, W. Green, 1900-1930, 176v. Reprinted edition by Fred B. Rothman & Co., South Hackensack, New Jersey, and Stevens & Sons, London. To be completed in 1970.

22 London, Sweet & Maxwell, Ltd.; Boston, Little, Brown and Company, 1891-1917, 149v.

report series not found in the Full Reprint. An example is *Wardell* v. *Usher,* 3 Scott's New Reports 508 (1841). There is a table of cases.

5. *Pre-1865 Law Reports: A New Publication in Microreproduction . . . (Those Reports Not Contained in the Present Set of English Reports, Reprint Edition).*[23] This is a microreproduction on cards, which aims to print those pre-1865 cases not reprinted in the English Reports, Full Reprint, either because the set of reports from which reproduced was wholly excluded from the Full Reprint or because the Full Reprint had selected for reproduction another report of a case. The present set on cards covers 191 report series in 330 volumes and 205,780 pages. For those libraries not possessing the original sets, it fills a gap left in the reprint sets listed above.

6. *All England Law Reports Reprint: Being a Selection From the Law Times Reports, 1843-1935, Revised and Annotated.*[24] This is a selection of cases reported in the Law Times Reports, comprising those reports which the present editors deem of sufficient general interest to warrant a place in the present-day practitioner's office. The reprint is intended to complement the All England Reports (see page 324, par. 3), for the use of those who do not have the complete Times Law Reports or other series antedating 1936, when the publication of the All England Reports began.

Although the subtitle of the series would seem to confine the reprinted cases to those taken from the Times Law Reports, in fact cases originally printed in all the standard reports series for the period covered are to be found if, in addition to the Times Law Reports coverage, such cases were originally printed also in one or more other series. That is, if a case was printed both in the Times Law Reports and in duplicating series, that case can be found by its case name in this reprint, because the table of cases will give all the parallel citations for each case reprinted.

The reports are reprinted verbatim as to text, but there are extensive Notes which serve the purpose of citators.

§24.7.    **English law reports: 1865 to date.**

1. *Court of Appeal cases.* A frequent cause of confusion and uncertainty is the reporting of cases decided on appeal by the Court of Appeal, and marked "C.A." in the reports. *There is no Court of Appeal series of reports.* Here is what happens: The decisions of the Court of Appeal are reported in the appropriate "divisional" series. That is, if a case comes up to the Court of Appeal from the King's Bench Division, for example, the decision

---

23 New York, Oceana Publications, 1960-1962.  4500 cards.
24 London, Butterworth & Co., Ltd., 1961 —.  31 unnumbered, dated volumes.

of the Court of Appeal is reported as a King's Bench (C.A.) report. Thus *Milmo* v. *Carreras*, [1946] 1 K.B. 306 (C.A.), arose originally in the King's Bench Division, was decided on appeal to the Court of Appeal, and is reported in the King's Bench Division of the Law Reports (described below). The Appeal Cases series of the Law Reports are not to be confused with the C.A. cases above. The Appeal Cases series reports the decisions of the House of Lords and of the Judicial Committee of the Privy Council, something entirely different.

Appeals from the County Courts also will appear in the divisional (e.g., Queen's Bench) reports. If the subject matter would be within the Queen's Bench jurisdiction if it were not for the amount involved, then if the appeal is reported it will appear in Queen's Bench. E.g., *Lewisham Borough Council* v. *Maloney*, [1948] 1 Q.B. 50. Similarly appeals by way of case stated from Magistrates' Courts to a divisional court are reported in the appropriate divisional reports. The Queen's Bench also includes reports of the Court of Criminal Appeal and the Court Martial Appeals Court.

2. *Law Reports.* Since their inception in 1865 these reports have comprised the principal body of English law reports.

a. *Authority.* The Law Reports are not "official" in the American sense, though they have often been mistakenly called so.[25] They have also often been called semiofficial. The judges revise and approve the reports of their own decisions before they are published, and it is the general custom of the courts to require citation of the Law Reports only, when a case has been published in one of the series.[26]

b. *Different series.*

(1) *Current series.* There are four current series: Appeal cases (covering the House of Lords and the Judicial Committee of the Privy Council); Queen's Bench Division (including cases appealed to the Court of Appeal as mentioned above, and decisions of the Court of Criminal Appeal); Chancery Division (equity, lunacy, and, on appeal, cases heard in the Court of Appeal); and the Probate, Divorce and Admiralty Division (with appeals in the Court of Appeal and decisions in the Ecclesiastical Courts).

The Law Reports are issued in monthly parts, with annual indexes and tables. Each volume contains a Table of Cases Judicially Noticed, and a table of Statutes Judicially Considered by cases printed therein — case and statutory citators, in other

---

[25] Lord Chancellor's Department, Report of the Law Reporting Committee, London, H. M. Stationery Office, 1940, p. 17.
[26] *Ibid.*

words — which tables formerly cumulated in the Law Reports Digest, which was discontinued in 1951. Since then, these tables have been cumulated in a Consolidated Index, covering 1951-1960 and supplemented by a pink-paper consolidation of the tables in the Weekly Law Reports.

(2) *Earlier Series.* There have been many different series of the Law Reports since their beginning in 1865, reflecting the various court organizations. Originally there were twelve series, reduced after the reorganization of courts under the Judicature Act of 1875 to seven, further reduced in 1881 to five and in 1950 (with the discontinuance of the Indian Appeals with volume 77) to the present four series. These are described in some detail in Price and Bitner, Effective Legal Research (1953), at page 285.

c. *Weekly Notes.* This periodical from 1860 to 1952 printed reports of cases decided in all courts covered by the Law Reports. It was a sort of advance sheet for the Law Reports, but it printed many other cases (marked by an asterisk) which were not reported in the Law Reports at all. Thus the periodical reported more cases than the main Law Reports series itself.

d. *Weekly Law Reports.* Beginning in 1953, after it had absorbed the Weekly Notes and the Times Law Reports, the Weekly Law Reports is probably the most complete of all current English law reports series in its coverage of general reports. As stated by F. Hudson, Secretary of the Incorporated Council of Law Reporting for England (the publishers of the Law Reports), Weekly Law Reports covers *every* decision likely to appear in any general series of reports.[27] (Reports not "general" are for example, tax and commercial cases, local government cases, reports of patent cases, etc.) Each issue is in two parts. Part I prints reports (starred) which will not later appear in the Law Reports. These are prepared by barristers and so may be cited, but are not revised by the judges. Part II prints the reports as they will later appear in the Law Reports, except that the arguments of counsel, prefacing the Law Reports publication of the decisions, are omitted. These reports are revised by the judges, as noted by the Secretary in the above letters.

Reports are published about three weeks after decision date. Each issue has a cumulative table of cases for the volume to date and an Index of Subject Matter digesting cases in that particular issue. These indexes cumulate annually; a Consolidated Index, covering 1951-1960, superseding all earlier forms of index for the period, was published in 1961.

e. *Inclusiveness of Law Reports and Weekly Law Reports*

[27] Letters to the authors, from Mr. Hudson, in 1953 and 1961.

*coverage.* These current reports aim to report "every reportable case of general interest." The Council also has published since 1958 the Restrictive Practices Reports, covering decisions of the Restrictive Trade Practices Court. The editor for the Law Reports and Weekly Law Reports is the final arbiter as to inclusion. According to his criteria, questions of fact alone are not reportable at all; cases of temporary interest, or which are a fresh illustration of an old principle, are not included in the Law Reports but may be printed as starred cases in the Weekly Law Reports. The cases printed in the Law Reports "consist of new points of law and are therefore cases of permanent interest to the legal profession." [28]

3. *All England Law Reports, Incorporating Law Times and Law Journal Reports.*[29] This is a series of weekly reports, beginning in 1936. They cover the superior courts and courts of special jurisdiction; they report about eight hundred cases a year, as compared to about three hundred in the Law Reports proper. Through 1946 they were annotated by brief notes, usually of a citator character. Beginning with October 23, 1952, the first issue of each month cross-references to cases reported in the appropriate sections of Halsbury's Laws of England wherein the subject matter of the cases is discussed. No attempt is made to give arguments of counsel preceding the opinions.

a. *Indexes.* Each weekly issue of the All England Law Reports contains a cumulative table of cases for the year to date and a table which "notes up" (Shepardizes) cases and statutes referred to in the reported decisions. There are Permanent Index, 1951-1956 and 1957-1965, covering the cases reported for the years stated. They are supplemented by an annual cumulative index listing, in the same way, cases subsequently reported. These "permanent" indexes are frequently recompiled.

The annual cumulative index also contains tables of statutes judicially construed, of words and phrases judicially considered, and of cases affected by subsequent decision (the Noter-Up). There is thus readily available at all times a combined table of cases from 1936 to date, a subject index and a citator.

b. *Reprint series for Law Times Reports.* See §24.6.

4. *Miscellaneous English law reports.* These were of two kinds: general, such as the Law Journal, Law Times and Times Law Reports; and special, such as Patent, Design, Trade Mark and Other Cases, election cases, tax cases, etc. The general reports

28 See Note 27, page 323.
29 London, Butterworth & Co., Ltd., 1936 to date.

competed directly with the Law Reports, and published many reports not contained in that series, but most of the cases printed in the special reports were not elsewhere reported. The general reports have all been merged with other current reports series, but they are still cited.

The Solicitors' Journal (1875 to date) prints brief reports of some four hundred cases each year. The Law Times and the Law Journal, though they have discontinued their separate reports series, still publish brief reports of cases in the periodicals themselves.

§24.8. **English search books and indexes.** The aids to finding English law parallel to a considerable extent their American counterparts, with perhaps greater emphasis on statutory indexes and citators. These latter likely to be of less interest to American law students than are the case digests and legal encyclopedias.

1. *Current Law, Scottish Current Law and Year Book*.[30] This monthly periodical has as a subtitle *"all* the law from *every* source." It is at once a statutory digest and citator, a case digest and citator, and an index of sorts to British legal periodicals and treatises. For the period covered, it is the nearest approach to a complete and convenient index of current English law in one place. There is a separate Scottish edition, duplicating the English, but with the addition of a blue-paper section covering statutes, statutory instruments and cases applicable to Scotland only.

This publication began in 1947, cumulates annually into a Current Law Year Book and a Scottish Current Law Year Book. There was a Current Law Consolidation for 1947-1951. The Scottish Current Law Year Book 1956: Master Volume, is a "complete statement of all the law of 1956 from every source, and a master volume for the years 1952-1956 (United Kingdom and England only) and 1947-1956 (Scotland only)." This is at once a table of cases for the period covered, a table of statutory instruments for 1956, and a subject index to cases, statutes, legal periodicals and treatises for the periods noted above. For many of the cases included, it is a good digest as well as an index. The current annual Year Books digest every case, often at considerable length.

a. *Digests.* In a single alphabet of about two hundred main topics, Current Law digests (1) statutes, (2) statutory instruments, and (3) cases construing them. New statutes are digested at some length, older ones only to the extent necessary to understand the digested cases construing them. Cases digested include not only

[30] London, Sweet & Maxwell, Ltd., 1947 to date. Monthly, cumulating annually.

those from English superior courts but also a selection from Irish, Dominion and English county courts.

b. *Statute lists.* Under Statutes and Orders, acts receiving the Royal Assent during the year are listed by title; there is also a separate Table of Statutory Instruments.

c. *Citators for Current Law.* There are two editions of a combined citator for the years covering 1948-1959: Current Law Citator and Scottish Current Law Citator. The Scottish Current Law Citator for cases is in two parts covering, respectively, cases reported in England during 1947-1959 and cases reported in Scotland during 1948-1959. This is indeed a most useful citator for the period covered.

d. *Case citator in Scottish Current Law Citator, 1947-1959.* As noted above, cases reported in England during 1947-1965 and in Scotland during 1948-1959 are considered. In addition, *cases of any date (cited cases)* which have been judicially considered by English or Scottish courts during the above periods, or affected by statutes during those years, are listed alphabetically by case name. Parallel citations to all reports series printing the case are given, with references to the sections in Current Law or Scottish Current Law where they are digested. Also, if a case has been commented upon in legal periodicals or modified by statute that fact is noted, something no American citator does.

e. *Statute citator in Scottish Current Law Citator, 1947-1965.* This is arranged in chronological order and gives references to the following: (1) summaries in Scottish Current Law of any statute passed between 1948 and 1965; (2) repeals, amendments or other modification of any act of any date; (3) rules or orders made since 1948 with respect to any act of any date; (4) cases since 1948 construing any act of any date; and (5) articles written since 1948 on the subject matter of any act of any date.

For legislative or judicial action from 1948 on, this is perhaps the most useful — and most used — case and statutory citator for English and Scottish materials. In using it, the searcher goes to the citator to get reference to Year Book paragraphs; then to the Year Book paragraphs, where the complete citator material is found. The citator comes out yearly, and is kept up to date by the monthly issues of Current Law in both the English and Scottish editions. It is thus possible to Shepardize all statutes and cases construed during the respective periods covered by Current Law from 1947 to date.

f. *Index to legal literature.* The final numbered paragraph under each main topic lists legal periodicals and books in point.

Any case which has been the subject of an article or case comment is noted in the Case Citator.

g. *Subject index.* Each volume contains a cumulative subject index to topics covered, continued in the monthly issues by a similar table for the current year.

2. *Digests of English case law.* English case digests differ in only one essential respect from American digests: They also serve as citators, in some instances for cases only, in others for both statutes and cases. The same approach to case law through the table of cases, legal analysis and fact situation is applicable as with American digests. Although there have been numerous case digests, those of current practical interest are limited to the following:

a. *Current Law.* As case digests, Current Law includes only those for English cases printed from 1947 on, and for Scottish only those from 1948 on. These digests — often of considerable length — are easily found through the Current Law Citator table of cases described above. Cases reported since the above dates are digested and listed in the annual and monthly issues. For the limited periods covered, this is perhaps the most used and most useful case digest of English and Scottish case law.

b. *English and Empire Digest.*[31] This has the most complete coverage of all English digests, claiming to be a complete digest of every English case, with additional cases from the courts of Scotland, Ireland, the Colonies and the Dominions. The first edition published from 1919 to 1930 is being replaced by the "Blue-Band" edition begun in 1961 and when completed in 1969 will comprise 56 volumes. Volumes 1-51 will cover all subjects in alphabetical order under approximately 164 main topics, Volumes 52, 53 and 54 will contain the Consolidated Tables of Cases and Volumes 55 and 56 will contain the Consolidated Index.

The digest paragraphs are rather long, compared to those in the Decennial Digests; following each there is an "annotation," which is a case citator, as seen in the specimen in Exhibit 72. A given case is digested in only one place but cross references to that place are given from other pertinent digest topics where the case is listed but not digested. Some cases, not digested at all, are listed and given case numbers and are annotated. All digest paragraphs are numbered consecutively for each separate topic. Scottish, Irish or Commonwealth cases are starred and are found in small type at the end of each sub-topic. The case

---

[31] London, Butterworth & Co., Ltd., 1961 to date. 51v., supplements.

262     DEEDS AND OTHER INSTRUMENTS     [Vol. XVII

Sect. 3. *Rules of construction : Sub-sect.* 3, cont.]

prevent a multiplicity of action (BULLER, J.).—SMITH *v.* MAPLEBACK (1786), 1 Term Rep. 441 ; 99 E. R. 1186.

*Annotation :*—Refd. Ford *v.* Beech (1848), 11 Q. B. 852.

**663.** ——.]—The ct. will construe a settlement according to the intent of the parties, though the literal expression be otherwise.—WOODCOCK *v.* DORSET (DUKE) (1792), 3 Bro. C. C. 569 ; 29 E. R. 704, L. C.

*Annotations :*—Consd. Bulmer *v.* Jay (1830), 4 Sim. 48 ; Jeyes *v.* Savage (1875), 10 Ch. App. 555. Refd. Hope *v.* Clifden (1801), 6 Ves. 499 ; Powis *v.* Burdett (1804), 9 Ves. 428 ; Schenck *v.* Legh (1804), 9 Ves. 300 ; Howgrave *v.* Cartier (1814), 3 Ves. & B. 79 ; Spencer *v.* Spencer (1836), 5 L. J. Ch. 310 ; Whatford *v.* Moore (1837), 3 My. & Cr. 270 ; Woodhouse *v.* Woodhouse (1841), 5 Jur. 404 ; Bythesea *v.* Bythesea (1854), 23 L. J. Ch. 1004 ; Jopp *v.* Wood (1860), 28 Beav. 53 ; Currie *v.* Larkins (1864), 4 De G. J. & Sm. 245 ; *Re* Watson's Trusts (1870), 39 L. J. Ch. 770 ; Day *v.* Radcliffe (1876), 3 Ch. D. 654 ; *Re* Ball, Slattery *v.* Ball (1887), 36 Ch. D. 508 ; *Re* Hamlet, Stephen *v.* Cunningham (1888), 38 Ch. D. 183.

**664.** ——.]—(1) In the construction of agreements & covenants the intention of the parties is principally to be attended to (BULLER, J.).

(2) We do not do justice to the parties unless we look to the whole deed, & infer from that their real intention (BULLER, J.).

(3) It is certainly true that the words of a covenant are to be taken most strongly against the covenantor, but that must be qualified by the observation that a due regard must be paid to the intention of the parties as collected from the whole context of the instrument (LORD ELDON, C.J.).—BROWNING *v.* WRIGHT (1799), 2 Bos. & P. 13 ; 126 E. R. 1128.

*Annotations :*—*As to* (1) Consd. Foord *v.* Wilson (1818), 8 Taunt. 543. Refd. Howell *v.* Richards (1809), 11 East. 633 ; Barton *v.* Fitzgerald (1812), 15 East. 530 ; Milner *v.* Horton (1824), M'Cle. 647. *As to* (3) Consd. Hesse *v.* Stevenson (1803), 3 Bos. & P. 565 ; Sicklemore *v.* Thistleton (1817), 6 M. & S. 9. Refd. Nind *v.* Marshall (1819), 1 Brod. & Bing. 319 ; Saward *v.* Anstey (1851), 10 Moore, C. P. 55 ; Smith *v.* Compton (1832), 3 B. & Ad. 189 ; Tenlon *v.* Curtis (1832), You, 610 ; Stannard *v.* Forbes (1837), 6 Ad. & El. 572 ; Young *v.* Raincock (1849), 7 C. B. 310. *Generally,* Refd. Farrall *v.* Hilditch (1859), 28 L. J. C. P. 221.

Jur. 404 ; Bouverie *v.* Bouverie (1847), 2 Ph. 349 ; Bailie *v.* Jackson (1853), 1 Sm. & G. 175 ; *Re* Morse's Settlmt. (1855), 21 Beav. 174 ; Swallow *v.* Binns (1855), 1 K. & J. 417 ; Remnant *v.* Hood (1859), 27 Beav. 74 ; *Re* Wollaston's Settlmt. (1860), 27 Beav. 642 ; Dalton *v.* Hill (1862), 6 L. T. 446 ; Currie *v.* Larkins (1863), 9 L. T. 638 ; Jackson *v.* Dover (1864), 2 Hem. & M. 209 ; Dixon *v.* Barkshire (1865), 34 Beav. 537 ; Jeyes *v.* Savage (1875), 10 Ch. App. 555 ; Wakefield *v.* Maffet (1885), 10 App. Cas. 422 ; *Re* Hamlet, Stephen *v.* Cunningham (1888), 39 Ch. D. 426 ; *Re* Poultney, Poultney *v.* Poultney, [1912] 1 Ch. 245.

**669.** ——.]—Lease for years by indenture rendering rent, & lessee covenants with lessor that he will pay the rent, & will not assign without leave of lessor, provided that if the rent be in arrear, or if all or any of the covenants hereinafter contained on the part of lessee shall be broken, it shall be lawful for lessor to re-enter ; & there were no covenants on the part of lessee after the proviso, but only a covenant by lessor that lessee paying, etc., & performing all & every the covenants hereinbefore contained on his part to be performed, etc., should quietly enjoy :—*Held :* lessor could not re-enter for breach of the covenant not to assign, for the proviso is restrained by the word " hereinafter " to subsequent covenants, & though there were none such, yet the ct. could not reject the word.

If we could clearly see the intention of the parties we ought to adopt that construction which would best give effect to the intention (BAYLEY, J.).—DOE d. SPENCER *v.* GODWIN (1815), 4 M. & S. 265 ; 105 E. R. 833.

*Annotations :*—Refd. Doe d. Abdy *v.* Stevens (1832), 3 B. & Ad. 299 ; Strickland *v.* Maxwell (1834), 4 Tyr. 346.

**670.** ——.]—COLMORE *v.* TYNDALL (1828), 2 Y. & J. 605 ; 148 E. R. 1060, Ex. Ch.

*Annotations :*—Apld. Beaumont *v.* Salisbury (1854), 19 Beav. 198. Refd. Lewis *v.* Rees (1856), 3 K. & J. 132 ; *Re* Sassoon, I. R. Comrs. *v.* Raphael, *Re* Sassoon, I. R. Comrs. *v.* Ezra, [1933] Ch. 858.

**671.** ——.]—It is a good rule of construction that deeds should be construed so as to give effect to the intention of the parties (ABBOTT, C. J.).—EVANS *v.* VAUGHAN (1825), 4 B. & C. 261 ; 6 Dow. & Ry. K. B. 349 ; 3 L. J. O. S. K. B. 213 ; 107 E. R. 1056.

Exhibit 72

number (as "Deeds 664" in Exhibit 72) is not a classification number covering a group of like cases, as in the American Digest System, but a serial number only, uniquely identifying a single case.

(1) *Supplementation.* In order to keep down the size of the Cumulative Supplements heretofore published, the publishers have placed the digests of cases subsequent to the publication of the permanent subject volumes "in separate permanent continuation volumes." This will make it unnecessary to reprint the same material year after year.

Two continuation volumes, A and B, have been published; Continuation Volume A relates to Volumes 1 to 40 and covers cases for 1952 through 1963; Continuation Volume B relates to Volumes 1 to 49 and covers the cases for 1964 through 1966. The Continuation Volumes A and B are implemented by the 1968 Cumulative Supplement covering cases 1952 through 1967. This latest supplement contains the "catchwords" of cases in Continuation Volumes A and B; additional annotations to cases in Volumes 1 to 51; and annotations to cases in Continuation Volumes A and B.

Since the volume and paragraph numbers in the 1968 Cumula-

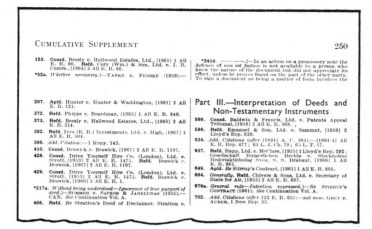

**Exhibit 73**

tive Supplement and in the Continuation Volumes A and B are identical to those in the main texts, the searcher has to go to the 1968 volume only to ascertain if there have been any changes in a topic or a case since the publication of the main volume. In Exhibit 73 he will note the additional information about the main case supplied in the 1968 volume under Deeds 664. If there has been a new case, he will be told where to find it. Note the reference in Exhibit 73 under 679a. The 1968 volume can be said to serve as a citator to the main volumes.

(2) *Table of Cases.* Each Continuation volume and the supplement has its table of cases for cases covered therein. The table of cases for the original edition was the most complete of all English case tables, and there is a like table for the new edition which appeared in late 1968.

(3) *Descriptive-word index.* The "Consolidated Index" for the first edition is typical of its kind and purpose and will be replaced by a similar index in 1969. Each replacement volume has its own index, arranged by and covering that volume similar to the volume indexes in American Jurisprudence, Am. Jur. 2d and Corpus Juris Secundum. There is an Interim Index covering Volumes 1 to 36 (Actions to Patents). In using these indexes one should remember that English terminology frequently differs from American. Examples are "running down cases" for injuries to pedestrians on highways; "winding up" for liquidation; and "death duties" for inheritance taxes.

c. *Mews' Digest . . . to the End of 1924.*[32] This digest has

[32] London, Sweet & Maxwell, Ltd. 2d ed., 1925-1928, 24v.; continued by annual supplements, 1925-1951, and two ten-year supplements, from 1925-1935 and from 1936-1945. Annual supplements to date.

cumulative supplements covering 1925-1935 and 1936-1945, with annual supplements from 1946 to date.

This is a selective digest; in contrast to the English and Empire Digest it makes no attempt to list all reported cases, but only those regarded by its editors as of substantial legal interest. The case digests are, in most instances, much longer than those in any other comparable work. In all respects but two it is a typical digest after the American fashion: It is a case citator and, beginning with 1925, it is a statute citator. Cases are Shepardized by a table of Cases Judicially Noticed, arranged alphabetically by case name. Statutes are Shepardized in a table by regnal years. Beginning in 1952 it has been supplied on order to subscribers to the Law Reports, in place of the discontinued Law Reports Digest.

d. *All England Law Reports digest.*[33] Although not entitled a digest, the Permanent Indexes, 1936-1956 and 1957-1965, and the Index and Noter-Up, described at page 324, par. a, combine to perform the functions of an "index-digest" for reports published from 1936 on. An index-digest is in the form of a subject index but giving more information in the entries than is found in the conventional index. The cases are not, however, digested. A separate Noter-Up covers Australian cases to 1950.

e. *Law Reports Digest of Cases and Statutes.*[34] This digest, in its various units from 1865 through 1950, was an excellent one. It was discontinued in its original form and in its place there is now a Consolidated Index covering the period beginning with 1951. This index is cumulated annually, each annual issue superseding the issue for the preceding year, which is then discarded. During each year it is kept up to date by the Cumulative Index to Subject Matter in issues of the Weekly Law Reports, beginning with January 1, 1960.

The Consolidated Index is an index-digest, indexing by both broad subject — as Evidence or Landlord and Tenant — and by catchword. It indexes every point of law, including dicta, in every case reported in the Weekly Law Reports. A main entry in the subject index is "Words and Phrases" judicially defined in the cases indexed.

The table of cases is not restricted to the Law Reports and Weekly Law Reports, in that parallel citations are given for Law Reports and Weekly Law Reports cases reported also in other series, such as the All England Law Reports and the Times Law Reports.

[33] London, Butterworth & Co., Ltd., 1957. Frequent supplements.
[34] London, Incorporated Council of Law Reporting for England and Wales. Consisted of six units covering 1865-1890, 1891-1900, 1901-1910, 1911-1920, 1921-1930, 1931-1950. Continued by Consolidated Index, 1951-1959 and supplements to date.

The tables of cases, statutes and statutory orders "considered" cover those of any date if construed by cases since January 1, 1951, and are thus case and statutory citators.

It is said by the publisher that the combined Law Reports Digest in its various units and the Consolidated Index provide "continuous indexing from 1865 to date."

f. *Current Law.* The digest functions of this legal periodical are described at page 325, par. 1.

3. *Encyclopedias of English Law.* The purpose, organization and use of an English legal encyclopedia are so like those of its American counterpart that the searcher familiar with the one will have no difficulty with the other. With the exception of Halsbury's Laws of England, all general encyclopedias of English law became casualties either of the First or the Second World War.

a. *Halsbury's Laws of England, Being a Complete Restatement of the Whole Law of England.*[35] This is an excellent encyclopedia, the editors and contributors being distinguished judges and lawyers. It is put together and used exactly as are similar American works, with two exceptions: A great deal more attention is paid to statutes than in any American encyclopedia and it has tables of cases and of statutes cited. The cases cited as authority are cross-referenced to the appropriate titles and sections of the English and Empire Digest where their subject matter is treated. This is done through the table of cases, and is an aid to working up the whole law on a given case or point. Conversely, if the case is first found in the English and Empire Digest it can easily be traced into Halsbury's by means of the table of cases; or, in the Replacement Volumes of the Digest, through direct citations to Halsbury's.

(1) *Tables.* Each volume of Halsbury's 3d edition contains a table of Statutes cited in the text, which cumulates in a single one for the entire set. There is also a table of cases cited, in each volume, which does cumulate into a single Consolidated Table of Cases for the entire set. There is also a General Index, which is a descriptive-word index in the usual form.

(2) *Supplementation.* The supplementation scheme is similar to that already described for the English and Empire Digest, in that it involves matching up main volume numbers and paragraph numbers in the main text with like numbers in the supplements.

An annual cumulative supplement to the Third Edition, arranged by the same volume, page and paragraph notations as those in the main work, keeps the encyclopedia up to date.

---

[35] London, Butterworth & Co., Ltd. 3d ed., 1952 to 1962, 43v.; 2d ed. 1931-1939, 37v. Annual cumulative supplement.

**15. Claim to benefit from plaintiff's crime.** It is contrary to public policy that a man should be allowed to claim a benefit resulting from his own crime whether under a contract or a gift or otherwise (o).

Thus a person who feloniously kills (p) another cannot benefit under the will (q) or on the intestacy (r) of his victim or under any insurance policy effected in his favour on the life of his victim (s). Nor, in general, can he or his representative claim to participate in the administration of his victim's estate (t). The rule that the guilty party cannot benefit does

---

(o) *Beresford* v. *Royal Insurance Co., Ltd.*, [1938] A. C. 586, H. L., at pp. 596–599; [1938] 2 All E. R. 602, at pp. 605–607, approving statements of principle by FRY, L.J., in *Cleaver* v. *Mutual Reserve Fund Life Association*, [1892] 1 Q. B. 147, C. A., at p. 156, and by Sir SAMUEL EVANS, P., in *In the Estate of Crippen*, [1911] P. 108, at p. 112. In relation to benefits under wills, the rules, similar to that stated in the text, adopted in other systems of jurisprudence in general depend on the principle that the donee is unworthy to take as a beneficiary, and that the deceased would presumably have disinherited his slayer or revoked the bequest to him, but this principle is unknown to English law; see title WILLS. The rule laid down in the cases cited above is, it appears, restricted to a claim by the criminal or his representatives, and third parties bona fide acquiring a title to personal property through the criminal may in some cases have protection; see note (c), p. 11, *post*, and see titles AGENCY, p. 214, *post* (dispositions under the Factors Act, 1889 (52 & 53 Vict. c. 45)); BILLS OF EXCHANGE; CRIMINAL LAW (limits on restitution of property under the Larceny Act, 1916 (6 & 7 Geo. 5 c. 50), s. 45); PERSONAL PROPERTY (rights annexed to mere possession); SALE OF GOODS (revesting of property in stolen goods under the Sale of Goods Act, 1893 (56 & 57 Vict. c. 71), s. 24).

---

**Vol. 1] 14–19**          **LAWS OF ENGLAND (3RD EDN.)—SUPPT.**

PARA.
NOS.

---

**15          Claim to benefit from plaintiff's crime.**

NOTE (o).—First case distinguished in *St. John Shipping Corpn.* v. *Joseph Rank, Ltd.*, [1957] 1 Q. B. 267; [1956] 3 All E. R. 683; *Pigney* v. *Pointers Transport Services, Ltd.*, [1957] 2 All E. R. 807.

NOTE (b).—The point left undecided in *Re Sigsworth* was reluctantly decided against the Crown by VAISEY, J., in *Re Callaway, Callaway* v. *Treasury Solicitor*, [1956] Ch. 559; [1956] 2 All E. R. 451, where the guilty party was the sole beneficiary under her victim's will and, on an intestacy, would have been entitled to share the estate equally with her brother. In the result the brother took the whole. In *Re Peacock, Midland Bank Executor and Trustee Co., Ltd.* v. *Peacock*, [1957] Ch. 310; [1957] 2 All E. R. 98, the residuary gift was to a group, including the guilty party. The other beneficiaries took the residue in equal shares, the Crown disclaiming any interest.

NOTE (c).—See however *Pigney* v. *Pointers Transport Services, Ltd.*, [1957] 2 All E. R. 807 (wife could recover damages under the Fatal Accidents Acts as these did not form part of the suicide's estate).

Exhibit 74

---

Tracing supplementary material is a simple matter of matching numbers. For example, bringing up to date the discussion of the liability of a principal for misrepresentation of an agent, from the main volume to date, requires only the matching of volume 1, page 10, paragraph 15 (3d edition), with the same numbers in the cumulative supplements. In the example in Exhibit 74 note how the supplement Shepardizes cases and statutes in paragraph 15.

(3) *Approach to the law through Halsbury's Laws of England.* The analytical approach (by means of the topical analysis or classification scheme) to the discussion of a point of law is exactly the same as in American encyclopedias. So is the fact or descriptive-word approach. The table of cases approach is also available, however, which is not true of American encyclopedias. If the general topic of law decided in a given case is known, for example, "Landlord and Tenant," "Companies," or "Deeds," a search in the case table in the volume covering that topic leads to the exact page in the encyclopedia where the case is used as authority for a statement in the text. The table of cases in each volume refers, as noted above, to the exact spot in the English and Empire Digest and supplements where other cases in point may be found. Also, an approach not found in American general legal encyclopedias is through statutes: If it is desired to find a discussion of a statute, the tables of statutes in the respective volumes refer to the proper page. Halsbury's Statutes of England also contains cross references to Halsbury's Laws.

(4) *Commonwealth editions.* For some of the member nations of the Commonwealth, Halsbury's provides special editions in which supplementary volumes annotating to the cases and statutes of the particular nation covered. Examples are the Australian Pilot and the Canadian Converter, in which "the reader will have before him the statement of the law with dual supporting footnotes; the English statutes and cases, and, in the Pilot [for example] the Australian Commonwealth and State statutes and cases."

4. *Tables of cases approach to English case law.* What is said in §25.1 about the table of cases approach to American law applies for the most part to English materials also, with the important addition that this approach is available in English law for statutes, to some extent. The case tables listed below have all been noted in describing the sets of which they are a part.

    a. *From the earliest times to date.*

        English and Empire Digest (the most complete single table).

        Mews' Digest (a selective case table).

        Halsbury's Laws of England (cases cited in the text as authority).

    b. *Limited period coverage.*

        English Reports, Full Reprint (1378-1865).

        Revised Reports (1785-1865).

Law Reports Digest (1865-1951, continued by Consoli-
dated Index, 1951-1959 and supplements to date).
All England Law Reports (1936 to date).
Current Law (1947 to date).

c. *Law review comments on cases.*

Index to Legal Periodicals (1917 to date).
Law Quarterly Review (volume 2, 1887, to date).
Current Law (1947 to date).
Scholarly law reviews in addition to Law Quarterly Re-
view.

d. *Statutes and the table of cases approach.*

Halsbury's Statutes of England (cases construing statutes
are listed).

5. *Words and phrases approach.* The English claim to have
originated this type of dictionary with Stroud's Judicial Dictionary
(1890; 3d ed. 1952). It is found in one form or another in many
English legal reference books.

6. *Citators for English statutes and cases.* One of the most frequent questions asked by law students is whether an English case
or statute can be Shepardized. This is possible to a limited extent.
There is no tabular system in England noting the legislative and
judicial treatment of statutes and cases, similar to Shepard's Citations, but there are numerous other means for finding the sources
of this information. All are incidental functions of some other
work, such as a digest, encyclopedia or table of cases. In general
they fall within three categories: (a) those, like the English and
Empire Digest, in which the annotations are printed as part of a
digest paragraph or syllabus, and "note up" the case digested by
indicating subsequent judicial action; (b) those in the form of case
and statute tables, in which the citation material follows the name
of the case or the date of the statute, much in the manner of the
Decennial Digest tables of cases; and (c) those in which the citation
is part of a legal encyclopedia footnote.

The citators listed below have been noted earlier in this chapter,
in describing the works of which they are a part; they are coordi-
nated here for convenience of reference.

a. *Statutory citators generally.*

Current Law and Current Law Statutes Citator, 1948 to
1959 (with annual and monthly supplements). Perhaps the most satisfactory table for the period covered.
Cited statutes from the earliest times are included;
citing cases are from 1948 to date.
Halsbury's Statutes of England. For statutes in force
which have been construed by the courts.

b. *Showing repeal, amendments, etc., of statutes.*

> Annotations in Halsbury's Statutes of England.
>
> Chronological Tables of Statutes, 1235 to date.

c. *Cases construing statutes.*

> Current Law, noted above.
>
> Digests. All but the English and Empire Digest have tables of statutes judicially construed.
>
> Encyclopedias. Halsbury's Statutes of England, in footnotes.

d. *Statutory instruments citators.*

> The tables in both the official editions of these instruments are citators. Digests (except the English and Empire) have citator tables, covering various periods from 1891 to date.

e. *Cases judicially considered.*

> All digests described in this chapter serve as case citators: the English and Empire Digest through the annotations to each digest paragraph (to be found through the table of cases); the rest through alphabetical tables of Cases Judicially Noticed, or the like. Current Law, published monthly, is the most frequently published of these citators. For construing cases 1947 to date (Scottish cases from 1948 to date), Current Law Citator is perhaps the most convenient; cited cases are of any date, that is, any case of any date which is cited by a case decided from 1947 to date is covered by case name.

Generally the law student will have comparatively little occasion to Shepardize English statutes, but he should certainly familiarize himself with the available means of Shepardizing cases. For cases prior to 1865, a limited amount of "noting up" is done in the reports published in the English Reports, Full Reprint, as shown in §24.6.

§24.9. **Canadian materials outlined.**[36] Canadian legal publications of all kinds so closely parallel their English and United States counterparts as to need little additional comment here. Accord-

---

[36] The authors are indebted to George A. Johnston, Q.C., Librarian of the Law Society of Upper Canada, Osgoode Hall, Toronto, for having read the notes for Effective Legal Research (1953) in manuscript, and for numerous helpful comments; to Miss Georgina M. Broad, of the library of the Law Society of Upper Canada, and Miss Anne Brown, Librarian of the Judges' Library of Osgoode Hall, for performing the same services for the Student Edition Revised; and to Miss Brown and Mr. Halevy for the same services of this edition. The responsibility for statements made and for appraisals of Canadian publications and for errors is, however, entirely that of the authors. The viewpoint throughout is that of the United States lawyer and law student, rather than of the Canadian.

ingly, only a bare outline of Canadian legislation, law reports and search books of current interest is attempted. The law student should by all means read the paper by George A. Johnston, Q.C., Librarian of the Law Society of Upper Canada, entitled Legal Research in Canada, 54 Law Lib. J. 360 (1961), which is the best survey of the subject.

Because of the federal character of Canada's political organization — with both federal and provincial legislatures and courts — much the same problems are encountered as in the United States.

1. *Federal legislation.* The United States lawyer in his search for the national legislation of Canada would probably begin with the Revised Statutes of Canada, 1952. He would then proceed to the Statutes of Canada (the session laws), and thence, if an administrative order were involved, to the Statutory Orders and Regulations, Consolidation 1955, and its current supplementation through the quarterly consolidated indexes and tables of the Consolidation and the fortnightly issues of the Canada Gazette, Part II.

a. *Revised Statutes of Canada, 1952.*[37] This work (cited as R.S.C. 1952) is a consolidation, a verbatim reprint of public general statutes in force. The Index volume includes such extra materials as the British North America Acts, and certain other statutes and Orders in Council dealing with the admission of provinces and territories to the Dominion. Many of the statutes are themselves consolidations of acts formerly in force, but re-enacted as positive law, in the manner of United States Code reenactments of certain Code titles, repealing in the process the earlier statutes from which they were derived. In other words, the R.S.C. 1952 has the status of the first edition of the United States Revised Statutes, as positive law and not merely prima facie the law. The arrangement of material is by subject. The last volume is a subject index. Appendices list all prior acts consolidated in this edition, with parallel citations to the R.S.C. 1952.

b. *Acts of the Parliament of Canada.*[38] These session laws are typical of their kind. Part I prints Public General Acts, and Part II Local and Private Acts, Not Including Divorce Acts. Divorce acts are listed in a separate table, however. Through 1946 they were printed in Part II, Local and Private Acts, but since then they have appeared in a separate second volume. Tables in the session laws include an alphabetical list of "acts proclaimed," an index of public general acts for the session, and table of Public Statutes

37 Ottawa, E. Cloutier, Queen's Printer, 1953, 6v.
38 Ottawa, E. Cloutier, Queen's Printer, 1841 to date. The title varies; that on the spine currently is Statutes of Canada.

1907 [to date] with amendments thereto, and their effect upon the current edition of the Revised Statutes of Canada.

c. *Statutory Orders and Regulations, Consolidation of 1955.*[39] This work is very similar to its English counterpart. Acts upon which orders are based are listed alphabetically by subject, beneath which are printed the orders and regulations issued thereunder, as in force in 1955. There is a brief subject index, and there are quarterly consolidated indexes and tables. New orders and regulations are currently printed in Part II of the fortnightly official Canada Gazette. Not all orders are printed, but only those regarded by the editors as of sufficient public general interest to justify it.

d. *Proclamations and Orders in Council Passed Under the Authority of the War Measures Act, R.S.C. (1927), Chap. 206.*[40] War orders were separately published in this series.

e. *Criminal Code.* Official editions[40a] appear at rather long intervals, but privately annotated editions are issued frequently and are the ones consulted by the legal profession. The Criminal Code also forms Chapter 51 of the Statutes of Canada, 1953-1954.

2. *Provincial legislation.* The provinces and territories have their own session laws, the provincial laws usually being entitled statutes, and the territorial laws ordinances. There are also the following compilations of current interest:

*Alberta,* 1906-1915, 1922, 1942, 1955. Ordinances of the North-West (now Northwest) Territories applying to Alberta through 1905 were separately published in 1907, 1911, and 1915.

*British Columbia,* 1871, 1888, 1897, 1911, 1924, 1936, 1948, 1960.

*Manitoba,* 1880, 1891, 1902, 1913, 1924, 1940, 1954 (1924 compilation called Consolidated Amendments).

*New Brunswick,* 1877, 1903, 1907, 1952.

*Newfoundland,* 1872, 1892, 1916, 1952. Local and Private Acts, 1873.

*Northwest Territories,* 1888, 1898, 1931, 1956. The annual Sessions Ordinances were formerly designated as of the "North West Territories," but are now uniformly "Northwest." The ordinances are published irregularly in mimeographed form, but some are later printed, like those for 1948 and 1949.

---

[39] Ottawa, E. Cloutier, Queen's Printer, 1955, 4v.

[40] Ottawa, E. Cloutier, Queen's Printer, 1940-September 1942, 8v., continued by Canadian War Orders and Regulations, 1942-1946, 13v.

[40a] Ottawa, Roger Duhamel, Queen's Printer, 1963; the latest edition available.

*Nova Scotia,* 1873, 1884, 1900, 1923, 1954.

*Ontario,* 1877, 1887, 1897, 1914, 1927, 1937, 1950, 1960.

*Prince Edward Island.* Revised Statutes of Prince Edward Island, 1951. There are several indexes: Crandall's Index to Statutes in Force 1845; Fraser's Index to Statutes 1869-1918; Fraser's Index to Statutes 1918-1928; and O'Donnell's Index to Statutes 1929-1944.

*Quebec,* 1888, 1909, 1925, 1941. 1964.

*Saskatchewan,* 1909, 1920, 1930, 1940, 1953, 1965.

*Yukon Territory,* 1902, 1914, 1958.

3. *Statutory indexes.* Although there have been numerous subject indexes to the federal legislation of Canada, few are of current value. For most practical purposes, the index to the R.S.C. 1952, as supplemented by the indexes to the Statutes of Canada to date, is used. A card index of both Dominion Local and Private Acts and Ontario Statutes has been kept since 1916 in the library of Osgoode Hall, in Toronto. A useful printed index covering all of Canada is the Index to Dominion and Provincial Statutes from the Earliest Period Down to 1916.[41] This index may be said to have been brought down to date by the R.S.C. 1952. Two other indexes are the Index to Eastern Provinces and Dominion Statute Amendments to 1926, and the Index to Western Provinces and Dominion Statute Amendments to 1926.[42] These are not subject indexes in the usual sense, however, but rather alphabetical lists of statutes by short titles, with citations to the original amending acts.

a. *Index, Local and Private Acts, Dominion of Canada, 1867-1941.*[43] This index, compiled by Maurice Ollivier, is a subject index under very broad headings. An appendix contains a Table of Public Statutes, 1907 to 1942; an alphabetical subject index to the R.S.C. 1927, showing amendments thereto; and certain other public acts and amendments.

4. *Law reports.* All Canada is covered by conventional law reports, and there are in addition legal periodicals printing reports, either in full or abridged. There is a present tendency to discontinue individual provincial reporters in favor of combined reporters for several provinces, as in the National Reporter System in the United States. The following reports are current.

a. *Covering all jurisdictions.* The Dominion Law Reports are said to be "reports of all reportable Canadian cases from all the courts of Canada . . . and Canadian decisions in the Privy Council," from 1912 to date. Through volume 70 (1922), the volumes

---

41 Montreal, Lovell, 1918.
42 Toronto, Garrett, 1927.
43 Ottawa, E. Cloutier, Queen's Printer, 1942.

were numbered consecutively, but from then through 1955 were renumbered each year, and are cited in the manner of the English Law Reports. Thus, [1950] 3 D.L.R. 118; [1951] 1 D.L.R. 361. With the start of the Dominion Law Reports, Second Series, in 1956, the consecutive volume numbering was resumed. Thus, 6 D.L.R.(2d) 118.

b. *Covering all criminal courts.* Canadian Criminal Cases Annotated is a "series of reports of important decisions in criminal and quasi-criminal cases in Canada . . . of the Dominion and of the provinces thereof," since 1898. The annotations consist of statements of "cases judicially considered," and "statutes considered" — in other words, the annotations serve a citator function. There are also occasional brief annotations in the A.L.R. manner. Criminal Reports (Canada) is a "series of reports with annotations and practice notes on criminal cases arising in the courts of the various provinces of Canada," 1946 to date. There are notations of cases referred to in the opinions, and of statutes construed. About half the cases are, in addition, briefly annotated in the A.L.R. manner. There is a cumulative subject index to volumes 1-32, 1946-1960, also a cumulative table of cases.

c. *Supreme Court of Canada.* This court is covered both by the Canada Law Reports, Supreme Court of Canada, and the Dominion Law Reports. The former reports, dating from 1923, continue the Reports of the Supreme Court of Canada covering 1876 through 1922. Cases "referred to" are noted following the syllabi and are indexed in a separate table. There are two additional tables contained in these reports: (1) Judgments rendered during the year and not reported; (2) motions decided. (Applications for leave to appeal granted are not included.) Statutes construed are listed under "Statutes" in the index-digest of each volume.

d. *Exchequer Court.* Canada Law Reports, Exchequer Court of Canada, is a reporter dating from 1923, continuing the older Reports of the Exchequer Court of Canada, covering 1891 through 1922. The Dominion Law Reports series also covers this court.

e. *Special-subject reports.* Current special-subject reports include Canadian Bankruptcy Reports Annotated, 1920 to date; Canadian Railway and Transport Cases, 1902 to date; Canadian Tax Cases Annotated, 1938 to date; Dominion Tax Cases, 1920 to date; Canada Tax Appeal Board Cases, 1949 to date; Canadian Patent Reporter, 1941 to date; Fox's Patent, Trade Mark, Design and Copyright Cases, 1941 to date; Insurance Law Reporter, 1934 to date; Canada Tax Cases, 1917 to date; and several reports series published in connection with loose-leaf services.

f. *Provincial courts.* Reporters cover all provinces. The Maritime Provinces Reports, 1929 to date, covers reports of cases from the courts of New Brunswick, Nova Scotia and Prince Edward Island, and, since 1947, Newfoundland. The Western Weekly Reports series (1911 to date) reports cases from Alberta, British Columbia, Manitoba and Saskatchewan. The earlier Western Law Reporter, v. 1-34, covered 1905-1916. Both also report some Privy Council, Supreme Court of Canada and Exchequer Court of Canada cases. Individual provincial reports are also currently issued for the courts of Ontario and Quebec.

5. *Digests.* There have been many such, some covering all of Canada, others restricted in scope to Dominion cases or to those of individual provinces. The following are of current interest.

a. *Canadian Abridgment system.*[44] The most complete digest, in jurisdictions and time covered, is a group composed of the Canadian Abridgment, the Canadian Abridgment Consolidation 1936-1955 [45] and the Canadian Abridgment Annual.[46] Through 1935 this system digests "decisions of the provincial and Dominion courts from the earliest times including appeals therefrom to the Privy Council, but excluding decisions based upon the Quebec Civil Code." Beginning with 1936 it includes Quebec Civil Code decisions.

This is a conventional digest except that it lacks a descriptive-word index. Cases are abridged at some length, rather than digested, for their point of chief legal interest, with cross references to that abridgment from other points considered in the opinion. The Consolidation is keyed to the main work by parenthetical references to topic, chapter and section of that work, thus enabling the searcher to find all cases in point in all units of the system, since this same cross-reference scheme is continued in the Canadian Abridgment Annual. Occasionally there are also cross references to Mews' Digest (2d edition), where English cases in point may be found. Each volume has its own table of cases, and there is a consolidated table for the entire set through 1955. This is probably the most complete of all Canadian tables of cases. There is an index of words and phrases judicially defined. The Index of Cases Judicially Noticed in Canadian Reports, by Leonard G. Wrinch, is perhaps the most complete Canadian case citator, kept up to date by loose-leaf supplements. This Index includes references to English as well as Canadian cases judicially noticed in Canadian courts. Beginning with the Consolidation (1936), there is also a Table of

44 Toronto, Burroughs & Co. (Eastern), Ltd., 1935-1946, 35v.; 2d ed., 1966 to date.
45 Toronto, Burroughs & Co. (Eastern), Ltd., 1956-1959, 10v.
46 Toronto, Burroughs & Co. (Eastern), Ltd., 1936 to date.

Statutes Judicially Considered, which is a statute citator.   The
Canadian Adridgment Annual supplements the Abridgment and
the Consolidation.   The second edition is presently being brought
out and to date six volumes have been published.   This edition
does not contain the Quebec (Canadian civil law) cases.

b. *All-Canada Digest system.*   From 1910 to 1961, this system
has purported to be "the key to every Canadian case and every current series of Canadian reports."   It consists of the All-Canada
Digest 1910-1934,[47] the First Decennial Supplement, 1935-1944,[48]
and the Canadian Annual Digest.[49]   For the period covered,
therefore, it traverses the same ground as the Canadian Abridgment system, though in considerably shorter compass.   It is a conventional digest.   The Supplement and the Annual Digest list
words and phrases, cases judicially noticed, and Dominion and
provincial statutes judicially considered, to 1957.

c. *Canadian Current Law.*[50]   This monthly digest of cases in all
Canadian courts has the unusual feature of digesting cases not yet
reported.   Each issue has a cumulative table of cases for the current year and there is a subject index.   Changes in federal legislation are noted, but since there is no tabular index to such statutes, material pertaining to them must be searched for through the
subject index.   Pertinent material from the Canada Gazette is
noted, such as new statutory rules and orders.   Cases decided in
the Supreme Court of Canada during the preceding month are also
listed and decisions noted.   References are made under the respective subject headings to Canadian law review articles in point.

d. *Dominion Report Service.*[51]   This is a loose-leaf digest, without English or United States counterpart in that form.   In scope
it is a "consolidation of the living law from the earliest times to
date," purporting to digest "every reported Canadian Case . . .
by the 11th of the month following" publication of the decision
digested.   In addition, it gives advance digests of "the important
decisions of the highest courts. . . ."   Digests include a statement
of facts and a fairly long digest of the case, with cross references to
allied topics.

Digest paragraphs are arranged under sixteen main topics,
under each of which there are several subtopics, the whole numbered consecutively.   Thus, "Commercial Law" 1-8; "Contracts"

[47] Title varies.   Toronto, Canada Law Book Co., 1935, 4v.
[48] Toronto, Canada Law Book Co., 1946, 2v.
[49] Annual Supplement to the All-Canada Digest, 1910-1934, and Consolidated
Supplement 1935-1944.   Toronto, Canada Law Book Co., 1945 to date.
[50] Toronto, Carswell Co., Ltd., 1948 to date.
[51] Toronto, CCH Canadian, Ltd.

9-14; "Criminal Law" 15-20, etc. Case digests are numbered consecutively under each topic and are filed thereunder by a paragraph number made up of the topic number, a hyphen, the case number and a jurisdiction abbreviation. For example, ¶1-482 Q denotes general commercial law, case number 482, from Quebec. Similar abbreviations indicate the Privy Council, Supreme or Exchequer Court of Canada, and the various provincial courts. At the present time, eight or more units must be consulted for complete coverage: the Consolidation, in four volumes; the current volume; and six biennial dated volumes, beginning with 1950-51. The original plan was to transfer cases from the current volumes to the Consolidation, but apparently that has not been done regularly.

(1) *Subject indexes.* In the Consolidation there is a Cumulative Topical Index following each of the sixteen main topic tables, which is revised whenever material is transferred from the current volumes. In the current volumes there is a combined index for all topics, revised monthly.

(2) *Case tables.* There are two case tables, a cumulative one covering the Consolidation, and revised whenever transfers of new material are made to it; and one covering the current volumes and revised monthly. Together these tables purport to cover all Canadian cases "from the earliest times."

(3) *Finding lists, statutory citators.* The current volumes contain finding lists of abbreviations employed in Canadian case reports, and Code Citators, by which the Canadian Criminal Code, Bankruptcy Act, Companies Act and Winding-Up Act, and the Quebec Civil, Civil Procedure and Municipal Codes may be Shepardized for cases construing them. These citators are only partially available in the Consolidation.

e. *Supreme Court of Canada cases.* There are two index-digests of Supreme Court cases. The index to Supreme Court Cases (1923-1950)[52] is a one-volume digest of "all decisions of the Supreme Court of Canada, published in the Canada Law Reports from 1923 to 1950, inclusive, with relevant annotations regarding appeals to the Privy Council." There is also an index of statutes and codes cited or discussed — a citator. The Index to Supreme Court of Canada Reports, 1876-1950 [53] is a two-volume index digest. It contains a consolidated table of cases and a subject index to Supreme Court of Canada cases for the whole period. The third cumulative supplement, 1951-1962, covers period to December, 1962.[53a]

---

[52] Montreal, Wilson et Lafleur, Ltd., 1951.
[53] Toronto, Butterworth & Co. (Canada), 1952.
[53a] Toronto, Butterworth & Co. (Canada), 1963.

f. *Chitty's Abridgment . . . Canadian Criminal Case Law.*[54] This is a digest of Canadian Criminal Cases. Both the main volume and the supplements contain a Criminal Code Citator.

g. *Repertoire Generale de Jurisprudence Canadienne.*[55] This is a conventional digest of Federal, Privy Council and Quebec cases through 1937, continued to date by the Annuaire de Jurisprudence de Québec.

h. *Index Judiciaire, 1900-1947.*[56] This is a subject index to Quebec cases rather than a digest.

i. *Butterworth's Ontario Digest Annotated.*[56a] This is a "statement of the case law of Ontario from 1901."

j. *Digest of Cases . . . in the Exchequer Court of Canada.*[57] This group of digests covers the Exchequer Court from its beginning.

6. *Encyclopedias.* There is no exact Canadian counterpart of Halsbury's Laws of England, American Jurisprudence or Corpus Juris Secundum, but there are current works which approach the conventional legal encyclopedia.

a. *Canadian Encyclopedic Digest.* There are two editions of this work (commonly referred to as C.E.D.): Canadian Encyclopedic Digest (Ontario),[58] now in its second edition; and Canadian Encyclopedic Digest (Western).[59]

The Ontario edition, covering cases from all Ontario and Maritime Provinces courts as well as from the Privy Council and Supreme Court of Canada applicable to this area, is an encyclopedia of the law as reflected in these cases. Federal law is treated when applicable. The second edition has a separate statute citator for 1859-1950, with loose-leaf supplement to date. The citator covers Ontario statutes judicially considered and, currently, synopses of Ontario legislation. There is no table of cases nor table of words and phrases in the Digest, reliance for these being placed upon the tables in the Canadian Abridgment.

The Western edition covers all Western Canada decisions and those of the Supreme Court of Canada and of the Privy Council applicable to the area.

---

[54] Toronto, Canada Law Book Co., 1925, with supplement 1925-1950.

[55] Montreal, Wilson et Lafleur, Ltd., 1914-1915, 4v.; Supplement, 1913-1925, 2v.; Supplement, 1926-1935, 2v.; Supplement, 1935-1955, 2v.

[56] Montreal, Denis, 1948, 2v.

[56a] Toronto, Butterworth & Co. (Canada), 1958-1966, 13v., annual supplements to date.

[57] From the beginning to 1922. Toronto, Carswell Co., Ltd., 1924; 1922-1946, compiled by Redmond Quain, 1948, with later supplements.

[58] Toronto, Carswell Co., Ltd., 1950 to date. As of July, 1961, 21v., cumulative supplement 1955, cumulative loose-leaf supplements to date.

[59] Calgary, Burroughs & Co., Ltd., 1919-1925, 7v.; 2d ed., 1956-1961, 11v. and supplements.

b. *Dominion Law Annotations Revised.*[60]  This is not, strictly speaking, an encyclopedia, but it performs much the same function for the material covered by the annotations.  It is a rewriting of the annotations originally printed in the Dominion Law Reports, incorporating changes necessitated by later decisions and statutes. Since the annotations are arranged in classified order, the work resembles a somewhat fragmentary legal encyclopedia.

7. *Citators.*  There are numerous Canadian citators, most of which are tables of statutes or cases "judicially considered."  The following list includes those of current interest.

a. *Federal statutes.*  The Canadian Statute and Criminal Code Citator, with its predecessor, Tremeear's Canada Statute Citator, covers Dominion statutes from 1906 to date.  It is now a loose-leaf service.  Amendments, additions and repeals are noted, including those pertaining to the R.S.C. 1927 and the R.S.C. 1952.  Cases construing federal legislation are cited and digested briefly.  The Criminal Code is also covered in the Code Citator in Chitty's Abridgment of Canadian Criminal Law, 1925-1949, and in those citators noted below which purport to cover all Canadian statutes, both Dominion and provincial.  Tables in the Revised Statutes of Canada, 1952 list consolidated acts contained in that revision and their subsequent legislative history.  The annual Statutes of Canada note all amendments of Dominion legislation from 1907 to date, by subject.

b. *Federal and provincial statutes.*  The Statute Citator in the All-Canada Digest 1935-1944 consolidation notes both statutory changes and cases construing Dominion and provincial statutes. This is continued in the Canadian Annual Digest to 1957.  The Canadian Abridgment Consolidation 1936-1955 and the Canadian Abridgment Annual have tables of statutes judicially considered to 1959, but these do not show statutory changes.  Statutory changes for the current year are noted, by subject, in the monthly Canadian Current Law.  As construed by the Supreme Court, foreign, Imperial, Dominion and provincial statutes are conveniently covered by the Index to Supreme Court Cases (1923-1950), in the Index of Statutes and Codes Cited or Discussed.

Quebec statutes are covered by the Table de Reference aux Codes in the Annuaire de Jurisprudence de Québec.  Ontario Statutes Judicially Considered and the Ontario Statute Citator 1960 cover Ontario statutes.  Both are kept up to date by loose-leaf supplements.  Ontario Statutes Judicially Considered briefly notes the effect of amendments; the Ontario Statute Citator prints the

---

[60] Annotations Consolidated from Dominion Law Reports, 1911-1950.  Toronto, Canada Law Book Co., 1928-1951, 3v.

amendments in full.   The table in the Canadian Encyclopedic Digest (Ontario), second edition, notes Ontario statutes judicially considered.   References to regulations under statutes are given in the Canadian Statute Citator, The Canadian Abridgment Statutes of Canada Judicially Considered, Ontario Statutes Judicially Considered, and the Ontario Statute Citator.   Citations of the Statutes of Alberta and Saskatchewan, 1886-1924,[61] covers those provinces. Loose-leaf supplements, published as appendices to the Western Weekly Reports, cover Alberta (1955 to date), Manitoba (1954 to date), and Saskatchewan (1954 to date).

c. *Case citators.*   The most complete case citator is in the Index of Cases Judicially Noticed in Canadian Reports . . . From the Earliest Times to [date], in the Canadian Abridgment, as kept up to date by supplements.   English cases judicially noticed in Canadian courts are also included.   Cases are listed by title, with citations to cases questioning, overruling, referring to, etc.   The All-Canada Digest 1935-1944 supplement also has such a table, continued in the Canadian Annual Digest.   Both citators cover Dominion and provincial courts.

d. *Loose-leaf services as citators.*   Particularly for statutes, the loose-leaf services for Canada are useful citators.

e. *How to Shepardize a Canadian statute.*   The citators to be consulted are noted above.   In these citators, the statutes are commonly listed by the short title of the original act or its consolidation — as County Courts Act, Dentistry Act, etc.   Exceptions are codes, such as the Canadian Criminal Code and the Quebec Civil Code, which are cited by code and section.   Having found the required statute and section in the citator, the searcher there sees that amendments, repeals, etc. are cited first under each section, followed by citations to cases construing the section.   Since there is merely a brief summary of what action the construing court took, the cases must be examined.

A feature of Canadian statute citators not found in those in the United States is the notation of statutory rules and orders (corresponding to our Code of Federal Regulations) promulgated under the authority of the statutes listed, and cases interpreting them. To find the interpretation of the order it is first necessary to look up the basic act under the authority of which the order was issued. Where a statute is involved in a decision, it is noted in the digests in Canadian Current Law, to be found under the subject matter, such as "Debtor and Creditor," "Real Property," etc., thus bringing the citation down to within a month or two of decision date. Ontario statute citators have loose-leaf supplements.

61 Toronto, Carswell Co., Ltd., 1924.

f. *How to Shepardize a Canadian case.* Case citators are described above. The approach is through the case title, as *Smith v. Jones,* rather than through jurisdiction and law reporter, as 5 D.L.R. 78. Thus any Canadian case may be Sheparized through the Table of Cases Judicially Noticed, in the Canadian Abridgment system, by consulting the bound volume and its supplements. Other citators are of somewhat smaller scope as to jurisdiction or period covered.

While Canadian digests note other cases referred to in the opinions digested, the digest paragraph is not itself a citator *for the case digested.* It thus differs from the English and Empire Digest, where the annotations following the digest paragraph Shepardize the digested case. A separate case table is therefore necessary for Shepardizing a Canadian case. With the exception noted below, citator material is not supplemented oftener than annually. The exception is the reversing or affirming of a decision by a court on appeal. Such action may be found through the cumulative table of cases in the monthly Canadian Current Law. For example, *Canadian Indemnity Co.* v. *Andrews & George Co.,* a case then as yet unreported, was noted in the November 1952 issue of this monthly as reversing the decision of the lower court as reported in 4 W.W.R. (N.S.) 37. In other words, action corresponding to the Shepard's Citations "history of the case" is available monthly, but that relating to the "treatment of the case" — whether referred to, applied, followed, etc., by another case — is supplemented only annually.

8. *Loose-leaf services.* Tax, labor and regulatory loose-leaf services perform the same functions in Canada, and in the same manner, as those in the United States, described in Chapter 23. The subject matter covered includes Dominion and provincial taxation, succession duties, companies, corporations, emergency control regulations, insurance and labor. As in the United States, the cases reported in connection with some of the services are later bound separately to form special-subject report series.

9. *Treatises.* The following, selected from many perhaps equally good, are, regardless of publication date, recommended to the United States lawyer and law student.

a. *Practice books.*

> Audette, Louis A., The Practice of the Exchequer Court of Canada. 2d ed., Ottawa, Copeland-Patterson-Crain, 1909.
>
> Cameron, Edward R., The Supreme Court of Canada Practice and Rules. 3d ed., Toronto, Carswell Co. Ltd., 1924.

Canadian Court Forms.  2d ed., Toronto, Canada Law Book Company Ltd., 1962.

Chitty, R. M. W., The Ontario Annual Practice.  Toronto, Canada Law Book Company Ltd.

Civil Code of the Province of Quebec.  Montreal, Kingsland (loose-leaf).

Crankshaw's Criminal Code of Canada.  7th ed., Toronto, Carswell Co. Ltd., 1959.  Cumulative Supplements.

Macklem, Douglas N. and Bristow, David I., Mechanics' Liens in Canada.  Toronto, Carswell Co. Ltd., 1962.

McKeon, Charles F., Division Court Handbook.  2d ed., Toronto, Carswell Co. Ltd., 1966.

Martin, John C., The Criminal Code of Canada.  Toronto, Cartwright & Sons, Ltd., 1955.

Martin, John C. and Mewett, Alan W., Martin's Annual Criminal Code and supplement to Martin's Criminal Code, 1955.  Toronto, Canada Law Book Company Ltd., 1966.  Annual to date.

Supreme Court Practice, 1967, 2v.  London, Sweet & Maxwell, Ltd.  Kept up to date by loose-leaf binder and sheets issued by Her Majesty's Stationary Office, London.

Tremeear's Ann. Crim. Code — Canada.  6th ed., Toronto, Carswell Co. Ltd., 1964.  Supp. 1964-1966.

b. *Substantive books.*

Anger, H. D., and Honsberger, John D., Canadian Law of Real Property.  Toronto, Canada Law Book Co., 1959.

Anger, William H., Anger's Digest of Canadian Law.  19th ed., Toronto, Canada Law Book Co., 1967.

Carrothers, Alfred William Rooke, Labour Arbitration in Canada.  Toronto, Butterworth & Co., 1961.

Castel, Jean-Gabriel, Private International Law.  Toronto, Canada Law Book Co., 1960.

Challies, George S., The Law of Expropriation.  Montreal, Wilson et Lafleur, Ltd., 2d ed., 1963.

Chrysler, Alfred C., Handbook on Canadian Labour Law.  Toronto, Carswell Co. Ltd., 1957.

Duncan, Lewis, and Honsberger, John D., Bankruptcy in Canada.  3d ed. Toronto, Canada Law Book Co., 1961.

Falconbridge, John D., The Law of Mortgages of Land.  3d ed., Toronto, Canada Law Book Co., 1942.

Fox, Harold G., Canadian Law and Practice Relating to Letters Patent for Inventions. 3d ed., Toronto, Carswell Co. Ltd., 1948, 2v.

——, The Canadian Law of Copyright. Toronto, Carswell Co. Ltd., 1944.

——, Canadian Law of Trade Marks and Unfair Competition. 2d ed., Toronto, Carswell Co. Ltd., 1956, 2v.

Goldsmith, Immanuel, Damages for Personal Injury and Death in Canada. Toronto, Carswell Co. Ltd., 1959; Supp. 1966.

Hall, Frank C., Digest of Automobile Accident Cases. 3d ed., Toronto, Carswell Co. Ltd., 1953.

Horsley, David B., Manual of Motor Vehicle Law. Toronto, Carswell Co. Ltd., 1963; Supp. 1967.

Jameson, Michael B., Canadian Estate Tax. Toronto, Butterworth & Co. (Canada), 1960.

——, Ontario Succession Duties. Toronto, Butterworth & Co. (Canada), 1959.

Loffmark, Ralph R., Estate Taxes. Toronto, Carswell Co. Ltd., 1960.

——, Tax and Estate Planning. Toronto, Carswell Co. Ltd. (loose-leaf). Kept up to date by releases.

Macaulay, Robert W., and Bruce, H. M., Handbook on Canadian Mechanics' Liens. Toronto, Carswell Co. Ltd., 1951.

Macdonell, I. M., and Sheard, Terence, Probate Practice. Toronto, Carswell Co. Ltd., 1953; Supp. 1961.

Magwood, W. Marsh, The Ontario Land Titles Act. Toronto, Carswell Co. Ltd., 1954.

Marriott, Alfred S., Practice in Mortgage Actions in Ontario. 2d ed., Toronto, Carswell Co. Ltd., 1955.

O'Brien, Arthur H., Conveyancing Law and Forms. 9th ed., Toronto, Canada Law Book Co., 1955. 3v.

Phelan, Roderick G., Highway Traffic Law. 2d ed., Toronto, Canada Law Book Co., 1961.

Power, W. K., Law and Practice Relating to Divorce and Other Matrimonial Causes in Canada. 2d ed., Calgary, Burroughs & Co. Ltd., 1964.

Rogers, Ian MacFee, The Law of Municipal Corporations. Toronto, Carswell Co. Ltd., 1959. 2v. Cum. Supp. 1966.

Sheard, Terence, Canadian Forms of Wills. 2d ed., Toronto, Carswell Co. Ltd., 1960.

————, The Drafting of Wills (Lectures).  Toronto, Carswell Co. Ltd., 1963.

Stewart, J. L., Handbook of Canadian Company Law. 5th ed., Toronto, Carswell Co. Ltd., 1960.

————, Company Law of Canada.  5th ed., Toronto, Carswell Co. Ltd., 1962.

Stikeman, Harry H., Income Tax Act, Annotated.  Toronto, Richard De Boo, 1927-1948 consolidated; Annual, 1949 to date.

Widdifield, Charles H., Executors' Accounts.  4th ed., Toronto, Carswell Co. Ltd., 1944.

Williams, Esten H., Notes on Canadian Law of Landlord and Tenant.  3d ed., Toronto, Carswell Co. Ltd., 1957.

10. *Legal directories.*  In Canada these are called Law Lists. They perform the same functions as in the United States, including the printing of abridgments of provincial laws.  The directory listed below is an annual publication.

Canadian Law List. Toronto, Cartwright & Sons, Ltd.

11. *Legal periodicals.*  Listed below are the principal Canadian law reviews.  They are currently indexed in Canadian Current Law; in the Index to Canadian Legal Literature[62] edited by Marianne Scott; and those in the English language (also Revue du Barreau de la Province de Québec), in the Index to Legal Periodicals.

Alberta Law Review.  Edmonton.

Canada Tax Journal.  Toronto.

Canadian Bar Journal.  Ottawa.

Canadian Bar Review.  Toronto.

Canadian Journal of Corrections.  Ottawa.

Chitty's Law Journal.  Toronto.

Criminal Law Quarterly.  Toronto.

Faculty of Law Review.  Toronto (vols. 1-13, School of Law Review).

McGill Law Journal.  Montreal.

Osgoode Hall Law Journal.  Toronto.

University of British Columbia Law Review.  Vancouver.

University of Toronto Law Journal.  Toronto.

Western Law Review.  London.

12. *Lists of current Canadian publications.*  Chitty's Law Journal, beginning with the issue for January 1953, lists Canadian Legal Publications of all kinds.  The Carswell Company, Limited, of Toronto, issues a monthly list of law publications.

[62] Montreal, Canadian Association of Law Libraries, 1963-1966, 2v.

# CHAPTER 25

# Coordinating the Research Techniques

**§25.1.  Approaches to finding the law.**  Finding the law may be compared to playing golf: seldom does a player make a hole in one, or cover the course by the use of a single club.  Similarly, most law-finding problems require the use of more than one source and index to the law.  Seldom is one approach a sufficient check upon either the scope or the completeness of a search.  The skillful and imaginative interplay of the various means of finding the law is the mark of the successful searcher.  Since the various techniques involved in finding and evaluating specific legislation and cases have been described in the preceding chapters, a knowledge of them is assumed here.  The aim of this chapter, accordingly, is to suggest some of the many possibilities of combining techniques in the solution of typical problems.

1. *Table of cases approach.*  This is perhaps the most nearly universal of all approaches to the case law.  Case tables are found in almost every publication which either prints, discusses or cites reported cases.  A case in point is the chief aim of most searches.  Once a case in point is found, some of the other approaches may usually be abandoned or modified.  One case in point leads, through a digest, to other cases in point; or to a detailed analysis of that and similar cases in a treatise, law review or annotation.  General legal encyclopedias and annotated statutes commonly lack tables of cases, however.

a. *Utility of case tables in the search for the law: Information supplied.*  Case tables supply the page number in the volume or advance sheet of law reports, casebook, periodical, treatise or annotation where a particular case is printed or commented upon.  They provide parallel case citations from one set of reports to another printing the same case.  Tables lacking the volume and page citation of the case, but referring to the place in a book where the case is printed or commented upon, lead by this one additional step to the full citation, which is usually on the page where the case is printed or referred to in the work served by the table. The case table in a digest lists the digest topic or topics and section numbers under which a case is digested. (If the Reporter is at hand for the searcher, it should be consulted for the topic and section or Key Number given in the headnote of the report.) The searcher, in some way, has found a case or the name of a case in point, and wants to read other like cases. The digest table of cases supplies the topics and section numbers under which these are digested.

Similarly, the case table may lead to the place in a treatise, legal periodical or annotation where a case is discussed. This table may be in the treatise pertinent to the topic, or it may be in the Index to Legal Periodicals, or it may be in the table of cases to the A.L.R. Digest, leading to an A.L.R. annotation.

The table of cases approach is not available for most legal encyclopedias and annotated statutes.

b. *Alphabeting case tables.* The alphabeting practices in case tables lack uniformity and consistency. Some frequently applied principles are described below, but the searcher must always be prepared to find that his particular case table does not apply them, and thus he must exercise his ingenuity. The material below follows the presentation order, though not the content, of the very full Explanatory Notes at pages v and vi of the table of cases volume of the A.L.R. Permanent Digest.

(1) *Corporations, associations and partnerships.* Alphabeting is by the full corporate or partnership name, as *American Brake Shoe Co. v. Bowles.* However, where such a name begins with the name of a person, as *E. I. Du Pont de Nemours & Co.,* there are three variant practices. (a) Index exactly as written above. (b) Place the initials at the end of the surname, and index by the surname: *Du Pont de Nemours (E. I.) & Co.* (c) Cross-reference from (a) above: *E. I. Du Pont de Nemours & Co. See Du Pont de Nemours (E. I.) & Co.*

(2) *Railroads, street railways, insurance companies.* The common practice here is to give the full name, in abbreviated form, always spelling out the first word of the title. *Chicago, R.I. & P.R. Co. v. Sampson; New York L. Ins. Co.*

(3) *Cities, counties, states, territories.* There is no consistency among indexes here. "City of New Orleans" in one table may be filed under "City"; in the other as "New Orleans." Most case tables are fairly liberal with cross references from one form to the other.

(4) *Ex rel., Use of.* Usually there is cross reference from the relator's name: that is, *State of New York ex rel. Zagayko* v. *Pechefsky* is filed under State of New York, but cross-referenced from *Zagayko* v. *Pechefsky. Use of* cases are similarly treated. Titles beginning with "State . . . ex rel." are filed at the end of other "State" cases, and thereunder are alphabeted by relator. Thus *State* v. *Zolantikis* precedes *State ex rel. Adams* v. *Lee.*

(5) *Ampersand (&).* This is alphabeted as "and" in most tables, but in some, titles containing it are filed after all others bearing the words preceding it. Thus *Borden's Will, Re* precedes *Borden & Co.* in such tables.

(6) *Abbreviations.* These are treated as though spelled out: Ft.-Fort; St.-Saint; Mt.-Mount. M,' Mc, and Mac are usually all treated as though spelled "Mac" and so alphabeted, but some tables file by the letters, with a cross reference from "Mac."

(7) *Ex parte, In re, Matter of, Estate of.* All are filed under the party's name, with cross reference from the prefix.

(8) *Numerals.* These are filed as though spelled out. Numbers (principally dates and street numbers) which are commonly expressed in hundreds, are filed as follows:

| | |
|---|---|
| 1690 Longfellow Ave. | Sixteen hundred ninety |
| 1676 Claremont Ave. | Sixteen hundred seventy-six |
| 1942 Chevrolet Motors Co. | Nineteen hundred forty-two |
| 19 Rector St. Corp. | Nineteen Rector St. Corp. |
| 1935 East 71st St. Corp. | Nineteen hundred thirty-five Seventy-first St. Corp. |

This results in case names being filed out of numerical order, but in many case tables it is done this way.

(9) *Filing by "letter" or by "word."* Filing according to the *exact succession of letters,* regardless of any ensuing word division, is called "filing by letters." "Filing by words" recognizes the word division, and results in a different filing order. It is the system employed by telephone directories. The two systems are illustrated below.

| By Letters | By Words |
|---|---|
| N. E. Wentworth Co. | N. E. Wentworth Co. |
| Newhart Mfg. Co. | New Haven |
| New Haven | New York |
| Newman | Newhart Mfg. Co. |
| New York | Newman |

(10) *"De," "Du," "Van," "Von."* Most case tables treat the prefix as an integral part of the name. Thus "De Groot," "Den-

nis," "Devlin," "De Witt," "Van Cott," "Vancouver," "Van de Carr," are filed in that order.

c. *Plaintiff-defendant tables.* This is the usual type of table of cases. Except in digest case tables, the only information commonly given in such tables is the page where the listed case is printed or referred to in the work containing the table — except that parallel citations to all standard reports of the case are also given, as official, National Reporter System and selective cases system (A.L.R.), in that order. In a digest table, the information usually includes not only the parallel citations but also the digest classification topics and sections under which the digest of the case is found. In many digests it also includes certain citator information — i.e., whether the case, within the period of time covered by the table, has been affirmed, reversed, etc., on appeal — the history of the case. Sometimes a digest table of cases fails to record the A.L.R. citation of a case, because the case was not printed in A.L.R. until after the digest table of cases was compiled. A surer parallel citation guide is in Shepard's Citations. A typical digest table of cases entry is Exhibit 75, from the Fifth Decennial Digest table of cases.

Kalb v. Feuerstein 228 Wis 525, 279 NW 687, reh den 228 Wis 525, 280 NW 726, appeal dism 59 SCt 107, 305 US 566, 83 LEd 356, foll in 231 Wis 185, 285 NW 431, rev 60 SCt 343, 308 US 433, 84 LEd 370, conformed to 234 Wis 507, 291 N W 840—Mtg 529(10).

Exhibit 75

Some digests omit the names of cases for which no printed opinion is given in the report, because there is then nothing to digest. Most digests, however, include the names of even memorandum cases which are not digested. The Decennial Digests list such a case when the memorandum decision is connected with another case which is digested.

d. *Defendant-plaintiff tables.* These tables, a comparatively recent development in case tables, frequently supply less information than the plaintiff-defendant tables, perhaps referring only to the plaintiff-defendant entry, which must then be searched in its table for the full information. The value of these tables is that when only the defendant's name is known, the case can still be found by case name.

e. *Popular-name tables.* Where the only available reference to a case is by some title such as *Hot Oil Case, Nitro-Glycerine Case,* or the like, a popular-name table is essential. Shepard's Acts and Cases by Popular Names, Federal and State, gives parallel citations to all standard report series for such cases. Beginning with the Second Decennial Digest, all Decennials have had such a table in the table of cases volume, and many regional and local digests have one. In some, as in the Digest of the United States Supreme Court Reports, the popular name appears with a cross reference in the regular plaintiff-defendant table. Thus: *Hot-Oil Case.* See *Panama Refining Co. v. Ryan.*

f. *Official-to-Reporter and Reporter-to-Official citation tables.* Where only the official or Reporter citation is known, parallel citations may be found in the appropriate Shepard's Citations unit. The transfer tables in the National Reporter System Blue Book and Blue and White Books, as described in §13.5, perform the same function.

g. *Patents and trade-marks tables.* Tables of adjudicated patents and trade-marks are found under "Patents" and "Trade-Marks," respectively, in the Decennial Digests, the Federal Digest and its successor, the Modern Federal Practice Digest, and in the Federal Supplement, Federal Reporter and Supreme Court Reporter. Shepard's United States Citations, Patents and Trademarks has a similar table, as do the digests of the United States Patents Quarterly.

h. *American Digest System case tables.* By far the most complete tables of American cases are those in the units of this system, purporting to list every case digested or connected with a case which is digested in all standard report series covered, from 1658 to date. If the case date is unknown, it may be necessary to search in all Decennial units. All cases, 1658 to 1906, are listed in volumes 21 to 25 of the First Decennial Digest. From 1906, each succeeding Decennial has its own table. Each monthly pamphlet and bound volume of the supplementing General Digest has its table of cases, which will cumulate into the next Decennial table, and a complete table of cases search may comprise all of the units above noted. Citation information given may include notice of affirmance, reversal, certiorari grant or refusal, dismissal, rehearing, and several other court actions on the listed case within the decennium. Beginning with the Second Decennial Digest, there has also been a table of cases by popular name, for cases digested in each decennium, printed in the table of cases volume. For some new topics, such as "Workman's Compensation," there have been provided special tables of cases embracing all case names from the earliest digest topics now included in the new ones.  How this is worked is described in §16.5.

i. *Legal periodicals tables of cases.*  Since 1917, cases commented upon in law reviews have been listed in the Index to Legal Periodicals.  Since 1928, case comments in the Legal Periodical Digest have been listed.  Individual legal periodicals, in both annual and cumulative indexes, commonly list case comments.

j. *Loose-leaf services case tables.*  Most loose-leaf services have case tables, plainly tabbed as such for easy finding.

k. *English and Canadian tables of cases.*  These are described in Chapter 24.

l. *Statutes through the case approach.*  Even when a statute is involved in the searcher's problem, he usually searches for a case in point interpreting that statute, and uses that case as his rallying point.  The searcher wants to know how the courts have construed legislation applicable to his problem.  A statute must be evaluated through judicial construction, which may be arrived at through annotated statutes or citators, but also through digests and other case indexes.  Digests do not afford a direct lead to the construction of specific statutes (with a few exceptions, such as the Table of Statutes Construed in the regional Reporter digests and similar tables in the Digest of the Supreme Court Reports).  However, cases construing statutes are digested by subject matter in the usual way: Whenever a statute is involved in a decision, it is cited in a headnote paragraph.  This often leads the searcher to statutes, the applicability of which was unsuspected by him, and so yields a better result than a statute search alone.

2. *Key Number approach.*  Since the Key Number in the Decennial Digests leads to all other cases in point, once you have found a Reporter case you have in its headnote the pertinent digest paragraph or paragraphs and Key Numbers without further ado.  As noted in §16.5, where an older digest topic has been expanded later or a new topic is created, the original Key Number has been discarded, and an additional step is necessary to find the presently applicable number.

3. *Annotated Reports System approach.*  Once you have found an A.L.R. or Lawyers' Edition case in point, you almost always have available an annotation on a point of law involved in it.  In the annotation, the publishers aim to examine all cases in point, as well as treatises, encyclopedias and other sources and reference books, so as to bring together in one place the cases in which this point has been adjudicated.  The editor carefully analyzes and criticizes the cases, and comments on the various rules extracted

from them, so that a great deal of preliminary work has already been done for you.

4. *Fact or descriptive-word index approach.* This approach is described in §16.6, under Digests, but while usually associated with digests, it is by no means confined to them. Every statutory index uses the fact approach, including the indexes in the Federal Register System and its state counterparts, for administrative regulations.

Annotated statutes combine a fact approach to the statutes directly through their general subject indexes, with a similar and more direct approach to the cases interpreting many of the individual sections of the statutes. This is done in connection with any statute section which contains a great many digest paragraphs, through special subject indexes to the cases construing that particular section. That is, the mass of digest paragraphs for that section is arranged according to a more or less detailed subject classification, and then indexed by catchword references to such minute subtopics as "change of basis," "death," "exhaustion," "severance damages," etc. An example from the United States Code Annotated is shown in Exhibit 76 below. It will be noted that in this instance there is both a combined fact index for the entire title and one for each subtopic.

In case law, the descriptive-word index approach is applicable to encyclopedias, treatises, loose-leaf services, legal periodicals, and A.L.I. Restatements. When A.L.R.2d and 3d annotations are of any length they are preceded by a fact index referring to the respective sections of the annotation. For example, the annotation to *Henningsen* v. *Bloomfield Motors,* 32 N.J. 358, 161 A.2d 69, 74 A.L.R.2d 1 (1960), on privity of contract as an element in products liability, has a three-page descriptive-word index in addition to a one-page table of jurisdictions represented. The subjects treated in the annotation, as listed in the index, range from "Abrasive wheel" to "Worm in canned food."

5. *Analytical or topic approach.* This approach has been discussed in detail in Chapters 16 and 17. Statutory compilations also make full use of the device, and the analysis preceding the text of the various titles and subtitles saves much time in arriving at the applicable section. See Exhibits 47 and 48, pages 207 and 208.

6. *Words and phrases approach.* This approach, described in Chapter 21, is used in nearly all digests and encyclopedias. The West Publishing Company's Words and Phrases is a dictionary of common words and legal words of art, as judicially defined. In most other similar works it is an alphabetical index to the page

**Notes of Decisions**

## VII. SUBD. (f). OBJECTIONS TO CLAIMS

*Subdivision Index*

**251. Law governing**

Where claim on note payable in Missouri was filed in bankruptcy court in Arkansas, statute of limitations governing note was the statute of Arkansas and not Missouri. In re Mays, D.C.Ark.1941, 38 F.Supp. 958, affirmed, 1942, 125 F.2d 693, 48 Am.Bankr.Rep.N.S. 716.

**Tit. 11, § 93**
Note 255

**255. Evidence—Admissibility**

In proceeding under this section, where claimant has attempted to establish by evidence the allegations of his proof of claim, he cannot be permitted to use such allegations to supply a deficiency in his evidence. In re Annin & Co., C.C.A.N.Y. 1938, 95 F.2d 381, 36 Am.Bankr.Rep.N.S. 381.

The general rule of law that a party can recover only on the cause of action alleged in his pleading, applies to claims presented in bankruptcy, and a claimant who has filed a statement of his demand under oath, as required under this title, cannot sustain it by evidence of an indebtedness arising in a different manner from that stated. In re Lansaw, D.C.Mo. 1902, 118 F. 365, 9 Am.Bankr.Rep. 167. See, also, Orr v. Park, Ga.1910, 183 F. 683, 106 C.C.A. 33, 25 Am.Bankr.Rep. 544.

The transcript of testimony taken during ancillary hearing before special master, pursuant to order of court before whom bankruptcy petition was filed, for purpose of ascertaining facts necessary to proper administration of bankrupt's estate with respect to claim against it was admissible in evidence at hearing on bankruptcy trustee's objection to allowance of claim. Hutson v. Coffman, C.C.A. Cal.1938, 100 F.2d 640.

Exhibit 76

where the listed work is defined. The approach is used when the definition of a word or term is a significant factor.

7. *Treatises approach.* The following simple problem illustrates a function of treatises in leading the searcher to other sources of authority, and in elaborating upon and making clearer the points of law involved in a case in your casebook.

Your torts casebook has the case of Mrs. X, who purchased at her butcher shop a sealed package of sausages manufactured by the Y company. Although no negligence on the part of the manufacturer was found, the sausages were, in fact, contaminated, resulting in the death of Mr. X, the husband. Mrs. X sues both the retailer and the manufacturer. Your casebook points out the possible grounds for the action and the defenses to it, but you are still somewhat at sea and wish a considerably fuller discussion of the issues, particularly that of privity of contract and warranty as between the consumer and the supplier of the product.

You are familiar with a typical student book, Prosser, Handbook of the Law of Torts.[1] The table of contents seems to indicate the pertinence of Chapter 19, Liability of Contracting Parties to Third Persons, but as that is a long chapter you try a shorter approach, the subject index. You look under "Food," but find nothing there. It should be noted here that the list of subjects and topics used in a treatise are not as extensive as in some other legal publications. After checking consumer and privity of contract you do find a lead under supplier of chattels. Under "Supplier of Chattels — Liability to third person — food and drink," you are referred to page 674, where the various ramifications of the topic are discussed.

Desiring a still more detailed discussions of the topic, with the latest cases in point and with indications of the jurisdictional trends, you consult a practitioners' book, such as Frumer and Friedman, Products Liability.[2] There, under the tab "Food and Beverages" in volume 1, a long chapter discusses in minute detail all aspects, with numerous citations to cases and to annotations.

§25.2.   **Order of search.** Although the mode of search in each case is a matter of common sense, varying somewhat with the fact situation, the following outline is suggested as a checklist of factors to bear in mind. The order given is logical, but often the circumstances of the search will dictate a different attack and the omission of some of the steps. All the steps in the outline below are necessary at one time or another, but seldom are all of them required in the solution of any single problem.

[1] 3d ed., St. Paul, Minn., West Publishing Co., 1964.
[2] Albany, N.Y., Matthew Bender & Company, Inc., 1960, 2v. (loose-leaf).

1. *Suggested outline of search.*
   a. *Analysis of the problem.*  Separation into aspects involved, including parties, procedure and substantive issues.
   b. *Preliminary review of the subject matter.*  Where needed for orientation, through treatises, encyclopedias, Restatements, etc.
   c. *Search of statutes and administrative regulations involved.*
      (1) Federal statutes.
      (2) Home state statutes.
      (3) Other state statutes: collections and indexes across state lines; persuasiveness of cases construing.
      (4) Administrative regulations implementing statutes.
      (5) Finding legislative intent where helpful.
   d. *Search for cases in point.*
      (1) Reading cases and orders cited by annotated statutes, treatises, etc.
      (2) Finding additional cases through digests.
         (a) Through Key Numbers in Reporter cases read.
         (b) Tables of cases approach.
         (c) Analytical or topical approach.
         (d) Fact approach.
         (e) Words and phrases approach.
      (3) Search of the Annotated Reports System.
      (4) As cited in administrative rulings.
   e. *Search of encyclopedias and treatises.*  To refresh memory, to supply additional cases, and to find analysis of subject matter.
   f. *Search of legal periodicals.*  For more detailed analysis of theoretical and controversial points, and for discussion of individual cases.
   g. *Search of loose-leaf services.*  To coordinate all material in tax and regulatory fields.
   h. *Search of miscellaneous materials.*  Study of A.L.I. Restatements, form books, government publications, etc.
   i. *Completing the search.*  Making certain that the latest editions and supplements have been consulted, including the digest portions of the National Reporter System advance sheets covering later cases than the General Digest.
   j. *Appraising the authorities found.*  Shepardizing statutes and cases.

The accompanying search checklist has been found useful by the students of Professor Albert P. Blaustein, Rutgers University School of Law, South Jersey Division.  It is reproduced here by his permission in Exhibit 77.

✓　Materials examined　　　　　　　　　　Researcher:＿＿＿＿＿＿＿＿＿
O　Materials not appropriate for examination　Memorandum for:＿＿＿＿＿＿＿

## LEGAL BIBLIOGRAPHY CHECK-LIST

TOPIC: ＿＿＿＿＿＿＿＿＿＿＿＿＿＿＿＿＿＿＿＿＿＿＿＿＿＿＿＿＿＿＿

Research begun: ＿＿＿＿＿＿＿＿＿＿　　Research completed: ＿＿＿＿＿＿＿

### Statutory Data

| | |
|---|---|
| ＿＿State Stat. Ann. | ＿＿U.S.C.A. (F.C.A.) |
| ＿＿State Code | ＿＿U.S. Code |
| ＿＿State Session Laws | ＿＿Stat. at Large |
| ＿＿Curr. Legis. Serv. | ＿＿U.S.C.C.A.N. |
| ＿＿State Legis. Hist. | ＿＿Fed. Legis. Hist. |
| ＿＿State Rules | ＿＿Fed. Rules |
| ＿＿Unif. L. Anno. | ＿＿C.F.R. & Fed.Reg. |

LATEST sources checked:

Pocket Part: Name＿＿＿＿＿　　Date＿＿＿＿＿
Pocket Part: Name＿＿＿＿＿　　Date＿＿＿＿＿
Pamphlet Supp.: Name＿＿＿　　Date＿＿＿＿＿
Pamphlet Supp.: Name＿＿＿　　Date＿＿＿＿＿

### Digests

| | |
|---|---|
| ＿＿State | ＿＿3rd Gen. Dig. |
| ＿＿Regional | ＿＿6th Decennial |
| ＿＿Sup. Ct. | ＿＿5th Decennial |
| ＿＿Federal | ＿＿4th Decennial |
| | ＿＿3rd Decennial |
| | ＿＿2nd Decennial |
| ＿＿Eng. & Empire | ＿＿Decennial |
| ＿＿Canadian | ＿＿Century |

List CATCH-WORDS & PHRASES checked:

＿＿＿＿＿＿＿＿＿　＿＿＿＿＿＿＿＿＿
＿＿＿＿＿＿＿＿＿　＿＿＿＿＿＿＿＿＿

List KEY NUMBERS checked:

＿＿＿＿＿＿＿＿＿　＿＿＿＿＿＿＿＿＿
＿＿＿＿＿＿＿＿＿　＿＿＿＿＿＿＿＿＿
＿＿＿＿＿＿＿＿＿　＿＿＿＿＿＿＿＿＿

LATEST sources checked:

Digest Pocket Part: Name＿＿＿＿　Date＿＿＿＿＿
Digest Pocket Part: Name＿＿＿＿　Date＿＿＿＿＿
Gen. Dig.: Vol.＿＿＿Month＿＿＿Year＿＿＿
Advance Sheets: Name＿＿＿＿　Date＿＿＿＿＿
Advance Sheets: Name＿＿＿＿　Date＿＿＿＿＿

### Annotated Reports

＿＿ALR 2d
＿＿ALR
＿＿LRA

List ANNOTATIONS checked:

＿＿＿＿＿＿＿＿＿　＿＿＿＿＿＿＿＿＿

LATEST sources checked:

ALR 2d Dig.-Index:　Vol.＿＿＿＿
ALR 2d Supp. Serv.:　Date＿＿＿＿
ALR Blue Book:　　　Date＿＿＿＿

### Miscellaneous

| | |
|---|---|
| ＿＿State Ency. | ＿＿Restatemen |
| ＿＿C.J.-C.J.S. | ＿＿Loose-Leaf |
| ＿＿Am. Jur. | ＿＿Serv. |
| ＿＿Words & Phrases | ＿＿Index |
| ＿＿Halsbury's Laws | ＿＿Leg. Peri |
| | ＿＿Treatises |
| | ＿＿Shepards |

List LEGAL PERIODICALS:

Articles checked　Topics checked

＿＿＿＿＿＿＿＿＿　＿＿＿＿＿＿＿＿＿
＿＿＿＿＿＿＿＿＿　＿＿＿＿＿＿＿＿＿

List TREATISES checked:
(with pages and section numbers)

＿＿＿＿＿＿＿＿＿＿＿＿＿＿＿＿＿＿＿
＿＿＿＿＿＿＿＿＿＿＿＿＿＿＿＿＿＿＿

LATEST sources checked:

Index Leg. Period.: Date＿＿＿＿＿
Shepards: Name＿＿＿＿　Date＿＿＿＿
Shepards: Name＿＿＿＿　Date＿＿＿＿
Loose-Leaf Serv.: Name＿＿＿Date＿＿
Other: Name＿＿＿＿　Date＿＿＿＿

Exhibit 77

2. *Resourcefulness.*  Since few extended legal searches progress smoothly, a most important weapon of the searcher is resourcefulness.  In the use of indexes he must remember that perhaps the indexer had a different point of view than he has, and he must cast about for other words or terms under which his fact situation might have been listed.  The same is true of the analytical approach.  Often, what seems to the searcher a perfectly obvious classification for his point of law did not seem so at all to the digester, with his much broader view of the whole topic.  Seldom can the searcher be certain that, even when he has found cases in point through either the fact or analytical approach, other cases just as applicable are not lurking under other entries or classifications.  It does not pay to be either too easily discouraged or too quickly satisfied.

3. *Other factors to be considered.*  Digest paragraphs, text expositions or annotations are not the law; the cases should always be read.  Note the parties involved, how the case arose, pertinent statutes, etc.  Most of the references found must be discarded: In case work there is much chaff and little wheat.

4. *Care and accuracy.*  The searcher should provide himself with some sort of checklist or reminder of things to look for in his search, to ensure completeness and accuracy.  The Blaustein checklist reproduced above is a good one.

Prominent in any list should be an admonition to *copy citations and other data accurately and with sufficient fullness to be clear — to you or to anybody else reading them.*  More time has probably been lost by lawyers and students because of inaccurate and incomplete copying of various data during searches than in any other way.  That cryptic notation of yours which saves a few seconds in recording and is so crystal clear to you when made will probably be incomprehensible at your desk later on when you wish to incorporate it in your brief or memorandum of law.  Write it down as though you expected somebody else to have to decipher it.

Copy with reasonable fullness.  That may sound like unnecessary advice, but is very far from it.  A check on accuracy is to copy down a complete statutory or case citation, including all parallel references.  Thus: *Cohen* v. *Wypiski,* 599 N.Y. 301, 201 N.E.2d 518, 275 N.Y.S. 93, 201 A.L.R.2d (1970), instead of only 599 N.Y. 301.  The more checks in the way of parallel references you have, the more chances there are that one or more of them will be correct.  Care should be taken that all necessary units — including supplements, advance sheets, etc. — of a publication consulted are covered.  In this connection, the careful searcher will *preserve a precise record of each publication and part thereof covered in a search,* as a measure of the completeness of the search and check against having to search the same publication twice.

**§25.3.   Illustrative problem involving statutes.**

1. *Problem stated.*   Your client, executor of the estate of a deceased partner, wishes to know his rights and duties, the partnership agreement having a clause providing for the carrying on of the business by the remaining partners after the death or retirement of one of them.   There is also the matter of the tax treatment of the partnership income.   There are thus involved the right, duties and personal liabilities of the executor, as well as the rights of the deceased partner's estate, of the partners, and of the federal government.   No question of procedure is involved.

2. *Preliminary review of the subject matter.*   Through an elementary treatise or legal encyclopedia you learn that in the United States, partnership, income taxation, and the liabilities of an executor are largely regulated by statute.   You therefore begin by examining the statutes.

3. *Search of applicable federal and home state statutes.*

a. *Federal statutes: Partnership income tax aspect.*   This is a matter of both federal and state jurisdiction, but for the purpose of this problem only the federal aspect is considered.   The subject index of the United States Code leads to Title 26, where a reading of the law shows the tax of partners to be covered by Section 702. The annotations in the U.S.C.A. and the F.C.A. digest several promising cases, which are read in full, including *Guaranty Trust Co. of N.Y.* v. *Commissioner,* 303 U.S. 493, 58 Sup. Ct. 673, 82 L. Ed. 975 (1938).

b. *Continuing the partnership business.*   The subject index of the annotated statutes of your state leads to the applicable section covering your problems, but the absence of case annotations shows that your courts have never construed these sections.

c. *Executor's personal liabilities aspect.*   The search here might begin with the annotated statutes of your state, with a local book on executors and administrators, or with a loose-leaf service on wills, trusts and estates.   As for the other aspects of the problem, the techniques are the same throughout and will not be further commented upon here.

4. *Search of the statutes and decisions of other states.*   You wonder if other states than your own have similar statutes which their courts have construed; and if so, whether their decisions have any weight as precedent in your state.   You remember that there are numerous collections and indexes of statutes across state lines, and that one of them is the Uniform Laws Annotated.   From volume

7, Partnership, you learn that your state statute is copied from the Uniform Partnership Act.

a. *Authority of the decisions of other states.*    You learn from the discussion in the topic "Statutes" in Am. Jur. or C.J.S. that the general rule of law is that where a question of statutory construction is one of first impression in a state, the courts will consider the construction of like statutes in other states by their courts.    You therefore return to the Uniform Laws Annotated, where the index leads to Section 41 or Section 42 as probably covering the continuation of a partnership after the death of a partner.    You observe that in searching the statute (as well as other search books), it is advisable to examine the material of more than one possibly applicable provision — that in practice your problems are rarely pinpointed.

The annotations turn up several cases reasonably in point, in different states.    One, *Froess v. Froess,* 289 Pa. 69, 137 Atl. 124 (1927), seems especially promising, and you read it.

5. *Search of other indexes.*    Since there is so much overlapping of subject matter in the law, there may be applicable cases not digested under the exact statutory section which in your opinion logically covers the matter.    Also, some points raised by apparently inconsistent cases are not clear to you, so you decide to search other indexes to the law.

6. *Digest search.*

a. *Key Number approach.*    Your reading of the *Froess* and *Guaranty Trust* cases in the Atlantic Reporter and the Supreme Court Reporter has given you the applicable headnotes, with their pertinent Key Numbers.    You then proceed directly to any appropriate West digest employing the Key Number classification. An exception is when the Key Number classification has been expanded or a new title has been added to the classification since the publication of your case, into which that case has been newly allocated.    In such circumstances the Key Number found in the headnote of the case as published years ago no longer applies. Thus, in the American Digest System, the original Internal Revenue ☞ 7(3) of the *Guaranty Trust* case has been changed to Internal Revenue ☞ 834, following the great expansion of the Internal Revenue title after the adoption of the Internal Revenue Codes of 1939 and 1954.    How to find the current Key Number classification in such cases is discussed in §16.5.

b. *Table of cases approach.*    This approach is described in §25.1.    No matter what digest is consulted, the table of cases will note all classification numbers under which a case is digested.    In the American Digest System, with its many units, knowing the date of the decision is a time-saving lead to the proper table of cases unit.

c. *Fact and analytical approaches.* Our partnership problem here presents no special difficulties. Note, however, that in the income tax aspect, the Key Number found (Internal Revenue ☜ 834) turns up a case in point, *Heiner* v. *Mellon*, 304 U.S. 271, 58 Sup. Ct. 926, 82 L. Ed. 1337 (1938), decided, not under the Internal Revenue Code §182, but under a section of the Revenue Act of 1918 not in the Code at all. This shows that even in searching statutes, the digest subject analysis often leads to cases in point involving unsuspected applicable statutes or sections.

d. *Words and phrases approach.* Our problem does not seem to hinge in any way upon the judicial definition of a word or term.

7. *Annotated reports search.* Your task has been partly performed for you if you can find your problem treated in an A.L.R. annotation. Accordingly, you turn to the A.L.R. and A.L.R.2d Digests, and to the Word Indexes to Annotations, where you find several annotations on partnership taxation. One in particular, "Construction of §42 of the Uniform Partnership Act as to the rights of parties where business is continued after a partner retires or dies," in 2 A.L.R.2d 1084, seems exactly in point. In it, the cases are analyzed from various aspects, including the effect of consent on continuation of the business (§2 of the annotation), and the effect of particular agreements (§4). The A.L.R.2d Supplement Service lists several later cases in point on these precise sections.

8. *Legal encyclopedias and treatises search.* No special problems are posed here.

9. *Legal periodicals search.* After reading the cases and treatises found through the above means, you are still not clear in your mind as to some aspects of your client's problem. In particular, *Guaranty Trust* and *Heiner* seem inconsistent and you are not certain of the doctrine applied. You know that legal periodicals provide a forum of discussion of legal theory and that, in addition, specific cases are often commented upon in detail. A search of the Index to Legal Periodicals reveals at least six leading articles dealing with various aspects of your problem. Weyher and Flom, Death and Income Taxes — The Demise of a Partner, 52 Colum. L. Rev. 695 (1952), sounds particularly good, and you find in it that your cases and others in point are analyzed and the issues discussed at length. As is common in law review articles, this one in its footnotes gives a rather extensive review of the earlier literature. The Index to Legal Periodicals, under the heading of "Partner-

ship," lists law review comments upon several other cases in point.

10. *Loose-leaf service or reporter search.* Because your problem involves both tax and estate matters, the loose-leaf publications described in Chapter 23 are particularly applicable.

11. *Appraising the value of authorities found.* Before writing your brief or memorandum of law, you Shepardize all cases and statutes, searching all supplements to date. For statutes, do not forget the Statutes Construed tables, because they may give you a later case than you have found elsewhere.

§25.4.  **Illustrative problem involving administrative law.**

1. *Problem stated.* Your client has purchased a dairy farm and dairy which until the purchase had distributed general milk products in the New York marketing area. Desiring to add a line of frozen desserts, your client asks whether this new activity affects his legal status. You consider only the federal aspect.

2. *Analysis of the problem.* This problem involves the production, processing and marketing of milk and milk products in a given area. Among other possible issues is whether this marketing activity is regulated by federal legislation.

3. *Search of statutes and administrative regulations involved.*

a. *Federal statutes.* As this is a matter of "public, general and permanent interest," and so incorporated in the United States Code, you examine the index to the Code, where, under "Milk and Cream," you note several entries which lead you to 7 U.S.C. §608c. The text of §608c(5) suggests that your client, because of his new marketing activity, may be subject to regulation as a "handler" of milk products, regulated under the Code. Case annotations in both the U.S.C.A. and F.C.A. turn up cases close to the point, but you are still doubtful as to whether a processor of his own milk into frozen desserts is a "handler" under the statute. Hoping that the regulations of the government agency concerned are more explicit, you search them.

b. *Administrative regulations.* Administrative regulations and the agency decisions implementing and interpreting them change so rapidly that any outline of problem solving through them must describe only means and procedures. What follows, therefore, while typical of the procedures followed may not be accurate as you read it here as to the designation of specific C.F.R. regulations in point, and is to be regarded only as showing a typical search, by way of example.

The United States Government Organization Manual, described in §14.4, reveals that the regulatory body involved in our problem is the Agricultural Marketing and Consumers Service of the Department of Agriculture. You know, therefore, that the regulations you seek will be in the Code of Federal Regulations, Title 7, "Agriculture." Since this is an enormous title, you consult the annual General Index of the C.F.R., under "Milk and Milk Products," which refers you to Title 7, Parts 1001-1137. You then discover that Title 7 has, for your convenience, been split into numerous "use units," one of which, covering the "Eastern Region," prints Regulations 7:1000 to 10029. A table in the front of this small volume tells you that New York regulations are in Part 1002. The separate and detailed table of contents for this Part tells you that "Handler" is treated in Part 1002.7, and "Frozen desserts" in Part 1002.121. Nothing that the pamphlet you have consulted covers references as of January 1, 1967, you may examine two more tables to determine if the form of your two regulations has changed since that date: the List of Sections Affected at the back of the pamphlet you are using and the Codification Guide, monthly, quarterly and daily, in the Federal Register. Through these, you check down to yesterday the present form of the two regulations in which you are interested.

Another way to find this regulation is through the parallel table leading from the United States Code sections to the corresponding regulations of the C.F.R. This table is found in 2 C.F.R., as described in §14.6. Here the entry under 7 U.S.C. §608c (the section covering federal regulation of milk and cream) cites the regulations issued under authority of the statute. Checking (1) the C.F.R. latest pamphlet, (2) the annual List of Sections Affected, and (3) the Federal Register Codification Guide, as indicated above, for the current year, you find that the regulation has not been renumbered or changed in text since 1967 and is still in force in the form in which it was printed in the 1967 revision of Title 7.

4. *Agency and judicial rulings search.* Since yours is a Department of Agriculture matter, your search leads to that Department's Agriculture Decisions. This is a series of reports printing both agency and court rulings construing both the above statute and the regulations issued under it. Each volume of Agriculture Decisions has an elaborate cumulative citator, by both federal statute and departmental regulation construed, and by subject, covering all court and agency decisions under the act in which you are concerned. The agency rulings give both the agency interpretation of "handler," and citations to Congressional hearings, reports, etc., indicating the legislative intent. Such citators, however, are found in but few reports of administrative rulings, and constructions of regulations must ordinarily be sought indirectly, through digests or tax or regulatory loose-leaf services; or, for the ten series of administrative decisions covered by Shepard's U.S.

Administrative Citations.   This Shepard's unit, however, does not cover the Department of Agriculture decisions.

5. *Remainder of the search.*   The rest of the search follows the outline already given above.   Note, however, that since this case involves the judicial definition of what constitutes a milk "handler," the words and phrases approach is available.   Several cases are listed in digests under this word.   Although the statute here and the court decisions construing it can be Shepardized in the usual manner, the regulations are not directly covered by Shepard's Citations.   If the regulations have been construed by federal courts, however, they will be listed in the Statutes Construed tables of the Federal Supplement and the Federal Reporter.   These tables do not cumulate from volume to volume.

§25.5.   **Illustrative problem involving a treaty-state law conflict.**

1. *Problem stated.*   *A, B,* and *C,* brothers residing and doing business in your state, were killed in an accident, leaving wills bequeathing their property situated in your state to their mother, a national and resident of Denmark.   *A* was an American citizen; *B* a national of Denmark; and *C* a national of Belovia, a newly constituted political entity.   Your state inheritance tax imposes a discriminatory tax on personal property passing to alien nonresident beneficiaries.   Your client, the mother, resists this tax.

2. *Analysis of the problem.*   Consider only the state inheritance tax aspect.   (a) The property passing is physically within the state, but is to be removed to Denmark.   (b) *A* was an American citizen, but *B, C,* and their mother were aliens.   (c) There was a mother-son relationship between the parties.   (d) Is the state law valid, and does it affect all parties alike?

3. *Preliminary review of the subject matter.*   Treatises and legal encyclopedias agree that the state wherein the decedent's property is situated may discriminate in inheritance taxation against alien beneficiaries, but there is a caveat to the effect that the right has been impaired to a considerable extent by treaty.   Through encyclopedias and annotations on the relation of treaty to state and federal law, in 4 A.L.R. 1377, 183, 134 A.L.R. 882, 885, 3 A.L.R.2d 484, and 14 A.L.R.2d 992 (the latter 242 pages in length), you learn that where there is a conflict between a treaty and a state constitution or statute, whether enacted prior to or subsequent to the making of the treaty, the treaty controls.   (In federal law, the latest legislation, whether treaty or Act of Congress, controls.)

4. *Federal statutes search.*   Although this is a state tax matter, the treaty caveat sends you in search of an applicable treaty be-

tween the United States and Denmark.  Through the means described in Chapter 4 you find and read the Treaty of April 26, 1826, with Denmark on friendship, commerce and consular rights, 8 Stat. 340, T.S. 65, 3 Miller 239, 1 Malloy 373.  Article 7 of that treaty, concerning inheritance taxation and the removal of property from one country by resident nationals of the other country, seems repugnant to your state inheritance tax statute, but you seek judicial construction.

In practice, at this time, you would now skip several steps in the search outline in §25.2 and Shepardize this treaty to see if the Supreme Court of the United States has ever construed it.  How this is done for treaties is shown in Chapter 4.  You discover that the Court has construed this section three times, and you read the cases.  Two of them, *Nielsen* v. *Johnson*, 279 U.S. 47, 49 Sup. Ct. 233, 73 L. Ed. 607 (1929), and *Petersen* v. *Iowa*, 245 U.S. 170, 38 Sup. Ct. 109, 62 L. Ed. 225 (1917), both involving Iowa statutes, seem to be in point.  Since treaties are uncodified, this one is not covered by the annotations in U.S.C.A., but F.C.A. has a special volume covering uncodified federal laws — including treaties — and the above cases are noted in the annotations to treaties in this special volume.

5. *Home state statute search.*  A search of the annotated statutes of your state reveals that this inheritance tax provision which we are considering has not been construed by your state courts.  You therefore seek a like statute in another state, which has been construed.

6. *Other state statute search.*  Statutes in point and their construction by the respective state courts may be found in at least four ways.  Since this problem involves state inheritance taxation, the first and speediest solution is through loose-leaf services covering the topic for all states.  Here a uniform classification scheme for state statutes leads to the appropriate section for each state having inheritance taxes discriminating against aliens.  In the services, all the law — federal and state, statutory and case — relative to this situation, is collected in one place.

Second, treatises frequently cite the pertinent statutory provisions.  Third, and hardest, the statutes of the various states may be checked, one by one.  Finally, as in our problem, if a treaty is involved, the cases found through Shepardizing it cite the state statutes construed.

An Iowa statute is cited in the two cases above, but one of them is Section 1467 of the Iowa Code of 1907, and the other includes Sections 7311, 7313 and 7315 of the Iowa Code of 1927, making it necessary to translate these sections of older codes into those for the current edition, so as to compare all with your state statute. Transferring into the present Iowa citation form may be done through the Iowa Code Annotated subject index, and more exactly through the elaborate parallel transfer tables from earlier to corresponding statute forms. Both of these methods lead to Sections 450.10 and 450.11 of the present Iowa Code, but you find that Section 450.11, exactly in point as discussed in the Supreme Court decisions, has been repealed (probably as a result of those decisions).

In addition, a History and Source of the Law note cites all earlier forms of the section, affording another check on the correspondence of the 1907 and 1927 sections to the present form. Furthermore, Iowa Law Review comments in point are listed (as they are in Shepard's Iowa Citations also). The transfer table technique enables you to convert the 1907 and 1927 Code sections into the later forms as found in the current Shepard's Iowa Citations, where all cases construing all forms of the statute presently in force are listed.

7. *Other cases in point search: Reading the cases found.* From the digest paragraphs in their headnotes, the *Petersen* and *Nielsen* cases seem irreconcilable. A careful reading of the full reports, however, indicates that Section 7 of the treaty seems to protect the *estate of the transferor* who was a national of the country to which the property to be transferred (Denmark here), rather than the *transferee* (the mother). Therefore it would seem that the estate of *A,* the American citizen, is not protected, since he is not a national of Denmark seeking to remove property, so that the transfer of his property by succession is subject to the discriminatory tax; that the estate of *B,* a national of Denmark, is so protected, and that *B*'s property is not subject to the tax; and that the estate of *C,* with whose country the United States has not yet concluded such a treaty as is here involved, has no such transfer protection.

8. *Remainder of the search.* This follows conventional lines. The Key Number covering the topic, as noted in the *Nielsen* case headnote, is Treaties ⬅ 11, "Operation as to laws inconsistent with or repugnant to treaty provisions," where all such cases are digested. As the treaty has been thoroughly Shepardized by you, it is doubtful that more cases reasonably in point will be found, but to make certain, the Statutes Construed tables in the Federal Supplement, Federal Reporter, and North Western Reporter advance sheets (the unit reporting Iowa) should be consulted. In

the Digest of the United States Supreme Court Reports statutory tables, in volume 14, cases construing this treaty are listed both under the laws of Denmark construed, and under United States treaties construed. In spite of the decisions by the Supreme Court in *Nielsen* and *Petersen,* the above digest section reveals many later cases on the point at issue.

# CHAPTER 26

# Standard Legal Citation Forms[1]

**§26.1. Function and construction of a good citation.** A legal citation has only one purpose: to lead its reader to the work cited, and this without enforced recourse to any other source of information, for data which should be given in the citation itself. This chapter hopes to provide rules and examples sufficient to enable the user to combine utility with good form so as to produce the perfect citation.

A good case citation, no matter what its form, possesses the following elements: an abbreviation of recognizable meaning, a date, the notation of the court deciding the cited case (if not evident from the report), and a parallel citation if there is one. The date is both a check against error (and errors in citations are unbelievably frequent) and a means of appraising the cited reference. The parallel citation serves the dual purpose of a check against error (one citation may be incorrect but probably not all) and an assurance that the reader will have available one of the forms cited. The time and space saved by curtailing are as nothing compared to the trouble caused by an insufficient or inaccurate reference.

[1] This chapter is abridged from Price, A Practical Manual of Standard Legal Citations (2d ed. 1958), by permission of the copyright owner, Oceana Publications, Inc.

In compiling this chapter on citations form, some three hundred briefs and as many opinions, about evenly divided among federal and state courts and federal administrative agencies, have been examined for form, as well as the output of some forty different law reviews, and the resulting analysis is responsible for what is believed to be a statement of good standard practice in brief writing. In addition, courts, attorneys general, and administrative agencies have cooperated by supplying forms of citations preferred by them. The United States Government Printing Office Manual of style has been the arbiter wherever pertinent, and any departures from it have been noted.

Law review practice, as formulated in A Uniform System of Citation, Forms of Citation and Abbreviations,[1] though it agrees in the great majority of respects with the rules laid down in this chapter for briefs, is often more complicated. The practices among law book publishers are not uniform. For example, the rules regarding the italicizing of the titles of books and periodical articles, observed by the publisher of this book and followed to a considerable extent in the text of the book, differ in some details from those advocated in this chapter. For written work in law schools and for briefs in law practice, however, the rules presented in this chapter are believed to be those applied by the great majority of lawyers and legal departments; they are acceptable in all law courts.

§26.2. **Section and chapter designations in statute citations.**

1. *In general.* There is little uniformity in the treatment of chapter, article and section designations in statute citations, either in abbreviation or capitalization, but the forms given below follow the preferred practice.

2. *Suggested form.*

a. *Quotations:* Follow copy quoted as to section designations.

b. *Main text:* Spell out and capitalize "section" as the first word of a sentence, and in references in a sentence to a specific section and act.

> Section 321 of the Act provides . . .
> It was provided in Section 321 of the Act . . .
> It was provided (Section 321) that . . .

In casual main text references to a section formerly cited:

> In referring to that section he said . . .

In parenthetical full citations, use "§" ("§§" for "sections").

---

1 Cambridge. Mass. The Harvard Law Review Association.

This provision, 58 Stat. 631, §8, that . . .
. . . of this statute, 58 Stat. 631, §8.
This provision (58 Stat. 631, §8), that . . .
. . . does not constitute reversible error.  Rev. Civ. Code, §2414.

c. *Footnotes.*  Spell out "section" as the first word of a sentence; otherwise use "§" except in *comment on a section,* when the same form as for text references should be used.

3. *Section references to the United States Code.*  The Supreme Court preference in its opinions is in the style of 28 U.S.C. §18 (no comma), which is recommended.

4. *"Sec."*  Uncapitalized, "sec." is seldom found except in quotations.  "Sec." capitalized, is more common.  The majority rule follows the forms suggested above, however.

5. *Chapter and clause designations.*  For "Chapter" use "c," as the prevailing practice.  The plural of "c" is "cc."  "Clause" is abbreviated "cl." and is seldom capitalized except as the first word of a sentence or as a proper noun, e.g., "Commerce Clause."

§26.3.   Constitutions.

1. *General considerations.*  Constitutions are cited by article, section and clause (if given).  In text references, when set off by parentheses or by commas, and in footnotes, the symbol "§" is frequently used.

"Constitution" is capitalized only when used as a proper name, i.e., when the United States Constitution or a state constitution is clearly indicated.  Conservative practice is to capitalize "article," "section," and "clause" (or their abbreviations) only when they form the first word of a sentence, or in headings.  In parenthetical citations, "§" for section is the majority rule.

The date of the United States Constitution is not given in citing it; there has been only one.  Although the prevailing rule in citing state constitutions is to give the date only of those not presently in force, it is better to date all.

Amendment citations or citations of particular clauses by name are spelled out in full except in parenthetical or footnote references, but are not capitalized when used with the word "Constitution."

2. *Text references.*

the Constitution [meaning of the United States].
the United States Constitution.
Article V, section 18, of the Constitution of Indiana.
The fourteenth amendment of the Constitution provides.
The Fourteenth Amendment provides.
the commerce clause of the Constitution.
the Commerce Clause.

The Constitution provides (Art. I, §8, cl. 8) for a patent system.
The Constitution provides for patents. Art. I, §8, cl. 8.

### 3. Footnote references.

U.S. Const., Art. I, §8, cl. 8.
U.S. Const., Amend. XVIII.
Ind. Const., Art. IV, §5.
N.Y. Const., Art. 2, §1 (1847).

## §26.4. Congressional publications.

### 1. Congressional bills.

| | | |
|---|---|---|
| House and Senate bills | H.R. | S. |
| House and Senate resolutions | H. Res. | S. Res. |
| Concurrent resolutions | H. Con. Res. | S. Con. Res. |
| Joint resolutions | H.J. Res. | S.J. Res. |

(Note that when the abbreviation consists of two single letters, as H.R., no space is left between the individual components; but that when one component has more than a single letter, a space is left, as H. Res.)

H.R. 70, 81st Cong., 1st Sess. (1949), p. 3.
S. 1201, 81st Cong., 1st Sess. (1949), p. 2. [Date and page references are usually omitted in bills.]

### a. Repeating citations.

. . . hereinafter cited as H.R. 70.

### 2. Congressional hearings.

Hearings before Senate Committee on H.R. 5327 (Import Duty on Virgin Copper), 81st Cong., 1st Sess. (1949), p. 56.

### 3. Congressional committee reports.

H. Rept. No. 19, 81st Cong., 1st Sess. (1949), p. 7.

### 4. Congressional debates and proceedings.

a. Annals of Congress ("Debates and Proceedings in the Congress of the United States"), 1789-1824.

18 Annals of Cong. 1763 (1819).

b. Register of Debates ("Gales and Seaton") (1824-1837).

11 Reg. Deb. 127 (1835).

c. Congressional Globe, 1833-1873. Cite by Congress and session.

Cong. Globe, 41st Cong., 1st Sess. (1869), p. 499.

d. Congressional Record, 1873 to date. The page numbers of the daily edition and of the bound edition do not match. Cite the bound volume if available.   In citing the daily edition, give the full date.

> *Bound volume:* 94 Cong. Rec. 9761 (1948).
> *Daily edition:* 94 Cong. Rec. 9917 (Aug. 4, 1948). [The same material.]

5. *Congressional documents.*

> H.R. Doc. No. 75, 81st Cong., 1st Sess. (1949), p. 25.
> S. Exec. Doc. No. 23, 81st Cong., 1st Sess. (1949), p. 19.

6. *Bulletin or report bearing a document number.*

> Parking Lots in the District of Columbia.   Report . . . (S. Doc. No. 209, 81st Cong., 2d Sess. (1949)), p. 56.

## §26.5.   Congressional legislation.

1. *Current or slip laws.*   Give the public or private law number, Congress and (before the 83d Congress, 1957) session, and date of approval.   The Statutes at Large citation is now printed in the margin of the official slip laws and may be added to the slip law citation, for convenience in future reference.   Beginning with the Eighty-third Congress, the session designation is omitted.

> Pub. L. No. 101, 80th Cong., 1st Sess. (June 23, 1947).   [Pre-1957 form.]
> Pub. L. 83-315 (Sept. 9, 1957).   [1957 to date form.]

2. *Statutes at Large.*   As soon as the Statutes at Large form is published, cite it instead of the law number.

> 47 Stat. 1470 (1933), 11 U.S.C. §909 (1958 ed.).

Here the Code is cited only for added convenience.   However, for those Code titles reenacted into positive law, it is neither necessary nor proper to cite the Statutes at Large, except for historical purposes, since they are no longer in force in that form.   The proper citation, therefore, is simply by title, section and edition of the Code.

In citing the Statutes at Large, it is customary to cite also the act from which the Statute is derived, by date, unless it can be readily identified from the context.   Where footnotes are employed, the full citation of a statute is rarely found in the main text, but usually only the name and section of the act, as the Clayton Act, Section 7, etc., the volume and page references being footnoted.   Where the section number of the Code is cited as part of the complete footnote citation, the section number of the act is usually omitted, to avoid needless repetition.

a. *Dating Statutes at Large citations.*   When the Statute citation alone is given, it should be dated, as 61 Stat. 37 (1947).   Where the date of the Statute and of the cited edition of the United States Code is the same, give only the latter when citing both forms; otherwise give both dates.

> 47 Stat. 1470 (1933), 11 U.S.C. §908 (1958 ed.).
> 60 Stat. 89, 47 U.S.C. §506 (1946 ed.).  [A 1946 act.]

b. *Citing an untitled act.*

> Act of July 23, 1947, c. 302, 61 Stat. 413.  [Date is in the act here.]
> The act for payment of fees, 61 Stat. 413 (1947), provided . . . [Context identifies the statute.]

c. *Citing a particular section or page.*

> The Second Decontrol Act of 1947, Section 6(a), 61 Stat. 321, 323, empowered . . . [The reference to page 321, where the act begins, is usually omitted.  In a footnoted brief, 61 Stat. 321, 323 would appear as a footnote.]

d. *Citing an earlier act amended.*

> Act of March 4, 1934, c. 84, §7, 48 Stat. 460, as amended Aug. 2, 1946, c. 753, §601(a), 60 Stat. 850.

e. *Citing an act by popular name.*

> The Labor Management Relations Act, 1947 (Taft-Hartley Act), Act of June 23, 1947, c. 120, 61 Stat. 136, hereinafter cited as LMRA (or, the Act).  [With footnotes, only the title would appear in the main text.]

f. *Treaties.*  Treaties before 1950 are cited in briefs as Statutes at Large, because up to that time they were printed in the Statutes at Large.  The last volume containing treaties is volume 64.  Beginning with 1950 (printing T.I.A.S. No. 2010), treaties and executive agreements of international import are published in the new series, United States Treaties and Other International Acts. The component parts of a treaty or executive agreement citation should ordinarily include the short title or a paraphrase thereof, the type of agreement (i.e., treaty, convention, etc.), subject (peace, commerce), countries signing, and date of signature, *not* of Senate approval, the designated "effective date," or the date proclaimed.

(1) *Cited as a Statute at Large in a brief.*

> Treaty of Peace with Rumania, Feb. 18, 1947, Part II, 61 Stat. 1801 (1948).

(2) *Cited as United States Treaties and other International Acts.*

> 1 U.S.T.I.A. 1 (1952).  [1 UST 1 (1952) is the Department of State preference.]

(3) *Cited in a periodical.*

> Treaty of Friendship, Commerce and Consular Rights, with Germany, Dec. 8, 1923.[1]  [Text.]

> [1] 44 Stat. 2132, U.S. Treaty Ser. 725, 4 Trenwith 4191.  [Footnote.]

g. *Reorganization plans as printed in the Statutes at Large.*

> Reorganization Plan No. 1 of 1947 . . . [Main text reference.]

h. *Presidential proclamations as printed in the Statutes at Large.* These may also be cited to the Federal Register and to the Code of Federal Regulations.

> Proc. No. 2899, Aug. 8, 1946, 61 Stat. 1033.

i. *Concurrent resolutions as printed in the Statutes at Large.*

> H. Con. Res. 49, 80th Cong., 1st Sess., 61 Stat. 1023 (1947).
> S. Con. Res. 21, 80th Cong., 1st Sess., 61 Stat. 1023 (1947).

3. *United States Revised Statutes.* The edition is a necessary part of the citation (1875; or second, 1878).  Do not cite "1873" as the date of the first edition.  Chapter and page references are omitted.  "U.S." is omitted, except in states which themselves have "Revised Statutes."  Then it should be included to avoid ambiguity.  In briefs, the usual abbreviation is R.S.; in legal periodicals, Rev. Stat., but either is acceptable in briefs.

> Congress expressly provided, R.S. §1 (1875), 1 U.S.C. 1 (1958 ed.) . . .

4. *United States Code.* Except where a Code title has been re-enacted into positive law, specifically repealing the original act from which it was derived, include the original act, since it, not the Code, is still the authority.  The date and supplement number of the edition are necessary parts of the citation.  In citing the supplement, give the supplement number also.  (The 1960 supplement, for example, contains only 1959 legislation.)

a. *Code citation to latest edition, with Supplement citations.* In the citations below, if the "Act" citation is omitted, date the Statutes at Large citation.

> Act of June 29, 1959, Pub. L. 86-72, 73 Stat. 155, 49 U.S.C. §1112 (Supp. I, 1959), hereinafter cited as Code §1112.

b. *Code citation where original act has been amended once.*

> Act of June 8, 1938, c. 328, §1(c), 52 Stat. 633, as amended Sept. 5, 1940, c. 715, §11, 54 Stat. 876, 23 U.S.C. §10b (1958 ed.).

c. *Code citation where original act has been amended several times.*

> Act of Nov. 9, 1921, c. 199, §11, 42 Stat. 214, as amended 23 U.S.C. §12 (1958 ed.).

*d. Code citation of legislation of current year.*   The unofficial United States Code Annotated and Federal Code Annotated pamphlet supplements may be cited when covering a period for which there is as yet no official supplement.

> 63 Stat. 98, 18 U.S.C.A. §3771 (Aug. 1961 pam.).

*e. Code title, enacted into positive law.*   The edition date should form part of the citation.   The Internal Revenue Code is an example of a Code title enacted into positive law.

> Int. Rev. Code of 1939, §811(g) (Sec. 404, Revenue Act of 1942).

Although  in the above citation the Revenue Act of 1942 is no longer in force as to Section 404, it is cited for convenience.

The Treasury Department, in its briefs, has an appendix to each brief, in which the exact provisions of the Internal Revenue Code relied upon are quoted in full, a good practice.

> Internal Revenue Code.
> Sec. 713.
> (d) [Quoting the statute.]

*5. Quoting the act in a footnote.*   Where the cited provisions are short, copy them in a footnote, the first time cited, and thereafter refer to them by section number.

> 1 The pertinent provisions are as follows:
> "Sec. 5(a) [quoting the section].
> "Sec. 15 [quoting the section]."

**§26.6.   Subordinate legislation: Administrative rules and regulations.**

*1. Federal Register.*

> 14 Fed. Reg. 6190 (1949).

*2. Code of Federal Regulations.*   The date of the supplement should be given.   The form "CFR" is common, but "C.F.R." should be used.

> 24 C.F.R. §202.13 (1959).

*3. Presidential proclamations and executive orders.*

> Proc. No. 2855, 14 Fed. Reg. 5413 (1949).   [Pre-Statute at Large citation.]
> Proc. No. 2454, 55 Stat. 608 (1941).
> Exec. Order No. 9662, 10 Fed. Reg. 14653 (1945).

*4. Rules of practice.*   In briefs intended for courts, the initial citation should make the name of the agency clear.   Agencies themselves frequently cite the Federal Register or Code of Federal Regulations form of a rule.

Patent Office, Rule 122 (Patents 1949).
F.T.C. Rules of Practice, Rule 7(c), 16 C.F.R. §2.7(c) (1949 ed.).

5. *Administrative regulations.* Begin the citation with the agency's name or abbreviation thereof, giving also the date.

U.S. Treas. Regs. 105, §81.24 (1943).    [Footnote form.]
Bureau of Land Management, Classification Order, Aug. 24, 1949, 14 Fed. Reg. 5346.

6. *Court rules.* The citations below are from official briefs.

Federal Rules of Criminal Procedure, Rule 18.
General Orders in Bankruptcy, No. 26.
Admiralty Rules, No. 54 (as amended July 21, 1948).
Mich. Court Rules, No. 51.
Rules, No. 51 (318 Mich. XII).    [Giving place of publication.]
Ill. Sup. Ct. Rule 49.

## §26.7.   State legislation.

1. *Legislative history.*

1 Cal. Senate Jour. 317, 56th Sess. (1945).
Neb. Legis. Jour., 68th Sess. (1947), p. 793.

2. *Miscellaneous documents.* Reports of state departments, when cited by numbered volume, follow the form of volume and page citation of law reports and periodicals; where not numbered by volume, the page citation follows the date, preceded by a comma, or follows the same form as the multi-volume citation, as desired.

Louisiana Revenue Code Comm., *Project of a Revenue Code . . .* (1949), p. 916. ·
N.Y. Law Revision Comm., *Act, Recommendations and Study . . .* Legis. Doc. No. 65(F) (1949).

3. *Dating state session law and statute citations.* Dating state statute citations is usual.   Session laws (except perhaps in Ohio, where the volumes are numbered consecutively and are often so cited) are always dated.

a. *Dating session laws in the middle.* This is usual and recommended, with no comma between the title and date.

Wash. Laws 1941, c. 1, §9, p. 8.

b. *Dating statutes.*

S.C. Code of Laws, §53-252 (1952).

4. *State constitutions.*   See §26.3.
5. *Slip laws and session laws.*

a. *General form.*

> Me. Laws 1945, P. & S., c. 96.
> Mass. Resolves 1945, c. 35. [For Acts: Stat. 1938, c. 136.]
> Tenn. Private Acts 1945, c. 69.
> Ohio Laws 1947, c. 119, 113 O.L. 179.

b. *Extra sessions.* These should be clearly indicated.

> Ala. Laws, 2d E.S. 1947, No. 16.
> Ga. Laws, E.S. Nov. 1948, No. 2.

c. *Advance sheet citations.* These may be shown if desired.

> N.Y. Laws 1950, c. 11 (1950 N.Y. Sess. L. Serv. 91).

d. *Earlier editions of session laws.* Some of these reprints are cited by the name of their editor, and by volume and page.

> N.Y. Laws 1779, c. 25, 1 Laws of New York 26 (Greenleaf, 1792).
> Va. Acts of Assembly 1647, Act 11, 1 Laws of Virginia 341 (Hening, 1823).

6. *State statutes.* Where they exist, the latest official editions of statutes, as amended by session laws, are usually cited in briefs, rather than the unofficial annotated editions, even when the latter bear a much later publication date. This is because the official edition is still the "best evidence" of the law. In legal writing generally, however, the tendency is to cite the unofficial, if later. A good and safe practice is to cite both the official and the unofficial, in parallel, in both a brief and a memorandum of law.

a. *Recommended standard form for state statutes.* In briefs addressed to your own state courts, follow their preferred form, as found in the judicial opinions of the forum; in citing statutes of other states, the standard citation form below is advised.

> Ore. Rev. Stat., §554.010 (1953), as amended by . . .
> N.J. Stat. Ann., §54:10 A-32 (West, 1960).
> Kan. Gen. Stat. 1949, §10-801 (Supp. 1959).
> Conn. Gen. Stat. Ann. 1959, §9-174 (West, 1960).

As of 1958, a list of statutory citation forms as preferred by each of the several state courts is found in Price, *A Practical Manual of Standard Legal Citations* (2d ed. 1958), pp. 24-27. Since editions constantly change, the Harvard Law Review Association, Cambridge, Massachusetts, issues an annual mimeographed chart showing current titles and suggested citation forms for statutes of all states.

§26.8.   **English and Canadian statutory material.**

1. *Parliamentary debates.* In some fashion, these are published from 1066 to date. The series name and number and the date are parts of the citation.

7 Parl. Hist. of Eng. 356 (Hansard's 1716).
118 Parl. Deb. 678 (Hansard's 3d Ser. 1891).
230 H.C. Deb. 721 (Hansard's 5th Ser. 1929).

2. *English statutes and court rules.*

a. *Session laws.* Cite by title (if any), regnal year, date, chapter, section and schedule (if any). Unofficial editions of the statutes (as Halsbury's) are not cited as such.

Supreme Court of Judicature Act, 1925, c. 49, s. 226, Sched. 6.

Where the title of the statute is not otherwise given, add the date, in parentheses.

19 & 20 Geo. V, c. 34, s. 2(2) (1929).

In tabular citations, by year, the title is enclosed in parentheses.

12 & 13 Geo. VI, c. 38 (Companies Act, 1948), s. 101.
12 & 13 Geo. VI, c. 58 (Criminal Justice Act, 1948), s. 38(2).

b. *Statutory rules and orders and Instruments.* Cite by year, number, volume and page.

S.R. & Order 1914 (No. 1629).
S.I. 1948 (No. 2357) I, p. 101 [in which I is the volume number].

c. *Supreme Court rules.*

R.S.C., Ord. 46, r. 4.

3. *Canadian statutes and court rules.*

a. *Statutes.* Citation of Canadian statutes generally is much the same as the citation of English statutes, but in Canada revised statutes, as in the United States, are the rule, and these are cited very much as here. The citations below are from official opinions.

Emergency Gold Mining Assistance Act, 1948, 11 & 12 Geo. VI, s. 4(1).
Section 37(24) of the Interpretation Act, 1927 Rev. Stats. Canada, c. 1, as amended by . . .
Ontario Rev. Stat. (1937), c. 18, as amended, 1939 Stats. c. 25.
Farm Security Act (Sask. 2d Sess.), c. 39, as amended 1945 (Sask.).

b. *Supreme Court rules.*

Rules of the Supreme Court, Order IV, rule 1 (Alberta).

## §26.9. Case material.

1. *Italics.* Italics are employed in the following examples of case citations, as is the majority practice with respect to briefs. Indicate italics by underlining the material to be italicized. Thus: Gruyger v. Burke.

2. *Elements of a case citation.*  Case reports are commonly cited by names of the parties, volume and page of reporter, the date of the decision and, when not otherwise entirely clear from the citation, the name of the court deciding the case.

3. *Case names.*

a. *Common form.*  Give only so much of the case name as makes the name entirely clear.  Thus: *Gryger v. Burke,* not *Francis Joseph Gryger, Petitioner v. C. J. Burke, Warden, Eastern State Penitentiary.*

b. *Abbreviations of case names.*

(1) *"United States" as a party.*  Abbreviate only when "United States" forms part of the name of a Government vessel.

> *United States v. Maryland & Va. Milk Assn.*
> *The U.S.S. Texas.*

(2) *The first word of a corporate or trade name.*  Write out in full.  But see also "omissions," par. h. below.

(3) *Exception.*  In legal writing other than briefs, the initials of Government administrative agencies, and organizations such as labor unions, commonly known by these initials, may be substituted for the complete name when there is no danger of confusion.  It should be borne in mind, however, that many such initials, perfectly clear in their meaning at one time, are definitely not so at a later date.  Legal periodicals and frequently the agencies themselves omit periods in the case title, but seldom in the report series abbreviation.

> *NLRB v. Hearst Publications.*
> *United States v. CIO.*

c. *Railroad names.*  The common practice is to give the full name in abbreviated form, always spelling out the first name in the title.

> *Chicago, R. I. & P. Ry. v. Chicago, M. & St. P.R.R. Co.*

d. *Ex parte, In re, Matter of.*  Cite as written, but index under party.

> *Ex parte Sterba.*  [Text or footnote reference.]
> *Ex parte.*  See name of party.  [Index reference.]
> *Sterba, Ex parte.*  [Index reference.]

e. *Ex rel.*  Cite *United States ex rel. Greathouse v. Smith* as written.  For alphabeting, see §26.14.

f. *Abbreviated parts of case names.*  The following are commonly abbreviated in case titles except when they form the first word of the name of a party.

| Administrator (Admr.) | Company (Co.) | Limited (Ltd.) |
| Association (Assn.) | Corporation (Corp.) | Railroad (R.R.) |
| Commissioner (Commr.) | Incorporated (Inc.) | Railway (Ry.) |

Contractions (Comm'r for Commissioner, Dep't for Department, etc.) are frequently employed instead of abbreviations. They require no period, because they end with the same letter as the full word. The abbreviated form is simpler and preferred.

g. *Corporate titles beginning with an initial.* Give the corporate name in full, but alphabet under *both* the initial and the surname.

> *H. J. Heinz Co. v. NLRB*

h. *Omissions from case names.*

(1) *Et al., et ux., deceased.* Omit.

(2) *Title containing both "Co." and "Inc." or "Ltd."* Use only "Co."

> *Brown Co. v. Jones,* not *Brown Co., Inc. v. Jones.*

(3) *Title of the position occupied by a party.* Omit.

> *Durkee Foods, Inc.* v. *Harrison* [omitting "Collector of Internal Revenue."]

(4) *"City" and "State."* Omit unless word needed to avoid ambiguity.

> *City of Washington* v. *Hodges.*       *Washington* v. *Oregon.*
> *Coyle* v. *New York.*              *Morral* v. *City of New York.*

(5) *The first word of the name of a corporation or association.* Do not omit.

> *McElroy* v. *Boise Valley Traction Co.*  [Not "Traction Co."]
> *United States* v. *United Mine Workers.*  [Not "Mine Workers."]

i. *Case name changed on appeal.* Where the name has been altered or the case reversed on appeal or certiorari granted, it is cited as follows:

> *Colver* v. *Skeffington,* 265 Fed. 17 (D. Mass. 1920), reversed sub nom. *Skeffington* v. *Katzoff,* 277 Fed. 129 (1st Cir. 1922).

Exceptions to the "sub nom." device are (1) where certiorari has been denied or the appeal dismissed under another name; and (2) where one of the parties was an official, replaced by another by the time the case on appeal is argued. For example, if Robertson were replaced by Ooms as Commissioner of Patents, *Jones* v. *Robertson,* would become on appeal *Ooms* v. *Jones.*

j. *Popular name case citations.* Capitalize "case" only when it

is part of the official title.   Once a case has been fully cited, later
text references may be made by short title.

> *Slade's Case.*  [Official title.]
> *Slaughter-House* cases.  [Popular title.]
> *Williams* v. *North Carolina* . . . the *Williams* case.

4. *Citing judicial opinions.*   It is customary to cite both official
or unofficial reports in most courts except the Supreme Court of
the United States, where only the official reports of *federal* courts
are preferred.

a. *Unreported decisions.*   Cite by name, docket number, court
and date.

> *Jones* v. *Smith,* no. 152, U.S. Sup. Ct., Jan. 10, 1950.
> *Eber* v. *Katz,* no. 137, S.D. Ill., Feb. 10, 1950.
> *Neuberger* v. *Halevy,* no. 1738, Sup. Ct. Mo., Feb. 23, 1950.

b. *Slip decisions.*   Cite advance sheets as bound volumes.   Citation may include docket number, court and date (not term).

> *Wade* v. *Mayo,* no. 40, U.S. Sup. Ct., June 14, 1943.  [Giving docket
> number and date of argument of a case not yet decided.]
> *Trupiano* v. *United States,* no. 427, U.S. Sup. Ct., June 14, 1948
> (8 CCH Sup. Ct. Bull. 2052).  [A decided case not yet published
> in official advance sheets.]

c. *Legal newspapers.*   Cite a newspaper report only when the
standard reports are not available.

> *Smith* v. *Jones,* 124 N.Y.L.J. 1709, col. 2 (N.Y. 2d Dept. Nov. 19,
> 1950).  [Date is of decision.   In New York, omit the "N.Y.," as
> superfluous.]

d. *Advance sheets.*   Advance sheets have the same volume and
page numbers as the bound volume, and so are cited as bound
volumes.

> *Commissioner* v. *Estate of Church,* 335 U.S. 632 (1949).
> *United States* v. *Capital Transit Co.,* 70 Sup. Ct. 115 (1949).  [If the
> official advance sheets had been published by the time this case
> was found in the Supreme Court Reporter advance sheets, they
> would have been cited preceding the Supreme Court Reporter
> citation.]

5. *United States Supreme Court Reports.*

a. *Dating Supreme Court decisions.*   In briefs to the Supreme
Court, date only unpublished decisions. Date all forms, for other
legal writing.

b. *Official edition of reports.*   Cite the first ninety volumes by
reporters' names.

*Smith* v. *Orton,* 21 How. 241, 16 L. Ed. 104 (1858).
*United States* v. *United Shoe Machinery Co.,* 247 U.S. 62, 38 Sup. Ct. 473, 63 L. Ed. 968 (1918).

c. *Opinions of Supreme Court justices sitting in chambers as circuit judges.* Certain opinions of Supreme Court justices, sitting in chambers as circuit judges, are reported.

*In re Rosenberg,* 346 U.S. 313, 73 Sup. Ct. 1173, 97 L. Ed. 1629 (1953) (order by Douglas, J., sitting as Circuit Judge).

6. *Lower federal court reports.*

a. *Early circuit courts (abolished June 1, 1912).* Cite the district but not the division thereof.

*Micon* v. *Lamar,* 1 Fed. 14 (C.C. S.D. N.Y. 1880).
*Smith* v. *Jones,* 21 Fed. Cas. 770, No. 12,505 (C.C. D. Pa. 1812).

b. *District courts.*

*Edwards* v. *Brown,* 85 F. Supp. 290 (N.D. W. Va. 1949).

c. *Federal cases.*

24 Fed. Cas. 784, No. 14,1441 (C.C. D. Mass. 1845).

d. *Circuit Courts of Appeals (to August 31, 1948).* Cite by circuit number and date.

143 F.2d 531 (9th Cir. 1944). [The abbreviation "C.C.A. 9th" has been largely superseded by "9th Cir."]

e. *Courts of Appeals (beginning Sept. 1, 1948).* Cite by circuit number and year.

171 F.2d 281 (9th Cir. 1948). [The abbreviation "C.A. 9th" has been largely superseded by "9th Cir."]

f. *United States Court of Appeals for the District of Columbia, now United States District Court of Appeals for the District of Columbia Circuit (new name adopted September 1, 1948).* The separate reporter, until November 10, 1941 (volumes 1-74), was known as Appeal Cases, but is better known as United States Court of Appeals, District of Columbia. In citing, however, prefer the Federal Reporter, except when citing to the court itself, because of its superior availability to most readers.

61 F.2d 404 (D.C. Cir. 1932). [Formerly cited as "App. D.C. 1932."]
175 F.2d 364 (D.C. Cir. (1949).

The court itself prefers its own reporter.

*Bacon* v. *Bacon,* 83 U.S. App. D.C. 313 (1948).

g. *Emergency Court of Appeals.*

*Herman* v. *Woods,* 175 F.2d 781 (Em. App. 1949).

h. *Court of Claims.*

> *Joseph Meltzner, Inc.* v. *United States,* 111 Ct. Cl. 389 (1949). More
> often cited as 77 F. Supp. 1018 (Ct. Cl. 1949) because of the supe-
> rior availability of the Federal Supplement.

i. *Court of Customs and Patent Appeals.* These reports are in
two series. In Supreme Court briefs, cite the official reports if
available; briefs to the Court of Customs and Patent Appeals
itself usually give parallel citations, if available.

> *In re Lobdell,* 35 C.C.P.A. (Patents) 1091 (1948).
> *United States* v. *Field,* 12 C.C.P.A. (Customs) 1202, 111 F.2d 902
> (1940).

j. *Federal Rules Decisions.*

> *Ratner* v. *Paramount Pictures,* 6 F.R.D. 618 (S.D. N.Y. 1942).

7. *State court reports.*
a. *Official reports by means of reporters.* Note the state and
court in parentheses, with the date.

> *Shivers* v. *Wilson,* 5 Harr. & John. 130 (Md. App. 1820).

b. *Official state reports covering several courts of the state.*
Where a plurality of courts are covered by a single reporter, the
court deciding the case is indicated in parentheses.

> *Sharp* v. *Hayes,* 43 Del. 494 (Super. Ct. 1946).

c. *Parallel citation of state reports.* State, court and date are
noted at some point.

> *Martin* v. *Post,* 92 Hun 133, 36 N.Y. Supp. 554 (Sup. Ct. 1895).

d. *Cases officially reported without opinion.* If only the unofficial report prints the opinion, cite as follows.

> *Blank* v. *Blank,* 59 Hun 1000, opinion in 5 N.Y. Supp. 200 (Sup. Ct.
> 1889).

e. *Cases not officially reported but reported unofficially.*

> *Lipman* v. *Martin,* 39 N.W.2d 69 (Mich. 1949).

8. *Annotated reports series.* These are not cited in federal court
briefs or in law reviews, as case reports, but frequently are in state
courts. They are often cited for their notes, preceded, however,
by "See."

> *Lively* v. *Munday,* 201 Ga. 409, 40 S.E.2d 62, 173 A.L.R. 1295 (1946).

9. *Federal administrative agency rulings as cited by the agencies
themselves.* Tables of typical modes of citation by federal agencies

of their rulings are printed in Price and Bitner, *Effective Legal Research*, (1953), pp. 342-345, and in Price, *A Practical Manual of Standard Legal Citations* (2d ed. 1958), pp. 43-51.

10. *Administrative material cited from legal newspapers.* Give the exact date of decision and docket number if available.

> *In re Transportation Activities of Midwest Transfer Co.,* 18 U.S.L.W. 2002, I.C.C. June 13, 1949.
> *In re Ryan Aeronautical Co.,* 85 N.L.R.B. No. 200, decided Sept. 6, 1949, 24 L.R.R.M. 1547.

11. *Collateral elements of case citations.*

a. *Dating case report citations.* Case citations should be dated because, other things being equal, the value of a recent case as authority is likely to be greater than that of earlier cases, and dating the citation provides an important element of appraisal; and it is also a check upon error in citations. For unpublished decisions, both the docket number and the exact date are given.

(1) *Place of the date citation.* Place in parentheses at the end of the citation. Where report volumes are dated but not numbered, the date precedes the series designation.

> *People* v. *Roth,* 128 Misc. 550, 220 N.Y. Supp. 167 (Gen. Sess. 1937).
> 1927 C.D. (Patents) 193. [An unnumbered but dated series.]
> *Wade* v. *Major,* no. 40, U.S. Sup. Ct., June 14, 1948. [Unpublished.]

b. *Designating the court deciding the case.* Clearly indicate when any chance of ambiguity exists.

(1) *Place for indicating the court.* This is in parentheses at the end of the citation, preceding the date. In parallel citations, indicate court only in one.

> *Application of Jacoby,* 33 N.Y.S.2d 621 (Sup. Ct. 1942).
> *Brady* v. *Brooklyn,* 1 Barb. 584 (N.Y. Sup. Ct. 1847).
> *De Bekker* v. *Stokes,* 219 N.Y. 573, 114 N.E. 1064 (1916).

c. *Named reporters.* In spite of the fact that most "nominatives" have been renumbered as parts of consecutively numbered series, it is still customary to cite them by their original designation: 2 Cranch instead of 6 U.S., for example.

(1) *Supreme Court reports.*

> *Watts* v. *Waddle,* 6 Pet. 389 (U.S. 1832).

(2) *Lower courts to 1880.* Cite as Federal Cases, omitting reporter's name.

(3) *State reports.*

> *Eames* v. *Prentice,* 8 Cush. 337 (Mass. 1851).

d. *Parallel citations.* These are not common in federal court briefs but are found in most state court briefs and in law reviews. They are always acceptable.

12. *Punctuation in case citation.*

a. *Commas.* Commas separate the case name from the volume, page and date citation, but are not used in the volume-and-page element itself except in multi-page references, as in citing dicta, or to separate this from the date and court notation in parentheses.

> *Doe* v. *Roe,* 154 F.2d 859 (9th Cir. 1946).
> *SEC* v. *Bourbon,* 47 F. Supp. 70, 73 (W.D. Ky. 1942).

b. *Citations in the main text.* Comma use depends upon the number, location and completeness of the citations to be set off. Note the punctuation below.

> These objections prevailed. *Brown* v. *Coumanis,* 135 F.2d 163 (9th Cir. 1943).
> These objections prevailed in *Brown* v. *Coumainis.*[1] [Text.]
>
> [1] 135 F.2d 163 (9th Cir. 1943). [Footnote.]

c. *Parentheses.* The parenthesis at the end of a citation is a catchall device for imparting information.

(1) *In the middle of a sentence.* Use a comma if it would have been necessary if the parentheses were not there.

> The case cited (401 Ill. 262) is not in point.
> The case cited (401 Ill. 262), not being in point . . .

(2) *Parenthetical matter closing a sentence.* Place the period outside and after the final parenthesis, with no comma preceding the parenthetical matter.

> These objections prevailed (*Brown* v. *Coumanis,* 135 F.2d 163).

3. *More than one parenthetical citation.* Note punctuation.

> The Court so said in that case (66 Mont. 100), but was reversed on appeal (264 U.S. 560).

(4) *A complete citation in the middle of a sentence.* Setting off by commas is preferred to parentheses.

> These objections prevailed, *Brown* v. *Coumanis,* 135 F.2d 163 (9th Cir. 1943), but that case is not in point.

(5) *In a separate sentence.* Place the period before the final parenthesis.

> These objections prevailed. (*Brown* v. *Coumanis.*)

(6) *Miscellaneous comments.* Except with "semble" and

"passim," brief comments made upon a case but not bearing upon its authority as precedent, may be enclosed in parentheses.

> *Bridges* v. *Wixon,* 326 U.S. 135, 65 Sup. Ct. 1443, 89 L. Ed. 2103 (1945) (deportation).
> *Wood Paper Co.* v. *Heft,* 8 Wall. 333, 19 L. Ed. 379 (U.S. 1869), semble.
> See *Gulf Oil Corp.* v. *Gilbert* (Mr. Justice Black dissenting, 330 U.S. 501, 512, 67 Sup. Ct. 839, 845, 91 L. Ed. 1055, 1064).

d. *Semicolons.* These are used to set off citations in a string.

> *Hargrave* v. *Turbeville,* 114 F.2d 33, 36 (2d Cir. 1940); *Salmon* v. *Leverett,* 201 Fed. 99, 100 (2d Cir. 1912).

13. *Purpose of citations: Signals and subsequent case history.* Briefs confine themselves for the most part to noting that a cited case was affirmed or reversed, was dismissed on appeal, or was a square holding or dictum, or should be compared with another case. In much theoretical writing, however, a more elaborate system is employed to indicate shades of authority.

a. *Square holding: No signal.* For a plurality of holdings, cite the initial page and the pages announcing each holding.

> *Boileau* v. *Williams,* 121 Conn. 432, 440, 185 Atl. 429, 431 (1936).

b. *Square holding: Contra.* A comma separates "contra" from the case cited.

> *In re La Porte,* 54 F. Supp. 911 (W.D.N.Y. 1943); contra, *In re Danby* [giving citation].

c. *Accord.* A square holding substantially in point but in some respects distinguishable is indicated by "accord," not often seen in briefs.

> *Cross* v. *Cross,* 110 Mont. 300, 102 Pac. 829 (1940); accord, *Doe* v. *Roe,* 212 Minn. 54, 2 N.W.2d 426 (1942).

d. *See: Dictum.* Precede the citation by "see," giving both the first page of the report cited and that (or those) upon which the dictum (or dicta) begins. Note the punctuation.

> See *Wright* v. *Cummins,* 109 Kan. 667, 668, 196 Pac. 246, 247 (1921).

e. *But see: Dictum contra.* Note the absence of a comma here.

> But see *Northern Pacific Ry. Co.* v. *Sanders.*

f. *Cf., But cf.* Where the dictum, though deriving from substantially different facts, is sufficiently in point to be cited in the discussion, substitute italicized "*Cf.*" for "See."

> *Cf. Thomas* v. *Collins,* 232 U.S. 516, 540 (1945).
> But *cf. Bailey* v. *Alabama,* 219 Ala. 220 (1911).

g. *E.g., See, e.g.*   Where only one or a few of many cases available are cited, use "e.g.," always beginning a sentence, always italicized, and always followed by a comma.

> *E.g., Smith v. Jones.*
> See, *e.g., Smith v. Jones.*

h. *Subsequent history of a case in the courts.*   Citations usually note later court action on a cited case.

> *Travis v. American Cities Co.,* 192 App. Div. 16, 182 N.Y. Supp. 394 (1st Dept. 1920), affirmed without opinion, 233 N.Y. 510, 135 N.E. 896 (1922).

i. *Abbreviating or contracting signals.*   Spell signal words out in full, except "cf." and e.g."

14. *Citation order.*   Primary authority is cited before secondary; higher courts before lower in the same jurisdiction; a statute before the case interpreting it; and in citing secondary authority, the descending order is from a book to a leading article, to a note, to a case comment.

a. *Primary authority.*

(1) *Statutes:* Cite in chronological order from earlier to later forms.

> Act of March 3, 1873, c. 234, §1, 17 Stat. 567, 38 U.S.C. §155 (1958 ed.).

Cite a statute which is positive law before one which is not.

> 49 Stat. 499 (1935), 29 U.S.C. §151 (1958 ed.).

In parallel citations, cite the official before the unofficial.

> Ohio Law of October 14, 1931, 114 O.L. 843, General Code of Ohio, §3294 (Throckmorton, 1940).

Cite the statute before the case interpreting it, separating by a comma.

> N.Y. Decedent Estate Law §78, *Stark v. National City Bank,* 278 N.Y. 388, 16 N.E.2d 376 (1938).

(2) *Case citations.*   Cite the official, National Reporter System unit (as Atlantic), Lawyers' Edition (of a Supreme Court report), and A.L.R., in that order.

> *Jones v. United States,* 362 U.S. 257, 80 Sup. Ct. 725, 4 L. Ed. 2d 697, 78 A.L.R.2d 233 (1960).

b. *Secondary authority: Purpose signals.*   Unless the material cited is in support of a settled point of law, "see" should precede the citation of such material.

15. *Repeating citations.* Legal writers have adopted such devices as *ibid., id., supra, infra, op. cit. supra,* etc. (always italicized) as short cuts, but they are to be used with great caution so as not to lead to confusion.

a. *Text references.* Once a case has been fully cited in the main text, or cited there by name with appropriate footnote reference to the reporter, it may thereafter within reasonable intervening space limitations be referred to by short title only. But if a particular page is referred to in the later reference, the full name must be given.

> In the *Hot Oil* case, the court said . . .
> As noted in *Halvey* v. *Halvey, supra* at 613 . . .

(1) *Supra.* Use to refer to a case previously cited on the same or preceding page, but if more pages than that intervene, repeat in full.

> *Halvey* v. *Halvey, supra.*

(2) *Quotation containing a citation.* Where the citation to a case in the text is in a quotation, cite the case fully in further references.

(3) *Ibid., Id.* Where, in a text or footnote reference, there is a complete case citation and upon the same page and without intervening citations (in footnotes, in succeeding notes), another reference is made to that case, *"ibid."* is sufficient. Where the citation is to a different page, cite *"id.* at page 119." This short cut is restricted to references on the same or opposite page of the text so that both references are visible to the reader at the same time. Note the punctuation below.

> "For this Court has declared in *Guaranty Trust Co.* v. *York,* 326 U.S. 99, 109, that a right without a remedy is not right. . . . The *York* case says this precludes a resort to the Federal court . . . [*ibid.*], so that Bullington's chance to get to the Federal court on such a basis was practically nil. [*id.* at 109.]"

In a footnoted brief the volume and page citation above, and the *"ibid."* and *"id."* following would be footnotes.

> [1] 326 U.S. 99, 108 (1946).
> [2] *Ibid.*
> [3] *Id.* at 109.

b. *Footnote references.* When a case is cited in a footnote relative to a statement in the main text but has not been mentioned in the text directly, repeat the citation in full in a later text reference to it.

If a case has been cited in a footnote and is referred to again in the same footnote, the case name, with *supra*, is sufficient, as in the text, for a square holding.   Indicate dictum by the usual means for a spot citation.

> *Quigg* v. *Newgrass Co., supra.*
> *Quigg* v. *Newgrass Co., supra* at 900, 286 N.Y. Supp. at 928.

A group of cases previously cited in a footnote may be indicated in another footnote by references to that note; if the note as a whole is referred to, omit the "cases cited."

> Note 16 *supra,* and cases cited.

In a footnote reference to a single case cited in the footnote immediately preceding, the case name is sufficient.

> [17] *Halvey* v. *Halvey, supra* note 16.

c. *Secondary material citations.* A limited use of *"op. cit. supra"* is permissible, but the device should never be employed where ambiguity is possible, as when two different works by the same author have been cited.   Do not use to repeat the title of a periodical, but only to refer to the work of an author, whether separately or in a periodical article.

> *Robertson, op. cit. supra* note 3, at 15.

d. *Shortened citation to avoid full repetition.*

> *Hearings before Senate Committee on Finance on H.R. 5327 (Import Duty on Virgin Copper),* 81st Cong., 1st Sess. (1949), p. 56 (hereinafter cited as *Hearings on H.R. 5327).*

e. *Punctuation.   Id.* at, *supra* at, *infra* at, *supra* note 17 at, require no comma following the italicized words.

16. *English law reports citation.*

a. *Indicating the court deciding the case.*   The court should be included except in report series where the court is plainly indicated in the series title.   In the Law Reports series the title usually indicates the court, but Court of Appeal cases (C.A.) and Judicial Committee of the Privy Council cases (P.C.) are exceptions.

> *Comber* v. *Jones,* 3 Bos. & Pull. 114, 127 Eng. Rep. 62 (C.P. 1802).
> *Fyfe* v. *Garden,* [1946] 1 All E.R. 366 (H.L.).

b. *Dating English case decisions.*   Put dates in parentheses at the end of the citation.   Exceptions are those Law Reports beginning in 1891, and the All England Reports, in which the date, in brackets, is an integral part of the citation, preceding the series volume and page notation.

> *Bain* v. *Central Vermont Ry. Co.,* [1921] 2 A.C. 412.
> *Fyfe* v. *Garden,* [1946] 1 All E.R. 366 (H.L.).

When the actual *decision* date differs in year from the bracketed *publication* or imprint date, then and only then is the decision date added, in parentheses, at the end of a bracketed date citation.

> *Petrie* v. *Mac Fisheries, Ltd.,* [1940] 1 K.B. 258 (C.A. 1939).

c. *Volume numbers.* For cases since 1891, be certain to cite both the bracketed date and the volume number of the Law Reports, as each series renumbers annually.

> *Hill* v. *Regem,* [1945] 1 K.B. 329.

d. *Parallel citations of English cases.* American practice is to give parallel citations for reports up to the Law Reports (through 1865); since then, citing only the Law Reports if the case is printed therein. If not so printed, then cite other reports in parallel, if any.

(1) *Original and English Report, Full Reprint parallel citations.*

> *Campbell* v. *French,* 6 T.R. 200, 101 Eng. Rep. 510 (K.B. 1795).

(2) *Law reports and other reports parallel citations.*

> *Smith* v. *Jones,* [1946] P. 31, 115 L.J. (N.S.) 29 (P.) 62 T.L.R. 16, 173 L.T.R. (N.S.) 305.

e. *Citing the Law Reports.* Citation is rather complicated. In the accompanying chart, note particularly the use or omission of "L.R." as part of the citation, the use of square brackets for dates, and, since 1891, the renumbering of volumes each year when there is more than one volume in any series for that year. English practice in each of the examples below would place the date at the beginning of the series citation, whether in parentheses or in brackets.

> *Hargrave* v. *Turbeville,* L.R. 2 Ex. 130 (1867).
> *Leverette* v. *Salmon,* L.R. 2 Ch. App. 100 (1866).
> *Stonaker* v. *Fiordalisi,* 7 Ch. D. 680 (1877).
> *Breuer* v. *Bloomfield,* L.R. 6 Q.B. 130 (1870).
> *Borner* v. *Nolan,* [1946] 1 K.B. 480.

Cite the present Queen's Bench Division reports as Q.B., not Q.B.D., as was done from 1876 to 1891. The "D" was dropped in 1891 for Probate and Chancery Division citations also.

f. *Law Journal, Law Times, Times Law, and All England Reports.* With the exception of the All England Reports, these have ceased publication, but are still cited.

> *Rex* v. *Knockaloe Camp,* 87 L.J.K.B. (N.S.) 46 (1918).
> *Beard* v. *Beard,* 174 L.T.R. (N.S.) 65 (C.A. 1845).
> *Lemon* v. *Lardeur,* [1947] 2 All E.R. 329 (C.A. 1946).

## THE LAW REPORTS, 1865 TO DATE

| Reporter | 1865-1875 | 1876-1881 | 1881-1891 | 1891-1926 | 1926-date |
|---|---|---|---|---|---|
| Admiralty and Ecclesiastical Cases | L.R.A. & E. | | | | |
| Chancery Appeal Cases | L.R. Ch. App. | | | | |
| Chancery Division | | 1 Ch. D. | 16 Ch. D. | L.R. [1891] Ch. | [1926] Ch. |
| Common Pleas Cases | L.R.C.P. | 1 C.P.D. | | | |
| Crown Cases Reserved | L.R.C.C. | | | | |
| English and Irish Appeal Cases | L.R.H.L. | | | | |
| Equity Cases | L.R. Eq. | | | | |
| Exchequer Cases | L.R. Ex. | 1 Ex. D. | | | |
| Privy Council Appeal Cases | L.R.P.C. | | | | |
| House of Lords Cases | | 1 App. Cas. | 6 App. Cas. | [1891] App. Cas. | [1926] App. Cas. |
| Privy Council Cases | | | | | |
| Probate and Divorce Cases | L.R.P. & D. | 1 P.D. | 6 P.D. | L.R. [1891] P. | [1926] P. |
| Queen's Bench Cases | L.R.Q.B. | | | | |
| Queen's Bench Division (inc. Crown Cases Reserved) | | 1 Q.B.D. | 6 Q.B.D. | L.R. [1891] 2 Q.B. | |
| King's Bench Division | | | | L.R. [1902] 2 K.B. | [1926] 2 K.B. |

g. *Court of Appeal cases.* There is no such report series, though there is such a court.

> *Milmo* v. *Carreras,* [1946] 1 K.B. 306 (C.A.).
> *Lemon* v. *Lardeur,* [1946] 2 All E.R. 329 (C.A.).

h. *Appeals Cases.* Do not confuse the House of Lords and Judicial Committee of the Privy Council cases with the Court of Appeal cases above.

17. *Canadian law reports.* Canadian case citation form, as employed in law reports, differs from the United States style in that the decision date precedes rather than follows the series citation. Where, as in the Canada Law Reports beginning with 1923, and the Dominion Law Reports, volumes are numbered anew each year instead of in a consecutive series, the date is in brackets, as is the English Law Reports style. Where the numbering is consecutive, the date is in parentheses.

> [1926] S.C.R. 412. [1926 has only one volume.]
> [1951] 3 D.L.R. 86; *but*
> (1906) 23 R.P.C. 66.
> (1951) 3 W.W.R. (N.S.) 169.

It is suggested, in the interest of uniformity, that when cited in the United States, the last two citations above read

> 23 R.P.C. 666 (1906).
> 3 W.W.R. (N.S.) 169 (1951).

18. *Foreign law citations.* While there is no uniform citation for all Civil Law countries, the following forms are suggested to the American user by Dr. Bruno H. Greene, formerly of the Vienna Bar, Professor of Law and Law Librarian of the University of Minnesota.

a. *Statutes.* Cite: (1) country, (2) the word "Law," (3) exact date, (4) number of official gazette or collection in which published.

> *France:* Law, July 14, 1819, Sec. VII B [Bulletin des Lois] 294.
> *Germany:* Law, March 30, 1892, R. Ges. Bl. 369.

b. *Codes.* Cite: (1) country, (2) article or section, (3) code name. If the edition is important, add date in parentheses at end of the citation.

> *Italy:* Art. 54, Cod. di Commercio.

c. *Law reports.* Cite: (1) country, (2) the word "Decision," (3) name of court and/or place (if given), (4) date, (5) docket number (if given), (6) name and number of collection in which case is contained. Parties' names are usually omitted.

> *Belgium:* Decision, Bruxelles, April 5, 1913, Pas[icrisie Belge], 1013, II; 334.
> *Austria:* Decision, March 17, 1914, R II 64, G[lasier] U[nger] 6865.

d. *Periodicals.* Cite: (1) author, (2) country (in parentheses), (3) title of article, (4) volume number, (5) name of periodical, (6) date, (7) number of issue, (8) page or other subdivision.

> Pogoda, Benon (Poland), *Niesluszne Zbogacenie*, 62 Gazeta Sadvowa Warszawska, Jan. 29, 1934, n. 5, pp. 65-67.
> Braun, Rudolf (Austria), *Zur Frage der Reformbeduerftigkeit des Dritten Rueckstellungsgesetzes*, J[uristische] Bl[aetter], Jan. 7, 1950, n. 1, pp. 1-3.

e. *Treatises and commentaries.* Cite: (1) author, (2) title, (3) place of publication, (4) date, (5) volume, (6) page or other subdivision.

> Demogue, *Les Notions Fondamentales du Droit Privé*, Paris, 1911, I, n. 246.

19. *Loose-leaf and other services.* For these see Price and Bitner, *Effective Legal Research* (1953), p. 354.

§26.10. **Treatises, reports, periodicals, etc.**

1. *Generally.* The material is cited by volume (if more than one), author (personal or corporate), title, page or section, edition, editor (when important), and date.

> 2 Pomeroy, *Equity Jurisprudence* 428 (5th ed., Symonds, 1941). [5th ed. 1941, if no editor is named, omitting commas.]

2. *Page or section references.* See §16.11.

3. *Author entry.* Authors are personal (as Wigmore, Powell), or corporate (as Columbia University, Department of State, New York Law Revision Commission). Many works (as monographs in series) have both kinds. The table below shows these forms.

| *Volume* | *Author* | *Title* | *Edition, date, etc.* |
|---|---|---|---|
| 6 | Williston | *Contracts* | (rev. ed. 1936) |
| | American Jewish Congress | *Survey of . . . Admissions* | (1947) |
| 33 | U.S. Dept. of Labor | Annual Report [no italics] | (1945) |
| | A.B.A. Special Committee on Assistance to Lawyers | Report | (1944) |
| 6 | N.Y. Judicial Council | Annual Report | (1940) |

a. *Personal author.* Legal citation practice omits given names or initials unless their inclusion is necessary for clarity: Wigmore, but T. R. Powell, R. R. B. Powell.

> Stieber, *Ten Years of Minnesota Labor Relations Act* (1949), p. 9. [Text or footnote reference.]
> Stieber, Jack W., *Ten Years of Minnesota Labor Relations Act* (Bull. No. 9, University of Minnesota Industrial Relations Center 1949), p. 9. [Index to brief.]

b. *Corporate author.* Many reports and pamphlets lack a personal author. Cite the significant author, whether personal or corporate, first. Note that in the table above, all but Williston are corporate authors.

Occasionally a report which is better known by title than by the agency producing it may be cited by title, but this is not recommended. The title may be forgotten, while the agency continues.

> *Investment Trusts and Investment Companies:* Part 5, *Conclusions and Recommendations* (SEC 1942).

c. *Both a personal and a corporate author.* Generally cite by the personal author, with a parenthetical reference to the publishing agency.

> Walton Hamilton, *Patents and Free Enterprise* (TNEC Monograph No. 31, 1941), p. 19. [Note that the author's name is not inverted.]

If several T.N.E.C. Monographs are to be cited in the same brief and collected in the index as such, cite there as Monographs, by number.

> Temporary National Economic Committee: Monograph No. 31 (Walton Hamilton, *Patents and Free Enterprise,* 1940), p. 19. Monograph No. 36 [giving title, etc.].

4. *Title.* Cite by title only when it is better known than the author. Cite the title as on the title page, giving it in full, with "A," "An," and "The," except that where unduly long or complicated, or where it is so well known that "Contracts" or "Evidence" or the like is all that is necessary to identify the work. "Treatise on" is usually omitted. Do not cite as "Williston on Contracts," unless that is the exact title. Cite as "Williston, *Contracts.*"

a. *Editor's name as part of the title.* Cite by the editor's name only when it has become better known than the original author's.

> Brannan, *Negotiable Instrument Law* (7th ed., Beutel, 1948), but *Medina's Bostwick's Forms.*

b. *Annual reports.*

> 6 N.Y. Jud. Council Ann. Rept. 17 (Leg. Doc. No. 48, 1940).

5. *Edition.* Note the capitalization and punctuation below.

> Gray, *Rule against Perpetuities* (4th ed., Roland Gray, 1942).
> Williston, *Contracts* (rev. ed. 1936). [No comma.]
> Walker, *Patents* (Deller's ed. 1937). [No comma here.]

6. *Translators.* These are shown in parentheses.

> Hatschek, *An Outline of International Law* (Manning trans. 1930).

7. *Periodic reports.* Cite by agency and title. The tradition of citing the publications of the Attorney General of the United States by title (Ops. Atty. Gen.) is still too strong to break, however.

A periodic report is cited as is a law report, with the title not italicized.

a. *If the volumes are numbered.*

> 73 A.B.A. Rept. 207 (1948).
> 33 Dept. of Labor Ann. Rept. 19 (1948).

b. *If the volumes are not numbered.*

> 1947 Attorney Gen. Ann. Rept. 49.

8. *Numbered bulletins lacking a personal author.*
a. *If cited singly.*

> *Characteristics of Company Unions* (U.S. Bureau of Labor Statistics, Bull. No. 634, 1935), p. 37.

b. *If cited as one of several.*

> Bull. No. 634 (*Characteristics of Company Unions,* 1935), p. 37.
> Bull. No. 770 [giving title, etc.].

9. *Collected essays.*
a. *Collected essays of one author.*

> Bohlen, *Landlord and Tenant,* in his *Studies in the Law of Torts* (1926), p. 202.

b. *Collected essays of several authors.*

> Corwin, *Judicial Review in Action,* in 1 *Selected Essays in Constitutional Law* 449 (1938).

10. *American Law Institute publications.* For citation purpose in briefs the Restatements should be assimilated to statutes, and not italicized.

> 21 A.L.I. Proceedings 157 (1944).
> A.L.I. Restatement, Torts §18 (1934).
> A.L.I. Restatement, Agency §390, comment (1933).
> A.L.I. Model Code of Evidence, Rule 399 (1942).
> Uniform Commercial Code §76 (1949).

11. *Legal encyclopedias.* Cite to volume, page, topic, section

and note, and date.    The date takes care of replacement volumes of C.J.S. and Am. Jur.

> 47 C.J. 644, Partnership, Section 7, n. 30.    [Main text, index.]
> 47 C.J. 644, Partnership §7, n. 30.    [Footnote.]
> 43 C.J.S. 768, Injunctions, Section 156.
> 43 C.J.S., Injunctions, Section 156 (Ann. Cum. Part 1957).
> 36 Am. Jur., Mechanics' Liens §206 (Cum. Supp. 1957).

*When omitting the subject heading:*

> 47 C.J. 644, n. 30; 36 Am. Jur. 136.

12. *Briefs.*    Parts of the briefs, transcript of the record below, etc., are usually cited in parentheses in other briefs.    Do not italicize the references.    Examples of citations in briefs are given below.

> The formula in Appellant's brief (p. 4) is inoperable.
> The Appellant's formula is alleged to contain kaolin (Br. 4).
> It is alleged that this is operable (Appellant's Brief 17), but . . .
> Brief for the United States as *amicus curiae*, p. 17, *Smith* v. *Jones* . . .
> Brief for Appellees, pp. 17, 27, *Doe* v. *Roe*, 300 N.Y. 19 (1948).
> Transcript of Record, p. 10, *Jackson* v. *Clayton & Durante*, 60 F.2d 18 (1932).
> The Appellant is licensed to do business in Canada (R. 17).
> Appellant does business in Canada (R. 17) and in . . .
> Appellant argues (Br. 53) that . . .
> The agreement (Appellant's Exhibit 19, not printed in the record) was . . .
> . . . were assigned against Defendant (Defendant's Exhibit 27, R. 29, f. 1).
> Is it true that Defendant's formula contains kaolin? (R. 21).

13. *Department of State publications.*    Routine Publications are cited by series number and title.

> Dept. of State Pub. No. 1288, *Communications to the Mexican Ambassador at Washington* (1939).

More important publications may be cited by title.

> *United States Relations with China* . . . (U.S. Dept. of State Pub. No. 3673, Far Eastern Series No. 30, 1949).

*Foreign Relations of the United States* (a series).

> Foreign Rel. U.S. 1912 (Dept. of State 1937), p. 616.
> 2 Foreign Rel. U.S. 1932, at 473 (Dept. of State 1947).    [There were two volumes of the series this year.]

*Department of State Bulletin.*

> 20 Dept. of State Bull. 577 (1949).

14. *Press releases.* These are usually cited by title, and if mimeographed, the citation should so indicate.

> Proposed New Rules of Practice, Treasury Dept. Press Release No. 793, Nov. 27, 1949 (mimeographed).

15. *Purpose signals.* Use sparingly in briefs, in the same manner as in case citations.

16. *Law reviews.*

a. *Volume and page references.*

> 49 Colum. L. Rev. 344 (1949).
> 1948 Wis. L. Rev. 528.   [Where volumes are unnumbered.]

b. *Leading articles.* Cite by author, title, volume and page. In the main text, the author's name may be copied there in full, but in footnote references cite as below, with initials given only when their omission might cause uncertainty.

> Browder, *Testamentary Conditions Against Contest* . . . 49 Colum. L. Rev. 321, 327 (1949). [Spotting material on page 327, of an article beginning on page 321.]
> W. A. Hamilton, *Safety in Airline Maintenance,* 9 J. Air L. 275 (1938). [Where more than one Hamilton.]

c. *Notes.* As distinguished from case comments, these are variously called by law reviews "Notes," "Comments," "Notes and Comments," etc. When citing, follow the periodical's own nomenclature. Notes are cited with or without title.

> Note, 34 Va. L. Rev. 944 (1948).   [Footnote style.]
> Note, *Constitutionality of Proposed Legislation,* 34 Va. L. Rev. 944 (1948).
> Notes, 49 Colum. L. Rev. 363 (1949), 27 Tex. L. Rev. 337 (1949). [In consecutive notes from different reviews, all are designated as "Notes."]

d. *Legislation notes.*

> Legis., *Merger and Consolidation in Iowa,* 34 Iowa L. Rev. 67 (1948).

e. *Case comments.* Cite either by volume and page alone or by the case commented upon. In the latter instance, the case comment citation is given as a parallel citation to the case itself. Give both the law review publication date and the decision date if they differ. Follow the review's own nomenclature.

> Recent Decisions, 47 Mich. L. Rev. 109 (1948).
> *Pope* v. *Garrett,* 204 S.W.2d 867 (1947), 37 Ky. L. Rev. 113 (1948).

17. *Newspapers.* Cite by title, page, column and date. When there are several sections not continuously paged, add the section number before the page number.

> *Smith* v. *Jones,* U.S. Sup. Ct., New York Times, Feb. 5, 1950, p. 6, col. 3.
>
> Krock, *How the Super-Bomb Was Disclosed,* New York Times, Feb. 2, 1950, p. 26, col. 5.  [A signed article.]

18. *Capitalization of titles of leading articles and notes.*  Capitalize first words, nouns, pronouns, adjectives, adverbs and verbs. Do not capitalize, except as first words, articles, conjunctions or prepositions.

> *Bargain and Sale under Power in Deeds of Trust.*
> *Distress and Execution in Pennsylvania.*

19. *Government periodicals.*  Cite as any other periodical.

> 94 Cong. Record 9761 (1948).

## §26.11.  Page citations.

1. *Multi-volume works.*  Where the reference is to sections rather than pages, the same principles govern as in page citations, with no comma separating the title of the reporter, treatise or document from either the page or section designation.

> 330 U.S. 219 (1948).
> 49 Colum. L. Rev. 927 (1949).
> 4 Walker, *Patents* 28 (Deller's ed. 1947).
> 6 Fed. Res. Bd. Ann. Rept. 36 (1919).
> 8 Wigmore, *Evidence* §2195 (3d ed. 1940).

2. *Single-volume works.*

a. *Law reports.*  Pages are referred to in the same manner as in multi-volume works.

> *Gilbert* v. *Cooley,* Walk. Ch. 494 (Mich. 1844).

b. *Unnumbered treatises, bulletins, reports, etc.*

> S. Rept. No. 1631, 77th Cong., 2d Sess. (1942), p. 51.
> Prosser, *Torts* (2d ed. 1955), p. 193.  [Or pp. 193-198.]
> Prosser, *Torts* (2d ed. 1955), §95.
> Secretary of Labor Ann. Rept. (1946), p. 40.

3. *Citations to more than one page.*

> Where numbers are consecutive: 69-83.  [Or pp. 69-83.]
> Where numbers are not consecutive: 69, 70, 73.  [Or pp. 69, 70, 73.]
> Where numbers are consecutive and above 100: 169-173, *not* 169-73.

4. *Spot page references.*

a. *Law reports.  Edmonds* v. *Heil,* 333 Ill. App. 497, 77 N.E.2d 863 (1948), is to the entire case beginning on the pages noted.  A citation to 333 Ill. App. 497, 501, 77 N.E.2d 863, 866 (1948), is to the matter on pages 501 and 866 of the reporters cited.

b. *"At" in spot page references.*  This convention is now usually confined to one of the following situations, to avoid the use of "p." or "page" as a part of a citation.

(1) *In case citation.* Further references to a different page of a case already cited may be made as follows. Note punctuation.

> 297 N.Y. 315.
> *Id.* at 319.
> *Jones* v. *Smith, supra* at 321.

(2) *In further citation to a different page.* Where a treatise or periodical article has already been fully cited, "at" may be used as follows. Note the punctuation.

> 4 Wigmore, *op. cit. supra* note 23, at 18.
> 4 Wigmore, *op. cit. supra* note 23, §2817. [Since the section symbol is necessary here anyway, no purpose is served by adding "at."]

c. *Annotations.* The citation is to the first and other page of the *annotation*, not to the case.

> Annot. 157 A.L.R. 315, 321 (1945).

5. *Parenthetical page citations.*

a. *A citation which is a sentence by itself.* The period in the parenthetical sentence is inside the parenthesis.

> The formula is copied from Appellant's brief. (See p. 17.)

b. *A page citation which is at the end of a sentence but is part of it.* The period follows the parenthesis.

> This was cited in the Appellant's brief (p. 17).

c. *A page citation in the middle of a sentence.*

> The case cited (401 Ill. 262) is not in point.
> The case cited (401 Ill. 262), not being in point . . .

d. *Where there is more than one parenthetical page reference in a sentence.*

> The court held (p. 319) as the State claims, but the Appellant's brief denies it (p. 2).

e. *Where the parenthetical citation follows a question.* Avoid ambiguity as follows.

> Did the formula in Appellant's brief contain kaolin? (See p. 4.)

6. *Briefs.* For page references in briefs, see page 393.

7. *Statutes.* Except in some state session laws and in the United States Statutes at Large, statutes are seldom cited by page.

a. *United States Statutes at Large.* Cite by volume and page, plus something else, which may be the title of the act, the chapter, section, or a specific page, if the context does not identify the reference.

> 38 Stat. 730 (1914).  Alone, it is insufficient.
> The Clayton Act, 38 Stat. 730 (1914), identifies the act by name.
> Section 6 of the Clayton Act, 38 Stat. 731 (1914), refers to the exact page where the section is printed.
> 38 Stat. 731, §6 (1914).

b. *United States Code.*  Page citations are rare.

c. *State session laws.*  See §26.7.

**§26.12.  Numerals.**

1. *Cardinal and ordinal.*  One, two, six are cardinals; first, second, sixth are ordinals.  The contractions 1st, 2d, 6th etc. are not abbreviations, and need no following period except when they close a sentence.

2. *Figures.*

a. *Serial numbers.*  Cite in figures.

> Bulletin 725          Document 71          pages 352-357, *not* 352-57.

b. *Dates, quantities and measurements are expressed in figures.*

> June 1935, *not* June, 1935          March 6 to April 15, 1935
> 1st day of May [in forms] *but* the last of May          6 acres

c. *Isolated numbers of 10 or more are expressed in figures.*

> 50 ballots          10 times as large          about 40 men

d. Use figures with "per cent."

3. *Numbers spelled out.*

a. *At the beginning of a sentence.*  Spell out.

b. *In a sentence in the main text.*

> Eighty-first Congress, *but* in a statute or report, 81st Cong., 1st Sess.

c. *Numbers less than ten are spelled out.*

> six horses          eight times as large          *but* $3\frac{1}{3}$ cans

d. *Fractions standing alone are generally spelled out.*

> three-fourths of an inch, *but* $\frac{1}{2}$ to $1\frac{3}{4}$ cans

**§26.13.  Quotations in briefs.**

1. *In general.*  Quoted matter is reproduced verbatim, even to errors in spelling, etc.  Some matter, however, is usually deleted in a quotation, page references may be added, emphasis supplied, and obvious errors noted (but not corrected).  Whenever any of these actions is taken, it should be precisely indicated.

2. *Citing the source: Cases.*  In quoting from an opinion not previously cited, the quotation is preceded or followed by a cita-

tion to the quoted source, including the exact page upon which the quotation begins.

> "It is likewise generally recognized law . . . that negligence exists toward a pedestrian using a passive path . . ." *Erie Railroad Co.* v. *Tompkins,* 304 U.S. 64, 70 (1938).

Generally, page references should precede the quotation.

> Mr. Justice Holmes stated in his dissent (page 273) that the doctrine was outmoded: [quoting].

3. *Short quotations.* Set off in the main text by quotation marks.

> The defendant contended "that by the common law . . . the only duty owed to the plaintiff was to refrain from wilful or wanton injury" (*id.* at 80).

4. *Long quotations.* A quotation of more than three or four lines becomes cumbersome in the body of a brief and should be set off by itself, by a wide indention on both sides. The quotation is dropped two spaces and is typed single space, with double spaces between the paragraphs quoted. Omit quotation marks.

> Mr. Justice Reed in his dissent discussed the application of *Swift* v. *Tyson* (p. 9):
>
> The "doctrine of *Swift* v. *Tyson,*" as I understand it, is that the words "the laws," as used in §34, line one, of the Federal Judiciary Act of September 24, 1789, do not include in their meaning "the decisions of the local tribunals." Mr. Justice Story, in deciding that point, said . . .
>
> To decide the case now before us and to "disapprove" the doctrine of *Swift* v. *Tyson* [continuing the quotation].

5. *Quotation within a quotation.* Where a quotation appears within a quotation, the primary quotation is enclosed by double marks, the secondary one by single marks.

> "In support of the above statement, the court quoted from the case of *State ex rel. Gwin* v. *Spencer,* 220 Ind. 337, 339, 43 N.E.2d 724 (1942), as follows:
> " 'Jurisdiction over the case must necessarily be in some court . . . for the protection of the rights of the parties litigant.' "

6. *Omissions from quoted matter.* It is customary and permissible to quote selectively, being careful that the meaning of the matter quoted is in no way altered, and that the original text is not garbled. Whenever something is omitted from a quotation the ellipsis should be indicated by three periods or by asterisks.

a. *Ellipsis within a sentence.* This is indicated by the three dots or asterisks, a space apart, separated one space from the rest of the quoted matter.

> We do not question the . . . holding of this court . . . that "the laws of the several states . . . do not include state court decisions as such."

b. *Omission of words at the beginning of a sentence.* Formerly this was always done by prefacing the omission by three dots or asterisks, as: He declared ". . . the operation of the writs has extended . . ." Increasingly popular, however, is the formerly impermissible use of brackets instead of dots. Thus: "[T]he operation of the writs has extended . . ."

c. *Omission of an entire sentence.* At the beginning of a quotation this is indicated by three dots, followed by a sentence beginning with a capitalized word.

> . . . There is no federal common law . . .

d. *When the final sentence of the quotation is incomplete.* Show this by dots, with one space before the first dot.

e. *When an ellipsis occurs following a complete sentence.* Give the complete sentence its usual period, followed by the three dots indicating ellipsis.

> Jones alleged he was not there. . . . However, he was there.

7. *Introducing a quotation.*

a. *In the main text.* When the quoted matter is made a part of the sentence but is not itself a sentence, only the quotation marks are necessary.

> The doctrine assumes "a transcendental body of law . . ." and . . .

b. *A longer quotation.* Where this is set off by itself by wide indention, the three dots are necessary when the quotation does not begin with the first word of a sentence.

> This court said in part (p. 82) that . . . as a general rule this court [continuing quotation].

8. *Dropping a paragraph in a quotation.* Indicate by using five dots to separate the paragraphs actually quoted, to take the place of the one or ones not quoted. Double space between the five dots and the paragraphs above and below.

> .    .    .    .    .

9. *When the quoted matter itself has dropped matter.* Indicate by *"sic."*

> Mr. Justice Butler quoted Mr. Justice Holmes to the effect that "a

> court of the United States was bound . . . [*sic*] before the state courts had rendered an authoritative decision."

10. *"Sic."*   *Sic,* a complete word, requires no period except at the end of a sentence.   It is italicized.

11. *Errors in quoted matter.*   Indicate by *"sic,"* in brackets, following the error.

> The statutes was [*sic*] held vaid [*sic*].

12. *Editorial interpolations.*   Extraneous matter supplied by the commentator is placed in brackets, and within the quotation marks.   Such matter (as page citations, for example), when it is outside the quotation marks, is placed in parentheses.   When using both brackets and parentheses together, brackets are always used outside the parentheses.

13. *Emphasis.*   Matter italicized in the quoted matter is of course italicized when quoted.   If it is desired to italicize quoted matter not italicized in the original text, do so as follows: At the end of the quotation, or in a footnote, use the form below.

> [Emphasis supplied.]   [Italics supplied.]

14. *Position of punctuation marks, relative to quotation marks.* The United States Government Printing Office rule is: The comma and the final period will be placed inside the quotation marks.   Other punctuation marks should be placed inside the quotation marks only if they are a part of the quotation.

> Mr. Justice Holmes said, "I dissent from the decision. . . ."
> Was it "just one of those things"?
> Who asked, "Why?" [A question part of the quotation.]
> The appellant said, "No!"
> He said that belonged to "The Star"; that it was his.

15. *Citing the source: Statutes.*

a. *In the main text.*   References are likely to be casual, as part of a sentence.

> Section 303 requires notice "in writing."

b. *In parenthetical citations in the main text.*   Whether set off by parentheses or commas, or as a separate citation at the end of the sentence, use the form of designation (Sec., sec., §) used in printing the act itself.

> According to that section [Sec., sec., §303] "notice is required to be in writing."
> ". . . notice is required to be in writing" (Sec. 303).
> ". . . notice is required to be in writing." (Sec. 303.)

c. *A verbatim quotation from a statute in the main text.*   Where this requires more than three or four lines, it is blocked off by wide indentions on both sides and dropped two spaces below the preceding text. In federal briefs it is common to make a footnote of the first reference to an act, quoting verbatim, and referring to it thereafter only by section. In such footnote citations quotation marks for the cited matter are the rule.

> The pertinent provisions are as follows:
> "Sec. 5(a). Unfair methods of competition [quoting] 52 Stat. 111-112, 15 U.S.C. §15(a) (1958 ed.)."

Where several rather lengthy sections are to be quoted, a common federal brief practice is to place them all together in an appendix, without quotation marks.

### APPENDIX I

> Relevant provisions of Sec. 5, Sec. 12, and Sec. 15 of the Federal Trade Commission Act (Act of September 26, 1914, 38 Stat. 717, as amended by Act of March 21, 1938, 52 Stat. 111-115, and by Sec. 1107(f) of Act of June 23, 1938, 52 Stat. 1028, 15 U.S.C. Sec. 45, Sec. 52, and Sec. 55):
> Sec. 5(a). Unfair methods of competition [quoting].
> Sec. 12(a). It shall be unlawful [quoting].
> Sec. 15. For the purposes of section 12 [quoting].

## §26.14.   Indexes to briefs.

1. *Scope.* The so-called index is really (a) a table of contents, followed by (b) a résumé of counsel's argument, and closing with (c) a list of authorities cited. Exhibits are best listed in the table of contents part.

2. *Table of contents.* This follows the order of the brief.

3. *Capitalization.* The first word of each new entry is capitalized, thereafter only those words capitalized in the brief itself. Section, chapter and clause references, however, are not capitalized except in tabular citations. (See the Fair Labor Standards Act in the index on page 409, compared with other statutory citations there.)

4. *Table of authorities cited.*

a. *Cases.* List alphabetically, in the same form as in the brief. Court action (usually certiorari granted or denied, or affirmance of appeal) is noted. If certiorari is pending, give the case docket number and the term of court. Dates and a notation of the court deciding are sometimes omitted. Pages in the brief where the case is cited are noted in the right-hand column. Case names are italicized or not, as in the brief itself.

(1) *Alphabeting case names.* Alphabet by significant name, ignoring corporate initials, *ex parte, in re,* etc., but make cross-references as needed. See page 351, par. b and page 353, par. c.

b. *Federal Constitution and statutes.* List the Constitution, then statutes chronologically.

> Act of June 23, 1947, c. 120, 61 Stat. 136, 29 U.S.C. (1958 ed.)
> (Labor Management Relations Act of 1947).

Most federal agency briefs list acts by title, if any. Note the Fair Labor Standards Act of 1938, under "Authorities Cited," below.

c. *State constitutions and statutes.* List constitutions alphabetically by states, followed by statutes listed alphabetically by states.

d. *Miscellaneous material.* List alphabetically by author or title, following the form used in the brief itself. It is common to give the author's full name in the index, however, even though cited only by surname in the brief.

5. *Typography.* Follow the form used in the brief itself. Briefs printed all in roman except the case names are common in all courts.

## INDEX

## AUTHORITIES CITED

*Cases*

## §26.15.  Capitalization.

1. *In general.*  The tendency is to capitalize too much; be conservative.

2. *Proper names and their derivatives.*  Capitalize unless the
derivative has acquired an independent meaning no longer closely
identified with the original.

> Italy, Italian, *but* italics.
> Rome, Roman, *but* roman type.

3. *"The."*  Capitalize when part of an official name.

> *The Queen Mary* [in a case name].
> the Attorney General.

4. *Names of organized bodies.*

> Congress, House, Senate.
> Committee of the Whole, *but* the committee.
> Virginia Assembly, the assembly.
> State Highway Commission, the highway commission.

5. *First words of an independent clause or sentence.*

> The question is, Shall the bill pass?

**a.** *Following a colon, exclamation point or interrogation point.* The first is not capitalized if merely a supplementary remark follows.

> Revolutions are not made: they come.

**b.** *Where the first word following a colon is an independent passage or sentence, or where it is tabular matter.*

> The decision was as follows: That Jones is liable.
> Section 8 provides for these things:
>     1. For a notice in writing.
>     2. For a hearing.
>     3. For an appeal.

**6.** *Suggested capitalization of words frequently used.*

Act: The Merrill Act, Section 13 of that Act; *but* the act, an act of Congress.

Bill: Bill of Rights; *but* the Ives bill, a Congressional bill.

Brief: Brief for Respondent; *but* as said in Apellant's brief.

Circuit: Circuit Court of Appeals; *but* the circuit courts.

Clause: as a heading or title: the Commerce Clause; *but* the commerce clause of the Constitution.

Court: The Supreme Court of the United States, the Court; *but* the Court of Appeals, the court.

District: United States Court for the Southern District of New York; *but* the district courts.

*Ex parte:* in a case name: *Ex parte Smith; but* an *ex parte* hearing.

Federal: capitalize only when part of a proper name: Federal Constitution; *but* federal courts, federal judges.

*Ibid., id.:* capitalize only at beginning of sentence.

*In re* (no period): capitalize only when part of a case report: *In re Perkins.*

Law: as a heading or title: Public Law No. 1.

Number: only as a heading or as part of a title: House Document number 17, page 3; *but* H. Doc. No. 17, 81st Cong., 1st Sess.

Report: only as a title or a proper name: Attorney General's Report, House Report No. 18; *but* the report of the Attorney General for 1949.

Session: as part of a title: Eighty-first Congress, first session, 81st Cong., 1st Sess.; *but* a special session of Congress.

Volume: as a heading only: Volume 2: Rule against perpetuities; *but* volume 2 of Williston, *supra.*

## §26.16.   Abbreviations.

**1.** *Caution.* In employing the short cut which abbreviations provide, the legal writer must never lose sight of the sole object of a citation — to lead its reader to the work cited, without error, ambiguity, or the necessity of consulting additional conversion tables, tables of cases, or the like, for data which the citation itself should have provided. There is never a legitimate choice between brevity and time-saving for the writer on the one hand and clarity for the citation user on the other.

2. *Contractions.* Distinguish these from abbreviations. Dep't, Adm'r, Ass'n, and the like are contractions, not followed by a period unless closing a sentence. A contraction begins and ends with the same letter as the full word; an abbreviation often ends on a different letter: Rev., Stat., La., Wis., etc., are examples. Abbreviations are the preferred style.

3. *Spacing abbreviations.*

a. *Omit spacing between elements generally.* But space between elements of abbreviations consisting of more than one letter; the ampersand (&) is considered a multiliteral abbreviaton.

| | | |
|---|---|---|
| 301 U.S. 15 | 175 S.E. 81 | *NLRB* v. *Jones* |
| C.C. S.D. N.Y. | Sup. Ct. | Fed. Cas. |

b. *Space the following.* The initials of a personal name; before and after unabbreviated words or abbreviations of more than one letter.

*United States* v. *H. J. Heinz Co.*          S.D. Ohio

4. *Second series of law reports.* Many law reports series have gone into their second series, some of which are differently abbreviated than the first series: Fed., F.2d; Atl., A.2d; N.Y. Supp., N.Y.S.2d; Pac., P.2d, etc. When the abbreviation unit next to the figures is multiliteral, space: So. 2d, *not* So.2d.

135 F.2d          69 S.W.2d          13 So. 2d

Unofficial reports often designate their second series as "new series."

29 P.U.R. (N.S.) 18 (1948).

5. *Periods.* With a few exceptions, every abbreviation which stands for a single word is followed by a period.

N.Y.          Ind. App.          App. Div.          LL.B.

The exceptions are:

R.R. (for railroad, a single word); S.S. (for steamship);
WGY (radio call letters); SOS (distress signal);
NLRB, ICC, FTC, CIO (for government agencies and labor unions).

6. *Words not abbreviated.* Some words are not abbreviated in legal writing. A few of them follow.

| day | mount | fort | point | Senator | port |
|------|--------|-------|-------|---------|--------|
| March | April | May | June | July | Figure |
| Alaska | Hawaii | Idaho | Iowa | Ohio | Utah |

7. *Corporate, firm and railway names.*

a. *Corporate titles beginning with an initial.* Give the name in full, but alphabet under both the initial and the surname in the index.

*H. J. Heinz Co.* v. *NLRB*

b. *Railroads' first names.* Spell out the first name, but the rest may commonly be abbreviated. The ampersand (&) should be used for "and" where it is part of the corporate title.

*Chicago, R.I. & P. Ry. Co.* v. *Chicago, M. & St. P.R.R. Co.*

8. *Ampersand (&).* Use this in place of "and" only where it is part of the corporate or firm name, as found in legal documents (incorporation or partnership papers, etc.) or letterheads.

9. *Table of frequently used American abbreviations.* A full table from abbreviation to complete word is found in Price and Bitner, Effective Legal Research (1953), pp. 511-620. An abridged table is included as Appendix III in this book.

### §26.17. Typography.

The type styles recommended below are intended for use in briefs and in student papers, which conform to the style of briefs. They are the styles most commonly found in printed briefs. Publishers of law books, however, vary in their typographical practices, and each issues its own manual of them for use by its authors. The type styles of the publisher of this book do not always agree with those prescribed in this chapter, particularly as to italicizing titles of books and periodical articles.

1. *Function of type styles.* The great majority of briefs print only the case names (except the "v.") in italics, whether in text, footnote or index references, with everything else in roman, and a brief so printed is acceptable in any court or quasi-judicial tribunal. This is simple and easy and reduces the possibility of error.

The use of italics to make more vivid on the printed page the titles of secondary material cited is growing in briefs, however, especially those presented to federal agencies and courts, and that is the style adopted in this chapter. The only problem involved is the determination of what, for the purpose of italics, is a title. Some suggested rules are stated below. In typing, italics are indicated by underlining the words to be italicized.

2. *Statutes and session laws.* All references to section, article, chapter, clause, session laws, statutes etc., are customarily printed

in roman in most legal writing, without large and small caps. In quoting a statute, the typographical style of the matter quoted is adopted.

Law review footnote style is to print the titles of session laws in roman ("New York Laws 1942, c. 387"), but titles of statutes in large and small caps ("CONST.," *not* "Const."; "STAT.," *not* "Stat."; "INT. REV. CODE," *not* "Int. Rev. Code"). This book follows the more usual style, printing both session laws and statutes in roman, without small caps. (Large and small caps are indicated in manuscript by double underscoring the part to be in small caps.)

3. *Case reports: Case names.* Except for the "v." italicize, case names, whether in the main text, footnote or index references. Law reviews italicize case names when commented upon, whether in main text or footnote — including the "v." — but not when merely cited and not commented upon, in the footnotes.

a. *Initials standing for persons.* "A," "B," etc., standing for persons, are capitalized and italicized: *A, B*.

b. *Ex parte, ex rel., In re, Matter of.* In briefs which italicize case names in text or footnote, these terms are also italicized. If case names are not italicized, the Latin terms, but not the English "Matter of" are italicized. *Ex rel.* (an abbreviation) requires a period. *In re* (complete words) does not.

Law reviews differentiate Latin elements of case names typographically from the rest. Thus Ex parte *Sterba* in the text becomes *Ex parte* Sterba in the footnote; *United States* ex rel. *Greathouse* v. *Smith* in the text becomes United States *ex rel.* Greathouse v. Smith in the footnote. Briefs seldom are so complex in their typography.

4. *Case reports: Subsequent history of a case.* When noting that a cited case was later *affirmed, reversed, reversed on other grounds, affirmed* or *reversed sub nom.,* or that *certiorari* or *rehearing* was *denied* or *granted,* the significant words may be italicized. Briefs practically never do this, however. Thus:

> *Joseph A. Holpuch Co.* v. *United States,* 104 Ct. Cl. 67, 67 F. Supp. 949 (1945), certiorari granted sub nom. *United States* v. *Joseph A. Holpuch Co.,* 327 U.S. 772, reversed, 328 U.S. 237 (1946).

5. *Treatises, bulletins, reports.* Most briefs print the entire entry, author and title, in roman type, which is simple and acceptable to courts. Many government briefs, however, following the usual scholarly practice, italicize the title (not including the edition and editor's name), with the rest of the entry in roman. This book recommends the government style.

> Gray, *Rule against Perpetuities* (4th ed., Roland Gray, 1942).

Where the title is that of a periodic report or of a publication assimilated to a statute, print the whole entry in roman; that is, do not italicize "Report," "Annual Report," "Restatement," etc.

> 1947 Atty. Gen. Ann. Rep. 19.
> A.L.I. Restatement, Agency §18 (1933).

Where the title of a series, other than a periodical, forms part of a citation, print in roman.

> Walton Hamilton, *Patents and Free Enterprise* (TNEC Monograph No. 31, 1941), p. 19.

6. *Periodicals and newspapers.* Cite the name of the author of a cited article in roman type, whether the author is a person or an impersonal agency. The majority of briefs cite the title in roman, also, properly enclosed in quotation marks. A substantial number of government briefs, however, italicize the title, wherever appearing, as in text, footnote or index, and that form is recommended. No confusion can result as to the title of the article, as sometime results with other type styles.

> Lathrop, *The Racial Covenant Cases,* 1948 Wis. L. Rev. 509.

Everything in a newspaper citation is printed in roman, except that the title of a signed article is italicized, as in a periodical article.

7. *Congressional publications.* Titles of hearings, committee reports with titles other than "Report," Congressional documents, etc., are italicized.

8. *Italics.* For the use of italics in case names, treatises, periodicals and Congressional publications, see the material immediately preceding this paragraph.

    a. *Capital letters indicating persons.*

> *A* went to see *B* about it.

    b. *Conventional words in legislation and legal documents.*

> *Whereas, Resolved, Provided, Ordered, Be it enacted*

    c. *Latin and other foreign words and phrases.* Few foreign legal words or phrases are now italicized, as most of them have been taken over into the language and it is an unnecessary affectation to italicize.

    (1) *Words not to be italicized.*

| | | | |
|---|---|---|---|
| ad valorem | in toto | nisi | res judicata |
| bona fide | in transitu | nol-pros | stare decisis |
| certiorari | ipso facto | pendente lite | subpoena |
| circa | laissez faire | post mortem | sub nom. |
| contra | mandamus | pro rata | ultra vires |
| habeas corpus | | | |

(2) *Words to be italicized.*

| | | | |
|---|---|---|---|
| *ab initio* | *ex parte* | *infra* | *loc. cit.* |
| *a fortiori* | *ex rel.* | *in limine* | *nunc pro tunc* |
| *amicus curiae* | *ibid.* | *in loco parentis* | *op. cit.* |
| *ante* | *id.* | *in re* | *sic* |
| *coram nobis* | *idem* | *in rem* | *sua sponte* |
| *e.g.* | *i.e.* | *inter se* | *sui generis* |
| *et seq.* | *in extenso* | *inter sese* | *supra* |

# Standard Form of Appellate Brief [1]

[COVER TITLE.]

No. 387

# Supreme Court of the United States

OCTOBER TERM, 1951

---

JONES & COMPANY, *Petitioner,*

*v.*

SMITH CORPORATION, *Respondent*

---

*ON WRIT OF CERTIORARI TO THE UNITED STATES COURT OF APPEALS FOR THE EIGHTH CIRCUIT*

---

**BRIEF FOR PETITIONER**

JOHN JONES SMITH,
*Attorney for Petitioner*

---

[1] This form is reprinted here by permission of a prominent law firm. It is the form supplied to its own attorneys for use by them in writing briefs. It is, of course, only an outline of a complete brief.

# INDEX

## CITATIONS

[FIRST PAGE OF BRIEF]

# Supreme Court of the United States

## OCTOBER TERM, 1951

---

No. 387

JONES & COMPANY, *Petitioner,*

*v.*

SMITH CORPORATION, *Respondent*

---

*ON WRIT OF CERTIORARI TO THE UNITED STATES COURT OF
APPEALS FOR THE EIGHTH CIRCUIT*

---

### BRIEF FOR PETITIONER

---

#### OPINIONS BELOW

The opinion of the District Court (R. 202) is unreported.
The opinion and dissenting opinion in the Court of Appeals
(R. 276) are reported at 182 F.2d 841.

#### JURISDICTION

This is an action for breach of contract, brought in the
District Court of the United States for the Western District of Missouri. The District Court had jurisdiction under
28 U. S. Code Sec. 1332, the plaintiff Smith Corporation
being organized under the laws of the State of Missouri
(R. 36), the defendant Jones & Company being a partnership all of whose members are citizens of the State of Oklahoma (R. 48), and the matter in controversy exceeding the
sum of $3,000 exclusive of interest and costs (R. 171).

The final judgment of the District Court, in favor of the plaintiff for the sum of $4,325.76 and costs, was entered on January 16, 1949 (R. 204). Notice of appeal to the United States Court of Appeals for the Eighth Circuit was filed on March 3, 1949 (R. 207), that Court having jurisdiction of the appeal under 28 U. S. Code Sec. 1291.

The final judgment of the Court of Appeals affirming the judgment of the District Court was entered on August 24, 1951 (R. 282). The petition for a writ of certiorari was filed on October 14, 1951, and was granted on November 20, 1951. The jurisdiction of this Court rests on 28 U. S. Code Sec. 1254(1).

### QUESTIONS PRESENTED

\*     \*     \*     \*

### STATUTE INVOLVED

The pertinent provisions of the Missouri Sale of Goods Law, Missouri Revised Code, Sections 4226-4240 (1936), are set out in full in Appendix A to this brief, pp. i-iii, *infra.*

\*     \*     \*     \*

### STATEMENT

\*     \*     \*     \*

#### History of the Litigation

\*     \*     \*     \*

#### Findings of Fact and Judgment

\*     \*     \*     \*

### SPECIFICATION OF ERRORS TO BE URGED

\*     \*     \*     \*

### SUMMARY OF ARGUMENT

\*     \*     \*     \*

**ARGUMENT**

\* \* \* \*

I

THIS CASE "INVOLVES OR GROWS OUT OF A LABOR DISPUTE" AND THEREFORE IS GOVERNED BY THE NORRIS-LAGUARDIA ACT

Section 1 of the Norris-LaGuardia Act is plain and unambiguous:

> "... no court of the United States ... shall have jurisdiction to issue any restraining order or temporary or permanent injunction in a case involving or growing out of a labor dispute, except in a strict conformity with the provisions of this Act. ..."

The "labor dispute" involved in this case consists primarily of three fundamental issues, etc., etc., etc.

\* \* \* \*

A. *VIOLENCE AGAINST CUSTOMERS IS NEITHER CHARGED, PROVED NOR FOUND*

\* \* \* \*

1. THE FINDING THAT THE POLICE WERE UNABLE AND UNWILLING TO FURNISH ADEQUATE PROTECTION MUST BE SET ASIDE

\* \* \* \*

a. *Upon This Record the District Court Was Clearly Wrong in Finding that any Effort by Plaintiffs to Settle the Dispute Would Have Been Impossible, Useless, or Unreasonable, and upon the Basis of this Finding, in Excusing the Making of any Effort*

\* \* \* \*

# II

ALL CLAUSES OF THE DECREE ENJOINING USE OR THREATS
OF FRAUD MUST BE REVERSED

\*   \*   \*   \*

*A. DISCRIMINATION AGAINST THE INTERNATIONAL*

\*   \*   \*   \*

1.  FINDINGS REQUIRED BY SECTION 7(a)

\*   \*   \*   \*

*a. Speed-up System*

\*   \*   \*   \*

**CONCLUSION**

Wherefore, it is respectfully submitted that the judgment of the court below should be reversed and the cause remanded with instructions to grant the motion to dismiss the complaint.

August 1, 1953

Respectfully submitted,

JOHN JONES SMITH,
*Attorney for Petitioner*

## APPENDIX A

## PERTINENT PROVISIONS OF STATUTES

*1. AGRICULTURAL ADJUSTMENT ACT OF MAY 12, 1933, C. 25, 48 STAT. 31, AS AMENDED, 48 STAT. 676, 49 STAT. 48, 770, 1739, 7 U.S.C. § 617 (1946)*

Sec. 17 (a) Upon the exportation to any foreign country (and/or to the Philippine Islands, the Virgin Islands, American Samoa, the Canal Zone, and the island of Guam) of any product processed wholly or partly from a commodity with respect to which product or commodity a tax has been paid or is payable under this title, the tax due and payable or due and paid shall be credited or refunded. Under regulations prescribed by the Commissioner of Internal Revenue, with the approval of the Secretary of the Treasury, the credit or refund shall be allowed to the consignor named in the bill of lading under which the product is exported or to the shipper or to the person liable for the tax provided the consignor waives any claim thereto in favor of such shipper or person liable for the tax. In the case of rice, a tax due under this title which has been paid by a tax-payment warrant shall be deemed for the purposes of this subsection to have been paid; and with respect to any refund authorized under this section, the amount scheduled by the Commissioner of Internal Revenue. . . .

\* \* \* \*

*2. INTERNAL REVENUE CODE, § 1112*

In any proceeding involving the issue whether the petitioner has been guilty of fraud with intent to evade tax, the burden of proof in respect of such issue shall be upon the Commissioner.

\* \* \* \*

## APPENDIX B

## LEGISLATIVE HISTORY

*1. REPORT OF THE HOUSE COMMITTEE ON WAYS AND MEANS, H. REPT. NO. 2475, 74TH CONG., 2D SESS. (1934), p. 13.*

It is the purpose of Section 601 of Title IV to reenact into law certain sections of the Agricultural Adjustment Act.

# Memorandum of Law [1]

## Question Presented

Under the terms of a will governed by Rhode Island law, does a gift in trust to the testator's daughter for life with a testamentary power of appointment and a gift to "her own right heirs, of my blood" in default of appointment mean that the daughter's heirs take *per stirpes* or *per capita* upon the death of the daughter failing to exercise the power of appointment?

## Conclusion

The Rhode Island cases indicate that the gift would be construed to require a stirpital division.

## Facts

Joseph Paul Jones died a resident of the State of Rhode Island, and his will was proved on February 15, 1911. By the terms of his will, the testator after making certain specific bequests gave the residue of his estate to trustees in trust. He directed that the corpus be divided into five equal shares, one such share to be held in trust for each of his two sons and each of his two daughters, and one share to be held in trust for his wife. The share for each daughter was to be held for her for life, and upon her death, as she might appoint by her will, and in default of such appointment, "to her own right heirs, of my blood." One of the daughters of Joseph Paul Jones died failing to exercise the power of appointment. The question arises, do the heirs of the daughter take *per stirpes* or *per capita.*

## Applicable Statutes

The applicable provisions of the Rhode Island statute of descent and distribution are found in Rhode Island General Laws 1938, ch. 567.

### Course of Descent

§1. Whenever any person having title to any real estate or inheritance shall die intestate as to such estate, it shall descend and pass, in equal portions to his kindred, in the following course:

*First.* To his children or their descendants, if any there be.

*Second.* If there be no children nor their descendants, then to the parents in equal shares, or to the surviving parent of such intestate.

*Third.* If there be no parent, then to the brothers and sisters of such intestate, and their descendants, or such of them as there be.

(As amended by ch. 1283, Public Laws 1943.)

---

[1] An important function of the junior attorneys in a law firm is to submit memoranda of law to seniors, on request. The one here reproduced is an actual memorandum from such a junior to his senior, reproduced here by permission. It shows the form and style desired, though it is somewhat shorter and simpler than most memoranda. Note that the conclusion is given immediately following the statement of the problem, not at the end of the memorandum. The same form and techniques may profitably be employed by law students in their written work.

Section 2 of ch. 567 makes provisions for the event that there be no parent nor brother nor sister.

### Inheritance by Descendants

§5. The descendants of any person deceased shall inherit the estate which such person would have inherited had such person survived the intestate, subject to the express provisions of these canons of descent.

### Distribution of Surplus Property Not Bequeathed

§9. The surplus of any chattels or personal estate of a deceased person, not bequeathed, after the payment of his just debts, funeral charges, and expenses of settling his estate, shall be distributed by order of the probate court which shall have granted administration in manner following:

*First.* — The sum of $3,000.00 from said surplus and one-half of the remainder to the widow or surviving husband forever, if the intestate died without issue.

*Second.* — One-half of said surplus to the widow or surviving husband forever, if the intestate died leaving issue.

*Third.* The residue shall be distributed among the heirs of the intestate in the same manner real estates descend and pass by this chapter but without having any respect to the life estate and discretionary allowance provided by section 4 of this chapter. (As amended by ch. 1283, Public Laws 1943.)

## Case Law

From this it can be seen that the statute itself provides in section 7 for stirpital provision. The descendants are to inherit the share which their deceased ancestor would have taken. However, this statutory direction can be overcome if the will of the person making a gift to "heirs" indicates an intent that the division be *per capita*. For example, in *Oulton* v. *Kidder,* — R.I. —, 128 Atl. 674 (1925), where a testatrix gave the residue of her estate to her brother for life, and upon his death "to Helen E. Oulton and my legal heirs," it was held that Helen Oulton and the legal heirs of the testatrix took *per capita* and not *per stirpes.* The Court said, at 128 Atl. 675,

> The general rules controlling whether a gift to "legal heirs" is to be distributed per capita or per stirpes had been considered at length in *Branch* v. *DeWolf,* 38 R.I. 395, 95 A. 857, and *Turbitt* v. *Carney,* 43 R.I. 582, 114 A. 134. The court said: "heirs at law" commonly not only designated the beneficiaries as those who would inherit in case of intestacy but the quantum of interest each should take. This is determined per stirpes and not per capita, unless a contrary intention appears. If Helen E. Oulton had not been interjected into the residuary clause, there would be good ground for the application of the usual rules calling for a per stirpes distribution. Does the will show any facts indicating a contrary intention?

The Court answers its own question in the affirmative, and finds that the testatrix intended the distribution to be *per capita.* Helen E. Oulton received a specific gift under a separate clause of the will, and the Court found no intention to prefer her, through a stirpital division of the residue, to other nephews and nieces.

Another case in which a gift to "heirs" was held to require a *per capita* division is *Dodge* v. *Slate*, 71 R.I. 191, 43 A.2d 242 (1945). The testator left his entire estate to "my heirs now living, share and share alike." The Court says at 43 A.2d 244,

> In both sentences which constitute clause "First" of the will, the testator leaves the estate to his "heirs." Although there are decisions to the contrary, it is generally held that, in the absence of language in the will indicating a different intention, a devise or bequest to a testator's "heirs," without qualification, designates not only the persons who are to take, but also the manner in which the estate shall be distributed, both being in accordance with the statute of intestate succession. The determining issue on this point therefore is whether the testator intended a distribution to his estate to be different from the one prescribed by such statute.

By singling out the words "share and share alike" and "equally among the heirs," the Court finds an intention that the estate be distributed to the heirs *per capita*. Great stress is laid on the word "among" as indicative of an intention that the distribution be *per capita*.

The will of Joseph Paul Jones appears to contain not the slightest hint of an intention that the distribution to the heirs of his daughter should be other than that provided by the statute, that is, stirpital. It is assumed, that at the time the will was executed, the daughters of the testator were unmarried and childless, consequently it cannot be argued that there were any particular individuals in mind when he used the word "heirs." It would seem that here, the general rule of a *per stirpes* provision should apply. No significance can be attached to the word "right" or the words "of my blood" used in the phrase "to her own right heirs, of my blood." These words in no way connote a *per capita* provision. The words "right heirs" are synonymous with "legal heirs," or just "heirs," *Starrett* v. *Botsford*, 64 R.I. 1, 9 A.2d 871 (1931). The cases of *Oulton* v. *Kidder, supra,* and *Dodge* v. *Slate, supra,* which found an intention that there be a *per capita* distribution are clearly distinquishable on their facts from the situation at hand.

A recent case, *Powers* v. *Dossett,* — R.I. —, 81 A.2d 275 (1951), held that a gift to heirs at law required a *per stirpes* distribution. In this case a testatrix established by her will a trust for her father-in-law and mother-in-law for life, and upon the death of the survivor directed her trustee "to pay over to my heirs at law all [the] trust estate." In a construction proceeding, the Court said,

> In construing the meaning of heirs at law as used in the instant will, we find nothing therein to show clearly that the testatrix intended that those answering such description should be determined at a time other than at her death. We therefore apply the general rule to the will before us and decide that the testatrix' heirs at law are those to whom her estate and property would pass immediately upon her death by operation of law under the statutes of descent and distribution of this state. It follows that our answer to the first question is that the balance of the trust estate should be distributed among the heirs at law of the testatrix *per stirpes*.

As previously said, no intention can be found in the will of Joseph Paul Jones that the distribution to the heirs of his daughter should be other than *per stirpes*. His daughter's heirs will naturally be ascertained at the time of her death.

February 10, 1953

# APPENDIX III

# Abbreviations Commonly Used in Anglo-American Law

*Scope of definitions.* The abbreviations defined in this list are those which the law student is most likely to encounter in his course work. No attempt is made at such complete coverage as is required for extensive research. The most complete list of abbreviations for Anglo-American law is found in Price and Bitner, Effective Legal Research (1953), Appendix VI, to which the student is referred when confronted by a less common abbreviation.

The present list aims to include practically all United States — federal and state — law reports; all English law reports of general interest, and the principal Canadian law reports of general interest. Excluded law reports are Scottish, Irish, as well as English and Canadian election, bail, bankruptcy, most ecclesiastical reports and others of restricted scope.

Legal periodical abbreviations included are those referring to periodicals of general interest in law school instruction. Where the abbreviation is self-explanatory, it is not defined in this list; where some doubt as to its meaning may exist, the abbreviation is defined. Thus, Harv. L. Rev. is not defined, but H.L.R. is; Georget. L.J. is not defined, but Geo. L.J. is.

*Alphabetical arrangement.* In order to follow the forms of abbreviations as found in the literature, the abbreviations are listed herein in three different sequences for each initial letter.

1. Abbreviations of which the *first* element is a single letter and the *second* element is not an ampersand (&). Thus:

      A.B.C.      A.R.R.      A.Ins.Co.      A.T.&T.Co.

2. Next come abbreviations of which the *first* element is a single letter and the *second* is an ampersand. Thus:

      A.&B.      A.&E.      A.&E.Pat.Cas.

3. Last come abbreviations, the *first* element of which is composed of two or more letters, as:

      Ab.Eq.Cas.      Am.L.Rev.      Ad.&El.

*Abbreviations employed in the definitions.* In the definitions themselves in this list, certain standard abbreviations are sometimes employed, among which are the following:

| | | | |
|---|---|---|---|
| Admin. | Administration | H.L. | House of Lords |
| Cas. | Cases | Jour. | Journal |
| Ch. | Chancery | K.B. | King's Bench |
| C.P. | Common Pleas | N.P. | Nisi Prius |
| Comm. | Commission | P.C. | Privy Council |
| Cr.Cas.Res. | Crown Cases Reserved | Pr.R. | Practice Reports |
| Ct. | Court | Q.B. | Queen's Bench |
| Div. | Division | R.C. | Rolls Court |
| Eq. | Equity | Rep. | Reports |
| Ex. | Exchequer | UN | United Nations |

**A.** Abbott
Alabama
American
Arkansas
Atlantic Reporter
Louisiana Annuals

**A.2d** Atlantic Reporter, Second Series

**AAA** Agricultural Adjustment Admin., *U.S.*

**A.B.** Anonymous Rep. at end of Benloe, *Eng.*

**A.B.A.J[o].** American Bar Assn. Jour.

**A.B.A.Rep.** American Bar Assn. Rep.

**A.B.C.** Australian Bankruptcy Cas.

**A.C.** Advance Cal. Rep.
Law Rep., Appeal Cas., *Eng.*

**A.C.A.** Advance Cal. Appellate Rep.

**A.C.L.J.** American Civil Law Jour.

**A.C.M.** Court-Martial Rep. Air Force Cas.

**A.C.M.S.** Special Court-Martial, U.S. Air Force

**A.D.** Agriculture Dec., *U.S.*
American Dec.
New York Sup. Ct. Appellate Div. Rep.

**AEC** Atomic Energy Comm., *U.S.*

**A.E.L.R.** All England Law Rep.

**A.F.Rep.** Alaska Fed. Rep.

**AFTR** American Fed. Tax Rep. (P-H)

**A.G.** Attorney General's Opinions, *U.S.*

**A.G.O.** Same as above

**AGO** Adjutant General's Office, *U.S.*

**A.J.** American Jurist

**A.K.Marsh.** A. K. Marshall (8-10 Ky.)

**A.L.C. (or ALC)** American Labor Cas. (P-H)

**A.L.J.** Albany Law Jour.

**A.L.R.** American Labor Cas. (P-H)
American Law Rep., Annot.

**A.L.Reg.** American Law Register

**AMS** Agricultural Marketing Service, *U.S.*

**A.M.C.** American Maritime Cas.

**A.M.S.,P.&S.** Agricultural Marketing Service, P.&S. Docket, *U.S.*

**A.Moo.** A. Moore Rep., in 1 Bosanquet & Puller, *Eng.*

**A.N.C.** Abbott's New Cas., *N.Y.*
American Negligence Cas.

**A.N.R.** American Negligence Rep.

**AO** Admin. Order, *U.S.*

**A.R.** American Rep.
Atlantic Reporter

**A.Rep.** American Rep.
Atlantic Reporter

**A.S.R.** American State Rep.

**A.&E.** Admiralty and Ecclesiastical, *Eng.*
Adolphus & Ellis, Q.B. Rep., *Eng.*

**A.&E. Ann.Cas.** American and English Annot. Cas.

**A.&E.N.S.** Adolphus & Ellis, New Series, *Eng.*

**A.&H.** Arnold & Hodges, Q.B. Rep., *Eng.*

**Abb.** Abbott, Cir. and Dist. Ct. Rep., *U.S.*

**Abb.Adm.** Abbott's Admiralty Rep., *U.S.*

**Abb.App.Dec.** Abbott Ct. of Appeals Dec., *N.Y.*

**Abb.C.C.** Abbott's Cir. Ct. Rep., *U.S.*

**Abb.Ct.App.** Abbott's Ct. of Appeals Dec., *N.Y.*

**Abb.Dec.** Same as above

**Abb.N.Cas.** Abbott's New Cas., *N.Y.*

**Abb.N.Y.App.** Abbott's Ct. of Appeals Dec., *N.Y.*

**Abb.Pr.** Abbott's Practice Rep., *N.Y.*

**Abb.Pr.N.S.** Same, New Series

**Abb.U.S.** Abbott's Cir. Ct. Rep., *U.S.*

**Acq.** Acquiescence by Commissioner in Tax Court or Board of Tax Appeals decision, *U.S.*

**Act.P.C.** Acts of the Privy Council (Dasent), *Eng.*

**Act.P.C.N.S.** Same, New Series

**Act.Pr.C.** Acton's Rep., Prize Cas., *Eng.*

**Ad.&El.** Adolphus & Ellis, K.B. Rep., *Eng.*

**Ad.&El.N.S.** Same, New Series

**Adams** Adams' Rep. (41, 42 Me.)
Adams' Rep. (1 N.H.)

**Add.** Addison's Rep. (Pa. Sup. Ct.)

**Add.Pa.** Addison's County Ct. Rep., *Pa.*

**Ad. L. Rev.** Admin. Law Review

**Adm.&Ecc.** Law Rep., Admiralty and Ecclesiastical, *Eng.*

**Adol.&El.** Adolphus & Ellis, Q.B. Rep., *Eng.*

**Adol.&El.N.S.** Same, New Series

**Aik.** Aiken's Rep., *Vt.*

**Air L.R.** Air Law Rev.

**Al.** Alabama
Aleyn, K.B. Rep., *Eng.*

**Ala.** Alabama Sup. Ct.
Minor's Ala. Rep. 1820-26

**Ala.App.** Alabama Appeals Rep.

**Ala.Law.** Alabama Lawyer

**Ala.N.S.** Alabama Rep., New Series, 1840-date

**Ala.Sel.Cas.** Alabama Select Cas. (and in 37-39 Ala.)

**Alaska** Alaska Rep.

**Alaska Fed.** Alaska Fed. Rep.

**Alb.L.J.** Albany Law Jour.

**Alb.L.R.** Alberta Law Rep.

**Alb.L.Rev.** Albany Law Rev.

**Ald.** Alden's Condensed Rep., *Pa.*

**Alexander** Alexander's Rep. (66-72 Miss.)

**Aleyn** Aleyn's K.B. Rep., *Eng.*

**All.E.R.** All England Law Rep. (formerly All England Law Rep. Annot.)

**Allen** Allen's Rep. (83-96 Mass.)
Allen's Rep. (6-11 New Brunswick)
Allen's Rep. (1-2 Washington Terr. 1854-85)

**Allin.** Allinson's Pa. Super. and Dist. Ct. Rep.

**Alta.L.R.** Alberta Law Rep.

**Am.B.A.** American Bar Assn.

**Am.B.R.** American Bankruptcy Rep.

**Am.B.R.N.S.** Same, New Series

**Am.Bank.Rev.** American Bankruptcy Rev.

**Am.Bar.Ass.J.** American Bar Assn. Jour.

**Am.Dec.** American Dec.

**Am.Dig.** American Digest

**Am.Fed.TaxR.** American Fed. Tax Rep. (P-H)

**Am.Ins.Rep.** American Insolvency Rep.

**Am.J.Comp.Law** American Jour. of Comparative Law

**Am.J.Int.L.** American Jour. of International Law

**Am.Jud.Soc.** American Judicature Soc. (Bulletins or Jour.)

**Am.Jur.** American Jurisprudence
American Jurist

**Am.Lab.Cas.** American Labor Cas. (P-H)

**Am.Lab.Arb.Cas.** American Labor Arbitration Cas. (P-H)

**Am.Lab.Leg.Rev.** American Labor Legis. Rev.

**Am.LawReg.** American Law Register

**Am.Mar.Cas.** American Maritime Cas.

**Am.Neg.Cas.** American Negligence Cas.

**Am.St.P.** American State Papers

**Am.St.Rep.** American State Rep. (Annot. Cases System)

**Am.Tr.M.Cas.** American Trade Mark Cas. (Cox)

**Amb.** Ambler's English Ch. Rep.

**Amer.** American
Amerman's Rep. (111-115 Pa.)

**Amer.LawReg.(N.S.)** American Law Register, New Series

**Amer.LawReg.(O.S.)** Same, Old Series

**Ames** Ames' Rep. (1 Minn.)
Ames' Rep. (4-7 R.I.)

**Ames,K&B.** Ames, Knowles & Bradley (8 R.I.)

**An.** Anonymous, at end of Benloe Rep., *Eng.*

**And.** Anderson's C.P. Rep. *temp.* Eliz., *Eng.*
Andrews' K.B. Rep., *Eng.*
Andrews' Rep. (63-73 Conn.)

**Andr.** Andrews' K.B. Rep., *Eng.*

**Ang.** Angell's R.I. Rep.
Angell & Durfee Reports (1 R.I.)

**Ang.&Dur.** Same as above

**Ann.** Cunningham's Rep. *temp.* Hardwicke, K.B., 7-10 Geo. II

**Ann.Cas.** American and English Annot. Cas.
American Annot. Cases
New York Annot. Cases

**Annaly**   Lee's K.B. Rep. *temp.*
Hardwicke, Annaly ed., *Eng.*

**Anst.**   Anstruther's Rep., Ex., *Eng.*

**Anth.**   Anthon's N.Y.N.P. Rep.

**Anth.N.P.**   Same as above

**Ap.Bre.**   Breese's Ill. Rep., Appendix

**App.**   Appleton's Rep. (19, 20 Me.)
Ohio Appellate Rep.

**App.Bd.O.C.S.**   Office of Contract
Settlement, Appeal Board Decisions, *U.S.*

**App.Cas.**   Law Rep., Appeal Cas.,
*Eng.*

**App.D.C.**   Appeal Cases, District of
Columbia

**App.Div.**   Appellate Div. Rep., *N.Y.*

**App.Rep.**   Ontario Appeal Rep.

**Appleton**   Appleton's Rep. (19, 20
Me.)

**Arb.J.**   Arbitration Jour.

**Arb.J.N.S.**   Same, New Series

**Archer**   Archer's Rep. (2 Fla.)

**Archer&Hogue**   Archer & Hogue (2
Fla.)

**Armour**   Manitoba Q.B. Rep. *temp.*
Wood

**Arn.**   Arnold's Rep., C.P., *Eng.*

**Arn&H.**   Arnold & Hodges' Q.B.
Rep., *Eng.*

**Arn.&Hod.**   Same as above

**Ash[m].**   Ashmead Pa. Rep. 1808-41

**Asp.**   Aspinall's Maritime Cas., *Eng.*

**Asp.Cas.**   Same as above

**Asp.M.C.**   Same as above

**Asp.M.L.C.**   Aspinall's Maritime
Law Cas., *Eng.*

**Atk.**   Atkyn's Ch. Rep., *Eng.*

**Atl.**   Atlantic Reporter

**Atty.Gen.Op.**   Attorney General's
Opinions

**Atw[ater]**   Atwater's Rep. (1 Minn.)

**B**   Barbour's N.Y. Rep.
Weekly Law Bulletin (Ohio)

**B.Bar**   Bench and Bar

**B.C.**   Bail Court
Bankruptcy Cases
British Columbia Rep.

**B.C.A.**   Board of Contract Appeals
Dec., *U.S.*

**B.C.Ind.&Com.L.R.**   Boston College
Ind. & Com. Law Rev.

**B.C.R.**   British Columbia Rep.

**B.Ch.**   Barbour's Ch. Rep., *N.Y.*

**BIS**   Bank for International Settle-
ments

**BLS**   Bureau of Labor Statistics, *U.S.*

**B.M.**   Burrow's Rep. *temp.* Mansfield, *Eng.*

**B.Mon.**   Ben Monroe Rep. (40-57
Ky.)

**B.Moore**   Moore C.P. Rep., *Eng.*

**B.N.A.**   Bureau of National Affairs
(unofficial), *U.S.*

**B.N.C.**   Bingham's New Cas., C.P.,
*Eng.*
Brook's New Cas., K.B., *Eng.*
Busbee's Rep. (44, 45 N.C.)

**B.P.N.R.**   Bosanquet & Puller, New
Rep., C.P., *Eng.*

**B.R.**   Bancus Regis [King's Bench]
Bankruptcy Rep.
Bankruptcy Register
Board of Review, U.S. Army

**B.R.C.**   British Ruling Cases

**B.R.H.**   Cases *temp.* Hardwicke,
K.B., *Eng.*

**B.T.A.**   Board of Tax Appeals, *U.S.*

**B.U.L.Rev.**   Boston Univ. Law Rev.

**B.&A.**   Barnewall & Adolphus' K.B.
Rep., *Eng.*
Barnewall & Alderson's K.B. Rep.,
*Eng.*

**B.&Ad.**   Barnewall   and   Adolphus
K.B. Rep., *Eng.*

**B.&Ald.**   Barnewall   and   Alderson,
K.B. Rep., *Eng.*

**B.&B.**   Broderip & Bingham's C.P.
Rep., *Eng.*

**B.&Bar**   Bench and Bar

**B.&C.**   Barnewall & Cresswell, K.B.
Rep., *Eng.*

**B.&D.**   Benloe & Dalison's C.P. Rep.,
*Eng.*

**B.&G.**   Brownlow & Goldesborough's
N.P. Rep., *Eng.*

**B.&H.**   Blatchford & Howland Dist.
Ct. Rep., *U.S.*

**B.&L.**   Browning & Lushington's Admiralty Rep., *Eng.*

**B.&M.[acn].**   Browne & Macnamara's
Rep., *Eng.*

**B.&P.**   Bosanquet & Puller C.P., Ex.
and H.L. Rep., *Eng.*

**B.&P.N.R.**   Bosanquet & Puller, New
Rep., *Eng.*

**B.&S.** Best & Smith's Q.B. Rep., *Eng.*

**Bac.Abr.** Bacon's Abridgement, *Eng.*

**Bac.Rep.** Bacon's Dec. (Ritchie), *Eng.*

**Bach** Bach's Rep. (19-21 Mont.)

**Bagl.** Bagley's Rep. (16 Cal.)

**Bagl.&Har.** Bagley & Harman Rep. (17-19 Cal.)

**Bai[l].** Bailey's Law Rep., *S.C.*

**Bai[l].Eq.** Bailey's Eq. Rep., *S.C.*

**Bail.** Bailey's Equity or Law Rep., *S.C.*

**Baild.** Baildon's Select Cases in Chancery, *Eng.*

**Bailey** Bailey's Rep., *S.C.*

**Bald[w].** Baldwin's Rep., Cir. Ct., *U.S.*

**Bald.App.** Appendix to 11 Peters, *U.S.*

**Bald.C.C.** Baldwin's Cir. Ct. Rep., *U.S.*

**Balt.C.Rep.** Baltimore City Rep.

**Bank.L.J.** Banking Law Jour.

**Banks** Banks Rep. ((1-5 Kan.)

**Bann.** Bannister's C.P. Rep., *Eng.*

**Bann.Br.** Bannister's O. Bridgman's C.P. Rep., *Eng.*

**Bann.&A[rd].** Banning & Arden's Patent Cas., *U.S.*

**Bar.** Barbour, N.Y. Rep.
Barnardiston, Ch. and K.B. Rep., *Eng.*

**Bar.&Ad.** Barnewall & Adolphus' K.B. Rep., *Eng.*

**Bar.&Al.** Barnewall & Alderson, K.B. Rep., *Eng.*

**Bar.&Cr.** Barnewall & Cresswell, K.B. Rep., *Eng.*

**Barb.** Arkansas Rep. (14-42 Ark.)
Barbour's N.Y. Sup. Ct. Rep.
Barbour's Ch. Cas. (Contracts), *Eng.*

**Barb.Ch.** Barbour's N.Y. Ch. Rep.

**Barb.S.C.** Barbour's N.Y. Sup. Ct. Rep.

**Barber** Barber's Rep. (14-42 Ark.)

**Barn.** Barnardiston, Ch. and K.B. Rep., *Eng.*
Barnes' C.P. Rep., *Eng.*

**Barn.Ch.** Barnardiston's Ch. Rep., *Eng.*

**Barn.K.B.** Barnardiston's K.B. Rep., *Eng.*

**Barn.&A[dol].** Barnewall & Adolphus' K.B. Rep., *Eng.*

**Barn.&A[ld].** Barnewall & Alderson, K.B. Rep., *Eng.*

**Barn.&Cr.** Barnewall & Cresswell, K.B. Rep., *Eng.*

**Barnf.&S.** Barnfield & Stiness' Rep. (20 R.I.)

**Barr.** Barr Rep. (1-10 Pa. State)
Barrows' Rep. (18 R.I.)

**Barr.Mss.** Barradall's Manuscript Rep., *Va.*

**Bates** Bates' Del. Ch. Rep.

**Bax[t].** Baxter's Rep. (60-68 Tenn.)

**Bay** Bay's Rep. (1-3, 5-8 Mo.)
Bay's S.C. Rep.

**Beasl.** Beasley's N.J. Eq. Rep.

**Beck** Beck's Col. Rep.

**Bedell** Bedell's Rep. (163-191 N.Y.)

**Bee** Bee's Dist. Ct. Rep., *U.S.*

**Bee Alm.** Bee's Dist. Ct. Rep., *U.S.*

**Bee C.C.R.** Bee's Crown Cas. Res., *Eng.*

**Bel.** Bellewe's K.B. Rep., *Eng.*

**Bel.Ca.t.H.VIII.** Bellewe's Cas. *temp.* Henry VIII (Brooke's New Cas.), *Eng.*

**Bell.** Bell's Crown Cas. Res., *Eng.*
Bellewe's K.B. Rep., *Eng.*
Bellinger's Rep. (4-8 Ore.)

**Bell C.C.** T. Bell's Crown Cas. Res., *Eng.*

**Bell.Cas.t.H.VIII.** Brooke's New Cas., *Eng.*

**Bell.Cas.t.R.II** Bellewe's K.B. Rep. *temp.* Rich. II, *Eng.*

**Bell Cr.Cas.** Bell's Crown Cas. Res., *Eng.*

**Bell H.L.** Bell's H.L. Cas., *Eng.*

**Bellewe** Bellewe's Cas. *temp.* Rich. II, *Eng.*

**Bellewe t.H.VIII** Brooke's New Cas., *Eng.*

**Bellinger** Bellinger's Rep. (4-8 Ore.)

**Belt Bro.** Brown's Ch. Cases, by Belt, *Eng.*

**Belt's Sup.** Belt's Supplement to Vesey Senior's Ch. Rep., *Eng.*

**Belt Ves.Sen.** Belt's ed. of Vesey Senior's Ch. Rep., *Eng.*

**Ben.** Benedict's Dist. Ct. Rep., *U.S.*

Benloe's C.P. and K.B. Rep., *Eng.*

**Ben.Monroe**　Ben Monroe's Rep. (40-57 Ky.)

**Ben.&Dal.**　Benloe & Dalison's C.P. Rep., *Eng.*

**Bendl.**　*See* Benloe

**Bened.**　Benedict's Dist. Ct. Rep., *U.S.*

**Benl.**　*See* Benloe

**Benl.inKeil.**　Benloe in Keilway Rep., *Eng.*

**Benl.New**　Benloe's K.B. and C.P. Rep., 1661 ed., *Eng.*

**Benl.Old**　Benloe & Dalison Com. Pl. C.P. Rep., *Eng.*

**Benl.&Dal.**　Benloe & Dalison's C.P. Rep., *Eng.*

**Benloe**　Benloe's K.B. & C.P. Rep., *Eng.*

**Benn.**　Bennett's Rep. (1 Cal.)
Bennett's Rep. (1 Dak.)
Bennett's Rep. (16-21 Mo.)

**Benne.**　Modern Rep., v. 7, *Eng.*

**Bennett**　*See* Benn.

**Ber.**　Berton's New Brunswick Rep.

**Berks**　Berks County Law Jour., *Pa.*

**Berry**　Berry's Rep. (1-28 Mo. App.)

**Bert.**　Berton's New Brunswick Rep.

**Best&Sm.**　Best & Smith's Q.B. Rep., *Eng.*

**Betts.Dec.**　Blatchford & Howland Dist. Ct. Rep., *U.S.*
Olcott's Dist. Ct. Rep., *U.S.*

**Bibb.**　Bibb's Rep. (4-7 Ky.)

**Bick.**　Bicknell & Hawley's Rep. (10-20 Nev.)

**Bick.&Hawl.**　Bicknell & Hawley's Rep. (10-20 Nev.)

**Big.Plac.**　Bigelow's Placita Anglo-Normanica, *Eng.*

**Bin.**　Binney's Rep. (Pa. 1799-1814)

**Bing.**　Bingham's C.P. Rep., *Eng.*

**Bing.N.C.**　Bingham's New Cas., *Eng.*

**Binn.**　Binney's Rep., *Pa.*

**Birk.J.**　Birkenhead's Judgments (H.L. 1919-22), *Eng.*

**Bis[s].**　Bissell's Cir. Ct. Rep., *U.S.*

**Bk.**　Black's Sup. Ct. Rep. (66, 67 U.S.)

**Bl.**　Same as above
Blackford's Ind. Rep. (1817–47)

**Blackstone's Commentaries**
Henry Blackstone's C.P. Rep., *Eng.*
William Blackstone's K.B. Rep., *Eng.*
Blatchford's Cir. Ct. Rep., *U.S.*

**Bl.C.C.**　Blatchford's Cir. Ct. Rep., *U.S.*

**Bl.Comm.**　Blackstone's Commentaries

**Bl.N.S.**　Bligh's H.L. Rep., New Series, *Eng.*

**Bl.Pr.Cas.**　Blatchford's Prize Cas., *U.S.*

**Bl.R.**　William Blackstone's K.B. Rep., *Eng.*

**Bl.W.**　Same as above

**Bl.&H.**　Blake & Hedges' Rep. (2, 3 Ind.)
Blatchford & Howland's Dist. Ct. Rep., *U.S.*

**Bl.&How.**　Blatchford & Howland's Admiralty Rep., *U.S.*

**Bla.Ch.**　Bland's Chancery Rep., *Md.*

**Bla.H.**　Henry Blackstone's C.P. Rep., *Eng.*

**Bla.W.**　William Blackstone's K.B. Rep., *Eng.*

**Black.**　Black's Rep. (30-53 Ind.)
Black's Sup. Ct. Rep. (66, 67 U.S.)
Blackford's Rep. (Ind. 1817-47)
Henry Blackstone's C.P. Rep., *Eng.*
William Blackstone's K.B. Rep., *Eng.*
Blackstone's Rep., K.B., *temp.* Geo. II, III; C.P., *temp.* Geo III, *Eng.*

**Black.Cond.Rep.**　Blackwell's Condensed Rep., *Ill.*

**Black.H.**　Henry Blackstone's C.P., Rep., *Eng.*

**Black.Jus.**　Blackerby's Justices' Cas., *Eng.*

**Black.R.**　*See* Black.

**Black.W.**　William Blackstone's K.B. Rep., *Eng.*

**Blackf.**　Blackford's Rep. (Ind. 1817-47)

**Blackst.**　Blackstone's Rep., K.B., *temp.* Geo. II, III; C.P., *temp.* Geo. III, *Eng.*

**Blackw.Cond.**　Blackwell's Condensed Rep., *Ill.*

**Blair Co.L.R.** Blair County Law Rep., *Pa.*

**Blake** Blake's Rep. (1 Mont.).

**Blake&H.** Blake & Hedges' Mont. Rep.

**Bland** Bland's Ch. Rep. (Md. 1811-32)

**Blatch.** Blatchford's Cir. Ct. Rep., *U.S.*

**Blatch.Pr.Cas.** Blatchford's Prize Cas., *U.S.*

**Blatch.&H.** Blatchford & Howard's Dist. Ct. Rep., *U.S.*

**Bleck[ley].** Bleckley's Rep. (34, 35 Ga.)

**Bli.** Bligh's Rep., H.L., *Eng.*

**Bli.N.S.** *Same,* New Series

**Bligh.** *See* Bli.

**Bliss.** Delaware County Rep., *Pa.*

**Bloom.Man.** Bloomfield's Manumission Cas., *N.J.*

**Blm.Neg.** Bloomfield's Negro Cas., *N.J.*

**Bond** Bond's Cir. Ct. Rep.,*U. S.*

**Bond Md.App.** Proceedings of Court of Appeal of Maryland (in American Legal Records, v. 1)

**Boor[aem]** Booraem's Rep. (6-8 Cal.)

**Booth** Chester Palatine Courts 1811, *Eng.*

**Bos.** Bosworth's Super. Ct. Rep. *N.Y.*

**Bos.&P[u].** Bosanquet & Puller's C.P. Rep., *Eng.*

**Bos.&Pul.N.R.** Bosanquet & Puller's New Rep., C.P., *Eng.*

**Bosw.** Bosworth's N.Y. Sup. Ct. Rep.

**Bow.** Bowler & Bowers (U.S. Comptroller's Dec., v. 2, 3)

**Boyce** Boyce's Rep. (24-30 Del.).

**Br.** Bracton; Bradford; Bradwell; Brayton; Breese; Brevard; Brewster; Bridgman; British; Brockenbrough; Brooke; Brown; Browne; Brownlow

**Br.Abr.** Brooke's Abridgement, *Eng.*

**Br.C.C.** British Crown Cas.
Brown's Ch. Cas., *Eng.*

**Br.Cr.Ca.** British Crown Cas.

**Br.N.C.** Brook's New Cas., K.B., *Eng.*

**Br.P.C.** Brown's Ch. Cas., *Eng.*

**Br.&B.** Broderip & Bingham's C.P. Rep., *Eng.*

**Br.&Col.Pr.Cas.** British and Colonial Prize Cas.

**Br.&G[old].** Brownlow & Goldesborough's C.P. Rep., *Eng.*

**Br.&L[ush].** Browning & Lushington's Admiralty Rep., *Eng.*

**Br.&R.** Brown & Rader's Rep. (137 Mo.)

**Bra.** Bracton's De Legibus Angliae, *Eng.*

**Bract.** Same as above

**Brad.** Bradford's Rep. (Iowa, 1838-41)
Bradford's N. Y. Surrogate Rep.
Bradford's Somerset Star Chamber, *Eng.*
Bradwell's Rep. (1-20 Ill. App.)

**Bradb.** Bradbury's Pleading and Practice Rep., *N.Y.*

**Bradf.** *See* Brad.

**Bradw.** Bradwell's Ill., Appellate Rep.

**Brame** Brame's Rep. (66-72 Miss.)

**Branch** Branch's Rep. (1 Fla.)

**Brant.** Brantley's Rep. (80-116 Md.)

**Brayt.** Brayton's Rep. (Vt. 1815-19)

**Breese** Breese's Rep. (1 Ill.)

**Brev.** Brevard's Rep. (2, 3 S.C.)

**Brew[er].** Brewer's Rep. (19-26 Md.)

**Brew[st].** Brewster's Rep. (Pa. 1856-73).

**Brew.(Md)**. Brewer's Md. Rep.

**Bridg.J.** J. Bridgman's C.P. Rep., *Eng.*

**Bridg.O.** O. Bridgman's C.P. Rep., *Eng.*

**Brief** Brief of Phi Delta Phi

**Bright.** Brightly's N.P. Rep., *Pa.*

**Bright,N.P.** Same as above

**Brisbin** Brisbin's Rep. (in 1 Minn.)

**Bro.** Brooke. *See* Brooke
Brown's English Ch. Rep.
Brown's Parliamentary Cas., *Eng.*
Brown's Mich. N.P. Rep.
Brown's Rep. (53-65; 80-136 Mo.)
Browne's Rep. (Pa. 1801-14)

**Bro.Ab.** Brooke's Abridgement, *Eng.*

**Bro.A.&R.** Brown's Dist. Ct. (Admiralty and Revenue) Rep., *U.S.*

**Bro.Adm.** Brown's Admiralty Rep., *U.S.*

**Bro.C.C.**  W. Brown's Ch. Cas., *Eng.*

**Bro.Ch.**  Brown's Ch. Rep., *Eng.*

**Bro.N.C.**  R. Brooke's New Cas., *Eng.*

**Bro.N.P.**  Brown's Mich. N.P. Rep.

**Bro.P.C.**  J. Brown's Cases in Parliament, *Eng.*

**Bro.Pa.**  Browne's Pa. Rep.

**Bro.&G.**  Brownlow & Goldesborough's C.P. Rep., *Eng.*

**Bro.&H.**  Brown & Hemingway's Rep. (53-65 Miss.)

**Bro.&L[ush].**  Browning & Lushington's Admiralty Cas., *Eng.*

**Brock.**  Brockenbrough's Marshall's Dec., U.S. Cir. Ct.

**Brock. Cas.**  Brockenbrough's Va. Cas.

**Brock.&H[ol].**  Brockenbrough & Holmes Va. Cas.

**Brod.&Bing.**  Broderip & Bingham's C.P. Rep., *Eng.*

**Brooke**  Brooke's New Cas., K.B., *Eng.*

**Brooke N.C.**  Brooke's New Cas., *Eng.*

**Brooke(Petit)**  Brooke's New Cas., *Eng.*

**Brooks**  Brooks' Rep. (106-119 Mich.)

**Brown**  Brown's Dist. Ct. Rep., *U.S.*
Brown's Ch. Rep., *Eng.*
Brown's Rep. (Mich. N.P.)
Brown's Reports (53-65 Miss.)
Brown's Reports (4-25 Neb.)
Brown's Parliamentary Cas., *Eng.*
Brownlow & Goldesborough's C.P. Rep., Eng.

**Brown A.&R.**  Brown's Dist. Ct. Rep. (Admiralty and Revenue Cas.), *U.S.*

**Brown Adm.**  Brown's Admiralty Rep.

**Brown C.**  Brown's Ch. Cas. *temp.* Lord Thurlow, *Eng.*

**Brown N.P.**  Brown's Mich. N.P. Rep.

**Brown.&Gold.**  Brownlow & Goldesborough's C.P. Rep., *Eng.*

**Brown&H.**  Brown & Hemingway's Rep. (53-58 Miss.)

**Brown&Lush.**  Browning & Lushington's Rep., Admiralty, *Eng.*
Brown's Rep. (97-109 Mass.)

**Browne**  Browne's Civil Procedure Rep., *N.Y.*
Browne's Rep. (Pa. 1801-14)

**Browne&Gray**  Browne & Gray's Rep. (110-114 Mass.)

**Brownl.**  Brownlow & Goldesborough's C.P. Rep., *Eng.*

**Buch.**  Buchanan's Rep. (71-85 N.J. Eq.)

**Buchan.**  *See* Buch.

**Buchanan**  *See* Buch.

**Buck**  Buck's Rep. (7-8 Mont.)

**Buck.Dec.**  Buckner's Dec. (in Freeman's Miss. Ch. Rep. 1839-43)

**Buff.Super.Ct.**  Buffalo (N.Y.), Sup. Ct. Rep., Sheldon

**Bull.**  Bulletin
Weekly Law Bulletin, Ohio

**Bull.Cr.Soc.**  Bull. Copyright Soc. of U.S.A.

**Bull.JAG**  Bulletin of Judge Advocate General of Army, *U.S.*

**Bull.N.P.**  Buller's N.P.,*Eng.*

**Bull.O.**  Weekly Law Bulletin, Ohio

**Bulst.**  Bulstrode's K.B. Rep., *Eng.*

**Bunb.**  Bunbury's Ex. Rep., *Eng.*

**Bur.**  Burnett's Rep. (Wis. 1841-43)
Burnett's K.B. Rep., *Eng.*

**Bur.M.**  Burrow's Rep. *temp.* Mansfield, *Eng.*

**Bur.S.C.**  Burrow's Settlement Cas., *Eng.*

**Burf.**  Burford's Rep. (6-18 Okla.)

**Burgess**  Burgess' Rep. (46-51 Ohio St.)

**Burn**  High Commission Ct. 1865, *Eng.*
Star Chamber Proceedings, *Eng.*

**Burnett**  Burnett's Rep. (Wis. 1841-43)

**Burr.**  Burrow's K.B. Rep. *temp.* Mansfield, *Eng.*

**Burr.t.M.**  Burrow's Rep. *temp.* Mansfield, *Eng.*

**Burrell.**  Burrell's Admiralty Rep., *Eng.*

**Burrnett.**  Burrnett's Rep. (20-22 Ore.)

**Busb.**  Busbee's Law Rep. (44 N.C.)

**Busb.Eq.**  Busbee's Equity Rep. (45 N.C.)

**Bush.**  Bush's Reports (64-77 Ky.)

**Butt's Sh.** Butt's Shower's K.B. Rep., *Eng.*

**Buxton** Buxton's Rep. (123-29 N.C.)

**C.** Cowen's N.Y. Rep.

**C.A.** Court of Appeal; Court of Appeals.
Customs Appeals Rep., *U.S.*
U.S. Court of Appeals.

**C.A.A.** Civil Aeronautics Admin., *U.S.*
Civil Aeronautics Authority Rep., *U.S.*

**C.A.A.J.** Civil Aeronautics Jour.

**C.A.A.Op.** Civil Aeronautics Authority Opinions, *U.S.*

**C.A.B. (or CAB)** Civil Aeronautics Board, *U.S.*

**C.A.D.** Canadian Annual Digest

**C.A.R.** Criminal Appeal Rep., *Eng.*

**C.App.R.** Same as above

**C.B.** Common Bench Rep. (Manning, Granger & Scott), *Eng.*
Cumulative Bulletin, Internal Revenue Service, *U.S.*

**C.B.N.S.** Common Bench Rep., New Series, *Eng.*

**C.C.** Cases in Chancery, *Eng.*
Coleman's N.Y. Cas.
Ohio Cir. Ct. Rep.

**C.A.A.** Circuit Court of Appeals, *U.S.*
County Court Appeals
Court of Crim. Appeal, *Eng.*

**C.C.C.** Canadian Crim. Cas.
Central Crim. Ct. (Old Bailey), *Eng.*
Choyce Cases in Chancery, *Eng.*
Cox's Crim. Cas., *Eng.*

**C.C.Ct.Cas.** Central Crim. Ct. Cas., *Eng.*

**C.C.E.** Caine's Cases in Error, *N.Y.*
Caines' N.Y. Term Rep.

**C.C.H.** Commerce Clearing House

**C.C.N.S.** Circuit Ct. Rep., N.S.

**C.C.P.A.** Court of Customs and Patent Appeals, *U.S.*

**C.C.R.** Circuit Court Rep.
City Courts Rep.
County Courts Rep.
Crown Cas. Res., *Eng.*

**C.D.** Chancery Div.
Commissioner's Dec., U.S. Patent Office, *U.S.*
Customs Court Dec., *U.S.*
Customs Dec. (U.S. Treasury Dept.)

**C.E.D.** Canadian Encyclopedic Digest

**C.E.Gr.** Green's Rep. (16-27 N.J. Eq.)

**C.F.R.(or CFR)** Code of Fed. Regulations, *U.S.*

**C.G.O.** Comptroller General's Op., *U.S.*

**CGR** Coast Guard Regulations, *U.S.*

**C.H.&A.** Carro, Hamerton & Allen's New Session Cas., *Eng.*

**CIA** Central Intelligence Agency, *U.S.*

**C.J.** Corpus Juris

**C.J.Can.** Corpus Juris Canonici

**C.J.Civ.** Corpus Juris Civilis

**C.L.** Common Law Rep.

**C.L.Ch.** Common Law Chamber Rep., *Ont.*

**C.L.J.** Canada Law Jour.
Central Law Jour.
Chicago Law Jour.

**C.L.J.N.S.** Canada Law Jour., New Series

**C.L.J.O.S** Canada Law Jour., Old Series

**C.L.N.** Chicago Legal News

**C.L.R.** Canada Law Rep.
Columbia Law Rev.
Common Law Rep.

**C.L.R.Can.** Canada Law Rep.
Common Law Rep. (Canada)

**C.L.T.** Canadian Law Times

**CM** Court Martial Rep. Army Cases, *U.S.*

**C.M.O.** U.S. Judge Advocate General (Navy) Compilation of Court Martial Orders

**CMR** Court-Martial Rep., Judge Advocates General of the Armed Forces and the United States Court of Military Appeals.

**CMR(AF)** Court-Martial Rep., Air Force

**C.M.&R.** Crompton, Meeson & Roscoe's Ex. Rep., *Eng.*

**C.N.Conf.** Cameron & Norwood's Conference Rep., *N.C.*

**C.N.P.C.** Campbell's N.P. Cas., *Eng.*

**C.P.** Common Pleas Rep., Upper Canada Law Rep., C.P. Series

**C.P.C.[oop].** C. P. Cooper's Prac. Cas., *Eng.*

**C.P.C.*t*.Br.** C. P. Cooper's Ch. Rep. *temp.* Brougham, *Eng.*

**C.P.C.*t*.Cott.** C. P. Cooper's Ch. Rep. *temp.* Cottenham, *Eng.*

**C.P.D.** Law Reports, C.P. Div., *Eng.*

**C.P.R.** Canadian Patent Reporter

**C.P.Rept.** Common Pleas Rep., *Pa.*

**C.P.U.C.** Upper Canada C.P. Rep.

**C.R.** Canadian Rep., Appeal Cas.
Chancery Rep. *temp.* Car. I to Queen Anne
Central Reporter
Criminal Rep.

**C.R.[date]A.C.** Canadian Appeal Cas.

**C.R.C.** Criminal Rep. (Canada)

**C.R.N.S.** Code Rep., New Series, *N.Y.*

**C.Rob.** Robinson's Admiralty Rep., *Eng.*

**C.S.** Supreme Court Rep., *Quebec*

**CSAB** Contract Settlement Appeal Bd., *U.S.*

**C.S.A.B.** Civil Service Arbitration Awards, *U.S.*

**C.S.C.R** Cincinnati Super. Ct. Rep.

**CSJAG** Opinion of Judge Advocate General, U.S. Army

**CSJAGA** Military Affairs Div., Judge Advocate of U.S. Army

**CSJAGE** Assistant Judge Advocate General for Procurement (Army); Contract Div., Office of Judge Advocate General of Army

**C.T.C.** Canada Tax Cas.

**C.Tax C.** Canadian Tax Cas.

**C.*t*.K.** Macnaghten's Select Ch. Cas. *temp.* King, *Eng.*

**C.*t*.N.** Eden's Ch. Rep. *temp.* Northington, *Eng.*

**C.*t*.T.** Cases *temp.* Talbot, Ch., *Eng.*

**C.W.Dud.** Dudley's S.C. Rep.

**CZO** Canal Zone Order

**C.Z.Rep.** Canal Zone Rep., *U.S.*

**C.&.C.** Case and Comment
Coleman & Caines' N.Y. Cas.

**C.&E.** Cababé & Ellis Rep., *Eng.*

**C.&F.** Clark & Finnelly's H.L. Cas., *Eng.*

**C.&J.** Crompton & Jervis Ex. Rep., *Eng.*

**C.&K.** Carrington & Kirwan's N.P. Rep., *Eng.*

**C.&L.C.C.** Cane & Leigh's Crown Cas., *Eng.*

**C.&M.** Carrington & Marshman's N.P. Rep., *Eng.*
Crompton & Meeson Ex. Rep., *Eng.*

**C.&Marsh.** Carrington & Marshman's N.P. Rep., *Eng.*

**C.&N.** Cameron & Norwood's Conference Rep., *N.C.*

**C.&P.** Carrington & Payne's N.P. Rep., *Eng.*
Craig & Phillips' Ch. Rep., *Eng.*

**Ca.*temp*.F.** Cases *temp.* Finch, *Eng.*

**Ca.*temp*.H.** Cases *temp.* Hardwicke, *Eng.*

**Ca.*temp*.Holt** Cases *temp.* Holt, *Eng.*

**Ca.*temp*.K.** Cases in Ch. *temp.* King, *Eng.*

**Ca.*temp*.Talb.** Cases in Ch. *temp.* Talbot, *Eng.*

**Cab.&E.** Cababé & Ellis Rep., Q.B.D., *Eng.*

**Cadwalader** Cadwalader's Dist. Ct. Cas. (E.D. Pa.), *U.S.*

**Cai.** Caines' N.Y. Term Rep.

**Cai.Cas.** Caine's Cases in Error, *N.Y.*

**Cai.T.R.** Caines' Term Rep., *N.Y.*

**Cal.** Caldecott's K.B. Rep., *Eng.*
California Law Rep.
Calthrop K.B. Rep., *Eng.*

**Cal.App.** California Appeals Rep.

**Cal.App.Sup.** California Super. Ct., Appellate Dept. (with Cal. Appeals)

**Cal.Dec.** California Dec.

**Cal.Jur.** California Jurisprudence

**Cal.L.J.** California Law Jour.

**Cal.Rep.** California Rep.
California Reporter
Calthrop's K.B. Rep., *Eng.*

**Cal.Rptr.** California Reporter

**Cal.Sup.** California Super. Court, Rep.

**Cal.Unrep.** California Unreported Cas.

**Cald.** Caldwell's Rep. (25-36 W. Va.)

**Cald.J.P.** Caldecott's Magistrates' Cas. *Eng.*

**Cald.Mag.Cas.** Same as above.

**Call** Call's Rep. (5-10 Va.)

**Calth.** Calthrop's K.B. Rep., *Eng.*

**Cam.** Cameron's Rep., Upper Canada

**Cam.Cas.** Cameron's Sup. Ct. Cas., *Can.*

**Cam.Op.** Cameron's Legal Opinions, *Can.*

**Cam.Prac.** Cameron's Sup. Ct. Practice, *Can.*

**Cam.Scacc.** Camera Scaccarii (Ex. Chamber), *Eng.*

**Cam.Stell.** Camera Stellate (Star Chamber), *Eng.*

**Cam.&N[or].** Cameron & Norwood's N.C. Conference Rep.

**Cameron** *See* Cam.

**Camp** Camp's Rep. (1 N.D.)

**Camp.** Campbell's N.P. Rep., *Eng.*
Campbell's Rep. (26-58 Neb.)

**Camp.Dec.** Taney's · U.S. Cir. Ct. Dec. by Campbell

**Camp.N.P.** Campbell's N.P. Rep., *Eng.*

**Campbell** Campbell's Legal Gazette (27-58 Neb.)
Campbell's N.P. Rep., *Eng.*
Taney's Cir. Ct. Dec., *U.S.*

**Can.Abr.** Canadian Abridgement

**Can.C.C.** Canada Crim. Cas. Annot.

**Can.Crim.Cas.** Same as above

**Can.Exch.** Reports, Ex. Ct. *Can.*

**Can.Gaz.** Canadian Gazette

**Can.L.R.** Canada Law Rep.

**Can.R.A.C.** Canadian Rep., Appeal Cas.

**Can.S.C.Rep.** Canada Sup. Ct. Rep.

**Can.Sup.Ct.** Same as above

**Cane&L.** Cane & Leigh's Crown Cas. Res., *Eng.*

**Car.H.&A.** Carrow, Hamerton & Allen Session Cas., *Eng.*

**Car.L.Rep.** Carolina Law Repository (4 N.C.)

**Car.&Kir.** Carrington & Kirwan's N.P. Rep., *Eng.*

**Car.&Mar.** Carrington & Marshman's N.P. Rep., *Eng.*

**Car.&P.** Carrington & Payne's N.P. Rep., *Eng.*

**Carey,M.R.** Carey's Manitoba Rep: *temp.* Wood

**Carl.** Carleton's New Brunswick Rep.

**Carpenter** Carpenter's Rep. (52, 53 Cal.)

**Cart.** Carter's Rep., C.P., *Eng.*
Carter's Rep. (1, 2 Ind.)

**Carter** Carter's C.P. Rep., *Eng.*
Carter's Rep. (1, 2 Ind.)

**Carth.** Carthew's K.B. Rep., *Eng.*

**Cary** Cary's Ch. Rep., *Eng.*

**Cas.** Casey's Rep. (25-36 Pa. St.)

**Cas.App.** Cases of Appeal to House of Lords, *Eng.*

**Cas.Arg.&Dec.** Cases Argued and Decreed in Chancery, *Eng.*

**Cas.B.R.** Cases Banco Regis *temp.* Wm. III (12 Modern Rep.), *Eng.*

**Cas.C.L.** Cases in Crown Law, *Eng.*

**Cas.C.R.** Cases *temp.* Wm. III (12 Modern Rep.)

**Cas.Ch.** (*or* Cas. in Ch.) Cases in Chancery 1660-88, *Eng.*
Cases in Chancery 1660-97, *Eng.*
Select Cases in Chancery, *Eng.*
Cases in Chancery *temp.* Car. II, *Eng.*

**Cas.Eq.** Gilbert's Cases in Equity, *Eng.*

**Cas.L.Eq.** Cases in Law & Eq. (10 Modern Rep.), *Eng.*

**Cas.F.T.** Cases in Chancery, *temp.* Talbot, by Forester, *Eng.*

**Cas.H.L.** Cases in the House of Lords, *Eng.*

**Cas.in Ch.** *See* Cas. Ch.

**Cas.K.B.** Cases in King's Bench (8 Modern Rep.), *Eng.*

**Cas.K.B.*t*.H.** Cases *temp.* Hardwicke (Kelynge's K.B. Rep.), *Eng.*

**Cas.Prac.C.P.** Cases of Practice, C.P., *Eng.*

**Cas.P.** Cases in Parliament, *Eng.*

**Cas.R.** Casey's Rep. (25-36 Pa. St.)

**Cas.*t*.Ch.II** Reports in Chancery, Cas. *temp.* Charles II, *Eng.*

**Cas.*t*.F.** Chancery Cas. *temp.* Finch, *Eng.*

**Cas.*t*.Geo.I.** Chancery Cas. *temp.* Geo. I (8, 9 Modern Rep.), *Eng.*

**Cas.*t*.H.** King's Bench Cas. *temp* Hardwicke, *Eng.*

Chancery Rep. *temp.* Hardwicke (West), *Eng.*

King's Bench Rep. *temp.* Holt (7, 11 Modern Rep.), *Eng.*

**Cas.***t***.K.** Chancery Cas. *temp.* King, *Eng.*

Chancery Rep. *temp.* King, (Mosley), *Eng.*

**Cas.***t***.Mac[cl].** Cases *temp.* Macclesfield (10 Modern Rep.), *Eng.*

**Cas.***t***.Q.Anne** (11 Modern Rep.), *Eng.*

**Cas.***t***.Talb.** Chancery Cas. *temp.* Talbot, *Eng.*

**Cas.***t***.Wm.III** Casas *temp.* Wm. III (12 Modern Rep.), *Eng.*

**Cas.***temp***.** *See* Cas.*t*.

**Cas. Wm.I** Cases, Wm. I to Rich. I (Bigelow), *Eng.*

**Casey** Casey's Rep. (25-36 Pa. St.)

**Cates** Cates' Rep. (109-127 Tenn.)

**Cent[r].Crim.C.R.** Central Crim. Ct. Rep., *Eng.*

**Cent.Dig.** Century Digest

**Cert.** Certiorari

**Ch.App.** Law Rep. Ch. Appeals, *Eng.*

**Ch.App.Cas.** Same as above

**Ch.Cas.** Cases in Chancery 1660-88, *Eng.*

Select Cases in Chancery *temp.* King, *Eng.*

**Ch.Ch.** Upper Canada Chancery Chambers Rep.

**Ch.Cham.** Same as above

**Ch.D.[iv].** Law Rep., Ch. Div., *Eng.*

**Ch.Pre.** Precedents in Chancery, *Eng.*

**Ch.R.** Chitty's K.B. Rep., *Eng.*

Reports in Chancery 1615-1712, *Eng.*

Upper Canada Chancery Chambers Rep.

**Ch.Rep.** *See* Ch.R.

**Ch.R.M.** R. M. Charlton's Ga. Rep. (1811-37)

**Ch.Rob.** Christopher Robinson's Admiralty Rep., *Eng.*

**Ch.Sent.** Chancery Sentinel, *U.S.*

**Ch.T.U.P.** T. U. P. Charlton's Ga. Rep.

**Cham.** Chambers' Upper Canada Rep.

**Chamb.Rep.** Chambers' Ch. Rep., *Ontario*

**Chan.** Chaney's Rep. (37-58 Mich.)

**Chand.** Chandler's Rep. (20, 38-44 N.H.)

Chandler's Rep. (Wis. 1849-52)

**Chaney** Chaney's Rep. (37-58 Mich.)

**Charl.R.M.** R. M. Charlton's Ga. Rep.

**Charl.T.U.P.** T. U. P. Charlton's Ga. Rep.

**Chase** Chase's Cir. Ct. Dec., *U.S.*

**Chest.Co.Rep.** Chester County Rep., *Pa.*

**Chev.** Cheves' Rep. (S.C. 1839-40)

**Chev.Ch.** Cheves' Eq. Rep. (S.C. 1839-40)

**Chip.** Chipman's Rep., New Brunswick.

Chipman's Rep. (Vt. 1789-1824)

**Chip.D.** D. Chipman's Vt. Rep.

**Chip.N.** N. Chipman's Vt. Rep.

**Cho.Ca.Ch.** Choyce Cases in Chancery, *Eng.*

**Chr.Rep.** Chambers' Rep., Upper Canada

**Chr.Rob.** Christopher Robinson's Admiralty Rep., *Eng.*

**Cin.Rep.** Cincinnati Super. Ct. Rep.

**Cin.S.C.Rep.** Same as above

**Cir.Ct.Dec.** Ohio Cir. Ct. Dec.

**City Ct.R.Supp.** New York, City Court Rep. Supplement

**City Ct.Rep.** New York, City Court Rep.

**City H.Rep.** City Hall Reporter, *N.Y.*

**Civ.Pr.Rep.** Civil Procedure Rep., *N.Y.*

**Cl.** *See* Clark; Clarke

**Cl.App.** Clark's H.L. Appeal Cas., *Eng.*

**Cl.Ch.** Clarke's Ch. Rep.,*N.Y.*

**Cl.&Fin.** Clark & Finnelly's H.L. Cas., *Eng.*

**Cl.&Fin.N.S.** Same, New Series

**Clark** Clark's H.L. Cas., *Eng.*

Clark's Rep. (58 Ala.)

**Clark(Pa.)** Clark's Pa. Law Jour. Rep.

**Clark&Fin.** *See* Cl. & Fin.

**Clarke** Clarke's N.Y. Ch. Rep.

Clarke's Rep. (19-22 Mich.)

Clarke's Rep. (Pa. 1842-52)

**Clarke Ch.** Clarke's N.Y. Ch. Rep.

**Clay.** Clayton's Rep. and Pleas of Assizes at York, 1631-50, *Eng.*

**Clayton** Same as above

**Clem.** Clemens' Rep. (57-59 Kan.)

**Cliff.** Clifford's First Cir. Rep., *U.S.*

**Clk.Mag.** Clerk's Magazine, London Rhode Island Clerk's Magazine

**Co.** Coke's Institutes
Coke's K.B. Rep., *Eng.*

**Co.Ct.Rep.** Pennsylvania County Ct. Rep.

**Co.Cts.** Coke's Courts (4th Institute), *Eng.*

**Co.Ent.** Coke's Entries, *Eng.*

**Co.G.** G. Coke's Practice Rep., *Eng.* Cooke's Practice Rep., *Eng.*

**Co.Inst.** Coke's Institutes, *Eng.*

**Co.Litt.** Coke on Littleton, *Eng.*

**Co. on Courts** Coke's 4th Institute, *Eng.*

**Co.P.C.** Coke's Pleas of the Crown, *Eng.*

**Co.Rep.** New York City Code Reporter
Coke's K.B. Rep., *Eng.*

**Cobb** Cobb's Rep. (121 Ala.; 4-20 Ga.)

**Coch.** Cochran's Nova Scotia Rep.

**Cochr.** Cochran's Nova Scotia Rep. Cochran's Rep. (3-10 N.D.)

**Cochran** Same as Coch.

**Cocke** Cocke's Rep. (16-18 Ala.; 14, 15 Fla.)

**Code Rep.** New York City Code Reporter

**Code Rep.N.S.** New York Code Reporter, N.S.

**Coffey.** Coffey's Probate Dec. (Cal.)

**Coke** *See* Co.

**Col.** Coldwell's Rep. (41-47 Tenn.)
Coleman's Rep., *Ala.*
Colorado Rep.
Colonial
Columbia

**Col.App.** Colorado Appeals Rep.

**Col.C.C.** Collyer's Ch. Cas., *Eng.*

**Col.Cas.** Coleman's Practice Cas., *N.Y.*

**Col.L.Rep.** Colorado Law Reporter

**Col.N.P.** Colorado N.P. Dec.

**Col.&Cai.Cas.** Coleman & Caines' Cas., *N.Y.*

**Cold.** Coldwell's Rep. (41-47 Tenn.)

**Cole.** Coleman's Rep., *Ala.*

**Colem.Cas.** Coleman's Cas., *N.Y.*

**Coll.C.R.** Collyer's Ch. Rep., *Eng.*

**Colo.** Colorado

**Colo.App.** Colorado Appeals Rep.

**Colo.Dec.** Colorado Dec.

**Colo.L.Rep.** Colorado Law Reporter

**Colo.N.P.Dec.** Colorado N.P. Dec. 1900-02

**Colq.** Colquit's Rep. (1 Modern Rep.) *Eng.*

**Colum.** Columbia

**Colum.J.L.&Soc.Prob.** Columbia Jour. Law & Soc. Problems

**Colum.J.Transnat.L.** Columbia Journ. of Transnational Law

**Com.** Blackstone's Commentaries
Comberbach's Rep., K.B., *Eng.*
Comstock's Rep. (1-5 N.Y.)
Comyns' Rep. K.B., C.P., Ex., *Eng.*

**Com.B.** Common Bench Rep. 1845-65, *Eng.*

**Com.B.N.S.** Common Bench Rep., New Series, *Eng.*

**Com.L.R.** Common Law Rep. 1853-55, *Eng.*

**Com.L.Rep.** Same as above

**Com.Pl.** Common Pleas

**Com.Pl.Div.** Law Rep. C.P. Div., *Eng.*

**Comb.** Comberbach's K.B. Rep., *Eng.*

**Comp.Dec.** Comptroller of the Treasury Dec., *U.S.*

**Comp.Gen.** Comptroller General's Dec., *U.S.*

**Comp.Rev.** Compensation Rev.

**Comst.** Comstock's Rep. (1-4 N.Y.)

**Comyns** Comyns' K.B. Rep., *Eng.*

**Con.** Conover's Rep. (16-153 Wis.)
Connoly's Crim. Rep., *N.Y.*

**Con.Sur.** Connoly's Surrogate's Rep. *N.Y.*

**Conf.** North Carolina Conference Rep. (Cameron & Norwood)

**Cong.Deb.** Congressional Debates, *U.S.*

**Cong.Dig.** Congdon's Digest, Can.

**Cong.Rec.** Congressional Record, *U.S.*

**Conn.** Connecticut [Reports]

Connolly's N.Y. Surrogate's Rep.

**Conn.S.** Connecticut Supplement

**Connolly** Connolly's Surrogate's Rep., *N.Y.*

**Conover** Conover's Rep. (16-153 Wis.)

**Const.** Constitutional Rep. by Harper, Mill, Treadway (S.C.)

**Const.N.S.** Same as above, New Series

**Const.R.S.C.** Constitutional Rep. of S.C., by Treadway

**Const.Rep.** Constitutional Rep., S.C.

**Const.S.C.** South Carolina Constitutional Rep., New Series

**Convey.** Conveyancer

**Cooke** Cooke's Rep. (3 Tenn.)

**Cooke C.P.** Cooke's C.P. Rep., *Eng.*

**Cooke Pr.Cas.** Cooke's Practice Rep., C.P., *Eng.*

**Cooley** Cooley's Rep. (5-12 Mich.)

**Coop.** Cooper's Ch. Rep., *Eng.*

Cooper's Ch. Rep. *temp.* Cottenham, *Eng.*

Cooper's Rep. (21-24 Fla.)

Cooper's Tennessee Ch. Rep.

**Coop.C.C.** Cooper's Ch. Cas. temp. Cottenham, *Eng.*

**Coop.Ch.** Cooper's Tenn. Ch. Rep.

**Coop.Ch.Pr.** Cooper's Ch. Practice Rep., *Eng.*

**Coop.G.** G. Cooper's Ch. Rep., *Eng.*

**Coop.Pr.Cas.** C. P. Cooper's Ch. Practice Cas., *Eng.*

**Coop.Ten.Chy.** Cooper's Tenn. Ch. Rep.

**Cooper** Cooper's Tenn. Ch. Rep.

**Cope** Cope's Rep. (63-73 Cal.)

**Corp.Rep.** Pennsylvania Corp. Reporter

**Counsellor** The Counsellor

**Count.Cts.Chron.** County Courts Chronicle

**Court Cl.** Court of Claims, *U.S.*

**Cout.** Coutlee's Unreported Cas., *Can.*

**Cout.S.C.** Notes of Unreported Cas., Sup. Ct., of Canada (Coutlee)

**Cow.** Cowen's N.Y. Rep. 1823-29

Cowper's K.B. Rep., *Eng.*

**Cow.Cr.Rep.** Cowen's Crim. Rep., *N.Y.*

**Cowp.** Cowper's K.B. Rep., *Eng.*

**Cox** Cox's Ch. Rep.,, *Eng.*

Cox's Crim. Cas., *Eng.*

Cox's Rep. (25-27 Ark.)

**Cox Am.T.M.Cas.** Cox's American Trade Mark Cas.

**Cox C.C.** Cox's Crim. Law Cas., *Eng.*

**Cox Ch.** Cox's Ch. Cas., *Eng.*

**Cox Cr. Ca.** Cox's Crim. Cas., *Eng.*

**Coxe** Coxe's Rep. (1 N.J. Law)

**Cr.** Cranch's Sup. Ct. Rep. (5-13 U. S.)

Cranch's Cir. Ct. Rep., *U.S.*

**Cr.Cas.Res.** Crown Cases Res., *Eng.*

**Cr.M.&R.** Crompton, Meeson & Roscoe Rep., *Eng.*

**Cr.&J.** Crompton & Jervis Ex. Rep., *Eng.*

**Cr.&M.** Crompton & Meeson's Ex. Rep., *Eng.*

**Cr.&Ph.** Craig & Phillips Ch. Rep., *Eng.*

**Crabbe** Crabbe's Dist. Ct. Rep., *U.S.*

**Craig&Ph.** Craig & Phillips Ch. Rep., *Eng.*

**Cranch** Cranch's Sup. Ct. Rep. (5-13 U.S.)

**Cranch C.C.** Cranch's Cir. Ct. Rep. District of Columbia App. Cas. (v. 1-5)

**Cranch D.C.** Same as above

**Cranch Pat.Dec.** Cranch's Patent Dec., *U.S.*

**Crane** Crane's Rep. (22-29 Mont.)

**Craw.** Crawford's Rep. (53-69, 72-101 Ark.)

**Crim.Rec.** Criminal Recorder, Philadelphia

Criminal Recorder, London

Criminal Recorder (1 Wheeler's N.Y. Crim. Rep.)

**Critch.** Critchfield's Rep. (5-21 Ohio St.)

**Cro.** Croke's K.B. Rep., *Eng.*

Keilway's K.B. Rep. 1496-1531, *Eng.*

**Cro.Car.** Croke's K.B. Rep. *temp.* Car. I, *Eng.*

**Cro.Eliz.** Croke's Rep. *temp.* Eliz., *Eng.*

**Cro.Jac.** Croke's K.B. Rep. *temp.* James I, *Eng.*

**Crockford** Crockford's Maritime Law Rep., *Eng.*

**Croke** *See* Cro.

**Crom.[p.]** Crompton's Star Chamber Cas., *Eng.*

**Cromp.Ex.R.** Crompton's Ex. Rep., *Eng.*

**Cromp.M.&R.** Crompton, Meeson & Roscoe's Ex. Rep., *Eng.*

**Cromp.&Jerv.** Crompton & Jervis' Ex. Rep., *Eng.*

**Cromp.&Mees.** Crompton & Meeson's Ex. Rep., *Eng.*

**Crounse** Crounse's Rep. (3 Neb.)

**Crumrine** Crumrine's Rep. (116-146 Pa.)

Pittsburgh Rep., ed. Crumrine

**Ct.Cl.** Court of Claims, *U.S.*

**Ct.Cl.N.Y.** Court of Claims Rep., *N.Y.*

**Ct.Cls.** Court of Claims, *U.S.*

**Ct.Com.Pl.** Court of Common Pleas

**Ct.Crim.App.** Court of Criminal Appeals, *Eng.*

**Ct.Errors&App.** Court of Errors & Appeals

**Ct.Just.** Court of Justiciary

**Cum.Bull.** Cumulative Bulletin, Internal Revenue Service, *U.S.*

**Cummins** Cummins' Rep. (Idaho 1866-67)

**Cun.** Cunningham's K.B. Rep., *Eng.*

**Cur.** Curtis' Cir. Ct. Rep., *U.S.*

**Cur.Dec.** Curtis' Edition, U.S. Sup. Ct. Rep.

**Cur.Ov.Ca.** Curwen, Overruled Cases, *Ohio*

**Cur.Reg.R.** Curia Regis Rolls, *Eng.*

**Curry** Curry's Rep. (6-19 La.)

**Curt.** Curtis Cir. Ct. Rep., *U.S.*

Curtis' Edition, U.S. Sup. Ct. Rep.

**Curt.C.C.** Curtis' Cir. Ct. Rep., *U.S.*

**Curt.Cond.** Curtis' Edition, U.S. Sup. Ct. Rep.

**Curt.Dec.** Same as above

**Curtis** Curtis' Cir. Ct. Rep., *U.S.*

Curtis' Edition, U.S. Sup. Ct. Rep.

**Curw.Ov.Cas.** Curwen's Overruled Ohio Cas.

**Cush.** Cushing's Rep. (55-66 Mass.)

**Cushing** Same as above

**Cushman** Cushman's Rep. (23-29 Miss.)

**Cut.Pat.Cas.** Cutler's Trademark and Patent Cases, U.S.

**D.** Dallas' U.S. Sup. Ct. Rep. (1-4 U.S.)

Dallas' Pa. Rep. 1754-1806

Delaware Rep.

Denio's Rep., *N.Y.*

Denison's Crown Cas., *Eng.*

Dictionary

Duxbury

Digest, Justinian's

Dowling. *See* Dow.

Dyer's Rep., *Eng.*

Disney's Ohio Superior Court Reports.

**D.B.** Domesday Book

**D.C.** District Court; District of Columbia; Treasury Department Circular, *U.S.*

**D.C.** (no.) Bull. Memo. U.S. Internal Revenue Service, Cumulative Bulletin, Treasury Dept. Circular.

**D.C.A.** Dorion's Q.B. Bench Rep., *Can.*

**D.C.App.** District of Columbia Appeals Rep.

**D.Chip.** D. Chipman's Rep. (Vt. 1789-1824)

**D.Ct.** District Ct. (usually U.S.)

**D.F.&J.** DeGex, Fisher & Jones' Ch. Rep., *Eng.*

**D.J.&S.** DeGex, Jones & Smith's Ch. Rep., *Eng.*

**D.L.R.** Dominion Law Rep., *Can.*

**D.M.&G.** DeGex, Macnaghten & Gordon Ch. Rep., *Eng.*

**D.N.S.** Dow, New Series (H.L. Cas.), *Eng.*

**D.P.R.** Porto Rico Reports (Spanish ed.)

**D.R.S.** Dominion Rep. Service (CCH), *Can.*

**D.&B.** Dearsley & Bell's Crown Cas.,, *Eng.*

Devereux & Battle's Rep. (18-20 N.C.)

**D.&C.** District and County Rep., *Pa.*

**D.&E.** Durnford & East's K.B. Rep. (Term Rep.), *Eng.*

**D.&J.** DeGex & Jones' Ch. Rep., *Eng.*

**D.&M.** Davison & Merivale's Q.B. Rep., *Eng.*

**D.&.P.** Dearsley & Pearce's Crown Cas., *Eng.*

**D.&R.** Dowling & Ryland's K.B. Rep., *Eng.*

**D.&R.N.P.** Dowling & Ryland's N.P. Cas., *Eng.*

**D.&S.** Drewry & Smale's Ch. Rep., *Eng.*

**Dak.** Dakota

**Dal.** Dalison's C.P. Rep., *Eng.*
  Dallas' U.S. Sup. Ct. Rep. (1-4 U.S.)
  Dallas' Pa. Rep. 1754-1806

**Dale** Dale's Rep. (2-4 Okla.)

**Dall.** Dallam's Tex. Sup. Ct. Dec.
  Dallas' U.S. Sup. Ct. Rep. (1-4 U.S.)
  Dallas' Pa. Rep. 1754-1806

**Dall.(Tex.)** Dallam's Tex. Sup. Ct. Dec.

**Dall. in Keil.** Dallison's Rep. in Keilway's K.B. Rep., *Eng.*

**Dall.S.C.** Dallas' U.S. Rep. (1-4 *U.S.*)

**Dallas** *See* Dall.

**Daly** Daly's N.Y.C.P. Rep.

**Dan.** Dana's Rep. (31-39 Ky.)
  Danner's Rep. (42 Ala.)

**Dan.&Ll.** Danson & Lloyd's Mercantile Cas., *Eng.*

**Dana** Dana's Rep. (31-39 Ky.)

**Dann.** Dann's Rep. (1 Ariz.)
  Dann's Rep. (in 22 Cal.)
  Danner's Rep. (42 Ala.)

**Danner** Danner's Rep. (42 Ala.)

**Dans.&L.L.** Danson & Lloyd's Mercantile Cas., *Eng.*

**Danv.** Danvers' Abridgment, *Eng.*

**Das.** Common Law Rep. v.3, *Eng.*

**Dauph.Co.Rep.** Dauphin County Rep., *Pa.*

**Dav.** Davies' Dist. Ct. Rep.
  Davis' Hawaiian Rep., *Eng.*
  Davis' Abridgement of Coke's Rep., *Eng.*

**Dav.Coke** Same as above

**Dav.&Mer.** Davison & Merivale's Q.B. Rep., *Eng.*

**Dav.(U.S.)** Daveis Dist. Ct. Rep. (v. 2 of Ware), *U.S.*

**Daveis (U.S.)** Same as above

**Davis Rep.** Davis' Hawaiian Rep.

**Day** Day's Rep. Conn. 1802-13

**Dayton** Dayton (Laning) Rep., *Ohio*
  Dayton Super. and C.P. Rep., *Ohio*

**DeG.F.&J.** DeGex, Fisher & Jones Ch. Rep., *Eng.*

**DeG.J.&S.** DeGex, Jones & Smith Ch. Rep., *Eng.*

**DeG.M.&G.** DeGex, Macnaghten & Gordon Ch. Rep., *Eng.*

**DeG.&J.** DeGex & Jones' Ch. Rep., *Eng.*

**DeG.&Sm.** DeGex & Smale's Ch. Rep., *Eng.*

**DeWitt** De Witt's Rep. (24-42 Ohio St.)

**Dea.** Deady's Cir. and Dist. Ct. Rep., *U.S.*

**Deady** Deady's Cir. and Dist. Ct. Rep., *U.S.*

**Deane** Deane's Rep. (24-26 Vt.)
  Deane & Swabey's Probate and Divorce Rep., *Eng.*
  Deane's Blockade Cas., *Eng.*

**Dears.C.C.** Dearsly's Crown Cas., *Eng.*

**Dears.&B.C.C.** Dearsley & Bell's Crown Cas., *Eng.*

**Dec.O.** Ohio Dec.

**Dec.*t*.H.&M.** Admiralty Decisions *temp.* Hay and Marriott, *Eng.*

**Del.** Delaware Rep.

**Del.Ch.** Delaware Ch. Rep.

**Del.Co.R.** Delaware Co. (Pa.) Rep.

**Del.Cr.Cas.** Houston's Crim. Cas., *Del.*

**Delane** Delane's Revision Courts Dec., *Eng.*

**Delehanty** New York Miscellaneous Rep.

**Dem.** Demarest's Surrogate Rep., *N.Y.*

**Den.** Denio's N. Y. Rep.
  Denis' Rep. (32-46 La. Annual
  Denison's Crown Cases Res. *Eng.*

**Den.C.C.** Same as above

**Den.&P.** Denison & Pearce's Crown Cas., *Eng.*

**Denio** Denio's N.Y. Rep.

**Denis** Denis' Rep. (32-46 La. Annual)

**Denver L.N.** Denver Legal News

**Des.** Desaussure's Eq. Rep., *S.C.*

**Desaus.Eq.** Same as above

**Det.Leg.N.** Detroit Legal News

**Dev.** Devereux' Rep. (N.C. Law and Eq.)

Devereux' Court of Claims Rep., *U.S.*

**Dev.Ct.Cl.** Devereux' Court of Claims Rep., *U.S.*

**Dev.Eq.** Devereux' Rep. (16, 17 N.C. Eq.)

**Dev.L.** Devereux' Rep. (12-15 N.C. Law)

**Dev.&Bat.** Devereux & Battle's Rep. (17-20 N.C. Law)

**Dev.&Bat.** Devereux & Battle's Rep. (21, 22 N.C. Eq.)

**Dew.** Dewey's Rep. (60-70 Kan.)

Dewey's Kan. Court of Appeals Rep.

**Di.** Dyer's K.B. Rep., *Eng.*

**Dice** Dice's Rep. (71-99 Ind.)

**Dick.** Dickens' Ch. Rep., *Eng.*

Dickinson's Rep. (46-66 N.J. Eq.)

**Dick.L.R.** Dickinson Law Rev.

**Dicta** Dicta of the Denver Bar Assn.

**Dill.** Dillon's Cir. Ct. Rep., *U.S.*

**Disn.** Disney's Ohio Super. Ct. Rep.

**Div.Ct.** Divisional Ct.

**Docket** The Docket

**Doct.&St.** Doctor and Student, *Eng.*

**Dod[s].** Dodson's Admiralty Rep., *Eng.*

**Donaker** Donaker's Rep. (154 Ind.)

**Donn.** Donnelly's Ch. Rep., *Eng.*

**Donnelly** Same as above

**Dorion** Dorion's Q.B. Rep., *Quebec*

**Doug.** Douglas' K.B. Rep., *Eng.*

Douglas' Rep. (Mich. 1843-47)

**Doug.K.B.** Douglas' K.B. Rep., *Eng.*

**Dow** Dow's H.L. Rep., *Eng.*

**Dow N.S.** Dow & Clark's H.L. Cas., *Eng.*

**Dow&Cl.** Same as above

**Dow.&Ry.** Dowling & Ryland's K.B. Rep., *Eng.*

Dowling & Ryland's N.P. Cas., *Eng.*

**Dow.&Ry.K.B.** Dowling & Ryland's K.B. Rep., *Eng.*

**Dow.&Ry.N.P.** Dowling & Ryland's N.P. Rep., *Eng.*

**Dr.** Drewry's Vice-Chancellors, Rep., *Eng.*

**Dr.&Sm.** Drewry & Smale's Vice-Chancellors' Rep., *Eng.*

**Dra[per]** Draper's K.B. Rep., *Can.*

**Drew.** Drew's Rep. (13 Fla.)

Drewry's Vice-Chancellors' Rep., *Eng.*

**Drew.&Sm.** Drewry & Smale's Ch. Rep., *Eng.*

**Drink.** Drinkwater's C.P. Rep., *Eng.*

**Dud.** Dudley's Ga. Rep. 1830-35

**Dud.Ch.** Dudley's S.C. Eq. Rep. 1837-38

**Dud.L.** Dudley's S.C. Law Rep. 1837-38

**Duer** Duer's Super. Ct. Rep., *N.Y.*

**Dug.Orig.** Dugdale's Origines Juridiciales

**Dugd.** Same as above

**Dunn.** Dunning's K.B. Rep., *Eng.*

**Durf[ee]** Durfee's Rep. (2 R.I.)

**Durn.&E.** Durnford & East's (Term) Rep., *Eng.*

**Dutch.** Dutcher's Rep. (25-29 N.J. Law)

**Duv.** Duvall's Rep. (62, 63 Ky.)

Duvall's Sup. Ct. Rep., *Can.*

**Dy.** Dyer's K.B. Rep., *Eng.*

**Dyer** Same as above

**E.** East's Rep., *Eng.*

**E.B.&E.** Ellis, Blackburn, & Ellis' Rep., *Eng.*

**E.C.** English Chancery

**E.D.** Exchequer Div.

**E.D.Smith** E. D. Smith's C.P. Rep., *N.Y.*

**E.E.** Equity Exchequer

**E.L.R.** Eastern Law Rep., *Can.*

**E.O.** Presidential Executive Order, *U.S.*

**E.P.C.** East's Pleas of the Crown, *Eng.*

**E.R.** East's K.B. Rep., *Eng.*

English Rep., Full Reprint

**E.R.C.** English Ruling Cases

**E.T.** Estate and Gift Tax Ruling, (Internal Revenue Service), *U.S.*

**E.&A.** Ecclesiastical & Admiralty Rep. (Spinks), *Eng.*

Upper Canada Error & Appeal Rep.

**E.&A.R.** Same as above

**E.&A.W.C.** Grant's Error & Appeal Rep., *Ontario*

**E.&B.** Ellis & Blackburn's Q.B. Rep., *Eng.*

**E.&E.** Ellis & Ellis' Q.B. Rep., *Eng.*

**Ea.** East's K.B. Rep., *Eng.*

**East** Same as above

Eastern Law Reporter, *Can.*

**East.L.R.** Eastern Law Reporter, *Can.*

**East P.C.** East's Pleas of the Crown, *Eng.*

**East.Rep.** Eastern Law Reporter, *Can.*

**Ebersole** Ebersole's Rep. (59-80 Iowa)

**Ed.** Eden's Ch. Rep., *Eng.*

**Ed.Bro.** Brown's Ch. Rep., *Eng.*

**Ed.C.R.** Edwards' Ch. Rep., *N.Y.*

**Ed.L.J.** Edinburgh Law Jour.

**Eden** Eden's Ch. Rep., *Eng.*

**Edinb.L.J.** Edinburgh Law Jour.

**Edw.** Edwards' Admiralty Rep., *Eng.*

Edwards' N.Y. Ch. Rep.

Edwards' Rep. (2, 3 Mo.)

**Edw.** Edwards' Admiralty Rep., *Eng.*

**Edw.Ch.** Edward's Ch. Rep., *N.Y.*

**Edw.P.C.** Edwards' Prize Cas., *Eng.*

**Edw.(Tho.)** Edwards' Admiralty Rep., *Eng.*

**Efird** Efird Rep. (46-51 S.C.)

**El.B.&E.** Ellis, Blackburn & Ellis' Q.B. Rep., *Eng.*

**El.&Bl.** Ellis & Blackburn's Q.B. Rep., *Eng.*

**Ell.&Bl.** Same as above

**Ell.&Ell.** Ellis & Ellis' Q.B. Rep., *Eng.*

**Ell.B.&S.** Ellis, Best & Smith's Q.B. Rep., *Eng.*

**Ell.Bl.&Ell.** Ellis, Blackburn & Ellis' Q.B. Rep., *Eng.*

**Eng.** English's Rep. (6-13 Ark.)

**Eng.Pr.Cas.** Roscoe's English Prize Cas.

**Eng.Rep.** English Rep., Full Reprint

English's Rep. (6-13 Ark.)

**Eng.Ru.Cas.** English Ruling Cases

**English** English's Rep. (6-13 Ark.)

**Eq.Cas.** Equity Cases in 9, 10 Modern Rep., *Eng.*

**Eq.Rep.** Equity Rep. 1835-55, *Eng.*

Gilbert's Equity Rep., *Eng.*

Harper's Rep. (S.C. Eq. 1824)

**E.R.** English Rep.; English Rep., Full Reprint

**Erie Co.L.J.** Erie County Law Jour., *Pa.*

**Err.&App.** Error & Appeals Rep., Upper Canada (Grant)

**Ersk.Dec.** Erskine's U.S. Cir. Ct. Dec. (in 35 Ga.)

**Esp.** Espinasse's N.P. Rep., *Eng.*

**Estee** Estee's Dist. Ct. of Hawaii Rep., *U.S.*

**Evans** Lord Mansfield's Dec., *Eng.*

**Ex.** Exchequer Rep. 1848-56, *Eng.*

**Ex.C.R.** Canada Ex. Ct. Rep. Canada Law Rep. (Ex. Ct.)

**Ex.D.** Law Rep., Ex. Div., *Eng.*

**Ex.Div.** Same as above

**Exch.** Same as above

Exchequer Rep. (Welsby, Hurlstone & Gordon), *Eng.*

**Exch.C.** Canada Law Rep., Ex. Ct.

**Exch.C.R.** Exchequer Ct. Rep., *Can.*

**Exch.Can.** Same as above

**Exch.Div.** Law Rep. Ex. Div., *Eng.*

**Exch.Rep.** English Ex. Rep., Reprint

Exchequer Rep. (Welsby, Hurlstone & Gordon), *Eng.*

**Exec.Order** Presidential Executive Order, *U.S.*

**Exter.Ca.** Lobingier's Extraterritorial Cases, U.S. Court for China

**Extra.Ca.** Same as above

**Eyre** Eyre's K.B. Rep. *temp.* Wm. III, *Eng.*

**F.** Federal Reporter, *U.S.*

**F.2d** Federal Reporter, Second Series

**F.A.D.** Federal Anti-Trust Dec., *U.S.*

**FAO** Food & Agriculture Organization, *UN*

**F.C.** Federal Cas., *U.S.*

**F.C.A.** Farm Credit Admin., *U.S.*

**F.C.C.(or FCC)** Federal Communications Comm., *U.S.*

**FDA** Food & Drug Admin., *U.S.*

**FEA** Foreign Economic Admin., *U.S.*

**FEB** Fair Employment Bd., *U.S.*

**F.L.J.** Canada Fortnightly Law Jour.

**F.P.C.** Federal Power Comm., *U.S.*

**F.R.** Federal Register, *U.S.*

**FRB** Federal Reserve Bd., *U.S.*

**F.R.D.** Federal Rules Dec., *U.S.*

**F.R.S.** Federal Reserve System, *U.S.*

**F.Supp.** Federal Supplement, *U.S.*

**F.S.A.** Federal Security Agency, *U.S.*

**FSA** Farm Security Admin., *U.S.*

**FTC** Federal Trade Comm., *U.S.*

**F.&F.** Foster & Finlason's N.P. Rep., *Eng.*

**Fac.L.Rev.** Faculty Law Rev., Toronto

**Fairchild** Fairchild's Rep. (10–12 Me.)

**Far.** Farresley (7 Modern Rep.), *Eng.*

**Farresley** Farresley's Rep. (7 Modern Rep.), *Eng.*

Holt's K.B. Rep. (Farresley Cases), *Eng.*

**Fawc.** Fawcett's Ct. of Referees Rep., *Eng.*

**Fed.** Federal Reporter, *U.S.*

The Federalist

**Fed.2d** Federal Reporter, Second Series, *U.S.*

**Fed.Anti-Tr.Dec.** Federal Anti-Trust Dec., *U.S.*

**Fed.B.A.J[o].** Federal Bar Assn. Jour.

**Fed.B.J.** Federal Bar Jour.

**Fed.Cas.** Federal Cas., *U.S.*

**Fed.Com.B.J.** Federal Communications Bar Jour.

**Fed.R.D.** Federal Rules Dec., *U.S.*

**Fed.Rep.** Federal Reporter, *U.S.*

**Fed.Supp.** Federal Supplement, *U.S.*

**Fin.** Finch's Ch. Rep., *Eng.*

**Fin.H.** H. Finch's Ch. Rep., *Eng.*

**Finch** Finch's Ch. Rep., *Eng.*

Finch's Precedents in Chancery, *Eng.*

**Fish.** Fisher's Prize Cas., Dist. Ct., *U.S.*

Fisher's Patent Cas., *U.S.*

**Fish.Pat.Cas.** Fisher's Patent Cas., *U.S.*

**Fish.Pat.Rep.** Fisher's Patent Rep., *U.S.*

**Fish.Pr.Cas.** Fisher's Prize Cas., Dist. Ct., *U.S.*

**Fits.Nat.Brev.** Fitzherbert's Natura Brevium, *Eng.*

**Fitz.** Fitzgibbon's K.B. Rep., *Eng.*

**Fitzh.Abr.** Fitzherbert's Abridgement, *Eng.*

**Fitzh.N.B.** Fitzherbert's New Natura Brevium, *Eng.*

**Fl.** Fleta, *Eng.*

**Fla.** Florida

**Fla.L.J.** Florida Law Jour.

**Fla.Supp.** Florida Supplement

**Flip.** Flippin's Cir. Ct. Rep., *U.S.*

**Fogg** Fogg's Rep. (32-37 N.H.)

**Fonbl.N.R.** Fonblanque's Cases in Chancery, *Eng.*

**For.** Forrest's Ex. Rep., *Eng.*

Forrester's Ch. Rep. *temp.* Talbot, *Eng.*

**For.Aff.** Foreign Affairs

**Fordh.L.Rev.** Fordham Law Rev.

**Forman** Forman's Rep. (1 Scammon, 2 Ill.)

**Forr.** Chancery Cas. *temp.* Talbot, *Eng.*

Forrest's Ex. Rep., *Eng.*

**Fort.** Fortescue's K.B. Rep., *Eng.*

**Fort. de Laud.** Fortesque, De Laudibus Legum Angliae, *Eng.*

**Fortes Rep.** Fortescue's K.B. Rep., *Eng.*

**Fortn.L.J.** Fortnightly Law Jour.

**Forum** Forum: Bench and Bar Rev.

Forum Law Rev.

Forum, Dickinson School of Law

**Fost.** Foster's Crown Cas., *Eng.*

Foster's Legal Chronicle Rep., *Pa.*

Foster's Rep. (21-31 N.H.)

Foster's Rep. (5, 6, 8 Hawaii)

**Fost.&Fin.** Foster & Finlason's N.P., Rep., *Eng.*

**Fox** Fox's Patent, Trade Mark, Design and Copyright Cas., *Can.*

Fox's Cir. and Dist. Ct. Dec., *U.S.*

**Fox Pat.Cas.** Fox's Patent, Trade Mark, Design and Copyright Cas., *Can.*

**Fr.** Freeman's K.B. and Ch. Rep., *Eng.*

**Fr.Chy.** Freeman's Ch. Rep., *Eng.*

**France** France's Rep. (3-11 Colo.)

**Free.** Freeman's Ch. Rep., *Eng.*

Freeman's K.B. Rep., *Eng.*

Freeman's Rep. (31-96 Ill.)

**Free.Ch.** Freeman's Ch. Rep., *Eng.*

Freeman's Rep. (Miss. Ch. 1839-43)

**Freem.C.C.**   Freeman's   Ch.   Cas., *Eng.*

**Freem.Ch.**   Freeman's   Ch.   Rep., *Eng.*

**Freem.(Ill.)**   Freeman's Rep. (31-96 Ill.)

**Freem.K.B.**   Freeman's K.B. and C.P. Rep., *Eng.*

**Freem.(Miss.)**   Freeman's Miss. Ch. Rep.

**French**   French's Rep. (6 N.H.)

**Fuller**   Fuller's Rep. (59-105 Mich.)


**G.**   Georgia
Gale's Ex. Rep., *Eng.*

**GA**   General Assembly, *U.N.*

**G.A.**   General Appraisers' Dec., *U.S.*

**G.A.O.**   General Accounting Office, *U.S.*

**GATT/CP**   General Agreement Tariffs and Trade, Contracting Parties, *U.S.*

**G.C.M.**   General Counsel's Memorandum, Internal Revenue Service, *U.S.*

**G.Gr.**   G. Green's Rep. (Iowa 1847-54)

**G.M.Dud.**   Dudley's Rep. (Ga. 1830-33)

**GSA**   General Services Admin., *U.S.*

**G.&D.**   Gale & Davison's Q.B. Rep., *Eng.*

**G.&G.**   Goldsmith & Guthrie's Rep. (36-67 Mo. App.)

**G.&J.**   Gill & Johnson's Rep., *Md.*
Glyn & Jameson's Bankruptcy Rep., *Eng.*

**G.&R.**   Geldert & Russell's Nova Scotia Rep.

**Ga.**   Georgia

**Ga.App.**   Georgia Appeals Rep.

**Ga.Dec.**   Georgia Dec.

**Ga.L.**   Georgia Lawyer

**Ga.L.J.**   Georgia Law Jour.

**Ga.L.Rep.**   Georgia Law Reporter

**Ga.L.Rev.**   Georgia Law Rev.

**Ga.Supp.**   Lester's Supplement to 33 Ga.

**Gal.&Dav.**   Gale & Davison's Q.B. Rep., *Eng.*

**Galb.&M.**   Galbraith & Meek's Rep. (12 Fla.)

**Galbraith**   Galbraith's Rep. (9-12 Fla.)

**Gale**   Gale's Ex. Rep., *Eng.*
Gale's New Forest Dec., *Eng.*

**Gale&Dav.**   Gale & Davison's Q.B. Rep., *Eng.*

**Gall.**   Gallison's Cir. Ct. Rep., *U.S.*

**Gard.N.Y.Rep.**   Gardiner's N.Y. Reporter

**Gardenhire**   Gardenhire's Rep. (14, 15 Mo.)

**Gay.(La.)**   Gayarre's Rep. (25-28 La. Annual)

**Gayarre**   Same as above

**Gaz.**   Weekly Law Gazette, Cincinnati

**Geld.&Ox.**   Geldert & Oxley's Nova Scotia Dec.

**Geld.&R.**   Geldert & Russell's Nova Scotia Rep.

**Geldart**   Geldart & Maddock's Ch. Rep. (6 Maddock), *Eng.*

**Gen.Dig.**   General Digest

**Geo.**   Georgia

**Geo.Coop.**   G. Cooper's Ch. Cas. *temp.* Eldon, *Eng.*

**Geo.Dec.**   Georgia Dec.

**Geo.L.J.**   Georgetown Law Jour.

**Geo.Wash.L.Rev.**   George Washington Law Rev.

**George**   George's Rep. (30-39 Miss.)

**Georget.L.J.**   Georgetown Law Jour.

**Gibbons**   Gibbons' Surrogate's Rep., *N.Y.*

**Gibbs**   Gibbs' Rep. (2-4 Michigan)

**Giff.**   Giffard's Ch. Rep., *Eng.*

**Giff.&H.**   Giffard & Hemming's Ch. Rep., *Eng.*

**Gil.**   Gilbert's Cases in Law and Equity, *Eng.*
Gilbert's Ch. Rep., *Eng.*
Gilman's Rep. (6-10 Ill.)
Gilmer's Rep. (21 Va.)

**Gilb.**   Gilbert's Cases in Law and Equity, *Eng.*

**Gilb.Cas.**   Gilbert's Cases in Law and Equity

**Gilb.Ch.**   Gilbert's Ch. and Ex. Rep., *Eng.*

**Gilb.Eq.Rep.**   Gilbert's Ch. and Eq. Rep., *Eng.*

**Gilb.Rep.** Gilbert's Ch. Rep., *Eng.*

**Gildersleeve** Gildersleeve's Rep. (1-10 N.M.)

**Gilfillan.** Minnesota Rep., Gilfillan ed.

**Gill.** Gill's Rep. (Md. App.)

**Gill&Johns.** Gill & Johnson's Md. Rep.

**Gilm.** Gilman's Rep. (6-10 Ill.)
Gilmer's Rep. (21 Va.)

**Gilmer** Gilmer's Rep. (21 Va.)

**Gilp.** Gilpin's Dist. Ct. Rep., *U.S.*

**Glanv.** Glanville's De Legibus et Consuetudinibus Regni Angliae, *Eng.*

**Glenn** Glenn's Rep. (16-18 La. Annual)

**Goldb.** Goldbolt's K.B., C.P. and Ex., *Eng.*

**Goebel** Goebel's Ohio Probate Cas.

**Gold.** Goldesborough's K.B. Rep., *Eng.*

**Gold.&G.** Goldsmith & Guthrie's Rep. (36, 37 Mo. App.)

**Gordon** Gordon's Rep. (24-26 Colo.)
Gordon's Rep. (10-13 Colo. App.)

**Gouldsb.** Gouldsborough's K.B. Rep., *Eng.*
Gouldsborough's Q.B. Rep., *Eng.*

**Gour.** Gourick's Patent Digest 1889-91, *U.S.*

**Gow** Gow's N.P. Rep., *Eng.*

**Gr.** Grant's Upper Canada Ch. Rep.
Grant's Pa. Cas. 1814-63
Green's Rep. (N.J. Law and Eq.)
Greenleaf's Rep. (1-9 Me.)

**Gr.Eq.** Green's Rep. (16-27 N.J. Eq.)

**Gra.** Graham's Rep. (98-139 Ga.)

**Granger** Granger's Rep. (22, 23 Ohio St.)

**Grant** Grant's Upper Canada Ch. Rep.
Grant's Pa. Cas. 1814-63

**Grant Cas.** Grant's Pa. Cas.

**Grant Ch.** Grant's Upper Canada Ch. Rep.

**Grant E.&A.** Grant's Ontario Error and Appeal Rep.

**Grant(Pa.)** Grant's Pa. Cas.

**Grant U.C.** Grant's Upper Canada Ch. Rep.

**Grat.** Grattan's Rep. (42-74 Va.)

**Gray** Gray's Rep. (67-82 Mass.)
Gray's Rep. (112-22 N.C.)

**Graya** Graya (periodical)

**Green** Green's Rep. (N.J. Law and Eq.)
Green's Rep. (1-9 Me.)
Green's Rep. (1 Okla.)
Green's Rep. (11-17 R.I.)

**Green Bag** Green Bag, Boston

**Green C.E.** Green's Rep. (16-27 N.J. Eq.)

**Green Ch.** H. W. Green's Rep. (2-4 N.J. Eq.)

**Green L.** Green's Rep. (13-15 N.J. Law)

**Green R.I.** Green's Rep. (11-17 R.I.)

**Greene** Greene's Iowa Rep. 1847-54
Greene's Reports (7 N.Y. Ann. Cas.)

**Greenl.** Greenleaf's Rep. (1-9 Me.)

**Greenl.Ov.Cas.** Greenleaf's Overruled Cas.

**Griffith** Griffith's Rep. (117-32 Ind.)
Griffith's Rep. (1-5 Ind. App.)

**Grisw[old]** Griswold's Rep. (14-19 Ohio)

**Gunby** Gunby's Dist. Ct. Rep. (La. 1885)

**Guthrie** Guthrie's Rep. (33-83 Mo. App.)


**H.** Hare's Ch. Rep., *Eng.*
Hill N.Y. Rep. 1841-44
Howard Sup. Ct. Rep. (42-65 U.S.)

**H.B.** House of Representatives Bill

**H.Bl.** H. Blackstone's C.P. Rep., *Eng.*

**H.Con.Res.** House of Representatives Concurrent Resolution

**H.Doc.** House of Representatives Document

**H.J.Res.** House of Representatives Joint Res.

**H.L.** House of Lords
Clark's H.L. Cas., *Eng.*

**H.L.Cas.** Same as above

**H.L.R.** Harvard Law Rev.

**HOLC** Home Owner's Loan Corp., *U.S.*

**H.P.C.** Hale's Pleas of the Crown, *Eng.*

**H.R.** House of Representatives Bill

House Roll, *U.S.*

**H.R.Rep.** House of Representatives Rep.

**H.Rept.** House of Representatives Rep.

**H.Res.** House of Representatives Resolution

**H.W.Gr.** H. W. Green's Rep. (2-4 N.J. Eq.)

**H.&C.** Hurlstone & Coltman's Ex. Rep., *Eng.*

**H.&G.** Harris & Gill's Md. Rep. 1826-29

Hurlstone's & Gordon's Rep., *Eng.*

**H.&H.** Horn & Hurlstone's Ex. Rep., *Eng.*

**H.&J.** Harris & Johnson's Rep. (Md. App.)

**H.&M.** Hemming & Miller's Vice-Chancellor's Rep., *Eng.*

Hening & Munford's Rep. (11-14 Va.)

**H.&McH.** Harris & McHenry's Md. Rep.

**H.&N.** Hurlstone & Norman's Ex. Rep., *Eng.*

**H.&R.** Harrison & Rutherford's C.P. Rep., *Eng.*

**H.&S.** Harris & Simrall's Rep. (49-52 Miss.)

**H.&T.** Hall & Twell's Ch. Rep., *Eng.*

**H.&W.** Harrison & Wollaston's K.B. Rep., *Eng.*

Hurlstone & Walmsley's Ex. Rep., *Eng.*

**Ha.** Hare's Vice-Chancellors' Rep., *Eng.*

**Ha.&Tw.** Hall & Twell's Ch. Rep., *Eng.*

**Had.** Hadley's Rep. (45-48 N.H.)

**Hadley** Hadley's Rep. (45-48 N.H.)

**Hag.** Hagans' Rep. (1-5 W.Va.)

Haggard's Admiralty Rep., *Eng.*

**Hag.Adm.** Same as above

**Hag.Con.** Haggard's Consistory Rep., *Eng.*

**Hagan** Hagan's Rep. (1, 2 Utah)

**Hagans** Hagans' Rep. (1-5 W.Va.)

**Hagn.&Mill.** Hagner & Miller's Rep. (2 Md. Ch.)

**Hal.Law** Halsted's Rep. (6-12 N.J. Law)

**Hale P.C.** Hale's Pleas of the Crown, *Eng.*

**Hall** Hall's Rep. (56, 57 N.H.)

Hall's Rep. (1, 2 N.Y. Super.)

Hallett's Rep. (1, 2 Colo.)

**Hall N.H.** Hall's Rep. (56, 57 N.H.)

**Hall&Tw.** Hall & Twell's Ch. Cas., *Eng.*

**Hallett** Hallett's Rep. (1, 2 Colo.)

**Hals.** Halsted's Rep. (6-12 N.J. Law)

**Hals.Ch.** Halsted's Rep. (5-8 N.J. Eq.)

**Ham.** Hammond's Rep. (1-9 Ohio St.)

**Hamlin** Hamlin's Rep. (81-99 Me.)

**Hammond** Hammond's Rep. (36-45 Ga.)

Hammond's Rep. (1-9 Ohio)

**Hammond&Jackson** Hammond & Jackson's Rep. (45 Ga.)

**Han.** Handy's Ohio Rep. (12 Ohio Dec.)

**Hand.** Hand's Rep. (40-45 N.Y.)

**Handy** Handy's Ohio Rep. (12 Ohio Dec.)

**Hans.Deb.** Hansard's Parliamentary Debates, *Eng.*

**Hansb.** Hansbrough's Rep. (76-90 Va.)

**Har.Del.** Harrington's Rep. (1-5 Del.)

**Har.St.Tr.** Hargrave's State Trials, *Eng.*

**Har.&Gil.** Harris & Gill's Rep. (1826-29 Md.)

**Har.&John.** Harris & Johnston's Rep. (Md. App.)

**Har.&McH.** Harris & McHenry (Md. Gen. Ct.)

**Har.&Ruth.** Harrison & Rutherfurd's C.P. Rep., *Eng.*

**Hard.** Hardin's Rep. (3 Ky.)

Hardres' Ex. Rep., *Eng.*

Kelyngs (W.), Ch. Rep., *Eng.*

**Hardes.** Hardesty's Rep. (Delaware Term)

**Hardw.** Cases *temp.* Hardwicke, Lee's, *Eng.*

Cases *temp.* Hardwicke, Ridgeway's, *Eng.*

**Hare** Hare's Vice-Chancellors' Rep., *Eng.*

**Harg.** Hargrave's State Trials, *Eng.*
Hargrove's Rep. (68-75 N.C.)

**Hargrove** Hargrove's Rep. (68-75 N.C.)

**Harm.** Harmon's Rep. (13-15 Cal.)
Harmon's Upper Canada C.P. Rep.

**Harp.Con.Cas.** Harper's Md. Conspiracy Cas.

**Harp.Eq.** Harper's Rep. (1824 S.C. Eq.)

**Harp.L.** Harper's Rep. (1823-30 S.C. Law)

**Harr.** Harrington's Rep. (1-5 Del.)
Harrington's Ch. Rep. (Mich. 1836-42)
Harris' Rep. (13-24 Pa. St.)
Harrison's Rep. (15-17, 23-29 Ind.)
Harrison's Rep. (16-19 N.J. Law)

**Harr.Ch.** Harrington's Mich. Ch. Rep.

**Harr.Con.La.R.** Harrison's Condensed La. Rep.

**Harr.N.J.** Harrison's Rep. (16-19 N.J. Law)

**Harr.&G.** Harris & Gill's Rep. (Md. 1826-29)

**Harr.&J.** Harris & Johnson's Rep. (Md. 1800-26)

**Harr.&Ruth.** Harrison & Rutherfurd's C.P. Rep., *Eng.*

**Harr.&Sim.** Harris & Simrall's Rep. (49-52 Miss.)

**Harring.** Harrington's Rep. (1-5 Del.)
Harrington's Mich. Ch. Rep.

**Harris** Harris' Rep. (13-24 Pa. St.)

**Harris&Sim.** Harris & Simrall's Rep. (49-52 Miss.)

**Harrison** Harrison's Rep. (15-17, 23-29 Ind.)
Harrison's Reports (16-19 N.J. Law)

**Hartley** Hartley's Rep. (4-10 Tex.)

**Hartley&Hartley** Rep. (11-21 Tex.)

**Hask.** Haskell's Rep. for U.S. Courts in Maine (Fox's Dec.)

**Hast.** Hastings' Rep. (69, 70 Me.)

**Hast.L.J.** Hastings Law Jour.

**Haw.** Hawkins' Pleas of the Crown, *Eng.*
Hawkins' Rep. (19-24 La. Annual)
Hawaii (Sandwich Islands) Rep.
Hawley's Rep. (10-20 Nev.)

**Hawaii** Hawaii Rep.

**Hawarde** Hawarde's Star Chamber Cas., *Eng.*

**Hawarde St. Ch.** Same as above

**Hawk.P.C.** Hawkins' Plea of the Crown, *Eng.*

**Hawkins** Same as above
Hawkins' Rep. (19-24 La. Annual)

**Hawks** Hawks' Rep. (8-11 N.C.)

**Hawley** Hawley's Rep. (10-20 Nev.)

**Hay.** Haywood's Rep. (4-6 Tenn.)
Haywood's Rep. (2-3 N.C.)

**Hayw.** Haywood's Rep. (2, 3 N.C.)
Haywood's Rep. (4-6 Tenn.)

**Hayw.N.C.** Haywood's Rep. (2, 3 N.C.)

**Hayw.Tenn.** Haywood's Rep. 4-6 Tenn.)

**Hayw.&H.** Hayward & Hazelton's District of Columbia Rep. 1840-63

**Head** Head's Rep. (38-40 Tenn.)

**Heath** Heath's Rep. (36-40 Me.)

**Hedges** Hedges' Rep. (2-6 Mont.)

**Heisk.** Heiskell's Rep. (48-59 Tenn.)

**Helm** Helm's Rep. (2-9 Nev.)

**Hem.&M.** Hemming & Miller's Ch. Rep., *Eng.*

**Heming.** Hemingway's Rep. (53-65 Miss.)

**Hemp.** Hempstead's Cir. Ct. Rep., *U.S.*

**Hen.Bl.** H. Blackstone's C.P. Rep., *Eng.*

**Hen.&Mun.** Hening & Munford's Rep. (11-14 Va.)

**Hennepin Law.** Hennepin Lawyer

**Hepb.** Hepburn's Rep. (3, 4 Cal.)

**Het.** Hetley's C.P. Rep., *Eng.*

**Hibb.** Hibbard's Rep. (67 N.H.)

**Higgins** Higgins Rep. (Tenn. Civil App.)

**Hight** Hight's Rep. (57-58 Iowa)

**Hill.** Hill's N.Y. Rep. 1841-44
Hill's Reports (S.C. Law 1883-37)

**Hill&Den.** Hill & Denio Supplement (Lalor) 1842-44, *N.Y.*

**Hill Eq.** Hill's Rep. (S.C. Eq.)

**Hill S.C.** Hill's Rep. (S.C. Law or Eq.)

**Hillyer** Hillyer's Rep. (20-22 Cal.)

**Hilt.** Hilton's N.Y. C.P. Rep.

**Hines** Hines' Rep. (83-98 Ky.)

**Ho.L.Cas.**   Clark's H.L. Cas., *Eng.*
**Hob.**   Hobart's K.B. Rep., *Eng.*
**Hodg.**   Hodges' C.P. Rep., *Eng.*
**Hoff.**   Hoffman's N.Y. Ch. Rep.
**Hoff.Ch.**   Same as above
**Hoff.L.C.**   Hoffman's Land Cases, U.S. Dist. Ct.
**Hoff.N.Y.**   Hoffman's N.Y. Ch. Rep.
**Hoffm.Ch.**   Same as above
**Hogue**   Hogue's Rep. (1-4 Fla.)
**Holl.**   Hollinshead's Rep. (1 Minn.)
**Holm.**   Holmes' Cir. Ct. Rep., *U.S.* Holmes' Rep. (15-17 Ore.)
**Holt**   Holt's Equity Rep., *Eng.* Holt's K.B. Rep., *Eng.* Holt's N.P. Rep., *Eng.*
**Holt Adm.**   W. Holt's Rule of the Road Cases (Admiralty), *Eng.*
**Holt Eq.**   W. Holt's Eq. Rep., *Eng.*
**Holt K.B.**   John Holt's K.B. Rep., *Eng.*
**Holt N.P.**   F. Holt's N.P. Rep., *Eng.*
**Hook.**   Hooker's Rep. (25-62 Conn.)
**Hop.**   Hopkins
**Hopk.Adm.**   Hopkinson's Judgments in Admiralty (Pa. 1779-89)
**Hopk.Adm.Dec.**   Hopkinson's Admiralty Dec. (*see* Gilpin's U.S. Dist. Ct. Rep.)
**Hopk.Ch.**   Hopkins' N.Y. Ch. Rep.
**Horn&H.**   Horn & Hurlstone's Ex. Rep. *Eng.*
**Horner**   Horner's Rep. (11-28 S.D.)
**Hosea**   Hosea's Rep. (Ohio)
**Hoskins**   Hoskins' Rep. (2 N.D.)
**Houghton**   Houghton's Rep. (97 Ala.)
**Houst.**   Houston's Rep. (6-14 Del.)
**How.**   Howard's Rep. (2-8 Miss.) Howard's N.Y. Practice Rep. Howard's Rep. (42-65 U.S.) Howell Rep. (22-26 Nev.)
**How.App.**   Howard's Appeal Cas. (N.Y. 1847-48)
**How.Cas.**   Same as above
**How.Cr.Tr.**   Howison's Crim. Trials (Va. 1850-51)
**How.N.S.**   Howard's N.Y. Practice Rep., New Series
**How.Pr.**   Howard's N.Y. Practice Rep.
**How.St.Tr.**   Howell's State Trials, *Eng.*

**How.&Beat.**   Howell & Beatty's Nev. Rep.
**Howard S.C.**   U.S. Sup. Ct. Rep. 42-65 U.S.
**Howell N.P.**   Howell's N.P. Cas. (Mich. 1868-84)
**Hu.**   Hughes
**Hubbard**   Hubbard's Rep. (45-51 Me.)
**Hugh.**   Hughes' Cir. Ct. Rep., *U.S.* Hughes' Rep. (1 Ky.)
**Hum.**   Humphrey's Rep. (20-30 Tenn.)
**Humph.**   Humphrey's Rep. (20-30 Tenn.)
**Hun**   New York Sup. Ct. Rep. Hun's N.Y. Appellate Div. Rep.
**Hurl.&Colt.**   Hurlstone & Coltman's Ex. Rep., *Eng.*
**Hurl.&Gord.**   Hurlstone & Gordon's Rep. (10, 11 Ex. Rep.), *Eng.*
**Hurl.&Nor.**   Hurlstone & Norman's Ex. Rep., *Eng.*
**Hurl.&Walm.**   Hurlstone & Walmsley's Ex. Rep., *Eng.*
**Hut.**   Hutton's C.P. Rep., *Eng.*
**Hutch.**   Hutcheson's Rep. (81 Ala.)
**Hutt.**   Hutton's C.P. Rep., *Eng.*
**Hy.Bl.**   Henry Blackstone's C.P. Rep., *Eng.*

**ICAO**   International Civil Aviation Organization, *UN*
**I.C.C.Pract.J.**   I.C.C. Practitioners' Jour.
**I.C.Rep.**   Interstate Commerce Commission Rep., *U.S.*
**I.D.**   Interior Department Dec., *U.S.*
**I.J.**   Irish Jurist
**ILO**   International Labor Organization, *UN*
**I.L.T.**   Irish Law Times
**I.R.B.**   Internal Revenue Bulletin, *U.S.*
**I.R.C.**   Internal Revenue Code, *U.S.*
**I.T.**   Income Tax Division Ruling (U.S. Internal Revenue Service)
**ITO**   International Trade Organization, *UN*
**ITU**   International Telecommunication Union, *UN*
**I.&N.**   Immigration and Nationality Laws Administrative Dec. (Justice Dept.), *U.S.*

**I.&N.S.** Immigration and Naturalization Services, *U.S.*

**Ia.** Iowa

**Ia.L.Rev.** Iowa Law Rev.

**Id.L.J.** Idaho Law Jour.

**Ida.** Idaho

**Idaho** Idaho Rep.

**Iddings T.R.D.** Iddings' Dayton (Ohio) Term Rep.

**Idea.** Pat. Tradem. & Copyr. J. of Research & Ec.

**Ill.** Illinois

**Ill.App.** Illinois Appellate Court Rep.

**Ill.Ct.Cl.** Illinois Court of Claims

**Ill.L.B.** Illinois Law Bulletin

**Ill.L.Q.** Illinois Law Quarterly

**Ind.** Indiana

**Ind.App.** Indiana Appellate Ct. Rep.

**Ind.L.J.** Indiana Law Jour.

**Ind.Super.** Wilson's Ind. Sup. Ct. Rep. 1871-74

**Ind.T.** Indian Territory

**Ind.&L.Rel.Rev.** Industrial and Labor Relations Rev.

**Ins.Counsel J.** Insurance Counsel Jour.

**Ins.L.J.** Insurance Law Jour.

**Inst.** Coke's Institutes, *Eng.* Justinian's Institutes

**Inst.Com.Com.** Interstate Commerce Comm., *U.S.*

**Inst.Min.L.** Inst. on Mineral Law, La.

**Int.Com.Rep.** Interstate Commerce Comm. Rep., *U.S.*

**Interst.Com.R.** Same as above

**Iowa** Iowa Rep.

**Ired.** Iredell's Rep. (23-35 N.C. Law)

**Ired.Eq.** Iredell's Rep. (36-43 N.C. Eq.)

**Irish L.T.** Irish Law Times

**J.** Johnson's Cases or Rep., *N.Y.*

**J.Account.** Journal of Accountancy

**JAGA** Military Affairs Division, Office of Judge Advocate General, U.S. Army

**J.Am.Jud.Soc.** Journal of American Judicature Soc.

**J.A.T.L.A.** J. Am. Trial Lawyers Assn.

**J.B.Moo.** J. B. Moore's C.P. Rep., *Eng.*

**J.Bridge.** J. Bridgman's C.P. Rep., *Eng.*

**J.C.** Johnson's Cases or Rep., *N.Y.*

**J.Ch.** Johnson's Ch. Rep., *N.Y.*

**J.C.L.&I.L.** Journal of Comparative Legislation and International Law

**J.C.R.** Judicial Council Rep.

**J.Comp.Leg.** Journal of Society of Comparative Legislation

**J.Comp.Leg.&Int.Law** Journal of Comparative Legislation and International Law

**J.Crim.L.** Journal of American Institute of Criminal Law and Criminology

**J.For.Med.** Jour. Forensic Med.

**J.For.Sci.** Jour. Forensic Sci.

**J.H.** Journal, House of Representatives, *U.S.*

**J.J.Mar.** Marshall's Rep. (24-30 Ky.)

**J.Kel.** John Kelyng's Crown Cas., *Eng.*

**J.Land&Pub.Util.Econ.** Journal of Land and Public Utility Economics.

**J.Legal Ed.** Journal of Legal Education

**J.P.** Justice of the Peace

**J.P.L.** Journal of Public Law

**J.P.O.S.** Journal of the Patent Office Soc.

**J.P.Sm.** J. P. Smith's K.B. Rep., *Eng.*

**J.Pl.L.** Journal of Planning Law

**J.Pub.L.** Journal of Public Law

**J.R.** Johnson's Rep., *N.Y.*

**J.S.Gr.** J. S. Green's Rep. (13-15 N.J. Law)

**J.Soc.Pub.Teach.Law** Journal of the Society of Public Teachers of Law

**J.Soc.Pub.Teach.LawN.S.** Same, New Series

**J.&H.** Johnson & Hemming's Vice-Chancery Rep., *Eng.*

**J.&S.** Jones & Spencer's Rep. (33-61 N.Y. Super.)

**J.&W.** Jacob & Walker's Ch. Rep., *Eng.*

**Jac.**   Jacob's Ch. Rep., *Eng.*

**Jac.&W.**   Jacob & Walker's Ch. Rep., *Eng.*

**Jack.Tex.App.**   Jackson's Rep. (1-29 Tex. Court of Appeals Rep.)

**Jackson**   Jackson's Rep. (46-58 Ga.) Jackson's Rep. (1-29 Tex. App.)

**Jackson&Lumpkin**   Jackson & Lumpkin's Rep. (59-64 Ga.)

**James**   James' Rep. (2 Nova Scotia)

**Jeff.**   Jefferson's Rep. (Va. Genl. Ct.)

**Jenk.**   Jenkins' Rep. 1220-1623, *Eng.* Jenkins' Ex. Rep., *Eng.*

**Jenk.Cent.**   Same as above

**Jenks**   Jenks' Rep. (58 N.H.)

**Jenn.**   Jennison's Rep. (14-18 Mich.)

**Jo.Jur.**   Journal of Jurisprudence

**Jo.T.**   T. Jones' K.B. Rep., *Eng.*

**John[s].**   Johnson's Rep. (Md. Ch.) Johnson's Rep. (N.Y. Sup. or Ch.) Chase's Cir. Ct. Dec., ed. by Johnson, *U.S.* Johnson's Vice-Chancery Rep., *Eng.*

**John.&H.**   Johnson & Hemming Ch. Rep., *Eng.*

**Johns.Cas.**   Johnson's Cas. (N.Y. 1799-1803)

**Johns.Ch.**   Johnson's Md. Ch. Dec. Johnson's Ch. Rep. (N.Y. 1814-23) Johnson's Vice-Chancery Rep., *Eng.*

**Johns.Ct.Err.**   Johnson's Rep. (N.Y. Ct. of Errors)

**Johns.Dec.**   Johnson's Ch. Dec., *Md.*

**Johns.Eng.Ch.**   Johnson's Ch. Rep., *Eng.*

**Johns.Rep.**   Johnson's Rep. (N.Y. Sup. or Ch.)

**Johns.U.S.**   Chase's Cir. Ct. Dec., ed. by Johnson, *U.S.*

**Johns.V.C.**   Johnson's Vice-Chancery Rep., *Eng.*

**Johns.&Hem.**   Johnson & Hemming's Ch. Rep., *Eng.*

**Jon.**   T. Jones' K.B. and C.P. Rep., *Eng.* W. Jones' K.B. and C.P. Rep., *Eng.*

**Jones**   Jones' Rep. (43-48, 52-57, 61, 62 Ala.) Jones' Rep. (22-30 Mo.) Jones' Rep. (11, 12 Pa.) Jones' Rep. (N.C. Law or Eq.)

Jones' Upper Canada C.P. Rep.

**Jones 1**   W. Jones' K.B. Rep., *Eng.*

**Jones 2**   T. Jones' K.B. Rep., *Eng.*

**Jones, Barclay & Whittlesey** (31 Mo.)

**Jones Eq.**   Jones' Rep. (54-59 N.C. Eq.)

**Jones N.C.**   Jones' Rep. (46-53 N.C. Law)

**Jones Pa.**   Jones' Rep. (11, 12 Pa. St.)

**Jones T.(or 2)**   T. Jones' K.B. Rep., *Eng.*

**Jones W.(or 1)**   W. Jones' K.B. Rep., *Eng.*

**Jones&McM.**   Jones & McMurtrie's Pa. Sup. Ct. Rep.

**Jones&Sp.**   Jones & Spencer's Rep. (33-61 N.Y. Super.)

**Jos.**   Joseph's Rep. (21 Nev.)

**Jud.Chr.**   Judicial Chronicle

**Jud.Rep.**   Judicial Repository, *N.Y.*

**Judd**   Judd's Rep. (4 Hawaii)

**Judg.U.B.**   Judgments of Upper Bench, *Eng.*

**Jur.Rev.**   Juridical Review

**Jurid.Rev.**   Juridical Rev.

**Jurispr.**   The Jurisprudent

**Just.L.R.**   Justices' Law Reporter (Pa. 1902-18)

**Just.Peace**   Justice of the Peace

**K.**   Keyes' Court of Appeals Rep. (40-43 N.Y.) Kenyon's K.B. Rep., *Eng.*

**K.B.**   Law Rep. K.B., *Eng.* Law Reports, K.B. Div., *Eng.*

**K.B.U.C.**   Upper Canada K.B. Rep.

**K.C.R.**   Reports *temp.* King, *Eng.*

**K.&J.**   Kay & Johnson's Ch. Rep., *Eng.*

**Kan.**   Kansas

**Kan.App.**   Kansas Appeals Rep.

**Kan.C.L.Rep.**   Kansas City Law Reporter

**Kan.L.J.**   Kansas Law Jour.

**Kan.L.Rev.**   University of Kansas Law Rev.

**Kans.App.**   Kansas Appeals Rep.

**Kay**   Kay's Ch. Rep., *Eng.*

**Kay&John.**   Kay & Johnson's Vice-Chancellors' Rep., *Eng.*

**Keb.**   Keble's K.B. Rep., *Eng.*

**Keil.** Keilway's K.B. Rep., *Eng.*

**Keilw.** Same as above

**Keith Ch. Pa.** Registrar's Book, Keith's Court of Chancery, *Pa.*

**Kel.** John Kelyng's Crown Case Rep., *Eng.*

**Kel.1(*or* J.)** John Kelyng's Crown Cas., *Eng.*

**Kel.2(*or* W.)** W. Kelynge's Ch. Rep., *Eng.*

**Kel.Ga.** Kelly's Rep. (1-3 Ga.)

**Kel.J.** Same as Kel. 1

**Kel.W.** Same as Kel. 2

**Kellen** Kellen's Rep. (146-55 Mass.)

**Kelly** Kelly's Rep. (1-3 Ga.)

**Kelly&Cobb** Kelly & Cobb's Rep. (4, 5 Ga.)

**Kelyng J.** Kelyng's Crown Cas., *Eng.*

**Ken.** Kenyon's K.B. Rep., *Eng.*

**Ken.Dec.** Kentucky Dec., Sneed (2 Ky.)

**Ken.L.Re.** Kentucky Law Reporter

**Ken.Opin.** Kentucky Opinions 1864-86

**Kenan** Kenan's Rep. (76-91 N.C.)

**Keny.** Kenyon's K.B. Rep., *Eng.*

**Keny.Ch.** Chancery Cas. (v. 2 of Notes of K.B. Cas., *Eng.*

**Keny.Chy.(3 Keny.)** Chancery Rep., at end of 2 Kenyon, *Eng.*

**Kern.** Kern's Rep. (100-116 Ind.) Kernan's Rep. (11-14 N.Y.)

**Kerr** Kerr's Rep. (18-22 Ind.) Kerr's Rep. (27-29 N.Y. Civil Procedure Rep.)

**Key.** Keyes' Rep. (40-43 N.Y.)

**Keyl.** Keilway's English Bench Rep.

**King** King's Rep. (5, 6 La. Annual)

**King** Select Cas. *temp.* King, Ch., *Eng.*

**King's Conf.Ca.** King's Conflicting Cas. (Tex. 1840-1911)

**Kir.** Kirby's Rep. and Supplement (Conn. 1785-89)

**Kn.** Knapp's P.C. Cas., *Eng.*

**Kn.A.C.** Knapp's Appeal Cas. (P.C.), *Eng.*

**Kn.P.C.** Knapp's P.C. Cas., *Eng.*

**Kn.&Moo.** 3 Knapp's P.C. Rep., *Eng.*

**Knapp** Knapp's P.C. Rep., *Eng.*

**Knowles** Knowles' Rep. (3 R.I.)

**Kreider** Kreider's Rep. (1-23 Wash.)

**Kress** Kress's Rep. (166-194 Pa. St.) Kress's Rep. (2-12 Pa. Super.)

**Kulp** Kulp's Luzerne Legal Register Rep., *Pa.*

**Ky.** Kentucky

**Ky.Dec.** Sneed's Ky. Dec. (2 Ky.)

**Ky.L.Rep.** Kentucky Law Reporter

**Ky.Op.** Kentucky Court of Appeals Opinions


**L.** Lansing's Select Cases in Chancery (N.Y. 1824, 1826)

**L.Abr.** Lilly's Abridgement, *Eng.*

**L.C.** Lord Chancellor

**L.C.J.** Lower Canada Jurist

**L.C.L.J.** Lower Canada Law Jour.

**L.C.R.** Lower Canada Rep.

**L.D.** Land Office Dec., *U.S.*

**L.Ed.** Lawyers' Edition, U.S. Sup. Ct. Rep.

**L.I.** Legal Intelligence, *Pa.*

**L.In.Trans.J.** Law in Transition Jour.

**L.J.** Law Jour. Hall's Law Jour. House of Lords Jour. New York Law Jour.

**L.J.Adm.** Law Jour. Rep., Admiralty, *Eng.*

**L.J.App.** Law Jour. Rep., New Series, Appeals

**L.J.C.** Law Jour. Rep., New Series, C.P., *Eng.*

**L.J.C.C.R.** Law Jour. Rep., New Series, Crown Cas. Res., *Eng.*

**L.J.C.P.** Law Jour. Rep., C.P., *Eng.*

**L.J.C.P.D.** Law Jour. Rep., New Series, C.P. Dec., *Eng.*

**L.J.Ch.** Law Jour. Rep., New Series, Ch. *Eng.*

**L.J.Ch.(O.S.)** Law Jour. Rep., Ch., Old Series, *Eng.*

**L.J.D.&M.** Law Jour. Rep., New Series, Divorce and Matrimonial, *Eng.*

**L.J.Eccl.** Law Jour. Ecclesiastical Cas., *Eng.*

**L.J.Exch.** Law Jour. Rep., New Series, Ex., *Eng.*

**L.J.Ex.D.** Law Jour. Rep., New Series, Ex. Div., *Eng.*

**L.J.Ex.Eq.**  Law Jour., Ex. in Eq. *Eng.*

**L.J.H.L.**  Law Jour. Rep., New Series, H.L., *Eng.*

**L.J.K.B.**  Law Jour. Rep., K. or Q. B., *Eng.*

**L.J.L.C.**  Law Jour., Lower Canada

**L.J.M.P.A.**  Law Jour. Rep., Matrimonial, Probate and Admiralty, *Eng.*

**L.J.Mat.Cas.**  Law Jour. Rep., New Series, Divorce and Matrimonial, *Eng.*

**L.J.N.S.**  Law Jour., New Series, *Eng.*

**L.J.O.S.**  Law Jour., Old Series, *Eng.*

**L.J.P.**  Law Jour. Rep., New Series, P.C., *Eng.*
  Law Jour. Rep., Probate, Divorce, and Admiralty, *Eng.*

**L.J.P.C.**  Law Jour. Rep., P.C., *Eng.*

**L.J.P.C.N.S.**  Law Jour. Rep., New Series, P.C., *Eng.*

**L.J.P.D.&A.**  Law Jour. Rep., New Series, Probate, Divorce, and Admiralty, *Eng.*

**L.J.P.M.&A.**  Law Jour. Rep., New Series, Probate, Matrimonial, and Admiralty, *Eng.*

**L.J.P.&M.**  Law Jour., Probate and Admiralty Cas., *Eng.*

**L.J.Q.B.**  Law Jour. Rep., New Series, Q.B., *Eng.*

**L.J.Q.B.D.**  Law Jour. Rep., New Series, Q.B. Div., *Eng.*

**L.J.R.[ep.]**  Law Jour. Rep., *Eng.*

**L.J.Rep.N.S.**  Law Jour. Rep., New Series (from 1831), *Eng.*

**L.J.U.C.**  Law Jour. of Upper Canada

**L.Jo.**  Law Jour. (newspaper), *Eng.*

**L.L.J.**  Law Library Jour.

**L.Lib.J.**  Law Library Jour.

**L.O.**  Legal Observer
  Solicitor's Law Opinion (U.S. Internal Revenue Service)

**L.Q.Rev.**  Law Quarterly Rev.

**L.R.**  Louisiana Rep.

**L.R.A.**  Lawyers' Rep. Annot.

**L.R.A.C.**  Law Rep., Appeal Cas., *Eng.*

**L.R.A.&E.**  Law Rep., Admiralty and Ecclesiastical Cas., *Eng.*

**L.R.App.**  Law Rep., Appeal Cas., H.L., *Eng.*

**L.R.A.N.S.**  Lawyers' Rep. Annot., New Series, *U.S.*

**L.R.C.C.R.**  Law Rep., Crown Cas Res., *Eng.*

**L.R.C.P.**  Law Rep. C.P., *Eng.*

**L.R.C.P.D.**  Law Rep., C.P. Div., *Eng.*

**L.R.Ch.**  Law Rep., Ch. Appeal Cas. *Eng.*

**L.R.Ch.D.**  Law Rep., Ch. Div., *Eng.*

**L.R.E.&I.App.**  Law Rep., H.L. (English and Irish Appeals)

**L.R.Eq.**  Law Rep., Eq., *Eng.*

**L.R.Ex.**  Law Rep., Ex., *Eng.*

**L.R.Ex.Div.**  Law Rep., Ex. Div., *Eng.*

**L.R.H.L.**  Law Rep., English and Irish Appeals and Peerage Claims, H.L., *Eng.*

**L.R.K.B.**  Law Rep., K.B. Div., *Eng.*

**L.R.Misc.D.**  Law Rep., Miscellaneous Div., *Eng.*

**L.R.P.**  Law Rep., Probate Div., *Eng.*

**L.R.P.C.**  Law Rep., P.C., *Eng.*

**L.R.P.Div.**  Law Rep., Probate, Divorce and Admiralty Div., *Eng.*

**L.R.P.&D.**  Law Rep., Probate, Divorce, *Eng.*

**L.R.P.&M.**  Law Rep., Probate, Matrimonial, *Eng.*

**L.R.Q.B.**  Law Rep., Q.B., *Eng.*
  Quebec Rep., Q.B.

**L.R.Q.B.D.**  Law Rep., Q.B. Div., *Eng.*

**LRR**  Labor Relations Reporter (B.N.A.), *U.S.*

**LRRM**  Labor Relations Reporter: Labor-Management Relations, *U.S.*

**L.R.Sess.Cas.**  Law Rep., Session Cas., *Eng.*

**L.Rep.Mont.**  Law Reporter, Montreal

**L.Repos.**  Law Repository

**L.Rev.&Quart.J.**  Law Review and Quarterly Jour.

**L.Soc.J.**  Law Society Jour.

**L.T.**  Law Times (Luzerne Law Times, Pa.)
  Law Times Rep., *Eng.*

**L.T.Jo.**  Law Times Jour. (newspaper), *Eng.*

**L.T.N.S.** Law Times Rep., New Series, *Eng.*

**L.T.O.S.** Law Times Rep., Old Series, *Eng.*

**L.T.R.** Law Times Rep., *Eng.*

**L.V.Rep.** Lehigh Valley Law Reporter (Pa. 1885-87)

**L.&C.** Leigh & Cave's Crown Cas. Res., *Eng.*

**L.&E.Rep.** Law and Equity Reporter, *N.Y.*

**L.&M.** Lowndes & Maxwell's Practice Cas., *Eng.*

**L.&W.** Lloyd & Welsby's Mercantile Cas., *Eng.*

**L.&Welsb.** Lloyd & Welsby's Commercial and Mercantile Cas., *Eng.*

**La.** Lane's Ex. Rep., *Eng.*
Louisiana

**La.A.** Louisiana Court of Appeals (Orleans)
Louisiana Annual Rep.

**La.Ann.** Louisiana Annual Rep.

**La.App.** Louisiana Courts of Appeal Rep.

**La.App.(Orleans)** Orleans Court of Appeals Rep., by Teissier (La. 1903-17)

**La.L.J.** Louisiana Law Jour.

**La.L.Rev.** Louisiana Law Rev.

**La.T.R.** Louisiana Term Rep. (Martin)

**Lab.** Labatt's Dist. Ct. Rep. (Cal. 1857-58)

**Lac.Jur.** Lackawanna Jurist, *Pa.*

**Lack.Leg.N.** Lackawanna Legal News, *Pa.*

**Lack.Leg.R.** Lackawanna Legal Record, *Pa.*

**Ladd.** Ladd's Rep. (59-64 N.H.)

**Lalor** Lalor's Supplement to Hill & Denio's N.Y. Rep.

**Lamar** Lamar's Rep. (25-42 Fla.)

**Lamb** Lamb's Rep. (103-105 Wis.)

**Lanc.Bar** Lancaster Bar (Pa. 1869-83)

**Lanc.L.Rev.** Lancaster Law Rev. (Pa. 1883-date)

**Land.Est.C.** Landed Estate Ct., *Eng.*

**Lane** Lane's Ex. Rep., *Eng.*

**Lans.** Lansing's Sup. Ct. Rep. (N.Y. 1869-73)

**Lans.Ch.** Lansing's Select Cas., Ch. (N.Y. 1824, 1826)

**Lans.Sel.Cas.** Same as above

**Lat.** Latch's K.B. Rep., *Eng.*

**Lath[rop]** Lathrop's Rep. (115-145 Mass.)

**Law Cas. Wm.I.** Law Cas., Wm. I to Rich. I, *Eng.*

**Law Chr.** Law Chronicle

**Law Chr.&Jour.Jur.** Law Chronicle and Journal of Jurisprudence

**Law.Ed.** Lawyers' Edition, U.S. Sup. Ct. Rep.

**Law Gaz.** Law Gazette

**Law.Guild Rev.** Lawyers' Guild Rev.

**Law Inst.J.** Law Institute Jour.

**Law J.** Law Jour. Rep. For various series *see* L.J.

**Law Jour.** Law Jour. Rep. For various series *see* L.J.

**Law Lib.J.** Law Liberty Jour.

**Law Q.Rev.** Law Quarterly Rev.

**Law Reg.** Law Register, Chicago
American Law Register, Philadelphia

**Law Rep.** Law Rep. *See* abbreviations under L.R.

**Law Rep.N.S.** Monthly Law Reporter

**Law Rep.** Law Reporter (Ramsey & Morin), *Can.*
Law Reporter, *Eng.*

**Law Repos.** Carolina Law Repository

**Law Rev.&Qu.J.** Law Rev. and Quarterly Jour.

**Law Soc.Jo.** Law Society of Massachusetts, Jour.

**Law Soc.Gaz.** Law Society's Gazette (London or Regina)

**Law Times** (London; Scranton, Pa.)

**Law T.Rep.N.S.** Law Times Rep., New Series, *Eng.*

**Law T.Rep.O.S.** Law Times Rep., Old Series, *Eng.*

**Law.&Bank.** Lawyer and Banker (New Orleans)
Lawyers' & Bankers' Quarterly (St. Louis)

**Law&Contemp.Prob.** Law and Contemporary Problems

**Law.&L.N.** Lawyer and Law Notes, *Eng.*

**Lawrence** Lawrence's Rep. (20 Ohio)

**Lawrence Comp.Dec.** Lawrence's Comptroller's Dec.

**Lay** Lay's Ch. Rep., *Eng.*

**Ld.Birk.** Lord Birkenhead's Judgments, H.L., *Eng.*

**Ld.Ken.** Lord Kenyon's K.B. Rep., *Eng.*

**Ld.Raym.** Lord Raymond's K.B. and C.P. Rep., *Eng.*

**Le.&Ca.** Leigh & Cave's Crown Cas. Res., *Eng.*

**Lea.** Lea's Rep. (69-84 Tenn.)

**Leach** Leach's Crown Cas., *Eng.*

**Lee** Lee's Rep. (9-12 Cal.)

**Lee *t*.Hard.** Lee's Cases *temp.* Hardwicke, in King's Bench and Chancery, *Eng.*

**Leese** Leese's Rep. (26 Neb.)

**Legal Adv.** Legal Advertiser (Chicago)

Legal Adviser (Chicago, Denver)

**Leg.Chron.** Legal Chronicle (Foster's Pa. Rep.)

**Leg.Gaz.Rep.** Campbell's Legal Gazette Rep. (Pa. 1869-71)

**Leg.Int.** Legal Intelligencer (Philadelphia)

**Leg.News** Legal News (Montreal; Sunbury, Pa.; Toledo, Ohio)

**Leg.Op.** Legal Opinion (Harrisburg, Pa.)

**Leg.Rec.** Legal Record (Detroit)

**Leg.Rec.Rep.** Legal Record Rep. (1-2 Schuykill County, Pa.)

**Lehigh Co.L.J.** Lehigh (Pa.) Law Jour.

**Lehigh Val.L.Rep.** Lehigh Valley (Pa.) Law Reporter

**Leigh** Leigh's Rep. (28-39 Va.)

**Leigh&C.** Leigh & Cave's Crown Cas., *Eng.*

**Leo.** Leonard's K.B. Rep., *Eng.*

**Leon.** Leonard's K.B., C.P. Ex. Rep., *Eng.*

**Lest.P.L.** Lester's Public Land Dec.

**Lester** Lester's Rep. (31-33 Ga.)

**Lester Supp.** Supplement to 33 Ga. Rep.

**Lev.** Levinz's K.B. and C.P. Rep., *Eng.*

**Lev.Ent.** Levinz's Entries, *Eng.*

**Lew.** Lewin's Crown Cas. Res., *Eng.*

Lewis' Rep. (29-35 Mo. App.)

Lewis' Rep. (1 Nev.)

**Lew.C.C.** Lewin's Crown Cas. Res., *Eng.*

**Lewis** Lewis' Rep. (1 Nev.)

Lewis' Rep. (29-35 Mo. App.)

Kentucky Law Reporter

**Ley** Ley's K.B. Rep., *Eng.*

Ley's Court of Wards Rep., *Eng.*

**Lib.Ass.** Liber Assisarum, Year Books, 1-51 Edw. III, *Eng.*

**Lil.** Lilly's Assize Rep., *Eng.*

**Lill.Ent.** Lilly's Entries, *Eng.*

**Lilly** Lilly's Cases in Assize, *Eng.*

**Lit.** Littell's Rep. (11-15 Ky.) Littleton's C.P. Rep., *Eng.*

**Lit.Brooke** Brooke's New Cas., K.B., *Eng.*

**Litt.** Littleton's C.P. Rep., *Eng.*

**Littell** Littell's Rep. (11-15 Ky.)

**Little Brooke** Brooke's New Cas., *Eng.*

**Liv.Cas.** Livingston's Cases in Error, *N.Y.*

**Liv.Jud.Op.** Livingston's Judicial Opinions, *N.Y.*

**Ll.L.Pr.Cas.** Lloyd's List Prize Cas., *Eng.*

**Ll.L.Rep.** Lloyd's List Law Rep., *Eng.*

**Ll.List.L.R.** Same as above

**Ll.&W[els].** Lloyd & Welsby's Mercantile Cas., *Eng.*

**Lloyd,L.R.** Lloyd's List Law Rep., *Eng.*

**Lloyd List** Lloyd's List, *Eng.*

**Lloyd's Pr.Cas.** Lloyd's Prize Cas. Rep., *Eng.*

**Lloyd's Rep.** Lloyd's List Law Rep., *Eng.*

**Lobin.** Lobingier's Extraterritorial Cas., U.S. Court for China

**Locus Standi** Locus Standi Rep., *Eng.*

**Lofft** Lofft's K.B. Rep., *Eng.*

**Lond.Gaz.** London Gazette, *Eng.*

**Lond.Jur.** London Jurist Rep., *Eng.*

**Loss&Dam.Rev.** Loss and Damage Rev.

**Lou.** Louisiana. *See* La.

**Lou.L.J.** Louisiana Law Jour.

**Lou.L.Rev.** Louisiana Law Rev.

**Lou. Leg. N.** Louisiana Legal News

**Low.** Lowell's Dist. Ct., Rep. (U.S., D. Mass.)

**Low.C.Seign.** Lower Canada Seignorial Rep.

**Low.Can.** Lower Canada Rep.

**Low.Can.Jur.** Lower Canada Jurist

**Low.Can.L.J.** Lower Canada Law Jour.

**Low.Can.Rep.** Lower Canada Rep.

**Low.Can.Rep.S.Q.** Lower Canada Rep., Seignorial Questions

**Lower Ct.Dec.** Ohio Lower Ct. Dec.

**Lower Ct.Dec.** Ohio Lower Ct. Dec.

**Luc.** Lucas' Rep. (Modern Rep., pt. X), *Eng.*

**Lucas** Same as above

**Ludden** Ludden's Rep. (43, 44 Me.)

**Lumpkin** Lumpkin's Rep. (59-77 Ga.)

**Lush.** Lushington's Admiralty Rep., *Eng.*

**Lut.** E. Lutwyche's Entries and Rep., C.P., *Eng.*

**Luz.L.J.** Luzerne Law Jour., *Pa.*

**Luz.L.T.** Luzerne Law Times, *Pa.*

**Luz.Leg.Obs.** Luzerne Legal Observer, *Pa.*

**Luz.Leg.Reg.** Luzerne Legal Register, *Pa.*

**Luz.Leg.Reg.Rep.** Luzerne Legal Register Rep., *Pa.*


**M.** Maine; Manitoba; Maryland; Massachusetts; Michigan; Minnesota; Mississippi; Missouri; Montana

Miles' Pa. Rep.

New York Miscellaneous Rep.

**M'** *See* Mac and Mc.

**MA** Maritime Admin., *U.S.*

**M.A.** Missouri Appeals Rep.

**M.B.** Miscellaneous Branch, Internal Revenue Service, *U.S.*

**M.C.** Mayor's Court

**M.C.C.** Interstate Commerce Comm. Rep., Motor Carrier Cas., *U.S.*

Moody's Crown Cas. Res., *Eng.*

**MCM 1951** Manual for Courts-Martial, *U.S.*

**M.D.&D.(or DeG.)** Montagu, Deacon & DeGex's Bankruptcy Rep., *Eng.*

**M.G.&S.** Manning, Granger & Scott's C.P. Rep., *Eng.*

**MLB** Maritime Labor Bd., *U.S.*

**M.L.Dig.&R.** Monthly Law Digest and Reporter, *Can.*

**M.L.J.** Memphis Law Jour.

**M.L.R.** Maryland Law Record

Montreal Law Rep.

Modern Law Rev.

**M.L.R.Q.B.** Montreal Law Rep., Q.B.

**M.L.R.S.C** Montreal Law Rep., Super. Ct.

**MO-JAGA** Memorandum Opinions, Judge Advocate General of the Army, *U.S.*

**M.P.C.** Moore's P.C. Cas., *Eng.*

**M.P.R.** Maritime Provinces Rep., *Can.*

**M.R.** Manitoba Law Rep.

Master of the Rolls, *Eng.*

**MSA** Mutual Security Agency, *U.S.*

**MT** Miscellaneous Branch Ruling, Internal Revenue Service, *U.S.*

**M.U.L.R.** Melbourne U. Law Rev.

**M.&C.** Mylne's & Craig's Ch. Rep., *Eng.*

**M.&G.** Macnaghten & Gordon's Ch. Rep., *Eng.*

Maddock & Geldart's Ch. Rep., *Eng.*

Manning & Granger's C.P. Rep., *Eng.*

**M.&Gel.** Maddock & Geldart's Ch. Rep., *Eng.*

**M.&Gord.** Macnaghten & Gordon's Ch. Rep., *Eng.*

**M.&H.** Murphy & Hurlstone's Ex. Rep., *Eng.*

**M.&K.** Mylne & Keen's Ch. Rep., *Eng.*

**M.&M.** Moody & Malkin's N.P. Rep., *Eng.*

**M.&P.** Moore & Payne's C.P. Rep., *Eng.*

**M.&R.** Manning & Ryland's K.B. Rep., *Eng.*

Moody & Robinson's N.P. Rep., *Eng.*

**M.&Rob.** Same as above

**M.&S.**   Manning & Scott's Rep. (9 Common Bench), *Eng.*
Maule & Selwyn's K.B. Rep., *Eng.*
Moore & Scott's C.P. Rep., *Eng.*

**M.&Scott**   Moore & Scott's C.P. Rep., *Eng.*

**M.&W.**   Meeson & Welsby's Ex. Rep., *Eng.*

**M.&Y.**   Martin & Yerger's Rep. (8 Tenn.)

**Mac.**   *See also* Mc

**Mac.&G.**   Macnaghten & Gordon's Ch. Rep., *Eng.*

**Macall.**   McAllister's Cir. Ct. Rep., *U.S.*

**MacArth.**   MacArthur's Rep. (8-10 District of Columbia)

**MacArth.&M.**   MacArthur & Mackey's Rep. (11 District of Columbia)

**M'Cl.**   M'Clelland's Ex. Rep., *Eng.*

**M'Cle.**   Same as above

**M'Cl.&Y.**   M'Clelland & Younge's Ex. Rep., *Eng.*

**McCl.&Y.**   Same as above

**M'Cle.&Yo.**   Same as above

**Maccl.**   Macclesfield's Rep. (Modern Rep., pt. X), *Eng.*

**MacG.C.C.**   MacGillivray's Copyright Cas., *Eng.*

**Mackey**   Mackey's Rep. (12-20 District of Columbia)

**Macl.**   McLean's Cir. Ct. Rep., *U.S.*

**Macn.**   Macnaghten's Select Cases in Chancery *temp.* King, *Eng.*

**Macn.Sel.Cas.**   Same as above

**Macn.&G.**   Macnaghten & Gordon's Ch. Rep., *Eng.*

**Mad.**   Maddock's Ch. Rep., *Eng.*
Maddock's Rep. (9-18 Mont.)

**Mad.&B.**   Maddox & Bach's Rep. (19 Mont.)

**Mad.&Gel.**   Maddock & Geldart's Ch. Rep., *Eng.*

**Madd.**   Maddock's Ch. Rep., *Eng.*
Maddox's Rep. (9-18 Mont.)

**Madd.&G.**   Maddock & Geldart's Ch. Rep., *Eng.*

**Mag.**   Magruder's Rep. (1, 2 Md.)

**Magruder**   Same as above

**Maine**   Maine Rep.

**Mait.**   Maitland's Select Pleas of the Crown, *Eng.*

**Maitland**   *See also* Mait.
Maitland's Pleas of the Crown 1221, *Eng.*
Maitland's Select Pleas of the Crown, *Eng.*

**Malone**   Heiskell's Rep. (6, 9, 10 Tenn.)

**Man.**   Manitoba
Manning Rep., Revision Ct., *Eng.*
Manning Rep. (1 Mich.)

**Man.BarNews**   Manitoba Bar News

**Man.Gr.&S.**   Manning, Granger, & Scott's Common Bench Rep., Old Series, *Eng.*

**Man.L.J.**   Manitoba Law Jour.

**Man.L.R.**   Manitoba Law Rep.

**Man.R.**   Same as above

**Man.R.*t*.Wood**   Manitoba Rep., *temp.* Wood

**Man.Unrep.Cas.**   Manning's Unreported Cases (La.)

**Man.&G.**   Manning & Granger's C.P. Rep., *Eng.*

**Man.&Ry.**   Manning & Ryland's K.B. Rep., *Eng.*

**Man.&Sc.**   Manning & Scott's Common Bench Rep., Old Series, *Eng.*

**Manb.Coke**   Manby's Abridgement of Coke's Rep.

**Manitoba**   *See* Man.

**Mann.**   Manning's Rep. (1 Mich.)
Manning's Revision Ct. Rep., *Eng.*

**Manning**   Manning's Rep. (1 Mich.)

**Manning(La)**   Manning's Unreported Cases (La.)

**Mans.**   Mansfield's Rep. (49-52 Ark.)

**Manum.Cas.**   Bloomfield's Manumission Cas., *N.J.*

**Mar.**   Maritime
March's K.B. Rep., *Eng.*
Martin Rep. (La. 1809-30)
Martin's Rep. (1 N.C.)
Marshall's Cir. Ct. Rep., *U.S.*
Marshall's Rep. (24-30 Ky.)

**Mar.Br.**   March's Brooke's New Cas., *Eng.*

**Mar.Cas.**   Maritime Law Cas., *Eng.*

**Mar.L.C.**   Maritime Law Rep. (Crockford), *Eng.*

**Mar.L.C.N.S.**   Maritime Law Cas., New Series, by Aspinall, *Eng.*

**Mar.L.Rec.**   Maryland Law Record

**Mar.L.Rev.** Maryland Law Rev.

**Mar.(La.)** Martin's Rep., *La.*

**Mar.N.C.** Martin's Rep. (1 N.C.)
March's New Cas., K.B., *Eng.*

**Mar.N.S.** Martin's Rep., New Series, *La.*

**Mar.R.** Maritime Law Rep., *Eng.*

**March.** March's K.B. and C.P. Rep., *Eng.*

**March.N.C.** March's New Cas. K.B. *Eng.*

**March.N..** March's New Cas., K.B. and C.P., *Eng.*

**Marks&Sayre** Marks & Sayre's Rep. (108 Ala.)

**Marq.L.Rev.** Marquette Law Rev.

**Marr.** Hay & Marriott's Admiralty Dec., *Eng.*

**Marsh.** Marshall's Cir. Ct. Dec., *U.S.*
Marshall's C.P. Rep., *Eng.*
Marshall's Rep. (8-10, 24-30 Ky.)
Marshall's Rep. (4 Utah)

**Marsh.A.K.** A. K. Marshall's Rep. (8-10 Ky.)

**Marsh.C.P.** Marshall's C.P. Rep., *Eng.*

**Marsh.Dec.** Marshall's Cir. Ct. Dec., by Brockenbrough, *U.S.*

**Marsh.J.J.** J. J. Marshall's Rep. (24-30 Ky.)

**Mart.Ark.** Martin's Dec. in Equity, *Ark.*

**Mart.Cond.La.** Martin's Condensed Rep., *La.*

**Mart.Dec.** (1 N.C.; contains U.S. Cir. Ct. reports for N.C.)

**Mart.Ga.** Martin's Rep. (21-30 Ga.)

**Mart.Ind.** Martin's Rep. (54-70 Ind.)

**Mart.La.** Martin's Rep. (La., Old and New Series)

**Mart.N.C.** Martin's Rep. (1 N.C.)

**Mart.N.S.** Martin's La. Rep., New Series

**Mart.O.S.** Martin's La. Rep., Old Series

**Mart.U.S.C.C.** Martin's Cir. Ct. Rep. in 1 N.C.

**Mart.&Yerg.** Martin & Yerger's Rep. (8 Tenn.)

**Martin.** *See also* Mart.
Martin's Rep. (21-30, 54-70 Ga.)

Martin's Rep. (La. 1809-30)
Martin's Rep. (1 N.C.)

**Marvel,** Marvel's Rep. (15, 16 Del.)

**Maryland** Maryland Rep.

**Mas.** Mason's Cir. Ct. Rep., *U.S.*

**Mass.** Massachusetts Rep.

**Mass.App.Div.** Massachusetts Appellate Div. Rep. 1935-date

**Mass.L.Q.** Massachusetts Law Quarterly

**Mast.** Master's Sup. Ct. Rep., *Can.*

**Math.** Mathieu's Quebec Rep.

**Matson** Matson's Rep. (22-24 Conn.)

**Matthews** Matthews' Rep. (75 Va.)
Matthews' Rep. (6-9 West Va.)

**Mau.&Sel.** Maule & Selwyn's K.B. Rep., *Eng.*

**Mc.** *See also* Mac.

**M'Cl.** McClelland's Ex. Rep., *Eng.*

**M'Cle.** Same as above

**M'Cl.&Y.** McClelland & Younge's Ex. Rep., *Eng.*

**M'Cle.&Yo.** Same as above

**McCl.&Y.** Same as above

**M'Mul.Ch.S.C.** M'Mullan's Eq. Rep. (S.C. 1840-42)

**M'Mul.L.S.C.** M'Mullan's Law Rep. (S.C. 1840-42)

**McAl.** McAllister's Cir. Ct. Rep., *U.S.*

**McAll.** Same as above

**McCah.** McCahon's Rep. (Kan. 1858-68)

**McCahon** Same as above

**McCart.** McCarter's Rep. (14, 15 N.J. Eq.)
McCarty's N.Y. Civil Procedure Rep.

**McCl.** McClelland's Ex. Rep., *Eng.*

**McCl.&Y.** McClelland & Younge's Ex. Rep., *Eng.*

**McClel.** *See* McCl.

**McCook** McCook's Rep. (1 Ohio St.)

**McCord** McCord's Rep. (S.C. Law 1821-28)

**McCord Ch.** McCord's Rep. (S.C. Eq. 1825-27)

**McCord Eq.** Same as above

**McCorkle** McCorkle's Rep. (65 N.C.)

**McCr.** McCrary's Cir. Ct. Rep., *U.S.*

**McGl.**  McGloin's Court of Appeal Rep., *La.*

**McL.**  McLean's Cir. Ct. Rep., *U.S.*

**McMul.**  McMullan's Rep. (S.C. Law 1840-42)

**McMul.Eq.**  McMullan's Rep. (S.C. Eq. 1840-42)

**McNagh.**  *See* Macn.

**McWillie**  McWillie's Rep. (73-76 Miss.)

**Md.**  Maryland

**Md.Ch.**  Maryland Ch. Rep.

**Md.L.Rev.**  Maryland Law Rev.

**Me.**  Maine

**Meddaugh**  Meddaugh's Rep. (13 Mich.)

**Mees.&Ros.**  Meeson & Roscoe's Ex. Rep., *Eng.*

**Mees.&Wels.**  Meeson & Welsby's Ex. Rep., *Eng.*

**Meigs**  Meigs' Rep. (19 Tenn.)

**Menken**  Menken's Rep. (9 N.Y. Civil Procedure Rep.)

**Mer.**  Merivale's Ch. Rep., *Eng.*

**Mercer B.L.Rev.**  Mercer Beasley Law Rev.

**Mercer L.Rev.**  Mercer Law Rev.

**Met[c].**  Metcalf's Rep. (42-54 Mass.) Metcalf's Rep. (3 R.I.) Metcalfe's Rep. (58-61 Ky.)

**Metc.Ky.**  Metcalfe's Rep. (58-61 Ky.)

**Metc.Mass.**  Metcalf's Rep. (42-54 Mass.)

**Mews**  The Reports (1893-95), *Eng.* Mews' Digest of English Case Law

**Mich.**  Michigan; Michaelmas Term

**Mich.Jur.**  Michigan Jurisprudence

**Mich.L.Rev.**  Michigan Law Rev.

**Mich.N.P.**  Brown's or Howell's Mich. N.P. Reports or Cases

**Miles**  Miles' Dist. Ct. Rep. (Philadelphia 1825-41)

**Mill**  Mill's Constitutional Rep., *S.C.*

**Mill.**  Miller's Rep. (1-5 La.) Miller's Rep. (3-18 Md.)

**Mill Const.**  Mill's S.C. Constitutional Rep.

**Mill.Dec.**  Miller's Cir. Ct. Dec. (Woolworth's), *U.S.* Miller's U.S. Sup. Ct. Dec. (condensed, continuation of Curtis)

**Mill.La.**  Miller's Rep. (1-5 La.)

**Mill.Md.**  Miller's Rep. (3-18 Md.)

**Mill.Op.**  Miller's Cir. Ct. Dec. (Woolworth), *U.S.*

**Miller**  Miller's Rep. (1-5 La.) Miller's Rep. (3-18 Md.)

**Mills**  Mills' Surrogate Rep., *N.Y.*

**Mills' Surr.Ct.**  Same as above

**Min.**  Minor's Rep. (Ala. 1820-26)

**Minn.**  Minnesota

**Minor**  Minor's Institutes Minor's Rep. (Ala. 1820-26)

**Misc.**  Miscellaneous Rep. (N.J., N.Y.)

**Misc.Dec.**  Ohio Miscellaneous Dec. (Gottschall 1865-73)

**Miss.**  Mississippi

**Miss.Dec.**  Mississippi Dec.

**Miss.L.J.**  Mississippi Law Jour.

**Miss.L.Rev.**  Mississippi Law Rev.

**Miss.St.Ca.**  Morris' Miss. State Cas. (1818-72)

**Mister**  Mister's Rep. (17-32 Mo. App.)

**Mo.**  Missouri Modern Rep. 1669-1732, *Eng.* Moore's C.P. Rep., *Eng.* Moore's K.B. Rep., *Eng.* Moore's P.C. Rep., *Eng.*

**Mo.App.**  Missouri Appeals Rep.

**Mo.App.Rep.**  Same as above

**Mo.Dec.**  Missouri Dec.

**Mo.F.**  Francis Moore's K.B. Rep., *Eng.*

**Mo.J.B.**  J. B. Moore's C.P. Rep., *Eng.*

**Mo.Jur.**  Monthly Jurist

**Mo.L. Rev.**  Missouri Law Rev.

**Mo.P.C.**  Moore's P.C. Rep., *Eng.*

**Mo.W.Jur.**  Monthly Western Jurist

**Mo.&P.**  Moore & Payne's C.P. Rep., *Eng.*

**Mo.&R.**  Moody & Robinson's N.P. Rep., *Eng.*

**Mo.&S.**  Moore & Scott's C.P. Rep., *Eng.*

**Moak Eng.Rep.**  Moak's English Rep.

**Mod.**  Modern Rep. 1669-1732, *Eng.* Style's K.B. Rep. 1646-55, *Eng.*

**Mod.Cas.**  Modern Cases (6 Modern Rep.), *Eng.*

**Mod.Cas.L.&Eq.**  Modern Rep., pts. 8, 9, *Eng.*

**Mod.Cas.per Far.(*t*.Holt)** Modern Cases *temp*. Holt, by Farresby (6, 7 Modern Rep.)

**Mod.L.Rev.** Modern Law Rev.

**Mod.Rep.** Modern Rep. 1669-1732, *Eng.*
Style's K.B. Rep. 1646-55, *Eng.*

**Moly.** Molyneaux's Rep. *temp*. Car. I, *Eng.*

**Mon.** Monaghan's Unreported Cas. (Pa. Super.)
T. B. Monroe's Rep. (17-23 Ky.)
Montana

**Mon.B.** Monroe's Rep. (40-57 Ky.)

**Mon.T.B.** T. B. Monroe's Rep. (17-23 Ky.)

**Mon.W.J.** Monthly Western Jurist

**Monag.** Monaghan's Rep. (147-65 Pa. St.)
Monaghan's Rep. (Pa. 1888-90)

**Monr.** Monroe *See* Mon.

**Mont.** Montana

**Mont.L.R.** Montreal Law Rep.

**Mont.L.Rev.** Montana Law Rev.

**Mont.Leg.News** Montreal Legal News

**Mont.Co.L.Rep.** Montgomery County (Pa.) Law Reporter

**Montreal L.R.Q.B.** Montreal Law Rep., Q.B.

**Montreal L.R.S.C.** Montreal Law Rep., Super. Ct.

**Moo.** Moody's Crown Cas. Res., *Eng.*
F. Moore's K.B. Rep., *Eng.*
J. B. Moore's C.P. Rep., *Eng.*

**Moo.A.** Moore's Rep. (1 Bosanquet & Puller after p. 470)

**Moo.C.C.** Moody's Crown Cas. Res., *Eng.*

**Moo.C.P.** J. B. Moore's C.P. Rep., *Eng.*

**Moo.Cr.C.** Moody's Crown Cas. Res., *Eng.*

**Moo.F.** F. Moore's K.B. Rep., *Eng.*

**Moo.J.B.** J. B. Moore's C.P. Rep., *Eng.*

**Moo.K.B.** Moore's K.B. Rep., *Eng.*

**Moo.P.C.** Moore's P.C. Cas., *Eng.*

**Moo.** Same as above

**Moo.P.C.C.N.S** Moore's P.C. Cas., New Series. *Eng.*

**Moo.&Mal.** Moody & Malkin's N.P. Rep., *Eng.*

**Moo.&P[ay]** Moore & Payne's C.P. Rep., *Eng.*

**Moo.&Rob.** Moody & Robinson's N.P. Rep., *Eng.*

**Moo.&S.** Moore & Scott's C.P. Rep., *Eng.*

**Mood.** Moody's Crown Cas. Res., *Eng.*

**Mood.C.C.** Same as above

**Mood.&M[alk].** Moody & Malkin's N.P. Rep., *Eng.*

**Mood.&R.** Moody & Robinson's N.P. Rep., *Eng.*

**Moon** Moon's Rep. (133-144 Ind.; 6-14 Ind. App.)

**Moore** *See also* Moo.
Moore's C.P. Rep., *Eng.*
Moore's K.B. Rep., *Eng.*
Moore's P.C. Rep., *Eng.*
Moore's Rep. (67 Ala.)
Moore's Rep. (28-34 Ark.)
Moore's Rep. (22-24 Tex.)

**Moore.A.** Moore's Rep. (1 Bosanquet & Puller, after p. 470), *Eng.*

**Moore C.P.** Moore's C.P. Rep., *Eng.*

**Moore K.B.** F. Moore's K.B. Rep., *Eng.*

**Moore P.C.** Moore's P.C. Rep., *Eng.*

**Moore P.C.N.S.** Moore's P.C. Rep., New Series, *Eng.*

**Moore Q.B.** F. Moore's Q.B. Rep., *Eng.*

**Moore&P.** Moore & Payne's C.P. Rep., *Eng.*

**Moore&S.** Moore & Scott's C.P. Rep., *Eng.*

**Moore&Walker** Moore & Walker's Rep. (22-24 Tex.)

**Mor.Ia.** Morris' Rep. (Iowa 1839-46)

**Mor.Miss.** Morris' Rep. (43-48 Miss.)

**Mor.St.Ca.** Morris' State Cases (Miss. 1818-72)

**Morr.** Morris' Rep. (Iowa 1839-46)
Morris' Rep. (5 Cal.)
Morris' Rep. (23-26 Ore.)

**Morr.Cal.** Morris' Rep. (5 Cal.)

**Morr.Miss.** Morris' Rep. (43-48 Miss.)

**Morr.St.Cas.** Morris' State Cases (Miss.)

**Morris.**   Morris' Rep. (5 Cal.)
   Morris Rep. (Iowa 1839-46)
   Morris' Rep. (23-26 Ore.)
   Morrissett's Rep. (80, 98 Ala.)
**Morse**   Exch.Rep.   Morse's   Exch.
   Rep.
**Mos.**   Moseley's Ch. Rep., *Eng.*
**Ms.**   Manuscript Reports or Dec.
**Ms.D.**   Manuscript   Dec.,   Commis-
   sioner of Patents, *U.S.*
   Manuscript Dec., Comptroller Gen-
   eral, *U.S.*
**Mu.L.J.**   Municipal Law Jour.
**Mun.**   Munford's Rep. (15-20 Va.)
**Munf.**   Same as above
**Mur.**   Murphey's Rep. (5-7 N.C.)
**Mur.&Hurl.**   Murphy & Hurlstone's
   Ex. Rep., *Eng.*
**Murph.**   Murphey's Rep. (5-7 N.C.)
**Murph.&H.**   Murphy & Hurlstone's
   Ex. Rep., *Eng.*
**My.&Cr.**   Mylne & Craig's Ch. Rep.,
   *Eng.*
**My.&K.**   Mylne & Keen's Ch. Rep.,
   *Eng.*
**Myl.&Cr.**   Mylne   &   Craig's   Ch.
   Rep., *Eng.*
**Myl.&K.**   Mylne & Keen's Ch. Rep.,
   *Eng.*
**Myr.**   Myrick's Probate Rep. (Cal.
   1872-79)
**Myr. Prob.**   Same as above


**N.**   Nebraska; Nevada
**NACCA**   Law   Journal,   National
   Assn. of Claimants' Compensa-
   tion Attorneys
**NATO**   North Atlantic Treaty Or-
   ganization
**N.B.**   New Brunswick
   New Benloe (or Bendloe) K.B.
   Rep., *Eng.*
**N.B.J.**   National Bar Jour.
**N.B.R.**   New Brunswick Rep.
**N.Benl.**   New Benloe's K.B. Rep.,
   *Eng.*
**N.C.**   North Carolina Rep.
**N.C.L.Rev.**   North   Carolina   Law
   Rev.
**N.C.Law   Repos.**   North   Carolina
   Law Repository

**NCM**   Navy Board of Review Dec.,
   *U.S.*
   Court-Martial Rep., Navy Cases
**N.C.T.Rep.**   North   Carolina   Term
   Rep. (4 N.C.)
**N.Car.**   North Carolina
**N.Ch.R.**   Nelson's Ch. Rep., *Eng.*
   H. Finch's Ch. Rep. 1673-81, *Eng.*
**N.Chip**   N.   Chipman's   Rep.   (Vt.
   1789-91)
**N.D.**   North Dakota
**N.D.L.Rev.**   North Dakota Law Rev.
**N.E.**   North Eastern Reporter
**N.E.2d.**   Same, Second Series
**N.F.**   Newfoundland
**N.H.**   New Hampshire
**N.H.L.Rep.**   New Hampshire Law
   Reporter
**N.H.R.**   New Hampshire Rep.
**N.I.R.A.**   National Industrial Recov-
   ery Act, *U.S.*
**N.J.**   New Jersey
**N.J.Eq.**   New Jersey Eq. Rep.
**N.J.L.J.**   New Jersey Law Jour.
**N.J.L.Rev.**   New Jersey Law Rev.
**N.J.L.[aw]**   New Jersey Law Rep.
**NJ.Misc.**   New Jersey Miscellaneous
   Rep.
**N.J.Super.**   New   Jersey   Super.   Ct.
   Rep.
**NL**   Lutwych's   C.P.   Rep.   (Nelson),
   *Eng.*
**N.L.G.Q.**   National Lawyers' Guild
   Quarterly
**N.L.R.B.**   National Labor Relations
   Bd., *U.S.*
**N.L.Rev.**   Northeastern Law Rev.
**N.M.**   New Mexico
**NMB**   National Mediation Bd., *U.S.*
**N.P.**   Nisi Prius
**N.P.C.**   Nisi Prius Cases
**N.P.N.S.**   Ohio N.P. Rep., New Se-
   ries
**N.P.Ohio**   Ohio N.P. Rep.
**N.P.R.**   Nisi Prius Rep.
**N.R.**   Bosanquet   &   Puller's   New
   Rep., *Eng.*
   The New Reports 1862-65, *Eng.*
**NRA**   National   Recovery   Admin.,
   *U.S.*
**N.R.B.P.**   Bosanquet & Puller's New
   Reports, *Eng.*

**N.S.** New Series; Nova Scotia

**N.S.Dec.** Nova Scotia Dec.

**N.S.L.R.** Nova Scotia Law Rep.

**NS.R.** Nova Scotia Rep.

**N.Sc.Dec.** Nova Scotia Dec.

**N.T.Rep.** New Term Rep., Q.B., *Eng.*

**N.W.** North Western Reporter

**N.W.2d** Same, Second Series

**N.W.LawRev.** Northwestern Law Rev.

**N.W.T.R.[ep].** North-West Territories Rep., *Can.*

**N.W.U.L.Rev.** Northwestern University Law Rev.

**N.Y.** New York

**N.Y.Anno.Cas.** New York Annot. Cas.

**N.Y.App.Dec.** New York Court of Appeals Dec.

New York Appellate Div. Dec.

**N.Y.C.B.A.Bull.** Bulletin of the Association of the Bar of the City of New York

**N.Y.Cas.Err.** Caines' N.Y. Cas. in Error

**N.Y.City Ct.Rep.** New York City Ct. Rep.

**N.Y.Civ.Proc.R.** New York Civil Procedure Rep.

**N.Y.Civ.Proc.R.N.S.** Same, New Series

**N.Y.Code Reptr.** New York Code Reporter

**N.Y.Code Reptr.N.S.** Same, New Series

**N.Y.Cond.** New York Condensed Rep. 1881-82

**N.Y.Cr.R.** New York Crim. Rep. 1878-1924

**N.Y.Ct.App.** New York Court of Appeals (highest court)

**N.Y.Jud.Rep.** New York Judicial Repository

**N.Y.Jur.** New York Jurist

**N.Y.L.J.** New York Law Jour.

**N.Y.L.Rev.** New York Law Rev.

**N.Y.L.S.Rev.** New York Law School Rev.

**NY.Law Gaz.** New York Law Gazette

**N.Y.Law J.** New York Law Jour.

**N.Y.Law Rev.** New York Law Rev.

**N.Y.Leg.N.** New York Legal News 1880-82

**N.Y.Leg.Obs.** New York Legal Observer

**N.Y.Leg.Reg.** New York Legal Register 1850

**N.Y.Misc.** New York Miscellaneous Rep.

**N.Y.Pr.** New York Practice Rep.

**N.Y.Rep.** New York Rep. (Court of Appeals)

**N.Y.Reptr.** New York Reporter (Gardenier 1820)

**N.Y.S.** New York State Reporter New York Supplement

**N.Y.S.D.R.** New York State Dept. Rep.

**N.Y.Spec.Term.Rep.** Howard's Practice Rep., *N.Y.*

**N.Y.St.R.** New York State Rep. 1886-96

**N.Y.Super.Ct.** New York Super. Ct. Rep. (various reporters)

**N.Y.Supp.** New York Supplement

**N.Y.Supr.Ct.** New York Sup. Ct. Rep.

**N.Y.T.R.** New York Term Rep. (Caines)

**N.Y.Trans.** New York Transcript 1861

**N.Y.Trans.Rep.** New York Transcript Rep.

**N.Y.Trans.N.S.** New York Transcript Rep., New Series

**N.Y.U.L.Qu.Rev.** New York University Law Quarterly Rev.

**N.Y.U.L.Rev.** New York Univ. Law Rev.

**N.&H.** Nott & Huntington's Rep. (1-7 U.S. Court of Claims)

**N.&Hop.** Nott & Hopkins' Rep. (8-29 U.S. Court of Claims)

**N.&M.** Nevile & Manning's K.B. Rep., *Eng.*

**N.&Mc.** Nott & McCord's Rep. (S.C. Law)

**N.&P.** Nevile & Perry's K.B. Rep., *Eng.*

**N.Bruns.** New Brunswick Rep.

**N.Ch.R.** Nelson's Ch. Rep., *Eng.*

**Nacca L.J.** Nacca Law Journal, National Assn. of Claimants' Compensation Attorneys

**Napton**  Napton's Rep. (4 Mo.)

**Narr.Mod.**  Narrationes Modernae (Style's K.B. Rep. 1646-55), *Eng.*

**Nat.Corp.Rep.**  National Corporation Reporter

**Nat.L.Rev.**  National Law Rev.

**Nat.Law Guild Q.**  National Lawyers' Guild Quarterly

**Nat.Rept.Syst.**  National Reporter System

**Nat.U.L.Rev.**  National Univ. Law Rev.

**Nd.**  Newfoundland

**Neb.**  Nebraska

**Neb.L.B.**  Nebraska Law Bulletin

**Neb.L.Rev.**  Nebraska Law Rev.

**Neb.Unoff.**  Nebraska Unofficial Rep. 1901-04

**Neg.Cas.**  Bloomfield's Manumission (or Negro) Cas., *N.J.*

**Nel.**  Nelson's Ch. Rep., *Eng.*
  H. Finch's Ch. Rep., *Eng.*

**Nel.C.R.**  Nelson's Ch. Rep., *Eng.*

**Nels.**  Nelson's Ch. Rep., *Eng.*
  H. Finch's Ch. Rep., *Eng.*

**Nev.**  Nevada

**Nev.&M.K.B.**  Nevile & Manning's K.B. Rep., *Eng.*

**Nev.&Man.**  Same as above

**Nev.&P.**  Nevile & Perry's K.B. Rep., *Eng.*

**New.**  Newell's Rep. (48-90 Ill. App.)

**New B.Eq.Ca.**  New Brunswick Eq. Cas.

**New Benl.**  Benloe's K.B. Rep. 1531-1628, *Eng.*

**New Br.**  New Brunswick Rep.

**New Rep.**  New Rep. 1862-65, *Eng.*
  Bosanquet & Puller's New Rep. (4, 5 Bosanquet & Puller), *Eng.*

**New Sess. Cas.**  New Sessions Cas. (Carrow, Hamerton, Allen), *Eng.*

**New Term.Rep.**  New Term Rep. (East), *Eng.*
  Dowling & Tyland's K.B. Rep., *Eng.*

**New York**  *See* N.Y.

**Newb.**  Newberry's Admiralty Rep., *U.S.*

**Newell**  Newell's Rep. (48-90 Ill. App.)

**Newf.**  Newfoundland

**Newfld.L.R.**  Newfoundland Law Rep.

**Noble**  Noble's Current Court Dec., *N.Y.*

**Nonacq.(or NA)**  Nonacquiescence by Commissioner in Tax Court or Board of Tax Appeals decision, *U.S.*

**Norc.**  Norcross' Rep. (23, 24 Nev.)

**Norris**  Norris' Rep. (82-96 Pa. St.)

**North.**  Eden's Ch. Rep., *Eng.*
  Reports *temp.* Northington, by Eden, *Eng.*

**North.Co.Rep.**  Northampton County Reporter, *Pa.*

**North&G.**  North & Guthrie's Rep. (68-80 Mo. App.)

**Northam.**  Northampton Law Reporter, *Pa.*

**Northam.L.Rep.**  Same as above

**Northum.**  Northumberland County Legal News, *Pa.*

**Northum.Co.Leg.N.**  Same as above

**Northumb.L.N.**  Northumberland Legal Jour., *Pa.*

**Nott&Hop.**  Nott & Hopkins' Rep. (8-15 U.S. Court of Claims)

**Nott&Hunt.**  Nott & Huntington's Rep. (1-7 U.S. Court of Claims)

**Nott&McC.**  Nott & McCord's Rep. (S.C. Law)

**Nov.Sc.**  Nova Scotia

**Nov.Sc.Dec.**  Nova Scotia Dec.

**Nov.Sc.L.R.**  Nova Scotia Law Rep.

**Noy**  Noy's K.B. Rep., *Eng.*

**Nye**  Nye's Rep. (18-21 Utah)

**O.**  Ohio; Oregon; Ontario
  Otto's Rep. (91-107 U.S.)
  Solicitor's Law Opinion (U.S. Internal Revenue Service)

**O.A.G.**  Opinions of Attorney General, *U.S.*

**O.A.R.**  Ontario Appeal Rep.
  Ohio Appeals 1913-date

**OAS**  Organization of American States

**O.Ben.**  Old Benloe C.P. Rep., *Eng.*

**O.Bridg.**  Carter's Rep. *temp.* Bridgman, C.P. Rep., *Eng.*
  Orlando Bridgman's C.P. Rep., *Eng.*

**O.C.A.** Ohio Courts of Appeal Rep. 1915-22

**O.C.C.** Ohio Cir. Ct. Rep. or Dec.

**O.C.C.N.S.** Ohio Cir. Ct. Rep., New Series 1903-17

**O.C.D.** Ohio Cir. Ct. Dec. 1901-18

**O.C.S.** Office of Contract Settlement, *U.S.*

**O.D.** Office Decision (U.S. Internal Revenue Service)
Ohio Dec. 1894-1920

**O.D.C.C.** Ohio Dec., Cir. Ct.

**ODM** Office of Defense Mobilization, *U.S.*

**O.Dec.Rep.** Ohio Dec. Reprint

**O.F.D.** Ohio Federal Dec.

**O.G.(or O.G.Pat.Off.)** Official Gazette, U.S. Patent Office

**O.Jur.** Ohio Jurisprudence

**O.L.Abs.** Ohio Law Abstract

**O.L.B.** Ohio Law Bulletin

**O.L.D.** Ohio Lower Court Dec.

**O.L.J.** Ohio Law Jour.

**O.L.N** Ohio Legal News

**O.L.R.** Ontario Law Reporter
Ontario Law Rep.

**O.L.Rep.** Ohio Law Reporter

**O.N.P.** Ohio N.P. Rep. 1894-1901

**O.N.P.N.S.** Ohio N.P. Rep. New Series 1903-1913

**OPA** Office of Price Admin., *U.S.*

**O.P.R.** Ontario Practice Rep.

**O.P.S.** Office of Price Stabilization, *U.S.*

**O.S.** Ohio State Rep.
Upper Canada Queen's Bench Rep., Old Series

**O.S.C.D.** Ohio Sup. Ct. Dec., Unreported Cases

**OSS** Office of Strategic Services, *U.S.*

**O.St.** Ohio State Rep.

**O.Supp.** Ohio Supplement

**O.S.U.** Ohio Sup. Ct. Dec., Unreported Cases

**OWM** Office of War Mobilization, *U.S.*

**O'Brien** O'Brien's Upper Canada Rep.

**Odeneal** Odeneal's Rep. (9-11 Ore.)

**Off.Gaz.Pat.Off.** Official Gazette, U.S. Patent Office

**Officer** Officer's Rep. (1-9 Minn.)

**Ogden** Ogden's Rep. (12-15 La.)

**Ohio C.C.** Ohio Cir. Ct. Rep.

**Ohio C.C.Dec.** Ohio Cir. Ct. Dec.

**Ohio C.C.N.S.** Ohio Cir. Ct. Rep., New Series

**Ohio Cir.Ct.N.S.** Same as above

**Ohio Cir.Ct.R.** Ohio Cir. Ct. Rep.

**Ohio Cir.Dec.** Ohio Cir. Ct. Dec.

**Ohio Dec.** Ohio Dec. 1894-1920

**Ohio Leg.N.** Ohio Legal News

**Ohio Misc.Dec.** Ohio Miscellaneous Dec.

**Ohio N.P.** Ohio N.P. Rep.

**Ohio N.P.N.S.** Ohio N.P. Rep., New Series

**Ohio Op.** Ohio Opinions

**Ohio Prob.** Ohio Probate Rep. by Goebel

**Ohio S.L.J.** Ohio State Law Jour.

**Ohio St.** Ohio State Rep.

**Ohio Sup.&C.P.Dec.** Ohio Super. C.P. Dec.

**Ohio Unrept.Cas.** Ohio Unreported Cases (Pollack)

**Okla.Ap.Ct.Rep.** Oklahoma Appellate Court Reporter

**Okla.Crim.** Oklahoma Crim. Rep.

**Olc.** Olcott's Dist. Rep., *U.S.*

**Olc.Adm.** Same as above

**Old.** Oldright's Rep. (5, 6 Nova Scotia)

**Old Ben.** Benloe in Benloe & Dalison's C.P. Rep., *Eng.*

**Ont.** Ontario

**Ont.App.** Ontario Appeal Rep.

**Ont.L.Rep.** Ontario Law Rep.

**Ont.Pr.Rep.** Ontario Practice Rep.

**Ont.R.** Ontario Rep.

**Ops.A.G.** Opinions, Attorney General

**Ops.J.A.G.** Opinions, Judge Advocate General, U.S. Army

**Or.** Oregon

**Or.T.Rep.** Orleans Term Rep. (Martin, La.)

**Oreg.** Oregon

**Orl.Bridgman** Orlando Bridgman's C.P. Rep., *Eng.*

**Orl.T.R.** Martin's Orleans Term Reports, *La.*

**Ormond** Ormond's Rep. (19-107 Ala.)

**Otto** Otto's Sup. Ct. Rep. (91-107 U.S.)

**Out.** Outerbridge's Rep. (97-110 Pa. St.)
**Over.** Overton's Rep. (1-2 Tenn.)
**Ow.** Owens' K.B. Rep., *Eng.*
Owen's C.P. Rep., *Eng.*

**P.** Law Rep., Probate, Divorce, and Admiralty, since 1890, *Eng.*
Pacific Reporter
Pennsylvania
Peters' U.S. Sup. Ct. Rep. (26-41 U.S.)
Pickering (18-41 Mass.)
**P.2d.** Pacific Reporter, Second Series
**P.A.D.** Peters' Admiralty Dec., *U.S.*
**P.C.** Pleas of the Crown; Parliamentary Cases; Patent Cases; Practice Cases; Prize Cases; Privy Council; Probate Court; Precedents in Chancery
**P.C.A.** Acts of the Privy Council, *Eng.*
**P.C.App.** Law Rep. P.C. Appeals, *Eng.*
**P.C.C.** Privy Council Cases, *Eng.*
Peters' Cir. Ct. Rep., *U.S.*
**PCIJ** Permanent Court of International Justice
**P.C.L.J.** Pacific Coast Law Jour.
**P.C.R.** Parker's Crim. Rep., *N.Y.*
Pennsylvania Corporation Rep., *Eng.*
**P.C.Rep.** Privy Council Rep., *Eng.*
**P.Cas.** Prize Cases 1914-22, *Eng.*
Prize Cases (Trehearn, Grant), *Eng.*
**P.D.** Law Reports, Probate Div., *Eng.*
**P.D.A.** Probate, Divorce and Admiralty, *Eng.*
**P.E.A.L.Q.** Publishing Entertainment and Allied Fields Q.
**P.E.I.** Prince Edward Island Rep.
**P.F.S.** P. F. Smith's Rep. (51-81 Pa. St.)
**P.-H.** Prentice-Hall
**PHA** Public Housing Admin., *U.S.*
**P.-H.Cas.** American Federal Tax Rep. (P-H)
**P.-H.Unrep.Tr.Cas.** Prentice-Hall Unreported Trust Cases
**P.Jr.&H.** Patton, Jr., & Heath's Rep. (Va. Special Ct. of Appeals)

**P.L.** Public Law
**PLO** Public Land Order
**P.L.R.** Pennsylvania Law Record
**P.N.P** Peake's N.P. Cas., *Eng.*
**P.R.** Ontario Practice Rep.
Pacific Reporter
Parliamentary Rep., *Eng.*
Pennsylvania Rep. (Penrose & Watts)
Philadelphia Rep. (Pa. 1850-51)
Philippine Island, Rep.
Pittsburgh Rep. (Pa. 1853-73)
Press Release (U.S. Govt. Departments)
Probate Rep.
Pyke's Rep., *Can.*
Porto Rico (*now* Puerto Rico)
**P.R.C.P.** Practical Register, C.P., *Eng.*
**P.R.Ch.** Practical Register in Chancery, *Eng.*
**P.R.Fed.** Porto Rico Fed. Rep. (*now* Puerto Rico)
**P.R.R.** Porto Rico Sup. Ct. Rep. (*now* Puerto Rico)
**P.R.S.C.R.** Same as above
**P.R.U.C.** Upper Canada Practice Rep.
**P.S.C.** Public Service Comm.
**P.S.C.U.S.** Peters' U.S. Sup. Ct. Rep. (26-41 U.S.)
**P.S.R.** Pennsylvania State Rep.
**P.T** Processing Tax Div. U.S. Internal Revenue Service)
**P.U.R.** Public Utilities Rep., *U.S.*
**P.W.** Peere Williams' Ch. & K.B. Rep., *Eng.*
**P.Wms.** Same as above
**P.&B.** Pugsley & Burbidge's New Brunswick Rep.
**P.&D.** Perry & Davison's Q.B. Rep., *Eng.*
Law Reports, Probate and Divorce Series, *Eng.*
**P.&F.** Pike & Fischer's Administrative Law
Pike & Fischer's Federal Rules Service
Pike & Fischer's OPA Price Service
**P.&H.** Patton, Jr., & Heath's Rep. (Va. Special Ct. of Appeals)
**P.&M.** Law Rep., Probate and Matrimonial Cas., *Eng.*

**P.&T.** Pugsley & Trueman's New Brunswick Rep.

**P.&W.** Penrose & Watts' Rep. (Pa. 1829-32)

**Pa.** Paine's Cir. Ct. Rep., *U.S.*
Pennsylvania
Pennsylvania State Reports

**Pa.Co.Ct.R.** Pennsylvania County Ct. Rep.

**Pa.Corp.Rep.** Pennsylvania Corporation Reporter

**Pa.D.&C.** Pennsylvania Dist. and County Rep.

**Pa.D.&C.2d.** Same, Second Series

**Pa.Dist.R.** District Rep. (Pa. 1892-1921)

**Pa.Dist.&C.Rep.** Pennsylvania Dist. and County Rep.

**Pa.L.J.** Pennsylvania Law Jour.
Pennsylvania Law Jour. Rep. (1842-52)

**Pa.Rep.** Pennsylvania Rep.

**Pa.St.** Pennsylvania State Rep. (1845-date)

**Pa.Super.Ct.** Pennsylvania Super. Ct. Rep.

**Pac.** Pacific Reporter

**Pac.Law Reptr.** Pacific Law Reporter

**Pac.Leg.N.** Pacific Legal News

**Pai.** Paige's N.Y. Ch. Rep.
Paine's Cir. Ct. Rep., *U.S.*

**Pai.Ch.** Paige's N.Y. Ch. Rep.

**Paine C.C.** Paine's Cir. Ct. Rep., *U.S.*

**Pal[m].** Palmer's K.B. Rep., *Eng.*
Palmer's Rep. (53-60 Vt.)

**Palmer's** Palmer's K.B. Rep.,*Eng.*
Palmer's Reports (53-60 Vt.)

**Papy** Papy's Rep. (5-8 Fla.)

**Par.** Parker's Ex. Rep., *Eng.*
Parker's N.Y. Crim. Cas. 1823-68

**Par.Dec.** Parsons' Dec. (from 2-7 Mass.)

**Par.Eq.Cas.** Parson's Select Eq. Cas. (Pa. 1842-51)

**Park.** Parker's Ex. Rep., *Eng.*
Parker's N.Y. Crim. Cas. 1823-68
Parker's N.H. Rep.

**Park.Exch.** Parker's Ex. Rep., *Eng.*

**Park.N.H.** Parker's N.H. Rep.

**Parker** Parker's Ex. Rep., *Eng.*

Parker's N.H. Rep.
Parker's N.Y. Crim. Cas.

**Parl.Cas.** Parliamentary Cases (H. L.), *Eng.*

**Parl.Deb.** Parliamentary Debates (Cobbett, Hansard)

**Pars.Dec.** Parsons' Dec. (from 2-7 Mass.)

**Pars.Eq.Cas.** Parsons' Select Eq. Cas. (Pa. 1842-51)

**Pasc.** Paschal or Easter Term Paschal's Rep. (Supp. to 25, 28-31 Tex.)

**Paschal** Same as above

**Pat.Dec.** Decisions, Commissioner of Patents, *U.S.*

**Pat.Off.Gaz.** Official Gazette, U.S. Patent Office

**Pat.&H.** Patton Jr., & Heath's Rep. (Va. Special Ct. of Appeals)

**Patt.&H.** Same as above

**Pea.** Peake's N.P. Rep., *Eng.*

**Pea.Add.Cas.** Peake's N.P. Rep. (v. 2 of Peake)

**Peake N.P.** Peake's N.P. Rep., *Eng.*

**Pears.** Pearson's Rep. (Pa. 1850-80)

**Peck.** Peck's Rep. (24-30 Ill.)
Peck's Rep. (7 Tenn.)

**Peeples** Peeples' Rep. (78, 79 Ga.)

**Peeples&Stevens** (80-97 Ga.)

**Peere Wms.** Peere Williams' Ch. and K.B. Cas., *Eng.*

**Pen.** Pennington's Rep. (2, 3 N.J. Law)

**Pen.N.J.** Same as above

**Pen.&W.** Penrose & Watts' Rep. (Pa. 1829-32)

**Penn.** Pennsylvania. *See also* Pa.
Pennington's Rep. (2, 3 N.J. Law)
Pennypacker's Rep. (Pa. 1881-84)

**Penn.Co.Ct.Rep.** Pennsylvania County Ct. Rep.

**Penn.Corp.Rep.** Pennsylvania Corporation Reporter

**Penn.L.G.** Pennsylvania Legal Gazette
Pennsylvania Legal Gazette Rep. (Campbell)

**Pennewill** Pennewill's Rep. (17-23 Del.)

**Penning.** Pennington's Rep. (2, 3 N.J. Law)

**Penny.** Pennypacker's Rep. (Pa. Unreported, or Colonial Cases)

**Penr.&W.** Penrose & Watts' Rep. (Pa. 1829-32)

**Per.C.S.** Perrault's Conseil Supérieur, *Can.*

**Per.P.** Perrault's Prévosté de Québec

**Per.&Dav.** Perry & Davison's Q.B. Rep., *Eng.*

**Perrault** Perrault's Quebec Rep.
Perrault's Conseil Supérieur, *Can.*
Parrault's Prévosté de Québec

**Pet.** Peters
Peters' Admiralty Rep., Dist. Courts, *U.S.*
Peters' Cir. Ct. Rep., *U.S.*
Peters' U.S. Sup. Ct. Rep. (26-41 U.S.)
Peters' Prince Edward Island Rep.

**Pet.C.C.** Peters' U.S. Sup. Ct. Rep. Dist. Courts, *U.S.*

**Pet.Br.** Bellewe's Cases *temp.* Henry VIII,*Eng.*

**Pet.S.C.** Peters' U.S. Sup. Ct. Rep. (26-41 U.S.)

**Peters Adm.** Peters' Admiralty Rep., U.S. Dist. Courts, *U.S.*

**Peters C.C.** Peters' Cir. Ct. Rep., *U.S.*

**Petit Br.** Brooke's New Cases 1515-58, *Eng.*

**Ph.** Philipps' Ch. Rep., *Eng.*

**Pheney Rep.** Pheney's New Term Rep., *Eng.*

**Phi Delta Delta** Phi Delta Delta (periodical)

**Phil.** Phillips' Ch. Rep., *Eng.*
Phillips' Rep. (152-245 Ill.)
Philipps' Rep. (61-64 N.C.)
Philippine Rep.

**Phil.Eq.** Phillips Rep. (62 N.C. Eq.)

**Phil.L.J.** Philippine Law Jour.

**Phil.L.Rev.** Philippine Law Rev.

**Phil.Law** Phillips' Law Rep. (61 N.C.)

**Phil.N.C.** Phillips' Law Rep. (61 N.C.)

**Phil.St.Tr.** Phillipps' State Trials

**Phila.** Philadelphia Rep. (Pa. 1850-91)

**Phila.Leg.Int.** Philadelphia Legal Intelligencer

**Phill.** *See* Phil.

**Phillips** *See* Phil.

**Pick.** Pickering's Rep. (18-41 Mass.)

**Pickle** Pickle's Rep. (85-108 Tenn.)

**Pike** Pike's Rep. (1-5 Ark.)

**Pike&F.Adm.Law** Pike & Fischer's Administrative Law

**Pike&F.Fed.RulesService** Pike & Fischer's Federal Rules Service

**Pin[n].** Pinney's Rep. (Wis. Reprint)

**Pitts.L.J.** Pittsburgh Legal Jour.

**Pitts.L.Rev.** University of Pittsburgh Law Rev.

**Pitts.Rep.** Pittsburgh Rep. (Pa. 1853-73)

**Pittsb.** *See* Pitts.

**Pl.C.** Placita Coronae (Pleas of the Crown), *Eng.*

**Plow.** Plowden's Reports (and Queries), *Eng.*

**Pol.** Pollexfen's K.B. Rep., *Eng.*

**Poll.** Same as above
Pollack's Ohio Unreported Judicial Dec. Prior to 1823

**Pop.** Popham's K.B. Rep., *Eng.*

**Poph.** Same as above

**Poph.(2)** Cases at end of Popham's Rep.

**Port.** Porter's Rep. (Ala. 1834-39)

**Porter** Same as above
Porter's Rep. (3-7 Ind.)

**Porto Rico Fed.Rep.** Porto Rico Fed. Rep.

**Posey Unrep.Cas.** Texas Unreported Cases (1879-84)

**Post** Post's Rep. (23-26 Mich.)
Post's Rep. (42-64 Mo.)

**Potter** Potter's Rep. (4-7 Wyo.)

**Powers** Powers' New York Surrogate Ct. Rep.

**Pr.** Practice Rep. (various jurisdictions)
Price's Ex. Rep., *Eng.*

**Pr.Dec.** Kentucky Dec. (Sneed, 2 Ky.)

**Pr.Div.** Law Rep., Probate Div., *Eng.*

**Pr.Edw.I.** Prince Edward Island Rep.

**Pr.Exch.** Price's Ex. Rep., *Eng.*

**Pr.R.** Practice Rep. (various jurisdictions)

**Pr.&Div.** Law Rep. Probate and Divorce, *Eng.*

**Pri.** Price's Ex. Rep., *Eng.*

**Price** Same as above

**Prickett** Prickett's Rep. (1 Idaho)

**Prin.Dec.** Kentucky Dec. (Sneed, 2 Ky.)

**Priv.C.App.** Privy Council Appeals, *Eng.*

**Prob.** Law Rep., Probate Div., *Eng.*

**Prob.Ct.Rep.** Probate Ct. Rep.

**Prob.Div.** Law Rep., Probate Div., *Eng.*

**Prob.Rep.** Probate Rep.

**Prob.&Adm.Div.** Law Rep., Probate and Admiralty Div., *Eng.*

**Prob.&Div.** Law Rep., Probate and Divorce Div., *Eng.*

**Proc.** Proclamation

**Prouty** Prouty's Rep. (61-68 Vt.)

**Prt.Rep.** Practice Rep.

**Psych.&M.L.J.** Psychological and Medico-Legal Jour.

**Pub.Adm.Rev.** Public Admin. Rev.

**Pub. Util.Fort.** Public Utilities Fortnightly

**Pug[s].** Pugsley's Rep. (14-16 New Brunswick)

**Pugs.&Bur.** Pugsley & Burbidge Rep. (17-20 New Brunswick)

**Pulsifer** Pulsifer's Rep. (35-68 Me.)

**Py.R.** Pyke's Lower Canada Rep., K.B.

**Pyke** Same as above

**Q.** Year Books, pt. IV
Quebec

**Q.B.** Queen's Bench
Adolphus & Ellis' Q.B. Rep., New Series, *Eng.*
Law Rep., Q.B., from 1891, *Eng.*
Queen's Bench Rep., Quebec
Queen's Bench Rep., Upper Canada

**Q.B.D.[iv]** Queen's Bench Div.
Law Rep., Q.B. Div., *Eng.*

**Q.B.L.C.** Queen's Bench Rep., Lower Canada

**Q.B.R.** Queen's Bench Rep. (Adolphus & Ellis, New Series), *Eng.*

**Q.B.U.C.** Queen's Bench Rep., Upper Canada

**Q.L.R.** Quebec Law Rep.

**Q.R.K.B.(*or* Q.B.)** Quebec K. [*or* Q.] B. Rep.
Rapports Judiciaires de Québec, Cour du Banc du Roi

**Q.R.S.C.** Rapports Judiciaires de Québec, Cour Supérieure

**Que.K.B.(*or* Q.B.)** Quebec K. [*or* Q.] B. Rep.

**Que.S.C.** Quebec Super. Ct. Rep.

**Que.K.B.** Quebec K.R. Rep.

**Que.L.R.** Quebec Law Rep.

**Queb.Pr.** Quebec Practice Rep.

**Quin.** Quincy (Mass.) Superior Court of Judicature Rep.

**R.** Rawle's Rep. (Pa. 1828-35)
The Reports (1893-95), *Eng.*
Kentucky Law Reporter (1880-1908)

**R.A.C.** Ramsay's Appeal Cases, *Can.*

**RB** Renegotiation Board

**R.C.** Revue Critique de Législation et de Jurisprudence de Canada
Ruling Cases

**R.C.L.** Ruling Case Law (encyclopedia)

**R.C.&C.R.** Revenue, Civil and Criminal Reporter

**R.deD.** Revue de Droit, *Quebec*

**R.deJ.** Revue de Jurisprudence, *Can.*

**R.deL.** Revue de Législation et de Jurisprudence, *Can.*

**REA** Rural Electrification Admin., *U.S.*

**RFC** Reconstruction Finance Corp., *U. S.*

**R.G.** Regulae Generales of Ontario

**R.I.** Rhode Island

**R.J.Q.** Rapports Judiciaires, Quebec

**R.J.R.** Quebec Revised Rep. (Mathieu)

**R.J.R.Q.** Same as above

**R.L.** Revue Légale, *Can.*

**R.L.N.S.** Revue Légale, New Series, *Can.*

**R.L.O.S.** Revue Légale, Old Series, *Can.*

**R.L.Q.B.** Revue Légale Rep., Q.B., *Can.*

**R.L.S.C.** Revue Légale Rep., Q.B., *Can.*

**R.M.Ch.**   R. M. Charlton's Rep. (Ga. 1811-37)

**R.P.&W.**   Rawle, Penrose & Watts' Rep. (Pa. 1828-40)

**R.R.**   Revised Rep., *Eng.*
Pike & Fischer's Radio Regulations

**RRB**   Railroad Retirement Bd., *U.S.*

**R.S.**   Revised Statutes (various jurisdictions); Rolls Series

**R.S.C.**   Revised Statutes of Canada
Rules of the Supreme Court, *Eng.*

**R.t.F.**   Reports *temp.* Finch, Ch., *Eng.*

**R.t.H.**   Reports *temp.* Hardwicke, *Eng.*
Ridgway's Ch. and K.B. Rep., *temp.* Hardwicke, *Eng.*

**R.t.Q.A.**   Reports *temp.* Queen Anne (11 Modern Rep.), *Eng.*

**R.t.W.**   Manitoba Rep. *temp.* Wood

**R.&C.**   Russell & Chesley's Nova Scotia Rep.

**R.&G.**   Russell & Geldert's Nova Scotia Rep.

**R.&G.N.Sc.**   Same as above

**R.&M.**   Russell & Mylne's Ch. Rep., *Eng.*
Ryan & Moody's N.P. Rep., *Eng.*

**R.&M.C.C.**   Ryan & Moody's Crown Cas. Res., *Eng.*

**R.&M.N.P.**   Ryan & Moody's N.P. Rep., *Eng.*

**R.&My.**   Russell & Mylne's Ch. Rep., *Eng.*

**R.&R.**   Russell & Ryan's Crown Cas. Res., *Eng.*

**R.&R.C.C.**   Same as above

**Rader**   Rader's Rep. (138-163 Mo.)

**Ram.**   Ramsey's Quebec Appeal Cases

**Ram.&Mor.**   Ramsey & Morin's Montreal Law Reporter

**Rand.**   Randall's Rep. (62-71 Ohio St.)
Randolph's Rep. (21-56 Kan.)
Randolph's Rep. (7-11 La.)
Randolph's Rep. (22-27 Va.)

**Raney**   Raney's Rep. (16-20 Fla.)

**Raw[le]**   Rawle's Rep. (Pa. 1828-35)

**Rawle**   Rawle's Rep. (Pa. 1828-35)

**Rawle Pen.&W.**   Rawle, Penrose & Watts' Rep. (Pa. 1828-40)

**Raym.Ent.**   Lord Raymond's Entries, *Eng.*

**Raym.Ld.**   Lord Raymond's K.B. Rep., *Eng.*

**Raym.Sir T.**   T. Raymond's K.B. Rep., *Eng.*

**Raymond**   Raymond's Rep. (81-99 Iowa)

**Re.de L.**   Revue de Législation et de Jurisprudence, Montreal

**Reapp.Dec.**   Reappraisement Dec., U.S. Treasury

**Rec.Dec.**   Vaux' Recorders Dec. (Pa. 1841-45)

**Red.**   Redfield's New York Surrogate's Ct. Rep.
Redington's Rep. (31-35 Me.)

**Redf.**   Redfield's New York Surrogate's Ct. Rep.

**Redf.Surr.**   Same as above

**Redington**   Redington's Rep. (31-35 Me.)

**Reg.**   Daily Register, *N.Y.*

**Reg.Deb.**   Gales & Seaton's Register of Debates in Congress, 1824-37

**Remy**   Remy's Rep. (145-162 Ind.; 15-33 Ind. App.)

**Rep.**   Report or Reports
Coke's K.B. Rep. (commonly known as "The Reports"), *Eng.*
Reporter
Knapp's P.C. Rep., *Eng.*

**Rep.Cas.Eq.**   Gilbert's Ch. Rep., *Eng.*

**Rep.Ch.**   Reports in Chancery 1615-1710, *Eng.*

**Rep.Const.Ct.**   South Carolina Constitutional Ct. Rep.

**Rep.Eq.**   Gilbert's Reports in Equity, *Eng.*

**Rep.Pat.Cas.**   Reports of Patents, Designs and Trade-Mark Cas., *Eng.*

**Rep.Q.A.**   Reports *temp.* Queen Anne (11 Modern Rep.), *Eng.*

**Rep.t.Finch**   Finch's Ch. Rep., *Eng.*

**Rep.t.Hard.**   Lee's Rep. *temp.* Hardwicke, K.B., *Eng.*

**Rep.t.Holt**   Settlement Cases, Rep. *temp.* Holt, *Eng.*

**Rep.t.O.Br.**   Common Pleas Rep. *temp.* O. Bridgman, by Carter, *Eng.*

**Rep.*t*.Q.A.** Reports *temp.* Queen Anne (11 Modern Rep.), *Eng.*

**Rep.*t*.Talb.** Chancery Rep. *temp.* Talbot, *Eng.*

**Rep.*t*.Wood** Manitoba Rep. *temp.* Wood

**Reports** Coke's K.B. Rep., *Eng.*

**Res.** Resolution

**Res.Gamma Eta Gamma** Rescript of Gamma Eta Gamma

**Rev.Crit.** Revue Critique, Montreal

**Rev.Crit.de Légis.et Jur.** Revue Critique de Législation et de Jurisprudence, Montreal

**Rev.de Jur.** Revue de Jurisprudence, Quebec

**Rev.de Leg.** Revue de Législation et de Jurisprudence, Montreal

**Rev.du B.** Revue du Barreau de la Province de Québec

**Rev.du Dr.** Revue du Droit, Quebec

**Rev.du Not.** Revue du Notariat, Quebec

**Rev.Gen.Reg.** Revised General Regulation, General Accounting Office, *U.S.*

**Rev.Jur.U.P.R.** Revista Jurídica, Universidad de Puerto Rico

**Rev.Leg.** Revue Légale, Montreal

**Rev.Rep.** Revised Rep. (Reprint), *Eng.*

**Rev.Stat.** Revised Statutes (various jurisdictions)

**Rice** Rice's Rep. (S.C. Law 1838-39)

**Rice Eq.** Rice's Rep. (S.C. Eq. 1838-39)

**Rich.** Richardson's Rep. (S.C. Law)
Richardson's Rep. (3-5 N.H.)
Richardson's Rep. (18 U.S. Ct. of Claims)

**Rich.Ch.** Richardson's Rep. (S.C. Eq.)

**Rich.Ct.Cl.** Richardson's Rep. (18 U.S. Ct. of Claims)

**Rich.Eq.** Richardson's Rep. (S.C. Eq).

**Rich.Law** Richardson's Rep. (S.C. Law)

**Rich.N.H.** Richardson's Rep. (3-5 N.H.)

**Rich.N.S.** Richardson's Rep. New Series (S.C. Law and Eq. 1850-68)

**Rich.&W.** Richardson & Woodbury's Rep. (2 N.H.)

**Ridg.** Ridgeway's Rep. *temp.* Hardwicke, Ch. and K.B., *Eng.*

**Ridg.Cas.** Ridgeway's Rep. *temp.* Hardwicke, Ch. and K.B., *Eng.*

**Ridg.*t*.H[ard].** Same as above

**Ridg.&Hard.** Same as above

**Ried.** Riedell's Rep. (68, 69 N.H.)

**Ril[ey]** Riley's Rep. (Law and Eq.), *S.C.*
Riley's Rep. (37-42 W.Va.)

**Ril.Harp.** Harper's Rep., ed. Riley (S.C. Law and Eq.)

**Rin.** Riner's Rep. (2 Wyo.)

**Ritch.Eq.Rep.** Ritchie's Eq. Rep., Nova Scotia

**Ro.** Rolle's Abridgement

**Ro.Abr.** Same as above

**Ro.Rep.** Rolle's K.B. Rep., *Eng.*
Robards' Conscript Cases (Tex. 1862-65)

**Rob.** Robards' Rep. (12, 13 Mo.)
Roberts' Rep. (29-31 La. Annual)
Robertson's Rep. (1 Hawaii)
Robertsons Rep. (24-30 N.Y. Super. Ct.)
Robinson's Admiralty Rep., *Eng.*
Robinson's Rep. (38 Cal.)
Robinson's Rep. (2-9, 17-23 Colo. App.)
Robinson's Rep. (1-4 La. Annual; Sup. Ct. La. 1841-46)
Robinson's Rep. (1 Nev.)
Robinson's Rep. (40, 41 Va.)
Robinson's Rep. (1-8 Ontario)
Robinson's Upper Canada Rep.

**Rob.Adm.** Robinson's Admiralty Rep., *Eng.*

**Rob.Cal.** Robinson's Rep. (38 Cal.)

**Rob.Chr.** Chr. Robinson's Admiralty Rep., *Eng.*

**Rob.Colo.** Robinson's Rep. (2-9, 17-23 Colo. App.)

**Rob.Consc.Cas.** Robards' Texas Conscript Cases

**Rob.Hawaii** Robinson's Rep. (1 Hawaii)

**Rob.Jun.** Wm. Robinson's Admiralty Rep., *Eng.*

**Rob.La.** Robinson's Rep. (1-4 La. Annual; La. Sup. Ct. 1841-46)

**Rob.Mo.** Robards' Rep. (12, 13 Mo.)

**Rob.Nev.**   Robinson's Rep. (1 Nev.)

**Rob.N.Y.**   Robertson's Rep. (24-30 N.Y. Super. Ct.)

**Rob.Ont.**   Robinson's Rep. (1-8 Ont.)

**Rob.Super.Ct.**   Robertson's Rep. (24-30 N.Y. Super. Ct.)

**Rob.U.C.**   Robinson's Rep. (Upper Canada)

**Rob.Va.**   Robinson's Rep. (40, 41 Va.)

**Rob.Wm.Adm.**   Wm. Robinson's Admiralty Rep., *Eng.*

**Rob.&J.**   Robards' & Jackson's Rep. (26, 27 Tex.)

**Robards**   Robards' Rep. (12, 13 Mo.)

Robards' Conscript Cases (Tex. 1862-65)

**Robards&Jackson**   Texas Rep., v. 26, 27

**Robb.**   Robbins' Rep. (67-70 N.J. Eq.)

**Robb Pat.Cas.**   Robb's Patent Cas., *U.S.*

**Roberts**   Roberts' Rep. (29-31 La. Annual)

**Robertson**   *See also* Rob.

Robertson's Rep., *Hawaii*

Robertson's Rep., N.Y. Marine Ct.

Robertson's Rep. (24-30 N.Y. Super.)

**Robinson**   Chr. Robinson's Admiralty Rep.

W. Robinson's Admiralty Rep., *Eng.*

Robinson's Rep. (38 Cal.)

Robinson's Rep. (17-23 Colo.)

Robinson's Rep. (La. 1841-46)

Robinson's Rep. (1 Nev.)

Chr. Robinson's Rep., Ontario

J. L. Robinson's Upper Canada Rep.,

Robinson's Rep. (40-41 Va.)

**Robt.**   *See* Robertson

**Rodm.**   Rodman's Rep. (78-82 Ky.)

**Rog.C.H.R.**   Rogers' City Hall Recorder (N.Y. 1816-22)

**Rog.Rec.**   Rogers' New City Hall Recorder

**Rogers**   Rogers' Rep. (47-51 La. Annual)

**Rol[l].**   Rolle's Abridgement, *Eng.*

Rolle's K.B. Rep., *Eng.*

**Roll.Rep.**   Same as above

**Rolle**   Same as above

**Rolls Ct.Rep.**   Rolls Ct. Rep.

**Root**   Root's Rep. (Conn. 1774-89)

**Rose's Notes**   Rose's Notes on United States Rep.

**Rowe**   Rowe's Rep., *Eng.*

**Rowe's Rep.**   Rowe's Rep., *Eng.*

**Rowell**   Rowell's Rep. (45-52 Vt.)

**Rucker**   Rucker's Rep. (43-46 W.Va.)

**Ruff.**   Statutes at Large, Ruffhead's Ed., *Eng.*

Ruffin & Hawks' Rep. (8 N.C.)

**Ruff.&H.**   Ruffin & Hawks' Rep. (8 N.C.)

**Runn.**   Runnell's Rep. (38-56 Iowa)

**Runnell**   Runnell's Rep. (38-56 Iowa)

**Rus.**   *See* Russ.

**Russ.**   Russell's Ch. Rep., *Eng.*

**Russ.t.Eld.**   Russell's Ch. Cas. *temp.* Eldon, *Eng.*

**Russ.&M.**   Russell & Mylne's Ch. Rep., *Eng.*

**Russ.&Ry.**   Russell & Ryan's Crown Cas. Res., *Eng.*

**Russell N.S.**   Russell's Nova Scotia Eq. Dec.

**Rutg.L.Rev.**   Rutgers Law Rev.

**Ry.&M.**   Ryan & Moody's N.P. Rep.

**Ry.&M.N.P.**   Same as above

**S.**   Senate Bill

New York Supplement

Quebec Sup. Ct. Rep.

**S.C.**   Same Case

Superior Court

Supreme Court

South Carolina

Supreme Court Reporter

**S.C.D.C.**   Supreme Court Rep., District of Columbia

**S.C.D.C.N.S.**   Same, New Series

**S.C.Eq.**   South Carolina Eq. Rep.

**SC.L.**   South Carolina Law Rep.

**S.C.L.Q.**   South Carolina Law Quarterly

**S.C.R.**   Canada Sup. Ct. Rep.

Canada Law Rep., Sup. Ct.

South Carolina Rep.

**S.Car.**   South Carolina

**S.Con.Res.**   Senate Concurrent Resolution

**S.Ct.** Supreme Court; Supreme Court Reporter

**S.D.** South Dakota

**S.D.B.Jo.** South Dakota Bar Jour.

**S.D.K.** Si De Ka Quarterly

**S.D.R.** New York State Dept. Rep.

**S.Dak.** South Dakota

**S.Doc.** Senate Document

**S.E.** South Eastern Reporter

**S.E.2d** Same, Second Series

**S.E.C.** Securities and Exchange Comm., *U.S.*

**S.E.C.Jud.Dec.** Securities & Exchange Comm. Judicial Dec. 1934-39, *U.S.*

**S.J.** Solicitors' Jour.

**S.J.Res.** Senate Joint Resolution

**S.L.R.** Saskatchewan Law Rep.
Scottish Law Reporter
Scots Law Rev.
Southern Law Rev.

**S.L.R.B.** State Labor Relations Bd.

**S.L.T.** Scots Law Times; Scots Law Times Reports

**S.M.** Solicitor's Memorandum, Internal Revenue Service, *U.S.*

**S.R.** Solicitor's Recommendation, Internal Revenue Service, *U.S.*
New York State Reporter
Supreme Court of Quebec Rep.

**S.R.C.** Stuart's Lower Canada Rep.

**S.R.&O.** Statutory Rules & Orders, *Eng.*

**S.Rept.** Senate Report

**S.Res.** Senate Resolution

**S.S.** Silvernail's N.Y. Sup. Ct. Rep.
Synopsis Series, U.S. Treasury Dec.

**S.S.C.** Sanford's Super. Ct. Rep. New York City

**S.S.R.** Social Security Tax Ruling, Internal Revenue Service, *U.S.*

**S.T.C.** State Tax Cas. (CCH)

**S.T.D.** Synopsis Dec., U.S. Treas.

**S.T.L.J.** Southern Tex. Law Jour.

**S.W.** South Western Reporter

**S.W.2d** Same, Second Series

**S.W.L.Rev.** Southwestern Law Rev.

**S.&G.** Smale & Giffard's Vice-Chancery Rep., *Eng.*

**S.&M.** Shaw & Maclean's H.L. Cas., *Eng.*
Smedes & Marshall's Rep. (9-22 Miss.)
Smedes & Marshall's Ch. Rep., *Miss.*

**S.&M.Ch.** Same as above

**S.&Mar.** Smedes & Marshall's Rep. (9-22 Miss.)

**S.&R.** Sergeant & Rawles' Rep. (Pa. 1824-28)

**S.&S.** Simons & Stuart's Vice-Chancery Rep., *Eng.*

**Sad.Pa.Cas.** Sadley's Cas. (Pa. 1885-88)

**Sal.** Salinger's Rep. (88-117 Iowa)

**Salk.** Salkeld's K.B. Rep., *Eng.*

**San.** Sanford's Rep. (59 Ala.)

**Sand.** Sandford's Rep. (3-7 N.Y. Super. Ct.)

**Sand.Ch.** Sandford's Rep. (N.Y. Ch. 1843-47)

**Sand.I.Rep.** Sandwich Islands (Hawaiian) Rep.

**Sandf.** Sandford's Rep. (3-7 N.Y. Super. Ct.)

**Sandf.Ch.** Sandford's Rep. (N.Y. Ch.)

**Sanf.** Sanford's Rep. (59 Ala.)

**Sask.** Saskatchewan

**Sask.L.R.** Saskatchewan Law Rep.

**Sauls.** Reports time of Saulsbury (5, 6 Del.)

**Saund.** Saunders' K.B. Rep., *Eng.*

**Sav.** Savile's C.P. Rep., *Eng.*

**Saw.** Sawyer's Cir. Ct. Rep., *U.S.*

**Sax.** Saxton's Rep. (1 N.J. Eq.)

**Say.** Sayer's K.B. Rep., *Eng.*

**Sc.** Scammon's Rep. (2-5 Ill.)

**Sc.Jur.** Scottish Jurist

**Sc.L.T.** Scots Law Times

**Sc.N.R.** Scott's New Rep., C.P., *Eng.*

**Scam.** Scammon's Rep. (2-5 Ill.)

**Scher.** Scherer's Rep. (22-47 N.Y. Miscellaneous)

**Schm.L.J.** Schmidt's Law Jour.

**Schuyl.Leg.Rec.** Schuylkill Legal Record, *Pa.*

**Sco.** Scott's C.P. Rep., *Eng.*

**Sco.N.R.** Scott's New Rep., C.P., *Eng.*

**Scot.** Scotland; Scots; Scottish

**Scot.Jur.** Scottish Jurist

**Scot.L.Rev.** Scottish Law Rev.

**Scot.L.T.** Scots Law Times

**Scott** Scott's C.P. Rep., *Eng.*
Scott's Rep. (25, 26 N.Y. Civil Procedure)

**Scott N.R.** Scott's New C.P. Rep., *Eng.*

**Scr.L.T.** Scranton (Pa.) Law Times

**Sea.&Sm.** Searle & Smith's Probate and Divorce Rep., *Eng.*

**Searle&Sm.** Same as above

**Sec.&Ex.C.** Securities and Exchange Comm., *U.S.*

**Seign.Rep.** Lower Canada Seigniorial Rep.

**Seld.** Selden's Rep. (5-10 N.Y.)

**Seld.Soc.** Selden Society

**Selden** *See* Seld.

**Selw.&Barn.** Barnewall & Alderson's K.B. Rep., 1st part, *Eng.*

**Sen.Doc.** Senate Document

**Sen.Jo.** Senate Jour.

**Sen.Rep.** Senate Report

**Serg.&Lowb.** English Common Law Rep., ed. Sergeant and Lowber

**Serg.&Rawl.** Sergeant & Rawle's Rep. (Pa.1814-28)

**Sess.Cas.** Sessions Cases, K.B., *Eng.*

**Sh.** Shand's Rep. (11-41 S.C.)
G. B. Shaw's Rep. (10, 11 Vt.)
W.G. Shaw's Rep. (30-35 Vt.)
Sheldon's Rep. (Buffalo, N.Y., Super. Ct.)
Shepherd's Ala. Rep.
Shepley's Rep. (13-18, 21-30 Me.)
Shipp's Rep. (66, 67 N.C.)
Shirley's Rep. (49-55 N.H.)
Shower's K.B. Rep., *Eng.*

**Shan.** Shannon's Unreported Cases, *Tenn.*

**Shand** Shand's Rep. (11-41 N.C.)

**Shaw** G. B. Shaw's Rep. (10, 11 Vt.)
W. G. Shaw's Rep. (30-35 Vt.)

**Shaw(Vt.)** G. B. Shaw's Rep. (10, 11 Vt.)
W. G. Shaw's Rep. (30-35 Vt.)

**Shaw (W.G.)** W. G. Shaw's Rep. (30-35 Vt.)

**Sheld.** Sheldon's Rep. (Buffalo, N.Y., Super. Ct.)

**Shep.** Shepherd's Rep., *Ala.*
Select Cases (in 37-39 Ala.)
Shepley's Rep. (13-18, 21-30 Me.)

**Shep.Touch.** Sheppard's Touchstone, *Eng.*

**Shepley** Shepley's Rep. (13-18, 21-30 Me.)

**Shingle** The Shingle, Philadelphia Bar Assn.

**Shipp.** Shipp's Rep. (66, 67 N.C.)

**Shirley** Shirley's Rep. (49-55 N.H.)

**Show.** Shower's K.B. Rep., *Eng.*

**Show.K.B.** Shower's K.B. Rep., *Eng.*

**Sick.** Sickels' Rep. (46-85 N.Y.)

**Sick.Min.Dec.** Sickels' U.S. Mining Laws and Dec.

**Sid.** Siderfin's K.B., C.P. and Ex. Rep.

**Silv.** Silvernails Rep. (N.Y. 1886-92)
Silvernail's Rep. (9-14 N.Y. Crim. Rep.)
Silvernail's Sup. Ct. Rep. (N.Y. 1889-90)

**Sim.** Simmons' Rep. (99 Wis.)
Simons' Ch. Rep., *Eng.*

**Sim.N.S.** Simons' Ch. Rep. New Series, *Eng.*

**Sim.&C.** Simmons & Conover's Rep. (99-100 Wis.)

**Sim.&St.** Simons & Stuart's Ch. Rep., *Eng.*

**Sir J.S.** Sir John Strange's Rep., *Eng.*

**Sir T.J.** Sir Thomas Jones' Rep., K.B. and C.P., *Eng.*

**Sir T.Ray.** T. Raymond's K.B. Rep., *Eng.*

**Skin.** Skinner's K.B. Rep., *Eng.*

**Skinker** Skinker's Rep. (65-79 Mo.)

**Slade** Slade's Rep. (15 Vt.)

**Sloan Leg.Reg.** Sloan's Legal Register, *N.Y.*

**Sm.** Smith

**Sm.C.C.M.** Smith's Cir. Courts-Martial Rep., Maine, *U.S.*

**Sm.Cond.Ala.** Smith's Condensed Ala. Rep.

**Sm.E.D.** E. D. Smith's C.P. Rep., *N.Y.*

**Sm.Eng.** Smith's K.B. Rep., *Eng.*

**Sm.Ind.** Smith's Rep. (in 1-4 Ind.)

**Sm.K.B.** Smith's K.B. Rep., *Eng.*

**Sm.Me.** Smith's Rep. (61-84 Me.)

**Sm.&G.** Smale & Giffard's Ch. Rep., *Eng.*
Smith & Guthrie's Rep. (81-101 Mo. App.)

**Sm.&M.** Smedes & Marshall's Rep. (Miss. Ch. 1840-43)
Smedes & Marshall's Rep. (9-22 Miss.)

**Sm.&M.Ch.**  Same as above

**Smed.&M.**  Smedes & Marshall's Rep. (Miss. Ch. 1839-43, or 9-22 Miss.)

**Smed.&M.Ch.**  Smedes & Marshall's Miss. Ch. Rep.

**Smith.**  J. P. Smith's K.B. Rep., *Eng.*
Smith's Rep. (54-62 Cal.)
Smith's Rep. (in 1-4 Ind.)
Smith's Rep. (61-64 Me.)
Smith's Rep. (81-101 Mo. App.)
Smith's Rep. (N.H. 1796-1816)
E.D. Smith's Rep. (N.Y. C.P.)
E.P. Smith's Rep. (15-27, 47-62 N.Y.)
Smith's Rep. (51-81 Pa. St.)
Smith's Rep. (2-4 S.D.)
Smith's Rep. (7, 12 Tenn.)
Smith's Rep. (1-11 Wis.)

**Smith,E.D.**  E. D. Smith's Rep. (N.Y. C.P.)

**Smith,J.P.**  J. P. Smith's K.B. Rep., *Eng.*

**Smith K.B.**  Same as above

**Smith Me.**  Smith's Rep. (61-64 Me.)

**Smith N.H.**  Smith's Rep. (N.H. 1796-1816)

**Smith N.Y.**  E. P. Smith's Rep. (15-27, 47-62 N.Y.)

**Smith,P.F.**  P. F. Smith's Rep. (51-81 Pa. St.)

**Smith Wis.**  Smith's Rep. (1-11 Wis.)

**Smith&G.**  Smith & Guthrie's Rep. (81-101 Mo. App.)

**Sneed**  Sneed's Ky. Dec. (2 Ky.)
Sneed's Rep. (33-37 Tenn.)

**Sneed Dec.**  Sneed's Ky. Dec. (2 Ky.)

**Snow**  Snow's Rep. (3 Utah)

**So.**  Southern Reporter

**So.2d**  Same, Second Series

**So.Calif.L.Rev.**  Southern California Law Rev.

**So.Car.**  South Carolina

**So.Car.Const.**  South Carolina Constitutional Rep. by Treadway, Mill, or Harper

**So.East.Rep.**  South Eastern Reporter

**So.Rep.**  Southern Reporter

**So.West.Rep.**  South Western Reporter

**Sol.**  The Solicitor

**Sol.J.**  Solicitors' Jour.

**Sol. Op.**  Solicitors' Opinion

**Som.L.J.**  Somerset Legal Jour. (Pa. 1920-date)

**South.**  Southern Reporter

**Southard**  Southard's Rep. (4-5 N.J. Law)

**Sp.**  Spear's Rep. (S.C. Law 1842-44)

**Sp.CM**  Special Court-Martial (U.S. Navy)

**Sp.Eq.**  Spear's Rep. (S.C. Eq.)

**Spaulding**  Spaulding's Rep. (71-80 Me.)

**Spears**  Spears' Rep. (S.C. Law of Eq.)

**Spears Eq.**  Spears' Rep. (S.C. Eq.)

**Speers**  *See* Spears

**Spencer**  Spencer's Rep. (10-20 Minn.)
Spencer's Rep. (20 N.J. Law)

**Spooner**  Spooner's Rep. (12-15 Wis.)

**Spottis.C.L.&Eq.Rep.**  Spottiswoode's Common Law and Eq. Rep., *Eng.*

**Spr.**  Sprague's Dist. Ct. and Admiralty Dec., *U.S.*

**St.**  Story's Cir. Ct. Rep., *U.S.*

**St.Ab.**  Statham's Abridgement, *Eng.*

**St.Ch.Cas.**  Star Chamber Cases, *Eng.*

**St.Inst.**  Statutory Instruments, *Eng.*

**St.P.**  State Papers

**St.Pl.Cr.**  Staundford's Pleas of Crown, *Eng.*

**St.Rep.**  State Reports

**St.Tr.**  Howell's State Trials

**Stafford**  Stafford's Rep. (69-71 Vt.)

**Stanford**  Staundford's Pleas of the Crown, *Eng.*

**Stanton**  Stanton's Rep. (11-13 Ohio)

**Star.**  Starkie's N.P. Rep., *Eng.*

**Star Ch.Ca.**  Star Chamber Cases, *Eng.*

**Stark.**  Starkie's N.P. Rep., *Eng.*

**Stark.N.P.**  Same as above

**Stat.**  Statutes; Statutes at Large; Statutes Revised

**Stat. at L.**  Statutes at Large

**Stat.Realm**  Statutes of the Realm, *Eng.*

**State Tr.**  State Trials (Howell), *Eng.*

**State Tr.N.S.**  State Trials, New Series, ed. Macdonell, *Eng.*

**Staund.Pl.**  Staundford's Pleas of the Crown, *Eng.*

**Staundforde**    Same as above

**Stevens&G.**    Stevens & Graham's Rep. (98-139 Ga.)

**Stew.**    Stewart's Rep. (Ala. 1827-31)
Stewart's Rep. (28-45 N.J. Eq.)
Stewart's Rep. (1-10 S.D.)

**Stew.Adm.**    Stewart's Nova Scotia Admiralty Rep.

**Stew.Eq.**    Stewart's Rep. (28-45 N.J. Eq.)

**Stew.N.Sc.**    Stewart's Nova Scotia Admiralty Rep.

**Stew.V.A.**    Same as above

**Stew.&P.**    Stewart & Porter's Rep. (Ala. 1831-34)

**Stewart**    *See* Stew.

**Stiles**    Stiles Rep. (22-29 Iowa)

**Stiness**    Stiness' Rep. (20-34 R.I.)

**Sto.**    Story's Cir. Ct. Rep., *U.S.*

**Sto.C.C.**    Same as above

**Stock.Adm.**    Stockton's Vice-Admiralty Rep., *Can.*
Stockton's Rep. (9-11 N.J. Eq.)
Stockton's New Brunswick Rep.

**Stock.Adm.**    Stockton's Vice-Admiralty Rep., *Can.*

**Stockett**    Stockett's Rep. (27-79 Md.)

**Stockt.Ch.**    Stockton's Rep. (9-11 N.J. Eq.)

**Stockton**    *See* Stock.

**Story**    Story's Cir. Ct. Rep., *U.S.*

**Str.**    Strange's K.B. Rep., *Eng.*

**Stra.**    Strange; *see* Str.

**Strahan**    Strahan's Rep. (19 Ore.)

**Stran.**    Strange; *see* Str.

**Strange**    *See* Str.

**Stratton**    Stratton's Rep. (12-14, 19 Ore.)

**Stringfellow**    Stringfellow's Rep. (9-11 Mo. App.)

**Strob.**    Strobhart's Rep. (S.C. Law)

**Strob.Eq.**    Strobhart's Rep. (S.C. Eq.)

**Struve**    Struve's Rep. (Washington Territory 1854-88)

**Stuart K.B.**    Stuart's Lower Canada K.B. Rep.

**Sty.**    Style's K.B. Rep., *Eng.*

**Sum.**    Sumner's Cir. Ct. Rep., *U.S.*

**Summerfield**    Summerfield's Rep. (21 Nev.)

**Sumn.**    Sumner's Cir. Ct. Rep., *U.S.*

**Sup.Ct.**    Supreme Court
Supreme Court Reporter

**Super.**    Superior Court

**Super.Ct.Rep.**    Superior Court Rep. (N.Y., Pa., etc.)

**Supp.Ves.Jun.**    Supplement to Vesey, Junior Rep.

**Susq.L.C.**    Susquehanna Law Chronicle, *Pa.*

**Sw.**    Swabey's Admiralty Rep., *Eng.*
Swan's Rep. (31, 32 Tenn.)
Swanston's Ch. Rep., *Eng.*
Sweeney's N.Y. Super. Ct. Rep.

**Sw.&Tr.**    Swabey & Tristram's Probate and Divorce Rep., *Eng.*

**Swab.**    Swabey's Admiralty Rep., *Eng.*

**Swan.**    Swan's Rep. (31, 32 Tenn.)
Swanston's Ch. Rep., *Eng.*

**Swan.Ch.**    Swanston's Ch. Rep., *Eng.*

**Swans.**    Same as above

**Sween.**    Sweeny's N.Y. Super. Ct. Rep.

**Syl.**    The Syllabi (legal periodical)

**Syn.Ser.**    Synopsis Series, Treasury Dec., *U.S.*


**T.**    Tappan's C.P. Rep., *Ohio*

**T.B.M.**    Advisory Tax Board Memorandum (U.S. Internal Revenue Service)

**T.B.Mon.**    T. B. Monroe's Rep. (17-23 Ky.)

**T.B.R.**    Advisory Tax Board Recommendation (U.S. Internal Revenue Service)

**T.C.**    Tax Court of the United States Trade Cases (CCH)

**T.C.**    U.N. Trusteeship Council

**TCM**    Tax Court Memorandum Dec. (CCH)

**T.C.Memo.**    Tax Court Memorandum Dec. (P-H)

**T.D.**    Treasury Dec. (U.S. Treasury Dept.)

**T.I.A.S.**    Treaties and Other International Acts

**T.Jo.**    T. Jones' K.B. and C.P. Rep., *Eng.*

**T.Jones(2 Jones)**    Same as above

**T.L.R.**    Times Law Reports, *Eng.*

**T.M.Bull.**    Trade Mark Bulletin, New Series

**T.M.Rep.**    Trade Mark Reporter

**T.R.**    Term Rep. (Durnford & East), *Eng.*

Caine's Term Rep., *N.Y.*

**T.R.N.S.** Term Rep., New Series (East), *Eng.*

**T.Raym.** T. Raymond's K.B. Rep., *Eng.*

**T.U.P.Charlt.** T.U.P. Charlton's Rep., *Ga.*

**TVA** Tennessee Valley Authority

**T.&G.** Tyrwhitt's & Granger's Ex. Rep., *Eng.*

**T.&M.** Temple & Mew's Crim. Appeal Cas., *Eng.*

Temple & Mew's Crown Cas., *Eng.*

**T.&P.** Turner & Phillips' Ch. Rep., *Eng.*

**T.&R.** Turner & Russell's Ch. Rep., *Eng.*

**Tal[b]** Chancery Cases *temp.* Talbot, *Eng.*

**Tam.** Tamlyn's Rolls Ct. Rep., *Eng.*

**Tan.** Taney's Cir. Ct. Rep., *U.S.*

**Tanner** Tanner's Rep. (8-14 Ind.) Tanner's Rep. (13-17 Utah)

**Tapp.** Tappan's Ohio C.P. Rep.

**Taun.** Taunton's C.P. Rep., *Eng.*

**TaxCoun.Q.** Tax Counselor's Q.

**Taxes** Taxes—The Tax Magazine

**Tay.** Taylor

Taylor's K.B. Rep., *Can.*

Taylor's Reports (1 N.C.)

**Tay.J.L.** J. L. Taylor's Rep. (1 N.C.)

**Tay.N.C.** Same as above

**Tayl.N.C.** Taylor's Rep. (1 N.C.)

**Taylor** Taylor's K.B. Rep., *Can.*

Taylor's Rep. (1 N.C.)

**Temp.L.Q.** Temple Law Quarterly

**Temp.Wood** Manitoba Rep. *temp.* Wood

**Temp.&M.** Temple & Mew's Crown Cas., *Eng.*

**Tenn.** Tennessee

**Tenn.App.** Tennessee Civil Appeals Rep.

**Tenn.C.C.A.** Tennessee Court of Civil Appeals

**Tenn.Cas.** Shannon's Unreported Cas. (Tenn. 1847-94)

**Tenn.Ch.** Tennessee Ch. Rep. (Cooper)

**Tenn.Ch.App.** Tennessee Ch. Appeals (Wright)

**Term.** Term Rep. (Durnford & East K.B.), *Eng.*

**Term.N.C.** Term Rep. (Taylor, 4 N.C.)

**Term.Rep.** Term Rep. (Durnford & East), *Eng.*

**Terr.** Terrell's Rep. (52-71 Tex.)

**Terr.L.R.** Territories Law Rep., *Can.*

**Terr.&Walk.** Terrell & Walker's Rep. (38-51 Tex.)

**Tex.** Texas

**Tex.App.** Texas Crim. Appeals Rep.

**Tex.Cr.R.** Texas Crim. Rep.

**Tex.Ct.Rep.** Texas Court Reporter 1900-08

**Tex.Dec.** Texas Dec.

**Tex.Jur.** Texas Jurisprudence

**Tex.Supp.** Supplement to 25 Tex. Rep.

**Tex.Unrep.Cas.** Texas Unreported Cas. (Posey)

**Th.C.C.** Thacher's Crim. Cas. (Mass. 1823-42)

**Th.&C.** Thompson & Cook's Rep. (N.Y. Sup. Ct. 1873-75)

**Thac.Cr.Cas.** Thacher's Crim. Cas. (Mass. 1823-42)

**Thayer** Thayer's Rep. (18 Ore.)

**The Rep.** The Reporter, Phi Alpha Delta

The Reports, Coke's Rep., *Eng.*

**Thém** La Thémis, Montreal, Quebec

**Thom.** Thomas' Rep. (1 Wyo.)

Thomson's Nova Scotia Rep.

**Thom.Dec.** Thomson's Dec. (1 Nova Scotia)

**Thom.Rep.** Thomson's Rep. (3 Nova Scotia)

**Thom.&Fr.** Thomas & Franklin's Rep. (1 Md. Ch.)

**Thomas** Thomas' Rep. (1 Wyo.)

**Thomp.Cal.** Thompson's Rep. (39, 40 Cal.)

**Thomp.Ten.Cas.** Thompson's Unreported Cas. (Tenn. 1847-69)

**Thomp.&C.** Thompson & Cook's N.Y. Sup. Ct. Rep.

**Thompson** Thompson's Rep. (39, 40 Cal.)

**Thor.** Thorington's Rep. (107 Ala.)

**Thorpe** Thorpe's Rep. (52 La. Annual)

**Tiffany** Tiffany's Rep. (28-39 N.Y.)

**Tillman** Tillman's Rep. (68, 69, 71, 73, 75 Ala).

**Times L.R.** Times Law Rep., *Eng.*

**Tobey** Tobey's Rep. (9, 10 R.I.)

**Tot.** Tothill's Ch. Rep., *Eng.*

**Toth.** Same as above

**Tr.App.** Transcript Appeals (N.Y. 1867-68)

**Tr.&Est.** Trusts & Estates

**Trans.Ap.** Transcript Appeals (N.Y. 1867-68)

**Trade-MarkRep.** Trade-Mark Reporter

**Tread.** Treadway's Rep. (S.C. Constitutional)

**Trem.** Tremaine's Pleas of the Crown, *Eng.*

**Trem.P.C.** Same as above

**Trin.** Trinity Term

**Tripp** Tripp's Rep. (5, 6 Dak.)

**Tru.** Trueman's New Brunswick Rep.

**True.** Same as above

**Trusts&Est.** Trusts and Estates

**Tuck.** Tucker's Rep. (District of Columbia)
  Tucker's Rep. (156-175 Mass.)
  Tucker's N.Y. Surrogate Rep.

**Tuck.Surr.** Same as above

**Tuck.&Cl.** Tucker & Clephane's Rep. (21 District of Columbia)

**Tul.L.Rev.** Tulane Law Rev.

**Tup.App.** Tupper's Appeal Rep., *Ontario*

**Tupper** Same as above

**Tur.&Rus.** Turner & Russell's Ch. Rep., *Eng.*

**Turner** Turner's Rep. (35-48 Ark.)
  Turner's Reports (99-101 Ky.)

**Tuttle** Tuttle's Rep. (23-32, 41-51 Cal.)

**Tuttle&Carp.** Tuttle & Carpenter's Rep. (52 Cal.)

**Tyl.** Tyler's Rep. (Vt. 1800-03)

**Tyng** Tyng's Rep. (2-17 Mass.)

**Tyr.** Tyrwhitt's Ex. Rep., *Eng.*

**Tyr.&Gr.** Tyrwhitt & Granger's Ex. Rep., *Eng.*

**Tyrw.** Tyrwhitt, Tyr.


**U.** Utah

**U.C.App.** Upper Canada Appeal Rep.

**U.C.C.P.** Upper Canada C.P. Rep.

**U.C.C.P.D.** Upper Canada C.P. Div.

**U.C.Ch.** Upper Canada Ch. Rep.

**U.C.Cham.** Upper Canada Chambers Rep.

**U.C.Chan.** Upper Canada Ch. Rep.

**U.C.E.&A.** Upper Canada Error and Appeal Rep.

**U.C.Jur.** Upper Canada Jurist

**U.C.K.B.** Upper Canada K.B. Rep., Old Series

**UCMJ** Uniform Code of Military Justice, *U.S.*

**U.C.O.S.** Upper Canada K. [or Q.] B. Rep., Old Series

**U.C.Q.B.** Upper Canada Q.B. Rep.

**U.C.R.** Upper Canada Rep.

**U.Ill.L.F.** University of Illinois Law Forum

**U.L.A.** Uniform Laws Annotated

**U.M.K.C.L.R.** U. Missouri at K.C. L. Rev.

**UN** United Nations

**UNESCO** United Nations Educational, Scientific and Cultural Organization

**UNICEF** United Nations International Children's Emergency Fund

**U. of P.L.Rev.** University of Pennsylvania Law Rev.

**U.S.** United States or U.S. Sup. Ct. Rep.

**U.S.Ap.** United States Appeals (Circuit Courts or Courts of Appeals)

**U.S.App.** Same as above

**U.S.App.D.C.** United States Court of Appeals for District of Columbia beginning with v. 75

**U.S.Av.R.** United States Aviation Rep.

**U.S.C.** United States Code

**U.S.C.A.** United States Code Annotated

**U.S.C.C.A.** United States Circuit Court of Appeals Rep.

**U.S.C.C.&A.N.** United States Code Congressional and Administrative News (a periodical)

**USCMA** Official Reports, United States Court of Military Appeals

**U.S.Ct.Cl.** United States Court of Claims

**USDA** United States Dept. of Agriculture

**U.S.Daily** United States Daily, Washington, D.C.

**U.S.Dist.Ct.Haw.** District Court, Hawaii

**USHA** United States Housing Authority

**U.S.L.W.** United States Law Week (a newspaper)

**U.S.L.Ed.** United States Sup. Ct. Rep. Lawyers' Edition

**U.S.M.C.** United States Marine Corps
United States Maritime Comm.

**U.S.P.Q.** United States Patents Quarterly

**U.S.Rep.** United States Reports

**U.S.Sup.Ct.(L.Ed.)** United States Sup. Ct. Rep., Lawyers' Edition

**U.S.S.B.** United States Shipping Bd. [Decisions]

**U.S.S.C.Rep.** United States Sup. Ct. Rep.

**U.S.Sup.Ct.(L.Ed.)** United States Sup. Ct. Rep., Lawyers' Edition

**U.S.Sup.Ct.Rep.** United States Sup. Ct. Reporter

**U.S.T.** United States Treaties and Other International Agreements 1950-date

**U.S.T.I.T.** Same as above

**USTC** United States Tax Cases (CCH)

**U.S.Treas.Reg.** United States Treasury Regulations

**U.S.Treaty Ser.** United States Treaty Series

**Up.Ben.Pr.** Upper Bench Precedents *Temp.* Car. I, *Eng.*

**Utah B.Bull.** Utah Bar Bulletin

**V.** Vermont; Victoria; Virginia

**VA** Administrator of Veterans' Affairs, *U.S.*

**V.A.D.** Veterans' Affairs Decisions, Appealed Pension and Civil Service Retirement Cases, *U.S.*

**V.B.** Veterans' Bureau, *U.S.*

**V.C.Rep.** Vice-Chancellor's Rep. (English; Canadian)

**V.N.** Van Ness' Prize Cas., *U.S.*

**V.R.** Vermont (or Virginia) Rep.

**Va.** Virginia; Virginia Rep.

**Va.Cas.** Virginia Cases (Brockenbrough & Holmes)
Virginia Crim. Cases (3, 4 Va.)

**Va.Ch.Dec.** Wythe's Ch. (Va. 1788-99)

**Va.Col.Dec.** Virginia Colonial Dec. (Randolph & Barradall)

**Va.Dec.** Virginia Dec. (Unreported)

**Va.R.** Virginia Reports

**Val.Rep.I.C.C.** Valuation Rep., Interstate Commerce Comm.

**Vand.L.Rev.** Vanderbilt Law Rev.

**Van K** Van Koughnet's Rep. (15-21 Upper Canada C.P. Rep.)

**Van N.** Van Ness' Prize Cas., U.S. Dist. Ct., Dist. of N.Y.

**Vaugh.** Vaughan's C.P. Rep., *Eng.*

**Vaux** Vaux's Recorder's Dec. (Pa. 1841-45)

**Ve.** *See* Ves.

**Vea.** *See* Veazey

**Ve.&B.** Vesey & Beames' Ch. Rep., *Eng.*

**Veazey** Veazey's Rep. (36-44 Vt.)

**Vent.** Ventris' C.P. and K.B. Rep., *Eng.*

**Ver.** Vermont

**Verm.** Vermont

**Vern.** Vernon's Ch. Rep., *Eng.*

**Ves.** Vesey, Senior's Ch. Rep., *Eng.*

**Ves.Jr.** Vesey, Junior's Ch. Rep., *Eng.*

**Ves.Sen.** Vesey, Senior's Ch. Rep., *Eng.*

**Ves.&Bea.** Vesey & Beames' Ch. Rep., *Eng.*

**Vez.** Vezey's Ch. Rep. *temp.* Hardwicke, *Eng.*

**Vilas** Vilas' Rep. (1-5 N.Y. Crim. Rep.)

**Vin.Abr.** Viner's Abridgement of Law and Equity

**Vin.Supp.** Supplement to above

**Virg.** Virginia
Virginia Cases (Brockenbrough & Holmes)

**Virgin** Virgin's Rep. (52-60 Me.)

**Vr.** Vroom's Rep. (30-85 N.J. Law)

**Vt.** Vermont

**W.** Watt's Pa. Rep.
Wendell's Rep. (N.Y., 1826-41)

Wheaton's Rep. (14-25 U.S.)
Wisconsin Rep.
Wright's Ohio Rep. (1831-1834)
Wyoming Rep.

**W.Bl.**  William  Blackstone's  K.B. Rep., *Eng.*

**W.C.L.J.**  Workmen's Compensation Law Jour.

**W.C.Ops.**  Workmen's  Compensation Opinions, U.S. Dept. of Commerce

**W.H.Cas.**  Wage  &  Hour  Cases (BNA)

**WHO**  World Health Organization, *UN*

**W.H.&G.**  Welsby, Hurlstone & Gordon's Ex. Rep., *Eng.*

**W.H.R.**  Wage  &  Hour  Reporter (BNA)

**W.H.R.Man.**  Wage & Hour Reference Manual (BNA)

**W.Jo.**  William  Jones'  K.B.  Rep., *Eng.*

**W.Kel.**  William Kelynge's Ch. Rep., *Eng.*

**W.L.R.**  Washington Law Reporter (D.C.)

**W.N.**  Weekly  Notes  (of  English Law Rep.)

**W.R.**  Wendell's Rep. (N.Y. 1826-41)
West's Ch. Rep., *Eng.*
Wisconsin Rep.

**W.Rep.**  West's Rep. *temp.* Hardwicke, *Eng.*

**W.Rob.**  W. Robinson's Admiralty Rep., *Eng.*

**W.T.B.R.**  War Trade Board Rulings, *U.S.*

**W.Ty.R.**  Washington  Territory Rep. 1854-88

**W.Va.**  West Virginia

**W.W.Harr.Del.**  W. W. Harrington's Rep. (31-39 Del.)

**W.W.&D.**  Willmore, Wollaston & Davison's Q.B. Rep., *Eng.*

**W.W.&H.**  Willmore, Wollaston & Hodges' Q.B. Rep., *Eng.*

**W.&M.**  Woodbury & Minot's Cir. Ct. Rep., *U.S.*

**W.&S.**  Watts & Sergeant's Rep. (Pa. 1841-45)

**W.&W.**  White & Wilson's Tex. Civil Cases, Court of Appeals

**Wa.**  Watts' Rep. (Pa. 1832-40)

**Wal.**  Wallace;  usually  abbreviated as Wall.

**Walk.**  Walker

**Walk.Ch.**  Walker's Mich. Ch. Rep.

**Walk.Mich.**  Same as above

**Walk.Miss.**  Walker's Rep. (1 Miss.)

**Walk.Pa.**  Walker's  Rep.  (Pa. 1855-85)

**Walk.Tex.**  Walker's Rep. (22-25, 38-51, 72-88 Tex.; 1-10 Civil Appeals Tex.)

**Walker**  Walker's  Rep.  (96,  109 Ala.)
Walker's Mich. Ch. Rep.
Walker's Rep. (1 Miss.)
Walker's Rep. (Pa. 1855-85)
Walker's Rep. (22-25, 38-51, 72-88 Tex.; 1-10 Civil Appeals Tex.)

**Wall.**  Wallace; Wallis
Wallace's Cir. Ct. Rep., *U.S.*
Wallace's Philadelphia Rep. (Pa. 1855-85)
Wallace's U.S. Sup. Ct. Rep. (68-90 U.S.)

**Wall.C.C.**  Same as above

**Wall.Jr.**  J. W. Wallace's Cir. Ct. Rep., *U.S.*

**Wall.Rep.**  Wallace, The Reporters (treatise)
Wallace's U.S. Sup. Ct. Rep. (68-90 U.S.)

**Wall.S.C.**  Wallace's U.S. Sup. Ct. Rep. (68-90 U.S.)

**Wall.Sen.**  J. B. Wallace's Cir. Ct. Rep., *U.S.*

**Walter**  (14-16 N.M.)

**War Dept.B.C.A.**  United States War Department, Decisions of Board of Contract Adjustment

**War Trade Reg.**  War Trade Reg., *U.S.*

**Ward.**  Warden's Rep. (2, 4 Ohio St.)

**Warden**  Same as above

**Warden&Smith**  (3 Ohio St. Rep.)

**Ware**  Ware's Dist. Ct. Rep., *U.S.*

**Wash.**  Washburn; Washington
Washington's Rep. (16-23 Vt.)
Washington's Rep. (1, 2 Va.)
Washington's Cir. Ct. Rep., *U.S.*
Washington Territory or State Rep.

**Wash.C.C.**  Washington's  Cir.  Ct. Rep., *U.S.*

**Wash.Co.R.** Washington County Rep., *Pa.*

**Wash.Terr.** Washington Territory Opinions 1854-64

Washington Territory Rep. 1854-88

**Wash.Ter.N.S.** Allen's Washington Territory Rep., New Series

**Wash.Ty.** *See* Wash. Terr.

**Wash.Va.** Washington's Rep. (1, 2 Va.)

**Washburn** Washburn's Rep. (18-23 Vt.)

**Watts** Watts' Rep. (Pa. 1832-40)

Watts' Rep. (16-24 W.Va.)

**Watts&Serg.** Watts & Sergeant's Rep. (Pa. 1841-45)

**We.** West's Ch. Rep., *Eng.*

West's Rep., H.L., *Eng.*

**Webb** Webb's Rep. (6-20 Kan.)

Webb's Rep. (11-20 Tex. Civil App.)

**Webb&Duval** Webb & Duval's Rep. (1-3 Tex.)

**Week.No.** Weekly Notes of Cases (Law Rep.)

**Week.No.Cas.** Weekly Notes of Cases (Pa. 1874-99)

**Weekly Notes** Weekly Notes (of Law Rep.), *Eng.*

**Welsb.H.&G.** Welsby, Hurlstone & Gordon's Ex. Rep., *Eng.*

**Wend.** Wendell's Rep. (N.Y. 1826-41)

**Wenz.** Wenzell's Rep. (60-72 Minn.)

**West.Res.Law Rev.** Western Reserve Law Rev.

**West.** West's Ch. Rep., *Eng.*

West's Rep., H.L., *Eng.*

Weston's Rep. (11-14 Vt.)

**West.Chy.** West's Ch. Rep. *temp.* Hardwicke, *Eng.*

**West *t.*H.** Same as above

**West H.L.** West's Rep., H.L., *Eng.*

**West Va.** West Virginia

**Westmoreland Co.L.J.** Westmoreland County Law Jour. (Pa. 1911-date)

**Weston** Weston's Rep. (11-14 Vt.)

**Weth.U.C.** Wethey's Rep., Upper Canada Q.B.

**Wh.** Wharton's Rep. (Pa. 1835-41)

Wheaton's U.S. Sup. Ct. Rep. (14-25 U.S.)

**Wh.Cr.Cas.** Wheeler's Crim. Cas., *N.Y.*

**Whar.** Wharton's Rep. (Pa. 1835-41)

**Whart.Pa.** Same as above

**Wheat.** Wheaton's U.S. Sup. Ct. Rep. (14-25 U.S.)

**Wheel.** Wheelock's Rep. (32-37 Tex.)

Wheeler's Crim. Cas., *N.Y.*

**Wheel.Cr.Cas.** Same as above

**White** White's Rep. (31-44 Tex. App.)

White's Rep. (10-15 W.Va.)

**White&W.** White & Willson's Rep. (Tex. Civil Cases, Court of Appeals)

**White&W.Civ.Cas.Ct.App.** Same as above

**Whittlesey** Whittlesey's Rep. (32-41 Mo.)

**Wight.** Wightwick's Ex. Rep., *Eng.*

**Wightw.** Same as above

**Wil.** Williams, abbreviated as Will.; Wilson, abbreviated as Wils.

**Wilc.Cond.Rep.** Wilcox's Condensed Rep. (1-7 Ohio, Reprint)

**Wilcox** Wilcox's Rep. (10 Ohio)

Wilcox's Lackawanna County (Pa.) Rep.

**Wilk.** Wilkinson's Rep., Tex. Court of Appeals and Civil Appeals

**Will.** Willes' C.P. Rep., *Eng.*

**Will.Mass.** Williams' Rep. (1 Mass.)

**Will.P.** Peere Williams' Ch. Rep., *Eng.*

**Will.Vt.** Williams Rep. (27-29 Vt.)

**Will.Woll.&D.** Willmore, Wollaston & Davison's Q.B. Rep., *Eng.*

**Will.Woll.&Hodg.** Willmore, Wollaston & Hodges' Q.B. Rep., *Eng.*

**Willes** Willes' C.P. Rep., *Eng.*

**Williams** Peere Williams' Ch. Rep., *Eng.*

Williams' Rep. (1 Mass.)

Williams' Rep. (10-12 Utah)

Williams' Rep. (27-29 Vt.)

**Williams P.** Peere Williams' Ch. Rep., *Eng.*

**Willm.W.&D.** Willmore, Wollaston & Davison's Q.B. Rep., *Eng.*

**Wilm.W.&H.** Willmore, Wollaston & Hodges' Q.B. Rep., *Eng.*

**Willson** Willson's Rep. Texas Appeals

**Willson** Civ.Cas.Ct.App. White & Willson's Rep. (Tex. Civil Cases, Court of Appeals)

**Wils.** G. Wilson's Rep., K.B. and C.P., *Eng.*

**Wils.Ch.** Wilson's Ch. Rep., *Eng.*

**Wils.Exch.** Wilson's Ex., *Eng.*

**Wils.Ind.** Wilson's Rep., Ind. Super. Ct.

**Wils.K.B.** Wilson's K.B. Rep., *Eng.*

**Wils.Minn.** Wilson's Rep. (48-59 Minn.)

**Wils.Oreg.** Wilson's Rep. (1-3 Ore.)

**Wilson** Wilson's Ch. Rep.

Wilson's K.B. and C.P. Rep., *Eng.*

Wilson's Exchequer in Equity Rep., *Eng.*

Wilson's Rep. Ind. Super. Ct.

Wilson's Rep. (48-59 Minn.)

Wilson's Rep. (1-3 Ore.)

**Win.** Winch's C.P. Rep., *Eng.*

Winer's Unreported Opinions (N.Y. Sup. Ct., Erie County)

Winston's Rep. (60 N.C.)

**Win.Eq.** Winston's Rep. (60 N.C.)

**Winch** Winch's C.P. Rep., *Eng.*

**Winst.** Winston's Rep. (60 N.C.)

**Wis.** Wisconsin

**Withrow** Withrow's Rep. (9-21 Iowa)

**Wm.Bl.** William Blackstone's K.B. Rep., *Eng.*

**Wm.Rob.** William Robinson's Admiralty Rep., *Eng.*

**Wms.** Williams, commonly abbreviated as Will.

**Wms.Mass.** Williams' Rep. (1 Mass.)

**Wms.Peere** Peere Williams' Ch. Rep., *Eng.*

**Wms.Vt.** Williams' Rep. (27-29 Vt.)

**Wol.** Wolcott's Rep. (7 Del. Ch.)

**Wood.&M.** Woodbury & Minot's Cir. Ct. Rep.

**Woods** Wood's Cir. Ct. Rep., *U.S.*

**Woods C.C.** Same as above

**Wood's R.** Wood's Manitoba Rep. 1875-83

**Woodw.Dec.** Woodward's Dec. (Pa. 1861-74)

**Wool.** Woolworth's Cir. Ct. Rep., *U.S.*

**Wool.C.C.** Same as above

**Woolw.** Same as above

Woolworth's Rep. (1 Neb.)

**Wright** Wright's Rep. (Ohio 1831-34)

Wright's Rep. (37-50 Pa. St.)

**Wright Ch.** Wright's Rep. (Ohio 1831-34)

**Wright N.P.** Wright's N.P. Rep., *Ohio*

**Wy.** Wythe's Ch. Rep. (Va. 1788-99)

Wyoming Rep.

**Wyo.** Wyoming

**Wyo.T.** Wyoming Territory

**Wythe** Wythe's Ch. Rep. (Va. 1788-99)

**Y.** Yeates Rep. (Pa. 1791-1808)

**Y.A.D.** Young's Vice-Admiralty Dec., *Can.*

**Y.B.** Year Books. The Year Books are usually cited by the year of each King's reign, the initial letter of his name, and the folio and number of the *placita, e.g.,* 34 H. VI, 25.3.

**Y.L.R.** York Legal Record (Pa. 1880-date)

**Y.&C.** Younge & Collyer's Chancery or Exchequer Equity Reports, *Eng.*

**Y.&C.Ex.** Younge & Collyer's Exchequer in Equity Rep., *Eng.*

**Y.&J.** Young & Jervis' Ex. Rep., *Eng.*

**Yates Sel.Cas.** Yates' Select Cas. (N.Y. 1809)

**Yea.** Yeates' Rep. (Pa. 1791-1808)

**Year Books** *See* Y.B.

**Yeates** *See* Yea. above

**Yel.** Yelverton's K.B. Rep.

**Yelv.** Same as above

**Yerg.** Yerger's Rep. (9-18 Tenn.)

**Yo.** Younge's Exchequer in Equity Rep., *Eng.*

**You.** Same as above

**You.&Coll.Ch.** Younge & Collyer's Ch. Rep., *Eng.*

**You.&Coll.Ex.** Younge & Collyer's Exchequer in Equity Rep., *Eng.*

**You.&Jerv.** Younge & Jervis' Ex. Rep., *Eng.*

**Young** Young's Rep. (21-47 Minn.)

**Young Adm.Dec.** Young's Nova Scotia Vice-Admiralty Dec.

**Younge** Younge's Ex. Rep., *Eng.*

**Younge&Coll.Ch.** Younge & Collyer's Chancery or Exchequer Equity Rep., *Eng.*

**Younge&Coll.Ex.** Younge & Collyer's Exchequer in Equity Rep., *Eng.*

**Younge&Jerv.** Younge & Jervis' Ex. Rep., *Eng.*

**Zab.** Zabriskie's Rep. (21-24 N.J. Law)

**Zane** Zane's Rep. (4-9 Utah)

# Index